SALES
AND LEASES

Examples and Explanations

SALES
AND LEASES

Examples and Explanations

James Brook
Professor of Law
New York Law School

LITTLE, BROWN AND COMPANY
Boston   New York   Toronto   London

Library of Congress Catalog Card No. 94-75927

ISBN 0-316-10985-1

MV-NY
Published simultaneously in Canada by Little, Brown & Company (Canada) Limited

Printed in the United States of America

For Isabelle

Contents

Preface for All Students   ix
Preface for Contracts Students   xiii
Acknowledgments   xv
Introduction   xvii

**PART ONE: TRANSACTIONS GOVERNED BY ARTICLES 2
AND 2A, FORMATION, AND BASIC TERMS**   1

1.   The Scope of Article 2   3
2.   The Subject Is Leases   19
3.   Who Is a "Merchant" and Why It Matters   35
4.   Offer and Acceptance: The Basics   43
5.   Offer and Acceptance Advanced: The Battle of the Forms   53
6.   The Statute of Frauds   71
7.   Usage of Trade, Course of Dealing, and Course of
     Performance   87
8.   The Parol Evidence Rule   99
9.   Open Terms, Gap Fillers, and the Doctrine of
     Unconscionability   119
10. Modification and Waiver   139

PART TWO: WARRANTY TERMS   157

11. The Warranty of Title   161
12. Express Warranties of Quality   179
13. Implied Warranties of Quality   199
14. Disclaimer of Warranties and Limitation of Remedies   219
15. The "Privity" Puzzle   249
16. Warranties in the Lease of Goods   267

PART THREE: PERFORMANCE OF THE SALES CONTRACT   279

17. Identification of Goods and the Seller's Tender   283
18. Acceptance or Rejection of Goods   299
19. Cure   323
20. Revocation of Acceptance   335
21. Anticipatory Repudiation and Insecurity   351

22. Installment Sales   369
23. Sale on Approval, Sale or Return, and Consignments   383
24. Excuse of Performance   393

PART FOUR: RISK OF LOSS   **405**
25. Basic Treatment   409
26. Delivery Through Independent Third Parties   419
27. When There Has Been a Breach   431

PART FIVE: REMEDIES   **439**
28. Seller's Remedies   441
29. Buyer's Remedies   469
30. Remedies in Lease Transactions   495

PART SIX: DOCUMENTARY TRANSACTIONS   **503**
31. Bailment Basics and Documents of Title   507
32. "Payment Against Documents"   529

Table of UCC Sections   *551*
Index   *555*

Preface for All Students

I start with a simple assumption. You come to this book because for one reason or another you want to learn the basic law relating to the sale and lease of goods under Articles 2 and 2A of the Uniform Commercial Code, or at least some significant portion of this material. You may be trying to pick this up on your own. More likely you are in a course — either the first year Contracts course or an offering in the upper level commercial law curriculum — and you're looking for something to help you review or, possibly, to help you make sense of what's going on in that course. I hope this book is of help. If it is, it will not be simply because you bought the book (although I do appreciate that) but because you will have put your own energy into it. This is not a review text. Rather it is a kind of workbook, giving you an organized way of *working through* the various sections, definitions, concepts, and controversies that make up the modern law of sale and lease of goods. I have done my bit; now it's your turn to do yours.

This leads me to a second assumption. I take it for granted that anyone studying this material owns his or her own copy of the Uniform Commercial Code (including the Official Comments), that it is a current version of the Code, and furthermore that you will have it at your side whenever you're working in this book. If you don't have a copy, run out and get one now. It is indispensable. There will be times when I actually quote passages from the Code or the Comments, but often enough I'll just point you to some section or a particular bit of language (e.g., "Look at §2-606(2) again" or "Check out the last sentence in Comment 5") and expect that you can and will find it in your own personal codebook. I anticipate, in fact, that you will not resist the urge to mark up your own copy of Articles 2 and 2A as you go along — highlighting certain words, cross-referencing to other sections, putting your own comments in the margins. In my opinion this is one temptation that you should definitely surrender to. The purpose behind this book is to help you study an important part of the Uniform Commercial Code. This book should be of assistance, but remember you are studying the Code, not this book.

I have tried to include just about any topic that might be covered in a separate course on Sales and Leases or in the equivalent portion of a longer survey course on Commercial Law or Commercial Transactions. The overall result is probably more than most people will need and may initially be more daunting than intended. Don't feel that you have to work through every chapter, nor even that you necessarily should take them up in the order in which they appear. If you are currently enrolled in a course, you should be able to pretty much pick and choose the chapters here to follow the outlines of that course.

Most readers will want to start out with Chapter 1 on the Scope of Article 2, if for no other reason than that this sets the stage for all that follows and also gets you acquainted with how the book is put together. The first time you run across the *lease* of goods (either in your classroom work or in this book) you'll want to take time to work on Chapter 2. Similarly, you should call on Chapter 3 when you first run across an example of the special treatment reserved for parties designated as *merchants* under Article 2. Other than that, you are pretty much on your own. If your course starts out with the Statute of Frauds, you could go directly to Chapter 6 without experiencing any terrible sense of loss for having skipped the previous chapters. If instead you are first studying the law relating to warranties, feel free to go directly to Part II, reading first the introduction to that part and then plunging into either Chapter 11 (if you are covering the warranty of title first) or Chapter 12 (if you are going directly into warranties of quality).

Where I have had to refer to a topic covered earlier in the book, or to be covered later, I have tried to give you clear signals about where you can find this coverage if you do want to check it out right away. Otherwise, you at least know that this is something that is not being focused on for the moment. Although this has made for a lot of sentences starting something like, "As we saw in Chapter 17 . . ." or "Assuming there is no right to cure (on which see Chapter 19) . . . ," it will, I hope, make it easier for you to work through the book as it best suits your needs. Note also that the book is indexed at the back not only by topic but by UCC section number.

Once you do get to a chapter and commit yourself to working it through, it should not be hard to scope out the general lay of the land. With only a couple of exceptions each chapter is structured in the same way: an introductory text, a set of Examples, followed finally by my own analysis (Explanations) of the questions raised in the Examples. It is very important that you realize from the outset that the introductory text does *not* purport to outline or give a full account of the chapter's topic. This is *not* the type of book where you will be given all of the law up front and then asked to apply those rules and principles in the questions that follow. In some chapters the introduction can be very brief. In others it goes on for a while. But in any event the introductory text is meant to set the stage; its purpose is to put you in the best possible posture for learning *through the questions.* (If anything, I have tended to deal with issues or problems in the introductory text that may not be of the first order of importance and that can then be put to one side, freeing us to better focus on the real meaty stuff in the Examples and Explanations.) In other words, if you aren't prepared to go through the Examples thoroughly on your own — if not writing down a carefully constructed answer to each question then at least jotting down an idea or two on how you see the situation and how you expect the Code would deal with it — there's really not much point in your starting any given chapter to begin with.

One final note on the Examples: It will not surprise you if when you get to my analysis you find I cannot offer a simple yes or no in many cases. I am a law professor, after all, and this subject, like all you've studied, has its indeterminate moments, longstanding controversies, and "subtle" difficulties. On the other hand, don't think just because this is the study of law that the answer to even the simplest question must necessarily be open to argument or subject to divergent analyses. Sometimes a question can and should be answered in a word or two, directly and without any hedging. If the answer is "Yes," you should say "Yes." If "No," say "No." Beyond that, of course, you should say *why* — citing the Code chapter and verse — you respond as you do. I always give my students in Commercial Transactions some rules of thumb to follow in writing their examination answers, which also make sense when studying this material.

1. Where an answer is given or suggested by a specific section, make reference to that section.
2. Where a specific subsection is relevant, cite the subsection.
3. Where a particular word or phrase in the section or subsection is of importance to your answer, say exactly what that word or phrase is.
4. Where a Comment answers — or seems to answer — the question, refer to it, reporting as you do whether you have any qualms or questions about the position taken in that Comment.
5. Where the answer appears to be dictated by a single fact or a set of facts, make clear what facts those are.

If, as will sometimes be the case, the answer has to be a "that depends," say *on what* you see the outcome depending. If you need to know other facts to better analyze the situation, say *whom* would you ask and *what* would you want to know. If the answer seems to depend on how a court would interpret a particular provision or how it would resolve a potential dispute between two provisions, what are the various possible interpretations or resolutions? What argues for one resolution over the other?

As I have said, I hope and expect this book will be helpful. If at the same time you find it stimulating and even mildly entertaining, then so much the better.

James Brook

May 1994

Preface for Contracts Students

As you have undoubtedly already discovered, law professors are a notoriously diverse group, at least when it comes to what topics to cover in any given course, in what order, and in how much detail. At some schools the official curriculum may dictate for inclusion in the first-year Contracts course a fair amount of Article 2 material. In practice there's always the question — given all of the competing goals that the professor in a first-year course may have set his or her sights on achieving — of how fully this official agenda gets carried out. At other places the Curriculum Committee has given up any pretense of power and entrusted the decision to the individual professor. Similarly, if you look at the various Contracts casebooks there is no clear consensus among them as to exactly how much or how little of the modern law of sales under Article 2 is appropriate for the introductory course.

My advice to you at this stage is really the same thing I've suggested in the general preface, but it's worth repeating: If your professor assigns or recommends particular chapters in this book, use them as suggested and don't think you have to look at any or all of the others. If your instructor isn't keying his or her course to this book, once you've figured out what topic or what sections of Article 2 he or she is covering at any given moment, you should be able to pick out the chapters that are right for you fairly easily, using the table of contents or the indexes at the back. Other than starting out by giving Chapter 1 a thorough going-over, you should be able to dip into the book at just about any point.

I thought it might be helpful at the outset, however, if I reviewed some of the principal topics traditionally covered in Contracts and point to the chapters here that seem more likely to be of relevance to you as you move through that course. I presume, for example, that at some point you'll cover *offer and acceptance*. What would Contracts be without offer and acceptance? Once you've seen the basic common law treatment of those issues, you may find Chapter 4 helpful as it reviews the same stuff from the Article 2 perspective. Many Contracts teachers covering offer and acceptance take their classes all the way up to and through the horrifying spectacle of the *battle of the forms,* both as it was treated by the common law and as it is dealt with in §2-207. If this is your lot, continue on to Chapter 5.

Your professor may set aside a separate part of the course to deal with the *Statute of Frauds*. If he or she does, you might find Chapter 6 helpful. It does, however, go into the unique features of the Article 2 provision (§2-201), which differs in many respects from the traditional common law approach, and you may find it unnecessarily distracting to get into all of the intricacies of that Code section and that chapter unless your instructor has suggested you do so or focused on §2-201 explicitly.

The Article 2 provision covering the *parol evidence rule* (§2-202) does carry forward the basic features of the common law rule (if rule it be), so Chapter 8 should be of help to most everyone. You should also check out the previous chapter on the Code's treatment of the various trade terms. Your Contracts teacher will most likely be making vague references to the importance of *custom* and *trade usage* throughout your study, and while these common law concepts are not identical to the Code scheme, the underlying ideas are very much the same. Working through Chapter 7 may give you a much deeper appreciation of how these ideas actually come into play in the legal context, more than your professor may have time for in the rush of the first-year course.

You'll probably hear mention of the doctrine or notion of *unconscionability* sometime this year. You may find Chapter 9's textual treatment of that concept and of §2-302 helpful, to the extent that anyone or anything can be helpful on that subject.

Contracts courses vary widely as to whether and to what extent they cover *warranty law.* If your course does get into warranties, it will probably be enough for you to read the introduction to Part II followed by Chapters 12 and 13. (The Contracts course would rarely if ever deal with the *warranty of title,* so you can skip Chapter 11 unless told otherwise. The later chapters in Part II deal with subjects usually reserved for upper-level courses.)

The material covered in Part III is by and large unlikely to be dealt with in a typical Contracts course with only a few exceptions. Chapter 17 takes on the traditional *perfect tender rule of performance* in the law of sales. Contracts teachers sometimes have the time and energy to contrast this with Article 2's treatment of *installment sales,* which you'll find in Chapter 22. Similarly, if your teacher has made room for the Code provision on *cure* (§2-508), you'll find it in Chapter 19.

Over the past few years there has been a movement in the teaching of Contracts to put greater emphasis on the *remedies* available upon breach, and in fact some casebooks come close to structuring the whole course around this one aspect of the material. One way or another, many casebooks do go into some detail on the Article 2 remedies provisions. It's very likely that you'll make use of either Chapter 28 on Seller's Remedies or Chapter 29 on Buyer's Remedies or both. There's no particular reason why one came before the other in this book. Feel free to take these in whichever order fits in best with the material as you cover it in your coursework.

And when you're done with Contracts? Hold onto the book. Play your cards right, pick your courses well, and you should have use for it again in the years to come.

James Brook

May 1994

Acknowledgments

I would like to thank Deans Jim Simon and Harry Wellington and Associate Dean Ellen Ryerson, who have shown their support for this project in a variety of ways. Thanks as well to my colleagues on the faculty at New York Law School and to the vast numbers of students at that school who have given me the opportunity to practice my teaching methods (and madness) on them over the years. The feedback that I've been given on my classroom work as well as on various parts of these materials, in ways subtle and not so subtle, has been of enormous help even if I have not always recognized it at the time.

There is no question that this book would never have been brought to any kind of conclusion without the enthusiastic support and encouragement of any number of good people at Little, Brown and Company. I would particularly like to thank Rick Heuser, Carol McGeehan, Betsy Kenny, and Bob Caceres. I also have to single out for special mention Joe Glannon, who was a friend long before either of us even dreamt of going to law school much less making a career out of teaching law. His initial work on the Examples and Explanation series was the genesis for all that followed, including this effort.

Portions of the Official Text and Comments of the Uniform Commercial Code reproduced and quoted herein are copyright © 1990 by The American Law Institute and the National Conference of Commissioners on Uniform State Laws and are reprinted with the permission of the Permanent Editorial Board for the Uniform Commercial Code.

Introduction

A Very Brief History of the Common Law of Sales

People have been buying and selling stuff for a long time. The law governing this particular aspect of human functioning likewise has a long history. For our purposes, we pick up the story of the law of sales in medieval England. By the 1300s and 1400s, the system of common law courts acting in the name of the King had already taken shape and their far-reaching powers recognized. Disputes arising between people buying and selling stuff (parties to contracts for the sales of goods), however, would for the most part not have found their way into this national court system. Such disputes were the province of a separate set, or really a set of sets, of more narrowly focused courts operating at the local level. Such courts were usually to be found in one of the principal market towns or occurring in conjunction with the regional trading fairs that were held on a regular basis. They became the specialists in dealing with disagreements between merchants, applying a set of rules that came to be thought of as a coherent body of rules comprising the *law merchant* or *mercantile law.*

It was only later, during the seventeenth century, that the national network of common law courts began for reasons of its own to expand its competence and jurisdiction to encompass purely commercial disputes. Eventually "the common law of sales," which often but not always adopted the reasoning and results of the mercantile law, replaced that older system. The mercantile courts died out. The common law, as you have probably seen in other contexts, reached out to take within its fold yet another collection of cases and eventually to hold the monopoly on those as well.

So what we would think of as the common law of sales is a relatively new phenomenon. It was only in the middle of the 1800s that there appeared the first general treatises attempting to set out a systemized view of the common law as it related to the purchase and sales of goods. At the same time, however, one of the grandest features of the common law — its very commonality, the supposed uniformity and predictability that it offered to the country as a whole—was being sorely tested in the United States of America, which is after all one big patchwork quilt of common law jurisdictions. No doubt each of the states (with the notable exception of Louisiana, whose legal system was and still is beholden to the French civil law tradition) applied the common law of sales to purchase and sale transactions. Similarly, each state applied common law principles to other areas of commercial life. The problem was that as each state's common law in a given commercial field was advanced, refined, and further explicated by a steady stream of decisions (which is after all what the common law is all about), it was perhaps inevitable that there would be a growing disparity among the common law of the several states. Add to this the decision of the Supreme Court in *Swift v. Tyson*, 41 U.S. 1 (1842), that cases tried in federal courts based on diversity jurisdiction were to be decided not under the common law of any one state but on "general principles and doctrines of commercial jurisprudence." So in the United States lawyers (and, not incidentally, ordinary folks going about their daily commercial business) had to be acquainted with, or at least acknowledge that they were subject to, what had to be thought of as a federal common law along with the various compendia of common law in each of the several states.* So very, very much common law; so little time.

The Uniform Law Movement and the Uniform Commercial Code

In many fields of law the steadily increasing divergence, both stylistic and substantive, among the common law of the several states was troubling, and not just in a theoretical sense: It made life difficult. The whole arena of commercial endeavor felt this lack of uniformity and predictability most keenly. As more and more individuals and firms reached out to make contacts and do business in places farther and farther from their home base, it became increasingly apparent that the lack of uniformity of basic commercial law was more than just a minor nuisance. Throughout the nineteenth century pressure was building for change and some way out of this predicament.

One response was the origination and advancement of what is referred to as the "uniform law movement," which also tapped into the growing sentiment in favor of codification or statutory treatment of difficult areas of law. At the end of the last century a group was formed that still goes by the name the "National Conference of Commissioners on Uniform Laws," or more succinctly, the "Uniform Law Commissioners." The Uniform Law Commission, a kind of quasi-governmental group, is made up of representatives of each of the states. These representatives are chosen by different methods in each of the states but usually by the governor acting alone or with the state legislature. Each state casts a single vote as decisions are made within the Commission. *The Commission itself can make no law.* Its role is to investigate, argue over, and eventually adopt

---

*The doctrine of *Swift v. Tyson* was to be overturned in *Erie Railroad Co. v. Tompkins*, 304 U.S. 64 (1932), of course. But no one could have known that at the time. Nor would that have done anything about the problem of the differences in common law cutting across the states.

recommended legislation — the "Official Versions" of its recommended Uniform Acts — which are then sent out to the several states. The fate of any of the Uniform Acts is up to the legislative process in each of the states (and in Congress in its role as the legislative body for the District of Columbia). The idea is that if each and every one of the states adopts the suggested legislation, and adopts it in exactly the same form, then blessed uniformity can be achieved. You, I, and everyone else will have no trouble knowing the applicable rules of law in each of the many jurisdictions since we will have the comfort of working with the identical statutory law no matter where a problem arises or which state's law is to apply.

The earliest of the Uniform Acts proposed in the commercial field was the Negotiable Instruments Law of 1896. The N.I.L., which covered the law of bills and notes, was a big hit. By 1924 it had been adopted in all of the states. The Uniform Sales Act, drafted for the Uniform Law Commissioners by the eminent authority Professor Samuel Williston of Harvard, was promulgated in 1906 and later amended in 1922. This Act found wide but by no means unanimous acceptance, and was eventually adopted in more than 30 states. Several other uniform acts covering other commercial areas were introduced during the early part of the twentieth century with varying success.

By the late 1930s and into the 1940s the feeling began to grow in many quarters that the Uniform Sales Act as well as other of the uniform commercial acts was in need of revision and updating. The American Law Institute, whose work on the numerous Restatements you are no doubt familiar with, got into the act as a cosponsor along with the Uniform Law Commission of the revision efforts.* By 1942 it was determined that the goal would be a single Uniform Commercial Code bringing together in substantially revised form a number of the previous uniform acts as well as including some new topics. The noted Professor Karl Llewellyn of Columbia University was appointed Chief Reporter (a kind of editor-in-chief) for the project. He in turn named a series of bright lights to serve as principal drafters of the various articles contemplated. The principal drafter of both Article 1 (General Provisions) and Article 2 (Sales), the two parts of the original Code with which we will be most interested in this book, was Karl Llewellyn himself. The UCC has been referred to (sometimes with reverence, sometimes not) as "Karl's Kode" as a reflection of the immense influence he had during its preparation and over the form it eventually took. Nowhere is this more true than in Article 2's treatment of Sales.

The history of the drafting and redrafting, the politicking, namecalling,

---

*The ALI is, as you are undoubtedly aware, a completely nongovernmental entity. It is in essence a totally self-appointed and self-perpetuating body of legal bigwigs whose work gains respect through the power of reputation, by aggressive marketing, and, to be fair, as it reflects the considerable degree of expertise and massive amounts of work put into each project by that body.

and eventual compromises that led up to the Code in its final form is a story unto itself.* By 1957 the process had come up with an Official Version that was approved by both of the sponsoring agencies (the "1957 Official Text"). Minor changes responding to concerns raised in various states as the Code's adoption was being considered all over the country resulted in another Official Text in 1958 and yet another in 1962. The version that we think of as the first real text of the Uniform Commercial Code as generally adopted was the 1962 Official Text. By 1968, the Code basically in this form had been enacted in 49 states, the District of Columbia, and the Virgin Islands. Guam came aboard in 1977.†

And all to what purpose? See §1-102(2) in which the drafters‡ laid out the underlying purposes and policies of the Code:

(a) to simplify, clarify, and modernize the law governing commercial transactions;
(b) to permit the continued expansion of commercial practices through custom, usage, and agreement of the parties;
(c) to make uniform the law among the various jurisdictions.

As you go through these materials you will be able to form your own opinions as to how well the drafters met the first two of these goals. The degree to which the third goal of uniformity was met by the project should be easier to judge. As we have said, by the late 1960s virtually all of the states and the other relevant jurisdictions had passed the Uniform Commercial Code in more or less the same form.

Nonuniform Amendments

The "more or less" with which I ended the preceding section was necessary because even from the very beginning legislators in many of the states seemed to think it appropriate actually to have a hand in picking the exact content and the precise wording of the legislation that they were adopting. You know how legislators can be, and this was true even in the face of what was being handed to them on a silver platter by the ULC and the ALI as the latest word on commercial law. Each of the

---

*For those interested in reading about the history and development of the Uniform Commercial Code in more detail, albeit in a fairly tamed-down version, your copy of the Code itself probably has at the beginning the *General Comment of National Conference of Commissioners on Uniform State Laws and The American Law Institute,* issued in conjunction with the 1962 Official Version, to which you may refer. If nothing else, you've got to be impressed with the number of people involved.

†Louisiana is the only state not to have adopted the Code in all its parts, as you might expect given its civil law orientation. That state adopted Articles 1, 3, 4, 5, 7, and 8 substantially in the official form in the 1970s. Article 9 was adopted in 1989. It has not adopted Article 2 on Sales.

‡There is a tradition of referring to the sum total of all the people who worked on the project as "the drafters."

states (always excepting Louisiana, of course) adopted the Code pretty much as the sponsoring agencies had approved it in the final 1962 Official Text, but large numbers of so-called nonuniform amendments began to crop up in various state versions.

For the most part, these state nonuniform amendments probably did not and do not greatly affect the basic working of the Code as we will see it. They were thought appropriate in the given state to conform the language of the Code to traditional usage or other local statutes. In some cases, however, the changes wrought by a given state's legislature had a more substantive effect. You will always have to be on the lookout for nonuniform amendments in any jurisdiction in which you operate or whose law you are sent to research. In this book, as in the other materials that are typically used to study the Uniform Commercial Code, you are asked to focus on the Official Text as prepared by the drafters and adopted by the sponsoring bodies — what I sometimes think of as the "vanilla" or the "off-the-rack" version of the Code. But nobody anywhere is subject to the Official Text just because the drafters drafted it as they did, and no transaction is governed by that Text in that exact form. The Uniform Commercial Code is the law of the land, or rather the law of a state, because it was adopted as a part of the *statutory law* of that state. Its legal effect is to be determined from the language as it was enacted *in that particular state.*

Still, to look once again on the positive side, the work of the drafters was by and large accepted right across the board by the late 1960s. A blessed uniformity had blanketed the land. It even stayed that way for a few years.

Ongoing Revision

In 1961 the sponsoring agencies appointed a Permanent Editorial Board, the purpose of which was to monitor the adoption process, do what it could to keep nonuniform amendments to a minimum, and suggest changes in the overall scheme as the need arose. For the first decade of its existence, there was no substantial change in the UCC, and only a bit of very minor tinkering in 1962 and 1966. The 1962 Official Text remained basically intact. It consisted of Article 1 containing General Provisions applicable to all the other articles, the eight following articles (2 through 9) each of which dealt with a single area of commercial law, and a couple of concluding articles dealing with the effective date and so on. (This would be a good time to look at the table of contents in the codebook you are using and to acquaint yourself with the basic outline. If you are using the most up-to-date version the table will refer to the "1990 Official" text.)

Change came, however, as various articles were studied and found wanting in some respect, and proposed revisions were promulgated by the sponsoring agencies. In 1972, a new Official Text was adopted, which made substantial revisions to Article 9. These revisions would not automatically become law in any jurisdiction, of course. Each state was going to have to debate, consider, and eventually conclude legislative action. As we all know, the process of legislation at the state level is often excruciatingly slow and painful. By 1988 almost all of the states had adopted the 1972 revisions. Three states — Missouri, South Carolina, and Vermont — were still stuck in time with the 1962 version of the Code. Missouri and South Carolina were eventually goaded into action. As of this writing Vermont has yet to take the first step in updating.

A similar process resulted in a series of revised versions in 1978 (making changes in Article 8), 1987 (adding Article 2A),* 1988 (recommending revision or repeal of 6), 1989 (adding 4A), and 1990 (primarily revising Article 3 but also affecting Article 4). Some of these revisions have been quickly taken up by almost all of the states. The new Article 4A has been particularly popular. Others have been slower to catch on and for all we know may never get universal acceptance. The upshot is that as we look around the country (and into the Virgin Islands and Guam) the UCC of the 1990s is just not as uniform as we might wish it to be. You'll have to check into any state in which you have a particular interest to see exactly what version is in operation at this time, which revisions have been passed in that state, which have been considered and rejected, and which are languishing somewhere in the legislative process. And, of course, you'll have to be on the lookout for nonuniform amendments.

Fortunately, for the purposes of this volume, the various revisions and the possibility of nonuniform amendment will pose less of a burden than when you study other topics of commercial law. We will be concerned primarily with the workings of Article 2, and that article is one of the few that has never (or I should say not yet) been subjected to the revision process. Also, in the initial round of adoptions in the 1950s and 1960s, the states went relatively lightly on this article, making fewer nonuniform amendments than they did to other pieces of the overall package. So to a large extent we can place any concern about official uniform revision and piece-by-piece nonuniform amendment off to one side.

It's only fair to warn you, however, that for students of Article 2 the specter of change is lurking somewhere just beyond the horizon. During the last decade the sponsoring agencies commissioned a study committee, the conclusion of which was that Article 2 was in need of revision. As you read these words a drafting committee is hard at work considering what changes are to be recommended. It will be interesting to see what comes of this process. It may be only revision or clarification of some particularly troubling bits and pieces of Article 2 language — just the kinds of things you'll see as you work through the following chapters — or it could be a wholesale revision and rethinking that goes to the underlying structure of how the article looks on the page if not how it operates on

---

*Even before it could get off the ground Article 2A had to be later amended in 1990, and it still has been adopted in only about 40 of the states. We will look at 2A and its history in much more detail beginning in Chapter 2.

a daily basis. Only time, and the incessant in-fighting of all the various
interest groups and professional know-it-alls concerned with such things,
will tell. And these things do tend to take a number of years. For the
moment — unless you're holding an awfully old copy of this book, in
which case I'd suggest you see whether a later edition is available — it's
fairly safe to assume that you are still living in the comparatively placid
time of the 1962 Official Version, at least as far as Article 2 is concerned.

Working with the Code — The Text

Part of the purpose of this book, in addition to helping you learn the
basic elements of Article 2 and Article 2A law, is to assist you in familiariz-
ing yourself with the Uniform Commercial Code, with how it is laid out,
and with how it is used in the legal process to resolve disputes between
parties. Some authors use the fancy phrase "Code Methodology" to refer
to the tools, strategies, and the overall stylistics of how lawyers handle
situations arising under and to be settled by the Code's set of rules. Even
if I don't stress the phrase, I have no doubt that there is great value in
the underlying idea. Students have to get used to the notion of working
with the Code as a particular kind of task, similar in many respects but
in other ways quite different from what they have done before.*

From the very beginning of your legal studies you were doubtlessly
immersed in the methodology of common law decisionmaking. The
sources to which you looked to answer questions — the grist for the mill,
so to speak — were the accumulated prior cases that might be relevant
to the issue you had before you. No one of the cases necessarily stated
word for word what "the law" was on a given point. Even if a case did
seem to lay out in a nice neat sentence or two what was to be understood
as the law of the jurisdiction from that point forward, you had to learn
to be careful: The result of any case was what that case actually *did*, not
what it *said*, no matter how forcefully it said it. The techniques you learned
as you progressed in your appreciation of "common law methodology," in
addition to the research techniques helpful to ferreting out the better
cases, were those of careful case analysis, characterization of holdings and
of dictum, distinguishing cases, and arguing from analogy. All that kind
of thing was what was needed to work with case-made law.

I hope that you have had an introduction before this point to the
general techniques of working with statutory law. I hope this for your
own sake, quite apart from what we must do here, although the relevance
of this "statutory methodology" should be clear. We live, it has been
said, in an age of statutes. If you have had a chance to work on the

---

*It all depends, of course, on what you have done before. If you come to this book
having already done extensive study in one of the other Code areas, you can feel free
to skip this and the remaining sections of the Introduction. Of course, there's nothing
wrong with a little review and brushing-up on what you have studied before.

tasks of lawyering under a statutory regime, undoubtedly your professor stressed time and time again the importance of reading and rereading the text, the statute itself. There's no other place to start. The text of a statute does not suggest what the law is, nor does it serve as evidence of what the law is: The law *is* what the text says it is. If the statute was duly passed and it says that such-and-such is to be the result, then such-and-such it is.

The only problems emerge when the text of the statute is less than 100 percent clear.* How are we to deal with a portion of a statute whose wording is ambiguous or vague and, if the matter is to be of more than academic interest, where the different possible readings of the text in question would lead to different outcomes for the case at hand? The first stop in our quest must always be to look for clues to a proper reading in the text of the statute, in our case the UCC, itself. Words are to be read not abstractly or for their "dictionary definition" but as they occur in context as part of the overall statutory scheme. Beyond this, you should be aware of the other sections of the Code — parts of the text itself — that can be of enormous help in interpretation and to which we will often turn. On the most mundane level, §1-102(4) specifically provides that "words of the masculine gender include the feminine and the neuter," and so on.†

Of great help in understanding and interpreting the Code as you move through it will be the many statutory definitions scattered throughout the text. You should get used to referring to the Definitional Cross Reference, which comes at the tail end of the Comments to each section for leads in finding these definitions. We will repeatedly refer to one or another of the definitions in §1-201, which are part of the general provisions and applicable to all sections in the Code wherever located. In addition we will have to take account of some special definitions placed in Article 2, such as the definition of *merchant* in §2-104 or of *commercial unit* in §2-105(6), which are applicable to the provisions of that article only. In looking for reliable guides to interpretation of a statute, nothing can substitute for the careful reading of the text of that statute — read it over and over if that is necessary. The definitions in the UCC are not just interesting marginalia: They count as full-fledged textual material.

---

*We're not concerned here with those unusual cases when someone thinks it worth his or her while to challenge the operation of the statute on constitutional grounds. Any argument or decision along these lines would, in any event, not be carried out as a matter of statutory method, but at the different (I won't say higher) plane of constitutional method. No one, as far as I am aware, has ever thought of challenging the overall plan of the UCC on federal or state constitutional grounds. We can leave that be.

†In recent times the Uniform Law Commissioners have abandoned the practice of using the masculine pronoun to refer to the whole world. As a matter of interest, you may want to contrast the language in the pre-revision §3-117 (if your copy of the Code comes complete, as many do, with an Appendix containing the "Pre-Revision" version of Article 3) with the present (1990 Official Text) §3-110(c)(2).

On a more global level, a general maxim of statutory construction would have it that any ambiguity or vagary is to be resolved with reference to "the intention of the legislature." This intention, it is generally believed, is to be understood not only from the exact words chosen for the final outcome but by what we can decipher about the overall purposes and considerations of policy the legislators must have had in mind at the time of adoption. All of this serves as a sort of backdrop to the whole legislative mission and is supposed to inform our understanding of the ultimate result.

In working with the Code, this approach poses an interesting problem. To be perfectly correct, the legislators in question are in any individual instance the members of one particular state legislature operating at the precise moment of adoption. And yet unlike in the more typical state statutory situation, we cannot ignore the fact that neither the overall legislative scheme or the exact language that was enacted into law originated with this body. The drafting work was done by some collection of individuals whom we tend to refer to (loosely to be sure) as "the drafters." The drafters' work was adopted in each of the states in substantially the same form precisely because the legislators of that state wanted to cede if not some power at least some of the work to the national sponsoring organizations, the Uniform Law Commissioners and the American Law Institute. If there is one thing we can say with confidence about "the intention of the legislature" in any one state in adopting the UCC, it is that it was to adopt a response to the myriad problems of commercial law that would be *uniform* with that of the other states. Like it or not, we tend in discussing the Code to refer to "the intent of the drafters" when trying to ferret out the deeper or more elusive meanings of the sections as we come to them.

We gain some insight into the drafters' state of mind by looking at a bit of the statutory language that they proposed and that has been adopted in every jurisdiction pretty much unscathed. Section 1-102(1) carries the injunction that, "This Act shall be liberally construed and applied to promote its underlying purposes and policies." What are those purposes and policies, you ask. Look no further than subsection (2), which was quoted earlier in this Introduction and which you should now consult again. The language there, which you will encounter more than once in your studies, may seem very bland and unhelpful. The courts have, however, on more than one occasion cited and quoted just this section, along with the even more nebulous §1-106, in making a tough interpretative call.* The text of the Code is, as we will see again and

---

*I have always thought that the unexplained and apparently unexamined use of the word "liberally" in §§1-102 and 1-106 speaks as much about the period in which the principal drafting of the UCC took place (remember the 1950s?) as anything else. Note also that in their wording of §1-102(2)(a) the drafters have asked us to assume, as they apparently did, that we know what it is to "modernize" the law and furthermore that such modernization is unquestionably for the better. In retrospect it certainly was a simpler time to be living in.

again, very rich in material of all sorts to which we will have to refer as the first line of inquiry consistent with sound "Code Methodology."

Legislative History and the Comments

If even the most careful reading of the text of a statute does not lead to an unequivocal answer on a matter of interpretation, where are we then to turn? Traditional doctrine, at least in the United States, has been that the vast bulk of material collectively referred to as "legislative history" may appropriately be consulted for deeper and truer understanding of what the legislature at least *thought* it was up to.* Again, this creates some special problems in the case of the Uniform Commercial Code. The Code worked its way through the legislative process in each and every one of the jurisdictions that adopted it. Apparently in half of the states there are at least some documents that would count as traditional legislative history for that particular jurisdiction. But the process of adoption was much more complicated than this. Academics looking in greater depth at intricate Code matters have had some measure of success (and arguably justified their existence) by looking at just about any kind of paper generated during the uniform law drafting process: the many drafts that were produced at various stages, reports, the transcripts of hearings held on the Code in various places (most notably the lengthy and crucial hearings before the New York State Law Revision Commission), letters from one important personage to another, and so on. We will make little use of this type of material in this book, but you should be aware that it's out there. As a practical matter, should you later be researching a difficult point, you will probably be led to this type of material by looking for and carefully poring over law review articles on point. (And you will implicitly be justifying the existence of legal academics, thank you very much.)

In this book itself we will pay more attention to the "Official Comments," which you should find in your copy of the Code following each section.† These Comments have an interesting genesis. The earlier Uniform Laws came with no lush commentary; there was little besides the text itself on which anyone could rely. The Uniform Sales Act in particular, adopted in 1941, came in a barebones version, Comment-free. One consequence was that courts called upon to interpret ambiguous

---

*As you may be aware, the use of legislative history as a proper guide to statutory interpretation has not gone unquestioned either in Britain nor in this country. Please do not think that I am making light of these jurisprudential disputes if I put them to one side here. As far as the UCC is concerned, the real problem is deciding exactly *what* counts as "legislative history" in the first place in the uniform law context and then finding anything worthwhile wherever we may look.

†In several states you will also be able to find a separate set of "Official State X Comments" to at least some of the sections if you are following along in the appropriate volume of that state's statutes. We'll stick to the Official Comments adopted by the drafters of the off-the-rack Official Uniform Texts.

provisions of the Uniform Sales Act were very ready, for better or for worse, to look outside the Act entirely for help. One place they looked consistently was to the already influential treatise on Sales law prepared, and not coincidentally revised in the late 1940s, by Professor Samuel Williston. Since Williston was also the principal drafter of the Uniform Sales Act, this seemed to make perfect sense. The upshot was, however, that it also made one private individual practically the sole guru on what should or should not be taken as the "intention of the drafters" of the Sales Act. The later drafters of the UCC resolved to prevent the same thing from happening again. So we have the "Official Comments," which are meant to be something less than statutory text (of this there can be no question, in many instances the states adopted parts of the Code before the Comments were even available) and yet something more than the persuasive authority of any one treatise writer, no matter how well respected or highly connected.*

That being said, it has to be admitted that there is no one right way to treat the Comments to the UCC nor one clear path to divining their significance. For one thing, the degree of specificity of the Comments (and some would say their quality) varies greatly, from article to article and from section to section. Much, probably the vast majority, of what is said in the Comments is not even mildly controversial. We will read this material as a helpful guide to the various sections without any fear of being misled or unduly influenced. Most Comments are just, well, useful comments. In some instances, however, for one reason or another what is said by a particular Comment may go well beyond what can be justified by the text of the statute itself. In such a case we have to step back. The reading of the statute given in the Comment *may* be an appropriate one, but a careful analysis will have to take into account more than the reassuring tone of the anonymous individual or cadre of people who drafted the "official" commentary.

The last word on the Comments is the simplest. They are there. Lawyers refer to them, as well they should. Courts refer to them and quote them regularly. To ignore the Comments would be foolish. Still, we must always remember that the Official Comments do not make law, however interesting and appealing they may be. The Code—the text as adopted—is the law. All else, as the saying goes, truly is commentary.

Other Sources

This book is meant to offer a pretty much self-contained adventure. Other than a copy of the Code, which you are expected to have ever-ready at your side, you may not feel the need to go beyond the bounds of what you have here and what you have been assigned in any course you're

---

*For a very good recent round-up of everything you'd want to know about the Comments and then some, see Note: The Jurisprudence and Judicial Treatment of the Comments to the Uniform Commercial Code, 75 Cornell L. Rev. 962 (1990).

taking. If that's so, fine. There is no reason, however, why you might not want to see even more, why you may not be interested in looking at the same material from yet one more viewpoint or in greater detail. That's fine too. Also, as you may in later life be called upon to do further research on a particular topic, it's only fitting that you should be aware from the outset of some of the other major works that lawyers engaged in commercial law practice regularly refer to and rely upon. Even if you work through every chapter in this volume, you won't know *everything* there is to know about Articles 2 and 2A. One measure of your success in mastering what you have here and your general level of comfort with the law of sales and leases of goods is how prepared you are at the end of the day to admit when you don't know enough about a particular provision or situation and have some idea of where to look for more help.

Without any doubt the most influential and most often cited treatise in this area is that written by Professors James J. White and Robert S. Summers, which goes boldly under the title *Uniform Commercial Code* (3d ed. 1988). Beyond being big and bulky, it's clearly and convincingly written. Not the least of its charms (and I may be the first to use that adjective in connection with this work) is that the authors are open about their disagreements over some of the more arcane points, so that you get both sides of the issue and beyond that can appreciate the fact that well-informed respectable opinion may differ on some very fundamental matters. The White and Summers book is not organized directly by Code section, which in some instances may cause you trouble but overall shouldn't be a difficulty, and you can usually find in the footnotes a good citation or two that will serve as a starting point for further research.

A second treatise, which *is* organized by section and which is updated on a very regular basis, is that by Professor William D. Hawkland. This is found as Volumes 1 through 3 of the Uniform Commercial Code Series published by Clark Boardman Callaghan. Hawkland is one of the major commercial code authorities of the past decades, and his comments necessarily carry the ring of authority. Again, footnotes supply a way into the cases.

If you'd like to see a different treatment, I suggest you check out Professor Thomas Quinn's *Uniform Commercial Code Commentary & Digest* (2d ed. 1991), published by Warren, Gorham & Lamont. This work comes in two volumes along with periodic updates and is organized by Code sections. Here, the cases take center stage. Some have been chosen for their importance and some I suspect just for the fun of it. Quinn has some textual treatment of most sections, but its real worth is in the capsule versions of a good cross-section of cases, all of which is rendered in a most engaging style and with no doubt in most instances of what the author thinks of the results for good or ill. There are many places in the Code where the best way to get a handle on what is going on is to take in a number of examples, and my experience is that Quinn works particularly well in this regard.

Of course when you get right down to it, nothing beats looking at the full text of the cases themselves. So our bow to "other sources" necessarily ends with a reminder that the cases are out there and waiting to be read. Since the Code works as state statutory law, cases in this field will be scattered all over the place, in state reporters, the regional reporters, and in the federal reporters as well. Fortunately, early on one publishing company (Callaghan & Company, now merged into Clark Boardman Callaghan) saw that there was some money to be made in a reporter that brought all the cases on the UCC together in one place. It will be well worth your while to find whether whatever library you usually work in has and keeps current the set of blue-bound books called the Uniform Commercial Code Reporting Service. The editors of this service do a good job of finding and reproducing just about any case that comes down the pike that is relevant to the Code.* In addition, there are indexes for each volume and for the series overall as well as handy tables setting forth the status of revision adoptions and local variations from the Official Text for each of the states. If you can get your hands on this set of reports, or a table near where they are kept, it will save a lot of time and energy tearing around the library.

But enough of history, method, and a bevy of other sources. Enough of introduction. I suggest you turn now to the beginning of Chapter 1. Take out your copy of the Uniform Commercial Code. Article 2 awaits you.

---

*In this book I cite to this reporter service with a simple "U.C.C." or "U.C.C.2d." This may not be standard Bluebook form, but it should be clear enough and it does save a lot of typing.

SALES AND LEASES

Examples and Explanations

PART ONE

Transactions Governed by Articles 2 and 2A, Formation, and Basic Terms

1

The Scope of Article 2

By Way of Introduction

Let's start at the very beginning. Look at §2-101. Nothing startling there. For something meatier, move on to §2-102. Necessarily this section is of prime importance. If there is a reason for studying Article 2 of the Uniform Commercial Code—and as a user of this book you had better believe there is—it is because Article 2 is the *source of law* covering a large number of claims and controversies. Section 2-102 is the obvious starting point for our discussion because it states which situations are governed by the law as laid down in Article 2. If a situation is not "within the scope" of that Article (and furthermore is not within the scope of Article 2A, the subject of the next chapter), there is no reason to panic: There *is*, however, reason to buy another book, or at least reason to acknowledge that a book on the law pertaining to Sales and Leases of Goods isn't going to give you the help you seek. If it's situations governed by either Article 2 or Article 2A you're interested in, you've come to the right place.

Of course parties to actual controversies are interested in the proper scope of these Articles not simply to guide them in their bookbuying habits. They care because it can be vitally important which body of law governs their individual situation. If neither 2 nor 2A governs, there should be some perfectly good law out there waiting to be applied to the dispute. It may be found in some other part of the Uniform Commercial Code, in some other statute entirely, or in principles of common law. Reference to the appropriate rule may or may not generate the same result as would the Sales and Leases articles of the UCC, but often enough the results under varying bodies of law will differ, and the success or failure of a party's case will ride on which rules apply. That's the way the law works.

This is obviously not the place to recite all of the particular results generated by Article 2 and how its workings differ from other possibly applicable legal regimens. That is, in effect, what this entire book is about. By way of introduction, however, and to offer some context for the issues of scope that this chapter will explore, a few examples may be helpful. First, there is the Statute of Limitations. If a dispute is governed by the law laid down in Article 2, then the applicable Statute of Limitations is found in §2-725. If the dispute is outside the scope of Article 2 then the applicable Statute is to be found, well, somewhere else. It may provide for a longer limitation period, or the period could be shorter. It is almost assuredly going to be different in at least some respect. Especially given the all-or-nothing consequences that attach to the application of the Statute of Limitations, it is not surprising that many cases in which the scope of Article 2 is made an issue have dealt with the problem of which Statute of Limitation governs.

A second important aspect of Article 2 for which many litigants find it important to fight is the wide range of warranty protection granted to buyers under §§2-312–2-315. The details of warranty law under Article 2 will take us a number of chapters to master (see Part II). Suffice it to say for the present that being allowed to proceed on a warranty theory can be very powerful for a claimant. For example, holding a seller liable on an Article 2 warranty will not require any showing of negligence or other bad behavior on that seller's part. Obviously, that fact alone can easily spell the difference between success and defeat for a plaintiff. For many an aggrieved individual the most important part of his or her case may be establishing the right to go by the name of "buyer" under Article 2 of the UCC and to assert the buyer's rights.

So What's the Scope?

Chapter 2 will delve into the scope and history of Article 2A. We'll leave that aside for the moment and focus in this chapter exclusively on the scope of Article 2 which, as we've seen, is set forth in §2-102. Look at that section again. Stripped of some language around the edges (we'll get back to it in time), the core of the section is the pronouncement that Article 2 applies to "transactions in goods." So transactions in goods it is. The problem is that the drafters of the Code nowhere define the word *transactions,* nor do they leave a clear trail on exactly what it covers. In fact it is fairly curious that they used the word here. Life would be easier if they had said in this section that Article 2 covers "sales in goods." There certainly is a good argument to be made that this is all they meant and that the transactions with which we must be concerned are exactly those which we would term *sales.** After all, we saw that §2-101 invited us to call Article 2 the "Sales" article. The Official Comment to that section informs us that the entire article is arranged "in terms of contract

---

*For the drafters' totally conventional definition of *sale,* see §2-106(1).

for sale and the various steps of its performance." As you will see as you move through its sections, Article 2 always refers to the parties under its sway as the "buyer" and the "seller."

So perhaps it is safe simply to conclude that Article 2 covers the sale of goods and move on from there. This understanding does at least eliminate some kinds of dealings in goods which everyone seems to agree are not covered by Article 2. One example is the *gift*. Suppose Susan makes a gift of a brand new Cadillac to one Peter—a true gift just because he is the kind of grand guy he is. Should some problem come up, whatever it is, Article 2 does not govern. Similarly, if Susan *lent* her car to Peter for a few days just to be nice, Article 2 would not come into play. For the legal principles governing their situation, they'd have to look to the law of bailment and particularly the rules pertaining to what is termed a *gratuitous bailment*.

Courts have, however, taken advantage of the vagaries of the term *transaction* to expand the reach of Article 2 beyond the conventional sale in some instances. In *Mieske v. Bartell Drug Co.*, 92 Wash. 2d 40, 593 P.2d 1308, 26 U.C.C. 262 (1979), for example, Mrs. Mieske was parting only temporarily with property that she would never in a million years have thought of selling: a collection of 32 reels of home movies that chronicled a long period of her family's life together, from their wedding right through their son's Little League games, not to mention the vacations in Mexico, Hawaii, and other places. Mrs. Mieske handed this treasure trove over to the camera department of her local store in order to have them spliced together into four large reels "for convenience of viewing." Her parting words were, "Don't lose these. They are my life." When they never returned from the processing lab, the Mieskes brought suit. "The best guess," the court concluded, "is that the plaintiffs' film went from [the] lab to the garbage dumpster to a truck to a barge to an up-Sound landfill where it may yet repose." In an attempt to limit the measure of its financial responsibility, the defendant attempted to rely on some exculpatory language on the receipt which had been handed to Mrs. Mieske and the effect to be given that language under a provision of Article 2. (We'll deal with §2-719 on the enforceability of such a provision in Chapter 14.) The plaintiffs argued that Article 2 was not applicable to this transaction, but the court held otherwise. While clearly not a sale, the court looked to the wording of §2-102 and to some prior cases dealing with commercial bailments for a finding that Article 2 could be applied to the Mieskes' case. For the Supreme Court of Washington, "Obviously 'transactions in goods'—the scope of Article 2—is broader than 'sales.' Had the drafters of the Code intended to limit Article 2 to sales they could have easily so stated. They did not." A decision on the applicability of Article 2 did not end the case, of course, but only set the ground rules. For the record we should note that a judgment of $7,500 in favor of the Mieskes was eventually affirmed. It must also be noted that the opinion in this case did not signal some vast new expansion of the scope of Article 2 law. Bailments are still treated as bailments, which observe a law unto themselves.

Besides the occasional commercial bailment, another type of situation outside of the pure sale which has been held by a majority of courts (but not by all) to come within the scope of Article 2 is the agreement creating a dealership or distributorship set up to forward the sale of goods. In *United Wholesale Liquor Co. v. Brown-Forman Distillers Corp.*, 108 N.M. 467, 775 P.2d 233, 9 U.C.C.2d 18 (1989), for example, the New Mexico Supreme Court noted that

> A majority of the jurisdictions that have looked at this issue . . . have concluded that a distributor contract is subject to the provisions of the UCC. . . . The purpose of distributorship agreements is to provide a contract for the sale of a product from a manufacturer at wholesale prices that is to be marketed in a specific area by the distributor. . . . As such, a distributorship agreement should be subject to the provisions of the UCC.

Thus, while the distributorship agreement is not in and of itself a traditional sale, it is all wrapped up in sales, and Article 2 is thought to apply.

By far the greatest number of instances where Article 2 has been invoked outside of the sales area have involved leases of personal property. This topic is sufficiently important, in fact, to warrant a chapter of its own. It gets its due in the next chapter.

The Language Around the Edges

Our reading of §2-102 necessarily focused on the core language and the meaning to be given to the term *transactions in goods*. That phrase is, however, found amid some other bits of language, and we consider them here. The entire section is introduced with the warning that Article 2 will not apply where "the context otherwise requires." Perhaps because the word *transactions* built sufficient (or more than sufficient) play into the scope section, little has been made of this introductory phrase. Perhaps it is just the drafters' way of hedging their bets a bit, and at least suggesting that a practical and not a literal approach to this section is to be preferred.

Next consider the injunction that the article "does not apply to any transaction which although in the form of an unconditional contract to sell or present sale is intended to operate only as a security transaction." We must first be aware of what a "security transaction" is, for which the Comment refers us to Article 9 of the Code. The topic of secured transactions under Article 9 is an entire book in itself. Do not worry about it here. For a glimmer of what is meant, read the first sentence *only* of §1-201(37). Suppose that Sheldon, a retail car dealer, sells Betty a car on credit. Betty will owe him money, to be paid over time. In order to get this loan, Betty will have given Sheldon a security interest in the car itself; she will have used it as *collateral*, as we say. If she does not repay, Sheldon can repossess. If it were all as simple as this, we wouldn't need a whole separate Article and a whole book just on secured transactions. But for the present this example will do. As the Comment says, the *sales aspects* of this transaction are indeed governed by Article 2; the *secured transaction* part of the deal is governed by Article 9. In some instances, a party will give a security interest in goods to another even when there is no underlying sale. The forms and terminology they use may make it appear that a sale is involved, but the language in §2-102 itself makes clear that the form does not control. If the transaction is intended "to operate *only* as a security transaction," then Article 2 has no part to play.

The final phrase of the section is a recognition that various states and the federal government have passed specialized legislation for the purposes of consumer protection, regulation of farming, and so on. Article 2 applies to those transactions, of course, but it does not "impair or repeal" any such specific legislation. It works in tandem.

What the adoption of Article 2 did explicitly repeal (see §§10-102 and 10-103) was the prior Uniform Sales Act where it had been in effect and any other state statute regulating the sale of goods generally. As a matter of course it also superseded a great bulk of what general common law remained in the states on the sale of goods. That's doing plenty.

Extension by Analogy

Good law can be hard to find, and by and large Article 2 of the Uniform Commercial Code is thought to be a recitation of some good law. It is the product of much labor by a lot of learned people. Whatever criticisms and quibbles you'll read in this book and elsewhere, it really is a remarkable accomplishment. It has the advantage of being a modern rethinking and a modern retelling all packaged in a relatively nice neat format. No wonder attorneys often refer to it for arguments and courts often go to it for answers even when faced with controversies acknowledged to be outside its scope. For similar reasons, legislators have often drafted statutes covering different realms incorporating terms and ideas first used and developed in Article 2 and the understanding which flowed from it. Article 2 of the Uniform Commercial Code has had influence far beyond its direct application.

It is important to be aware of this possibility and to be prepared for what is referred to as *argument by analogy* to Article 2. At the same time it is well to remember that what you're seeing in such statutes and in such cases is work done by analogy only. When a court decides a case involving real property or the delivery of services by reference to Article 2, it is not making Article 2 law. Nor is it reinterpreting §2-102 out of all bounds. The decision rests on the common law of whatever field is being discussed. The decision to apply a certain rule or principle is a decision of common law, with Article 2 serving as *persuasive authority* only. If the words and ideas of Article 2 are incorporated into another statute, all fine and good, but it is that statute which must be and will be interpreted in the future and serve as authority for its results. Article 2 is *primary authority* only on those controversies within its scope.

On "Goods"

We return to the central proposition that Article 2 covers "transactions in good," but now focusing on the meaning to be given the word *goods*. Look at the definition of *goods* in §2-105(1). Note that you are also led to some special rules for special types of property to be found in §2-107. The Examples and Explanations that follow will lead you through the application of these sections. Problems and subtleties there will be, but as you go through the questions, don't lose sight of the big (and comforting) picture. As you yourself have experienced, the study of law tends to focus on the so-called "grey areas"—the matters on the fringes. Don't take from this that nothing is ever certain and that everything is always up for grabs. In most real-life situations whether you are dealing with a sale of goods or not will be entirely clear-cut. Rarely will you (or your adversary) find something to argue about here. But the grey areas are interesting for any number of reasons and deserve our attention. And, as is always true in the law, once an issue is legitimately in doubt its resolution is anything but academic to the parties involved. The grey areas can make a great difference to those particular people.

EXAMPLES

1.   The question in each instance is the same: Is the transaction governed by Article 2?

a. On the advice of a number of her friends, Annie visits her local bookstore where she buys a copy of a book, *Sales and Leases: Examples and Explanations,* published by Little, Brown and Company and written by one Professor Brook.

b. Because of an amazing demand, the bookstore runs out of the Brook book and must contract to buy a large number of copies from the publisher. Is your answer changed by the fact that the publisher informs the store that all previous printings of the book have been completely sold out and that it will fill this order only when a later printing is completed sometime in the next month?

c. In light of his success with the book, Professor Brook is hired to give a series of lectures on the law of sales (and leases) by a group representing all of the commercial law students in the Metropolitan New York area.

d. Brook decides to move out of his rental apartment and move into a larger home. He enters into an agreement to buy a house, 789 Widget Lane.

e. Assume Brook holds the copyright to the book in his own name. He enters into an agreement with Megalith Pictures Incorporated, giving that company the right to produce a television miniseries based on the book.

f. With just a small part of his accumulated fortune, Brook buys some stocks and bonds through a newly acquired stockbroker.

      g. Before he leaves on a triumphal around-the-world tour, Brook contacts a dealer in foreign currency and arranges to buy 10,000 British pounds.

2.   But enough about me. Consider the following transaction: Bob contracts to buy a cocker spaniel from Sally's Pooch Emporium. Would it matter if the contract was for a puppy not yet born? Not yet conceived?

3.   Mrs. Carroll needs a pair of dentures. She orders a set of teeth out of a mail order catalog from a firm called Dentures-R-Us, sending that firm some measurements of her mouth as they request.

      a. If she has trouble with the teeth, can she sue under Article 2?

      b. Suppose that Mrs. Carroll instead went to a dentist to fill her need. Over a series of visits the dentist prepares a set of false teeth for her and fits them to her mouth. At the end of the final visit, she takes the new teeth home. Would this change your answer to the previous question?

4.   Bigelow decides to fix up the kitchen in his bungalow. He enters into an agreement with Hammer for the construction and installation of a new set of kitchen cabinets. The specifications call for a particular type of knotty pine and designated brass handles and hinges. The agreed price is $3,000, which covers all materials and labor. Is the transaction governed by Article 2?

5.   Bigelow goes to a local carpet store and picks out a style of "100% wool" wall-to-wall carpeting for his living room. He buys it from the store for a price that includes installation by the store's personnel. If he later finds that the carpet is not all wool as warranted, can he bring suit under Article 2? What if he has problems with the carpeting not because of its make-up but because it was installed improperly?

6.   Kitty, the owner of the East End Café, decides to get out of the business and agrees to sell the restaurant as a package to one Kathy. Under the agreement Kathy gets all of the liquor inventory and all of the chairs, tables, dinnerware, and other furnishings. She also gets an assignment of the liquor license, an assignment of the lease, and the right to continue using the name. Kathy discovers that much of the liquor she gets has been watered down. Can she sue under Article 2?

7.   Wimpy goes into a local diner and orders a hamburger, some fries, and a soda. Is this simple act covered by Article 2? See particularly §2-314.

8.   Jones owns some land on which there is a lot of gravel. He enters into an agreement with Grady under which Grady may enter onto the land and with her equipment take as much gravel as she wishes paying a stated amount per ton. Does Article 2 govern? Would your answer be the same if Jones was expected to dig and bag the gravel, so that Grady could just come and pick it up as needed? You'll want to check out §2-107 for this and the next question.

9.   There is also a stand of timber on Jones's land. He enters into an agreement with Woody under which Woody can enter onto the land, fell some trees, and remove them. Again and finally, does Article 2 apply to this transaction?

EXPLANATIONS

1a. Yes. This is a sale of goods governed by Article 2. The book clearly qualifies as goods under the definition of §2-105(1): It is a "thing" which is "moveable at the time of identification to the contract for sale." You don't know what "identification" means in this context, and you won't have to know until Chapter 17, but that's no problem here. If ever anything was "goods" a book like this is. (By the way, you'll just have to get used to the awkwardness of *goods* seeming to function as a singular as well as a plural noun. You say "the book is goods" for the purposes of Article 2, not "the book is a good" or "the book is good." The last statement has meaning, of course, but not in the Article 2 sense.)

1b. Yes. The large order of books is a contract for the sale of goods. Notice that Article 2 covers the single consumer transaction of the type Annie entered into and the larger commercial, business-type of deal referred to here. Article 2 covers any sale, no matter how small or how large, as long as the subject is goods.

It should make no difference to your answer if the books which were to be sold didn't even exist at the time of the contract. By the time they are to be "identified to the contract" they will exist, and at that time they will be moveable. Look at subsection (2) of §2-105. "Goods which are not both existing and identified are 'future' goods." The important thing here is that *future goods are goods,* and it makes no difference for the applicability of Article 2.

1c. No. Brook's contract is for the provision of services, not for the sale of goods. True, he is and will be "moveable" when the time for the lectures comes around, but that's obviously not the test. His lectures are not "moveable" simply because they don't have a physical, a tangible form which goods must have. (The notes that Brook uses to give the lectures are, of course, goods. So if many years hence these notes were sold to a collector of valuable Brook memorabilia, that transaction *would* be covered by Article 2.) Contracts for services are a major category of contract not covered by the UCC, but still left to the common law of the states.

1d. No. This is a sale of real property. Real property isn't moveable and thus can't be considered goods. Contracts dealing with the purchase and sale of real property are another big chunk of legal activity outside the scope of the UCC.

1e. No. Brook's deal involves what is usually referred to as a *chose in action,* but which §2-105(1) Anglicizes to a *thing in action* and which is directly read out of the definition of goods. A traditional definition of a chose in action is something like "an incorporeal right, a right not reduced to possession but recoverable by bringing and maintaining an action." My right to prevent others from trading on the success of this book is just such a right. It has no tangible form. True, I might have received a Certificate of Copyright Registration at some point, but should that be lost or burned up in a fire all my rights would remain. (Compare this to the value of the Certificate itself as goods when Brook memorabilia becomes popular.) A right such as a copyright can, of course, be bought and sold. It's just that Article 2 will not govern the transaction.

1f. No. "Investment securities" are expressly excluded from the scope of Article 2 by language in §2-105(1). Transactions in such things are governed by Article 8 of the Code and not by Article 2. You can look at §8-102 for an idea of what these include, but your basic instincts probably are on target on this one.

1g. Yes. The sale of foreign currency is covered by Article 2. See Comment 1 to §2-105. The dollars with which Brook will pay for the pounds cannot be goods, but the pounds themselves are. Compare the situation if Brook agrees to buy some dollars, taking delivery in the present, in exchange for his agreement to repay a greater number of dollars in the future. This is what we call a "loan," not a sale of goods, and is perforce not covered by Article 2.

2.   Bob's transaction with Sally is governed by Article 2. The fact that the object of the sale is a living thing makes no difference, and in fact we'll see many cases decided under Article 2 dealing with animals as goods. If the contract was for a puppy not yet born or even conceived, Article 2 still governs. This is specifically provided for in the second sentence of §2-105(1). The puppy is *future goods,* but we remind ourselves that's just one type of goods. Under Article 2 (as indeed under the common law) one can legally bind oneself to sell something that is not yet possessed or which doesn't even exist yet. All that this means is that the seller assumes the risk of getting his or her hands on the thing in order to meet a contract obligation.

3a. It is not for us to comment on the wisdom of Mrs. Carroll's move, only on the law governing it. The answer should be clear: This is a sale of goods directly within the scope of Article 2.

3b. If Carroll's purchase from the mail order house was covered by Article 2, is there any question that the same is true when she gets her dentures from a dentist? As a matter of fact, in the actual case on which this is based, *Carroll v. Grabavoy,* 77 Ill. App. 3d 895, 396 N.E.2d 836, 27 U.C.C. 940 (1979), the court held that Article 2 did not govern. What is the difference? The argument is that the dentist is not primarily engaged in selling the dentures but is really rendering a professional service, of which only one part is the handing over of the finished product. The reason she went to a dentist was to get the benefit of such services, which presumably included examining her teeth, taking impressions, making professional judgments about how to proceed, and fitting the dentures. In *Carroll* the court, relying on an earlier pre-Code case, held that "the dentist was not engaged in selling false teeth to the patient but rather that his charges were for his skill and knowledge for his personal work in the examination and in the making of the dentures in question." In another case involving dentures, this holding was followed, the court concluding, "Without a doubt, plaintiff paid for and received a course of health care treatment and services, not merely a piece of merchandise." *Preston v. Thompson,* 53 N.C. App. 290, 280 S.E.2d 780, 31 U.C.C. 1592 (1981). You see the same reasoning and the same result where a patient tried to rely on Article 2 protection in a suit against her ophthalmologist following problems with a pair of contact lenses. *Lamb v. Newark Emergency Room, Inc.,* No. 82-JL-26 (Del. Sup. Ct., LEXIS 1983).

> Here, the plaintiff was purchasing a product but in the context of medical care and treatment for her vision deficiency. She consulted Dr. Hall in his capacity of a medical doctor trained in ophthalmology. The acceptability of the product he dispensed depended on the degree of skill and acumen he applied to the examination of the eyes, the prescription he developed and the fitting and care of the patient after insertion. If a breach of care occurred in any of these areas the remedy is through an action for negligence, not breach of warranty.

See also *Cutler v. General Electric Co.,* 4 U.C.C. 300 (N.Y. Sup. Ct. 1967), which held that the insertion of a pacemaker into a patient did not constitute a sale by the doctor who performed the operation. Nor was it a sale by the hospital, even though the hospital had been paid for the cost of the device.

It's important to note in such a case that the court is not saying that there has been no sale of the offending product, but only that the doctor who delivered over the product to the ultimate user was not making such a sale, even if the cost of the product was a big factor in the doctor's fee. There was presumably a sale by the manufacturer of its product somewhere up the line, and as we will see (in Chapter 15) the patient may well be able to sue that manufacturer based on Article 2 warranties. But the doctor, in providing the product as part of a package of professional services, is not making a sale. He or she is primarily providing a service, and any action by the patient presumably will be governed by the local law of medical malpractice. Again, it is perfectly good law—just not part of the Uniform Commercial Code.

Should the result be the same if a patient, having once been fitted with a pair of prescription lenses but having lost them, orders a replacement pair through the ophthalmologist and they are found to be improperly made or contaminated? Should the doctor in that situation be treated any differently from the typical retail seller, who *does* warrant whatever he sells to his buyer, even if he is in no way responsible for the problem but only passing on what he bought from the manufacturer or wholesaler? Would it matter if the doctor made some profit from supplying replacement lenses or if it were done only as a convenience for patients? Certainly if an individual orders a pair of contacts from an independent supply house, that seller's liability is grounded in Article 2 and the law of sales.

The difficulty in such cases comes from the fact that the doctor's activities are in some sense a mix of sales and service. Both aspects of the transaction are important to the patient's health, and it is awfully hard to disentangle them. More generally, the problem is whether Article 2 applies to so-called hybrid transactions, where sale or delivery of some goods is part of a package including at least some nonsales activity. We focus on this problem in the two following questions.

4. Bigelow's argument, if he wanted to rely on Article 2 law, would be that the contract involved the sale of wood and hardware and that at least if there is some problem with the quality of these he is suing on a "sale of goods." Hammer, if he wants to avoid the sweep of Article 2, will counter that he is engaged in a construction service, and service contracts are not covered by the Code. Clearly, the transaction is a mixture of sales and service, or what is often referred to as a *hybrid transaction*. We need some way of deciding whether Article 2 governs, and if so, how much.

The courts are not perfectly in agreement on how to handle such situations, but basically there are two schools of thought. The majority of decisions rely on the so-called *predominant factors test*. A minority of jurisdictions, responding to a fair amount of academic criticism of the predominant factors approach, have adopted what is sometimes referred to as the *gravamen test*. Let's lay these two approaches out in turn.

A court applying the predominant factors test is basically making an all-or-nothing decision. The entire transaction is reviewed and judged to be either a sales contract or a service contract. It's one or the other. Which is it? The question is whether, when all factors are considered, it is more like a sales contract with a little service on the side or a service contract with some sales thrown in. One aspect will dominate and that will determine whether Article 2 governs or not. A well-known case putting forth this test is *Bonebrake v. Cox*, 499 F.2d 951, 14 U.C.C. 1318 (8th Cir. 1974), where the court said

> The test for inclusion or exclusion is not whether [the sales and service aspects of a contract] are mixed, but granting they are mixed, whether their predominant factor, their thrust, their purpose reasonably stated, is the rendition of service with goods incidentally involved (e.g., contract with artist for painting) or is it a transaction of sale, with labor incidentally involved (e.g., installation of a water heater in a bathroom).

Utilizing this distinction, the court in *Bonebrake* held Article 2 applicable to a contract for the sale and installation of some used bowling alley equipment. The fact that the contract involved a significant amount of labor did not prevent its being found to be within the scope of Article 2 in its entirety.

If the predominant factors test is being applied to our hypothetical, it seems fairly easy to conclude that Bigelow and Hammer's agreement was not for a sale of goods, but was for service of the type typically performed by a workman. Article 2 would not govern. Such is usually found to be the case when a construction contractor is performing services, even if a good deal of what he or she charges for is the cost of materials. The relative "cost" or "value" of the sales versus the service component is not necessarily the decisive factor. If the crafting of the materials is the primary reason, that is, the thrust of why the agreement has been made by the buyer, then it is services he or she is after and not a sale of goods.

Contracts for repair are also usually viewed as not covered by Article 2, even if the cost of parts is significant. See, e.g., *Northwestern Equipment, Inc. v. Cudmore,* 312 N.W.2d 347, 33 U.C.C. 160 (N.D. 1981), where the repair of a bulldozer by a sales agency was held not to be within Article 2 even though the cost of the repair parts was almost three times what was charged for labor. The court concluded that "the primary purpose" of the contract in the minds of the parties was the repair of the bulldozer, the sale of parts being incidental to this purpose. "The essence of the contract between the parties was the skill and judgment to be employed by Northwestern's employees in repairing the transmission, torque converter, and hydraulic control box." To the same effect, see *Stafford v. International Harvester Co.,* 668 F.2d 142, 32 U.C.C. 1331 (2d Cir. 1981).

As another example of the predominant factors test in action, I offer *Missouri Farmers Association v. McBee,* 787 S.W.2d 756, 12 U.C.C.2d 32 (Mo. Ct. App. 1990). Farmer McBee contracted with MFA to have his soybean crop sprayed for cocklebur. MFA selected the chemical to be sprayed and how and when the beans were to be sprayed. Within a day after the spraying the beans, which had been of "good color and good height," were brown, crumbly, and dry. Within two days they were dead. Farmer McBee brought suit alleging breach of warranty by MFA. The court held that he could not sue under Article 2 and a sales theory: "Applying [the predominant factors] test to the present facts, it appears that the dominant element of the contract was service. Mr. McBee contacted MFA about spraying his beans to eradicate cocklebur; MFA selected the chemicals used and when and how the spraying was to be done." McBee's action was for the breach of a contract for service. This being so, he would have to show negligence by MFA in order to hold it liable.

Application of the predominant factors test may not always be that easy, but the courts that abide by this analysis seem pretty satisfied with it and untroubled by the fact that sometimes its application may strike the observer as arbitrary. Still, by jamming every contract into one of two cubbyholes, no matter how complex the agreement and what the circumstances, this test strikes some as elevating form over substance. To such naysayers, a possible answer has been the second approach, the so-called gravamen test. This idea was first proposed by Professor Hawkland, who has written that

> Unless uniformity would be impaired thereby, it might be more sensible and facilitate administration, at least in this grey area [of the sales-service hybrid], to abandon the "predominant factor" test and focus instead on whether the gravamen of the action involves goods or services.

1 W. Hawkland, Uniform Commercial Code Series §2-102:04, at p. 12

(1982). Under such an analysis a single hybrid transaction would not have to be characterized as one thing or the other for all purposes. Only when an action is brought does the problem of characterization arise, and at that time the issue will be whether the gravamen (from the Latin *gravis*, meaning "heavy") or weight of the accusation is more like that reflecting dissatisfaction with goods or dissatisfaction with the rendition of services. A case often used to illustrate the use of this approach is *Newmark v. Gimbel's Inc.*, 54 N.J. 585, 258 A.2d 697, 6 U.C.C. 1205 (1969). Mrs. Newmark sued the proprietors of a beauty salon in which she had been given a permanent wave. Apparently there was something seriously wrong with the wave solution used, and she suffered considerable harm to her hair and scalp. The trial court dismissed her claim based on a breach of warranty, concluding that her contract with the beauty parlor had been predominantly one of service. Some prior cases in other states had indeed held that there were no implied sales warranties in the case of beauty treatments. The New Jersey Supreme Court reversed.

> The transaction, in our judgment, is a hybrid partaking of incidents of a sale and a service. It is really partly the rendering of service, and partly the supplying of goods for a consideration. Accordingly, . . . an implied warranty of fitness of the products used in giving the permanent wave exists with no less force than it would have in the case of a simple sale.

The sales component of this transaction was to be governed by the law of sales. Presumably, by extension, had Mrs. Newmark's complaint been grounded not on any problem with the chemical solution applied but with *how* it was applied (say if the hairdresser had wrenched her neck much too hard or scraped her scalp with a utensil), the operative rules would be those applicable to a service contract.

We can explore how the gravamen test would apply to the *McBee* case (the case of the all-too-potent herbicide). Had that court attempted to use this alternative analysis, the question would have come down to whether the alleged problem was with the herbicide (i.e., it had been incorrectly mixed by the manufacturer and contained a toxin it should not have) or with the manner in which it was applied. If the problem was with the stuff, then Article 2 should apply; if it was how the stuff was handled, then Article 2 would not, and the applicable rules would be found in the common law governing service arrangements.

When the hypothetical with which we started—concerning Bigelow, his cabinets, and Hammer—is addressed under the gravamen test, the answer whether Article 2 applies is not clear. First we have to assume that something has gone wrong and that there is some controversy between Bigelow and Hammer. Is Bigelow complaining about the type of wood used? Is he mad because the handles are not made of brass? Then Article 2 would apply. If instead his grievance was with the workmanship, Article 2 would not apply. But this line might not always be so easy to draw. What if he was bringing suit because the hinges squeaked? This could be because the hinges themselves were defective in some way or it could be that they were poorly installed. Is there any sense to saying that the cause of the squeaking must be determined *before* we can say which law governs? Cases that have adopted something like the gravamen test have usually focused on the issue of what substantive standard should apply to the contractor's obligation and in particular whether the whole battery of sales warranties can be relied upon (instead of the common law principles of negligence) by the complaining party who got some goods as part of a hybrid transaction. But the law of Article 2 goes beyond these questions. Should the questions of what Statute of Limitations, what Statute of Frauds, what rules of contract formation, and so on apply all remain in limbo until Bigelow can establish—or is made to pick—a theory of why he keeps hearing that squeak?

5.   We can consider this situation under each of the two approaches presented above. Under the predominant factors test, a court would probably find this was predominantly a sale of goods with the installation service incidental. This was the result in *Snyder v. Herbert Greenbaum & Assocs. Inc.*, 38 Md. App. 144, 380 A.2d 618, 22 U.C.C. 1104 (1977), and *Colorado Carpet Installation, Inc. v. Palermo*, 87 Nev. 204, 668 P.2d 1384, 36 U.C.C. 1516 (1983). (The *Palermo* case contains a particularly good review of the application of the predominant factors test.) Notice that once the situation is found to be governed by Article 2 under this test then it would not matter whether the gist of Bigelow's complaint was about the quality of the carpeting itself or the manner of its installation.

Now approach this problem from the point of view of the gravamen test. Presumably if Bigelow's complaint were about the quality of composition of the carpet, his suit would be governed by Article 2. If he were complaining about something that was wrong with the installation, Article 2 would not govern. He'd proceed and defenses would be available under the law governing service contracts. Again, the use of the gravamen test may be helpful if the carpet seller is trying to argue that it can't be held to the normal seller's warranties just because installation was part of the package. But then the predominant factors test meets this problem as well. If the issue is which Statute of Limitations governs any action between Bigelow and the carpet store based on this contract, isn't there some value to having a single answer which can be stated with some certainty from the moment the contract is entered into?

6.   Here we have a hybrid transaction where the mix is not of sales and services, but of the sale of goods with the sale of a bunch of other stuff that is not goods. If the jurisdiction has adopted a predominant factors test, it would seem likely that this would be seen as a single contract for "the sale of a business" with the transfer of goods incidentally involved. Thus Article 2 would not apply. This was the result in *DG Porter, Inc. v. Fridley*, 373 N.W.2d 917, 41 U.C.C. 1823 (N.D. 1985), on which this question is based. Of course there may be instances in which the court concludes that the negotiated sale of a business is exclusively or predominantly the sale of a collection of things which are moveable and truly goods. In such a case, Article 2 would apply. See, e.g., *Wikler v. Mar-Van Industries, Inc.*, 39 Pa. D. & C. 3d 136, 2 U.C.C.2d 1190 (Pa. C.P.

1984), where it was estimated that $49,500 out of a total purchase price of $50,000 represented moveable items of factory equipment and inventory.

Were this problem to come up in a jurisdiction committed to a gravamen test approach, we would have to know what type of action is being brought. If Kathy sues because the inventory of liquor had been watered down or the tables were not fit for use, then Article 2 would apply. If Kathy sues because of some problem with the liquor license or the lease, then Article 2 would not. Again, does it make sense to think of the contract as broken up so? Especially in this situation, if Kathy were stuck with the general contract law governing the sale of a business and could not rely on the warranties found in Article 2, is there such a problem? If she carefully negotiated a written agreement for the purchase, Kathy presumably will have gotten explicit warranties about the quality of all the various assets. She isn't anything like a typical buyer under Article 2 and there seems little reason for adding the confusion of the gravamen approach just to deal with this problem.

7. The last sentence of §2-314(1) leaves no question that at least *that* section applies to Wimpy's purchase. Since a dinner at a diner or a restaurant is such a medley of sales and service, the prior law was not consistent as to whether sales law applied. The drafters of the Code gave us this answer in §2-314. But are we to take the location of this sentence in §2-314 as meaning that the rest of Article 2 does *not* apply to such a situation or that there is some doubt whether it does? This question isn't particularly troubling, since it is hard to think of a real situation where a suit would be brought other than when the warranties of quality are involved. And I know of no court questioning the application of the other two warranty sections (§§2-313 and 2-315) to the sale of food.

8. Under §2-107(1) Grady's purchase is not governed by Article 2 if she is to sever it from the land. If Jones, the seller, is to do the severing, Article 2 does cover. This all follows from the fact that gravel constitutes "minerals or the like."

9. Sale of standing timber is governed by §2-107(2). It is covered by Article 2 "whether or not the subject matter is to be severed by the buyer or by the seller." Notice this rule applies not only to timber but to "growing crops or other things attached to realty and capable of severance without material harm thereto but not described in subsection (1)" of the section.

2

The Subject Is Leases

There are no questions in this chapter for you to work on, just text, as the material seemed best handled that way. Still, you will want to go through what follows carefully the first time you read a case about or your instructor refers to a lease of goods, the practice of equipment leasing, or Article 2A.

An Explosion of Leases

Anyone who has ever rented a car or taken a canoe out for the day knows that personal property, just as it can be bought and sold, can be the subject of a lease. What not everyone is aware of, however, is the extent to which transactions in goods of every kind are under current practice cast as leases. Histories of the subject inevitably (and rightly) refer to the explosive increase in the amount of equipment leasing since the Second World War and particularly in the last decade. This phenomenon is evident not just in the consumer rental of things like automobiles and canoes but in the leasing of equipment by large industrial firms where in the past they might have entered into straight purchases and sales. For example, many airlines rent all or most of the planes that make up their fleets. Major manufacturers regularly enter into multimillion dollar leases for the massive pieces of industrial machinery which pound away in their factories.*

---

*For a good overview of this history, as well as the coming of Article 2A, see Amelia Boss, The History of Article 2A: A Lesson for Practitioner and Scholar Alike, 39 Ala. L. Rev. 575 (1988). Professor Boss cites studies for the proposition that, "Equipment leasing grew at an estimated rate of thirty percent a year during the 1950s and has

What's behind this accelerating interest in the lease of goods? There are a number of explanations. Some have to do with the intricacies (to put it politely) of federal income tax law. Other considerations that encourage large corporations, their counsel, and their financial advisers to structure transactions as leases have meaning only to those who recognize and appreciate the subtleties of corporate accounting. Fortunately we do not have to delve into these matters. It is enough for us to acknowledge the importance of the lease of goods in the modern business environment.

Our concern is solely with how disputes between the parties themselves are to be resolved. Here we are less fortunate. As the practice of leasing has burgeoned, the legal landscape has revealed itself to be rough going at best.

Presumably most leases, either of the consumer or the commercial variety, work out splendidly and all concerned find themselves perfectly contented. But if even a small percentage of these transactions end up in controversy, plenty of business will result for the lawyers and the courts. What quickly became apparent with the mushrooming number of such disputes was that the common law does not have a particularly good handle on these problems. Unlike real property leasing, where the common law has developed a fairly rich repertoire of doctrine, the lease of personal property has never been given much consistent attention by the courts. Issues of rights and responsibilities arising under the lease of goods have had to be decided, and the courts found themselves struggling, in the relatively unexplored and often archaic territory of the so-called chattel mortgage or the common law bailment for hire.

From this perspective it might have been expected that the adoption of the Uniform Commercial Code, and particularly of its Article 2, would have been seen as offering some help. Here was a new rendering of commercial law designed for the modern era. From the first, however, it was far from clear what applicability—if any—Article 2 had to the lease transaction. Courts that have been importuned by counsel to apply bits and pieces of Article 2 to the lease situation or that have found themselves understandably attracted to the idea in the absence of anything else to rely on have met the challenge in a variety of ways. In the well-known case of *Barco Auto Leasing Corp. v. PSI Cosmetics, Inc.,* 125 Misc. 2d 68, 478 N.Y.S.2d 505, 39 U.C.C. 840 (1984), Judge Edward Lehner of the Civil Court of the City of New York cataloged what he saw as the four distinct approaches that courts have taken to the possible interplay between Article 2 and the lease. His catalog is helpful, and we will follow it here. One bit of warning: The names that have been given to the four approaches are perhaps as serviceable as any could be, but they still are not all that helpful. Indeed they are particularly unhelpful in distinguishing

---

exceeded the thirty percent per annum growth rate several times during the past two decades." As a result, by the late 1980s, "approximately twenty percent of all capital investment in the United States [was] directly attributable to equipment leasing with over 310 billion dollars in lease receivables [then] outstanding."

the third and fourth modes of analysis listed below (the so-called analogy approach and the policy approach). As you will see, the analogy approach obviously has policy justifications and implications, and the policy approach makes use of the legal technique of analogy. In any event, the courts themselves rarely use these descriptive terms with any consistency. Indeed, in many if not most of the decided cases the court seems to be either unaware of or unclear on exactly which approach it is following, or concocting a blend of more than one. In what follows I will not try to restyle the various modes of analysis—it will be enough to untangle them.

The "Inclusionary" View

What may have been initially the most appealing answer to the question of whether Article 2 is applicable to lease transactions is the simplest to state: Just say yes. After all, §2-102 proclaims that the article is applicable to "transactions" in goods, and a lease is certainly a transaction. Indeed a few courts have taken this line. The problem, as we noted in the previous chapter, is that while §2-102 speaks in terms of a "transaction," everything else in the article from its short title on down (see §2-101) fairly shouts the language of sales. Except for that one place in §2-102, nothing is made in Article 2 of the broader term *transaction*. Everything is stated in terms of the *sale*. The parties whose rights are the subject of Article 2 are consistently and insistently referred to therein as the "seller" and the "buyer" and nothing else.

In any event it is simply not reasonable to expect all the answers to the myriad problems with leases could ever be found in Article 2. The sale and the lease are indeed both transactions, but there are significant differences between them. As just one example, the lessor expects the return of the leased goods at the end of the lease term. The seller expects and hopes never to see again the goods which it has sold. These observations naturally lead to the second diametrically opposed approach which can be taken to the whole controversy.

The "Exclusionary" View

In what is sometimes also referred to as the "strict constructionist's" resolution of the matter, some courts have resolutely held Article 2 applicable only to the classic sales situation, excluding completely any consideration of leases or other nonsales transactions. Taking this tack, we simply say no. Seen as a rejection of the broad "inclusionary" view first noted, this stance has much to recommend it. In the words of the Supreme Court of South Carolina in the recent case of *D & D Leasing Co. of South Carolina, Inc. v. Gentry*, 298 S.C. 342, 380 S.E.2d 823, 9 U.C.C.2d 461 (1989), "Legislative intent is best determined from the language of the statute itself. . . . Article 2 is replete with references to sales, not leases. To apply Article 2 to leases in general would be to ignore the intent of the legislature as expressed in the plain language of the statute."*

If this exclusionary approach is itself taken too literally, however, it may be a case of protesting too much (or at least more than is absolutely necessary). A rigid adherence to the exclusionary view presumably makes any and every provision of Article 2 simply irrelevant when a lease of personal property is the subject of dispute. Questions relating to leases are then to be answered exclusively by reliance on the existing common law, however feeble, as if Article 2 had never been created. Most courts confronted with a lease but also with a problem on which the wisdom of Article 2 has something to say are understandably loath simply to turn their backs on the whole Code enterprise. Some use or reference to Article 2 may be irresistible when the right case comes along. This leads to the two intermediate approaches to the question of leases, which have been suggested in the literature and the case law. Please note that even if the courts of a particular state often seem to be judging these next two approaches one against the other, the two (as will be discussed below) are not really in any inherent conflict. True, they come at the question from different angles, but when properly understood they are perhaps better seen as treating different aspects of the same problem.

The "Analogy" Approach

This approach begins with a simple, if initially strange, proposition: Not every lease really is a lease. By this what is meant is that many transactions that are carefully drawn up to appear as leases—with documents headed "Lease" repeatedly referring to the "Lessor," the "Lessee," the "Rent," and so on—may not actually be intended by the parties to operate *in an economic or business sense* in the way we expect a lease to operate. If form is not to dominate totally over substance, the title on the paper cannot control. We have to have some idea of what distinguishes transactions in goods that as a real economic or business proposition constitute a lease. We will return to this problem in the last section of this chapter. For the moment it is enough to suggest an answer. A lease that is a lease in more than just name (what the analysts end up calling in a somewhat curious fashion a "true lease") is distinguished by the lessor's continuing interest in the economic value of the goods even as they are in the hands of the lessee. The lessee is paying for the *use* of the goods for some period of time *less than* what is anticipated to be the full economic life of the goods. The lessor intends that it will get the goods back at the end of the term

---

*Indeed, accepting such a broad reading of the word *transaction* in §2-102 would seem particularly difficult now in light of the fact that the various powers responsible for Code upkeep have seen fit in recent years (as we will discuss in a section to follow) to expend enormous time and energy on the formulation of a separate Article 2A covering leases. In all this process, as far as I am aware, no one has bothered to suggest redrafting of §2-102 to avoid an overlap of the two articles.

and expects that the goods will return with some (economic) life left in them.

Why would parties enter into a transaction structured as a lease if something else—something which is for all intents and purposes economically indistinguishable from a sale—is intended in fact? Again, we have the tax laws and principles of accounting to thank. And again, for our purposes it is enough to let the tax lawyers and accountants have their way—as long as the issues involved are issues of taxation and corporate finance. When core issues arise about the rights of the two parties to the transaction as they relate to each other, however, it seems only fitting that the law of leases (whatever that may be) be applied only to those true leases in which the parties have entered into not only the form but the substance of that relationship.

If a transaction that purports in all its finery to be a lease is really what we can call a "disguised sale," then it is understandable that the courts may unmask the intruder and call a sale a sale, whatever its superficial appearance. This explains what the *Barco* opinion calls the "analogy" approach, an approach which in fact that court saw itself constrained by prior New York cases to follow:

> Though eloquently advocated, . . . the inclusive approach has not been accepted. While it has been noted that "transactions in goods" encompasses a wider area of activity than a "sale", . . . this had been more in the way of judicial lip service. The cases in New York have not specifically relied on the Article 2 scope provision alone, most preferring instead to analyze the underlying facts of the transaction in issue in order to determine whether it [that is, the instant transaction] sufficiently approximates a sale.
>
> Therefore, much as this court might prefer to indulge in the flexible and inclusive approach in determining whether the lease transaction herein is subject to the provisions of Article 2, the inquiry will be limited to an analysis of the transaction in order to determine whether or not it is analogous to a sale.

Applying this test to the particular transaction, the court found Article 2 applicable. "While the lessor retains title and a security interest, the fact that the lessee is saddled with both the risks and the headaches of ownership [and, one might add, any possibility of gain and unbridled happiness] suggests that there is no significant economic difference between full title ownership and the instant lease."

For another example of this approach, see *Pactel Finance v. D.C. Marine Service Corp.*, 136 Misc. 2d 194, 518 N.Y.S.2d 317, 4 U.C.C.2d 665 (N.Y. Dist. Ct. 1987), where the court notes the "persuasive argument" that "courts should look to the economic reality of the transaction, rather than to its form, in determining whether there has been a sale or a true lease." This way of stating the problem makes clear what is really going on here. A court such as *Barco* or *Pactel,* deciding under this theory that Article 2 applies to the transaction in question, is merely doing the necessary job of statutory construction. It in effect concludes that the legislature in adopting Article 2 meant to and did enact a statute to govern all "transactions in goods" which in economic reality were intended to act as the classic sale, whatever the paperwork was made to look like. Article 2 governs such purported "lease" transactions just as it governs transactions that openly declare themselves to be sales. It is a matter of legislative fiat, now correctly understood and interpreted, to put substance ahead of foolish form. Seen in this way, it is clear that if a transaction is found to have what the *Pactel* court refers to as "the essential nature" of a sale rather than a true lease, then each and every section of Article 2 applies to it just as it would to any other transaction coming within the scope of that Article. This notion is to be contrasted with our final approach, which itself works by the ways of analogy but in an altogether different manner.

The "Policy" Approach

In the words of the *Barco* opinion, a court is using the policy approach when it engages in "the selective application of particular provisions of Article 2 whenever the policies underlying such provisions are appropriate to the transaction in issue." Note that unlike the analogy approach, which first examines transactions for their fundamental nature and then at least in theory either applies Article 2 to them in toto or leaves them completely untouched by that enactment, the so-called policy approach works on a case-by-case and, more importantly, on a section-by-section basis. Furthermore, this approach is unlike the analogy approach in that it can bring various sections into play even when the transaction in question is clearly a "true lease" in every sense of that curious phrase.

The distinction between the two approaches is made more difficult by the fact that the policy approach is itself clearly grounded in the venerable legal concept of reasoning by analogy. The court, in searching for the correct way to handle a problem between a lessor and lessee, finds wisdom and guidance by looking at how the analogous question is dealt with in the law of sales. And that law is now to be found in the pages of the UCC's Article 2. Perhaps the best known language propounding this policy approach is from the case of *Glenn Dick Equipment Co. v. Galey Construction, Inc.,* 97 Idaho 216, 541 P.2d 1184, 18 U.C.C. 340 (1975), which indeed stresses the notion of legal analogy:

> Reasoning by analogy does not require us to apply Article 2 in toto to a lease; rather, we need apply only those provisions which are sufficiently analogous. In order to determine which provisions are applicable, we will look to the commercial setting in which the problem arises and contrast the relevant common law with Article 2—we will use Article 2 as a *premise for reasoning* only when the case involves the same considerations that gave rise to the Code provisions and an analogy is not rebutted by additional antithetical circumstances. (Emphasis added)

Using such an approach courts have found a wide variety of Article 2 provisions (or rather, perfectly analogous common law principles) applicable even to the truest of true leases. Without by any means exhausting the list, one can easily find cases where this type of treatment has resulted in judicial extension to leases of Article 2's warranty provisions, its Statute of Frauds, and its treatment of unconscionability.

In theory at least, application of this approach is not a matter of statutory interpretation at all. The court, concluding that the instant transaction does not come under the authority of Article 2, is left to its own devices (i.e., common law decisionmaking techniques) to decide the case. Among the most venerable of common law mechanisms is a court's ability to survey the law as it applies to other related or analogous problems. And the Uniform Commercial Code is, as more than one court has pointed out, an embodiment of "the foremost modern legal thought concerning commercial transactions." This at least is the policy behind the so-called policy approach.

One Curious Decision

If a court applies a provision of Article 2 to a lease, is it merely enforcing the legislative will as set out in that enactment? Or is it instead enunciating common law principles on its own authority—which principles just happen to be analogous in every way to a particular section or sections of Article 2? The distinction may seem a question as academic as they come. If the result is the same, why engage in such theorizing, particularly since many courts seem unclear as to exactly what it is they are doing as they are (in a perfectly uncontroversial manner) doing it? But then consider the bewildering result in *Cucchi v. Rollins Protective Services Co.,* 524 Pa. 514, 574 A.2d 565, 11 U.C.C.2d 737 (1990), decided by the Supreme Court of Pennsylvania not that long ago. The facts at least are very straightforward. In July of 1973 Anthony and Grace Cucchi leased from the Rollins Protective Service Company a burglar alarm system to protect their home. They paid a set sum for installation and thereafter regularly paid a monthly fee for service and maintenance of the system. Unfortunately, when their home was burglarized in February of 1984 and approximately $36,000 worth of personal property taken, the system did not raise an alarm. On October 30, 1985, the Cucchis filed suit against the company alleging, among other grounds, breach of the implied warranties of merchantability and fitness for intended use. These warranties, as you will see in Chapter 13, are central to Article 2 law. But then the applicable Article 2 sections speak only of the existence of such warranties as implied "in any contract of sale." And this contract, all members of the Supreme Court agreed, was not a sale of goods, nor even a disguised sale. The contract had provided that the entire system "shall remain personal property and title thereto shall continue in Rollins," that the homeowners were to refrain from damaging the system, and furthermore that upon termination of the lease the system was to be returned to Rollins.

That the contract was not a classic sale of goods was just about the only thing on which the members of the Supreme Court could agree. As it turned out, the real problem had to do with the Statute of Limitations: Which Statute applied and how was it to be applied to the facts of the case? At trial the jury, having been given the case on a warranty theory, awarded the Cucchis a total of $30,000. Judgment was entered in this amount and Rollins appealed, contending that any action on a warranty theory had been effectively barred by the Statute of Limitations. Rollins' argument, to put it in a nutshell, was that the applicable Statute was that found in §2-725 of the Code. Under this section any action on a breach of warranty theory had to have been brought within four years from when "tender of delivery" had been made. Delivery had been in 1973, argued Rollins, and thus the suit in 1985 was far, far too late. The Cucchis on the other hand argued that the applicable limitation was not that to be found in Article 2 but the more general Statute of Limitations covering contract actions appearing in Pennsylvania's Commercial Statutes. This Statute also had a term of four years but, important to the Cucchis, could be read as beginning to run only when the breach of contract occurred or was discovered. If this was the correct analysis, the Statute began to run only in 1984 and their action was not have time-barred.

So who was right? A fractionalized Supreme Court of Pennsylvania gave the day to the homeowners, by a vote of 4 to 3, but exactly *why* they won is far from clear. Three principal opinions have to be considered. The opinion of the court, written by Justice Larsen, was joined in by only one other member of the court. (One of the stranger aspects of the case is that the other two opinions continually refer to Larsen's two-person opinion as that of "the majority.") Larsen first determined that under Pennsylvania law, while Article 2 "does not by its terms apply to contracts for the lease of goods," it can be applied on a section-by-section basis, using what we have seen termed the *policy approach*.

> [W]e will extend by analogy selected provisions of [Article 2] to transactions involving the lease of goods on a case by case basis, considering the nature of the specific transaction (lease), the language, purpose, and intent of the UCC provision under consideration, and the practicality of applying the particular provision(s) at issue to the particular transaction in goods.

There can be no serious question, Larsen continues, that under this approach the warranty provisions of Article 2 apply to a lease of goods such as in the instant case. So the Cucchis had a warranty cause of action. What limitation governed? Larsen concludes that all breach of warranty actions "brought under the UCC, including breach of warranties in sales-analogous transactions (i.e., conventional leases of goods) are governed by the statute of limitations set forth in §2-725." If this is so, how can Larsen and his one cohort still find in favor of the Cucchis? He reads §2-725(2) in its entirety and relies on the language that in the exceptional situation where "a warranty explicitly extends to future performance of the goods and discovery of the breach must await the time of such performance" the Statute begins to run only when the breach is or should have been discovered. This exception had previously been read very narrowly by the Pennsylvania courts, relying particularly on the section's use of the word "explicitly," but Larsen, commenting that "the parties in a conventional lease of goods transaction presumably barter for the future performance of the goods," holds that the cause of action accrued—and the four-year Statute of Limitations began to run—only when the breach was discovered in 1984. So the suit was timely filed.

Larsen's opinion and analysis garnered only two votes for the Cucchis. Their ultimate victory depended as much on the concurring opinion filed by Justice Nix, with whom one other justice joined. Nix begins by chiding Larsen's opinion for its "unnecessary examination of the applicability of the U.C.C. statute of limitations." Instead his concurring analysis is that the Cucchis' complaint was really a complaint about the *service* they got from the alarm company and that therefore "the provisions of the U.C.C. were irrelevant to this transaction which was a contract for the sale of services, not a contract for the lease or sale of the equipment." Concerned that Larsen has muddled the distinction between tort and contract law, Nix concludes, "The effect of the majority's [sic] reasoning is to breach the sanctity of contractual relationships and to contravene the constitutional protection against the impairment of contracts." On a more prosaic level, he would hold that the action was clearly not barred by the general Statute of Limitations which began to run only at the time when the alarm service failed to operate properly. So here are two votes for the Cucchis but against Article 2, the warranty sections as well as its distinctive Statute of Limitations.

We turn finally to the principal dissent, joined in by the remaining three justices and written by Justice Zappala. Zappala first expresses his disapproval of the whole tack taken by "the majority" and accuses them of having engaged in inappropriate judicial activism in their extension of Article 2 to leases.* He goes on, however, to opine that even assuming Article 2 could be applied in this way, the resolution made by Larsen of the Statute of Limitations issue was faulty. Section 2-725 generally calls for the Statute to begin running at the time of delivery of the goods. The exceptional treatment accorded warranties "explicitly" extended to future performance cannot be invoked in the instant case. An implied warranty, argues Zappala with the backing of some good Code authority, "by nature cannot be explicit."

---

*Zappala noted that the UCC revisions proposed by Article 2A, to be discussed shortly, had not at the time been enacted in Pennsylvania. Larsen's opinion found support in how the drafters of 2A would deal with the Statute of Limitations problem. Zappala reprimands Larsen for his extension of the dictates of the UCC to leases, "a 'wisdom' that has not yet befallen the legislature." On this point he concludes, "I must state that I find it unwise to effect sweeping changes in lease transactions merely because the judiciary is impatient with the legislature's failure to do so." One Justice, Cappy, who joined in this dissent filed a separate even more stinging dissenting opinion to register his disapproval of "such blatant judicial interference." And you thought such passion was reserved by judges only for matters of constitutional law?

So three justices conclude that, even given all of the help that Article 2 can afford a lessee, the Cucchis sued too late.

I leave you to ponder (but not too hard or for too long) exactly *what* was the operative law relating to leases of goods in Pennsylvania following this result in the highest court of that state. Did Article 2 apply to leases, at least on a section-by-section "policy" basis? If so, and suit were brought to enforce a lessor's or a lessee's substantive right established in this way, would Article 2 govern the suit in all its particulars? Or only in selected provisions? Just to add to the muddle, ask yourself what the court in *Cucchi* did to the general jurisprudence of §2-725. That section, after all, must be applied regularly and predictably to any number of cases, almost all of which will be straightforward sales. Has an important aspect of run-of-the-mill application of §2-725 been unnecessarily put into question by the *Cucchi* court? In my opinion, you would be perfectly justified in wondering if any good whatsoever came out of the labors of the courts of Pennsylvania in what should have been a relatively minor case. But perhaps there is something that can be said on its behalf. If nothing else, *Cucchi* makes abundantly clear how poor is the fit between Article 2 and lease transactions, no matter how carefully we approach the problem. Article 2 just wasn't written with leases in mind. Fortunately, help is on the way, at least if the legislatures of the several states take the proposed Article 2A, newly arrived on the scene, to their collective hearts.*

Enter Article 2A

Meanwhile, as the practice of commercial leasing boomed and the courts struggled with the awkward working of Article 2 when the subject was leases, various forces among the powers-that-be in the uniform law movement (the ABA, the ALI, and the National Conference of Commissioners on Uniform State Laws) were coming to a uniform conclusion: Some change was needed in the uniform laws. Either the Commercial Code had to be amended to take leases into account or an entirely independent uniform statute dealing exclusively with the leasing of goods had to be promulgated. Starting in the early 1980s a number of special committees were established, drafts drafted, and meetings convened.† All this activity culminated in a decision to go forward with an entirely new article to be

---

*Help arrived for the citizens of Pennsylvania with the very recent adoption of 2A effective July 1, 1993. The *Cucchi* holding, whatever it was, will eventually be only a memory. But that will take some time. To see an intermediate court in Pennsylvania making its way warily through the strange netherworld between the Supreme Court's decision in *Cucchi* and the effective date of 2A, you could look at *Keblish v. Thomas Equipment, Ltd.,* — Pa. Super. — , 21 U.C.C.2d 41 (1993).

†The early history is laid out in detail in Professor Amelia Boss's article, cited above. Unfortunately, her article only goes through promulgation of the 1987 version of 2A and does not cover the most recent developments.

made part of the UCC—the first new article ever proposed!—to be squeezed in right after Article 2. And so we have been given Article 2A. An official draft of this article was completed by the National Conference of Commissioners in 1986 and approved in final form by the ALI in late 1987, thus becoming an official recommendation to the several states.

This measure, which now has to be referred to as the "Original Official Text" or the "1987 Official Version" of 2A, was first enacted in Oklahoma. Had the rest of the states followed Oklahoma's lead, a blessed uniformity would have blanketed the land. That is, after all, the underlying justification for the entire uniform law movement. Unfortunately for the drafters and for us, things have not worked out so simply. At the moment we are left more with a patchwork quilt of state action and inaction. The problems began immediately when California in 1988 enacted Article 2A, but with a number of significant amendments to both the article's language and the comments. In Massachusetts a bill was introduced to adopt Article 2A with some, but not all, of the California amendments. At the same time the New York Law Revision Commission began its own study and analysis of the 1987 Official Version and seemed ready to announce its own impressions about what was wrong with it and on how to proceed.

In an effort to return to the spirit of uniformity, the National Conference of Commissioners established a Standby Committee to monitor developments and recommend action (to anyone who would listen). After extensive negotiation that brought in, among others, representatives of California, New York, and Massachusetts, this Standby Committee drafted a compromise set of amendments to 2A (the "Official Amendments") which were then themselves adopted by the sponsoring organizations in 1990. This official version of 2A as now amended is referred to as the "1990 Amended Version."

So where do things stand now? Well, that depends where you are standing. So far 39 states and the District of Columbia had adopted Article 2A.* Other states are still thinking about what to do, with some more actively considering it than others. This situation continues to change; where it will all end is far from certain. The Code sponsors obviously hope that within a short time every jurisdiction will have picked up Article 2 in the 1990 Amended Version, but for the moment we are left in limbo.†

In this book, references to Article 2A are to the 1990 Amended

---

*As of March 1994, Florida and South Dakota, two of the states that had been among those most quickly to get on the Oklahoma bandwagon, have not yet adopted all of the 1990 Amendments, and are thus being blessed at least temporarily with 2A in the old repudiated Original Official Text. South Dakota has adopted some of the official amendments but not all. Oklahoma itself adopted the 1990 Amendments in 1991, as did California. As of June 1993, no action had been taken in either Massachusetts or New York.

†Notice that if Article 2A is not quickly picked up by a particular state's legislature, that fact in and of itself conceivably could make things even tougher for that state's

Version. (You should obviously check now that this is the version in the copy of the Code you are using.) Remember as you refer to it that, however much it appears in the pages of your copy of the Code as of equal stature with the other articles and particularly Article 2, this is a very different beast and has to be treated differently. Article 2 is not simply a part of the Code, interesting for its own sake and because the drafters drafted it. It represents the authoritative law of sales as it has been adopted and continuously applied in virtually all of the United States for just about 30 years. Article 2A, on the other hand, for all its virtues is a text in the process of becoming.

You should take the time now to read the drafters' Foreword at the very beginning of Article 2A. You may also want to read the History section of the Official Comment to §2A-101. The rest of that Comment is a good overview of Article 2A but is probably much more than you need right now and can be daunting, especially if you have not yet studied Article 9 of the Code.

When Is a Lease a Lease?

An introduction to Article 2A is now in order. Look at §2A-102. The new article "applies to any transaction, regardless of form, that creates a lease." For the definition of *lease* see §2A-103(j). What's of immediate importance here is what is said in the negative. A "sale" or "the creation of a security interest" is not a lease. Now go back and read at least the first two paragraphs of the Official Comment to §2A-102. Again, while the Comment is clear that Article 2A covers a wide diversity of leases, "sales and security interests are governed by other Articles of this Act." Sales we know are governed by Article 2. Creation and enforcement of security interests come under Article 9, which is the subject of a whole other area of commercial transactions (and a whole other book). If 2A is an article designed exclusively for and about leases, why all the talk about transactions which are *not* leases? The answer is that, as we have previously noted, parties for a variety of reasons often enter into an agreement that has the *form* of a lease but that is in *substance* something

---

courts confronted with what to do about leases of goods. Should the judges read such a rejection as an indication that the legislature considers the rules laid down in 2A as poor policy to be rejected in that state? Or should such inaction be taken to mean that the legislature expects the courts to continue importing Article 2 concepts by analogy and that this will deal with the problem just fine? Is legislative inaction best understood merely as a reflection of the fact that state legislators are often busy with other more glamorous matters? If so, what result? The difficulty inherent in this intricate relationship between the courts and the legislature is a theme running through the various opinions in the *Cucchi* case discussed above and may account for the vehemence of some of the statements made there.

very different. Article 2A is intended to govern only the arrangement that we sometimes refer to as the *true lease,* which has not just the form of a lease but also establishes a relationship that actually operates in the economic sense as a traditional lease of goods. Parties are not allowed to import wholesale the law of Article 2A into a nonlease relationship, even if both should wish it, simply by casting their documents in terms of "lessor," "lessee," and "rents due."

As we discussed earlier, the true lease should be distinguished from what is often called the *disguised sale,* but which must more fully be thought of as a "disguised sale with a disguised retained security interest attached." To understand what all this is about, follow me through a simple (if admittedly farfetched) example: Suppose that Sue owns a special pass which will allow the holder to get into the movies free for the entire year of 1994. It is late 1993. Sue doesn't think she'll use the pass that much, but her friend Bob (an inveterate movie-goer) would love to have just such an item. Sue could sell the pass to Bob. If she sold it in December 1993 for the cash price of say $720, that would be a sale pure and simple. She would end up with the cash and Bob with the pass. The value of the pass as it may be affected for good or ill (for example, by a raising or lowering of the standard price of admission in their area) is now totally Bob's concern. Sue has no conceivable interest in the pass anymore, neither in the legal sense nor in the economic sense that she couldn't care less what value anyone else (or the impersonal market) would ever put on it. It's no longer any of her business.

Now suppose that in late 1993 Bob does not have that kind of cash on him, but that he expects to come into funds early in the next year. If Sue is willing, they may enter into an agreement for the present sale of the pass to Bob on credit. In exchange for the pass Bob agrees to pay the $720 on February 1. This is still a sale, and in fact a very typical kind of sale of which we'll see plenty of examples in this book. Does Sue have any continuing interest in the value of the pass over time? No. Sue has traded her ownership interest in the pass for an interest in good old cash. What would happen if Bob cannot or does not pay when he is supposed to? Sue will then have a right to sue him for the price. Her action would have nothing to do with the pass per se—there is simply a debt owed to her. Even if Bob were to go bankrupt, Sue would have no special right simply to reclaim the pass. Bob's debt to her is what is called an *unsecured debt.* In any bankruptcy proceeding she would be what is termed a *general creditor* (which is another way of saying, "pretty much out of luck").

To protect herself to a degree against the risk of Bob's nonpayment, Sue might ask that as part of the sale Bob give her a *security interest* in the pass to secure this debt. Look at the first sentence *only* of §1-201(37). This is the basic Code definition of a "security interest." In older days, before Article 9, we might have said he would give her a lien on his property or something called a "chattel mortgage." The idea is that Bob would give Sue an interest in some property of his (the pass) as collateral securing the payment of his obligation (the $720 he must pay her in

February). Should Bob fail in his obligation to Sue, she could still bring a simple contract action on the debt, but in addition she would have the right to "go against" the collateral. That is, as a secured creditor she could foreclose on that particular piece of the debtor's property, take it into her possession, and then sell it to someone else and use the money from that sale to satisfy Bob's debt to her.

The important point for our purposes right now is that in this situation there *still has been a sale* to Bob. Sue does retain an interest in the goods, but it is not an ownership interest, merely a secondary security interest. If over the course of 1993 the pass becomes much more valuable (say a lot of really fine films are coming out), she does not share in the bonanza. She can ask for no more than $720 from Bob. Even if Bob fails to pay and she repossesses the collateral, any value in the pass over and above the amount of the $720 still owed her would legally be Bob's, not hers. If the value of the pass should plummet, she is still owed her $720 and could, if she chose, sue on that debt ignoring the pass and its value entirely.

Change the facts just a bit. Suppose their agreement is that Bob will pay $180 on the last of each month January through April. Spreading out payment of the price in this way is what is sometimes referred to as an *installment sale* and is nothing unusual. This is still a sale on credit with a reserved security interest in the seller, only now with a different credit term and payment schedule. Change the situation once again to where Bob will pay the full price but in twelve installments of $60 each at the end of each month in 1994. Again we have an installment sale. From the time they enter into this agreement in late 1993 it is Bob, as the buyer, who would have to anticipate any gain or loss from the fluctuating value in movie passes over the coming year. Sue has effectively rid herself of any investment in movie-pass property.

Now imagine that for some arcane reason Sue's lawyer suggests that they structure this last deal as a "lease." Bob's lawyer understands the (arcane) reasoning of this approach and doesn't object. The two sign a lease. Sue as lessor agrees to lease the pass for the term of twelve months starting in January 1994 to Bob for a "monthly rental payment" of $60. Bob agrees to make his rent payments and has no right to terminate the lease before the end of the year. The economic reality of what they have now done is, as you can see, no different from what we had when they entered into a sale with payment on a one year installment plan. Of course at the end of the "lease" term Sue as lessor would have the right to the return of the property, a right she would not have if she were the seller. But this right to the eventual return of the pass is meaningless. It's hard to imagine that Sue would even care if she never got it back. She'd probably tell Bob to toss it out when he is done with it. What is the value of a 1994 pass in January of 1995? Its worth may only be the value of the paper it's written on.

This hypothetical serves as a simple if farfetched example of leases for a term exactly equal to what we would call the full economic life of the article. It is in just such situations, where the supposed lease term is chosen to extend at least through the full anticipated economic life of the collateral, that a "lease" is not a lease.

Note that it would be perfectly possible for Sue and Bob to create a true lease covering this pass. If Bob were only going to be in town for the first half of 1994, he could lease the pass for the months of January through June at a rental of $60 a month. But we see here that at the end of the lease term the item would still have economic life left in it. Six months of free movie-going remains. Sue would undoubtedly insist on its return on July 1. Beyond this, from the very beginning Sue would have known that the market value of movie passes for the second half of 1994 continued to be of direct economic importance to her. Now it is Bob who has no stake in the value of the property following the end of the lease term.

I've given an example where it should be easy to tell whether what purports to be a lease is one in reality. What makes this one so easy is that the item has such a defined and indisputable economic life—an unusual situation. More typically the economic life of a piece of goods can only be estimated or anticipated at the time the agreement is entered into.* Courts looking into the issue, either prior to Article 2A or especially now after its enactment, will rarely have such a clear-cut case.

To offer assistance for the real cases, the drafters of Article 2A also offered up to the states a revised (and considerably lengthened) version of §1-201(37). Not exactly hidden in this lengthy definitional section are some guides to help the courts determine when what purports to be a leasing arrangement is in fact such and hence governed by 2A. As we noted earlier, even without the adoption of 2A in any particular state the courts have often had to decide whether a purported lease is in fact a sale and hence govern by Article 2. The new version of §1-201(37) is presumably helpful even when that is the chore, and indeed several states have adopted this definitional change even when they have not yet enacted 2A.

Glance over §1-201(37) in your copy of the Code. If you see a single subsection covering almost a full two pages of the book, you are looking at the new updated version. (The prior version was just one long paragraph.) Read the first part of the second paragraph, just up to the semicolon: "Whether a transaction creates a lease or security interest is determined by the facts of each case. . . ." That's the basic rule. All else that follows is in effect a series of guidelines or rules of thumb that the courts can use in scrutinizing the facts of an individual case. You may

---

*Notice that the so-called useful economic life of goods or personal property will presumably always be some finite amount of time. Everything eventually wears out or becomes useless. Compare this to the value of real property, which we assume will go on having at least some value as long as there is an earth and people who want a place on it.

want to look this over now, but it certainly isn't necessary and you shouldn't let the details distract you from the basic idea.* The determination hinges not on the intent of the parties, and certainly not on how they chose to characterize it, but on the economic realities that surround their transaction. The distinguishing feature of a true lease is the reservation of some economically significant ownership interest in the lessor and an expectation that at the end of the lease term the subject property will have some useful life left on its return to the lessor. Then, and only then, is a lease a lease.

Onward with Article 2A

In the chapters that follow I will be making reference to Article 2A when the need arises. Sometimes the rules adopted by 2A are virtually identical to analogous sections in Article 2 and we can study the two as if they were one. Other times 2A diverges from 2 and the differences will be noted. In these instances different rules have been proposed for leases just because leases—when they are true leases—are different not just in form but in substance from sales and the rules of the game must reflect these different economic realities.

---

*If you do find the subject fascinating or it is something you have to go more deeply into, you will also want to look at the new, lengthy comment to §1-201(37).

3

Who Is a "Merchant" and Why It Matters

Why Care Who's a Merchant?

Article 2 of the Uniform Commercial Code rules over all of us. Each and every person selling or buying goods in a jurisdiction that has adopted Article 2 of the Uniform Commercial Code is subject to the provisions of that article. Buyers and sellers of goods are governed by the Code's provisions simply because of who they are: buyers and sellers of goods. It makes no difference that people might not think of themselves as engaging in a "business" or "commercial" transaction when, for example, they buy a burger at a fastfood restaurant or pick up a paperback at the local bookstore. Anyone who is a participant in a transaction within the scope of Article 2 (a subject on which Chapter 1 had plenty to say) is governed by the provisions of that article.

Article 2 lays out some special rules for a unique set of players, however: those it defines and refers to very carefully as "merchants." The important point initially is just that—there need be no guesswork involved in deciding when a distinct rule or standard of Article 2 law applies to a merchant. You need only look for the word *merchant*. If a special rule applies to merchants, it is because the Code language clearly states that this is so. It is not for you or me to decide whether in a particular situation someone we think of as a merchant has any different responsibility than a mere mortal nonmerchant. Those decisions have already been made by the drafters of the Code.*

---

*The definition of "merchant" in Article 2 is made applicable to Article 2A by §2A-103(3). Presumably it will be interpreted in the same manner as it has been for the sales article. Note also the definition of "merchant lessee" in §2A-103(1)(t).

This chapter is not intended as a full discussion of the special rules governing merchants under Article 2. That discussion must necessarily be woven into the following chapters and our coverage of individual topics. I will not even attempt here a full listing of all of the places in Article 2 where merchant status can make a difference. The purpose of this chapter is simply to alert you to the significance placed on this definition by the drafters. This is as good a place as any to study (even if it initially must be out of any fuller context) the definition set out in §2-104. You may well find yourself referring back to this chapter when particular rules for merchants are invoked in later material.

For the purposes of this discussion, however, a few examples may be in order. A quick look at §2-314 (which gets the full treatment in Chapter 13) lets you see that a buyer only benefits from what we will call the "warranty of merchantability" when "the seller is a merchant with respect to goods of that kind." In Chapter 6 we will go into the details of the Statute of Frauds as it has been incorporated into Article 2 in §2-201. We will see there that an important provision of that section is its subsection (2), which applies only in the case of agreements made "between merchants." The term *between merchants,* as you see in §2-104(3), is defined as meaning "any transaction with respect to which both parties are chargeable with the knowledge or skill of merchants." Which leads us to the definition of *merchant* itself.

The Merchant Class

The definition of *merchant* in §2-104(1) is sufficiently important to be quoted in full.

> "Merchant" means a person who deals in goods of the kind *or* otherwise by his occupation holds himself out as having knowledge or skill peculiar to the practices *or* goods involved in the transaction *or* to whom such knowledge or skill may be attributed by his employment of an agent or broker or other intermediary who by his occupation holds himself out as having such knowledge or skill.

As you probably could guess, the emphasis on the repeated use of *or* is mine. It is important to stress that the way §2-104(1) is written there is not necessarily a single test for whether a person is a merchant. In fact, as the section has been applied a person may well be a merchant for the purposes of one section of the Code and not a merchant with respect to another. Take time now to read in full Comment 2 to this section. It should help you in analyzing the questions which follow.

EXAMPLES

1.   Ned, a lawyer, is the proud owner of a purebred female cocker spaniel which he arranges to have mated with a purebred male owned by a neighbor. When the puppies are born, he posts a handwritten "Puppies

For Sale" notice on bulletin boards around town and places a small ad in the want ads section of the local newspaper. Would a buyer of one of the puppies get the §2-314 warranty of merchantability along with the puppy?

2. It turns out that Ned, while keeping his lawyering job, had expanded his dog breeding activities considerably. He now owns several females which he regularly breeds, advertising and selling the offspring under the name of "Spaniels of Springfield." Would your answer to the previous question be any different?

3. The Wauwatosa High School Band Mothers Association organized a fundraising luncheon at which they served turkey salad and a dessert. Pearl Samson attended the lunch, ate some of the food (for which she paid $1.25), and by the next day was seriously ill. Eventually she was diagnosed as having contracted salmonella food poisoning. There was evidence that the turkey salad was to blame. Can Pearl bring an action against the Mothers Association based on §2-314 and the warranty of merchantability?

4. Dr. Newbolt had been a dentist for many years when she decided to give it all up and try something else. She opens a furniture store. During the "Grand Opening Sale" on her first day in business, she sells a sofa to one Sophie. Does Sophie get a warranty of merchantability along with the sofa? Would it make any difference if Sophie had long known Dr. Newbolt and had, in fact, discussed with her the whole idea of her going into the furniture business?

5. In the process of building a vacation home on some land that he owned in Maine, Joe heard about some new "super efficient" insulation manufactured by a California company called Newtech. Joe contacted his local building supply store, Sarah's Supply of Portland. Sarah said she had never heard of the product but that she would contact the NewTech company and try to order some for Joe. Eventually just enough insulation to fill Joe's order is shipped to Sarah, who duly delivers it to Joe's building location and bills Joe for the price, which she calculates as the cost of the material to her plus a customary markup. Later it turns out that the insulation is defective. If Joe sues Sarah, can she defend on the basis that she had never ordered the new product before or since and had not held herself out as having any special knowledge or expertise about it?

6. Flora owns a flower shop. Whenever she sells any flowers her buyer would, of course, be getting a warranty that they were merchantable. Suppose that in remodelling her store Flora decides to get rid of her old refrigeration unit and buy a new one. She sells the old unit to a dealer in used refrigeration equipment. Does *this* buyer get the warranty of merchantability from Flora?

7. Flora enters into an oral agreement with a salesperson from Chillers, Inc. under which she will buy an expensive new refrigerated display case. She later tries to get out of the deal using an argument based on the Statute of Frauds and the lack of any writing signed by her. For reasons

that we will explore in Chapter 6, Chillers argues that she is bound in spite of a lack of a writing signed by her. This argument will only work for Chillers if it can show this agreement was "between merchants." Does Chillers succeed?

8.   Farmer Jones is, as you might expect, a farmer. During the summer of 1992 he harvests a large crop of summer squash, of which a small portion he sells to the public at a roadside stand. The rest of the harvest is claimed by a large company, Agribuyer, Inc., on the basis of an agreement it entered into with Jones earlier in the year. Jones would like to get out of the deal with Agribuyer, relying on the Statute of Frauds.

a.   When a few squash are purchased by Dan Urban, a city-dweller out for a drive in the country, does Urban get a warranty of merchantability?

b.   Will Agribuyer have any success invoking the "between merchants" exception to the Statute of Frauds as applicable to its dealing with Jones?

EXPLANATIONS

1.   No, Ned would not be considered a merchant on these facts. The buyer would not get the warranty of merchantability. (As you'll see in later chapters, this doesn't mean the buyer doesn't get any warranty protection, only that the particular warranty of merchantability isn't available to him or her.) In the language of the section, Ned does not "deal in goods of the kind" or "hold himself out" as having any "special knowledge or skill." As Comment 1 sets out, the definition of the term "merchant" is supposed to distinguish between the "professional" on the one hand and the "casual or inexperienced seller or buyer" on the other. See also Comment 3 to §2-314, which states that "[a] person making an isolated sale of goods is not a 'merchant' within the meaning of the full scope of the section, and, thus, no warranty of merchantability would apply." In *Nuijens v. Novy*, 144 Misc. 2d 453, 543 N.Y.S.2d 887, 10 U.C.C.2d 1179 (1989), a town justice in New York, faced with a disgruntled puppy buyer, held that the warranty of merchantability did not apply when there was no evidence that the seller, a self-employed farrier, had engaged in the sale of more than one litter in the course of the year.

2.   Under these facts buyers would get the warranty of merchantability. It is not necessarily the larger scale of Ned's venture that makes the difference. It becomes relevant, however, that he is in fact running it as an ongoing business and holding it out to the public as such by his use of the name "Spaniels of Springfield" and, presumably, such indicia of a professional business venture as letterhead using this name and a telephone listing under it.

It should be obvious that drawing the line between the "professional" dealer and the "casual or inexperienced" individual who is making only an "isolated" sale is not always so easy to draw. In some situations it will seem something like a toss-up. Then it's got to be a judgment call. What we can say is that the more "professional" the party appears to be the more likely it is that he or she will fall within the merchant class. The more "casual or inexperienced," the less likely.

3. The Wisconsin Supreme Court (Wauwatosa is in Wisconsin) held that the Mothers Association was not a merchant in *Samson v. Riesing,* 62 Wis. 2d 698, 215 N.W.2d 662, 14 U.C.C. 618 (1974). The court distinguished between folks like the Mothers Association and the "commercial restauranteur." But does this make a difference to Pearl? It's best to reserve judgment until we study the merchantability idea in Chapter 13. Of course the result might well have been different if it had been shown that the Association sponsored meals on some kind of regular or continuing basis.

4. Newbolt is a merchant of furniture from the moment she opens up the store. Even as a new entrant in the business world, she "holds herself out" as having the kind of knowledge and skill which others in the field have. If Newbolt doesn't have this degree of expertise, it's her problem and she can't shift the risk to her buyers. Under the language of §2-104(1), it shouldn't make any difference that the particular buyer might know she is new to the field or that she doesn't have the requisite knowledge or skill. In *Golden Needles Knitting & Glove Co, Inc. v. Dynamic Marketing Enterprises, Inc.,* 766 F. Supp. 421, 14 U.C.C.2d 1069 (W.D. N.C. 1991), the defendant, which had entered into an agreement to be the exclusive distributor of plaintiff's surgical gloves, claimed not to be a merchant since the company was new in the business. The court noted:

> Such an argument is undermined in light of a letter by [the defendant's] President, Victor Ragucci, to Plaintiff's marketing manager, Roger Sutton, on December 20, 1989. In that letter, Ragucci states, "Dynamic Medical (the predecessor of defendant) has presently dealers in Massachusetts, Michigan, and California, promoting our quality latex glove lines." . . . The letter demonstrates that Victor Ragucci, the alter-ego of defendant, had extensive experience distributing goods similar to the ones manufactured by plaintiff. Therefore, the court finds that defendant, through Ragucci, was a merchant for the purposes of the UCC.

The important point, of course, is not that Ragucci did in fact have this expertise, but that he "held himself out" as having it in his business dealings.

In this context consider also *Miller v. Badgley,* 51 Wash. App. 285, 753 P.2d 530, 6 U.C.C.2d 1082 (1988). Earl Miller was a well-known racer, sailor, and builder of sailboats. According to one expert witness, Miller "built the biggest, fanciest fiberglass boats that had ever been seen in Seattle." He and his wife owned the *Bonnie,* which they sold to Ms. Badgley. The buyer claimed a breach of the warranty of merchantability. The sellers argued that this was a personal sale, not one through Mr.

Miller's company, Miller Marine, and that as an "isolated sale" it was not covered by §2-314. The court would have little of this argument.

> Miller built and sold sailboats for a living. He held himself out to Badgley as having professional knowledge and skill in this field. To hold under the circumstances here that Miller was not a merchant merely because the transaction was carried out privately rather than through the corporate entity would be to elevate form over substance.

5.   Sarah would probably be liable on the warranty of merchantability. Her argument against liability is based on the language in §2-314 that requires that the seller be a merchant "with respect to goods of that kind." She argues she does not normally deal in nor did she hold herself out as having any special expertise with respect to this type of insulating material. But a court would most likely read the "goods of that kind" requirement more broadly. Sarah does regularly deal in building materials, and that should be enough. After all, her supply company is in business to make money; Joe contacted her because of her general experience in the area, and she was willing to deal with him and make money off of this sale. The question is based on *Ashley Square, Ltd. v. Contractors Supply of Orlando, Inc.,* 532 So. 2d 710, 6 U.C.C.2d 1100 (Fla. Dist. Ct. App. 1988), which held the supply company to be "a merchant with respect to goods of that kind" in a similar situation having to do with some special stucco it ordered at the request of a buyer.

6.   The buyer of the refrigerator would presumably not get the warranty of merchantability because Flora is not a "merchant with respect to goods" of the refrigerator kind. As far as the trade in refrigerators goes, this seems to be a particularly good example of the "isolated sale" which in and of itself does not make the seller a merchant who gives the warranty of merchantability.

The distinction between flowers and refrigeration equipment is pretty clear. In other situations, sellers have tried to draw a very fine line with the "goods of that kind" language in §2-314, with some success. In *Fear Ranches Inc. v. Berry,* 470 F.2d 905, 12 U.C.C. 27 (10th Cir. 1972), the defendant ranchers had previously sold all of the cattle they raised to packers. Because of financial difficulties they were forced to sell some of the animals to the plaintiff buyer who, supposedly unknown to the sellers, was to use them for breeding. The court held that the sellers had not given any warranty of merchantability which would protect the plaintiff when the cattle sold turned out to be unfit for breeding. Contrast this to the case of *Alpert v. Thomas,* 643 F. Supp. 1406, 2 U.C.C.2d 99 (D. Vt. 1986). The sellers, operating under the name Georgian Hill Arabians, were engaged in the business of training, breeding, and selling Arabian horses. They sold one such horse, a twenty-month old Russian-Arabian stallion named Raxx, to the buyer for a price of $175,000. The sellers understood that the buyer was buying Raxx for breeding purposes. Over time, and after many examinations by a series of expert veterinarians, Raxx was found (while having "excellent libido") to fall under guidelines established by the Society of Theriogenology in the category of "unsatisfactory prospective breeder." So much for Raxx, at least in the eyes of the buyers, who sought relief under the doctrine of the warranty of merchantability. The sellers argued that, under the *Fear Ranches* case, they could not be held to have given the warranty of merchantability as they had never before sold a stallion for this purpose. However, the cases were easily distinguishable on the facts. Here the sellers had known of the buyer's intention to try to breed Raxx. They had previously been involved in the sale of seven or eight mares for breeding purposes, and they had sold shares in a breeding stallion. The court had no difficulty in finding that these sellers, unlike the ranchers in *Fear Ranches,* were merchants for the purposes of §2-314.

While Flora the florist is almost assuredly not a merchant with respect to the refrigerator, it would not be right to conclude that a seller will never be held to have given the warranty of merchantability unless it makes a sale of exactly that stuff which it is in business to sell. The Massachusetts Supreme Judicial Court has held that the Massachusetts Bay Transportation Authority, which is presumably in the business of providing mass transit services, was a merchant and gave the warranty of merchantability in connection with its sale of eight used trolly cars to a dealer in scrap metals. *Ferragamo v. Massachusetts Bay Transportation Authority,* 395 Mass. 581, 481 N.E.2d 477, 41 U.C.C. 304 (1985). The suit was brought in the name of a worker who died following his work dismantling the cars, allegedly because of the level of certain materials in them which gave off deadly fumes when exposed to the worker's acetylene torch. The MBTA had argued that the sale was "incidental" to its primary business and, hence, was not made by it as a merchant. The Supreme Judicial Court, however, noted that

> the MBTA was highly "experienced and knowledgeable" with respect to the goods involved. The MBTA had, through its employees, a long-term and thorough acquaintance with the cars sold to the plaintiff: MBTA employees had contributed to the manufacture of the cars, had operated, repaired, refurbished, and maintained them for twenty-five years. [W]hile the MBTA may not be a merchant of scrap, there was sufficient evidence to conclude that it was a merchant of used trolly cars.

Nor did the MBTA's sale of these used trollies rightly fall within the category of an "isolated sale." The court found that the jury could have rightly concluded that the MBTA routinely sold off its used and discarded cars.

7. After analyzing the previous question, we concluded that Flora was not a merchant, so what's the problem here? Comment 2 to §2-104, which is widely quoted and respected, informs us (even if the actual language of the section does not) that a person can be a merchant for one purpose and not for another.

> The professional status under the definition may be based upon specialized knowledge as to the goods, specialized knowledge as to business practices, or specialized knowledge as to both and which

kind of specialized knowledge may be sufficient to establish
merchant status is indicated by the nature of the provision.

Read the rest of this Comment if you have not already done so. The
question of whether Flora sold the old refrigerator as a merchant for the
purposes of §2-314 was, we are told, a much narrower question than
whether she should be classified a merchant for the purposes of the Statute
of Frauds of §2-201. For purposes of that section, "almost every person
in business" would be deemed to be a merchant. Flora is in business; she
owns and operates a flower shop; the transaction was undertaken by her
in that business capacity. Chiller should win on its argument that this
deal took place "between merchants."

The Comment's statement that for purposes of provisions like the
Statute of Frauds "banks or universities, for example, may well be 'merchants' " is made real in the recent case of *National Microsales Corp. v.
Chase Manhattan Bank N.A.*, 761 F. Supp. 304, 14 U.C.C.2d 995
(1991). The court held Chase Manhattan subject to the so-called merchants' exception of §2-201(2) in conjunction with its alleged sale of
used computer output microfilming equipment.

8. Here again we face the possibility that the question whether Jones
fits under the Code definition of merchant will be answered differently
depending on what section of Article 2 is being invoked. In (a) the
question is one for §2-314, and the answer is fairly straightforward: Jones
is a merchant selling his squash to Dan Urban at the roadside stand.
Urban gets the warranty of merchantability. The issue in (b) is more tricky
and has no easy answer. There are an amazing number of cases dealing
with just this issue, that is, whether a farmer is to be considered a merchant
for the purposes of §2-201(2). The results are split just about down the
middle. Some courts hold that a farmer's once-a-year sale of his or her
entire crop is rightly an "isolated sale" by a nonprofessional. Others see
the modern farmer as more than a simple hayseed. He or she must be as
sophisticated in business as other actors on the commercial scene. Those
states which have held that a farmer can be a merchant for the purposes
of this section typically say that whether a *particular* farmer is a merchant
is a question of fact, and that the court has to look into the degree of
business acumen he or she has shown, length of time in the trade, and
so on. For all their talk of "the intention of the drafters," the cases seem
to turn on the individual court's attitude towards farmers and farming
as much as on anything else. There is no reason to think that there will
be any agreement in the foreseeable future on whether a farmer is a
merchant under Article 2.

4

Offer and Acceptance: The Basics

Contract Formation Under Article 2

In the basic Contracts course, much time and energy is invariably spent on what are generically referred to by Contracts teachers as "problems of contract formation." Students more regularly refer to this material as simply "the offer and acceptance stuff." Here the totally innocent student can be excused for feeling that he or she is being hit by a veritable blizzard of rules, subrules, generalizations and exceptions not just about offers and acceptances but all manners of revocations, rejections, counteroffers, "deviant acceptances," and what-not. And any or all of these can come in the form of a letter, a telegram, a phone conversation, a nod, or a shrug, not to mention the intriguing possibility of communication by silence. The whole topic can easily begin to seem like a grotesque dance of innumerable intricate (and dizzying) steps.

You might therefore initially be surprised at how *few* sections Article 2 devotes to contract formation issues. To a large measure this is because of the overall approach the drafters took—and wished us to take—to such problems. Look at §2-204 on Formation in General, and particularly at the first subsection: "A contract for sale of goods may be made in any manner sufficient to show agreement, including conduct by both parties which recognizes the existence of such a contract." We are encouraged to conceive of the necessary "mutual assent" in a much more flexible way than was true in the traditional or classical common law of contract, where formal structure and a myriad of technicalities took center stage.* As a matter of fact, this more laissez-faire attitude of the Code is not so far from more recent thinking about contract law in general. As I hope you see in studying this material, many of the more recent common law contracts cases (and certainly recent commentators) tend to downplay the technicalities and, like the Code, instead focus on the fact of agreement, using the notions of offer, acceptance, and so on not as ends in themselves but to delve into the (reasonable) reality of the situation in which the two communicating parties find themselves. This so-called modern law of contract had its influence on the drafting of Article 2 and has in turn itself been influenced by that article's overall success.

There is a second related reason why Article 2 does not go into all of the details of offer and acceptance law as you might have expected. It cannot ignore these problems entirely but, to the extent that the sections we are discussing in this and the next chapter don't answer a particular question, there will always be the general common law of offer and acceptance to fall back on. Note the effect of §1-103. The drafters of Article 2 did not purport to be codifying all of the minutia of the law of contract formation. What was left uncodified remains governed by the general principles of contract law. As an example, you will find no mention in the Code of that old stand-by, the mailbox rule. But that's just the point. You really can think of it as a stand-by. In the unlikely event you are ever called upon to deal with a potential sale of goods in which an unambiguous revocation of an offer and an equally unambiguous acceptance of that offer cross in the mails, then by all means refer to your notes on the common law's way of sorting out the mess. Otherwise, be glad that the Code drafters did not clutter up their work with each and every detail. Focus your thoughts, as they would have you in §2-204 and the following sections, on *why* such communications matter. The question is whether or not the parties have as a practical matter reached sufficient agreement for contract liability to arise. If they have in fact reached agreement, *how* they did so is of secondary or no importance.† In this regard, note also §2-204(2).

The third subsection of §2-204 deserves a bit more comment. *Indefiniteness* has always been itself a particularly indefinite and troublesome term for the common law of contracts, but if anything the drafters seem to be saying that some greater degree of indefiniteness may be possible in the negotiations for the sale of goods without putting the formation of a legally binding contract into jeopardy. Read by itself this statement may seem like just so much handwaving and in that respect not particularly

---

*I probably should not even dignify by mention an even earlier and now totally discredited style of dealing with formation issues, that supposedly captured in the charming but hopelessly archaic phrase "the meeting of the minds." So I won't mention it. Forget about this note.

†The one place where this last generalization doesn't really hold is in the so-called "Battle of the Forms," an advanced topic to be dealt with in the next chapter. And, as you will see there, it is just the situation where the drafters' willingness to go deeper into the details got them into so much trouble.

helpful. But §2-204(3) is not left to work on its own. See the last two paragraphs of the comment to this section. As we will discuss in later chapters, Article 2 takes particular note of how often negotiations that would seem hopelessly indefinite or merely bizarre to the observing layperson will be perfectly clear to the parties themselves. (The crucial role of so-called trade terms is left to Chapter 7. A set of particular sections, the so-called gap fillers of Article 2, are dealt with in Chapter 9.) For the moment it is enough to take to heart the comment's message that *commercial* standards of indefiniteness, not the standards of an uninformed layperson and certainly not the standards of a pettifogging lawyer, are what are relevant to the question of contract formation.

A note on leases: As you can check, §2A-204 on the formation of lease contracts in general tracks §2-204 word for word. No doubt the drafters of Article 2A meant whatever jurisprudence of §2-204 there is to be followed when the transaction is a lease. There may be, however, one potential difference between the two sections in practice: The gap-filling provisions of Article 2, which can make up for a good measure of indefiniteness in many circumstances, were not carried over into Article 2A. Though it is too soon to tell, this does suggest that the measure of detail necessary to avoid failure for indefiniteness in negotiation for a lease may turn out to be somewhat greater, or at least different in some respects, than in the case of a sale.

Agreement Seen in Conduct

Both §2-204(1) and §2A-204(1) specify that an agreement can be established by "conduct by both parties which recognizes the existence of such a contract." This provision can be of particular importance when the parties never quite get all the paperwork in order and one is later trying to rely on this fact alone to establish that a contract never existed. The drafters recognized that all too often contracting parties, either through lack of diligence or because they continue to squabble over minor details none of which would be a "deal breaker," fail to produce a nice neat package of terms all written up and signed. At the same time both parties may be well into performance of their obligations, speaking and acting for all the world as if there was a binding agreement. The law of the Code is that if this is the case (and if there is "a reasonably certain basis for giving an appropriate remedy" in the event of a breach), then there actually *is* a binding agreement. No one gets out of his or her deal on this particular technicality.

In *Nebraska Builders Products Co. v. The Industrial Erectors, Inc.,* 239 Neb. 744, 478 N.W.2d 257, 16 U.C.C.2d 568 (1992), for example, the parties entered into an agreement for the purchase and sale of some industrial cranes, which were to be prepared according to detailed specifications. The parties never executed a formal writing. Industrial, the seller, claimed that as a result it was not bound by any contract. The trial court agreed, ruling that no contract had been formed, but the Supreme Court of Nebraska held this to be error. The key was §2-204. While the buyer may or may not have accepted the seller's written sales proposal over the telephone soon after it was made, the court noted that for several months after it sent its proposal the seller acted *as if* a contract existed, preparing shop drawings and corresponding with the buyer about obtaining approval for minor variances in the specifications. In addition, a representative of Industrial had visited the buyer's offices almost five months "after the alleged agreement was made," in the words of the court, "to answer questions on the crane system that Industrial would supply." On behalf of Industrial, of course, it could be argued that all this activity was carried out not in accordance with an obligation already undertaken but in pursuit of a possible deal. But that is exactly the point. Under §2-204 the question is to be decided as one of fact—did sufficient agreement exist?—and the facts are to be viewed in their own unique commercial context. In another case, *American Plastic Equipment, Inc. v. CBS Inc.,* 886 F.2d 521, 9 U.C.C.2d 848 (2d Cir. 1989), the court stressed among other facts that at the conclusion of a negotiation session between representatives of the two parties, the buyer's negotiator "asserted that a deal had been made and the two thereupon shook hands—a formality indicating intent to be bound." Of course not every handshake concludes a legally binding contract, but this court rightly took note of the fact that in such a situation parties do not take an offered handshake lightly. Along with other activities on the part of the seller, it formed "conduct which recognize[d]" the existence of a contract.

Two final points about contracts established in this way by conduct. First of all, note that the "conduct" called for in this section presumably need not rise to the level of what is studied in Contracts as *detrimental reliance*. The point of finding the conduct relevant here is really informational or evidentiary—not as is the case with true detrimental reliance that it significantly alters the balance of equities between the parties because of one's conduct influenced by the fact of the contract. For example, imagine that after a period of negotiation between a prospective Buyer and Seller, Buyer contacts the head of his purchasing department and directs that a computer file be initiated "to handle this account" including information such as where payments are to be sent and so on. Meanwhile, Seller tells her billing and shipping departments to put Buyer in their computer files. Further assume that she tells these departments to get all pertinent information from the sales department, which will be putting in deep computer storage its own relevant file on Buyer, as its practice is to keep current files only on "active prospects." Here I have posited a whole mess of conduct consistent with a contract having been entered into on both parties' parts. And yet it would take a very watered-down view of "detrimental reliance" to find it on either Seller's or Buyer's part here, at least if their computer systems come equipped with the delete function.*

---

*As this discussion suggests, the Code's concept of establishing a contract for sale by conduct rather than through the rigid regime of communicated offer and acceptance

A second point is that, while behavior of the type we have been discussing may be sufficient to establish a contract under §2-204, it is not necessary. This section (and Article 2 in general) does not preclude finding a contract in the more old-fashioned way, by identifying an offer and an acceptance and leaving it at that. If one party can establish the existence of a contract by the mechanism of offer and acceptance, further conduct evidencing the existence of the contract is icing on the cake, but it is not required. Certainly no reliance on the deal need be shown to make it enforceable. The parties having agreed to a purchase and sale, that is enough.

Matters of Offer and Acceptance

While the drafters of Article 2 did not think it necessary to restate all of the law of offer and acceptance, they did apparently find some tinkering in order. The three sections beginning with §2-205 are the result. Section 2-205 concerns what the Code refers to as *firm offers*. As you know, the traditional contract law held as sacred the principle that an offer could be revoked by the offeror at any time before its acceptance. At the same time this result could create a dilemma for even the most honest, diligent and cooperative offeror and offeree. How could the offeree be given sufficient confidence that the offer would be held open for a length of time necessary for the offeree to explore the advisability of taking up the offer or to put in place other related plans? Presumably you studied or will soon study the principal common law mechanism for dealing with this problem, the *option contract*. The Code's approach, as set forth in §2-205 (and the analogous §2A-205), is explored in the first Example that follows.

The remaining Examples address some particular "fixes" to the common law which are found in §2-206 and the parallel §2A-206. You may have seen how the common law approach—at least in its most traditional mechanistic mood—can actually thwart the intentions of the parties. As I have already noted, since the adoption of Article 2 the common law of contract has been "modernized" partly through the Code's influence. The results of §2-206 will probably not strike you as unusual or remarkable as they would someone who had studied Contracts prior to the 1960s and to Article 2's widespread acceptance.

The final of the Code's three special sections on offer and acceptance, §2-207, is sufficiently tricky to warrant its own chapter, which follows.

---

is, if anything, more like the notion of the *contract implied-in-fact* which you may have discussed in your Contracts study. Even here there may be a difference, however. The notion of a contract implied-in-fact usually still involves manifestations made by one party to the other, even if not in the clearest of words or in the most formal manner. By contrast, conduct evidencing an agreement under Article 2 could presumably be strictly internal to the party but later discoverable, as for example the instance I have given in the text of internal filekeeping.

EXAMPLES

1. Sam, a used car dealer, offers to sell a certain 1984 Chevy to Beth for $1,000. She tells him that she can't make up her mind right away. Sam says to her, "Don't worry. I'll keep the offer open for the next week. You can accept any time until then." The very next day Beth decides to buy the car, but before she can get over to Sam's she receives a message from him on her telephone answering machine in which he says that he has decided not to sell the car to her at this price. His message concludes, "I would sell at $1,200."

    a. Can Beth still get the car for $1,000?

    b. Suppose that at their initial meeting Sam had scribbled on a memo pad bearing his company's logo the following: "Offer to sell 1984 Chevy to Beth for $1,000. Good for one week as of today." The only other marking on the piece of paper was the day's date. Does this change your answer to the question?

    c. Bonnie, who happens to be a bank president, drives her car into Sam's looking to sell it. She is asking $2,400. Sam says he'll consider this deal, but only if she signs a piece of paper he writes out that says, "Bonnie offers to sell her car to Sam for $2,400, this offer to remain open and irrevocable for a period of one month from this date." Sam dates the paper. Bonnie signs it. Is Bonnie bound to keep this offer open for the full month? Would your answer be any different if Bonnie were herself a dealer in automobiles and not a banker?

2. Seller sends a telegram to Buyer making a definite offer to sell. Buyer immediately sends back a letter clearly stating that she accepts the offer? It arrives in the normal course of post. Has a contract been formed?

3. After some preliminary and inconclusive negotiations over the telephone, Buyer sends Seller a letter setting forth the terms of a proposed deal. The letter ends with the statement, "This offer may be accepted by Seller only by his returning to Buyer a copy of this letter signed and dated by him." At the bottom of the letter is a line for the Seller's signature under the heading "Accepted on _____ by Seller." Seller never returns this letter, but instead calls and leaves a message with Buyer's secretary that he accepts the offer mailed to him. Has a contract been formed?

4. Betrand, a maker of appliances, needs some electrical switches. He reviews a catalog and price list that he had received from Switches International, a major vendor of such things, and concludes that he wants their switch #XR7, which is listed at a price of $5 per unit. He sends Switches a Purchase Order form he filled out that calls for 2,000 of the #XR7 switches. Under "Date of Delivery" on the form, he puts "Immediate Delivery."

    a. When Switches receives this order, what may it do in order to accept this offer?

    b. Suppose that Switches accidentally ships 2,000 of its #XR9 switches. Betrand cannot use this model, does not accept the shipment, and is hurt by the delay. If Betrand sues Switches for breach, can that firm argue that there never was a contract for the #XR7 switches as it never accepted the order?

c. Suppose instead that the shipment of the #XR9s was not a mistake. When it received Betand's order it found itself temporarily low on the #XR7 switch. Believing that the buyer could use the more advanced #XR9 in its place, and being willing to accept the same price for them, it shipped the newer switches in response to this order. Is Switches in breach of contract?

EXPLANATIONS

1a. No. Sam has effectively revoked the original offer. Beth would want to argue that his promise to keep the offer open was binding on him under §2-205, but she loses because it was not in writing. Reading this section you find a number of criteria which must be met in order for an ordinary, revocable offer to be made into a firm offer: The offeror must be a merchant, the offer must be made in a signed writing, and the writing must "by its terms give assurances that it will be held open" for some time. Note that if no exact period of time is stated, the offer will be firm for "a reasonable time." If a time limit is stated, it must be no longer than three months.

What happens if an offer is made meeting all of these criteria but purporting to be irrevocable for a longer period, say six months? Does this failed attempt to take advantage of §2-205 mean that the offer is revocable from its inception? Comment 3 says no. "A promise made for a longer period will operate under this section to bind the offeror only for the first three months of the period but may of course be renewed." Is there any way under Article 2 that an offeror can bind him or herself to a longer period of irrevocability? The Comment goes on to remind us that an offer "supported by consideration" may continue for a longer period. This is just the old common law option, the possibility of which presumably survives the passage of Article 2—at least if the consideration is real and of some value and not merely a token amount or the recitation of a purported consideration like "one dollar in hand paid."

1b. Here all the criteria appear to be met and the offer would be irrevocable for the week. The language on the memo sheet is a bit vague, but it should be enough to constitute an "assurance" that the offer would be held open for that period of time. Note that if Sam had written instead something like, "Offer will lapse one week from today," this would probably not constitute a firm offer. That language would be taken as meaning only that the offer would lapse naturally of its own accord after a week, not as a promise that the buyer couldn't make it lapse earlier by a revocation effectively communicated.

The one problem Beth might have here is establishing that this was a *signed* writing, as Sam never did add his personal signature to the paper. But look at the definition in §1-201(39) and the comment to that subsection. The fact that the paper had Sam's logo on it and was given by him to record something to do with his business should be enough. See also Comment 2 to §2-205 itself, which supports this conclusion.

1c. Bonnie cannot be held to her promise not to revoke the offer. Her case is easy since she is not a merchant. On who is and who is not a "merchant" under Article 2, see §2-104 as discussed in Chapter 3. Note in the second comment to that section that for the purposes of §2-205 almost every person in business would be a merchant. But the comment goes on to say that even if Bonnie is president of a bank, if she is here buying in a personal capacity she need not worry about making a firm offer.

If Bonnie deals in cars, she would be a merchant and could presumably make a firm offer to sell one under §2-205. In that case the final language of that section becomes crucial. Read it. The idea here, as noted in Comment 4, is to prevent any offeror, even a merchant, from "inadvertently" giving up the precious right to revoke by too casually signing a paper put in front of him or her.

2.   Yes, *if* responding with a letter was a medium "reasonable in the circumstances" under §2-206(1)(a). Of course if in the particular situation the buyer should have recognized that the seller would expect a speedier response, then the ordinary post might not be a reasonable medium. Presumably a fax or a telephone call would be. Maybe even a letter sent by special overnight delivery. It all depends on the particular circumstances. As Comment 1 suggests, this language in §2-206(1)(a) was included to do away with any lingering adherence to an older set of highly technical (and often "unreasonable") rules about offer and acceptance. (This comment's reference to the possibility of new media of communication developing is particularly interesting in light of the recent explosive rise in faxes and faxing quite beyond what would have been anticipated even a few years ago. People who before led perfectly productive lives now are wondering how they ever got along without it.) I hope that in your study of the modern law of contract formation you saw this more flexible and realistic approach as it has been adopted more generally, thanks in part to the influence of Article 2's drafters.

3.   No. This section does not do away with the old idea that the offeror is "master of his or her offer." Here the offer unambiguously indicates a particular mode of acceptance and §2-206(1) allows this to control. Courts have upheld this result. In fact in an interesting set of circumstances this provision can work to the advantage of an offeree who later changes his or her mind. Sales made by travelling and door-to-door salespeople often are written up by the seller's representative filling out a Purchase Order on the spot and getting the buyer to sign it. The buyer will be given the impression that he or she is committed from that moment on. Somewhere on the Purchase Order form, however, is language to the effect that a contract will be entered into only when the form is accepted or signed by a higher official of the seller at its home office. This is put there by the company, of course, to be sure that an overeager sales representative doesn't enter into a deal which he or she shouldn't have. But notice the result. Until the form is transmitted back to the home office, and until it is actually signed there, the paper is merely an offer made by the buyer. So the buyer has the right to get out of the deal by

revoking the offer before it has been accepted at the home office. Sellers sometimes are sloppy with their own internal paperwork and have to take the consequences. See, for example, *Beard Implement Co., Inc. v. Krusa*, 208 Ill. App. 3d 953, 567 N.E.2d 345, 15 U.C.C.2d 750 (1991).

4a. Switches has several options on how to accept. Read §2-206(1)(b) and §2-206(2). It can promptly reply with a promissory acceptance, either in writing or orally. It can promptly ship the switches off to Betrand. It may even be able to accept by "the beginning of [the] requested performance," although what that might be in this instance is unclear. If, for example, Switches ran its business not with a large inventory on hand but began to fabricate switches only when they were ordered, it might be deemed to have accepted once it starts making up the #XR7's needed to fill this order. Would it be enough if Switches had itself ordered from its own suppliers the component parts it would need to make up these units? What if Switches did sell from inventory and had already begun to "make up" Betrand's order by pulling the switches from the shelves, packaging them, and labelling the packages? This would not be an acceptance by shipment under §2-206(1)(b), at least according to Comment 2, but could it constitute the beginning of performance under subsection (2)? Betrand, if he tried to revoke before actual shipment, would argue that this was not the beginning of performance but only preparation for performance. After all, Switches would have felt free to unpack the goods or change the address on the packages if a more lucrative deal came along. Comment 3 suggests that in such a situation the court should look to the developing common law in this area. In any event, if a seller later wants to claim under §2-206 that the beginning of performance made for its acceptance, note that it must have notified the buyer of its acceptance within a reasonable time. Good advice, of course, would be to notify buyer as soon as possible and take no chances.

4b. Switches will be bound to the contract for the #XR7 switches. Note in §2-206(1)(b) that prompt shipment of *nonconforming goods* can act as an acceptance of the original offer. So Switches has accepted and breached the contract both at the same time! This result may seem odd, but look at it from Betrand's point of view. Should Switches be able to get out of all obligation to him because it made this mistake? Even worse, what if the seller *intentionally* shipped nonconforming goods? The common law would have it that this constituted a counteroffer. The buyer, faced with having to make a quick decision when this shipment arrived at the door might be under pressure to accept the shipment. The consequence would be that he ended up buying some things he never ordered and never really intended to buy. An argument in favor of the Code result is that it takes away from the seller this possibility of what is called *strategic behavior*.

Notice that while in this hypo the nonconformity involves the actual type of good ordered, the result would be the same if the shipment was non-conforming in some other way. For example, suppose Switches had indeed shipped the #XR7 chip, but only 1,850 of them. This too would be an acceptance and a breach.

4c. Again, by shipping nonconforming goods Switches would be both accepting and breaching a contract for the goods ordered by Betrand. Under §2-206(1)(b) Switches could avoid this result if it "seasonably notifies the buyer that the shipment is offered only as an accommodation to the buyer." Betrand, of course, would not then have to accept the shipment—it would be merely in the nature of a counteroffer—but if he did there would be a contract for the #XR9 switches. For a case involving the accommodation notion, which the court itself acknowledges to be, despite its lengthy recitation of facts, "a straightforward sale of goods problem resembling those found in a contracts or sale of goods casebook," see *Corinthian Pharmaceutical Systems, Inc. v. Lederle Laboratories,* 724 F. Supp. 605, 11 U.C.C.2d 463 (S.D. Ind. 1989).

If you found the matters of offer and acceptance in this chapter too straightforward, wait for the next chapter. Things soon begin to fall apart.

5

Offer and Acceptance Advanced: The Battle of the Forms

The Battle Joined

As we saw in the previous chapter, the drafters of Article 2 did not mean to codify, much less to revamp, all of the common law of offer and acceptance. They did hope to push it along a bit in a more modern, less mechanistic direction, and that they did with what is said in §2-204. There was also some minor tinkering in §§2-205 and 2-206, but nothing terribly radical or difficult.*

Some changes were not so uncomplicated nor so neat. This chapter concerns what is universally referred to as *the Battle of the Forms*. The considerable problems that we will encounter come about because actual contracting parties tend not to order their affairs just to make things easy for their lawyers or for law students. They don't conveniently label their documents "Offer" and "Acceptance" and follow the rules of the offer and acceptance game, whatever version is in operation. Instead people in business tend to rely heavily on form documents that they have had preprinted for their use, detailing all manner of terms and conditions

---

*If you have not worked through Chapter 4, you might want to do so now, before you jump into this "advanced" material. At the very least, prepare for what lies ahead by looking at §2-204 and reading its Official Comment.

which not surprisingly suit them just fine. They will title their forms in whatever manner they choose. But it takes two to tango and two to make a deal. If each party relies upon or insists upon its own form, and the two forms differ as they almost invariably will, what have we? From the time of the drafting of Article 2 the answer was pretty clear: We have a situation which does not lend itself well to traditional analysis. The drafters, as we will see, get credit for facing the problem squarely. How successful their end product, the revolutionary §2-207, is—that's another matter altogether.

Our first order of business must be to review how the common law dealt* with the battle of the forms. Only then can we turn in the questions to the workings of §2-207. As you work through the questions you may come to your own conclusion about why the later drafters of Article 2A chose not to include anything like §2-207 in their work.†

A Common Law Nutshell

Imagine that Buyer sends one of his standard forms captioned "PURCHASE ORDER" to Seller. The form is mostly boilerplate of terms and conditions drafted to Buyer's liking. It does have a few blank spaces on it, which Buyer fills in with the item number and description of the goods he is ordering, the price per unit, and the requested time of delivery. He gets the information about the item from a catalog and price list that Seller had previously sent him. Seller receives this purchase order. Under the common law, would a contract for purchase and sale have been formed as of this point? The answer was almost certainly no. You may remember the old saw about how a catalog or a price list generally does not constitute an offer, but only an invitation to the recipient to make an offer. So Buyer's sending of the form is the making of an offer. That's as far as they've gotten.

Suppose now that Seller responds in a timely fashion by sending

---

*The past tense is used here because, of course, this common law has now been displaced for the sale of goods by §2-207. We are concerned here solely with the battle when the prize is a contract for the sale of goods. When the proposed contract is for something other than the sale of goods, the common law naturally still applies. There has been some suggestion in recent Contracts cases and in the Restatement of Contracts Second that the "wisdom" of §2-207 should be adopted more generally. As many have begun to sour on §2-207, at least in its present form, it is unclear how far its influence will carry.

†See Huddleston, Old Wine in New Bottles: UCC Article 2A—Leases, 39 Ala. L. Rev. 615, 620 (1988): "To its credit, Article 2A does not contain any provision corresponding to section 2-207, the sales provision that has engendered much wasteful 'battle of the forms' litigation over contract formation." This tells you something about how much respect §2-207 gets in some quarters nowadays. Others are somewhat more charitable. In any event it *is* part of Article 2, and will be until further notice, so we can't avoid working it through.

Buyer its own form, headed with "ACKNOWLEDGMENT." This form was printed up for Seller's use and, as you by now expect, has its own boilerplate, here tailored to Seller's position. The few places on the Acknowledgment which call for insertion of particularized information have been filled in with the item number, description, price and so on. All of these bits of information specific to this deal—what we will end up referring to as the "dickered terms"—are consistent with what Buyer put into the Purchase Order. Once Seller sends off this Acknowledgment form and Buyer has received it, has a contract been formed?

The short answer is that under the common law it was very unlikely that such an exchange of forms would result in a binding contract. This was true even though Buyer and Seller, being perfectly reasonable types, would probably think that they were bound, they had a done deal, or however you want to phrase it. The common law of offer and acceptance took a very rigid approach to a lot of things which ordinary business people, having to get along in the hustle and bustle of commerce and not the idealized realm of classical theory, reacted to very differently. In particular the common law rule was that for an acceptance to be an acceptance (that is, for it to conclude a binding agreement) it had to be the "mirror image" of the offer. Any additional or different terms in the response, even if seemingly trivial to the parties involved, made that response into a counteroffer. There could be no contract unless that counteroffer was itself accepted by a perfectly conforming mirror image acceptance. It's a pretty fair assumption that the boilerplate on Seller's Acknowledgment contains some provision that isn't found on Buyer's form. It's also likely that neither party noticed this and even more likely that if they did notice they didn't care. Buyer wanted to buy. Seller wanted to sell. They might have thought they had a done deal, but under the common law they did not.

The upshot of this was that if later, before the time for performance, one of them wanted to back out of the deal, even if the reason had nothing to do with anything printed on the forms, his or her lawyer would be able to make a perfectly good legal argument that there never was a contract. The Acknowledgment not being the mirror image of the Purchase Order, that offer was never accepted. The Acknowledgment was itself a counteroffer, but *that* offer was never accepted, the buyer never having responded to it. Neither could legally be held to the deal. Not to put too fine a point on it, the result of the common law rule was to allow a party who had for all practical purposes committed itself to later wriggle out of the deal on what can most charitably be called a technicality. This hardly seems fair. More than that, it's not what Buyer and Seller themselves would have expected.

To continue with our review, imagine that neither Buyer nor Seller tries to welsh on the deal. Seller ships the goods and Buyer accepts them. Now is there a contract? If so, what are its terms? Obviously, if controversy later develops about the goods or payment of the price, the precise terms of the contract can be vitally important. The common law answer was, again, fairly consistent: Now there is a contract. Seller's shipment of the goods arrived at the Buyer's door as a very tangible offer to sell on the terms and conditions on which Seller had, through its Acknowledgment, expressed its willingness to sell. Buyer could, of course, have summarily rejected this offer, but if as we posited he accepted the goods, he accepted the offer. There is a contract between the two, and its terms are to be found in Seller's Acknowledgment form. What of the special terms Buyer placed in the PURCHASE ORDER? They go for nought. As we saw, that form was just an offer that was never accepted. That's past history; it has no legal effect.

So the Seller's later form gets to lay out the terms of the deal. This result is an example of what was characterized as the *last shot rule* (or perhaps we should say the "last shot" result) of the common law. It does not always work to the benefit of the seller, as it did in this hypothetical; in some situations it was the buyer whose form document was the last to travel between the parties before performance actually began. In such a situation the analysis was that this buyer's form constituted an offer to buy on a strict set of terms laid out therein and the seller's shipment was an acceptance of all of those terms. That's the way the last shot rule worked. One party, the one whose overzealous form was the last in the series, won the grand prize. The other party was out of luck.

A First Look at §2-207

Even a quick glance at §2-207 makes clear that the drafters of Article 2 were trying to make some changes from the common law approach. What they were trying to do and what in fact they wound up doing is the matter that can no longer be avoided. Let's look at what they came up with. In its entirety, §2-207 has been referred to by one court as "a murky bit of prose," and I know of no one who would violently disagree. Still, a bit of creative typography might help. First look at §2-207(1) as it appears in your copy of the Code. Try to parse it if you can. The result should be something like this:

[A COMMUNICATION which is either]

(i) a definite and seasonable expression of acceptance

or

(ii) a written confirmation which is sent within a reasonable time

OPERATES AS AN ACCEPTANCE

even though [that communication] states terms additional to or different from those offered or agreed upon

UNLESS . . .

I have left the concluding "unless" part out for the moment, because my experience has shown that students are always rushing to worry over that language and not paying attention to what comes before. The concluding language is after all only an exception to the general rule first expressed. That general rule will give you enough to think about for the moment as you look at the first Example. I'll point you to other parts of the section as they become important for later questions.

EXAMPLES

1.   Boston Universal Yoyos ("BUY") is a major manufacturer of the popular children's toy. Finding that she needed to order a shipment of string, BUY's Purchasing Director reviewed the catalogs and price lists she always kept on hand from various string suppliers. She decided to order from a company called String Emporium of Lexington ("SEL") and instructed a clerk to place the order. That clerk took from his desk a copy of BUY's standard purchase order form. This form, which BUY had been using for a number of years, came preprinted with a lot of legal looking material (what the clerk always thought of as "our terms") as well as blank spaces calling for the item, amount, and so on. In the spaces provided he filled in SEL's item number for the kind of string he was told to order, the amount required, and the price listed in SEL's most recent price list, and indicated "For Immediate Delivery." He mailed this off to the address given on SEL's materials. A week later he received back from SEL a copy of that firm's acknowledgment form. He checked that this form had been filled in with the same item number and description, amount, price and delivery terms as he had put into the Purchase Order. He did not bother to read all of the other stuff on the Acknowledgment (what he always discounted as simply the seller's "boilerplate"). He put this Acknowledgment along with a copy of his Purchase Order in the files, told the Purchasing Director that the order had been placed, and notified the head of manufacturing that the string would be arriving shortly. If SEL never delivers the string (e.g., because it realizes the price it stated was too low), will it be in breach of contract? If SEL does deliver the string but BUY no longer wants it, can that firm simply refuse the shipment without being in breach of contract?

2.   Would the result be any different if it were shown that SEL's acknowledgment form contained on the reverse the following language in print no different from all the rest of the terms?

> SEL hereby agrees to sell only on the terms and conditions expressly stated herein. No other terms apply. SEL's agreement to this order is made conditional on purchaser's acceptance of all of the terms and conditions of this Acknowledgment form.

What if in addition the front of the Acknowledgment had printed on it in big bold letters "SEE REVERSE FOR TERMS AND CONDITIONS"? You are now given permission to look at the concluding language of §2-207(1), beginning with the word "unless."

3.   Imagine that SEL came to you asking for advice. There was a particular term on its Acknowledgment which it really did care deeply about. It

was willing to sacrifice a sale rather than enter into a contract without this particular provision. What advice would you give?

4. Assume you conclude that BUY and SEL have entered into a contract for the purchase and sale of string. What are the terms of that contract? In particular, imagine that the string is delivered and used by BUY in its manufacturing process. Many yoyos are returned to BUY because of defective strings which keep snapping.

a. BUY wants to sue SEL for damages, but that firm points to a provision on its Acknowledgment stating

> Buyer's rights in the event any product delivered pursuant to this agreement proves defective are limited to the replacement of any defective goods. Buyer agrees that SEL is not responsible for any consequential damages.

Is this clause binding upon BUY? For this question and the two that follow you'll have to move on to §2-207(2).

b. Suppose that the Acknowledgment had no language relating to a disgruntled buyer's remedies. Instead the clause of concern is one found in BUY's Purchase Order form. It states

> Seller agrees that BUY may return any product found defective for a full cash refund, and that such right to return shall continue in BUY for no less than two years from date of delivery.

Is this enforceable against SEL?

c. Would your answer to the previous question be any different if the following language had appeared in SEL's Acknowledgment?

> Purchaser agrees that it shall have no remedy for a claimed defect in the goods provided pursuant to this agreement unless demand and proof of defect has been made to SEL no later than one year from the date of delivery of said product.

5. We now change the hypothetical fundamentally. Assume that the various differences in the printed matter on the two forms are in fact spotted by employees of the parties when the forms were first exchanged. Someone from BUY calls someone at SEL and says that her firm wants the string but can't agree to several terms, including the one-year limitation. The man from SEL says he is happy to take BUY's order, but "under company policy" has to insist on this term and indeed must object to certain others in the Purchase Order. This bickering continues over a period of months. Maybe some higher-ups from the two companies get involved. Meanwhile, life goes on. The string is shipped by SEL. The shipment is accepted by BUY's manufacturing unit without any comment. The string is used to make yoyos. Then some problem develops. Is there a contract at all? If so, what are the terms of that contract which will be referred to in settling the dispute? Look at §2-207(3).

EXPLANATIONS

1. As we noted in the introductory text, under the common law and its mirror image rule, neither party would have been bound at this point, and either could get out of the deal if it chose. It did not matter whether either or both of the parties believed that the purchase and sale had been finalized nor whether that belief was justified in the circumstances; a nice technical argument allowed for welshing on what was probably considered by both a done deal. The drafters of Article 2, in accordance with their general principle that the law of sales should comport with and support what people involved in doing the buying and selling would think their obligations to be, had in mind changing this result via their drafting of §2-207(1).

This subsection determines when a communication in response to an offer operates as an acceptance as a matter of Article 2 law. To "operate as an acceptance" is to *bind both parties*. As we know, the common law had it that the only thing that operated as an acceptance was an *actual acceptance*, by which it meant a response that mirrored the offer in each and every detail and provided for nothing new. Section 2-207(1) changes this. Now something called a "definite and seasonable expression of acceptance" will do the trick, and this is so "even though it states terms additional to or different from" those in the offer. So our first question is how to recognize a "definite and seasonable expression of acceptance" when we see one. The key is to be found at the beginning of Comment 2: "Under this Article a proposed deal which in commercial understanding has in fact been closed is recognized as a contract." Courts in making this determination must necessarily look to the real commercial world of the parties and how they themselves treated the communication. In our hypothetical the people at BUY took the Acknowledgment as the conclusion of a deal. We know that from their actions. No one was saying, "Well, maybe we have a deal with SEL for some string if we can work it out." We don't know firsthand how the people at SEL were viewing the situation and what they were doing, but certainly they gave BUY no reason to think that there was something iffy in the situation or that they expected negotiations to continue. In the commercial world a deal had been struck, and in the law of sales under Article 2 an effective acceptance had bound both parties.

In *Idaho Power Co. v. Westinghouse Electric Corp.,* 596 F.2d 924, 26 U.C.C. 638 (9th Cir. 1979), it was the seller Westinghouse which made the offer, on a form designated a Price Quotation. Idaho Power, the buyer, replied with a Purchase Order that the court found to operate as an acceptance.

> Here, Idaho Power referred to and accepted the price quoted in Westinghouse's offer. It requested shipment within the time limits specified by Westinghouse. No other correspondence ensued and the [machinery] was shipped and installed accordingly. In commercial transactions such an order, especially when followed by performance, would normally be understood to have closed the deal between the parties. Conse-

quently, it was a "definite and seasonable expression of acceptance," even though it contained the additional terms.

The fact that in our situation the parties have not yet actually begun to perform as if they had a contract should not make a difference. What the courts will look to in making the determination is, in effect, what the clerk in the BUY office looked at. Did the response he received give any hint that SEL wasn't willing to sell to them the particular stuff at the particular price on the particular delivery terms? What matters most is that the fill-in-the-blank items—what are sometimes referred to as the "dickered terms" unique to this specific transaction—have been approved and repeated in the return form.

Compare the situation if SEL's Acknowledgment had stated a higher figure under "Price Per Unit." Then the parties should know that the negotiations were not yet finalized and that more dickering would have to occur if there were ever to be agreement; there would be no acceptance, either in commercial understanding or under this section. Apparently in the battle of the forms nobody expects the boilerplate to match up, and now under Article 2 neither must the courts.

There are two other things to note about the language of §2-207(1) with which we are working. The first is nothing difficult nor new. To act as an acceptance a return communication, be it an expression of acceptance or a confirmation, must be "seasonable" or "sent within a reasonable time." Obviously an offeree cannot sit on an offer forever and then send something back in the mails expecting it to land the deal. The offeror may expressly set a time limit on his or her offer. If not, the offer will naturally lapse of its own accord after a reasonable time. On *reasonable time* generally see §1-204, which not surprisingly emphasizes both the principles of freedom of contract and the desirability of making judgments based on the circumstances of an individual transaction.

The second matter is not so simple. Though we have so far discussed acceptances arising out of the "definite and seasonable expression of acceptance," there is a second part to what we've seen. Under §2-207(1) a "written confirmation" may also "act as an acceptance even though. . . ." The first comment indicates this refers to situations where a written confirmation is sent by one party after an agreement has already been reached. But if an agreement has already been reached, this means that an acceptance had already been rendered in some form or another. So is the confirmation an acceptance piled on top of an already valid acceptance? The comment even suggests the possibility of both parties sending their own confirmatory memoranda. How many acceptances have we now? This is only one example of the clumsy way §2-207 has been put together, although at least this instance hasn't caused much trouble for the courts. Once there is an acceptance there is a deal, and confirmatory writings no matter what they say certainly aren't going to undo this result. The real problem with confirmations that state additional or different terms is whether those terms can possibly become part of the contractual relationship and, if so, how. But that's a problem for subsection (2), which we haven't even begun to tackle yet.

2.   SEL here would be arguing that by virtue of this language on its Acknowledgment form its acceptance was "expressly made conditional on assent to the additional or different terms." Therefore, it claims, its Acknowledgment never operated as an acceptance, only as a counteroffer. SEL never heard back from BUY acceding to these terms, and hence SEL was never legally obligated to make the delivery. (Of course in the abstract this argument could backfire on SEL since it would also imply that had SEL wanted to go through with the deal, BUY could have gotten out of it without any problem. But under the circumstances SEL couldn't care less. Is it too cynical to suggest that an argument like this only comes to light when one party has later decided to pull the plug on a deal to which it had, in all commercial reality, committed itself?)

Is SEL correct in its reliance on this language, which is often referred to as "the proviso to §2-207(1)?" That depends on whom you ask, although the overwhelming trend of decisions is not in its favor. The earliest decision interpreting this language was *Roto-Lith, Ltd. v. F. P. Bartlett & Co., Inc.*, 297 F.2d 497, 1 U.C.C. 73 (1st Cir. 1962), which is now universally referred to as the "infamous" *Roto-lith* case and credited with setting back a correct appreciation of this proviso language by at least a decade. In *Roto-Lith* the court held that any response that "states a condition materially altering the obligation solely to the disadvantage of the offeror" would trigger the proviso. But this broad a reading is clearly wrong. Virtually every form response will have something in the boilerplate which would fit this description, with the result that just about any form response would not operate as an acceptance under this view. In practice, this reading resurrects quite nicely the result if not the exact language of the old common law mirror image rule. And everyone recognizes that the whole idea of §2-207(1) was to do away with that outcome.

The *Roto-lith* result is today pretty much dead and laid to rest in most jurisdictions—even if generations of Sales professors insist on bringing it up if only as an example of horrid Code methodology. It should take more than differing terms in the return form to bring the proviso into play. What more? Some courts focus on the word *expressly* and find it enough that there is language on the form which states that the offeree intends his or her form to be taken as a counteroffer. A clear statement is said to suffice. If SEL is held to this standard, it should be able to make its argument stick. Read again the language it has put in its form.

But should this be enough? True, this language is very clear when you read it, but the whole point about boilerplate is that no one *does* read it. And more than that, no one truly expects that the recipient of the form will read it. A somewhat more realistic standard would at least require that any expression of the conditional nature of the acceptance be made somehow conspicuous so there is a better chance that it will come to the recipient's attention.* If that is what is called for, then

---

*We'll have more to say on "conspicuousness" and its consequences in Chapter 14. You can check out §1-201(10) now, but it's probably better left until later. For the moment the important thing to note is that the drafters did not put a conspicuousness

perhaps the bold legend on the front of the form would make a difference. But probably more is required than technical conspicuousness.

Most courts looking at this question recently have taken a fairly narrow view of the proviso, seeing this as essential if the overall philosophy of §2-207(1) is not to be undermined. One articulation that has gained a considerable following is that found in *Dorton v. Collins & Aikman Corp.*, 453 F.2d 1161, 10 U.C.C. 585 (6th Cir. 1972). There the court held that the proviso was intended to apply "only to an acceptance which clearly reveals that the offeree is unwilling to proceed with the transaction unless he is assured of the offeror's assent to the additional or different terms therein." For a purported acceptance to operate as a counteroffer under the proviso it must actually be a counteroffer, not just in words but in effect. It should be worded and presented in such a manner as is calculated to bring a reasonable recipient to the understanding that no deal has yet been concluded and none will be concluded until either it responds favorably to the new terms being presented or even more negotiation hammers out a compromise. Under the *Dorton* type of test, the question whether BUY and SEL have been bound to a contract is not merely a matter of what language appears somewhere in SEL's boilerplate. Was BUY put on some kind of reasonable notice that all was not well with this string deal, that it could not count on receiving string from SEL unless and until the final terms were settled? Even if upon consideration BUY may decide it can live with the terms SEL is pushing, the "Acknowledgment" should be such that BUY would have to realize that nothing more is going to happen until it in turn communicates its willingness to go along with those terms to SEL.

3.   There is no doubt that the offeree in the battle of the forms (SEL in our hypothetical) can if it truly wishes refuse to deal except on its own terms. But to do so it must make a true counteroffer and get an actual knowing acceptance of that counteroffer by the other party. It cannot count on this result simply because of some fancy language its lawyers have drafted up to include in its Acknowledgment form. If you were advising SEL, which was willing to insist on its own terms even if it meant losing a customer, you would tell it not merely to make perfectly clear that its response is a counteroffer (perhaps by a personalized letter stapled to the front of the Acknowledgment making clear you need to hear from BUY) but also by *acting* like an offeror. Above all, do not ship the stuff off on the assumption that you do have a deal on your terms. What an offeror does is sit and wait. It cannot assume that its offer will be taken up. Some, perhaps most offers are turned down.

of course, don't be too surprised if the people at sel are not terribly happy with this advice. How, they will ask you, can they run a business this way? You will have to respond (or perhaps more tactfully, only think to yourself), why do they expect they can have their cake and eat it too?

Finally, notice what is likely to happen if SEL immediately sends out

---

requirement into §2-207. This suggests that a more generalized test along the "reasonableness under the circumstances" line is what is called for here.

the Acknowledgment and the order of string, figuring that it can insist on its understanding of the contract later on. Under the common law's "last shot" rule, we know SEL would have been in a position to argue that the differing provisions in its Acknowledgment made for a counteroffer that BUY accepted by performance the minute it took delivery of the goods. Thus the common law could have allowed SEL a contract, and on its terms. It got to eat the cake and keep it too. Section 2-207, of course, does not allow for this analysis. Even if SEL had some gobbledegook in its Acknowledgment of the type suggested in the previous question, should it ship off the stuff without getting an actually acquiescing response to its Acknowledgment it will be hard for it later to argue that it had made an effective counteroffer under the proviso which was thereafter accepted. So a deal would have been struck before performance. But on what terms? We now turn to that issue in the questions that follow.

4a. The first subsection of §2-207 has to be deemed fairly successful measured against its principal objective, which was getting past the old and easily criticized common law mirror image rule. It is now clear that a contract for sale may be created by the parties' having exchanged forms which contain different terms as long as the differences are not of the type which in the commercial environment usually make or break a deal. But now the obvious question presents itself: What are the terms of the contract formed in this way? This is much trickier. We can no longer say, as we could in the good old days of the common law rule, that the terms must necessarily be those that were offered and which were then perfectly mirrored by the offeree in response. Almost everyone who has had anything to say on the matter (and just about everyone remotely interested in the Code has taken a whack at it) agrees that §2-207 is far less successful in laying out the answer to this question. But it is a question that will not go away.

As a starting point, of course, there is nothing for it but to look at the words of §2-207 itself, now focusing on both the first and second subsections. At the outset the conclusion seems unavoidable (although some courts and commentators have gone to great length to wriggle their way out of it) that all of the terms present in the form which constituted the offer, if that offer is found to have been accepted via subsection (1), are then binding terms of the contract. Section 2-207(1) says the acceptance "acts as an acceptance," and it's hard to understand what that could mean except that a deal has been formed on the terms offered. It has been suggested that the responding communication only accepts "those terms which it intends to accept" or some such idea, but there really is no statutory support for this argument beyond a generalized belief that the Code drafters must have intended to do what is in the particular commentator's opinion the obviously correct thing.

So the terms of the offer are the terms of the contract. Beyond that, §2-207(2) indicates that *some* "additional terms," which were in the "definite and seasonable expression of acceptance," or which are to be found in a later confirmation sent by one party to the other, may also become terms of the contract. But the passage of any such additional term through the tangle of §2-207(2) and into the heart of the contract is pretty tricky as we will see.

Under §2-207(2) there seem to be two ways that an additional term in the acceptance can become part of the contract. The first is implicit in the statement that such additional terms are to be "construed as proposals for additions to the contract." There's always the chance, even if it is slim, that such a proposal will be accepted. So, for example, if BUY had somehow become aware of the limitation of remedy clause that SEL put in its Acknowledgment and beyond that had communicated to SEL that this limitation was acceptable to it as a buyer, the term would become binding between the two. Of course there would be no obligation on BUY's part to acquiesce to this term (and we might wonder why on earth a buyer would), but you have to allow for the possibility. So an "additional term" can become part of the contract by its express acceptance by the original offeror.

The second mechanism for such a term to make its way into the contract is given by the second sentence of §2-207(2). Such a term may *automatically* become part of the contract *if* a series of conditions are met. The first condition is that such automatic inclusion is possible only in dealings "between merchants."* Once we establish that we are dealing only with merchants, it is further necessary that (a) the offeror not have expressly limited acceptance to the terms of the offer, (b) the new term not be a "material alteration" of the contract already formed, and (c) notice of objection to the new terms has not already been given by the offeree nor is it seasonably given after the offeror becomes aware of them. Take each of these requirements in turn.

In one sense every offer could be said to expressly limit acceptance to the terms contained therein. But reading clause (a) this way would effectively make the whole possibility of automatic inclusion meaningless. By analogy to the better reading of the proviso of subsection (1), this language in (2)(a) should probably be taken to refer only to those situations where the offeror has given the offeree clear reason to believe that it will under no circumstances consider even the most trivial addition to its terms and *won't proceed* with the deal as long as the offeree is even suggesting any. Again analogizing to the better understanding of the proviso, this condition will presumably not be met by the inclusion of some generalized boilerplate in the offer to the effect that the offeree deals on its terms and its terms only. The offeror will have to bring home to the offeree that it really would rather lose business than enter into a contract on any terms other than its own. The fact is, of course, that plenty of firms will say this is their position, but how many really can consistently take this high ground, act on it, and still stay in business?

In practical application, clause (b) is more important. There is no way a suggested additional term can be incorporated into the contract automatically (even between merchants) if it would work a "material

---

*On merchants and dealings "between merchants" generally, see §2-104 and Chapter 3.

alteration" to the contract as it stands without that term. This question of materiality has been heavily litigated, and the results are not easily characterized. For the drafters' attempt at drawing the line, see Comments 4 and 5. Language at the end of Comment 5 suggests that the clause SEL is trying to insist upon need not be considered material. (As we will see in Chapter 14, it is a kind of provision expressly allowed for as part of a sales agreement under §2-719.) The courts are not so sure. In *Burbic Contracting Co. v. Cement Asbestos Prods. Co.*, 409 So. 2d 1, 32 U.C.C. 1406 (Ala. 1982), the Alabama Supreme Court found that such a limitation of remedy clause was not material and hence could become part of the contract while conceding that "the courts are split on this issue." Moreover it held for Alabama that no blanket answer could be given for all such limitation provisions; the question had to be addressed on the facts of each case. Perhaps the determination should turn on how common such terms are in the particular industry involved, the extent to which its inclusion could work a hardship on the other party, and other such factors. But if the materiality question is to be determined on anything like a case-by-case basis, how are contracting parties ever to know with reasonable certainty what terms they have bound themselves to? In a more recent case, *Glyptal, Inc. v. Engelhard Corp.*, 801 F. Supp. 887, 18 U.C.C.2d 1059 (D. Mass. 1992), the federal district court applying Massachusetts law decided to follow what it characterized as a "recent trend . . . to find that such [remedy-limiting] provisions are material alterations" for the purposes of §2-207(2)(b).

Finally, under §2-207(2)(c), it is possible for the offeror to block the automatic inclusion of even the most immaterial and innocuous term by objecting to it. What constitutes an "objection" in this situation? Again, for this clause to make any real sense it has to be referring to something more than a boilerplate or prepackaged response. Would it be enough if BUY's clerk had a routine of sending out in response to any form Acknowledgment a preprinted letter that said in effect, "Thank you for your order and we object to any and all terms in your form that are in addition to any in our form?" I think not. If, however, the management of BUY did think it worth the time and expense for this clerk to go over SEL's Acknowledgment form in detail and then send out to that firm an individualized letter painstakingly objecting to each and every additional term, it seems clear BUY could keep out any and everything it didn't like.

4b. Yes. By the analysis given above, any term in the communication which makes up the offer is a term of the contract. The long and the short of it seems to be that BUY can get all its idiosyncratic boilerplate terms into the contract and SEL will have a devil of a time getting any of its terms in.

Some commentators are exceedingly troubled by this result. They question how in doing away with the common law's much criticized "last shot" rule the drafters could have in effect replaced it with an equally unbalanced and arbitrary "first shot" principle. Ideally, they argue, neither party should get an advantage simply because of the order in which the two standard forms were sent. They point to §2-207(3), which makes binding only "those terms on which the writings of the parties agree" as an example of a more principled approach. But the important point here is that subsection (3) does not as written apply to a situation where the parties accept each other's forms and only later are arguing terms. By its language, that subsection relates only to cases where "the writings of the parties do not otherwise establish a contract," and writings that contain different terms most assuredly *can* establish a contract. That's what subsection (1) is all about; that is what has happened to BUY and SEL here. Strict impartiality between the combatants in the battle of the forms may, indeed, be an ideal worth striving for—although others are not so sure—but unfortunately for its proponents the language of §2-207 doesn't leave much room for argument. Unless and until §2-207 is substantially revised, something like a "modified first shot" is the rule of the day.

4c. This would appear to be the toughest case yet: The two documents have distinctly differing terms on the same topic, herein the length of time the buyer has to complain of a problem with the goods. The courts have been all over the place on what to do with such differing terms under §2-207. At least three modes of analysis have been adopted. The first is simply to ignore differing terms found in the communication operating as an acceptance. The reasoning is very direct. There is simply no language in subsection (1) or (2) which even suggests that such differing terms could ever become part of the contract. Subsection (2) does make allowance for some terms of the acceptance being incorporated into the final contract, but it speaks only to "additional" terms. Since we know from (1) that the drafters considered additional and different terms to be two separate and distinct things—why else would they have mentioned both?—we have to read (2) as implicitly ruling out the possibility that "differing" terms can ever find their way into the agreement or even affect its contents. Under this analysis BUY's provision is enforceable and SEL's is simply ignored.

A second approach to the problem of differing terms argues that not so much should be made of the nitpicking distinction between "additional" and "different" terms in reading §2-207. After all, in many cases this will probably be as much a matter of degree as of kind. Note also that Comment 3 refers to subsection (2) as relating to "additional or different" terms. Several courts have adopted the position that subsection (2) does apply to so-called differing terms as well as to additional ones. But does this really help the offeree, SEL in this instance? It would seem that any term in the acceptance that differs from an explicit term of the offer would by its nature be an attempt to "materially alter" the terms of the contract. As such it could never automatically make its way into the agreement. BUY still wins and gets its term, only under a different technical analysis.

A third view does, at least, potentially come up with another result. It even has a colorful name. Under the so-called *knock-out approach,* conflicting terms in the offer and the acceptance in effect cancel each other out. Neither term becomes part of the contract. What's left are the terms on which the two writings do not conflict, presumably the dickered terms among them. These terms of agreement, as supplemented by various provisions of Article 2 itself, make up the terms of the contract.

This knock-out analysis has been receiving increasing adherence in the courts. A noted example is *Daitom, Inc. v. Pennwalt Corp.,* 741 F.2d 1569, 39 U.C.C. 1203 (10th Cir. 1984), the case which inspired this question. Seller submitted a proposal for the sale of some industrial machinery on September 7, 1976. Its typewritten proposal specified the equipment to be sold, the price term, and delivery and payment terms. Attached was a preprinted sheet containing a list of conditions of the sale and a statement that the conditions were to be considered an integral part of the proposal. Buyer responded with its own preprinted Purchase Order, containing plenty of its own boilerplate, on October 5, 1976. The machinery was delivered in May of the following year, but because of delay in the construction of buyer's plant, was not installed until June of 1978. Buyer soon notified seller of serious troubles with the machines. Seller responded by pointing to a condition in its printed list that gave the buyer a period of one year in which to bring any breach of warranty action. The district court granted summary judgment to the seller based on this clause in its offer, applying in effect a first-shot analysis. The circuit court reversed. It noted that in its responsive Purchase Order the buyer had its own boilerplate clause, this one expressly reserving all warranties and remedies available in law. The circuit court first held that this clause "impliedly reserves the statutory period of limitations," which under §2-725 would be four years, not one. The court then went on to apply the "knock-out" rule to what it now took to be conflicting express provisions of the offer and the acceptance.

> [T]he conflicting terms in Pennwalt's offer and Daitom's acceptance regarding the period of limitations and applicable warranties cancel one another out. Consequently, the other provisions of the U.C.C. must be used to provide the missing terms.

The relevant other provision of the Code in this case was of course the standard statute of limitations found in §2-725. Victory for the buyer. As you will note, use of the knock-out approach was particularly creative in *Daitom* since one of the "differing terms" with which the court claimed to be unavoidably confronted was at least partially of its own making. The buyer's reservation of a longer period in which to bring a warranty claim was nowhere near as explicit as I have made it in my hypothetical. It was found "impliedly" in a very general boilerplate reservation of right. One judge in dissent opined that whatever the value of the knock-out rule in dealing with differing terms in the offer and acceptance, its application should not extend to cases where there are no clear-cut conflicts between explicit provisions. In the particular situation, he noted, "there was no term in [the buyer's] purchase order in conflict with the express one-year limitation within which to bring warranty actions." Indeed, it's far from clear that the majority's result works a fair compromise. Certainly Article 2 does not take away from sellers the right to sell on the precise terms they wish. Setting shorter limitation periods, as the seller attempted to do in this instance, is specifically allowed for in §2-725. Should the buyer be able to block any limitation or modification of the seller's warranties merely by the inclusion of a generalized reservation of any and all rights stuck into the middle of its boilerplate?

The majority in *Daitom* believed its whole-hearted adoption of the knock-out principle to be "supported persuasively by the underlying rationale and purpose behind the adoption of §2-207. . . . To refuse to adopt the 'knock-out' approach and instead adopt one of the remaining two approaches would serve to re-enshrine the undue advantages derived solely from the fortuitous positions of when a party sent a form." The court's heart may indeed be in the right place. Perhaps §2-207 should have been drafted to get this result. But was it? There is precious little support, if any, in the text or comments for the knock-out way of doing things. At least one court has relied on §2-207(3) for authority, but this clearly won't work. As we have already noted, by its terms that subsection deals only with cases where the papers passing between the parties do not effectively create an agreement. That's not the case when one form responds to another so as to be "a definite and seasonable expression of acceptance." Knock-out proponents have taken some comfort in Comment 6, but even they must acknowledge that this comment seems to be speaking exclusively to conflicting terms in later written confirmations or a prior oral agreement, not to terms in a written offer and acceptance pair. The recent receptivity by the courts to the knock-out approach seems to be a reflection more of the increasing frustration with §2-207 in general than of any new brilliant flash of insight.

5.   There is a contract under §2-207(3) and the terms are as stated there. Here, finally, is an unarguably appropriate use of that subsection. The two parties' disagreement over terms is out in the open and it is never resolved. The writings cannot be said to establish a contract for sale, but the conduct of both parties clearly does. In such a case, the terms of the contract are "those terms on which the writings of the parties agree, together with any supplementary terms incorporated under any other provisions of this Act." Where are such other provisions to be found? Patience. As you progress through the book you'll get a chance to explore terms incorporated by custom and usage (Chapter 7), the so-called "gap-filler" provisions (Chapter 9), and the Code's elaborate warranty regime (Part II).

In Conclusion

A final word or two on the battle of the forms and how Article 2 deals with it. Everyone pretty much agrees that, for all its noble intentions, §2-207, at least when it is called upon to decide what terms the parties have bound themselves to, is a bit of a muddle. You may have found yourself particularly frustrated working through this material, but as I've suggested the courts and commentators share this feeling. Certainly your author does. At least there is something to knowing you are not alone.

Repeated calls for the revision or simple out-and-out repeal of §2-207 have been heard since soon after the adoption of Article 2. And there is some reason to hope that help is on the way. One conclusion of the Committee which recently undertook a study of Article 2 for the Permanent Editorial Board of the UCC was that *something* had to be done about §2-207. In the words of the Executive Summary of that Committee's report:

> The application of §2-207 has generated confusion in the courts, excessive litigation and continuing criticism from the commentators. In attempting to answer an important question, when do standard form terms become part of the agreement, §2-207 produces a complex overkill. A revision for both substance and clarity, if not a repeal, is required.

This Committee was not charged with making any particular recommendations as to what changes should be made. A good thing too, for not surprisingly the members who did voice an opinion were anything but uniform in what they would have happen. The matter now rests with another, a drafting committee. We will have to see what they come up with, and whether anything they do come up with will win any more favor than the present version. In the meantime we are left to make our way as best we can through the minefield and over the battleground, with only that current version of §2-207 as our guide.

6

The Statute of Frauds

And There Shall Be "Some Writing"

Anyone who has ever studied basic contract law—at least anyone who has done so since the English Parliamentary session of 1677—can be expected to have an acquaintance with the Statute of Frauds. The basic idea behind the Statute is relatively straightforward. Sometimes you have to produce some written evidence of a contract if you expect to enforce it in a court of law. The problems come when we try to firm up just when these "sometimes" are and what kind of writing will be sufficient.*

Contrary to what the uninformed layperson might think, there is no general requirement in the law that for a contract to be valid it must be put down in writing. *As a general proposition*, a contract which arises solely from oral communications and is in no way evidenced or memorialized by a writing is perfectly enforceable. Certainly, getting the other party to sign on the dotted line is nice, and no one would advise against it, but *generally* it is not a legal requirement. Even in those cases which defy this generalization, those classes of contracts which are said to "fall within the Statute of Frauds," there has never been a requirement that the contract *in and of itself* be in writing. In the words of the original enactment, what will be needed is only "some note or memorandum of the said bargain to be made and signed by the parties to be charged by such contract, or their agents thereunto lawfully authorized."

The long course of history has not been kind to the Statute of Frauds. Its enactment was originally intended to deter the "fraude and

---

*Of course today even though we tend to speak of "the" Statute of Frauds there is not a single Statute, but a whole slew of them relating to various types of contracts and applicable in various jurisdictions. While at a later point I will briefly point to other Statute of Frauds provisions in the UCC, our concern in this chapter will be principally with the Statute as it rears its head in §2-201.

perjurie" to be feared from those rascals bold enough to sue on a totally trumped up (and what they will be maintaining just happened to be a totally oral) agreement. The fear was of course that the rascal might actually win, once he or she got this fabrication in front of an easily deceived or overly sympathetic jury. Undoubtedly the Statute does stand in the way of such knavery, but this result is not without a price. The Statute of Frauds can be, and often is, criticized as a totally mindless mechanistic response to a problem which, at least in the present day, could be handled more effectively by other means. It cannot be denied that in many instances the Statute does provide a purely "technical" but highly effective defense to what would otherwise be a perfectly appropriate and meritorious contract action based on a valid and easily proven oral agreement.

In Great Britain such criticisms resulted in the 1954 repeal by Parliament of the Statute of Frauds in all instances covering the sale of goods. Meanwhile in the USA, during the course of drafting and eventual adoption of Article 2, there was substantial argument that the better course would be for the American law of sales to likewise say good riddance to what was to many simply an anachronism whose time had long passed. This, however, was not to be. As we will see in this chapter—indeed it is the very raison d'être for this chapter—the drafters of the Code retained the basic Statute of Frauds for sales at a price of $500 or more. It's found in §2-201. The core language is right there in the first sentence of subsection (1), as you should now check.

The drafters did, however, make some important changes to the Statute. Their attempt at a compromise solution was to concoct for Article 2 what they apparently hoped would be regarded as a less rigid, more pragmatic Statute of Frauds. Its positive effect would be to protect parties and the courts from even being bothered with contract claims which were too flimsy to be countenanced, if not to be believed. At the same time they codified in §2-201 a series of exceptions to the writing requirement which, they believed, would ameliorate some of the more egregious side-effects of that writing requirement. How well the drafters succeeded in crafting a workable and beneficial "modern" version of the Statute of Frauds is a question that necessarily runs throughout this chapter.

Some Other Statutes

Before the Examples and Explanations lead us through §2-201 in all its detail, there are two preliminary matters to attend to. First of all, it has to be noted that this section is not the only Statute of Frauds provision in the Uniform Commercial Code, even if it is the one which concerns us here. Separate provisions cover the sale of securities such as stocks and bonds (§8-319) and the creation of security interests of the type dealt with by Article 9 (§9-203). In §1-206 is to be found a Statute of Frauds provision covering the sale of personal property not otherwise covered by one of the more specific provisions of Articles 2, 8 or 9.* None of these other sections will be addressed here.

Of more immediate interest is the version of the Statute incorporated in the recently promulgated Article 2A. Perhaps the most important point initially is simply that there *is* such a section in 2A; once again Uniform law drafters have not taken the opportunity to jettison what seems to many an unnecessary and troubling bit of baggage. Section 2A-201 parallels in many respects §2-201, but in others the Article 2A creators have chosen to differ. We will note some of these differences as we proceed, even as our principal attention will be given to the provision in the Sales article and its established track record.

The Heart of the Matter

A second preliminary bit of business goes to the very heart of the Statute of Frauds and is crucial to understanding the Statute no matter where we find it or what the version. All too often students, and maybe just as often the courts, fail to make the distinction between two very different analytic issues. Quite apart from any Statute of Frauds concerns must be the elemental question, first in our hearts and minds, of *whether a contract exists at all*. This has to do with the whole notion of agreement, with all those matters of offer and acceptance with which we dealt in the previous two chapters. Whether a contract exists, and of course what its provisions are if it is found to exist, are questions to be answered on their own terms. These things are *not* what the Statute of Frauds is about.

Parties do not invoke a Statute of Frauds defense as a way of arguing that no contract was ever agreed to. Their contention is rather that *even if* a contract was entered into, of the nature and on the terms alleged by the party claiming under it, that contract is not enforceable against them in this court at this time. They escape enforcement, they contend, because of the lack of a sufficient writing or the lack of the right signature. Their position is not necessarily that they did not enter into the agreement the breach of which is being argued against them, but rather that the court lacks the power, under a rule of law, to do anything about it even if they did.

As a practical matter, of course, a Statute of Frauds defense if one is available is often among the very first arguments a defendant will advance. If you can get a complaint against you thrown out on a technicality quickly and easily, well then you do. Why go to all the bother of arguing and trying to prove that the alleged agreement never took place when you can get the whole thing resolved in your favor so very neatly? This is especially true when you consider how hard it can be to prove a negative, that is, to prove that an agreement never was. It is of course just this

---

*So, for instance, the sale of an interest in an insurance policy or a patent may be governed by this provision, since it involves personal property but not "goods" or an investment security.

difficulty of making such proof—and the prospect that a clever claimant could somehow make what never was appear to a jury to be all too believable—that has been the rationale for the Statute of Frauds from the seventeenth century through today.

To make sure you can distinguish between the issue of contract formation and the Statute of Frauds defense, consider the following two hypotheticals. In the first, two law students Andy and Betty are asked by their Sales professor to engage in a simulation of contract negotiation. The subject is to be the supposed sale by Andy of his used car to Betty. Their negotiations result in a "sale price" of $750. To complete their assignment the two draft up a Contract of Sale for the car. Each signs this document. Let's assume they both get A's not only for effort but because the document is well-drafted in all respects. Now assume further that Andy, for some reason known only to him, then brings suit against Betty *in a real court of law* charging her with failing to live up to this agreement. A copy of the Contract of Sale is appended to his complaint. Betty is going to have to defend herself. If there is any justice in this world she should be able to win, but it won't be through a Statute of Frauds defense. If she relies only on the Statute, the Court (with a signed document right before it) must give a decision for Andy. She will have to plead and prove (with no small help from the unimpeachable testimony of her professor) that no actual legal agreement for purchase and sale ever existed between her and Andy.

Now consider this situation: Carl and Donna are also two law students. Carl really does want to sell his old car to Donna, and Donna is really interested in buying it. In front of their Sales professor and a number of other witnesses they conclude an oral agreement for the purchase and sale of the car for $950. They shake hands on it. Later, Carl refuses to go through with the sale. Donna brings suit, again in *a real court of law*. If the facts are as simple as I've made them here, Carl wins easily with the §2-201 Statute of Frauds defense. Was there an agreement? Yes. There are all kinds of witnesses. Carl will forever be known as someone who doesn't stick to his bargains. Was it a contract under the Code? Yes, again. The agreement resulted in a contract governed by Article 2. Can Donna enforce this contract against Carl if he chooses to act this way and breach? No, not without some writing signed by him or something else that will satisfy the Article 2 Statute of Frauds. To convince yourself that there is a contract here, look at Comment 4 to §2-201. In the unlikely event a third party, say the evil Edmund, had somehow wrongfully induced Carl to breach his contract with Donna, Edmund could be held liable to Donna on a tort theory.

So much for the preliminaries. The following all deal with §2-201, which you should now look over in its entirety.

EXAMPLES

1. The "King Leopold Ferrari" was custom designed and built in 1954 for King Leopold III of Belgium, who had by that time abdicated his

throne and was living in exile in Switzerland. Through a series of perfectly lawful transactions the car ended up in the hands of one Wayne Golumb, a resident of Illinois, where he, his brother Larry, his parents and his girlfriend Graceia Voyles spent more than a decade restoring it to its original condition. Robert M. Lee, a big game hunter and exotic car fancier, took a shine to the Ferrari and desperately wanted to add it to his collection. Several times Golumb rebuffed his steadily increasing offers. Finally one day Lee said he would be willing to give $275,000 for the car. Golumb said, "OK, you've got yourself a deal," and the two shook hands on it. Several people, friends of both of the parties and just the types who would make excellent witnesses, were present at this exchange.

a. Two days later Golumb signed and sent a letter to Lee which stated, "I'm sorry that I cannot sell you the Ferrari for the price you offered." If Lee brings suit against Golumb, what result?

b. Would your answer to the previous question be any different if the letter sent by Golumb had contained the following language: "I don't know what I was thinking of agreeing to sell you the car at that price"?

c. What would your answer be if Golumb had sent no letter to Lee, but at the time of the oral agreement had written "K.L. Ferr. — R.M.L. — $275,000" on a piece of paper on which was printed "From the Desk of Wayne Golumb"? Would it matter whether Golumb had given this paper to Lee or if he had kept it himself in his desk?

2. Samantha, a manufacturer of gaskets, enters into an oral agreement to sell 100,000 of her Number 2 gaskets at a price of $.50 each to Buddy, who will use them in his widget assembly plant. They shake hands on the deal. The next day Buddy sends a letter to Samantha which reads

> This is to confirm our agreement entered into yesterday for the purchase and sale of 100,000 of your Number 2 widgets for immediate delivery at 50 cents per as discussed. Glad to be doing business with you.

a. Samantha receives this letter and files it away. If she later tries to go back on the deal, could she successfully defend in a suit brought by Buddy based on the fact that she never signed anything relating to this sale? Would your answer be any different if she could show to the satisfaction of the court that she had never received Buddy's letter?

b. What would be your answer to the previous question if Samantha had received Buddy's letter but had immediately written back

> Wait one minute, Buddy! We never agreed on immediate delivery. We'll have to work out a timetable or I can't do it. You'd better give me a call if you want those gaskets.

3. Lydia is a lawyer. She is visited in her office by Hal, a representative of Atomic Office Systems, the maker of a line of computerized office equipment. Lydia agrees to give Hal a few minutes of her time. He gives her a very detailed proposal for a complicated computer set-up which he

"recommends" to her. After a few minutes, Lydia shows him out of her office with the statement that she'll "think about" the proposal. The pesky salesman having been dealt with, she gets back to work. Several days later she receives a letter signed by Hal which states that "I am happy to confirm your order of the system as proposed and as detailed on the attached memorandum. I will call soon to arrange for payment and installation." Attached to this letter is a detailed description of a system which is if anything even more complicated (and more expensive) than what Hal had pitched to her in her office. Uttering a mild expletive, Lydia tosses this letter into the garbage. Six months later Lydia is served with papers in a suit bought by Atomic Office Systems, charging her with breach of contract. You can imagine what she says now. What is she to do? Can she get the suit dismissed on summary judgment based on the Statute of Frauds? Would it have helped her situation any if she had called Hal when she got his letter and given him a piece of her mind?

4.   Lydia, the lawyer from the previous Example, decides to add a second fax number to the letterhead she uses in her business. She calls up Pam the printer who has done work for her before and over the phone orders 25 boxes of letterhead identical to her previous orders (a copy of which Pam has on file) but with the one addition. Pam tells her that the cost will be $30 a box, to which Lydia agrees. Pam creates the printing plate necessary for doing the work and runs off the first box. Before she does any more, she receives a call from Lydia who says that she has changed her mind and will not require any new letterhead. If Pam decides to sue Lydia for breach of contract, will she have any Statute of Frauds problem?

5.   Sam and Dave are both model railroad enthusiasts. At a convention held for such types, they discuss a particular antique caboose which Sam owns and Dave craves. No paper changes hands. Dave is willing to swear that they did agree to a sale at $1250 and believes he can find some witnesses who would confirm that the two parted with a hearty handshake. Sam refuses to sell. When confronted by Dave he does not deny their deal but says, "Oh yeah, let's see you prove it in court." When Dave does sue, Sam moves for summary judgment based on the Statute of Frauds. Is that the end of it? Or can you see an argument for Dave that the case should proceed at least long enough for him to take Sam's deposition? What result?

6.   Tidwell enters into an oral agreement with Anthony to purchase 100 head of cattle for $500 each. He delivers a check for $1,000 which Anthony holds on to but does not immediately put into his bank account. There are no special markings on the check.
    a. The value of the cattle starts to climb to at least $570 a head. Anthony returns the check, refusing to go through with the deal. Will Tidwell have an action for damages good as against the Statute of Frauds? For how much?
    b. Suppose instead that the market value of the cattle drops to $480. Anthony has already delivered 12 head of cattle, which have been taken onto Tidwell's ranch where they reside. No payments

have been made by Tidwell. Can Tidwell demand Anthony take the return of these twelve? If Anthony sues for damages, will he have a Statute of Frauds problem?

7.   Robert X. Lee, a relative of Robert M. Lee from Example 1, is a collector of antique salt and pepper shakers. The shakers are, needless to say, worth much more when they are in their matched sets. One day Lee spots in Saul's antique shop the salt half of a famous set, the "King Leopold Salt and Pepper," which had long been thought lost. As a connoisseur of such things he is aware that the matching pepper is owned by one Paul. Saying something about how he intends to buy the pepper now that he's found the sale, he enters into an oral agreement with Saul to buy the salt shaker for $550. They shake hands on the deal. Lee is to bring in the money and to pick up the shaker within the week. As soon as he leaves Saul's store, Lee contacts Paul and offers to buy the pepper from him. Paul, figuring that Lee must have some good reason to buy it, drives a hard bargain and eventually gets Lee to agree to a price of $3,800. Lee and Paul sign a contract for sale. Lee returns to Saul's shop only to find that Saul is refusing to sell the salt at the $550 price. Will Lee be able to enforce his agreement with Saul in a court of law? What argument will he make? Will he succeed? Should he?

EXPLANATIONS

1a. Golumb should be able to get the action dismissed under §2-201. As you might have suspected, this question is based on an actual case. In *Lee v. Voyles*, 898 F.2d 76, 11 U.C.C.2d 7 (7th Cir. 1990), the circumstances were only a little more complex than I've related here. As Judge Easterbrook noted, "Sometimes fascinating facts bring with them exciting legal issues. This is not such an occasion." There being no writing signed by Golumb evidencing the agreement and no exception to §2-201 being available, the contract "is not enforceable by way of action or defense" against Golumb.

Note that Lee does in fact have a writing signed by Golumb, but it does not fit the bill as it is not "sufficient to indicate that a contract for sale has been made between the parties." The letter in and of itself indicates that an offer had been made by Lee, but not that it had ever been accepted. Does Lee have a right to introduce other evidence to show that the letter meant something else, that there had in fact been an agreement and that it was now being repudiated? No. The writing on its own must meet a certain standard. That's what the Statute of Frauds is all about. In the words of the Court of Appeals of New York in the case of *Bazak International Corp. v. Mast Industries, Inc.*, 73 N.Y.2d 113, 535 N.E.2d 633, 7 U.C.C.2d 1380 (1989):

> Parol evidence, even in affidavit form, is immaterial to the threshold issue whether the documents are sufficient on their face to satisfy the Statute of Frauds. Consideration of parol evidence in assessing the adequacy of a writing for Statute of Frauds purposes would

otherwise undermine the very reason for the Statute of Frauds in the first instance. That issue must be determined from the documents themselves, as a matter of law.

It is interesting that the court speaks here of "the documents" in the plural. Several courts have held that two or more documents taken together can satisfy the Statute even if no one of them would on its own. For example, suppose Seller sends a written offer replete with terms, including a quantity term, to Buyer. Buyer sends back a signed note saying only, "I accept." Neither piece by itself satisfies the requirements of §2-201(1). Taken together they do.

1b. If this were the language in Golumb's letter, Lee should be able to get past the Statute of Frauds. It is important to focus on the fact that the writing need not set out all details of the agreement but can be something far less formal. It need not be what a layperson thinks of as "a written contract" which the other side has signed. Read Comment 1 to §2-201. The last paragraph sets forth three definite and invariable requirements which the writing must meet. First of all it must "evidence a contract for the sale of goods." Earlier the comment says that in this regard all that is required "is that the writing afford *a basis for believing* that the offered oral evidence rests on a real transaction." Professor Karl Llewellyn, draftsman of §2-201, is often quoted for his statement, "What the section does . . . is require some objective guaranty, other than word of mouth that there really has been some deal." Here the letter surely meets the test. How likely is it that there would exist such a letter signed by Golumb saying what this one says if he had not in fact ever entered into an agreement with Lee about selling the car?

Remember, the issue here is not whether the offered writing is conclusive proof that an agreement was made or what its terms were. It is enough if there is some writing which backs up the claim. That will satisfy the Statute and get the litigation into a further stage. Lee still needs to prove that there was a contract for the sale of this Ferrari and at this price; Golumb will still have the opportunity to dispute this claim, but he will have to do so based on the facts of the situation, that is, on what transpired between them on the car lot, not on the lack of a writing.

We should check that the other two requirements mentioned in the comment are met here. The writing must be "signed," and that's been given. It also must specify a quantity. Here it says "the car," which should do as making for a quantity of one automobile.

A question arises as to why the drafters made the quantity term and not, say, the price term crucial to the writing. Apparently they thought that there was less of a problem that someone would assert a wholly fraudulent contract at a wholly fraudulent price designed to give him or her a huge advantage simply because there usually is some external "reality check" on what price could have been agreed upon. No amount of documentation is going to make believable my claim that you agreed to sell me something at one-tenth your usual price or your claim that I agreed to pay ten times market value. Contrast this to the question of quantity. There is no way of ferreting out even an approximately normal, usual, or reasonable amount that might be bought and sold in any given situation. One party may purchase ten widgets and another may want 10,000. See the second paragraph of Comment 1. Note also that in §2A-201(3) the drafters of that provision have made not only the quantity of goods leased but the lease term crucial to the writing.

An interesting variant of our Example you should consider is how the Statute of Frauds argument should come out if instead of writing a letter Golumb had called Lee and said these fatal words (in effect, admitting the existence of an agreement) as part of a message left on Golumb's answering machine. Clearly if he had gotten Lee in person and said what he did there would be no writing and nothing to satisfy the Statute. But does the tape-recorded message make a difference? First of all, is there a "writing"? Look at the definition in §1-201(46) and the comment to this definition. (Parenthetically, why is this definition not cross-referenced at the end of the Comments to §2-201? Presumably just a slip on the drafters' part. We are all human. But did you think to look for a definition in Article 1?) We are not talking here about a recording made without Golumb's knowledge but one he in effect creates intentionally. One court has held in a somewhat similar situation that a tape recording does suffice. *Ellis Canning Co. v. Bernstein,* 348 F. Supp. 1212, 11 U.C.C. 443 (D. Colo. 1972). But in our case, where is the "signing"? I'd argue that it comes when Golumb says something into the recorder like, "Hello, this is Golumb." Certainly this result would be in keeping with the underlying principle behind the Code's version of the Statute of Frauds, requiring only "some basis" for believing the alleged contract exists, not a full-blown legal looking document.

1c. This writing may well satisfy the Statute. Initially it may seem the signature requirement has not been met, but look at §1-201(39), the Comment to that definition, and then return to Comment 1 of §2-201. The writing and the signature requirements have obviously been loosened up considerably by Article 2. But query whether the language is "sufficient to indicate that a contract for sale has been made between the parties." Golumb would argue that a note like this is just as easily understood as his way of recording an offer made to him which he was going to consider. But again, the measure is whether the writing affords "some basis," not "an overwhelming basis," for believing an agreement had been entered into. This note should suffice.

On the question of whether the note had to have been delivered to Lee, see Comment 6. It is sufficient that some writing exists. As another example, suppose the only writing Golumb signs is a note to a friend saying, "I have gotten myself into terrible trouble by selling the King Leopold to a guy named Lee." It's the creation of this note which is his real trouble. If Lee becomes aware of it, he does not have to worry about Golumb's raising a Statute of Frauds defense.

2a. Samantha has never signed anything, but she won't be able to assert the Statute of Frauds thanks to the so-called "merchants' exception" found in §2-201(2). You should check for yourself and for Buddy that all of the criteria of that exception are met. If you have any doubt that this is a transaction "between merchants," you might want to review Chapter 3.

Incidentally, as was pointed out in that chapter, a major dispute in applying the Article 2 definition of "merchant" is whether a farmer falls within its scope. The issue has come up often, and in fact usually in the context of the §2-201(2) exception. A farmer allegedly enters into an oral agreement to sell his or her crop with the travelling representative of some large buyer of agricultural produce. On return to the home office, the agent sends out a "Confirmation Letter" to which the farmer never responds. The farmer has signed nothing, but has he or she lost the right to rely on the Statute of Frauds should a dispute arise? Obviously the drafter didn't think this was an unduly harsh result against a merchant, as opposed to your ordinary Joe or Jane consumer, as someone who is in business should know enough to read—and answer—his or her mail. As we noted in Chapter 3, the courts have come to no agreement whether a farmer should be held to this level of professionalism and responsibility.

In going through the numerous criteria of this merchant's exception you'll notice that it is necessary that the confirmation actually have been "received" by Samantha and to determine *when* it was received. For a working definition of *received* see §1-201(26). The contrast between receipt and the giving of *notice* or *notification* is important in the Code, and you should be sure to work through §1-201(26) carefully now if you have not done so before. (On the question of when a notification such as a confirmation would be considered received by a complex organization, see §1-201(27).) Note that in §2-201(2) the objection must be in writing but that it is sufficient that it be "given." Receipt of the objection is not necessary.

One issue that has divided the courts is the standard for determining whether a writing sent by one party to another can be considered "a writing in confirmation of the contract." The subsection goes on to require that the writing be one "sufficient against the seller" under §2-201(1). As we've seen, this can be a very loose standard requiring only that it offer "some basis" for believing a contract exists. Must a confirmation say anything more? A number of courts, troubled by the possibility of a party's being bound by a writing it did not itself sign, have held that there must be some clear language of confirmation in the writing, and that it must explicitly alert the recipient it is intended to confirm a previous agreement. In the *Bazak* case (cited in Example 1a), the New York Court of Appeals rejected this approach, placing itself in line with what it maintained to be a majority of courts and commentators.

> [I]n determining whether writings are confirmatory documents within UCC §2-201(2), neither explicit words of confirmation nor express references to the prior agreement are required, and the writings are sufficient as long as they afford a basis for believing that they reflect a real transaction between the parties.

In justification of its position, the court stressed that

> as additional protection against abuse and inequity . . . the conse-
> quence of a failure to give timely written notice . . . is only
> to remove the bar of the Statute of Frauds. The burden of proving
> that a contract was indeed made remains with [the party alleging one],
> as does the burden of proving the terms of the contract.

Look at Comment 3 to §2-201. In our particular example, of course, there is no doubt that Buddy's letter sets the merchants' exception in motion.

2b. Samantha will claim that her timely response effectively countered Buddy's reliance upon his confirmation. But is what she wrote "objection to its contents?" The courts and commentators have taken this language to mean that the writing must state an objection to the principal thrust of a confirmation, that is, that a contract in fact exists between the parties. Here Samantha's response in effect acknowledges a contract and is only contesting a term. The kind of objection contemplated in §2-201(2) is a response that does not merely quibble about terms or dispute who's to do what under the agreement, but a clear disavowal that any agreement was ever finalized. In order to preserve her Statute of Frauds defense, Samantha would have to reply not only in a timely fashion but object in no uncertain terms to the very idea that a contract had been concluded.

3. You understand why I put this example in: A word to the wise. If there is any justice in this world, Lydia should eventually win this suit, but she won't be able to do it that easily with a summary judgment based on the Statute of Frauds. She's going to have to establish that she and Hal never came to an agreement during their earlier meeting, which is a question of fact and looks like it will be her word against his. If you have any doubt that Lydia is a merchant for these purposes, see the second paragraph of Comment 2 to §2-104. Here a lawyer is alleged to be buying not fishing tackle for her own use but office equipment for her place of business. A phone call to Hal might have done Lydia some good psychologically, but it would not have helped her legal position. The objection must be in writing.

Finally on the merchants' exception, note that it does not appear in §2A-201. The comment to that section states that it was not included "as the number of such transactions involving leases, as opposed to sales, was thought to be small."

4. Pam will rely on the exception found in §2-201(3)(a) for contracts involving specially manufactured goods. The general idea behind this exception should be fairly obvious. As one court has said, "in these cases the very nature of the goods serves as a reliable indication that the contract had been formed." Furthermore, not only is the likelihood of a perjured claim significantly diminished, but "denying enforcement to such a contract would impose substantial hardship on the aggrieved party." *Impossible Electronic Techniques, Inc. v. Wackenhut Protection Systems, Inc.,* 669

F.2d 1026, 33 U.C.C. 809 (5th Cir. 1982). What's Pam going to do with all this stuff if she can't sell it to Lydia?

There are a number of distinct criteria in (3)(a), but it appears Pam meets most of them with no question. Her only problem would be in showing that he had made "a substantial beginning" of the manufacture of the letterhead. Is one box out of twenty-five substantial enough? It would seem so, especially since a large part of the cost must be tied up in the preparation of the plate that had also been completed. What if she had only made the plate but not put any ink to paper? She should get past the Statute. This does seem a significant part of the printing job and a particularly good basis for believing a contract had been previously formed. Making the plate also seems analogous, if not exactly the same thing, as "making commitments for . . . procurement" as mentioned in (3)(a).

Not all courts have given such an expansive reading to this language. In one noted case, *Epprecht v. IBM Corp.*, 36 U.C.C. 391 (E.D. Pa. 1983), the plaintiff alleged that IBM had ordered 50,000 print-head assemblies to be made to that company's specifications, but there was no written instrument to that effect. Seven thousand were delivered. IBM accepted 4,000 of them but rejected the rest and refused to take any more, claiming quality problems. Epprecht's suit to make IBM pay for the rejected units and acknowledge the full extent of the deal was dismissed on Statute of Fraud grounds. The court ruled that manufacture of the 7,000 was not a substantial beginning on the alleged 50,000. (Apparently no work whatsoever had been done toward making the other 43,000. The result may well have been different if those units were all in production at the plaintiff's plant at the time IBM told them the deal was off.) The *Epprecht* court seems to have been concerned that to read this exception too broadly would open up a buyer of a small or reasonably sized purchase of specifically manufactured goods to potential perjured claims that the orders were for much, much larger amounts. It is true that the drafters of §2-201 suggest a particular anxiety about the possibility of exaggerated quantity terms, but this reading of the exception may be a bit too constrictive. Remember, once again, that had Epprecht's suit survived the Statute, it still would have had to prove as a matter of fact that a contract for the larger quantity had been entered into.

5.   Dave seeks to rely on the exception to the writing requirement found in §2-201(3)(b), the *admissions exception*. See also Comment 7. This provision has caused a good deal of concern and controversy. Note that not just any subsequent statement will do: The "admission" must be made in a particular legal setting. Voluntary admissions are not a big problem, although there is some question about exactly what constitutes an "admission." Suppose that Dave were to be deposed or testify in court that, yes, he and Sam did have the conversation Sam alleges and that, yes, they did shake hands. He further states under oath that he did not and does not see this as a completed deal. He claims they just had a productive and friendly negotiation session. Could the court look at what

admittedly happened and conclude that by admitting the details he had in effect admitted the existence of a contract, whether he admits to having so admitted it or not? The courts are not clear on this, although some have said yes.

The real problem, however, is whether an *involuntary* admission can sink a Statute of Frauds defense, and in particular how much leeway and time the complainant should be given to try to force such an admission—under penalty of perjury—out of the defendant. In our hypothetical, can Sam resist the motion for summary judgment, arguing that Dave should at least be made to file a complete answer to the complaint? The idea is that it may be hard for Dave to frame a truthful answer which doesn't admit the existence of the deal. Even if Dave can frame such an answer and *then* moves for summary judgment based on the Statute, does Sam have the right to insist on at least some time for discovery and the chance to depose Dave? At the deposition, of course, he would ask the pointed questions intended to put Dave between the proverbial rock and a hard place.

I think most authorities would say that the defendant should have the right to use and succeed with the Statute of Frauds defense in a summary fashion, at least if he has somewhere been willing to have recorded under oath his denial that a contract existed. Otherwise, if involuntary admissions can fit the bill, and if the complainant is given full court backing in trying to wring a confession out of the defendant no matter how long it takes, this exception might swallow up the whole Statute of Frauds idea. This has been the conclusion of several recent cases, most notably *DF Industries v. Brown,* 851 F.2d 920, 7 U.C.C.2d 1396 (7th Cir. 1988), in which Judge Posner opined

> When there is a bare motion to dismiss, or an answer with no evidentiary materials, the possibility remains a live one that, if asked under oath whether a contract had been made, the defendant would admit it had been. The only way to test the proposition is for the plaintiff to take the defendant's deposition, or, if there is no discovery to call the defendant as an adverse witness at trial. But where . . . the defendant swears in an affidavit that there was no contract, we see no point in keeping the lawsuit alive. Of course the defendant *may* blurt out an admission in a deposition, but this is hardly likely, especially since by doing so he may be admitting to having perjured himself in his affidavit. Stranger things have happened, but remote possibilities do not warrant subjecting the parties and the judiciary to proceedings almost certain to be futile.

What if Dave is willing to sign an affidavit that he and Sam never entered into a contract? Sam just *knows* this is not so and thinks he has great evidence that Dave has just perjured himself. What can he do? Perhaps he can get Dave ostracized by all right-thinking members of the community, but the Statute of Frauds seems to make clear this is the end of it as far as the courts and the law of sales are concerned. Is this any way to run a judicial system?

You should be aware that California never adopted this portion of the Article 2 Statute of Frauds, primarily on the argument that (3)(b) simply "reward[s] a defendant's perjured denial. If a defendant denies the existence of the oral contract, no matter how strong the proof he is lying, the contract remains unenforceable. The same contract would be enforceable against a defendant who truthfully admitted an oral contract had been made." California Code Comment, 23A Cal. Comm. Code §2201 at 131 (1964). Faced with all this controversy, the drafters of Article 2A choose to include the admissions exception, and in exactly the same form we've seen it in §2-201. See §2A-201(4)(b).

6a. Tidwell has an action good against the Statute of Frauds based on the "payment" exception found in §2-201(3)(c): "A contract which does not satisfy the requirements of subsection (1) but which is valid in all other respects is enforceable . . . with respect to goods for which payment has been made and accepted. . . ." The idea here is pretty well spelled out in Comment 2. Tidwell's delivery of the check and Anthony's holding on to it are both acts that give some basis for believing Tidwell's claim that a contract had been made. Tidwell's problem is that under the Code he will be able to enforce the contract only to the extent that goods have been paid for. This is a change from the prior law under which partial payment took the whole contract outside the Statute of Frauds. Under the Code's provision, with its particular passion for preventing fraudulent assertions of excessive quantities, a partial payment will in effect support only a partial contract. Tidwell paid $1,000, which will allow him a suit for two of the cattle but no more, as the court in fact held in *Anthony v. Tidwell*, 560 S.W.2d 908, 23 U.C.C. 561 (Tenn. 1977). The idea is that this amount of payment does support a conclusion that at least two head were contracted for at this price, but doesn't give any basis for believing that there was an agreement for 100 head any more than that they contracted for 200 or for 2,000 of the beasts.

What if Tidwell had given a check for only $400 in down payment? Would he be entitled to sue for only 80 percent of a cow? No, the courts have held that such a down payment would support the assertion that *at least one* animal was agreed to and Tidwell could sue for that one. In a situation that has come up many times, someone enters into an agreement to buy a car from an auto dealer but the dealer never signs any papers. The buyer gives a check in down payment. When the dealer later tries to renege on the deal, the delivery and acceptance of the down payment will serve to take the buyer's case out of the Statute of Frauds. While partial payment will normally only support a partial contract, when partial payment has been made on a single indivisible item the contract for that one unapportionable whole is supported. We don't usually think of a person's buying some percentage of an automobile, so a suit for the car is not blocked by the Statute of Frauds. See, for instance, *Sedmak v. Charlie's Chevrolet, Inc.*, 622 S.W.2d 694, 31 U.C.C. 851 (Mo. Ct. App. 1981).

If Tidwell's argument here is based on the idea that his payment had been "accepted" by Anthony, does it make a difference that the latter had never negotiated the check but just held on to it? Probably not.

Comment 2 says that "part payment may be made by money or check, accepted by the seller." Here Anthony did accept the check even if he did not immediately cash or deposit it. If, however, Anthony could show that the check had been delivered to him for some other reason entirely, such as another deal, then that presumably would make a difference.

6b. Now it's Anthony who would take advantage of subsection (3)(c) since the Statute cannot block enforcement of a contract "with respect to goods . . . which have been received and accepted." Again, he can sue only on a contract for the amount delivered—12 head of cattle and no more. Here there should be no problem in establishing that Tidwell accepted these 12. Sometimes, however, there will be a real question whether the delivered goods have been accepted. While the Code has no special provision relating to when a payment has been "accepted," it does go into considerable detail on when there has been an "acceptance of goods." This is all found in §2-602, which we will go over in scrupulous detail in Chapter 18. Don't worry about it for now.

7.   This set of facts I *did* make up, but you can see they make for a particularly troubling situation. If Lee does bring suit against Saul, he will run smack dab into the Statute of Frauds. The price is over $500. There is no writing signed by anybody, no specially manufactured goods, and no partial payment or delivery. If Saul is careful in his response to the suit, he'll admit nothing. Section 2-201 is fully in force and there is no exception provided for in that section that would help Lee. It seems that in spite of the fact that he had an oral contract with Saul he won't be able to enforce it.

   Lee's argument, of course, is that he so obviously and earnestly relied upon this contract, a possibility which Saul had good reason to expect, that it would be wrong for him to be left with no relief simply because of a technicality like the Statute of Frauds. You'll recall from your Contracts study the notion of a suit based on the doctrine of *promissory estoppel* (you'll recall it from that course because we can't and won't rehearse the whole idea here). The present problem is a relatively narrow one, but one which has given the courts and commentators a good deal of grief and over which there is no agreement whatsoever. Assuming for the moment that a plaintiff could make out a good cause of action under the doctrine of promissory estoppel, may that action be barred for lack of a writing under §2-201? If so, the result may seem very harsh against Lee. If not, then there must be a further exception to the §2-201(1) writing requirement that is not found in any language in Article 2 but inherent in the estoppel notion. Lee could sue and could win getting some relief (his loss incurred in reliance, if not the full value of the contract promise to him) based on his handshake agreement with Saul even though no writing was ever signed by anybody.

   As I've suggested, numerous academic writers have written on the question and several courts have had to address the issue head-on. There is no agreement on whether the Statute acts as a bar, or indeed is in any way relevant, to an action once promissory estoppel is the claimant's theme. At one extreme is the position that the Statute of Frauds is no bar whatsoever. Adherents of this view point out the language of §1-103, which specifically preserves the law relative to estoppel among other things. The Statute of Frauds bars *contract* actions, they would argue, but a suit brought on the reliance theory is something else altogether. At the other extreme are those of the opinion that there can be no exceptions to the §2-201 Statute of Frauds not explicitly provided for in that section. Note the introductory language of subsection (1): "Except as otherwise provided *in this section*. . . ." Those taking this position argue in effect that the Article 2 Statute of Frauds has been drafted with enough care and operates loosely enough through its various sensible exceptions that the potential harshness of mechanical application of a writing requirement has been sufficiently ameliorated. For the courts to start finding other exceptions not provided for by the drafters is just an invitation to judicial circumvention of the rule as adopted by the legislature. See, for example, *International Products & Technologies, Inc. v. Omega Corp.*, 10 U.C.C.2d 694 (E.D. Pa. 1989), where the federal district court, called upon to determine whether the courts of Pennsylvania would allow for an estoppel exception to §2-201, concluded that they would not.

> Since the statute allows three limited and express exceptions, other exceptions should not be allowed. These exceptions are sufficient to protect against unequitable results. If estoppel claims were not barred by the application of the statute of frauds, *every* promise satisfying §90 of the Restatement [of Contracts], but which was otherwise invalid under the statute of frauds, would be actionable under an estoppel claim. Such a reading would strip the statute of its purpose.

Some courts have tried to find some middle ground, such as: requiring that the potential injury to the claimant whose action would otherwise be barred be "particularly inequitable or harsh;" requiring a showing that the defendant had deceitfully promised; or looking for a distinct promise made, if never kept, to reduce the agreement to writing. The jury is still out on the interplay between promissory estoppel and the Statute of Frauds. For Lee the lesson is now painfully clear. He may win on such a theory, but think of how much easier it would be for him had he taken the time and effort to get something in writing before he went off and spent all that money on the King Leopold Pepper. There's a moral here.

7

Usage of Trade, Course of Dealing, and Course of Performance

The Terms of the Contract

The three previous chapters dealt with the fundamental issue of whether the parties had ever entered into a contract that could be enforced against either or both of them. But that is in general the easy question. We now turn to the often more troubling problem of exactly *what* the contracting parties have obliged themselves to do. Given that they have bound themselves by their actions and by the law of the Code into a contract, what are the precise terms of that contract to which they will be held? Believe it or not, the Code actually defines the term *term*. According to §1-201(42), when used in the Code it means "that portion of an agreement which relates to a particular matter." Admittedly this is, in itself, not very helpful, but it does remind us that any contractual relationship has to be thought of as a compendium of any number of individual terms covering all sorts of things, large and small. Where do these various contract terms come from? Or, putting it only slightly more legalistically, where does an advocate or a court go for authority that such-and-such is a term of the parties' contract?

Article 2 of the Code incorporates a scheme, often referred to as the *hierarchy of terms,* for testing and determining what ultimately are the enforceable aspects of the contract between the buyer and seller. It is worth the effort to review this scheme in broad outline before getting too involved in any of the details.

We start, naturally, with the agreement between the parties. First and foremost, of course, terms of a contract will be found in the explicit arrangement entered into by the parties. This express agreement is found in the specific language used by the parties, in their negotiations, and in their final words of commitment. The various bits of the negotiation may of course be in writing, or they may be oral. In addition the parties often, but not always, will in the end adopt a common writing or writings as setting forth their agreement. As you will no doubt remember from your study of the common law of contracts, the exact contours of a contract, even one memorialized (or *integrated*) in this formal written manner, are not always perfectly distinct. For one thing, not even the most meticulous use of language will eliminate all questions of interpretation. Beyond this, the common law saw fit to adopt *the parol evidence rule,* a particularly vexing doctrine (if not exactly a rule) which adds greatly to the complexity of the task. The parol evidence rule makes it possible for a party to argue that something to which he or she expressly *did in fact agree* has ultimately been rendered unenforceable because it was not later set forth in the writing adopted by the parties.

We reserve the intricacies of (and the frustration engendered by) the parol evidence rule for the next chapter. This chapter concentrates on something else. It introduces an integrated set of three concepts—trade usage, course of dealing, and course of performance—carefully laid out in Articles 1 and 2, which together make possible terms of the agreement *in addition to* those explicitly agreed to. Such *trade terms,* as they are sometimes collectively called, may be used by a party to argue for a better or more sophisticated understanding of the agreement (and hence the contract) by which he or she is bound. They help in interpretation. But beyond that, it is clear that authority for actual substantive terms of an agreement can be found not merely in the express overt conduct of the parties themselves, but in what we might think of as the underlying context in which their acts are to be judged. The Code makes the importance of these terms clear in its definition of *agreement* found in §1-201(3): " 'Agreement' means the bargain of the parties in fact as found in their language or by implication from other circumstances including course of dealing or usage of trade or course of performance. . . ." Under the Code, trade terms are *part of* the agreement as much as are those provisions explicitly dickered over by the buyer and seller.

Determining the dimensions of the agreement between the parties is, of course, not the end of the quest for the terms of the contract. *Contract,* in the language of the Code, means "the total legal obligation which results from the parties' agreement as affected by this Act and any other applicable rules of law." §1-201(11). The terms of the contract are the terms of the agreement (which we now know includes trade terms), subtracting those which the Code renders unenforceable for one reason or another and adding those for which the Code is itself authority irrespective of the parties' agreement. In later chapters we'll see examples of each of these. For instance, the operation of the parol evidence rule (of §2-202 and the next chapter) can in the right instance render unenforceable a term of the agreement. It reads a term of the agreement-in-fact out of the contract. The prime examples of those provisions of Article 2 which may actually add contract terms not found in the agreement as broadly understood are the so-called gap-filler provisions (which we will discuss in Chapter 9) and the whole structure of the Code's warranty provisions (to which all of Part II is devoted).

Thus ends our outline of the Code's hierarchy of terms. We will leave the additions and subtractions for the moment. This chapter is dedicated to a better understanding of the agreement of the parties, as that term is used in Article 2, and in particular the part that commercial usage and prior dealings play in marking and delineating the extent of that agreement.

The Ways of (the Parties') World

From your introductory study of the common law governing the interpretation and construction of contracts you will recall how often you were tempted (or cajoled by your instructor) to ask what was "always done" or "usually done" by experienced commercial actors in situations similar to the particular one before you. You may have heard this invocation of business practice referred to under the classic rubric of *custom*, a common law notion that some ways of doing things in a particular trade were so well-recognized, so certain, so unvarying, and above all so ancient that by these facts alone they became part of the contractual relationship between the parties. The doctrine of custom, as you may have seen, has always been ringed in by number of technicalities, qualifications, and limitations. Traditionally, it played a limited and uneasy part in classical contract theory. In more recent times, customary commercial practices have begun to take a more important role in much of the workings of contract law simply because so much of the standard formulation of general principles is now laced with references to "reasonable" expectations and "reasonable" ways of behaving. To a large measure, if such "reasonable" language means anything it is as an invitation to look at the larger social and commercial context in which the parties acted out their story and to take that context into account in judging the legal consequences of their behavior.

The trend towards greater receptivity of such real-world-based material in evaluating contracting behavior is everywhere in evidence in Article 2, and in fact the adoption of the entire Code has in itself been seen as giving additional momentum to development along these lines. Among the bedrock "underlying purposes and policies" of the Code, as set forth in §1-102, is that of "permit[ting] the continued expansion of commercial practices through custom, usage and agreement of the parties." An Official Comment to §1-205 declares that the Uniform Commercial Code rejects both the "lay-dictionary" and the "conveyancer's" reading of a commercial agreement. Instead the meaning of the agreement of the parties is to be determined by the language used by them and by their action, read and interpreted in the light of commercial practices and other surrounding circumstances. The measure and background for interpretation are set by the commercial context, which may explain and supplement even the language of a formal or final writing.

In actual operation, the drafter of the Code carried forward these goals by articulation of three distinct concepts. The first two, *course of dealing* and *usage of trade,* are defined and their operative power set forth in §1-205. As you might expect since these terms are found in Article 1 of the Code, they have applicability beyond their relevance to problems involving the sale of goods and Article 2 issues. The third concept, *course of performance,* is defined in §2-208, and hence is a term defined for Article 2 purposes only.*

Note initially that the power of these concepts extends to two related, but at least analytically distinct, tasks. First, trade terms will have a part to play in how the parties argue about the correct interpretation of the express agreement entered into, whether in writing or orally. Beyond this, however, you should recognize that adequate proof of this type of commercial background may under the Code actually *create* terms entirely supplemental to those of the express agreement. You see this in the expansive definition of "agreement" quoted in the previous section, as well as in the seemingly innumerable times the phrase "unless otherwise agreed" pops up in the various sections of Article 2. Finally we note that the drafters included in the general provisions of the Code a statement that, "The presence in certain provisions of this Act of the words 'unless otherwise agreed' or words of similar import does not imply that the effect of other provisions may not be varied by agreement. . . ." §1-102(4). The importance of usage of trade, course of dealing, and course of performance to the real working of Article 2 in the real world in which sales transactions take place cannot be overstated.

This chapter's Examples and Explanations are not intended to be a full and complete survey of how these concepts play their parts in Article 2. That would be impossible in such a limited space, and not very helpful in any event. In everything you study and in every problem involving the sale of goods, the possibility of trade terms coming into play must be borne in mind. The following questions and analysis are offered only as a way of introducing the broad outlines of each of the three concepts and discussing some of the principle issues their use brings forward. Fortunately, there are not many difficult issues of law involved in §1-205 and §2-208. Each offered instance of a usage or a course of dealing or performance may, of course, generate some very heated debate: Does such a usage actually exist? Has it been sufficiently proven? What exactly

---

*Of course the Article 1 definitions work for Article 2A and leases as well. You can check that §2-208 has its 2A analogy in §2A-207.

is the extent of and effect of the usage? Is it rightly applied in this situation or against this particular party? But such questions point to issues of fact important to resolution of the particular case, not intrinsic disagreement on what the law relevant to commercial practices is. The significance of trade terms as provided for in the Code was intended by the drafters not to engender complex discussion of legal norms or abstract jurisprudential theory. The idea was to some extent to get beyond all that and actually to facilitate the resolution of factual issues of real importance to the parties involved. All in all, the results seem to work well to this end.

If you have not done so yet, you should read over §1-205 and §2-208 carefully before going on to the questions.

EXAMPLES

1. The Knits Corporation is a manufacturer of knitwear located in Capitol City. Through one of its salesmen it enters into a contract to deliver 1,200 sweaters to Mazie's Department Store, also located in Capitol City. The written agreement contains specifications for the various numbers of sweaters to be delivered, by size and color, but no language pertaining to how the sweaters are to be packaged for delivery to Mazie's. When the sweaters are delivered, Mazie is angered to find that they are boxed according to size, with the colors all mixed together. She has expected them to be presorted by color which is much more in line with how she stores merchandise in her stockroom.

a. If she were to complain and to sue over this, would it be a sufficient defense on Knits' part if its distribution manager were to testify that The Knits Corporation always packaged and shipped its products sorted by size? That is, the manager insists (we will assume truthfully) that "That's the way we always do it." If this testimony alone would not vindicate Knits, what additional information would allow it to successfully argue that packing by size became a term of its contract with Mazie as an applicable trade usage?

b. Imagine that Knits is not able or chooses not to establish a trade usage to support its position. Would it still win if it could show that in the previous year it had entered into a similar contract for sale of scarves and mittens to Mazie's and furthermore that Mazie had accepted delivery of these—sorted by size—without complaint?

c. Suppose that Knits is able to establish a course of dealing between the parties that knitwear it sells to Mazie is to be sorted by size. Mazie, however, claims that she was legitimately surprised because there is a general usage of trade that when manufacturers sell clothes to retail stores the items are delivered presorted by color. Who wins?

d. Finally, suppose that the contract between Knits and Mazie called for delivery of 1,000 sweaters during each month for a year starting in May. Knits made deliveries in May and April, which remained unopened in Mazie's storehouse. When the June shipment arrived, Mazie decided it was time to break out all the sweaters in anticipation of the winter sales season. Only then does she discover that the goods are not packed in the way she expected. Is it too late for her to complain?

e. Would your answer to the previous question change if the written agreement between the parties contained a clause that read, "Items to be presorted by color?"

2. Sunny Toy Manufacturers and Bunny, the owner of a toy store, sign a contract for the purchase by Bunny of a specified number of talking dolls manufactured by Sunny. Sunny delivers the dolls on June 1. On June 17, Bunny attempts to return some of them to Sunny because there is something wrong with them. They will not talk. There is no language in the written agreement regarding how long after delivery the buyer has to return defective goods. Sunny is able to show that virtually all written contracts for the sale of toys by manufacturers to retail stores in the area contain language stating something to the effect that "All returns must be made no later than two weeks from the date of delivery." Sunny argues that this creates a trade usage which is binding on Bunny. Should Sunny win on this argument?

3. Williams, a Georgia farmer, contracted to sell all of the "slaw cabbage" to be grown on his land to one Curtin, a dealer working out of New York who intended to resell it to various cole slaw manufacturers. Because of poor growing conditions, most of the cabbages grown on Williams' land turned out to be fairly small. Meanwhile the value of all cabbage has risen. Curtin demands the delivery of all the cabbages grown by Williams. Williams offers to prove that in Georgia "slaw cabbage" refers particularly to larger cabbages which are generally used for making cole slaw. Curtin objects to the introduction of any such evidence claiming that it is not applicable to their deal. What result?

4. Assume instead that Williams in the previous Example had sold his "slaw cabbage" to one Tyro. Tyro is a former New York City law professor who, tired of the pace and pressure of his life, recently moved to rural Georgia and opened up a plant to make homemade cole slaw based on his mother's secret recipe. He entered into the contract with Williams and now wants all the cabbages, including the smaller ones which would work perfectly fine in his slaw-making process. Williams asserts that he is obligated to deliver only the larger cabbages, based on the trade usage for the Georgia area which he again offers to prove. Should Tyro be allowed to prove that he never knew of the existence of this usage? Even if he does prove this, should it make any difference in the contract between him and Williams?

EXPLANATIONS

1a. The fact that Knits itself "always does it this way" would presumably not be enough to establish a trade usage. Section 1-205(2) requires that the practice have "such a regularity of observance in a place, vocation or trade as to justify an expectation that it will be observed with respect to the transaction in question." To make their point crystal clear, the drafters went on to state specifically, "The existence and scope of such a usage are to be proved as facts." So what would Knits have to show and how would they show it?

First of all, of course, counsel for Knits would have to make clear in his or her own mind exactly *what* usage was to be established and, particularly, to what "place, vocation or trade" it was meant to apply. Knits could argue that packing goods sorted by size is a usage within the sweater trade, or the trade of knitwear sellers, or indeed the whole clothing manufacturing industry. It could argue that it was an established usage within the realm of Capitol City, or the whole country, or some other identifiable area of commerce. Assuming, for example, that counsel sought to establish that Knits had followed a usage well established in the knitwear industry within the entire United States, what evidence will it need to present? What witnesses should it be prepared to call and what should it hope these witnesses will say? The last sentence of §1-205(2) makes clear that Knits would do well if it were able to provide the court with something like a "Knitwear Manufacturer's of America Code of Uniform and Fair Dealing." See, for example, *Foxco Industries, Ltd. v. Fabric World, Inc.*, 595 F.2d 976, 26 U.C.C. 694 (5th Cir. 1979), where the court found admissible an industry group's standard definition of "first quality goods." If no such trade code exists, they'll try to find others who regularly deal within this industry who can testify, in effect, that sorting by size is "how it is always done," but they might have to be satisfied with statements that are a little less global. Would Knits' evidence have to establish that it *always* is done this way? No, but how close to always is a matter of fact and not easily quantified. Note the language in Comment 5 giving support to usages "currently observed by the great majority of decent dealers, even though dissidents ready to cut corners do not agree."

I find it interesting to think about exactly what it takes for some practice, even if it is clearly one regularly observed in an area, to "justify an expectation" that it will be observed in a given transaction. The language of the Code seems to say that regularity of observance is enough in and of itself to create such a justification, but I think there is a subtle (or maybe not so subtle) further requirement. There are after all practices or rituals that we regularly go through which are so common as to justify an expectation that they'll be followed, but which do not seem to justify an expectation or an argument that another party has a *right* to their observance each and every time. I give you the following example. I enter a fashionable restaurant, and order and enjoy a truly fine meal. The service has been more than adequate. I am presented with the bill. Legally, it's clear I owe this amount. Surely the waiter, and the establishment owner as well, have a reasonable expectation that I'm going to leave a tip. Almost certainly I will. But if I don't, would they have any legal right to insist on one? I argue that leaving a tip is something that is virtually always done, especially by those "decent dealers" that the Comment talks about, but it isn't a trade usage because there is no justifiable expectation that "it will be observed" *as a matter of law* "with respect to the transaction in question."

One final point is worth mentioning here. Notice that nothing in the definition of usage of trade or in the operative language in §1-205(3) makes it necessary that Knit prove that any usage of trade it is able to establish was actually known by Mazie, either at the time of contracting or the time of delivery. Look again at §1-205(3) and notice how many times *or* is used. We'll return to the problems this can create for a party new to the industry, and how the courts have responded, in explaining Example 4.

1b. Here Knits would be trying to establish a course of dealing between itself and Mazie. Check out the definition in §1-205(1). Knits would apparently lose because one prior incident would not be "a sequence of previous conduct." Neither the Code nor the Comments give us any help on how many prior incidents are necessary to make up a sequence, but presumably it would be at least two.

Even if Knits could show that it entered into two or more previous contracts for scarves and mittens, and that in each case deliveries had been packaged by size, you can see Mazie might still have an argument that this did not establish a course of dealing relevant to this transaction. All this evidence could do would be to establish a course of dealing in scarves and mittens, Mazie would argue, and now we're talking sweaters. Could a course of dealing in those other knit products "fairly be regarded as establishing a common basis of understanding" for interpreting their contract for the purchase and sale of sweaters? Here it would be helpful to know if practices and customs are generally the same across the whole larger knitwear industry. If so, then Knits would have established a course of dealing covering this transaction as well. If for some reason, or if only by tradition, scarves and mittens are sold, packaged and delivered in ways quite distinct from how sweaters are dealt with, Knits would not have a course of dealing to go on.

Note that the definition of "course of dealing" makes it clear that, unlike a usage of trade which at least theoretically could bind a party who was never even aware of it, a course of dealing depends on prior dealings of these particular parties—things of which they are themselves presumably intimately aware.

For a good example of the importance of a course of dealing (albeit in a very different context), see *Pearsall v. Alexander*, 572 A.2d 113, 11 U.C.C.2d 1081 (D.C. Ct. App. 1990). Pearsall and Alexander were friends of some 25 years standing who for several years were in the habit of meeting twice a week and going to a liquor store, where they would purchase what they liked to refer to as a "package"—a half-pint of vodka, orange juice, two cups and two lottery tickets. The two would then repair to Alexander's house to drink screwdrivers, watch TV, and "scratch" the tickets. On the evening of December 16, 1982, the pair made the journey to the liquor store twice. The second time was the charm. After some playful and not so playful pulling and tugging concerning the tickets, presumably enlivened by the vodka and the orange juice, each took a ticket and "scratched" it. Pearsall's proved worthless, but Alexander's was a $20,000 winner. There followed several years of pulling and tugging in the courts, wherein the parties raised a variety of issues including the enforceability of contracts arising from gambling transactions and the Statute of Frauds. By 1990, in the cited case, the District of Columbia Court of Appeals was able to conclude that there had been a valid and enforceable agreement between the two friends to share the $20,000 proceeds. The court noted, "this conduct took place within the context of a long-standing pattern of similar conduct, analogous to a 'course of conduct' as described in the Uniform Commercial Code. . . ."

1c. Knits wins. Its course of dealing controls over the usage of trade established by Mazie. See §1-205(4) and the hierarchy set forth therein.

1d. Mazie may have trouble complaining now. Knits will claim that the May and June deliveries established a course of performance for this particular contract under §2-208. Mazie could argue here that she did not have "knowledge of" the nature of the earlier deliveries and hence had no "opportunity for objection" to how the sweaters were packaged, but I doubt that would be successful. If Knits has been making its monthly deliveries for some time and Mazie has not made any mention of the shape they were in, doesn't Knits have the right to claim Mazie "accepted or acquiesced without objection?" The language of knowledge and the opportunity to object obviously adds something to the definition of "course of performance," but where as here Knits would be reasonable to assume that its having heard no objection to the earlier shipments meant that Mazie was at least "acquiescing," I'd think Knits would win. Perhaps the answer would be otherwise if Mazie could show that Knits would have or should have been aware that a buyer of its sweaters would not unpack any shipments made in the Spring immediately, but would rather open them up only when several shipments had arrived. But then, what was the point of the earlier deliveries?

1e. If express language of the written agreement calls for packaging by color, that should give Mazie what she wants. Neither a usage of trade, a course of dealing, nor a course of performance will overcome the express agreement. Review §1-205(4) and §2-208(2). This seems pretty clear-cut, and in most situations it will be. Remember the significance the Code gives to the parties' ability to vary "by agreement" just about any result and to tailor their contract as they see fit. But see §2-208(3) and Comments 3 and 4. Knits may make the argument that Mazie's acceptance of the earlier shipments sorted by size constituted a *waiver* of her right to insist on assortment by color. We will deal with waiver as a separate topic in Chapter 10, but you should see here how easily that idea shades into that of course of performance.

2. No. Sunny has not established a trade usage by showing that virtually all written agreements of the type he and Bunny entered into contain specific language like that quoted. What he'd have to show is that similarly situated parties usually consider themselves bound to this time limitation *even though* it is nowhere expressly agreed to. In fact, dealers in this market apparently think it sufficiently important to get it expressly and

explicitly in the written agreement. If anything, this should *hurt* Sunny's case. A court could (and I think should) make a negative inference from the fact that Sunny and Bunny did not write it in. This reminds us that a usage of trade is "what people usually do" in addition to or in elaboration of their explicit agreement. That's quite different from what people usually actually agree to in so many words. The express terms are just the stuff they implicitly don't want to leave to trade usage or course of dealing.

3. This Example, raising the issue of the geographical scope of a trade usage, is based on the case of *Williams v. Curtin*, 807 F.2d 1046, 2 U.C.C.2d 1169 (D.C. Cir. 1986). It is easy enough to say that a trade usage is good for the entire area for which the usage holds true, but that doesn't help here. We can assume that if both the buyer and the seller of the "slaw cabbages" were doing business in Georgia they would be bound by the Georgia usage of this term. But if it's a usage only good in Georgia, what weight does it carry when the seller is in Georgia and the buyer is not? The Code does not make clear the answer, nor do we have a batch of cases to help out. As to the particular cabbage involved in *Williams v. Curtin*, Williams, the seller, argued that "because the planting, nurturing, cutting, sizing, and bagging of the cabbage" all took place in Georgia, that state was the "focus of performance" and that hence the usage governed. This argument got nowhere with the court, which held that even if such a usage did exist in Georgia it was not applicable between these parties as "the relevant aspect of the performance is delivery" and delivery had been called for and taken place in "the interstate market." "Since the transaction is an interstate transaction," concluded the court, "it cannot fairly be expected that the parties contracted only with reference to the Georgia market." But is it all that simple? In the actual case the seller was not a farmer, but a dealer in cabbage, who the court notes did business with out-of-state buyers on a regular basis. Is this what made the difference? And did the court give sufficient attention to the fact that this was not simply a transaction made at long distance over the phone or by mail. The buyer had initially visited the Georgia cabbage fields before entering into the sales agreement and visited the cabbages as they grew on at least one occasion. Perhaps the court was most impressed in reality with the fact that the seller's reliance on the Georgia usage at this point if successful would have allowed it to make a killing off of the dramatic rise in the value of cabbage during 1982, and the large loss it would have imposed on the buyer who had had to cover on the open market.

4. Tyro would probably be stuck with the usage even if he truly had not known of it when he made the deal. Note again the language of §1-205(3). Parties are affected by any usage of trade "in the vocation or trade in which they are engaged *or* of which they are *or* should be aware." That is very expansive language, and presumably the drafters meant us to take it just that way. Recall also the articulation of general purposes of the Code in §1-102 and particularly subsection (2)(b). Here we could simply say that Tyro is engaged in the cabbage-buying trade in Georgia

and that would be that. The language of §1-205(3), with all those *or*'s makes clear that if anything people who are not themselves in the trade but who for other reasons are or should be aware of how the trade operates will be held to the usages in their own dealings outside the trade. So, for example, if Williams entered into a contract with one Baggott, who was in the business of manufacturing packaging material, for some bags to hold his "slaw cabbage," Baggott might be held to this usage even though he is not in the cabbage trade. A court could determine he actually knew what "slaw cabbage" meant in that trade, or that he "should have been aware" for some reason or another.

Returning to the original Example, we see that a literal reading of the Code puts a very heavy burden on anyone just starting out in a highly specialized business. (And what businesses nowadays are not highly specialized?) Should there be any leeway given to the new entrant? That argument was made in *Heggblade-Marguleas-Tenneco, Inc. v. Sunshine Biscuit, Inc.,* 59 Cal. App. 3d 948, 131 Cal. Rptr. 183, 19 U.C.C. 1067 (1976), but to no avail. The court answered that

> [P]ersons carrying on a particular trade are deemed to be aware of prominent trade customs applicable to their industry. The knowledge may be actual or constructive, and it is constructive if the custom is of such general and universal application that the party must be presumed to know of it.

The lesson would seem to be that the new entrant into any field should bone up thoroughly on exactly how things are done in the industry, or at least acknowledge that he or she is taking the risk of not learning of all the customs and usages. But should this always be so? In our example, would it make any difference if Williams actually knew that Tyro was innocently ignorant of the usage? Would this be enough to be some burden on Williams to straighten him out, or failing that, to later forego reliance on the usage? What if Williams knew only that Tyro was a first-time buyer and that most outsiders did not know and had no reason to know what people in the cabbage trade meant by "slaw cabbage?" Perhaps these difficulties are what justify a fairly rigid notion that once you hang out your shingle as being part of a trade you can be held to live by all of its most arcane mysteries.

8

The Parol Evidence Rule

The Agreement, The Writing, and The Result

In studying contracts under the common law, you almost certainly spent some time and a good deal of energy on a doctrine going under the name *the parol evidence rule*. Briefly put, the one thing that became clear was that this so-called rule could not be put briefly and still make much sense to the uninitiated reader. Learning how the law deals with parol evidence is a whole course of study and not the memorization of any short and tidy formula. Still, the drafters of Article 2 did about as good a job as anyone has in setting forth the rule in the English language, so we might as well start with a look at the Code's version of the "rule" in its entirety. It's found in §2-202, which I've "reformatted" below:

Terms

with respect to which the confirmatory memoranda of the parties agree

or

which are otherwise set forth in a writing intended by the parties as a final expression of their agreement with respect to such terms as are included therein

may not be contradicted by evidence of any prior agreement or of a contemporaneous oral agreement

but [such terms] may be explained or supplemented

(a) by course of dealing or usage of trade (Section 1-205) or by course of performance (Section 2-208);

and

(b)   by evidence of consistent additional terms unless the court finds
      the writing to have been intended also as a complete and exclusive
      statement of the terms of the agreement.

Now the question is what to make of all this. Section 2-202 is one of
those parts of Article 2 which has to be read and appreciated with an eye
to history and pre-Code law. The authors of §2-202 did not pull this
one out of thin air. (Who would?)

The drafters did give us considerable help in thinking about this
material, however, with their clear definition of the word *agreement* as
used in the Code. Look at §1-201(3). The *agreement* of the parties is
"the bargain of the parties in fact as found in their language or by
implication from other circumstances" including any applicable course
of dealing, usage of trade, or course of performance.* The agreement is
what really happened between the parties in the real world. How they
came to this agreement is the kind of thing we talked about in Chapters
4 and 5. It may have been at the moment the two signed a carefully
negotiated and minutely detailed piece of paper (or more probably a
number of sheets all stapled together) with all kinds of *whereas*'s and
herein agreed's, but that certainly is not required. Probably the great
majority of agreements for purchase and sale of goods are concluded
simply through an oral understanding, or even through nods, shrugs, or
other body language.

The agreement is simply what it is. It has an existence in fact, but
not a corporeal existence in our three-dimensional physical universe. The
parties' *agreement* could never be lost or stolen or burned up in a house
fire. To borrow from the world of the detective story, the parties'
agreement is the "what happened" to be deduced from the various clues
found lying about, but it itself is not something that the detective can
trip over or waggle in the face of a suspect. Yet many clues to the nature
and content of the agreement, of which we naturally want to take advantage, *are* in the tangible form of a writing. People in these situations will
often leave a paper trail, either on purpose or otherwise. Note, by the
way, the definition of *writing* in §1-207(46).† A writing is most definitely
a tangible thing. It takes up space.

If the parties to a contract for sale are arguing about the terms of
their agreement, pretty much any evidence they can bring to bear on the
question of fact—what did they agree to do?—is fair game and will be

---

*Throughout this Chapter, I will assume the reader is familiar with the terribly
important Code concepts of usage of trade, course of dealing, and course of performance. If you have not already worked through Chapter 7, I urge you to do so at
this time.

†We'll confine our work in what we do here to handwritings, things printed, and
such like. Under the Code, would the special place given to a writing apply to an
audiotape or a videotape intentionally used by the parties to reduce their agreement
"to tangible form?" In at least one case the answer was yes. A tape recording was
determined to constitute a writing under §1-201(46). *Ellis Canning Co. v. Bernstein,*
348 F. Supp. 1212, 11 U.C.C. 443 (D. Colo. 1972).

thrown into the mix. The history of the common law parol evidence rule, however, and its inclusion in pretty much the traditional form in Article 2, are premised on the idea that once some piece or pieces of evidence have this particular tangible form, once they are in writing, they have a specially privileged part to play. Even without a parol evidence rule, of course, written evidence presumably would have a powerful effect on the trier of fact. Our fictional detective would, we assume, be delighted to find that extraordinarily incriminating note in a suspect's handwriting or the will that has been so mysteriously missing. But then any detective worth his or her salt would also be aware how easily such scraps of paper can mislead, or at least how often they tell only part of the story. The detective, as he or she is always sure to explain to the somewhat slow-witted sidekick, is not constrained to take any one piece or any one kind of evidence at face value. All evidence is considered and valued for its own unique explanatory power whatever its form, size, or shape.

In ferreting out to what the parties to a contract of sale actually committed themselves, that is, what the Code refers to as their *contract* (§1-201(11)), however, the legal detective finds a strange constraint on his or her methods. The rules of the game have been changed. Written evidence *must* be given a special credence. In this endeavor, writings—or at least writings of a certain kind—get special pride of place and will perforce have special explanatory powers *as a matter of law* beyond what nature might have provided them. It is this special rule of law that is the parol evidence rule. At its most powerful the rule actually deletes from the enforceable contract terms undoubtedly included in the agreement and on which one or the other party might have heavily relied. On my assumption that you have already studied the rule in the common law context, I will not here rehearse the numerous objections which have been raised to it over the years and which are heard probably even more loudly today. The parol evidence idea is not without its critics, to say the least. Nor will I here recount the various justifications for it that have been advanced in the past and in the modern setting. The nature of this debate will soon be apparent as it appears in the particulars of application. It is these particulars that we explore in this chapter's questions. Before the questions, though, a couple of preliminary issues should be considered: On what writings does the parol evidence rule bestow its special favors, and who makes the decisions that make the rule run?

What Writings Count?

As you know, there is no absolute requirement under Article 2 that a contract for sale be in writing. In general, an oral agreement is perfectly fine and enforceable. Should the price of the goods equal or exceed $500, of course, the Article 2 Statute of Frauds may require that a party in order to hold a contract enforceable against another produce "some writing to indicate that a contract for sale has been made" signed by that other party. The full workings of this Statute of Frauds provision were explored in Chapter 6, and we will not repeat them here. Suffice it to recall for our present purposes that the writing requirement of §2-201 applies only in a specific subset of all sales situations. Beyond that, to "satisfy" the Statute of Frauds a writing need not be a document setting forth the contract itself. It may be, and often is, a writing prepared by only one of the parties and not a joint production. It need not state all of the material terms of the agreement, nor even recount those that it does state correctly. In the words of a comment to §2-201, the writing made necessary in some cases by the Statute must serve only as some "basis for believing" that the proffered agreement (the substance of which may be proven by entirely oral evidence) "rests on a real transaction."

The parol evidence rule is like the Statute of Frauds in that it deals in and with writings, but there the two part company. The parol evidence rule makes no demand on the parties that they produce any writing whatsoever in order to enter into an enforceable contract. The parties are free to write or not write as they wish. They may choose to enter into a writing because of Statute of Frauds concerns, or because it is convenient, or out of mere force of habit. Once, however, the parties *have* together brought into existence a writing memorializing all or some of the terms of the agreement, then the parol evidence rule comes into play.

Just because a proffered piece of evidence is in written form does not mean, however, that it triggers application of the rule. The rule traditionally takes special cognizance only of those writings which are so-called *integrations* of the agreement. In the words of §2-202, the writing must have been "intended by the parties as a final expression of their agreement with respect to such terms as are included therein." The important thing here is that writings which qualify as integrations are those that are produced or at least accepted by *both parties* as setting forth what they mean to put in writing about their agreement. Papers that are the exclusive work of one or the other of the parties usually will not do unless there is strong evidence of the other party's adoption of that writing as correct in some sense. So, for example, an internal memorandum produced by a seller for her own files that details what she took away from a negotiating session would not constitute an integration. If the seller wanted her document to have that special status, she would have to show it to the buyer and get the buyer to literally or figuratively "sign on" to the memo as correctly setting forth what has been agreed to. Similarly, early tentative drafts of proposed contract language of the type that are regularly exchanged by parties (often ad nauseam) in the course of negotiations cannot be seen as integrations.

Just because an offered writing is the only written evidence of the agreement it will not necessarily be an integration. So, for example, in *General Matters, Inc. v. Penny Products, Inc.*, 651 F.2d 1017, 31 U.C.C. 1556 (5th Cir. 1981), the buyer introduced a copy of its purchase order, which was acknowledged by all to be the only writing generated in the course of the transaction, and argued that testimony of an oral statement by the seller should therefore be barred under §2-202. The court rightly held that the purchase order had no such effect, as there was no evidence that the two parties together intended the particular piece of paper to be a joint memorial of their understanding. At the same time, for a writing to constitute an integration it is unnecessary for it to have any precise heading or format, or for it to carry any particular language of integration. It need not look like dozens of lawyers slaved over it in every detail. In *Intershoe, Inc. v. Bankers Trust Co.*, 77 N.Y.2d 517, 571 N.E.2d 641, 569 N.Y.S.2d 233, 14 U.C.C.2d 1 (1991), for example, a confirmation sent by the bank to the Intershoe corporation, which was then signed by that corporation's Treasurer and returned, was held to be an integration for the purposes of §2-202. The facts here, though interesting, are not easily related in terms of a "Seller" and a "Buyer," for the question of exactly who was doing the selling and who was buying lay at the very heart of the case. Both parties agreed that Intershoe had placed a telephone order with the foreign currency department of the bank for the purchase and sale of a stated quantity of Italian lira.* Following the conversation the Bank sent Intershoe a confirmation slip including, among others, the following terms: "WE HAVE BOUGHT FROM YOU ITL 537,750" and "WE HAVE SOLD TO YOU USD 250,000.00." Apparently other parts of the slip made it clear that the "We" referred to was the Bank and the "You" was Intershoe. Intershoe's Treasurer signed the slip and returned it to the Bank. Later Intershoe claimed that the confirmation was a mistake, that it had intended to *buy* the lira from the Bank and that such a deal was in fact what had been agreed to over the phone. It offered in support of this position an affidavit of its Treasurer stating in effect that, while he couldn't recall the particular conversation, he just knew he never had placed an order to sell lira to the Bank any time during that year. Obviously, if the confirmation slip was seen to be an integration, this offered statement was about as contradictory to the writing as you can get, so Intershoe was forced into the claim that the confirmation slip never was "a writing intended by the parties as a final expression of their agreement." They pointed out that no language in the slip said in so many words that it was intended as such. The Court of Appeals of New York showed little patience with this argument, saying

> We reject [Intershoe's] contentions that UCC §2-202 requires that there be some express indication in the writing itself or some other evidence that the parties intended it to be the final expression of their agreement. A holding that the writing must include express language that it represents the parties' final expression would introduce a technical, formal requirement not contemplated by the Code and one that would frustrate the Code's purpose of facilitating sales transactions by easing the process of contract formation. . . .

---

*As the New York Court of Appeals noted, "There seems to be no question that the UCC applies to foreign currency transactions (see UCC §2-105 Official Comment 1)." See Chapter 1, I might add.

Section 2-202 potentially adds a little something to the traditional parol evidence rule by its introductory language with its reference to "terms with respect to which the confirmatory memoranda of the parties agree." Unfortunately, we are hampered here by the drafters' failure to define "confirmatory memoranda" or "confirmation." Taken on its face, however, this language can be given meaning that is of some help. Suppose the buyer and seller make an agreement over the telephone. The buyer sends a confirmation letter to the seller, saying something like, "This will confirm the agreement entered into this day with you to buy 5,000 covered widgets at $5.62 per piece." He does not ask the seller to sign this letter, to check it, or to return it. He just sends it. Simultaneously, the seller sends a letter to the buyer reading in part, "This confirms our sale to you of 5,000 widgets (with covers) at $5.64 each." Neither of these letters would constitute an integration in the classical sense, nor would either be a "writing intended by the parties" in the words of §2-202. Should a dispute arise about the terms of the agreement, however, §2-202 will make it possible for either side to argue that the amount of 5,000 and the fact that the widgets are to be of the covered variety are not really debatable. Argument over what price had been agreed on is still open to proof by the two parties, of course, but neither piece of writing will have a special role to play in resolving that dispute, at least not by virtue of §2-202.*

One final problem: What if the buyer and the seller, egged on perhaps by overeager lawyers, simultaneously sign two or more writings to finalize their agreement? So, for example, at some kind of elaborate closing they both sign one document captioned "SALES AGREEMENT," another "DISTRIBUTION AGREEMENT," and a third denoted a "SERVICE AGREEMENT." All relate to the same purchase and sales transaction of a single set of goods. They all bear the same date, the date of the closing. Is there an integration? If so, what is it? Here the answer is straightforward. The parties have indeed prepared an integration. It is found in a single writing consisting of the three documents taken as one three-part written exposition. Staple them together and you have an integration. There is the potential, of course, that language in one of the three documents will conflict with what is said in one of the others. But then it is always perfectly possible for even the most careful negotiators (and even the most careful attorneys) unintentionally to throw contradictory language into a *single* written instrument. Should problems arise, whether the integration is crafted as one compact document or as several meant to be read as a package, these are problems of interpretation. They do not defeat the basic conclusion that an integration was intended and hence created.

---

*You may be tempted to race to §2-207 for help on the problem of the price (See Chapter 5), but would it help when the disagreement is so clearly over what would be a "dickered" term?

Who's in Charge Here?

One question that is easy to answer with regard to the parol evidence rule is who, judge or jury, makes the key decisions under the rule. Throughout its long pre-Code history, it had always been clear that the application of the rule was within the special province of the judge. To many commentators (especially those who would argue for what we will end up calling a very liberal application of the rule), this may be the most important feature of the rule in actual operation. It serves as a tool for the judge to keep from the jury certain arguments thought by him or her to contradict a writing intended by those parties to settle those arguments once and for all.

This special role for the court in the application of the rule was clearly intended to continue under §2-202. Note that subpart (b) hinges on "the court" making a finding about the completeness of the writing. Also, although it is nowhere specifically stated in the section, it seems to be assumed by everyone that the initial question of whether a writing was "intended by the parties as a final expression" of at least "such terms as are included therein" is for the judge alone. Of course, once the judge determines that certain evidence can be admitted over any parol evidence objection, it is for the jury as the trier of fact to decide whether that evidence is to be believed and whether it proves what the offering party claims it does about the nature of the parties agreement.

Because of this special role for the court in the day-to-day operation of the parol evidence rule, it is no surprise that when such decisions are brought up on appeal the appellate courts show little hesitancy to weigh in with their own determinations, almost as if they were making judgments de novo. The questions that follow explore a number of easy decisions—and some close calls—that have to be made in applying the rule. You be the judge.

EXAMPLES

1.   Bernice, who runs a clothing store, enters into a written agreement for the purchase of a large quantity of men's dress shirts from Shirtmakers of Boston. The written agreement says nothing about how the shirts are to be packaged. When they are delivered to Bernice she finds they are all simply jammed into the crates. They are wrinkled and will need to be ironed, folded, pinned up and labelled before she can put them out on her shelves.

a.   In an action against Shirtmakers, Bernice seeks to prove a usage in the apparel industry that shirts such as these are to be delivered properly folded, individually wrapped, and marked as to size. Is she barred from making such a presentation by the parol evidence rule?

b.   Will it make any difference if Bernice is seeking to show that the type of packaging she expected—and claims she had a right to expect—is based on a course of dealing established between herself and Shirtmakers?

c. What if the shirts are delivered in the individual packaging, to Bernice's satisfaction, but she discovers that the shipment contains no extra buttons? The agreement says nothing about Shirtmakers being obliged to send extra matching buttons along with the shirts, but Bernice claims that there is a usage of trade in the industry that gives her the right to insist upon getting them. May she prove *this* usage of trade, or is it barred by the parol evidence rule?

d. Assume that the packaging causes no problems between them; the shipment is just fine. The problem comes when Bernice receives the invoice. It calls for her to pay $10 per shirt. The written agreement, in the space provided for "Price" had been filled in with the figure "$10," but Bernice claims there is a well-established usage of the trade—which she assumed would apply—which gives buyers a ten percent discount off of the stated price if they take delivery immediately, which is what she did. Will she be allowed to prove this usage?

2a. Buyer and Seller enter into an agreement for the purchase and sale of some lumber. The number of feet of lumber is specified. The type of lumber is identified in the written agreement as "standard 2″ × 4″ pine." When the lumber arrives, Buyer measures it. It is exactly two inches by four inches in dimension. In a lawsuit against Seller, would he be allowed to show a general trade usage that so-called two-by-four lumber is actually supposed to measure 1½″ × 3½″?

b. Suppose the written agreement signed by Buyer and Seller specified a price of fifty cents per foot for "10,000 board feet of White Pine of Grade B." Prior to his signing, Buyer seemed hesitant to enter into the agreement, and Seller said to him, "Tell you what— I'll make that the better Grade A stuff at no extra charge." With this Buyer signs the agreement, although no change is made in its wording. Does Buyer have the right to insist on Grade A lumber?

c. What if Seller in the previous problem had instead said, "I'll let you upgrade that to Grade A stuff for only one cent more a foot." This is, in fact, practically a giveaway of the upgrade. Buyer eagerly signs the document. Again, no change is made in its wording; it still speaks only of Grade B lumber at a stated price. Does Buyer have the legal right to buy the Grade A lumber at 51 cents a foot?

3. The remaining Examples all involve sales made by Smiling Sol of Smiling Sol's Used-Car-O-Rama. Barry, visiting one Saturday, takes a fancy to a particular 1982 Oldsmobile. Sol sees his interest and offers to sell him the car for the price written on the windshield ($8,999) and writes up a standard Sales Agreement putting "$8999" in the blank provided for "Purchase Price." Barry is wavering on whether or not to sign the agreement. Trying to wrap up the sale, Sol makes the following statements:

(a) "If you buy it, I'll throw in a new set of tires."
(b) "If you buy it, I'll take the cost of your first tank of gas off the price."
(c) "I'm so sure you'll love it that if you don't you can return it and get your money back."

Barry then signs the agreement with no changes having been made in its language. Can Barry enforce any of these statements (a) through (c) against Sol?

4.   Suppose you discover that the Sales Agreement signed by Sol and Barry contains the following language:

> THIS SALES AGREEMENT IS INTENDED BY THE PARTIES HERETO AS A FINAL EXPRESSION OF ALL TERMS AGREED TO BY THE PARTIES AND IS A COMPLETE AND EXCLUSIVE STATEMENT OF THOSE TERMS.

Is your analysis of the previous question changed?

5.   On Monday, Andy enters into a written Sales Agreement with Sol to buy a used Chevy. When Andy picks up the car on Tuesday, Sol tells him, "That's the original paint job, you know." Sol had previously said nothing about the paint on the car and the Sales Agreement makes no mention of it. It turns out that, unknown to Sol, the Chevy had been repainted prior to its having arrived on his lot. Does Andy have rights against Sol based on the statement made on Tuesday?

6.   On Wednesday, Betty sees a Buick on Sol's lot which she likes very much. She tells him she will not be able to commit herself on buying the car until she knows whether she is getting a raise, which she won't know for about a week. Sol suggests to her that "to hold the car" she sign a Sales Agreement, telling her that "it won't mean a thing unless you do get that raise." Betty signs on that understanding. She does not get the raise. Sol comes against her relying on the Sales Agreement which she had signed. The Agreement reads as an absolute obligation on her part to buy and contains no mention of their oral understanding. Is Betty stuck with a contract to buy the car?

7.   Charles enters into a Sales Agreement with Sol to buy a used Pontiac. Prior to Charles's signing the agreement Sol told him that the car had been driven by "a little old gentleman who used it only on Sundays." Charles later finds out that this statement is patently untrue—it was previously owned by a teenage rock musician who spent a lot of time on the road—and furthermore that Charles knew what he was saying was false when he made the statement. Can Charles use the statement against Sol or is it barred by the parol evidence rule?

EXPLANATIONS

1a.   No. Bernice's argument based on a usage of trade (if she can successfully establish that such a usage exists and can be used against Shirtmakers) is not barred by the rule. From the hypothetical we know there is nothing in the written agreement about the method of packaging. She is not seeking to "contradict" the writing. Rather this is a case of her "supplementing" its terms by a usage of trade. Clause (a) of §2-202 specifically authorizes this.

1b. The result is no different if what Bernice is arguing is a course of dealing. Same result if this were some kind of installment contract calling for several deliveries over time and the first deliveries had established a course of performance. An important point to be made here is that trade terms such as these are, according to the drafters, to be allowed in to "explain or supplement" *whether or not* the language of the written instrument appears on its face to need explanation or supplementation. Prior to the Code, many courts held that trade custom would be allowed to vary or explain the terms of a written agreement only if that agreement was first found by the court to be "ambiguous." This condition is rejected by §2-202. See Comment 1 and particularly its subpart (c). The courts have been fairly good in following the intention of the drafters as set forth in this comment.

Of course, while a trade term can "explain or supplement" the writing, it cannot flat-out contradict it. But, as we'll see in what follows, you have to have a pretty flexible idea of what constitutes "contradiction" when it comes to the modern parol evidence rule.

1c. Bernice will try to argue, as she successfully did in Example 1a, that this is merely a matter of a usage of trade being allowed to "supplement" the written terms of the agreement. There would seem to be no particular problem for her here, other than her having to establish such a usage to the satisfaction of the court. Doubt creeps in only because of a recent case, *Latex Glove Co., Inc. v. Gruen,* 146 Ill. App. 3d 868, 497 N.E.2d 466, 2 U.C.C.2d 424 (1986). There the defendant, a printer, contracted to prepare a catalog for the plaintiff. Its services, according to its written quotation, included "complete typesetting, photos, keylines, separation plates and 4-color printing." The buyer's complaint (actually the argument first cropped up in its third amended complaint out of the total of five which it eventually managed to generate) alleged that trade usage gave it the right to obtain various by-products necessarily associated with the production of the catalog, such things as films, negatives, and color separations. The court held that, even if such a usage were provable, the buyer could not take advantage of it in the litigation. Why? The court adopted the defendant seller's argument that trade usage cannot be used "to create a new contract for separate, identifiable goods." According to the Illinois Appellate Court,

> Trade usage is used to fill a gap in the contract, such as terms regarding delivery, credit, and quality of performance. . . .
> The term for the sale of the by-products which the plaintiff wishes to have imposed on defendant here is not a gap filling term, but rather a new obligation for separate goods.

The buyer lost. It was not allowed to take advantage of the trade usage, even if it did indeed exist and even if it had been known to the seller. (Nor was the buyer allowed to file yet one more amended complaint, the court concluding that enough was enough.)

Is the distinction relied upon by the court in *Latex Glove* valid? Apparently some think it is, but I personally find it hard to see how it could be. No language in the section defining and dealing specifically with usage of trade (§1-205) supports the line the court tries to draw. And in §2-202 it merely says "supplement." To supplement is to supplement: There is no suggestion that some kinds of supplementations are valid and others are not. While there are some other cases which rely on a distinction like that enunciated in *Latex Glove*, I doubt many independent authorities would agree with the approach. The holding seems particularly crabbed when you recall that one of the "underlying purposes and policies" of the Uniform Commercial Code is "to permit the continued expansion of commercial practices through custom, usage and agreement of the parties." §1-102(2)(b). In a more recent case, *Capital Converting Equipment, Inc. v. LEP Transport, Inc.*, 750 F. Supp. 862, 14 U.C.C.2d 51 (N.D. Ill. 1990), the federal district court put considerable time and energy into debunking the *Latex Glove* analysis on its way to holding that even if that case had been correct on its facts, there need be no such limitation on the ability of a *course of dealing* to supplement the terms of an agreement.

1d. Now it appears that Bernice has gone too far. Shirtmakers will argue that in this instance she isn't just trying to explain or to supplement the writing, but rather directly to contradict it. If there is any point to the parol evidence rule, they will contend, it is to prevent just such arguments from getting anywhere.

But maybe Shirtmakers's case isn't as clear-cut as all that. *If* Bernice can show there is a well-established practice in the trade of giving such a discount (that is, that knowledgeable traders treat it as a matter of buyers' rights and not just a friendly gesture on the part of sellers and that this is so *even when* the price is as seemingly clear and unambiguous as it is here), then she might have a right to insist upon it. The extent to which many courts are disposed in favor of supplementation through trade usage, even where an initial reading appears to render the usage improperly contradictory, is often demonstrated by the well-known case of *Columbia Nitrogen Corp. v. Royster Co.*, 451 F.2d 3, 9 U.C.C. 977 (4th Cir. 1971). Both parties were in the fertilizer business. Royster was a producer of so-called mixed fertilizers, the primary components of which are nitrogen, phosphate, and potash. Columbia Nitrogen was, as you might expect, primarily a producer and seller of nitrogen. In fact, in past dealings Royster had itself purchased nitrogen from Columbia. The contract in question, however, involved a sale *by* Royster of some of its excess phosphate *to* Columbia, which was in need of some of this other stuff. The contract document recited "Products Supplied Under Contract—Minimum Tonnage Per Year" totalling 31,000 tons over a three-year period. A price per ton was specified, subject to an escalator clause based on the seller's production costs. After the contract was made, the market price of phosphate plunged. Columbia, the buyer, ordered only a small fraction (under ten percent) of the amount specified as a "minimum" for the first year. Royster brought suit for Columbia's failure to take the minimum.

At trial Columbia sought to introduce evidence of a usage of trade that, because of uncertain crop and weather conditions, farming practices, and government agricultural programs, quantity terms in contracts for materials in the fertilizer industry were regarded by the parties thereto as "mere projections to be adjusted according to market forces." Furthermore, Columbia offered to prove that in their past dealings with Royster, where Royster was the buyer and it, Columbia, was the seller, they had actually operated in keeping with this usage. In at least four instances, Columbia claimed, Royster took none of the goods for which it has contracted as buyer (presumably under language substantially the same as in the instant agreement) and had not been held in breach by Columbia.

The district court had held the proffered evidence of a trade usage inadmissable, reasoning that it was being offered to *contradict,* not merely supplement or explain, the writing. The Court of Appeals reversed on this issue, remanding the case for a retrial in which Columbia would be allowed to show "a practice of mutual adjustments so prevalent in the industry and in prior dealings between the parties that it formed a part of the agreement governing this transaction." This certainly is an expansive reading of the Code and the deference to be paid to trade terms. In defense of the result, note that one knowledgeable insider, addressing the unique characteristics of the fertilizer industry that would explain this seemingly bizarre contracting behavior, offered testimony that

> the contract is considered binding to the extent, on [the buyer] morally that if he uses the tonnage that he will execute the contract in good faith as the buyer. . . . I have never heard of a contract of this type being enforced legally. . . . Well, it undoubtedly sounds ridiculous to people from other industries, but there is a very definite, several very definite reasons why the fertilizer business is always operated under what we call gentlemen's agreements [sic].

But if evidence such as this were offered at the retrial, would it necessarily give the day to the buyer? Does the Uniform Commercial Code make every "gentlemen's agreement" enforceable? Consider the following language from a decision that declined to follow the *Royster* result. The case involved a sale of concrete to be used in construction of a building.

> The type of evidence which the *Royster* decision might allow and which the defendant here undoubtedly wishes to introduce would probably show that a very few contracts specifying quantity and price in a particular industry have been strictly enforced. . . . While in some industries it may be virtually impossible to predict future needs under a contract,

in other industries, such contracts may not be strictly adhered to for entirely different reasons. Lawsuits are costly and they do not facilitate good business relations with customers. A party to a contract may very much prefer to work out a renegotiation of a contract rather than rest on its strict legal rights. Yet the supplier or purchaser knows that he may resort to those enforceable contract rights if necessary. If the courts were to conclude that this reluctance to enforce legal rights resulted in an industry-wide waiver of such rights, then contracts would lose their utility as a means of assigning the risks of the market.

Southern Concrete Services, Inc. v. Mableton Contractors, Inc., 407 F. Supp. 581, 19 U.C.C. 79 (N.D. Ga. 1975). So no easy conclusion can be based on *Royster* read alone. Remember, it is one thing to say that because of trade practice some party has no legal right under a contract; it's something else to observe that a party in that position she has such-and-such a right but rarely if ever chooses to pursue it.

2a. I doubt Buyer would have any difficulty establishing this usage and its relevance to the contract here. I find many students, not necessarily in the lumber business, are aware of this usage and others are willing to accept it once told. Analysis of the last few questions might have made you uncomfortable with the apparent ease with which some courts appear to allow even direct contradiction of the writing by trade usage. To my mind at least this example serves to underscore how easy it is for people in a trade to live with a usage which would seem to the outsider so contrary to their very words.

This is as good a place as any to consider the relationship between this part of the parol evidence rule in §2-202 and the specific language of both §1-205(4) and §2-208(2) which deals with the hierarchy of terms when express provisions meet trade terms. You should reread these subsections and convince yourself that they are consistent with what we've been seeing in §2-202. Express terms are to dominate, yes, but only when a construction that finds those terms "consistent" with the trade terms is patently "unreasonable." If cases like *Royster* and hypotheticals like the one in this question are to be believed, a court can correctly be very liberal in finding consistency between express and trade terms. One question that remains is why, if these subsections are consistent with §2-202, they were needed at all. At least two explanations can be given. First note that §1-205(4) and §2-208(2) both refer to *express terms.* Express terms need not be in writing, but can be part of an oral agreement. If the express terms are all oral the parol evidence rule doesn't come into play at all, and these subsections are then needed to instruct us on how to reconcile those express oral terms with the various trade terms offered by the litigants. Secondly, even when the express terms are in writing, the subsections are still useful as a guide to interpretation once a whole variety of terms—written, oral, trade usage, course of dealing, and course of performance—are all on the table. Section 2-202 speaks more to the question of what evidence should be allowed into the contract interpretation mix by the court. If once all of the evidence is collected there still remains any question about how it is all to be reconciled and the contract interpreted, these subsections are intended as guides on interpretation in general.

2b. No. Buyer has no contract right to Grade A lumber. The result is really mandated by the introductory language of §2-202. That the subject of the contract was to be Grade B lumber is found in a term which is "set forth in a writing intended by the parties a final agreement with respect to such terms as are included therein." Hence this term may not be "contradicted by evidence of any prior agreement or of a contemporaneous oral agreement." Later we'll have to deal with exactly how to read the word *contradicted* in this context, but there doesn't seem to be any doubt that a claim for Grade A contradicts a writing which calls for "Grade B." If the parol evidence rule means anything (and there are those who wish it didn't, but for now it does) it would have to bar proof of the kind Buyer wants to make here.

2c. In this example, Buyer will argue he is not trying to contradict the writing with his claim of an upgrade term, but only to supplement it. At least as he has articulated it the upgrade is to be for an additional consideration of one cent per foot, so he'll claim this isn't trying to contradict either the price term or the quality term. If he clears that hurdle, does Buyer necessarily get to introduce evidence of a contemporaneous oral agreement which would only supplement what was in the writing? Not necessarily. The court must in addition find that the writing involved was not "intended also as a *complete and exclusive* statement of the terms of the agreement." (emphasis added). How does the court make such a determination? It can be a tough call. Comment 3 is often quoted:

> Under paragraph (b) consistent additional terms, not reduced to writing, may be proved unless the court finds that the writing was intended as a complete and exclusive statement of all the terms. If the additional terms would certainly have been included in the document in the view of the court, then evidence of their alleged making must be kept from the trier of fact.

A reading of this comment suggests that just about the only time a court could rule out of order an "alleged" oral term is when the court just doesn't believe the allegation. This reading doesn't make much of the parol evidence rule, of course, although it does give a judge some additional control over what a jury can hear and decide. Such a reading, however, goes against the long history of the parol evidence rule, which rests on the idea that something more is going on even if it isn't clear exactly what. Presumably the court will look not just to what it actually believes these parties did, but what it thinks other "reasonable" parties similarly situated (going back to an idea from the common law parol evidence rule) "would certainly have done" in like circumstances. A pretty flaccid notion, granted, but there must be something to it.

When such a question arises, the court will presumably take into account the situation in which the parties found themselves. Was it what we would call a formal setting or something fairly casual? Beyond that, the court will look at the writing itself. Was it the product of a long laborious negotiation process, during which every clause, every word was fought over? Were lawyers involved, working their tedious way through numerous drafts and innumerable details? If so, and if the argued supplemental term is anything of significance, it seems likely that parties such as these "would certainly" have put their energies into writing this into the document along with everything else. Compare this to the situation where the writing being relied upon is merely a preprinted blanket form with some details of the particular deal dropped into the few blank spaces. In such a situation, a court will much more easily find that the argued supplemental term could have been reasonably left out by parties such as these.

3.   Here, as in the previous question, the buyer will be arguing that the oral terms were merely "consistent" additions to the written agreement and should be considered part of their enforceable deal. If the Sales Agreement used by Sol is a fairly standard one, and if the two just signed it in Sol's office without much fuss and without making any variations to its printed language, it would seem pretty easy for Barry to argue that the writing can be supplemented by a wide range of terms not included in it. The language that ends subpart (b), "unless the court finds the writing to have been intended also as a complete and exclusive statement of the terms of the agreement," might suggest that the matter of so-called *complete* versus *partial integration* is an all-or-nothing kind of game. Either the writing is found to be a complete integration, in which case nothing can possibly supplement it, or it is found not to be complete, in which case maybe just about anything can be added. But the parol evidence rule doesn't work that way. A writing may in fact be found to be complete as to some aspects of the agreement and yet not complete as to others. Imagine, for example, if Sol had eventually promised Barry a lower price but had not changed it in the writing. Sol could argue that the writing was clearly complete as to the purchase price. Even if this is so, that doesn't mean it is necessarily complete as to how the car will be equipped when it is delivered. The real issue is whether the offered terms can be thought of as consistent with the writing. In effect, a totally one-hundred-percent "complete integration" is merely one which is found to be so thorough and detailed that absolutely no term not included in it could possibly be thought consistent with the very existence of such a long drawn-out document. Anything less is only a partial integration, which may be supplemented by (but only by) consistent terms. The question still centers on the notion of *consistency;* unfortunately this is a concept which, at least at the edges, will have to remain fairly nebulous.

Barry would probably win on the issue of the tires. He'd have a harder time with the promise in (b). Sol would argue that saying that the price would be anything but $8,999 is by its nature not consistent, and is in fact downright contradictory. Barry will answer that this is not a change in the purchase price, just a little supplemental perk thrown into the bargain. It's not clear who would win on this one. Barry would presumably have a much harder time still when it comes to the alleged buy-back provision. This is, after all, a fairly unusual term for a used car dealer to agree to, and it's of no small significance if it were ever to be invoked. Even if it believes Barry as to what transpired, I think a court would probably conclude that such a term "would certainly" have been included if the parties meant it to be effective and rule it not an enforceable part of their contract.

In terms of the language of §2-202 itself, Sol's argument must be that the alleged buy-back provision was not consistent with the other terms of the writing. True, there is no language in the document which says that Sol *won't* buy back the car on these terms, but isn't the whole idea that "a seller sells and a buyer buys for keeps" in a sense inconsistent with an understanding that one party can reverse the deal whenever he wants with no ramifications? This question of exactly how to determine when an alleged term is a consistent addition is one which has troubled the courts from the inception of the Code. Dealing as each will with a unique fact situation, it is unlikely that the cases will ever be terribly consistent on what exactly counts for consistency. An early case, *Hunt Foods & Industries, Inc. v. Doliner,* 26 A.D.2d 41, 270 N.Y.S.2d 937, 3 U.C.C. 597 (1966), took what was later to be criticized as a very narrow view on this issue. The court there held that to be inconsistent an offered term had to "contradict or negate a term of the writing." In other words, there had to be some particular language in the writing itself which was just flatly at odds with the offered term. If that standard were used, Barry would presumably be able to prove his unusual, but not flatly and expressly contradicted, buy-back provision.

Most commentators and courts have rejected the *Hunt Foods* test. Among other reasons is that this would make the consistency requirement in part (b) merely duplicative of the earlier language in §2-202 that rules out any contradictions generally. Most courts today use instead a standard under which an offered term is found inconsistent in "the absence of reasonable harmony in terms of the language *and* respective obligations of the parties." *Snyder v. Herbert Greenbaum & Associates, Inc.,* 38 Md. App. 144, 380 A.2d 618, 22 U.C.C. 1104 (1977) (emphasis in original). In *Snyder,* the Maryland Court of Appeals held that parol evidence of a contractual right to unilateral rescission was inconsistent with a written agreement for the sale and installation of carpeting. Following this line of reasoning, Barry's claim for enforcement of the offered buy-back provision would presumably fail.

Note, in comparison, that even if a court were to find a writing a "complete and exclusive statement of the terms," this would *not* bar the introduction of trade terms as set forth in subpart (a) unless they were found to be "contradictory" to the writing itself. The language of complete versus partial integration, for what it's worth, is found only in subpart (b) of the section.

4.   The presence of such language in the Sales Agreement might make a difference, but this result may not be as clear-cut as Sol (who wants us to read only that language and throw the case out of court) would have us believe. *Merger clauses* are common in written agreements, and in general it should be said that they are as enforceable as any other term agreed to by the parties. They serve a very useful function when the written instrument truly *is* what the merger clause says that it is, that is, a detailed and well-drafted final version of a written agreement over which the parties have been laboring. There is in such a situation every reason to think that the parties *did* intend to wrap every single thing up in the document and tie it with a bow, and the merger clause just makes this official.

It is a very different matter, however, when we have a consumer buyer signing a standard agreement provided by the seller without any dickering over the language. There a court will usually not be as impressed by the merger language. In such cases the clause is often viewed by the court as mere boilerplate with no independent legal effect just because it has been thrown in among the mass of verbiage. The intention of the parties is still the key. If the court is not favorably disposed towards the integration and to such a standard merger clause in a standard agreement, it can easily hold that even though the buyer signed a paper having such language in it he or she did not actually intend the paper to have the effect argued for. The court can determine, in effect, that the alleged merger clause was no more actually "agreed to" than was anything else.

In any situation, a party wishing to secure a valid and enforceable merger clause in a written contract would do well to follow a few simple guidelines: (1) make the language as conspicuous as possible (don't bury it); (2) provide evidence that the other party gave his or her considered assent to that clause in particular by having it separately signed or initialed; (3) draft the clause as carefully as possible to cover the specific concerns of the parties involved and tailor it to the particular situation. Faced with a clause meeting these criteria, a court will find it difficult (although still not impossible) to set it aside and will allow supplementation to the terms of the written agreement.

(Note that when language such as is suggested here is being argued to have disclaimed a warranty or to have limited the seller's liability in the event of a breach, Article 2 provides a set of special rules that must be applied. Disclaimers and limitations are special cases. We deal with them directly in Chapter 14.)

5.   The parol evidence rule would not bar this statement. This was a statement made *subsequent to* the parties entering into an integration of their agreement, so §2-202 is simply inapplicable. Andy may have a problem taking advantage of this statement, but there isn't a parol evidence issue. For one thing, Sol may claim that as a later modification of their agreement it is unenforceable as lacking "consideration," although this argument shouldn't go far because of §2-209(1). (Don't worry about

this now; it's in Chapter 10.) Also, as a claimed express warranty, Andy may have to worry about the timing and the "part of the basis of the bargain language" of §2-313 (see Chapter 12). The point here is simply that there is no parol evidence problem at all once Andy is relying on a later statement.

6.   Betty's argument is that, whatever may appear to someone viewing the paper, no final agreement of any kind was ever entered into between her and Sol because a condition to her acceptance of his offer never came to pass. This is often referred to as the *conditional delivery exception* to the parol evidence rule, but it is not really an exception at all. The concept is more rudimentary: There is simply no reason to invoke the rule whatsoever, because the parties never created an integration of an enforceable agreement; in fact, there never was an agreement in the first place. This argument is accepted by the courts. For example, in *King v. Fordice,* 776 S.W.2d 608, 10 U.C.C.2d 65 (Tex. Ct. App. 1989), the seller presented an exchange of mailgrams which he claimed set forth the agreement between himself and the buyer for the sale of a Cessna 414 aircraft. The alleged buyer presented a different view of the events. He claimed that he had agreed to an exchange of mailgrams solely for the purpose of the seller's getting the airplane to Dallas for his inspection, and that he had no intention at the time of entering into a binding agreement to buy the plane for $400,000. The buyer pointed out that, "in accordance with the understanding that the exchange of mailgrams was an inspection ticket and not a binding contract he did not send the $25,000.00 deposit as mentioned in the mailgrams." Prior to trial the seller filed a motion to suppress all evidence which would vary or expand the terms as they appeared in the pair of mailgrams. The Texas Court of Appeals upheld the trial court's decision to deny this motion and to allow into evidence the buyer's testimony about his oral understanding with the seller. The appellate court considered both the general common law notion of conditional delivery and how it was effected by the adoption of Article 2, concluding

> that parol evidence is always competent to show the nonexistence of a contract, or the invalidity of a contract even if there is a writing purporting to be an integration, and that such matters are outside the scope of the common law parol evidence rule and the ambit of §2-202, with regard to the sale of goods. These matters are admissible on their own merit and not as an exception to the parol evidence rule or §2-202. . . . The trial judge did not err in admitting the complained of testimony on a "no contract" or non-formation theory. Such oral testimony did not vary the terms of the mailgrams as contended by [the seller] but showed that the mailgrams were never intended to be a contract or of binding force between the parties.

Determining that this evidence was admissible and not barred by the parol evidence rule did not, of course, completely decide the case. The trial court's attention had to be directed toward whether it believed the characterization of events as related by the buyer. It did, and the buyer was found never to have entered into an agreement to buy the plane. The result thus turned not on the mechanics of the parol evidence rule but on a factual determination of what had actually transpired between the parties.

7.   Charles has a good case of fraudulent inducement. Such claims are generally not held to be barred by the parol evidence rule. Again, as in the last Example, the issue is not over identifying the terms of an agreement acknowledged to be enforceable between the parties, but rather whether the agreement is in fact enforceable at all, here in light of the fraud committed by one of the players. Section 2-202 is simply not applicable if for some reason recognized in law there is no enforceable agreement between the parties. Where does Charles find authority for his argument on the theory of fraud? See §1-103. Charles' case, if he can prove it, seems perfectly clear. The courts will be wary, of course, to be sure that claimants don't circumvent the effect of the parol evidence rule merely by framing their arguments in terms of fraud. Key here is that Charles will show that Sol intentionally misled him with a statement he knew to be untrue.

The only problem for Charles would be if the Sales Agreement he signed had a very powerful and broad-ranging merger clause, something like the following:

> THIS AGREEMENT SIGNED BY BOTH PARTIES AND SO INI-TIALED BY BOTH PARTIES IN THE MARGIN OPPOSITE THIS PARAGRAPH CONSTITUTES A FINAL WRITTEN EXPRESSION OF ALL THE TERMS OF THIS AGREEMENT AND IS A COM-PLETE AND EXCLUSIVE STATEMENT OF THOSE TERMS AND ANY AND ALL REPRESENTATIONS, PROMISES, WARRANTIES, OR STATEMENTS BY SELLER'S AGENT THAT DIFFER IN ANY WAY FROM THE TERMS OF THIS AGREEMENT SHALL BE GIVEN NO FORCE OR EFFECT.

This language is suggested by Professors White and Summers in their treatise. If it were to be found in Sol's standard form agreement, and if Charles had indeed signed the agreement and initialed the merger clause paragraph, would Sol be isolated from claims of fraudulent inducement? Should he be? I doubt you'd ever find a clear answer to what a court would do in this situation.

9

Open Terms, Gap Fillers, and the Doctrine of Unconscionability

The Agreement "as Affected by This Act"

A brief review is in order. The starting point for determining the terms of the sales contract is the agreement of the parties. As we noted in the introduction to Chapter 7, the Code uses the word *agreement* to refer to the "bargain of the parties in fact" (§1-201(3)). So first we have to piece together just what the operative agreement is. Chapters 4 and 5 focused on the parties' express agreement as it arises out of their direct communications one with the other. Chapter 7 added to the mix (and to the agreement) terms arising from trade usage, course of dealing, and course of performance.

But delineating the agreement is not the end of the story. The sales *contract* under the UCC is "the total legal obligation which arises from the parties' agreement as affected by this Act and any other applicable rules of law" (§1-201(11)). To find the terms of the contract we start with the terms agreed to—but then the Code giveth and the Code taketh away. Chapter 8 was all about one particular way in which an agreed term or terms might be taken out of the eventual contract by operation of law. In certain circumstances, Article 2's parol evidence rule §2-202 makes unenforceable a "prior agreement" or "contemporaneous oral agreement" reached by the parties. The buyer's and seller's agreement may include many a term which, given §2-202 and the fact that the term hasn't been included in a written integration, will not make it into the enforceable legal relationship, the contract.

This chapter is concerned with a further set of provisions in Article 2 which can work to add or subtract terms from the contract. They are variously referred to as the *gap fillers* of Article 2 or the sections allowing for and regulating *open terms*. One very special provision (that dealing with the doctrine of *unconscionability*) gets a separate, if not particularly exhaustive, treatment.

The Unconscionability Police

People are not necessarily fair. Certainly when they are out to make the best deal possible for themselves they may not be. People going into a bargain should plan to look out for themselves and try to get the best deal available. Furthermore a contracting party will normally expect that the opposing party will likewise be ruled by self-interest and take appropriate care. If some people drive hard bargains, well, more power to them: That's what freedom of contract is all about, and Comment 2 to §1-102 reminds us (if we needed any reminding) that "freedom of contract is a principle of the Code." There was no general rule in the common law of contracts, and there is certainly nothing in Article 2, which requires that parties to a sales agreement be fair to each other, or reasonable in what they ask for, or anything like that. As a general rule, it's "every man for himself," and we have to assume the drafters would have had it no other way.

But sometimes things get out of hand. Even under the common law, extracting a bargain by duress, coercion, or fraud is impermissible. These doctrines still apply to sales contracts governed by Article 2 by virtue of §1-103. Beyond this, will there be any limit to what parties may agree to? Does the law "police" the substance of the bargain itself? The traditional doctrinal response was no, even though the courts often found ways to accomplish what was not technically allowed. See the first two sentences of Comment 1 to §2-302. As the comment goes on to state, this section was intended to allow courts to do a bit of policing directly and out in the open. Under §2-302 an agreement which as a whole is *unconscionable* or which contains an unconscionable provision need not necessarily be enforced by the court. Unconscionability is a defense. In §2-302 the Code empowers a court to eliminate from the enforceable contract any unconscionable term or terms of the agreement, or even to refuse to enforce the agreement entirely.*

---

*The discussion that follows will deal with the doctrine of unconscionability in its general application. Unconscionability plays a special part when the provisions concerned are those which purport to disclaim warranties or limit a buyer's remedies in the event of a breach. Such terms are discussed in detail in Chapter 14.

Note that California has not adopted §2-302. There are, however, statements

You should read §2-302(1) now if you have not already done so. Clearly the court is given great leeway in dealing with unconscionability. Unfortunately what this section doesn't tell us is the one thing we most would like to know: What exactly does it mean for a clause or for an entire contract to be unconscionable? The word is never defined in the Code. Indeed most everyone seems to agree that a simple one-line definition is not possible (and probably not even desirable). Unconscionability is a doctrine, a thesis, a concept. Still we need to get some handle on what it's all about. Comment 1 is of limited help:

> The basic test is whether, in the light of the general commercial background and the commercial needs of the particular trade or case, the clauses involved are so one-sided as to be unconscionable under the circumstances existing at the time of the making of the contract.

This language is important in that it makes clear that unconscionability is to be measured at the time a contract is entered into and not in the light of later events. Beyond that it cautions that any determination has to be made in light of the overall commercial setting. We are dealing with the real world here, not some utopian community.

But we are still left with a "basic test" that seems to define unconscionability in terms of 'that which is unconscionable.' Not much help. Later language in this Comment is often cited:

> The principle is one of prevention of oppression and unfair surprise . . . and not of disturbance of allocation of risks because of superior bargaining power.

Is this any clearer? The Comment concludes with a recitation of some illustrations. You may look at them if you wish, but don't be surprised if you come away with the idea that for unconscionability, like some other things, the only test is that you are supposed to know it when you see it. Indeed not a few commentators, including many who heartily support the whole §2-302 agenda, have concluded that there's not much more that can be said on the matter and certainly no definition or precise set of criteria which separates the unconscionable from the merely naughty.

Perhaps more can be said about the substance of the doctrine of unconscionability, of what it is, and of how we spot it. Before venturing into those waters, however, there are some points to be made of a more procedural nature. At least here we can make some statements with confidence. Note first that under §2-302(1) and Comments 2 and 3 the unconscionability doctrine is firmly in the hands of the court; it will be

---

by California courts that the notion of unconscionability is to be found in that state's common law. What are we to make, then, of the legislature's very notorious decision to omit this section? Was it just being ornery?

Note also that §2A-108 is an analogous, albeit somewhat expanded, section covering leases. Subsection 2A-108(2), for example, covers a species of unconscionable *conduct* after the lease is entered into. Contrast this with §2-302, which deals only with terms unconscionable from the sales contract's inception.

up to the judge to apply its provisions. Decisions about unconscionability are not for a jury to make. This is, of course, of no small significance. Whatever the doctrine of unconscionability is about, §2-302 is not meant to be a means for the jury to roam freely over an agreement, striking those provisions it chooses as unfair or inappropriate, especially as those terms may affect a party who has gained its sympathy. Judges, we are to believe, are made of sterner stuff and are not so easily swayed. Beyond that, judges will not so readily be distracted from the underlying virtues and benefits of freedom of contract. The power to police via the notion of unconscionability is heady stuff, which is firmly in the control of the judiciary.

A second point of importance is found in the dictate of §2-302(2). Look at that subsection. Whether a particular contract or clause is unconscionable is not solely a matter of judicial instinct. The court in making the determination must be guided not just by first impressions but by *evidence*—evidence of the commercial setting, as well as the purpose and effect of the accused clause. Both parties must be given a reasonable opportunity to present such evidence. It would be a serious mistake to dismiss this statutory language as merely a vague incantation that courts which try cases should really try the cases. In fact, subsection (2) may be the most important part of §2-302 from the perspective of a party trying to defend a challenged clause. "Hear me out," he or she will be heard to say. "There is a legitimate and quite comprehensible reason for what I bargained for given the circumstances." In any number of cases, clauses that initially might seem like clear unconscionability (whatever that may be) will upon closer inspection take on a very different character. Depending on your overall view of the unconscionability doctrine, in fact, you may be among those who conclude that few if any challenged clauses will fail to stand up to scrutiny once the full facts are revealed and the commercial justification for the particular provision understood. Perhaps bargainers who later fall victim to the unconscionability doctrine are not doing such bad things after all; perhaps they are just having trouble helping a court see the commercial necessity of how they carry on business.

Of course you may well conclude that there is much more to unconscionability than this. Virtually all the commentators seem to acknowledge that there is *some* substance here, even if they can't exactly put their finger on what it is.* An age-old rubric has it that conduct is unconscionable if it "shocks the conscience." This language isn't very helpful and isn't heard that often anymore. Among other problems, it begs the question of whose conscience we are talking about. What is shocking to your run-

---

*But see Professor Leff, whose article in the Pennsylvania Law Review is rightfully regarded as a leading piece in the field and whose views will be noted shortly. He opined the unconscionability principle as set forth in §2-302 was merely "an emotionally satisfying incantation" having "no reality referent." This last phrase is, I believe, a scholarly way of saying that in fact the concept just doesn't mean anything when you get right down to it. Leff, Unconscionability and the Code—The Emperor's New Clause, 115 U. Pa. L. Rev. 485 (1967).

of-the-mill professor of ethics might look very different to a hardened businessman or woman who spends each and every day out in the real world.

The modern discussion of unconscionability usually starts out with some language from Judge Skelly Wright in the oft-discussed case of *Williams v. Walker-Thomas Furniture Co.,* 350 F.2d 445, 2 U.C.C. 955 (D.C. Cir. 1965):

> Unconscionability has generally been recognized to include an absence of meaningful choice on the part of one of the parties together with contract terms which are unreasonably favorable to the other party.

Following up on this, Professor Arthur Leff, writing soon after the adoption of the Code, suggested an analysis which distinguished between two types or flavors of unconscionability. He offered the term *procedural unconscionability* for what he saw as "bargaining naughtiness," that is, some significant taint in the process by which the agreement was extracted out of the innocent party. This ties in to Judge Wright's reference to "an absence of meaningful choice" on that party's part and the *means* by which the overreaching party put the other in this pickle. What Leff termed *substantive unconscionability,* on the other hand, calls for a focus on the *ends* which are achieved by the bargaining process. How one-sided or unfair did the contract turn out to be? Substantive unconscionability relates to Wright's requirement of "terms which are unreasonably favorable" to the one party at the expense of the other. The Leff analysis has stuck, partly because of its genuine usefulness and partly because nothing better has come along. Courts and commentators regularly make reference to it. We can pursue it a bit more here.

Procedural unconscionability can be found—and has been found—where one party knowingly takes advantage of the other's lack of education or unfamiliarity with the English language. It is found in too-fine print or in contractual gobbledygook which, however large on the printed page, is virtually impossible for any mere mortal to make sense out of. A court looking for signs of procedural unconscionability can usually find some high-pressure salesmanship thrown in as well. Procedural unconscionability is the sin of preying on the guileless and vulnerable consumer.

This raises an immediate question. Does the particular individual's economic position, that is, his or her clout in the marketplace, bear on the defense of unconscionability? Certainly courts often take pains to justify a determination of unconscionability with a showing of the lack of bargaining power by the injured party. Lack of bargaining power alone would presumably not be enough to call for an invocation of §2-302. Note the language previously quoted from Comment 1 that the principle is *not* "the disturbance of allocation of risk because of superior bargaining power." There is no reason to think the drafters meant to turn their backs on the basic assumption underlying the free-market economy and everything that is dear to capitalism. But unequal bargaining power does seem to play a part. How else could you explain the complaining party's having entered into such a grossly unfair and shocking deal? And yet we know that even a fairly sophisticated and intelligent consumer may later feel he or she was unfairly roped into a deal. Can that consumer call upon the principle of unconscionability? Possibly, but the instances where unconscionability would be found in favor of a sophisticated consumer will presumably be rare. For people such as this it will be hard to say there has been an "absence of meaningful choice." Your typical middle-class consumer always has the option of saying no to a deal and taking his or her business elsewhere—and would be wise to do so.

I have been writing so far as if questions of unconscionability can only come up in what we would think of as the "consumer protection situation." Could a party who has entered into an agreement as part of his or her business (a commercial actor) ever be successful in claiming unconscionability? Again the answer is that this is possible. Nothing in the language of or Comments to §2-302 limits its applicability, and there have been cases where business entities have been successful with this defense. But the instances of unconscionability in a commercial setting should be few. Certainly once both parties to a business arrangement have had legal counsel advising them during the negotiation and conclusion of an agreement the doctrine of unconscionability would seem inappropriate to the situation. Unconscionability is largely, albeit not exclusively, a doctrine intended to give some measure of protection to the poor and disadvantaged consumer who suffers unduly from the harsh realities of the marketplace.

So far we have been concentrating on so-called procedural uncon-scionability. Turning now to the notion of *substantive unconscionability,* the question becomes whether the results of bargaining (the terms which are agreed to) are so one-sided as to call into question their very enforce-ability. Note the various examples set forth in Comment 1.* It's hard to define or delineate substantively unconscionable terms in the abstract, and no one ever tries. Presumably the taint of substantive unconscionability lies in a term's (or an entire contract's) being not just a hard bargain nor a losing one, but something beyond that. Recall the use of the term *oppres-sion* in Comment 1 and the old *shocks the conscience* language.

In following Leff's popular and helpful two-branch analysis, we natu-rally ask what is the relationship between procedural and substantive unconscionability. Will one alone do to state a defense under §2-302? Here we have an issue on which the commentators disagree and the courts have not been all that clear. Certainly the typical case of unconscion-ability (at least the typically strong one) will exhibit both procedural and substantive problems. Furthermore, everyone seems to agree that the more of one you have, the less of the other is necessary to make out a case. As we've highlighted, unconscionability is to be addressed solely by the judge, and courts invariably look to the totality of the situation and the "mix" of factors in making such determinations. Rarely if ever does a

---

*As a matter of fact, almost all of these examples would now be subject to the more particularized treatment of §§2-316 and 2-719 which are discussed in Chapter 14.

court think it necessary or wise to parse too closely all of the considerations involved.

A particularly troubling question on which there is no agreement is whether the §2-302 power can be exercised by a court when there is no showing whatsoever of procedural unconscionability, but only what appears to be a substantively unconscionable *result*. The issue is seen in its most pristine form when it is reduced to the question of so-called *price unconscionability*. Imagine that a buyer has agreed to a price far in excess of what "should be" or "normally would be" charged for the product in question. Can this fact alone support a court's nullification of the agreement—or adjustment of the price—under §2-302?

The courts and the commentators are decidedly split on how they would handle such a situation. In several cases, the court explicitly stated that an excessive price in and of itself may render the deal unenforceable. In reality, of course, one suspects that the court in many if not all of these cases could easily have pointed to a questionable bargaining technique or two had it found the need to do so. Other courts and some commentators have stated just as confidently that an excessive price or other substantively unconscionable term can be excised by the court under §2-302 only if some discernable element of procedural unconscionability is also present. Notice that the previously quoted language of Judge Wright, which started out this whole line of attack, speaks of unconscionability being found in an absence of meaningful choice on one party's part *together with* a term or terms unreasonably favorable to the other party. Of course it may not be that hard for a court following this approach to find some procedural taint. How else to explain the buyer's agreement to such an "excessive" price or "outrageous" provision?

In point of fact it has been noted how relatively few claims of unconscionability based primarily on excessive pricing, at least as reflected in the published cases, have been brought in recent years. One possible reason for this relates back to an initial point made about §2-302(2). If the buyer asserts an unconscionably high price, the seller has to be given an opportunity to present evidence "as to its commercial setting, purpose and effect." Perhaps sellers are just getting wiser in their use of this provision. There may be perfectly legitimate reasons after all why the price charged to poor or disadvantaged consumers, the least powerful members of the community, ends up being significantly higher than what is charged for the same merchandise in a trendy suburban store or a rustic enclave. Once challenged by a buyer claiming price unconscionability, the seller may be able to justify this price based on the increased costs of doing business in the particular area. This would not, of course, justify sharp practices, "oppression" or the "unfair surprise" such as that which fits within our notion of procedural unconscionability. But a higher price alone may eventually have to be understood as a reflection of the prevailing conditions in certain segments of the economy and of forces quite beyond the power of the seller to influence even if he or she wanted to. And on this, an argument of unconscionability would presumably have to fail.

It remains to be seen whether the courts will ever come up with a single consistent answer to the question of the pure case of so-called price unconscionability. But then price unconscionability is only the most dramatic and perhaps the most troubling aspect of that more general mystery—the doctrine of unconscionability and its uneasy place in a law of sales fundamentally premised on traditional notions of freedom of contract.

Introduction to the Gap Fillers

As we saw in Chapter 5, Article 2 takes a more liberal (the drafters would say a more realistic) view of when a contract has been entered into than does the traditional common law of contract. The question is always that of intent. In particular recall §2-204(3), which holds that

> Even though one or more terms are left open a contract for sale does not fail for indefiniteness if the parties have intended to make a contract and there is a reasonably certain basis for giving an appropriate remedy.

If a contract can exist in this way, who or what sets the terms "left open" by the parties? For one thing, the Code's rich scheme for identifying any applicable trade usage or course of dealing and incorporating it into the agreement will fill in many of the holes. (On which refer back to Chapter 7.) Beyond this the drafters of Article 2 included an extensive set of rules (usually referred to as the *gap fillers*) to set the terms of the contract of sale which the parties themselves have otherwise left open. You should now glance over §§2-304 through 2-311.*

EXAMPLES

1. Hector has an exercise bicycle which he never uses. Cleo has been given an expensive hammock which she doesn't want at all. They agree to a trade. Is this transaction covered by Article 2? If so, who is the "seller" and who the "buyer"?

2. Arnold Moneybucks, the noted art patron, goes into Stella's gallery where he looks over the various paintings on display. Every artwork in the gallery is up for sale, but in keeping with the classy nature of the establishment no price tags are visible. A price list is kept discretely in Stella's office. Arnold spots a painting he particularly admires, and tells Stella, "I simply must have that one." Stella invites him to step into her

---

*These sections take on particular importance in the "Battle of the Forms" situation where the parties' conduct recognizes the existence of a contract although their writings do not. See §2-207(3) and the discussion in Chapter 5.

It is interesting to note that these sections do not have analogs in Article 2A. Apparently we are meant to take from this that parties to a lease of goods should, and regularly will, bargain out the details of price, quantity, and performance to a greater extent than your typical buyer and seller.

office, to which he responds, "That won't be necessary. I'll send my assistant around for it tomorrow. Have it ready." Stella is barely able to utter, "Anything you want, Mr. Moneybucks," before her flamboyant visitor is out the door. Is there a contract for the sale of the painting? If so, what is the contract price?

3.   On his lunch hour, the office clerk Benny is looking over the paintings in Stella's gallery. She approaches him as he is staring intently at a particular work and identifies herself. He tells her, "I'd really like to own this one." She grabs his hand, gives it a good shake, and says, "You've got yourself a deal. You're not going to be sorry." Is there a contract for sale here?

4.   We are still at Stella's gallery. A third individual, one Constance, is sitting with the owner in her private office discussing art. She points to a small statue on Stella's desk. "Now that," says Constance, "is something I'd love to have." Stella says that the statue was a gift from the artist, who was at the time just starting out but who has since become very popular, and that the piece is now undoubtedly worth a good deal of money. She had not intended to sell it, but if Constance is really interested she is willing to let her have it. The two sign a written Purchase and Sale agreement. Where the agreement calls for a "Price" they fill in "As fixed by Ken Clark." Ken is a noted authority on modern art who often acts as an appraiser in the local art market.

  a.   Under these circumstances is there a contract for sale, and if so at what price?

  b.   What if Stella and Constance find out the next day that Ken has left the country, saying he will have no more to do with the art market?

  c.   What result if instead Ken is available but Stella, regretting her agreement, tells Constance to forget about their deal and that she is not going to let Ken have a look at the statue?

5.   Buyer goes into Seller's bookstore and asks for a particular book. Seller says that he does not have the book in stock, that it is in fact out of print, but that he is sure he can find a used copy for Buyer. He says, "I'd get one if you are going to buy it. I don't know exactly how much a used copy will cost. I'd have to see what to charge you for it." Buyer says, "That's OK. I'll take it." Seller later contacts Buyer to tell him that he's obtained a copy of the book and that the price will be $125. Is Buyer obligated to buy the book at this price? What if Buyer could show that the original manufacturer's suggested price marked on the book had been $49.95?

6.   Candy is a candy manufacturer. One of the several candies she produces is the Pecan Supreme, for which she quite naturally needs pecans. She contacts Shelly, a major nut supplier. They enter into a written agreement under which Candy will purchase "all of her pecan requirements" from Shelly for a period of three years at a stated price. Under the agreement, Candy will notify Shelly by the 15th of any month how many nuts to deliver by the beginning of the following month. During

the course of their negotiations Candy has told Shelly that she anticipates a need for something like 1,000 to 1,200 pounds of pecans per month.

a. Is there a contract here? Would your answer be the same if the writing had not referred to "all" of Candy's pecan requirements?

b. Thanks to a very successful marketing campaign, sales of Pecan Supremes rise dramatically. Candy's order to Shelly begin to range around 2,000 pounds a month. Shelly is concerned because he finds he has made a bad deal with Candy and is losing money on every pound he delivers to her. Is he obligated to fill these larger orders?

c. Assume that the reason Candy's orders to Shelly had jumped was that Candy, realizing that (due to a world-wide pecan shortage) she had a particularly good deal on pecans, decided to add a new product to her line of treats. She plans to put together and distribute little packets of pecans under the name of Candy's Fresh Pecan Packets. Is Shelly obligated to fill these larger orders?

d. Suppose instead that during the second year of their agreement Candy looks at her sales figures and concludes that the Pecan Supreme is not a big seller. It is just barely breaking even. She decides to discontinue making it in favor of a new product, the Walnut Delight, which she anticipates will sell better. She notifies Shelly that she no longer needs any pecans from him. Does Shelly have any rights against Candy? Would it make a difference if Candy could show she was actually losing money on the pecan product? What if she were losing money just because her pecan costs under the deal with Shelly were higher than those of her competitors?

e. Looking again at the basic question of enforceability in Example 6(a), would the agreement between Candy and Shelly still be binding if the writing they signed had not been for a definite term of years and in fact had left its duration totally up in the air? See §2-309.

7. Babs is building her own house and has almost completed the job. She agrees to buy three truckloads of topsoil from Sol's garden supply firm. The written contract sets the price at $600 and calls for delivery "the week of May 15." Payment is to be made "On Delivery." On Monday, May 15 Sol arrives at Babs's, his truck loaded with topsoil. He says he is ready to dump the dirt wherever Babs tells him to and that he expects $200 right away. He plans to bring another truckload on Wednesday and the final one on Friday. Babs refuses to take the single truckload on Monday. At the most, she tells Sol, she would be willing to let Sam dump the dirt but will not pay him anything until the final load has been delivered on Friday. Is Babs within her rights to take this stand?

8. Bert contracts to buy a dinette set consisting of a table and four matching chairs from Selma's Table City, which is to make delivery the following week. When the truck from Selma's shows up at Bert's, the driver starts to unload the table but has only three chairs. He asks Bert to take and "sign for" these items, saying that he'll bring the last chair

the following day. Would Bert be within his rights to refuse the partial delivery?

9a. Over the telephone Sam and Dave enter into an agreement for the sale of Sam's used car to Dave for $450. They agree that Dave "can have the car next week" but say nothing more about delivery. When the following week comes around, Sam calls Dave and tells him to come and pick up the car. Dave insists that Sam should bring it over to his house. Who's got the better legal argument?

   b. Suppose instead that when Sam and Dave concluded their used car deal it was specifically agreed that Sam would deliver the car to Dave's house. There was no mention, however, of *when* he was to do so. A week passes and Sam has not shown up at Dave's. Is he in breach?

   c. Finally, assume that Sam does drive the car over to Dave's. He offers to hand over the registration certificate and the keys to the car in exchange for $450 cash from Dave. Dave tells him that he's waiting to get some money owed him in order to pay for the car, but that he will definitely mail Sam a check within a week. Does Sam have to accept this method of payment? What if Dave offers to give him a personal check for $450 then and there?

10. Ms. Blandings is in the process of organizing a new company which will manufacturer and sell widget holders. She realizes that she will need to have cardboard cartons to use in shipping the goods. She enters into an agreement with Shipshape's Cartons Unlimited for the purchase of 10,000 cartons to be delivered on or about April 1. Shipshape makes cartons in three standard sizes. The agreement states that Shipshape will deliver the cartons "in an assortment of sizes to be specified by Blandings no later than March 10." Under place of delivery the parties put in "Per Buyer's instructions." Is there a contract here? What result if Blandings contacts Shipshape on March 5 and asks for a shipment of all large boxes to be delivered to Mexico? See §2-311. What would be the consequences if Shipshape has not heard from Blandings by the end of the day on March 10?

EXPLANATIONS

1. The answer is clear from §2-304(1). This transaction is covered by Article 2. Hector is the seller of the exercise bicycle and the buyer of the hammock. Cleo sells the hammock and buys the bike. A typical situation where this result is relevant is the purchase by a consumer of a new car where he or she gives a trade-in as part of the deal. The buyer of the new car is a seller of the trade-in. As we'll discuss in Part II, as a seller he or she will almost certainly be giving some warranties about the trade-in along with turning over the used car itself.

   Note also the provision in §2-304(2) that makes clear that even if an interest in realty is part of the overall deal, Article 2 governs the transfer of the goods.

2.   There should be a contract here, and the price will be whatever was noted on Stella's list. We can harken back to §2-204(3) and the fundamental test of whether "the parties have intended to make a contract" as long as there is a "reasonably certain basis for giving a remedy." Perfectly in tune with this idea (and more directly to the point), §2-305(1) provides, "The parties if they so intend can conclude a contract for sale even though the price is not settled." You could argue here that although the price was never mentioned it was in fact "settled," at least if Arnold knew that galleries set prices in the way Stella does. Or you might conclude that the price hadn't been "settled" here, in which case the second sentence of this subsection holds that the price is to be "a reasonable price at the time of delivery." You could then maintain that this would be the price Stella listed it for, at least if that's the way sales of such artworks usually operate.

Suppose Arnold could show that buyers from such galleries or from Stella's in particular customarily paid some lower price (say, ten percent less) than what was actually listed in the seller's catalogue. First of all, would this defeat the existence of a contract? I think not. The question is still whether the parties intended to be bound, and there's no suggestion here that either had any reservations about that. Could Arnold argue that if he is so bound he should only have to pay 90 percent of the listed price? That's trickier. It would presumably depend on how the "customary ten percent discount" was arrived at. If it was because buyers typically do go into the gallery owner's office and haggle, even if only in a perfunctory way, then it seems Arnold by not even making this gesture can't argue for anything off in this instance. If Arnold were to show that the discount had in the past automatically been given, then it could be a usage of trade or a course of dealing between him and Stella and presumably would be part of this deal.

3.   Benny should not have to worry about being bound to a contract with Stella. Again, what is crucial is a question of fact. Do you find here that Benny and Stella both intended to be so bound? Section 2-305(4) just states the obvious. If "the parties intend not to be bound unless the price be fixed or agreed and it is not fixed or agreed there is no contract."

Notice also in §2-305 its treatment of the so-called "agreement to agree." There is a lot of question under the common law whether such an agreement can ever be enforceable, and if so, when. This section makes clear that the central issue is whether the parties themselves intend to be bound in such a situation. There is no rule of law barring them from being held to a contract if that is in fact what they wanted. What is the price? If the parties do later agree on a price, that is presumably that. If they fail to agree then §2-305(1) sets the price at a "reasonable price at the time [and, one would assume, the place] for delivery."

4a.   There is a contract for sale since the parties clearly so intend. The price will be whatever Ken fixes it at.

4b.   Under §2-305(1)(c) there would still be a contract and the price would be "a reasonable price at the time for delivery." If the parties cannot now agree on a price perhaps they can agree on a substitute appraiser. If not, then somewhere down the road a court would have to determine the statue's "reasonable price" taking into account whatever evidence the parties want to muster. An important point here is that under this section neither party could simply call the deal off because of Ken's unavailability.

4c. Look at §2-305(3). Constance now has an option. She can treat the contract as canceled or herself fix "a reasonable price." Of course this doesn't mean she can just pick a number out of the air. But look at Comment 5 and its reference to a "reasonable leeway."

5.   There is a contract and under §2-305(2) the price will be as set by the Seller, as long as he acts in good faith. Remember that good faith in the case of a merchant (which Seller clearly is) is defined in §2-103(1)(b) to require not merely honesty in fact but "the observance of reasonable commercial standards of fair dealing in the trade." Seller should be able to get the $125 if this is the kind of price he would have placed on the book had he simply put it out on his shelves in the hope of attracting a buyer. Look at Comment 3. Notice that while we normally think of used goods as being cheaper than new, this would not necessarily be true when it comes to a copy of an out-of-print book. So the original list price is only part of the story.

6a. Even though the quantity of nuts to be sold under this agreement has been left indefinite, there is a binding contract. This is a *requirements contract* and it is dealt with in §2-306(1). What is important here is that Candy's situation is such that it makes sense to talk of a "stated estimate" or a "normal or otherwise comparable prior . . . requirement." The parties can each have in contemplation at least some idea of roughly how many nuts they are talking about over the next three years. What if Candy were not a manufacturer with some kind of "pecan requirement" and could make no estimate of how many she might want over time. For instance, she could herself be a speculator and a dealer in nuts. She waits until the price is right and then buys as many as she can. If the price is not right she simply leaves them be. She never really *needs* any kind of nut at any time, although she may really *want* them. Comment 1 seems to say that there would still be a contract to bind Shelly for three years, but is that correct? How can you speak of a nut speculator's "requirements" for pecans? How can you measure what she needs in "good faith"?

In this Example you were also asked about how your answer might change if Candy had not agreed to buy her pecans exclusively from Shelly over the three years. It would at first appear that exclusivity is necessary to the very idea of a requirements contract. How can you say I will buy my "requirements" from you but also be free to buy the same stuff from others? At least one court confronted with a contract that did not have any language of exclusivity salvaged the agreement by concluding that exclusivity could be implied from the circumstances. *Cyril Bath Co. v. Winters Industries,* 892 F.2d 465, 10 U.C.C.2d 725 (6th Cir. 1989).

A second case went further. *Hoover's Hatchery, Inc. v. Utgaard,* 447 N.W.2d 684, 11 U.C.C.2d 477 (Iowa App. 1989), involved baby chicks—hundreds of thousands of them. Hoover alleged a contract under which his hatchery, which took such chicks and raised them, would supply substantially all of Utgaard's chick requirements for 1985. An initial estimate was that 400,000 chicks would be required. Utgaard took far fewer. Hoover ended up with hundreds of thousands of chicks on his hands which he could not easily resell. He sued for his damages. Utgaard argued that no contract for any number of chicks had ever arisen. Specifically he claimed that there could not be a requirements contract under §2-306(1) since he had nowhere agreed to use chicks only from Hoover. He pointed to the fact that Hoover would have been aware that he, Utgaard, would be raising some chicks that had been hatched in his own hatchery.

The Iowa Court of Appeals concluded that exclusivity was not an absolute prerequisite to the establishment of a requirements contract. How then could it ever be determined whether the buyer had kept to its end of the §2-306(1) bargain? The court concluded that "the inclusion of [the buyer's] expected requirements set forth in the correspondence which constitutes the agreement, is a sufficient standard by which the good faith of the parties may be measured." Under this type of analysis, if Candy did not promise to buy *all* of the pecans she required from Shelly, perhaps we could conclude that she did commit herself to buy something like 1,000 to 1,200 pounds a month from him, at least if she used that many in her ongoing business. Once she started needing many more, she would presumably be free to go to someone else and ask for a lower price on the rest of the nuts. Is that fair to Shelly? If he has committed himself to her, shouldn't she at least give him first crack at any larger orders? Cases like *Hoover's Hatchery* make for interesting discussion, but in practice the parties almost invariably will carefully express the exclusivity of a requirements deal and the issue should never arise.

6b. Shelly will probably be bound to deliver this larger amount of nuts. Section 2-306, having established that agreements with vague "requirements" quantity terms are enforceable, then sets forth two separate criteria as to how much can be or must be taken by the buyer. The first test is that of "good faith." Once again we recall that in Article 2 good faith requires not only honesty in fact but, in the case of a merchant, commercially reasonable behavior. Certainly Candy has not been dishonest here. She's telling no lies or anything like that. Is her behavior reasonable in light of her situation and commercial practices? It would help if we knew more about the commercial setting and what type of elasticity could have been anticipated here. I'd think it hard to find Candy guilty of bad faith just because her business was booming.

A second criterion enunciated in §2-306(1) is that "no quantity unreasonably disproportionate" to the stated estimates (if there were such estimates) may be demanded by the buyer. Here Candy is asking for something like twice as much as was estimated. Is that disproportionate? If so, is it *unreasonably disproportionate?* Look at Comment 2.

> [A] sudden expansion of the plant by which requirements are to be measured would not be included within the scope of the contract as made but normal expansion undertaken in good faith would be within the scope of this section.

Candy's recent success with the Pecan Supreme seems to me more a normal expansion than a sudden one, but you have to admit the difference is not all that obvious.

The courts have not come up with any single test to determine whether a request is unreasonably disproportionate so as to fail under §2-306(1). Indeed it would be unreasonable of us to expect that they could. One court enumerated the factors to be considered thusly:

> A number of factors should be taken into account in the event that a buyer's requirements greatly exceed the contract estimate. These include the following: (1) the amount by which the requirements exceed the contract estimate; (2) whether the seller had any reasonable basis on which to forecast or anticipate the requested increase . . . ; (3) the amount, if any, by which the market price of the goods in question exceeded the contract price; (4) whether such an increase in market price was itself fortuitous; and (5) the reason for the increase in requirements.

Orange & Rockland Utilities, Inc. v. Amerada Hess Corp., 59 App. Div. 2d 110, 397 N.Y.S.2d 814, 22 U.C.C. 310 (1977). In Candy's case the reason for the increase seems perfectly benign. And as far as we know Shelly is not claiming that his financial distress is the result of any increase in market value of the nuts, fortuitous or otherwise. It seems Candy is within her rights here to insist on the 2,000 pounds.

6c. Under this set of facts, Shelly probably would not be obligated to deliver the larger amount of nuts. Look again at the factors given by the court in the *Amerada Hess* case. Elsewhere in its opinion that court noted:

> It is well settled that a buyer in a rising market cannot use a fixed price in a requirements contract for speculation. . . . Nor can a buyer arbitrarily and unilaterally change certain conditions prevailing at the time of the contract so as to take advantage of market conditions at the seller's expense.

Note also the concern about the fact of a rising market price in Comment 2.

You might have a question about whether Candy's request, if it is found to be out-of-bounds here, fails because it is made in bad faith or because of its being "unreasonably disproportionate" to the estimate. In truth, while the subsection lays these out as two distinct concepts they quickly blend one into each other—at least when the buyer is a merchant and his or her good faith is subject to a test of commercial reasonableness. You can see that the two are not easily kept distinct in Comment 2. This is presumably nothing to worry about. The two concepts certainly don't conflict.

6d. The problem here is whether the buyer can in effect scale its requirements back to zero without being liable to its supplier under a requirements contract. There is no easy answer to this. Scaling back to zero is certainly possible. Comment 2 says, "A shut-down by a requirements buyer for lack of orders might be permissible when a shut-down merely to curtail losses would not." One court, dealing with the analogous situation of whether an outputs seller could stop making the single product involved even as it continued in business generally, set the test as whether "its losses from continuance would be more than trivial." *Feld v. Henry S. Levy & Sons,* 37 N.Y.2d 466, 335 N.E.2d 320, 17 U.C.C. 365 (1975). The court contrasted such a "trivial" loss or the "yield of less profit" with something like "a bankruptcy or genuine imperiling of the very existence of [the output producer's] entire business," which would presumably allow cessation of production without liability. If *Feld* is to be believed, it would be very hard for Candy to avoid liability should she stop making the pecan candies for any of the reasons given.

There are situations, of course, where the requirements buyer may actually end up buying nothing and still not be in breach of the contract. In *R. A. Weaver and Assocs., Inc. v. Asphalt Construction, Inc.,* 587 F.2d 1315, 25 U.C.C. 388 (D.C. Cir. 1978), the court determined that the parties had entered into a requirements contract under which the buyer, a construction company, had agreed to buy from the seller all of the limestone it would need on a particular project. When it later turned out that no limestone whatsoever was called for in the revised construction specifications, buyer notified seller that it would not need any of the stone. The buyer was held not to be in breach. It had acted in good faith. Furthermore, the Circuit Court held, while zero would seem to be "the quintessentially" disproportionate amount, §2-306(1) does not preclude reductions all the way to nothing if they are made in good faith.

A more recent case, *Empire Gas Corp. v. American Bakeries Co.,* 840 F.2d 1333, 5 U.C.C.2d 545 (7th Cir. 1988), went somewhat further. Judge Posner, writing for the majority, declared that the concluding language in §2-306(1) about disproportionality had been intended by the drafters to apply only where the requirements buyer was demanding *more than* had been estimated or anticipated. In the case of a *lowering* of the demand, even to the point of demanding nothing, the only test is that of good faith. This does not mean that the subsection has no bite when the buyer makes drastically reduced demands. In *Empire Gas* itself the buyer was found to be in bad faith for taking nothing under the contract, where throughout the lengthy litigation it offered no reason for its actions that would justify a conclusion other than that it had simply had "second thoughts" about the terms of the agreement. For a buyer's request for less than was anticipated to be in good faith "requires at a minimum that the reduction of requirements not have been motivated solely by a reassessment of the balance of advantages and disadvantages under the contract to the buyer."

In deciding the *Empire Gas* case, Judge Posner commented, as others have before and since, on how relatively few reported cases there are on the problem of scaled-back requirements. His observation is worth quoting.

> This is a good sign; it suggests that, while we might think it unsatisfactory for the law to be unclear on so fundamental a question, the people affected by the law are able to live with the lack of certainty. The reason may be that parties linked in an ongoing relationship—the usual situation under a requirements contract—have a strong incentive to work out their disagreements amicably rather than see the relationship destroyed by litigation.

As a student of Article 2, are you as sanguine about the lack of certainty here? But then if the parties involved can learn to live with it, shouldn't we?

6e. The problem now is not lack of certainty over quantity but the lack of a definite term. Under §2-309(2) the agreement is valid "for a reasonable time but unless otherwise agreed may be terminated at any time by either party." On the need for "reasonable notification" on the part of either Candy or Shelly to terminate, see subsection (3). So either could call an end to the agreement at any time but would have to give the other some reasonable warning. After several years of operation Candy could not, presumably, call Shelly on the 15th of a month and announce she wasn't taking any pecans the following month. Nor could Shelly take Candy's order in the regular manner and then on the 16th simply write her that he wasn't filling that order.

7.   Under §2-307 it is a question of fact whether "the circumstances give [Sol] the right to make . . . delivery in lots" apportioning the price among the lots. A *lot* is defined in §2-105(5). As you might remember from your Contracts course, under the common law it was regularly held that all of the goods had to be delivered or tendered before any money was due on any of them. This was the result, for example, in *Kelly Brick,* 91 N.J.L. 585, 103 A. 417 (1918), a case you may have studied. As you can see from Comment 3, the drafters' intention was to reject this result and to substitute a rule based on the facts of the particular situation. From the earlier part of that Comment it appears that Sol has a good argument here that Babs should take the single load and pay for it. Dirt is, after all, dirt.

8.   Bert shouldn't have to take the partial shipment. A dinette set is not the kind of thing which can be delivered in lots. The value of sets like this is that they match, and the buyer shouldn't have to accept any part until he or she can look at all of the pieces together to be sure they do in fact make up a good set. Nothing in §2-307 is to the contrary; the

general rule is still tender of a single delivery and there is nothing in "the circumstances" here which would change that result.

9a. Under §2-308(a), the place of delivery is Sam's place of business, or if he has none, his residence. Dave will have to come over and pick up the car. In reality it is probably the very rare situation where this tie-breaking provision comes into play. Note that §2-308 sets forth the place of delivery only where the parties have not "otherwise agreed." Remember that agreement on this point could be found in a trade usage, a course of dealing or a course of performance. The responsibility for delivery may also arise from reference to one of the so-called delivery terms, such as F.O.B. or F.A.S., which will be discussed in Chapter 26.

9b. Under §2-309(1) Sam must deliver within "a reasonable time." Is a week too late? You can make the call. If Dave plans to rely later on Sam's failure to deliver on time, wouldn't it be prudent for him to make some kind of demand for action before he uses Sam's lateness as an excuse to call the whole deal off? In *Lundy v. Low*, 200 Ga. App. 332, 408 S.E.2d 144, 16 U.C.C.2d 292 (1991), no time for delivery had been set and the buyer of some Christmas trees argued that those delivered on December 5 had come too late. The court had little patience with this argument, especially in light of the fact that the buyers had "expressed their gratitude for the trees on December 27" and had told the seller that they planned to purchase trees again from him in the following year. If timing is that important to the buyer, of course, he or she is best off setting a particular date for delivery in the agreement and insisting upon delivery by that date.

9c. Under §2-310(a) the assumption is that payment is due on delivery. Credit in favor of either the seller or the buyer must be mutually agreed upon. Of course in many situations such agreement can be found in trade terms, but that wouldn't seem to be the case here. The sale is for cash. Dave must pay cash to get the car. This is also found in §§2-507 and 2-511. Will giving a personal check be enough? See §2-511(2) and (3) and Comment 4 to that section. We are told payment by check is "commercially normal and proper" at least where the party giving the check is "seemingly solvent." It would have made sense for Sam to get Dave's express agreement that payment was to be made in cash or by an equivalent, say a certified check. If he did not, §2-511(2) gives him the right to demand payment in legal tender, but he's going to have to allow Dave a reasonable extension of time to produce the cash.

10. Under §2-311(1) there is a contract here even though the agreement leaves "particulars of performance" to be specified by Blandings. Here both the assortment and the place of delivery were left to her as buyer. She is then allowed to set the specifications "in good faith and within limits set by commercial reasonableness." It all depends on the facts. Is she being commercially reasonable in asking for shipment to Mexico? It isn't clear. If Shipshape is to pay for the shipping and if international shipment is much more expensive, maybe she is not within her rights. If

Shipshape is in Texas, of course, shipment to Mexico might be cheaper than to New England. Is it commercially reasonable to ask for all large boxes? Again, we'd have to know more about the situation.

If Blandings does not set the specifications in time, §2-311(3) gives Shipshape an excuse if his delivery is late because of this. In addition he may after a time be able to treat the failure on her part as a breach.

10

Modification and Waiver

Goodbye to Consideration

Once the parties have entered into a contract of sale, the terms of that contract are set. What each is supposed to do has been decided. In the words of §2-301, "The obligation of seller is to transfer and deliver and that of the buyer is to accept and pay in accordance with the contract." So that is that, and everything is set in stone. In the real world, however, changing circumstances are if not inevitable then at least fairly common, and either one or both of the parties may think it only right that the deal be revised in some way in light of later events. Section 2-209 is the part of Article 2 that deals directly with the possibility of a change in rights or responsibilities *agreed to by the parties* subsequent to their initial agreement to contract.*

As you will surely recall, the common law of contracts does not prohibit contracting parties from making a change in their respective obligations. There is, however, a significant qualification. The common law will not give effect to what we might call a "one-sided" modification, that is, a change in which only one of the two parties gets the advantage

---

*For the more limited possibility of a change in the contract claimed by one party in light of changing circumstances and arguably warranted by those changing circumstances alone, even if not agreed to by the other party, see §2-615. This is dealt with in Chapter 24.

As to leases, §2A-208 tracks the language of §2-209, with one notable exception: Subsection (3), dealing with the need to satisfy the Statute of Frauds in some situations, has been omitted. A comment to §2A-208 leaves the question up in the air when it comes to leases, concluding that "[r]esolution of the issue is left to the courts based on the facts of each case."

of a new term or terms. A modification must affect the rights and responsibilities of *both* parties to the contract if it is to be held binding. For the common law this result is all bound up with the fundamental (and fundamentally treacherous) need for *consideration* and with the *pre-existing duty rule* as a corollary to that principle. A promise made by one party to accept less or give more than originally called for under a binding agreement is itself binding only if given for consideration. Furthermore, the consideration given by the other party has to be more than simply promising to do (or even actually doing) that which he or she was already bound to do. The promise to do that which we are already legally obligated to do, we all know, cannot constitute consideration. In particular it cannot serve as consideration making enforceable another's promise to live with less out of an already binding agreement.

We need not deal here with the doctrine of consideration, the preexisting duty rule, or anything of the sort. In the context of modification, Article 2 (we can thank the drafters) has no use for the doctrine of consideration. Read and appreciate §2-209(1). Modification of any contract within the scope of Article 2 "needs no consideration to be binding."* It is true that §2-209(1) speaks only of "modifications," and not of the "rescission" and the "waiver" mentioned in the title of the section, but that is no real problem. The Code nowhere defines the word *rescission,* and it would be nice if it did. In this context, however, it would seem to mean a subsequent agreement by the buyer and seller to release each other totally and irretrievably from the whole deal. The buyer realizes he would rather not buy, the seller doesn't care to sell, and the two simply concur in undoing the pact they have made. If this is the meaning to be given *rescission,* we see why the drafters didn't bother dealing with it in §2-209(1). A rescission by its very nature would seem to have consideration on both sides: Each party gives up the ability to enforce the deal in return for freedom from his or her own end of the bargain.

Finally, what about *waiver?* The Code does not define this term either, and as we will soon discover the lack of a clear definition in some situations is more than a minor inconvenience. For present purposes, however, only the most fundamental understanding of waiver is necessary. Whatever a waiver is under the Code, it presumably doesn't need consideration to be binding. Why, even under the common law a right (at least if it were not a substantial one, which few would talk about "waiving" anyway) could be waived without any discussion of the hoary doctrine of consideration. So it is hard to see how consideration could be much of an issue

---

*Note parenthetically that Article 2 nowhere speaks of the need for consideration in order to make the original sales agreement binding. There is no need to. If, as we assume from the nature of a sale and as is set forth in §2-301, the agreement binds the seller to sell in exchange for the buyer's buying, there is necessarily the kind of bargained-for exchange with which the doctrine of consideration is so obsessed. This assumes, of course, that Article 2 deals only with sales of goods and perhaps to some degree with leases, but not with gifts. The assumption seems pretty good, even if §2-102 speaks in terms of "*transactions* in goods." See the discussion in Chapter 1.

when waiver is being discussed under Article 2. The notion of consideration, which took center stage through so much of your study of common law contracts has, in Article 2, been moved graciously out of the limelight.

The Modification Police

The common law's insistence on consideration to support modifications does, of course, have some method behind its madness. It serves as a means, albeit a very crude and imperfect one, of insuring that modifications are not obtained by one contracting party's improper coercion of the other. It is all too easy for the buyer, for example, to greet the cross-country delivery of a large shipment with a suggestion that the price be "made a bit more reasonable." The seller may very well accede to this "request" rather than face the prospect of having to trudge the long way home with all that stuff, even if he or she will also take home a nice neat contract action against the buyer. Legal actions are, after all, seldom nice and neat when it really comes time to bring them. In the best of circumstances it is costly, in time and money, to enforce your legal rights. A little pressure from the buyer can too easily get him or her a substantially better deal than that which was originally bargained.

Of course, buyers are not the only bad (or pushy) types around. Sellers, knowing how much their buyers are depending on a coming delivery, will understandably be tempted to ask for a bit more in the way of price, and buyers—faced not with a hypothetical in contract law but with a real world business crunch—may be understandably willing to let them have it.

The common law's pre-existing duty rule gives the party who does accede to this kind of coercive one-sided modification an argument against it when time comes to pay up. But, as you no doubt discussed in your study of the rule, it is a far from perfect tool for separating out this type of illegitimate pressure tactic from those other times when a modification (even a purely one-sided modification) is the result of a legitimate decision by both parties to change the shape of their original bargain in light of a new set of circumstances.

Article 2, as we have seen, does away with the need for consideration in modifications, but it was not the intention of the drafters that it simply wink at the possibility of illegitimately coerced one-sided modifications. Rather, the Code takes on the problem directly by insisting that any such behavior be judged by the standard of "good faith." Note the language in Comment 2 to §2-209:

> [M]odifications made [under subsection (1)] must meet the test of good faith imposed by this Act. The effective use of bad faith to escape performance on the original contract terms is barred, and the extortion of a "modification" without legitimate commercial reason is ineffective as a violation of the duty of good faith. Nor can a mere technical consideration support a modification made in bad faith.

The general obligation of good faith is found in §1-203, which reads in its entirety, "Every contract or duty within this Act imposes an obligation of good faith in its performance or enforcement." The term *good faith* is defined for all parts of the Code in §1-201(19) as "honesty in fact." Furthermore, there is found in §2-103(1)(b) a special Article 2 definition of good faith in the case of a merchant: An Article 2 merchant must meet the higher standard of not just honesty in fact but "the observance of reasonable commercial standards of fair dealing in the trade." Finally look to Comment 2 to §2-104. This special definition of good faith applies to the broadest range of people who could possibly be considered "merchants" under the Code's definition of that term.

There is, of course, no way to sum up neatly what will be required to show good faith in a modification or what conduct will be deemed a mark of bad faith. People, both the virtuous and the less than virtuous, work in an infinite variety of ways. One important criterion, however, is the rudimentary need for "honesty in fact." Getting the other party to agree to give a bit more or to accept a bit less on the basis of a lie clearly will not do. The seller who says that he must raise the price because of an unanticipated increase in the cost to him of parts or raw materials must be telling the truth if he is later going to assert that he acted in good faith. Similarly for the buyer who gets a break in price because of an asserted unanticipated increase in her distribution costs. Note that in either instance to be in good faith the party would have to be telling the truth about not only the rise in costs but that this increase was truly "unanticipated" when the original deal was struck.

Beyond the basic precept that lies make for bad faith, what more can be said, particularly when the standard is expanded to include "reasonable commercial standards of fair dealing" as it is for the wide range of parties who are merchants? The comment to §2-209 suggests that this standard

> may in some situations require an objectively demonstrable reason for seeking a modification. But such matters as a market shift which makes performance come to involve a loss may provide such a reason even though there is no such unforseen difficulty as would make out a legal excuse from performance [under the doctrine of impracticability].

Is it enough that one party tell the other—truthfully—that only now is it apparent that the deal as originally stuck would leave him or her with a loss instead of a profit? Remember, we are not asking whether this party has the *right* to a change in terms. There is no reason to think he or she would. But if the other party decides to give a little and agrees to a modification, is there any reason to upset the resulting modification on the grounds of bad faith?

One helpful analysis was offered by the Sixth Circuit in *Roth Steel Products v. Sharon Steel*, 705 F.2d 134, 35 U.C.C. 1435 (6th Cir. 1983):

> In determining whether a particular modification was obtained in good faith, a court must make two distinct inquiries: whether the party's conduct is consistent with "reasonable commercial standards of fair dealing in the trade" . . . , and whether the

parties were in fact motivated to seek modification by an honest desire to compensate for commercial exigencies. . . . The first inquiry is relatively straightforward; the party seeking the modification must demonstrate that this decision to seek modification was the result of a factor, such as an increased cost, which would cause an ordinary merchant to seek a modification of the contract. . . . The second inquiry, regarding the subjective honesty of the parties, is less clearly defined. Essentially, this inquiry requires the party asserting the modification to demonstrate that he was, in fact, motivated by a legitimate commercial reason and that such a reason is not offered as merely a pretext.

In *Roth Steel* the seller, asserting that it faced substantial losses under a long-term contract for the delivery of both cold- and hot-rolled steel, had obtained the buyer's concession that it would pay more than the initial contract price. While the modified price was in fact below the steadily advancing market price, the buyer refused to pay at this rate at the end of the term, claiming that it had acquiesced to the modification only because of its dire need for steel from the seller, its principal supplier. The district court held that the request for a modification had not been made in good faith. Central to its determination were three findings of fact: (1) that the seller had been partially insulated from raw material price increases, (2) that it had initially bargained for a contract with a slim profit margin and thus implicitly assumed the risk that performance might result in a loss, and (3) that its profits over the relevant period of time were inconsistent with its position that the modification was sought to avoid a loss.

The court of appeals held that these factors were in and of themselves not sufficient to support a finding that the seller had acted in bad faith by asking for a modification when an "ordinary merchant" would not. As the court noted, "[a] party who has not actually suffered a loss on the contract may still seek a modification if a future loss on the agreement was reasonably foreseeable." The appeals court, however, upheld the decision that the modification in the particular case had not been made in good faith, finding that the seller's actions did not meet the second prong of its test. In its view the justification given by the seller for its announcement of a price rise above what the contract called for had not been particularly strong and, more damaging, had not been advanced by the seller at the time but was (the court suggests) only thought up in time for the trial. The seller having failed to act "honestly in fact," the modification was not enforceable.

In a second case, *T & S Brass & Bronze Works, Inc. v. Pic-Air, Inc.,* 790 F.2d 1098, 1 U.C.C.2d 433 (4th Cir. 1986), the contract of sale had originally placed the burden of shipping charges and the risk of delay on the seller, by providing that shipping was to be "F.O.B. Destination" (see §2-319 or wait until Chapter 26) and that time was of the essence. Later at two separate times the buyer had agreed to pay air freight charges to get the goods on time. In holding the modification unenforceable, the Fourth Circuit noted that "[c]ourts have determined that a legitimate commercial reason is one outside the control of the party seeking the modification." Here the delays necessitating the extra air freight charges were the fault of the seller or its subcontractor. The seller had twice assured the buyer that the installments would be delivered on time, "only to retract these assurances and demand that [the buyer] pay air freight." Under these circumstances the delay was held not to be a legitimate commercial reason for the requested modification.

In what follows we will assume good faith all 'round. Unfortunately, this is not the end of the story.

Of Writings and Waivers

At least theoretically, the requirement that modifications be made in good faith deals with improper behavior at the time when a modification is asked for and arranged. A second kind of bad behavior with which §2-209 is meant to deal is the possibility that a party will after the fact assert that a modification took place when it never did. As Comment 3 suggests, it is all too easy for someone later to "conjure up" a modification, be willing to testify to it, and thereby hopefully rewrite his or her personal history. The section deals with this problem and allows the parties themselves to agree to avoid later arguments, as you might expect by the requirement of a writing in the more important situations. Section 2-209(3) invokes Article 2's own Statute of Frauds.* Section 2-209(2) gives effect to what is sometimes referred to as a "private" Statute of Frauds agreed to by the parties at the time of their initial contracting. The operation of these two subsections, intended as Comment 3 notes, "to protect against false allegations of oral modifications," is considered in the Examples that follow.

But that's not all. Read §2-209(4). Attempts at modification or rescission that somehow fail under either the public or private statutes may still have effect by operating as "waivers." The possibility of a party's arguing for a waiver when all else fails opens up a whole new can of worms, made all the more difficult because the Code nowhere defines and never exactly makes clear what a *waiver* is. We will have to deal with the modification and/or waiver puzzle, or at least puzzle through it, in the Example and their Explanations.

EXAMPLES

1.   In early December, lawyer Bill orders from Sally, a printer of business forms, a quantity of specially printed letterhead of the type he uses in his office. The order is made by the two signing one of Sally's Order Forms, which reflects the details of how the letterhead is to look, the paper on which it is to be printed, the quantity, and the price of the order. The form also contains the following clause:

---

*As to which see Chapter 6 if you have not already done so.

(15.1) No modification or change of the terms of this order shall
be valid except as such modification or change is set forth in a writing
signed by each of the parties hereto.

A week after this agreement is signed, Bill telephones Sally and asks her
if it is too late to make a change on the printing order. He wants to add
the name of a newly hired associate to the listing of lawyers. She responds,
"No problem. I'll make that change. Just give me the name." Bill carefully
spells the name for her over the phone. When the printing job arrives,
Bill finds that the letterhead is as he had originally specified; the new
associate's name does not appear. While Sally has to admit to the fact of
the telephone conversation, she points out that there was no writing
whatsoever setting forth the argued change.

    a. Is Sally in breach of their contract?

    b. Add the following facts: After Sally tells Bill she can and will
make the addition, he says to her, "I know we'll need this in writing,
so you should send me a new Order Form." Sally responds, "Oh,
there's no reason to bother with all that. I'll just make the change
right on the sample we laid out." No revised Order Form is ever
sent to Bill. Under these facts, can Bill successfully argue she was in
breach for failing to include the additional name?

    c. Suppose that no such conversation about the need for a writ-
ing ever took place. The situation is as it was initially given, but in
addition Bill will be able to show that on at least three prior occasions
when he had ordered from Sally he phoned in later changes and the
work delivered in each instance conformed to the changed order.
Based on these facts, can Bill show Sally was legally obligated to
include the new name on the letterhead? Would your answer be any
different if Bill and Sally had entered into a long-term installment
contract (which included Clause 15.1) and on at least two previous
occasions installments had been changed through an oral directive
with no new writing?

    d. Now go back and look at just the original facts. Does your
consideration of the previous two situations give you any new ideas
about how Bill, invoking the notion of a waiver, might argue against
Sally even with no additional facts? Would such an argument work?
Should it?

2a. Buyer and Seller enter into an oral contract for the sale of a used
motorcycle, the agreed purchase price being $495. Prior to delivery Seller
starts grumbling to Buyer that he'd "practically given the hog away,"
especially since he had just put a brand new seat on it "which by itself
cost me $50 bucks." Buyer had himself thought that the price of $495
was very low, and says, "Tell you what. I'll give you $520 for it. That's
certainly fair." Seller orally agrees to the sale at that price. No writing
evidencing the sale is ever signed by either party. Is there an enforceable
contract for sale, and if so at what price?

    b. Imagine that the original price had been $520 and the parties
had signed a written agreement to this effect. Now it's Buyer who's

grousing, and Seller orally agrees to reduce the price to $480. No new writing is ever signed by the parties. Under these circumstances, what is the binding contract price for the motorcycle?

3.   On December 1, Belle and Serge enter into a written contract for the purchase by Belle of a large quantity of fabric from Serge for a price of $2,300. As set forth in the Bill of Sale, delivery of the entire lot is due "on or before January 31." In the middle of December Belle calls Serge and tells him she would really like to have the fabric as early as possible. He says, "I can assure you that it will be delivered by January 15 at the latest." On January 16 the fabric still has not been delivered.

   a. Is Serge in breach of their agreement? Would it make any difference if Belle could show that she offered to come in to his office and sign a revised version of the Bill of Sale, and that Serge has told her not to bother? Is there any other waiver argument possible for Belle?

   b. Assume that the fabric is finally delivered to Belle on January 24, and she decides not to make a stink about the date of delivery. She gets an order for some work for which she would like to use the fabric she bought from Serge. Unfortunately, it is the wrong color. Some fabric takes well to dying and some does not. She and Serge have never had any discussion, nor is there any language in the Bill of Sale, about whether this particular fabric could be dyed. She calls up Serge and asks him. He says, "Yes, you can dye it without any problems." She does so, only to find that the fabric was warped and shrunk. It is unusable. Can she successfully argue that Serge had warranted that the fabric could be dyed without harm to it?

4.   Buyer and Seller enter into an installment contract covering one full year starting in January. According to the terms of the written agreement Seller is to make deliveries by the first of each month. He delivers on time in January, but each of his next six deliveries arrives around the tenth of the month. Buyer never objects and sends in her payments regularly. The August delivery arrives on August 8. Does Buyer have the right immediately to declare Seller in breach because of the late August delivery? Is Buyer within her rights if she informs Seller that the remaining deliveries starting with September's must come by the first of the month? Would it make any difference if Seller had contacted Buyer in January asking for some leeway in delivery dates and Buyer had written Seller back saying, "I will accept deliveries as long as they are not over twelve days late"?

EXPLANATIONS

1a.   Our first stop in analyzing this situation is §2-209(2), which states as clearly as possible that provisions such as Clause 15.1 are enforceable. (By the time we get to Example 1d we'll have reason to wonder whether this first stop can be the last stop, but for the moment let's assume that it is and concentrate on this subsection.) Note that under the second sentence of this subsection the clause would have to be separately signed by Bill except for the fact that this is a contract entered into "between merchants." For the purposes of this provision of Article 2, someone who should be familiar with "normal business practices" would be considered a merchant. See Comment 2 to §2-104. Bill is after all a lawyer, and would I assume be covered. Even if his practice weren't in any business or commercial field, a lawyer should know how to run his office, order supplies, and so forth.

As Comment 3 to §2-209 notes, subsection (2) "permits the parties in effect to make their own Statute of Frauds as regard any future modifications of the contract. . . ." An explanation of this section's background, given by Judge Posner in the well-known case of *Wisconsin Knife Works v. National Metal Crafters,* 781 F.2d 1280, 42 U.C.C. 830 (7th Cir. 1986), is worth quoting at length:

> The common law did not enforce agreements such as section 2-209(2) authorizes. The "reasoning" was that the parties were always free to agree orally to cancel their contract and the clause forbidding modifications not in writing would disappear with the rest of the contract when it was canceled. "The most ironclad written contract can always be cut by the acetylene torch of parol modification supported by adequate proof." [citation omitted] This is not reasoning; it is a conclusion disguised as a metaphor. It may have reflected a fear that such clauses, buried in the fine print of form contracts, were traps for the unwary; a sense that they were unnecessary because only modifications supported by consideration were enforceable; and a disinclination to allow parties in effect to extend the reach of the Statute of Frauds, which requires only some kinds of contracts to be in writing. But the framers of the Uniform Commercial Code, as part and parcel of rejecting the requirement of consideration for modifications, must have rejected the traditional view; must have believed that the protection which the doctrines of duress and bad faith give against extortionate modifications might need reinforcement—if not from a requirement of consideration, which had proved ineffective, then from a grant of power to include a clause requiring modifications to be in writing and signed.

More about the *Wisconsin Knife* case later on. For the moment it is enough to note that Bill signed the contract which included Clause 15.1 and such a clause would seem to be undeniably enforceable. Even though Bill may have done nothing improper in asking for the change, and Sally did say she would make it, he is seemingly out of luck. Sally was never legally bound to make the change. Sally may never get Bill's business ever again, but he's not going to be able to hold her liable for a breach on this printing job.

In one of the first cases to deal with this subsection, *C.I.T. Corp. v. Jonnet,* 419 Pa. 435, 214 A.2d 620, 3 U.C.C. 968 (1965), the Supreme Court of Pennsylvania found that a term such as we have in our Clause 15.1 "stands as a stone wall in the path of" any contention that a modification had been orally agreed to. Exactly how sturdy a stone wall this actually will be is the fundamental issue posed by the following questions.

1b. I think that Bill would and should have much more success in this situation, even though I know of no case where the facts are this clearcut. His argument would be that Sally's part of the phone conversation constituted a *waiver* on her part—a waiver of her rights to insist on a writing under Clause 15.1 itself, and so the change was effective in spite of the fact that there was no writing. He would point to §2-209(4) which states: "Although an attempt at modification or rescission does not satisfy the requirements of subsection (2) or (3) it can operate as a waiver." The Code does not define the word waiver, and this will cause us plenty of trouble later on, but if ever there was a waiver of a right to insist on a writing, this seems to be the situation. Even the court in the *C.I.T. Corp.* case previously quoted allowed that in the face of such a stonewall clause there can be a modification provided there is first a waiver of the no-oral-modification clause itself.

Would it make any difference if Clause 15.1 had specified that "no modifications or changes *or waivers*" would be effective unless in writing? Arguably not. Bill could argue that Sally expressly and knowingly waived her rights under 15.1 altogether, including her right to insist on only written waivers, so the whole clause is now simply irrelevant. And here we begin to glimpse the power—and the problem—of arguments based on the waiver idea. Taken to the extreme (something we haven't done yet, but soon will), they tend to swallow up everything in their path, no matter how specifically worded or carefully negotiated.

Before we move on, we might as well acknowledge one other vexing problem that haunts this whole field. It may be only a bit of wordplay or it may be something of importance (and even if it is important, it is not immediately apparent *what* its importance is). Assume that as the facts are given in this second question Bill wins, as it seems he should, and he has established his right to get the printing done with the amended listing. How do we characterize his victory? As I've analyzed it so far, we would presumably say that Sally by her actions waived her rights under Clause 15.1. A modification agreed to by both parties on the substance of the contract was therefore enforceable in spite of the inclusion of 15.1 So Bill wins because he is able to establish an enforceable oral modification.

The way some courts express their results, however, puts a different spin on it. They would say that Bill and Sally could not, and did not, modify their agreement without a writing. Clause 15.1 barred oral modifications in every case and it has done so here. The result in favor of Bill, however, is authorized because §2-209(4) permits waivers where modifications aren't allowed, and that is what happened here. Bill was able to establish a successful waiver by Sally of her substantive right to insist that he accept the letterhead with the new name missing. Bill wins by establishing a waiver, no modification ever having been made.

Is there a difference in the two ways of looking at it? That may depend on exactly what we see as the difference between a modification and a waiver in general. And there's the rub. The language of §2-209 taken as a whole suggests they are different things. Traditionally the words were not used as exact equivalents, but no one quite can spell out what the difference was and/or still is. Classically a *waiver* was said to be something like "the voluntary and intentional relinquishment of a known right, claim or privilege." If there was any true difference between a waiver and a *modification* it was that a waiver was usually considered only when there had been an argued sacrifice by one party of what we might think of as an incidental, insubstantial, or "technical" term or condition. (The Second Restatement of Contracts speaks of being able to relinquish only those conditions not "material to the agreed exchange.") Beyond that, the main difference historically between a waiver and a modification was that the issue of consideration did not come up when waiver was invoked, at least as to such an incidental term, and new consideration was crucial for a modification to be effective.

As we have seen, however, Article 2 cuts us loose from the anchor of the consideration doctrine. At the same time, some courts seem willing to think of a waiver of even the most basic and fundamental terms of a sales contract. Taken together, it is harder than ever to make any cogent statement about the difference between modification and waiver, except that they are spelled differently and §2-209 proceeds on the assumption we can tell them apart. But if we can't tell them apart, then there is at least an argument that anything that fails under subsection (2) or (3) to be an effective modification can simply be reclassified as a waiver and waltz right through the gates via §2-209(4). This reading of the term "waiver" and of that subsection can't be right, however, or the whole framework of the section collapses. The result is hardly satisfactory. But is there a principled way of distinguishing the two terms? We have come then to what some commentators have variously referred to as the modification/waiver maze or mystery—which I think qualifies as a muddle—with which we must deal. More on it as we proceed.

1c. Here Bill will be arguing that a waiver can be found in a course of dealing between the parties. The facts seem good for him, and he might well win. There is, however, no clear authority in Article 2 for that result. Compare this to the situation when the parties had entered into an installment contract and Bill's argument is based on a course of performance. (As to course of dealing and course of performance generally, you may want to review Chapter 7.) Section 2-208(3) specifically provides that

> Subject to the provisions of the next section on modification and waiver, such course of performance shall be relevant to show a waiver or modification of any term inconsistent with such course of performance.

That's not very clear, is it? It just throws us back into §2-209 and the middle of the muddle. Reading between the lines and the sections, however, there is a forceful argument that the drafters expected to see and would look favorably on waivers made by course of performance. But then does this mean that a course of dealing could never act to create or, as they say in §2-208, "be relevant to show" a waiver or a modification of an inconsistent express term? If the facts of a course of dealing are as strong for Bill as I first posited, it's hard to argue that the course of dealing—a course of conduct between Bill and Sally under which she repeatedly failed to insist on the niceties of Clause 15.1—can be ignored this time out.

1d. With the experience of the last couple of questions behind us, we now have an idea about how to argue for Bill even in the original barebones hypothetical. He can claim that Sally, knowing that she had a contractual right to have any change evidenced by a writing signed by both of them, must have knowingly and willingly "waived" her right to such a writing. She could have insisted on a writing, but she did not. That being so, Bill will argue, by the end of the phone call she had waived her right to later rely on Clause 15.1 to her benefit. And since it is only this private Statute of Frauds provision on which her defense relies—she acknowledges the fact of the phone agreement, and she can't make any stand under the doctrine of lack of consideration—she must lose. It's a nice and neat argument, but it may go too far. It virtually eliminates Clause 15.1 from the contract for all practical purposes, since any oral agreement to modify the contract would seem to be enforceable by like argument. And the parties did presumably write that clause into the document meaning it to have *some* effect. Beyond this, it would construe §2-209(4) in such a way as to do away with §2-209(2) for all practical purposes, except to say that when a party is having trouble proving a "modification" he or she should characterize it as a "waiver" in order to win. That hardly does justice to the drafters nor does it comport with common sense. Are all failed modifications just potential waivers waiting to be appreciated?

It was this conundrum that was directly addressed by Judge Posner in the *Wisconsin Knife Works* case cited above. The Knife Works as buyer claimed to have rightfully terminated a sales contract when the seller, National Metal Crafters, was late in its delivery of the specified goods. National's response was that the delivery dates initially specified in the contract had been extended by agreement. The written contract first entered into contained a clause reading "No modification of this contract, shall be binding upon the Buyer [Wisconsin Knife Works] unless made in writing and signed by Buyer's authorized representative." In spite of this clause, the trial jury had been allowed to find a modification and judgment had been for the seller. Judge Posner, writing for the Seventh Circuit, first held that the clause itself was valid and applicable under §2-209(2). Further it was found that there had been no written modification of the delivery dates. This, however, was not the end of the matter, for as the Judge Posner noted the jury may have "found waiver but called it modification." And so he headed straight into the maze.

> If section 2-209(4) . . . is interpreted so broadly that *any* oral modification is effective as a waiver notwithstanding section 2-209(2), both provisions become superfluous and we are back in the common law—only with not even a requirement of consideration to reduce the likelihood of fabricated or unintended oral modifications.

As the judge noted, one conceivable way out of this dilemma (which does in fact have some backing in the cases, which he failed to note) is to distinguish between

> a modification that substitutes a new term for an old, and a waiver, which merely removes an old term. On this interpretation National

Metal Crafters could not enforce an oral term of the allegedly modified contract but could be excused from one of the written terms.

Judge Posner was not convinced. "Whether the party claiming modification is seeking to impose an onerous term on the other party or to wriggle out of an onerous term that the original contract imposed on it is a distinction without a difference." His dismissal of this idea may have been a little too quick. After all, the traditional use of the term waiver has been in the context of one party's giving up or *losing* an existing right or claim, not a change in the status quo which *adds* to the terms or conditions. This might indeed be mere pettifogging and only an imagined difference, but how much of the common law (and maybe even some of Article 2) is based on just such imagined differences?

In any event, Judge Posner was not at a loss as to how to work through the maze.

> The path of reconciliation with subsection (4) is found by attending to the precise wording of (4). It does not say that an attempted modification "is" a waiver; it says that "it can operate as a waiver." It does not say in what circumstances it can operate as a waiver; but if an attempted modification is effective as a waiver only if there is reliance, then both 2-209(2) and 2-209(4) can be given effect. Reliance, if reasonably induced and reasonable in extent, is a common substitute for consideration in making a promise legally enforceable, in part because it adds something in the way of credibility to the mere say-so of one party.

In Posner's view *reliance* is the key. Since in the instance at hand it was impossible to tell whether the jury had found a true waiver (even if calling it modification) or something that fell short, the case was remanded for a new trial at which the question of whether the seller had actually relied to its detriment on the buyer's agreement to extend the delivery dates could be determined.

If a finding of reliance is what makes for a valid waiver, is the answer to our question (remember Bill and Sally?) so obvious? The concept of *detrimental reliance,* as it has developed in the common law, is not without its own difficulties. Indeed, it may be as elusive as *consideration* when you get right down to it. When exactly has a party relied on the other to his or her detriment? To bring it closer to home, did Bill rely on Sally's oral agreement to add the one name to the printed letterhead? Well, it's true he did not go out and enter into some other arrangement the success of which would be crucially dependent on his soon receiving some letterhead complete to each and every associate's name. But then again he apparently refrained from rushing down to her shop to give a written change order which would have avoided any potential problem in the most direct way, nor did he order new, updated letterhead from anyone else. Would this be sufficient reliance to meet Judge Posner's requirement? And if so, are we once again led down the road of finding every imperfect modification transmuted into a waiver? Presumably not, but only if the requirement of reliance is given some real heft by a fuller elaboration. To be fair to the judge, he does refer in making the remand to the need to show "*reliance* expenses." The emphasis on the first word is his. I might switch the emphasis to the second word, or at least give it equal emphasis. It would be hard to say that Bill had incurred "reliance *expenses*" because of Sally's oral agreement.

We'll return to the *Wisconsin Knife Works* case and Judge Posner's reliance analysis in our discussion of later questions. Feel free to withhold final judgment for a while.

2a. There is a contract for sale at $495. While there was no writing evidencing the original agreement, that would not defeat the contract since the Code's Statute of Frauds comes into play only when the goods are "for the price of $500 or more" (§2-201(1)). The parties agreed to a modification, but under §2-209(3) the requirements of §2-201 "must be satisfied if the contract as modified is within [that section's] provisions." The contract as modified is for a price more than $500, and so the Statute of Frauds would have to be satisfied. As to what satisfies that section, see Chapter 6. Basically some writing would be needed, signed by the party against whom enforcement is sought. Since neither signed any writing whatsoever, neither could enforce the contract at the higher price. Recall from your study of that earlier chapter that there are a number of exceptions to the writing requirement, situations where the Statute of Frauds is "satisfied" in some other way. These are available to make a modification enforceable just as they were to make an initial agreement binding. Unfortunately for Seller here, none seem applicable in this situation.

2b. There would be a binding agreement for $480. The original agreement was enforceable as the Statute was satisfied by the writing. There is no writing evidencing the modification, but §2-209(3) says that the Statute comes into play only "if the contract as modified comes within its provisions." The contract as modified is for a price of less than $500, and so it does not come within the Article 2 Statute of Frauds. Note that if the parties had agreed to a lower price of, say, $505 the modification would not be binding absent some writing which would satisfy the Statute or some exception from §2-201 coming into play.

There is some minor controversy about the correct reading of §2-209(3), but really it's more a controversy about how that subsection should have been written, since the language as it stands is pretty clear. You look at the contract as it has allegedly been modified. That new agreement needs to meet the Statute, by a writing or by falling within one of the exceptions to the writing requirement, if it is a contact for sale at a price of $500 or more. Perhaps the rule should have been that any agreement that originally had to be and was in writing could be modified only by a writing. Or you can make an argument that, since the quantity term is the only one the Statute of Frauds makes mandatory, only changes in quantity need to be in writing. But that isn't how the drafters framed §2-209(3), and most courts read and apply it literally.

3a. Belle would have a hard time arguing that the contract had been effectively modified to include an earlier delivery date. The contract she would be asserting (the contract as modified) would itself come within the Statute of Frauds, and under the literal reading of §2-209(3) it would have to satisfy that section. Here there is no writing and no obvious exception to the writing requirement, so presumably the oral modification has no binding effect.

But can Belle argue waiver? Section 2-209(4), which we've seen before in its application to attempted modifications which run afoul of a so-called "private" Statute of Frauds provision, states in addition that an attempt at modification that does not satisfy the requirements of subsection (3) "can operate as a waiver." We are back in the same muddle that we dealt with in the earlier questions: What exactly makes for a waiver? Is it possible that any attempted modification which fails, now because of subsection (3), can be recharacterized as a waiver and find enforcement heaven that way?

If Serge did explicitly tell her not to come in to produce a new writing, it would seem to be a good case for a waiver. Again, I know of no case where the facts are this clear. Here, I guess, you would say that Serge waived his rights to insist on a writing under the provisions of the Code. That being so, the oral modification cannot be barred by the Statute of Frauds requirement and so it comes into the contract if well proven.

Some courts have found waiver under §2-209(4) in the face of §2-209(3), even where there has been no specific reference to and dismissal of the need for a writing. In *Double-E Sportswear Corp. v. Girard Trust Bank*, 488 F.2d 292, 13 U.C.C. 577 (3d Cir. 1973), the court held that the parties had orally agreed to "waive the Statute of Frauds"; having done so, "there is no barrier to an oral modification of the terms of the contract under §2-209(1)." Under this analysis, of course, once a waiver is found there is no limitation on what changes could be made or what totally new terms could be added via this route. If there is no Statute of Frauds minding the gates, and no need for consideration either, then anything goes (as long as it's in good faith). Most troubling perhaps is that the court seemed to find this waiver of the Statute of Frauds based solely on the fact that the parties made a subsequent oral agreement to modify. By this analysis, it would seem, any modification barred only by the technicality of the Statute of Frauds could come in through subsection (4). A concurrence by Judge Garth criticized this reading of §2-209(4), and his points are well taken. The waiver referred to therein, he argued, is not what he characterized as "a wholesale waiver of the Statute of Frauds."

This reading of the term is indeed a strain. We generally don't conceive of a party's being able to "waive" a statutory requirement (anyone for waiving the Statute of Limitations?). The waiver of subsection (4), according to Garth, is "limited to the particular condition, term or portion of the written contract sought to be waived by a party entitled to waive it." Under this analysis, a party can waive—in the sense of give up—a right which he or she had according to the original writing, "but obviously no new or affirmative term can be substituted therefore without satisfaction of the Statute of Frauds."

Judge Garth's way of reading §2-209(4) has an appeal. Not the least of its virtues is that it reads the subsection in a way that prevents every disabled modification from qualifying as a waiver. Modifications that seek to augment the agreement with terms not mentioned or even dreamt of in the original writing cannot simply be depicted as the fallout from a blanket waiver and held enforceable that way. The difficulty comes when we try to apply this distinction. Take the Example we are working on: Had the seller, Serge, called Belle and asked if he could deliver the fabric later, and if she had consented, that probably would be seen as a waiver. In fact it's very typical of the kinds of things which the common law regularly took to be effective waivers. Belle waives delivery by the date originally specified by her explicit relinquishment of her right to insist on that date. So is Serge's agreement to deliver *earlier* than initially agreed similarly a waiver? Fairness and symmetry would seem to require it, but even if we think Belle should win, a statement that Serge had "waived his right to withhold delivery until the very end of January" is awkward to say the least.

There's more trouble still for Judge Garth's approach when we consider some of the toughest cases—those in which a later agreement is alleged that would tack on a warranty not part of the initial agreement. These cases, as we see in discussion of the next Example, are among those where the courts have seemed most disposed to find a waiver in spite of the lack of the required writing, the effect being to add a new affirmative term to the contract.

3b. We reserve the full discussion of warranty law for the next part of this book. For the moment it is sufficient to note that Serge's statement could be what we will term an *express warranty* arising under §2-313. In fact the answer under that section would be easy except for one little problem: A crucial element of §2-313 is that any expression by the seller, if it is to be the basis of an express warranty, must be "part of the basis of the bargain." As we will discuss in Chapter 12, a representation made well after the deal was concluded will rarely meet this criterion. The timing is simply wrong. Belle would want to argue here that there was an express warranty that the fabric could be dyed without harm, a warranty later added to the contract through a modification. But she runs into trouble because this modification is not in writing, and the contract as she would have it modified is for more than $500. Can she argue a waiver? If we applied the reasoning of the majority of the circuit court in the *Double-E* case, she would have no trouble. But then again, presumably any modification to which she actually got Serge's agreement could become enforceable in that way as long as she thought to frame her argument in terms of "a waiver of the Statute of Frauds." The open-endedness of that analysis is troubling. If we were to apply Judge Garth's reasoning in *Double-E,* Belle would presumably lose. She is arguing here for an additional affirmative obligation on Serge's part which she claims he took on after the original deal was set.

There are, however, several cases where an express warranty given after the initial contract was concluded was held enforceable. In *Moldex, Inc. v. Ogden Engineering Corp.,* 652 F. Supp. 584, 3 U.C.C.2d 572 (D. Conn. 1987), on which this question is loosely based, the buyer purchased a large quantity of what was called "oriented nylon." In August, after much of the fabric had been delivered, the buyer contacted the seller to ask whether the nylon could be dyed without changing its properties. The seller assured the buyer that this could be done. When the goods did not take well to the dying, the seller refused to pay for them. The court first noted that "while a statement made after an agreement may not constitute a warranty it, nevertheless, may be deemed a modification of the sales contract and thus binding on the parties." Under the particular circumstances, however, the court concluded that the alleged representation could not be considered a binding modification because it was not in writing and therefore failed under §2-209(2). In the end, however, the buyer won out—on the basis of a waiver. The court held that it had produced "sufficient facts to suggest that the parties' conduct in August and November of 1983 and during various other telephone conversations constituted a waiver or restatement of the parties' contractual intent and thus such representation may be binding and enforceable under UCC §2-209(4)." What this court could mean by a "waiver or restatement" is anything but apparent, but the result was a clean victory for the aggrieved buyer.

A similar result was reached in the earlier case of *Bigelow v. Agway, Inc.,* 506 F.2d 551, 15 U.C.C. 769 (2d Cir. 1974). Bigelow, who was eventually to be named "Vermont's Outstanding Farmer in 1972," knew as would all such accomplished farmers that hay must be allowed to dry before being baled. Failure to do so carries a risk of spontaneous combustion when the bales are stored in a confined area. Sometime prior to his receiving his undoubtedly much-deserved honor he purchased a chemical advertised as an "Improved Hay Savor" and related spraying equipment. Hay savor is a product which is sprayed onto hay at the time of baling, the purpose being to retard mold growth in the baled hay. After his purchase a representative of the seller told farmer Bigelow that the hay then in his fields could be safely baled if treated with the Hay Savor, even though its moisture content was higher than would allow for safe baling under general farming practice. Farmer Bigelow testified that he then baled the hay despite his better judgment that it was still too green. The resulting fire destroyed his barn. The circuit court held that Bigelow's evidence sustained a case on breach of an express warranty created by the later statement of the seller's representative. While perhaps not "part of the basis of the bargain," these statements "might constitute an actionable modification of the warranty." The court made no reference to the various criteria of §2-209, although the later representations were oral only.

If results like those in these two cases are justified, and they certainly seem to be, how can they be squared with the rigors of §2-209? One obvious factor in both of them is the reliance which the buyer placed on the later statements by the seller. The fabric would not have been dyed nor the hay baled when it was except for the additional assurances made by the seller or its representative. We return then to the notion advanced by Judge Posner in the *Wisconsin Knife Works* case discussed earlier. Recall that in trying to distinguish a waiver he first gave short shrift to the idea that we should distinguish, as Judge Garth would have us do, between "a modification that substitutes a new term for an old, and a waiver, which merely removes an old term." For Posner the principle feature that sets apart a waiver, and consequentially brings §2-209(4) into play, is the fact of actual reliance by one party on the later manifestations of the other. The cases which give hope to sellers that a later expression by their buyer can create a binding warranty in their favor, at least if they rely to their detriment on such an expression, give support to this suggested analysis. It is too early yet to tell if the idea most forcefully advanced by Judge Posner of waiver distinguished by reliance will catch on generally, but it does draw some line—arguably a workable one—with which we can thread our way through the muddle.

4.   Buyer could probably not hold Seller in breach for the late delivery in August. A course of performance "is relevant," in the language of §2-208(3), "to show a waiver or modification of any term inconsistent with such course of performance." Since there was no writing, and since Seller could claim reliance on the course of performance, this would seem to be a good case of an enforceable waiver. Buyer would be within her rights in insisting on a return to the original delivery obligation for the future, however. See §2-209(5). If she gives Seller a reasonable amount of notice and he has not otherwise been disabled from making deliveries on the first of the month, he should do so from now on.

If the change in delivery date had been agreed to in a writing by Buyer the situation is not as clear. Seller would argue this was a modification, not a waiver. It does meet the requirements of a modification under subsections (1), (2) and/or (3). There is nothing in §2-209 about the "retraction" of a modification. Certainly if Seller agrees to start delivering by the first of the month starting in September, we have a modification or waiver piled on top of the original modification. But if Seller won't agree? It seems Buyer is out of luck. She was generous to Seller when he asked for a change in February, but if Seller is unwilling (or, to be fair, he may be unable) to show generosity in return, Buyer will have to live content with the knowledge of her own admirable conduct even if it was not returned in kind.

PART TWO

Warranty Terms

This Introduction is intended primarily for those readers who are starting their study at this point with the law of warranties. There is nothing wrong if that is what you are doing. Many courses in Sales get into warranties right off the bat and Contracts teachers often first dip into Article 2 at this point. If, however, you have worked through most of Part I, you should be comfortable going right to Chapter 11 (if you are taking up title and the warranty of title) or Chapter 12 (if you are concentrating on the express and implied warranties of quality). Do what works for you.

A contract for the sale of goods sets out the plan for a swap: The buyer gets the goods, and the seller ends up with the price paid in pocket. Note the language of §2-301, which is entitled "General Obligations of the Parties." "The obligation of the seller is to transfer and deliver and that of the buyer is to accept and pay in accordance with the contract." That's it. But it is important to note that in this section the drafters have used the word *contract* and not *agreement*. What's the difference? *Agreement* is defined in §1-201(3) as "the bargain of the parties in fact as found in their language or by implication from other circumstances including course of dealing or usage of trade or course of performance. . . ." The agreement in any sale of goods is what the parties themselves bargained out and ultimately consented to. It is a private matter between the two of them. It is for the buyer and seller to say what their agreement is.

The *contract* is something else: It is the result of the private agreement as it enters the public arena. It is the bundle of *legal* rights and obligations that arise from the agreement. To delineate the contract is to say what the two parties must do, in the eyes of the law, as a consequence of their act of agreement. In the language of the Code, the *contract* is "the total legal obligation which results from the parties' agreement as affected by this Act and any other applicable rules of law" (§1-201(11)).

This difference is crucial for both parties. It is particularly significant, however, for the buyer in the situation in which he or she is now placed. "The buyer is to get the goods." Presumably this means that at some time he or she is to take possession or get control over them. If everything is as the buyer expects, this should be the end of our (and the buyer's) troubles. But what exactly does the buyer expect, and how is he or she to react if those expectations are not met? Presumably the buyer does not simply expect to get physical possession, but reasonably expects to end up with a true ownership interest in the items purchased—what we have come to know as *title*. Beyond that the buyer will undoubtedly have very concrete expectations about the quality of the goods, such as what color they will be, their size, how well they will function, and on and on.

Where do such expectations come from? How do they arise? To a large extent they are found in the agreement itself. The seller has agreed in so many words that the goods will meet certain standards. The seller has, by invoking explicit language of promise, or warranty, or guarantee, given the buyer his or her word. If this promise is broken, the buyer must have some legal recourse. The agreement has, after all, resulted in a contract, and the elemental law of contracts tells us plenty about how an aggrieved party is entitled to react to a contractual promise not kept, a *breach of contract*. As we will see, under Article 2 a breach of this kind may give the buyer the right to reject the goods or to revoke an acceptance already made. The buyer may also have the right to sue for damages.

But what if the seller has not in so many words promised the goods will meet certain expectations? In an earlier day, as you are probably aware, the rudimentary answer was summed up in the single phrase *caveat emptor*, "let the buyer beware." If the goods were not as the buyer expected them to be, then the seller could and would be expected to live up to any *express* promise he or she had made, but if the seller hadn't made any such promise the buyer was out of luck. If the buyer wanted the protection of being able to make the seller stand behind his or her product in any particular way (to get what we now can call a *warranty on the goods*), the buyer had to make sure to bargain for and obtain just such a direct and unreserved promise. In the modern terminology of the Code, the buyer would have to make sure that any warranties were expressly and explicitly made part of the *agreement* of sale. Otherwise, they would not be part of the buyer's contract.

We will have more to say about the bad old days of *caveat emptor*. For the purpose of introduction it is enough to note that we now live in a more progressive and enlightened era—at least, that is, as far as the buyer is concerned. Under the more mature law of sales (and as now codified in Article 2), the *contract* for sale, the legal relationship, includes a whole host of warranties upon which the buyer may rely, going well beyond those created through overt expressions of promise. The buyer gets these rights not necessarily because he or she bargained for them, or even thought about the possibility that they would be necessary, but because the law of Article 2 imports them into every contract for the sale of goods. How and when the warranties of sale are created, how they are to be interpreted, and how the seller may effectively get out from under them—these are what we deal with in the following chapters.

Chapter 11 deals with the passing of title to goods and the warranty of title given by the seller. The buyer will expect to get a true ownership interest in the subject of the contract, in what he or she buys. Section 2-312 basically protects the buyer in this expectation, but not without some complexity, brought on in the main from the very obscure concept of "title" itself. If you are not studying title or the warranty of title at this time, you can skip this chapter and go directly to Chapter 12. That chapter and the ones that follow deal with the warranties of quality provided for in §§2-313 to 2-315 of the Code. We will also have to consider how such warranties may be disclaimed, if at all, under §2-316, and the related issue of how a seller may effectively bargain under §2-719 for a limitation of his or her liability for breach of warranty. The material on warranties in sales concludes in Chapter 16 with a discussion of the (maddening) relationship between this seemingly compact and manageable system developed in the law of sales and the ever-burgeoning and devilishly complex law of products liability.

Analogous warranty protection is found for the lessee of goods who's entered into a contract to lease governed by Article 2A. We deal with these provisions separately in Chapter 17.

11

The Warranty of Title

This chapter deals with two related topics which are sometimes dealt with at different points in the Sales course. The first is the very concept of title and how title in goods passes from one party to another. The second topic is the warranty of title under §2-312. If you are now only dealing with preliminary title issues, you can skip the last section of text and work through only the first three Examples. When you later hit the warranty of title material, you can revisit this chapter concentrating on that last bit of text and the later Examples.

That "Intangible Something" and Practical People

Prior to the adoption of the Uniform Commercial Code, a whole host of issues in the law of sales were dominated by the concept of *title*. Title is basically a property notion. In a society where private ownership of property is not only possible but on the order of something sacred, the concept of title has come to sum up the whole complex relationship which a person has with the things he or she owns. Make that he, she, or *it* owns, for we know that under our law title to property can be held by "persons" neither male nor female—nonhuman legal constructs such as a corporation or a trust. Indeed the very idea of "legal personality" in the common law can be seen as a question of what manner of individual, organization, or collective can legally hold title to property in its own name.

That to which you hold title is the stuff which is yours—yours to possess, to use or dispose of as you please, and which you can protect against the claims of the rest of the world. If you have title to it, you can take it where you want and do with it what you will. You can give it to a friend, recover it from a thief, or toss it into a ravine. The word *title* encompasses a lot. Unfortunately, words that carry so much weight do not serve so well when precision is required. This, the drafters of the Code thought, was definitely true of "title." Whatever may have been its history or its value in property law, it never served with distinction in the law of sales. Cases on title were legion, concerning just about every issue in sales law. Even if one was able to work through and make sense of any particular line of cases, trying to use this learning to solve a different question (even if it too were said to hinge on "title") tended only to result in additional confusion, rarely insight or any measure of clarity. And it was said that the resourceful lawyer could always find authoritative statements about "title" to support just about any side of a proposition, no matter how tangentially related to the case at hand.

In the single comment to §2-101, the very first section of Article 2, the drafters make their position known in no uncertain terms:

> The arrangement of the present Article is in terms of contract for sale and the various steps of its performance. The legal consequences are stated as following directly from the contract and action taken under it without resorting to the idea of when property or title passed or was to pass as being the determining factor. The purpose is to avoid making practical issues between practical men turn upon the location of an intangible something, the passing of which no man can prove by evidence and to substitute for such abstractions proof of words and actions of a tangible nature.

The drafters meant to accomplish their goal by making the concept of title and even the use of the word simply irrelevant to a large number of important issues where previously, including under the Uniform Sales Act, title had been determinative. Note, most specifically, the preamble to §2-401:

> Each provision of this Article with regard to the rights, obligations and remedies of the seller, the buyer, purchasers or other third parties applies *irrespective of title to the goods* except where the provisions refers to title.

The emphasis is mine, but it might as well be that of the drafters. As examples of issues that were once mired in the world of title but which the Code now deals with directly and without reference to that concept, we can point to the problem of risk of loss (which will be dealt with in Part IV) and the seller's action for the price under §2-709 (to be considered along with other remedies in Chapter 28).*

---

*Just to make clear, there still are plenty of instances where our law relies on the concept of title, such as the right of a creditor to levy on property, the proper coverage of insurance, and criminal responsibility for stealing someone else's property. What is important (and fortunate) for our present study is that such problems are by and large outside of the law of sales.

Passing Title Around

Having observed the significant degree to which the Code downplays the abstraction of title, we now turn to the situations in which it *does* matter. Article 2 does not, indeed could not, avoid the notion altogether. In fact, the very definition of a *sale* in §2-106(1) says that it "consists in the passing of title from the seller to the buyer for a price," and points us to §2-401 which deals with "Passing of Title" among other things. For various purposes, the problem of who has title, whether it passes, and if so when it passes must be determined. The question of *when* title passes from the seller to the buyer is dealt with by §2-401, which you may want to glance over now. The basic idea is that the purchaser and seller may agree as they please regarding when title will pass, but in the absence of such an agreement the time of delivery of the goods or of a document of title covering the goods will be key. Fortunately, the time when title passes rarely causes much problem, as the issues to which it had once been so central (primarily risk of loss) are now resolved under Article 2 with no reference to title whatsoever.

The issues still remaining, and to which we must give some attention, have to do with not when but *whether* title passes at all. Did the seller have title? Does the buyer get title? This last question will obviously be crucial if the warranty of title is to mean anything. The initial questions of this chapter explore these fundamental concerns. In particular they explore the workings of §2-403, which you should read in conjunction with these questions.

Discussion of these issues seems inevitably (and unfortunately) to revolve around three phrases: *good title, void title,* and *voidable title.* A word of warning is in order. *Good title* or *real title* or *clear title* or any other such phrase can mean only one thing—just plain title. It is the legal position of ownership which we've been talking about. In theory at least, either you have title or you don't. Speaking of "good title" is a little bit like talking about the "real truth" or the "true facts."

On the other hand, what is sometimes referred to as *void title* isn't title at all. In fact it is the very absence of title. A person may claim whatever he or she wants, but whether the person making the claim knows it or not, if that person doesn't have title then he or she just doesn't have title. As you'll see in the analysis of the questions to follow, we tend to use the term *void title* when referring to an item in the hands of a thief or someone who has taken from a thief, but it would be just as correct to say that I, your author, have *void title* to the Chrysler Building. Believe me, I don't own it. I do not have title to it. Not even a bit. My guess is that you have *void title* to the Chrysler Building along with me.

The third phrase, *voidable title,* is most troublesome of all, not least because §2-403 uses the term without ever defining it. The wording suggests it is something in the middle, somewhere between all or nothing, and that may be one way to think about it. Best of all is to avoid worrying about *voidable title* in the abstract altogether. What will matter are the particulars, and the questions will run through the various possibilities to be considered. "Voidable title" is as "voidable title" does, and it shouldn't end up being too mysterious if you allow yourself to think about it on a case-by-case basis.

The Warranty of Title and Against Infringement

Whatever this strange thing title is, it is something that the buyer wants and expects to get from the seller as an integral part of the deal. If the seller cannot or does not provide title, the buyer obviously will be hurt and will deserve some legal right to respond. The buyer gets this protection as part of the contract of sale by virtue of §2-312. Basically the idea is pretty clear-cut. In a typical contract of sale the seller warrants that "the title conveyed shall be good, and its transfer rightful" and furthermore that that title is delivered free of any encumbrances of which the buyer is unaware. Buyers are to get what they expect—what any reasonable person in their situation would expect—they would be getting. The later questions in this chapter deal with the operation of §2-312 and the warranty protection it provides.

EXAMPLES

1.   Alice is the owner of a necklace. It has been in her family for years, and you may assume that she has title. She gives the necklace as a gift to her niece Betty. Betty wears it for some time before selling it to Clara.
    a. Did Betty have title? Does Clara?
    b. Suppose that instead of giving Betty the necklace as a gift, Alice only lent it to her to wear to a party. After the party Betty, who lost heavily at the gaming tables, sells it to Clara to raise money to pay her debts. In this situation, does Clara get title to the trinket?

2.   Among the several valuable paintings in his collection, Dan is the proud owner of a beautiful portrait called "Young Man with a Horn." One day he discovers the painting missing. It turns out it has been stolen by one Earl. Earl sold it to Felice, who had no reason to question how it came into Earl's possession. Felice in turn sold it to Gayle. Gayle happens to show her new acquisition to her friend Dan, who recognizes it as the piece missing from his collection.
    a. Other than Dan's friendship, does Gayle stand in jeopardy of losing anything else? That is, can Dan recover the painting from her?
    b. Suppose that Earl did not actually steal the painting. Instead he arranges to buy it from Dan at a very hefty but perfectly reasonable price. Earl picks up the painting, giving Dan in exchange a personal check for the entire purchase price. The check bounces. Dan tries to get in touch with Earl, but the rascal has disappeared. When he later sees the painting in Gayle's possession, will Dan be able legally to

get it back? Would it make any difference to your analysis if Dan could show that the only reason he took a personal check from Earl was that Dan thought him to be another person, also named Earl, who was known to be one of the wealthiest and most upstanding people in the community? Finally, suppose that instead of taking a check Dan had insisted on cash on delivery. At the time of sale Earl had picked up the rather bulky canvas and then said he was taking it out to his car to stow safely in the trunk. He said he'd be right back with the cash. Earl, of course, disappears. Now what result? There must be a lesson in all of this. What is it?

    c. In all of the situations considered above, would it make any difference if Felice could be shown to have been aware that Earl had obtained the painting in the way that he did and had used this information to buy it at a "steal" from Earl? What if Felice had no direct knowledge of Earl's way of doing business, but the price for which he sold it to her was very much below what such a painting would normally be worth?

3.   Rick has a rare and expensive electric guitar, which he values highly. The story is that it had once been played by Elvis. But it is on the blink. He takes it in for repair to Cathy's Music City, a retail store selling various musical instruments which also has a service department. When he goes to pick it up, an embarrassed Cathy tells him that one of her clerks mistakenly sold it to Chris. Can Rick just go to Chris's house and insist that he get the guitar back? What more do you need to know to advise Rick?

4.   Recall the situation in Example 2, the case of the purloined painting. If Gayle is made to give the painting back to Dan, what rights does she have against Felice? Should Felice be found liable, does she in turn have rights against anyone?

5.   Recall the situation in Example 3, where the "Elvis" guitar ended up in Chris' hands. When Rick comes calling, Chris might understandably decide to put up a fight to keep such a precious object. She engages a high-powered attorney in an effort to retain the instrument, but eventually loses the case and has to give it back to Rick.

    a. What amount can she now collect from her seller, Cathy's Music City? See §§2-714 and 2-715. Assume that Chris had originally paid $12,400 for the instrument but that she had soon thereafter been offered upwards of $16,000 for it. Assume further that she had to pay her attorney $2,560 for her unsuccessful defense.

    b. Assume instead that in the previous question Chris ultimately prevails and is allowed to keep the guitar. She wins! Of course, she is still out $2,560 in attorney's fees and maybe more as a result of all the hassle. Should she have any right to recover from Cathy for the costs of her *successful* defense?

6.   Harry buys an oriental rug from his friend Marv for a cost of $12,000. The rug is old and is worn in spots. The parties agree that the sale will be "as is," and a provision to this effect is written into the contract of

sale. It later turns out that the rug, unbeknownst to Marv, had once been stolen from a mansion in the community. Its true owner shows up to recover it from Harry.

a. Can Marv use the "as is" provision in defense against a breach of warranty claim by Harry?

b. Suppose instead that Harry bought the rug from Marv at a foreclosure sale. The rug had been the property of Joan, who had borrowed money from Marv putting up the valuable rug as collateral. When Joan did not repay Marv, he as a secured creditor was entitled to take possession of the rug and could sell it off to get at least part of his money back. It is in this capacity that Marv made the sale. When it turns out the rug had been stolen by Joan and is reclaimed by its rightful owner, can Harry go against Marv on the warranty of good title?

c. Finally, imagine that Marv is a stranger to Harry. In fact he's a bit of a mysterious stranger. He shows up at Harry's home one evening claiming that he's heard Harry is "the kind of man who appreciates fine oriental rugs." He offers to sell Harry the rug at a price that seems, to Harry, to be incredibly low. Marv explains that he has "low overhead," which does seem true since he appears to be operating out of the back of a pick-up truck. Harry buys the rug. Has he gotten any warranty protection if he should end up without good title?

EXPLANATIONS

1a. Alice has title to the necklace originally, at least, that's what I asked you to assume. (Of the things to which you would claim title, how many of these could you actually *prove* were truly yours? For the most part we tend to assume title in goods just because there's no reason to doubt it.) When Alice gives the bauble as a gift the effect is to vest title in Betty. This has nothing to do with the law of sales or even of contract. It comes from property law and the law pertaining to gifts, so we needn't get into any detail here. Suffice it to say that the real essence of a gift of personal property is not simply transferring possession (that isn't even absolutely necessary), but rather bestowing title on someone else. Once Betty has title, she can sell the thing and by doing so transfer the title to Clara. This last bit is just the direct application of the first sentence in §2-403(1): "A purchaser of goods acquires all title which [her] transferor had or had power to transfer. . . ." As a matter of fact, this language can be made to justify the first result we needed, that Betty had acquired title, since the Code's idea of a "purchaser" is pretty broad. See §1-201(33), which leads us to §1-201(32) and the notion that *purchase* under the Code includes taking by "gift or other voluntary transaction creating an interest in property."

1b. Under these facts Betty never got title to the necklace. Since her aunt let her have possession, at least temporarily, she would be a *bailee* but that's all, and we presume that this does not create "an interest in property" in Betty. This being so, and since the seller cannot normally pass on to her buyer better title than she has, Clara does not have title. Where does this leave Clara? Holding Alice's property, that's where. Jumping ahead just a bit, we recognize that in this situation if Alice becomes aware that Clara has the necklace she can get it back from her. Where does *that* leave Clara? It certainly isn't hard to see that Clara should have rights against Betty here. And, as we'll see, that's just what §2-312 will give her. Note also at this point that the so-called "entrusting" provision of §2-403(2), with which we deal in Example 3, is of no help to Clara, as Betty does not appear to be a merchant who deals in goods of the glittery kind.

It also isn't hard to see just from these first two simple examples that the question of who has title to a piece of personal property, even if in theory nice and neat, can be made very messy by the facts of a situation. The result in the second question, when the necklace is only loaned temporarily to Betty, does not depend on Betty's believing she does or does not have title to the piece of jewelry. The conversation between Alice and Betty may have been ambiguous, and Betty could have honestly thought that her aunt was giving it to her forever. We can assume that she never would have sold it to Clara if she had realized that eventually a court would determine that she hadn't been given an outright gift in the situation. But Betty's belief as to her status at the time she sells means nothing to Clara's interest. As you'll see from the following questions, law professors love to seize on the case of property that was at one time in its history the subject of an out-and-out theft when discussing problems of title. In truth, many of the actual cases that come up do have this intriguing element in them, but as the story of Alice, Betty, and Clara shows there can be genuine questions as to title, and an innocent person can try to pass on title that he or she does not legally have to give, even when there's been no such skullduggery in the past.*

2a. Dan can get the painting back from Gayle. In fact he can get it back from anyone who has it, whenever and wherever he finds it. In this Example we have a chain of possession involving theft. Earl obviously never had title. He didn't take by anything that the Code, or any other rule of law, would see as "creating an interest" (by which is presumably meant creating some legally legitimate interest) in the painting. When

---

*You may want to contrast this situation, where personal property is involved, with what you know about the passing of title (and the problems attendant thereto) when real property is at stake. The amounts at risk are typically much greater, and the law has developed a system of public recordation on which the issues of "who has title" will depend. The risks inherent in buying personal property are usually not as great, and we are left to make do without a uniform system of recording and proof. As you are probably aware, in one instance where the value of personal property can become considerable (that of the purchase and sale of motor vehicles), many states have adopted a formal measure for meeting these problems, the laws relating to certification of automobile title. We will not deal with such laws in this volume.

Earl sells it to Felice, she cannot and does not get title. Because Felice does not have title, Gayle can get none by purchase. It is as straightforward as that. As a practical matter we don't have to worry about how Dan goes about getting actual possession. Once he proves it's his painting that had been stolen, there shouldn't be any difficulty. His right to get it need not be found in the Code—it's a classic property action (*replevin*) to recover one's property wrongfully held by another. Notice again that this is so in spite of our assumption that neither Gayle nor Felice had any bad motive or any reason to know they were dealing in hot property.

You might think the result given here is hard on Gayle, who will be left with nothing of value and out the amount she paid to Felice. The answer, as we will see, is that she'll be able to sue Felice for her damages. Felice will have the right to go against Earl for *her* damages. To be sure, the right to go against a thief may not be all that comforting. People like Earl tend to disappear into the night and are rarely amenable to suit. So Felice may be left holding the bag. Again, this may not seem terribly fair to poor Felice. But remember that the alternative would be to conclude that Dan, whose property was stolen, could not recover it. What would we say to him? True, he could go after Earl and make him return the stolen property or pay the consequences. But why should Dan have to bear this terrible burden of tracking Earl down and suing him for every last penny? The real question in such cases, of course, is which of two innocent people (in our hypo, Dan or Felice) should have to bear the theft loss. The conventional wisdom, and the answer that the common law and the UCC supply, is that the person who purchases from the thief should bear this risk. The conventional explanation, for what it is worth, of this allocation of risk is that the purchaser in such a situation could presumably guard against buying stolen property by checking into the article's past history, asking the right questions, and asking to see proof of her seller's ownership. The person from whom the item is filched has presumably already done what could reasonably be done to prevent his or her stuff from being stolen. He or she would be unlikely to behave cavalierly with regard to possible thefts on the strength of a legal principle which says that the owner can get it back from whoever eventually has it. That all depends on the goods making an appearance again. Most stolen property just vanishes, and we expect owners will protect to the appropriate extent against this possibility. When it comes to dealing with thieves, at least, it definitely still is the case that the buyer must be wary.

2b. First the case of the bounced check. This may seem awfully similar to what we just saw, but in fact the result will be different. Gayle has good title in the painting. How could this be? Earl's behavior is perhaps a bit less monstrous, but why should that make such a difference? The answer is to be found in the concept of voidable title and its consequences as laid out in §2-403(1) in the material that follows the first sentence. Note the second sentence: "A person with voidable title has power to transfer a good title to a good faith purchaser for value." The final part of the subsection gives the four instances provided for in the Code when a person can get this thing called "voidable title." Here we're relying on clause (b). The painting was "delivered in exchange for a check which was later dishonored." Because this was so, Earl himself did *not* gain title; he did not have the *right* to sell what wasn't properly his to sell; what he did get was the *power* to transfer a good title to Felice, provided she is what the Code calls a *good faith purchaser for value*. We'll assume that in this situation she is such a person, whatever the term means. So upon purchase Felice had good title. Felice sells it to Gayle, who thereby gets good title.

An obvious question is why the outcome of this problem should be so different, in fact the exact opposite, of the prior one. Remember the justification that was suggested there. It is at least arguable that someone who buys from a thief should have been able to avoid doing so by using a little more care and circumspection. We do not say the same thing about someone who "allows" a thief to get at this property. But here Dan did not take all the precautions he could have to avoid losing the painting to Earl in this way. He took a personal check. In the real world that's got to be understood as taking a big risk. Personal checks can and sometimes do bounce. If Dan had wanted to further protect himself, he could have asked for cash, or for a certified check, or something of the sort. And it's also very possible in this situation that Dan allowed Earl to get his hands on the kind of documentation of ownership (for instance, a Bill of Sale signed by Dan and to all appearances perfectly valid) that Felice would expect to rely on to guard against buying something of doubtful pedigree. The equities between the two innocents, Dan and Felice, work out quite differently in this situation.

The same argument explains the parallel result when we find that Dan sold to Earl believing him to be someone else. Read §2-403(1)(a). The case where Earl is supposedly buying for cash but somehow manages to drive off with the goods without having paid the money is dealt with in §2-403(1)(c). Again, Dan will suffer the consequences of not protecting himself more successfully against this kind of behavior. And finally look at §2-403(1)(d), which states that the transferee gets voidable title whenever "the delivery was procured through fraud punishable as larcenous under the criminal law." The four instances given in this section where a transferee gets voidable title are not meant by the drafters of the Code to be exhaustive. They never actually define *voidable title* once and for all. The result is that there are apparently other situations, similar to those enumerated but not actually covered, in which the common law would give rise to such voidable title, and by virtue of the second sentence of §2-403(1) the holder in such an instance has the power to create good title in his or her purchaser. No one has explained precisely what these other situations are, but the authorities seem to agree that the common thread is that a person with good title will have made some kind of voluntary transfer to another, intended at least initially to part him- or herself from title. When it later turns out this transfer had been obtained by the person taking the goods in some nefarious way, true title does not pass, but voidable title may. The true thief can get nothing and can pass on nothing. The swindler, however, may be able to pass on good title to an innocent party. Apparently we are supposed to be able to guard ourselves against (or at least learn to live with the risks of) a little larceny, at least when the perpetrator confronts us face-to-face.

It's worth pointing out once more that none of this business about voidable title is saying that the person whose behavior is the direct cause of all the trouble—the person who gives the bum check, who somehow forgets to deliver the cash, and so on—can benefit or get any interest in the property by this type of behavior. Our concern is with the innocent third party who deals with, and buys from, the scoundrel. Which leads us to the following question and the issue of just exactly who is a good faith purchaser for value.

2c. If Felice knows how Earl came to have the painting, she cannot get good title from him. A person with voidable title can transfer good title only to a *good faith purchaser for value*. This creature plays an important role in the law of commercial transactions. He, she, or it is featured in several sections of the Uniform Commercial Code (most in other articles with which we are not concerned). We will not go here into all the details and all the controversy about how someone qualifies for this favored status. Note, however, that one must first be a *purchaser*, as defined in §1-201(33), and have given *value*, as defined in §1-201(44). Neither of these are a problem for Felice. The more difficult question here, and in most actual situations, is whether the purchaser had been acting in good faith in taking the goods. As we've seen before, *good faith* is a defined term under the Code. Whether or not Felice is a merchant for Article 2 purposes, for her to qualify as a good faith purchaser she will have had to act with "honesty in fact." See §1-201(19). Buying property which you actually know the seller does not rightfully own would not qualify.

A more difficult question is raised when we assume Felice has no direct knowledge of Earl's way of doing business, but does buy the painting at a price far below its worth. If she was well aware that the price was less than she would normally have to pay for such an item, it's probable that she wouldn't be able to qualify as a good faith purchaser. She would have a much better chance of qualifying if it were shown that she did not know she was getting such an unusual (and presumably suspicious) bargain. In such situations the courts and commentators get all wrapped up in questions of whether the issue is exclusively a question of the buyer's subjective knowledge and intent (the "pure-heart-and-empty-head" test) or a supposedly objective consideration of what a "reasonable person" would have or should have known under the circumstances. We can afford to skip an extended discussion of such disputes. We should note, however, that if Felice were a merchant under Article 2 her good faith would be judged by the possibly more demanding standard of §2-103(1)(b). A court would be justified in inquiring not only into her subjective honesty, but also into how the purchase should be viewed in light of "reasonable standards of fair dealing in the trade."

An interesting corollary to what has gone before is that *if* Felice does qualify as a good faith purchaser for value, hence actually herself getting good title, she will pass on good title to anyone who buys from her (in our case Gayle) even if *that* person does know of the improper way it got into her seller's hands. This *shelter principle* is a straightforward application of the first sentence §2-403(1). So Gayle could get good title from Felice even if Gayle knew all about Earl's larcenous behavior. Can you think of an explanation, apart from mere contrariness of the drafters, why this should work out the way it does?

3. If Rick is able to recover the guitar from Chris, it will be under the doctrine of *entrustment* as set forth in subsections (2) and (3) of §2-403. Clearly Cathy did not get title from Rick, nor is there any way for Chris to argue that Cathy had obtained voidable title. But under subsection (2), "Any entrusting of possession of goods to a merchant who deals in goods of that kind gives him power to transfer all rights of the entruster to a buyer in the ordinary course of business." Since Rick presumably had all the rights of a title holder, if this section applies to the situation Chris now has good title. Rick could not get the guitar back from Chris and would only have an action against Cathy for what she did.

There are several subsidiary questions apparent from these subsections, but none is especially tricky. First of all, did Rick actually "entrust" the goods to Cathy? It seems clear he did. The fact that he delivered the guitar to her only for the limited purpose of repair would not, by virtue of the language in (3), make any difference. Cathy seems clearly to be an Article 2 merchant, but is she a merchant "who deals in goods of this kind?" This is a factual question, and the answer is not obvious from the facts given. True, she runs a retail store which sells musical instruments, but would every such mom-and-pop store deal in rare memorabilia like this piece? Does Cathy's Music City normally deal in such precious objects? Presumably the question should be addressed from the point of view of the person entrusting the goods. Was there reason for Rick to realize that leaving the guitar in Cathy's possession put him at risk that just this kind of thing could happen, and that he could lose title this way?

The final question is whether Chris can qualify as a buyer in the ordinary course of business from Cathy. Such a person is, like the good faith purchaser for value, a type very important to commercial law. The two are not identical. Look at the definition of the *buyer in the ordinary course of business* in §1-201(9). He must be buying in good faith and "without knowledge that the sale to him is in violation of the ownership rights or security interest of a third party in the goods." So Chris could not have title to the goods if she were somehow acting in bad faith or if she had reason to know that the guitar was Rick's and he wasn't interested in giving it up. Beyond that the purchase must be from "a person in the business of selling goods of that kind." So again we come to the question of whether Cathy deals in goods "of the kind," but here more from the buyer's perspective. Was there any reason for Chris to doubt that this retail store would normally sell an item like this?

The fundamental idea of these entrustment provisions is that when any of us buys something in the ordinary course of *the seller's* business, that is, buys from a seller the things which that person is in business to sell, we need not worry that we might not be getting good title. If we buy stuff off the shelf, so to speak, we can be confident we're getting all the title we need. Notice how this doctrine would not apply if, for example, Cathy sold Chris a cash register which she had been using in her store. Cathy is a merchant, and Chris could be operating in complete good faith. Indeed Chris may actually get good title to the machine, but it won't be because she bought it in the ordinary course of business. Cathy is not in the business of selling business machines. (This also explains why Clara, from Example 1b, couldn't take advantage of the entrustment principle.)

A typical, if not very momentous, case that touches upon both the voidable title and entrustment concepts is *Atlas Auto Rental Corp. v. Weisberg,* 281 N.Y.S.2d 400, 4 U.C.C. 572 (N.Y. City Ct. 1967). Atlas Auto Rental, from time to time, would sell off its used autos. Herbert Schwartzman offered to purchase a two-year-old Chevrolet station wagon, which Atlas was offering for sale at $1,250. His offer of a personal check for this amount was, according to the testimony of Atlas's manager, rejected. Nevertheless, the manager allowed Schwartzman to take the car out for a test run. Schwartzman got in the car, drove off, and was never seen again, at least not by anyone at Atlas. Atlas's manager found that he still had Schwartzman's check around, but when he tried to cash it, it was returned marked "No Funds." A week later the car was traced to an establishment in the Bronx run by the defendant Weisberg, who was licensed to do business there as an auto wrecker and junk dealer. But the car was no longer there. Weisberg claimed that he had purchased it from Schwartzman for a price of $900, paying $300 down, the rest to be paid at a later time. Schwartzman had never been heard from again and never collected the rest of the $900. Weisberg had not received from him either a bill of sale or a registration certificate for the car. Where was the car? Weisberg had immediately resold it, for $1,200, to a dealer. That's the story.

Atlas brought suit against Weisberg for conversion, seeking to recover the value of the station wagon. Weisberg's defense was that he had acquired good title to the car. He made two arguments to support his claim. The first was based on §2-403(1) and the notion of voidable title. After all, the reason Atlas was aggrieved could be said to be the bounced check. But, the court reasoned, when Atlas actually delivered the car to Schwartzman it was "solely for the purpose of permitting a test run, not with any idea of conferring title upon him." Admittedly, the fact of the bounced check raised "troublesome questions as to whether or not plaintiff had in fact intended to convey a voidable title dependent on whether the check cleared," but at least if the manager's statements were to be believed, this intention did not exist when he gave Schwartzman the keys and allowed him to drive it away.

The defendant also made a claim that the auto had been entrusted to Schwartzman and that he, Weisberg, got good title under §2-403(2).

But this would all depend on Schwartzman's being a merchant who deals in goods of the kind of a used Chevy. The defendant was able to offer into evidence an invoice headed "Herbert Schwartzman, Wholesale Automobiles" which he later found in his files. But it did not appear that he was relying on this when he bought from Schwartzman. Beyond this, it in no way showed that *Atlas* would have believed Schwartzman to be such a merchant. "Since the 'entrusting' provisions of UCC §2-403 are an extension of the principle of estoppel," the court concluded, "it would appear to be essential that the actual vocational status of the merchant be established, but also that the original owner and the ultimate purchaser must be shown to have been aware of that status."

If there had been any hope for Weisberg at this point, it was dashed by the court's conclusion that under the circumstances he could qualify as neither a good faith purchaser for value (which would have been necessary to prevail on the voidable title idea) or a buyer in the ordinary course of business (which was crucial to the entrustment claim). After all, he was licensed in the Bronx only to do business in "junk." He had in effect paid only $300 in cash for an automobile which he was immediately able to sell for $1,200. He had apparently not been troubled that his seller could show him neither a bill of sale nor a certificate of registration. The court concluded

> It was [Weisberg] who had prior dealings with Schwartzman. Certainly if he was not working with him, he had every reason to be skeptical of Schwartzman's claim of ownership. The Uniform Commercial Code protects the innocent purchaser, but it is not a shield for the sly conniver, the blindly naive, or the hopelessly gullible.

4. Gayle can sue Felice for breach of warranty and should have no trouble winning. This is the heart of §2-312, and it is perfectly direct. There is nothing in the question to suggest that Felice in selling to Gayle attempted to exclude or modify the warranty of title, so subsection (2) doesn't come into play. Under subsection (1), therefore, the contract for sale between Felice and Gayle included a warranty by Felice that "the title conveyed shall be good, and its transfer rightful." Our assumption in this question is that Dan could get the painting back, which means that the title conveyed to Gayle was not good. Felice has breached the warranty of title. Note that this result does not depend on a finding that Felice knew she could not give good title, or even that she should have known this. It's simply a matter that she didn't give what she contracted to give. What can Felice do now? Since she bought from Earl, she'll be able to go against him on the warranty of title herself. So the responsibility under the Code is ultimately Earl's, as it should be. The problem, of course, will be finding him and getting him to live up to this responsibility. The risk that he can't be forced to make amends for what he's done thus falls on Felice, the person who directly took from him.

In the question as I've set it up, Gayle had already taken the painting and paid for it. When she has to give it back, the only sensible remedy for this breach of warranty will be an action for damages. In other situations, the breach (or an arguable breach) of the warranty of title plays out in different ways. If, for example, Gayle had purchased the painting from Felice on credit, the breach of warranty would be a good defense for her when Felice tries to collect on the contract.

Suppose instead that the two had simply contracted for the purchase and sale of the painting, delivery and payment to take place at a later date. When Felice delivers the painting, Gayle — for some reason or another, or simply because she's sensible and cautious — is worried about whether she'll get good title. She asks Felice for some form of proof that the painting is Felice's to sell. Felice cannot show her anything of the type that would normally be available for a valuable art work with a good pedigree. Gayle would want to argue that the delivery, lacking as it does assurances of good title, fails to conform to what was required under the contract. As we will see in Chapter 18, if the seller's delivery fails to conform, the buyer will ordinarily not have to accept the goods. Gayle may not have to take the painting. Beyond that, if Felice is never able to perform under the contract, Gayle would have an action for damages.

Note that the warranty of title will be breached not only where the buyer gets no interest in the goods whatsoever. He or she is also protected by a warranty that "the goods shall be delivered free from any security interest or other lien or encumbrance of which [he or she] at the time of contracting has no knowledge." Thus, if the goods are later found to be worth less because there is unknown to the buyer some security interest in the goods held by a third party and that third party must be paid off, the buyer will have an action for damages against the seller.

5a. Section 2-312 itself says nothing about the measure of damages for a breach of the warranty of title. We have to look at the general provision for damages in a breach of warranty action, which is found in §2-714. This in turn leads us to §2-715 on the buyer's incidental and consequential damages. These sections will be discussed fully in Chapter 29. We do not want to go into all the details now. Still, breach of the warranty of title is sufficiently distinct from the more typical breach of warranty action where a warranty of quality is involved, so it's worth some consideration here.

In the question as posed, clearly Chris can recover from Cathy for the loss of the guitar, but for what amount? Over the years the courts have not been terribly consistent in answering this question, first under the common law, then under the Uniform Sales Act, and now under the Code. Should Chris simply be entitled to the return of her purchase price plus any interest from the time of the sale? Or should she be able to prove that even at the time of the sale the guitar was worth more than the purchase price, say $13,400, and that she is entitled at least to "the benefit of her bargain"? Or is Chris right if she argues that the only way *now* to fully compensate her for the fact that she is left without the guitar is for her to be allowed to recover the full market value of the guitar as of the date it is taken away from her? Recently the courts seem to be moving in the direction of giving this last measure of value, at least where the goods are of the type which could have been expected to significantly appreciate in value and in fact have done so. In so ruling they often refer with approval to the noted case of *Menzel v. List*, 24 N.Y.2d 91, 298 N.Y.S.2d 979, 6 U.C.C. 330 (1969), which because of the date on which the contract was entered into was actually decided under the New York counterpart to the Uniform Sales Act. In *Menzel* a valuable painting, a Chagall, had been purchased by Albert List in 1955 from the Perls, proprietors of a New York art gallery, for a price of $4,000. The painting, it later turned out, was the rightful property of Mrs. Erna Menzel and her husband, who had purchased it in Belgium in 1932. When the Menzels fled Belgium at the time of the Nazi invasion in 1940, they left the picture behind. When they returned to their home six years later the picture was gone. Only a receipt had been left by the German authorities. What happened to the painting between the time of the Menzels' flight and early 1955, when the Perls purchased it from a Parisian art gallery, was unknown. Only in 1962 did Mrs. Menzel become aware that the painting was in the hands of Mr. List. She sued for its recovery and won. In the same action List brought a third-party complaint against the Perls for breach of the warranty of title. Even though the Perls were apparently unaware of the painting's history, having relied upon the reputation of the Paris gallery, they clearly were in breach of the seller's warranty. The jury assessed damages at $22,500, the value of the painting at the time of the trial. On appeal to the Appellate Division this amount was reduced to $4,000, the purchase price List had paid, plus interest from the date of the sale to List. On further appeal, the New York Court of Appeals reinstated the judgment for the higher amount. Mr. List was entitled to damages from the Perls for the full value of the painting as of the time of trial, when the painting was taken from his possession.

A second issue in the question is whether our claimant Chris can recover from Cathy her attorney's fees spent in her unsuccessful bid to retain possession. As a matter of fact, in *Menzel v. List* the party who had to give up possession (Mr. List) was awarded attorney's fees by the jury although the award of this amount was apparently never appealed and the court had little to say on it. A case that does consider the question in some detail, and which allows an award of the buyer's attorney's fees as legitimate consequential damages in a similar situation is *Universal C.I.T. Credit Corp. v. State Farm Mutual Automobile Ins. Co.*, 493 S.W.2d 385, 12 U.C.C. 648 (Mo. Ct. App. 1973).

A novel case worth noting is *De La Hoya v. Slim's Gun Shop*, 80 Cal. App. 3d 6, 146 Cal. Rptr. 68, 24 U.C.C. 45 (1978). The plaintiff had purchased what turned out to be a stolen handgun from the defendant, a licensed gun dealer, for $140. De La Hoya apparently did nothing illegal or untoward with the gun, but in any event the police became aware that he was in possession of a stolen gun and arrested him. It ultimately cost him $800 in legal fees to have the criminal charges against him dropped. In his suit for breach of the warranty of title, the gun shop was made to pay not only the $140 value of the gun but the $800 expense it had caused the plaintiff as well.

One way a buyer can avoid having to deal with the question of attorney's fees in such a situation is to take advantage of the so-called "vouching in" provision of Article 2. See §2-607(5).

5b. Chris should be able to recover the costs involved in a successful defense, although the authority for this is not that easy to find in the Code. In earlier law, and in the Uniform Sales Act, there was found a direct expression of *warranty of quiet possession* to deal with cases such as this. There is no such language in §2-312 and, in fact, Comment 1 to the section states that "[t]he warranty of quiet possession is abolished." However, the comment goes on to say, "Disturbance of quiet possession, although not mentioned specifically, is one way, among many, in which the breach of warranty of title may be established." It's hard to read this in any other way than that something pretty close to the historical warranty of quiet possession is still available to aggrieved buyers, even if they aren't allowed to call it exactly that. The courts support this understanding, the most famous language being from *American Container Corp. v. Hanley Trucking Corp.*, 111 N.J. Super. 322, 268 A.2d 313, 7 U.C.C. 1301 (1970):

> The purchaser of goods warranted as to title has a right to rely on the fact that he will not be required, at some later time, to enter into a contest over the validity of his ownership. The mere casting of a substantial shadow over his title, regardless of the ultimate outcome, is sufficient to violate the warranty of good title.

The Code does not answer the question of exactly how substantial a shadow must be in order to put the burden of defending against it on the seller under this theory. In one recent case, the court commented:

> [A] purchaser can recover for breach of warranty of title when he demonstrates the existence of a substantial cloud or shadow on his title, regardless of whether it eventually develops that any third party's title is superior. Whether a substantial cloud or shadow exists in relation to a purchaser's title is a mixed question of law and fact and must be determined on a case-by-case basis. Surely the cloud on the title must be predicated on some objective factor and the baseless anxiety of the hypersensitive purchaser regarding the validity of his title will not result in a breach of warranty.

Maroone Chevrolet, Inc. v. Nordstrom, 587 So. 2d 514, 15 U.C.C.2d 759 (Fla. Dist. Ct. App. 1991). So much for the question of how dark the shadow or how gloomy the clouds. Nor is it clear under §2-312 whether the buyer must show some way in which his seller's behavior helped create the difficulty. In other words, suppose that some stranger came to me with the allegation that the computer on which I'm writing this had in fact been stolen from him one year before I bought it from the retail dealer. Sounds pretty flimsy, but I'd still have to defend against this stranger's account if he persisted in his claim. (You can't just lay this off on my hypersensitivity. A suit has been filed against me.) We can assume that I would win eventually, but not without incurring some expense and a good deal of aggravation. If the claim were no stronger than appears from what I've just laid out, and if there were no reason to suspect that anything the dealer did or failed to do helped give rise to the claim or encourage this stranger's strange behavior, would I have any rights against the dealer? It's very unlikely. I do, indeed, have the right to the quiet possession of my computer, but not all disruptions of that quietude should be the responsibility of the dealer.

For another case where the notion of quiet possession was involved, see *Jefferson v. Jones,* 286 Md. 544, 408 A.2d 1036, 27 U.C.C. 1174 (1979), which arose out of the sale of a motorcycle. As part of the transaction, the seller delivered to the buyer a certificate of title covering the machine. Unfortunately, and due only to an innocent mistake on the seller's part, the serial number on the certificate was wrong. It didn't match that of the motorcycle. When a policeman became aware of this mismatch (some two years after the sale), the motorcycle was impounded. The buyer was ultimately successful in establishing title, but it took him a significant amount of time and money to prove the property was his and actually get it back. The court held that a breach of the warranty of title had occurred and that the buyer was to be compensated for his losses. Presumably this could include some measure of damages for the loss of use of the machine for a period of time.

6a. It is doubtful here that Marv has any defense based on the "as is" clause. Any argument by a seller that the warranty of title has been effectively "excluded or modified" is governed by §2-312(2). (Later, in Chapter 14, we will take an extended look at warranty disclaimers as they are governed by other sections, but the point here is that those sections deal only with the warranties of quality, *not* the warranty of title. See Comment 6 to §2-312.) The question then is whether the "as is" provision is the kind of "specific language" which will satisfy §2-312(2). As you can imagine, getting title and the warranty of title is of major importance to just about any buyer. It's rare that a buyer will pay good money for something which may or may not turn out to be his or hers at the end of the day. The courts respond to this by holding any language argued to disclaim the warranty of title up to a particularly high standard. "As is" was found not to be sufficiently specific in *Eccher v. Small Business Administration,* 643 F.2d 1388, 30 U.C.C. 1524 (10th Cir. 1981). In *Jones v. Linebaugh,* 34 Mich. App. 305, 191 N.W.2d 142, 9 U.C.C. 1187 (1971), the bill of sale given to the buyer by the seller of two Bugatti automobiles said that the seller was transferring all of his "right, title and interest" in the autos and that to the "best of [his] knowledge there [was] no title in existence by way of registration with the State of Michigan or with any other State or Nation." In the course of the earlier negotiations, the seller had acknowledged to the buyer that he didn't have title, but the buyer had asked him to get title and the seller had said that his attorney was working on it. Under the situation, the court held that the warranty of title had not been disclaimed by the language in the bill of sale.

6b. Harry will not have an action based on the warranty of title. Marv can argue that any such warranty was excluded in this instance because the sale was made under "circumstances which [gave] the buyer reason to know that the person selling does not claim title in himself or that he is purporting to sell only such right or title as he or a third person may have." The strength of Marv's position may not be obvious from this language, but he will point to Comment 5, which makes clear what kinds of "circumstances" the drafters were thinking of here. This result, of course, depends on Harry's having been aware, or having had reason to know, that Marv was selling only in the capacity of a foreclosing lienholder.

6c. The question here is whether the mysterious Marv can make the argument that the sale was made under "circumstances" which gave Harry reason to know that he, Marv, wasn't purporting that he could legitimately transfer good title. This is probably only an academic question, of course, since it's hard to imagine that Harry would ever be able to find Marv (if that is his real name) now and get an effective suit going against him. Not surprisingly, I know of no reported cases on point.

Before wrapping up matters on title and the warranty of title, we should at least refer to §2-312(3) and the Buyer's Obligation Against Infringement which is there set forth. I did not include any questions on this provision, as it is not really a matter of title and is truly tangential to the subject at hand. Comment 3 explains it pretty well if you find the language unclear. As far as I can tell there has never been any reported litigation involving this subsection.

12

Express Warranties of Quality

A Bit of History

Buyers buying particular goods expect to get something. They expect to get the tangible object itself, of course, and beyond that to be blessed with title to the property as we discussed in the previous chapter. It is important to recognize, however, the whole host of other expectations buyers will normally have. A buyer is not, we assume, dealing for a mysterious something hidden in a black box. He or she is making the purchase because of what the thing is, or at least because of what the buyer believes the thing is (what it is made out of, what it can do, etc.). The buyer wants the thing itself, but beyond that wants it for the *qualities* he or she understands it to have. If it does live up to these expectations (or if it is even more desirable), all well and good; if the goods are not as the buyer presumed them to be, he or she will naturally expect to have some rights against the seller. If such rights are available it is because he or she has, as a buyer, received certain *warranties of quality* along with actual delivery of and title to the goods. As the Code drafters say in Comment 4 to §2-313, the whole idea behind the law of warranty is "to determine what it is that the seller has in essence agreed to sell."

This and the following chapters will explore the law relating to warranties of quality as it now pertains to sales of goods under Article 2 of the Uniform Commercial Code.* We live, study, and practice law in the present. To make sense of the Article 2 approach, however, it is worthwhile to spend some time on a bit of ancient history. Actually, our history lesson

---

*Warranties taken by the lessee under Article 2A are dealt with separately in Chapter 16.

need not go back to ancient times, but only to seventeenth-century England and the heyday of the doctrine of *caveat emptor.* As a matter of fact, there is plenty of historical evidence that in even earlier times the English legal system afforded more protection to the buyer, albeit in forms that we would not easily recognize today as warranty law, than it would in the common law courts of the 1600s. But discussion of warranty law always seems to start then and there with the well-known case of *Chandelor v. Lopus,* 79 Eng. Rep. 3 (1625), and in this we can follow tradition.

In *Chandelor* the plaintiff had sold the defendant something which he had described as a "bezoar [or bezar] stone." A bezoar stone was apparently a hard object recovered from the internal organs of a goat believed at least by some at the time to have remarkable healing powers. The seller never received payment for this distinctive bit of goods. When he brought suit for the purchase price the buyer defended on the ground that what he had received was not what he thought he was getting. He claimed it wasn't a bezoar stone at all. Whether by this the buyer meant that he believed it hadn't come from a goat's innards or that even if it had it didn't work like a real bezoar stone should, we do not know. In any event, such subtleties would not have mattered to the Exchequer Chamber, which ruled that the seller had given no warranty of any kind that it was such a stone. Why? The seller may have referred to the item as a "bezoar stone." He may have affirmed that it was just such a thing. But, the court noted, he had never expressly and explicitly *promised* that it was a bezoar stone. That being the case, there could be no warranty. In the words of the court:

> [T]he bare affirmation that it was a bezar-stone, without warranting it to be so, is no cause of action; and although he knew it to be no bezar-stone, it is not material; for everyone in selling his wares will affirm that his wares are good, or the wares which he sells is sound; and yet if he does not warrant them to be so, it is no cause of action. . . .

We should be careful. The law in seventeenth-century England was not that a buyer had no hope of receiving warranty protection from his seller. The concept of warranty was around. If the buyer expected to get a warranty, however, he had to have elicited for his benefit a direct and explicit promise to that effect from the seller. A "mere description" of the goods as being such-and-such would not suffice. Use by the seller of the explicit language of promise was all important.

Moving forward in time and into this hemisphere, we find the highest court of New York following essentially the same line in *Seixas v. Woods,* 2 Caines 48 (1804). The defendant sold some wood to the plaintiff, which had been advertised as "brazilletto," a particular kind of expensive wood. The bill of sale delivered to the buyer called it "brazilletto." The invoice the seller had received from the person who sold it to *him,* a paper which he showed to the buyer, referred to it as "brazilletto." There was apparently no reason to doubt that the seller himself thought it was indeed the stuff. "In fact," said the court, "neither party knew it to be other than brazilletto, nor was any fraud imputed." It turned out of course that the wood was nothing of the kind but was instead peachum, an inferior type of wood "worth hardly anything." The buyer sued the seller for his money back, but recovered nothing. Again, the fact that the entire sale was made with reference to a particular description of the goods was of no avail for the buyer. It was, said the court, "a clear case for the defendant." As of 1804 a buyer can, we are told, protect himself and make sure he is getting exactly what he expects by his own vigilance. He can inspect the goods and make sure of what he is getting. "And even against his own want of vigilance, the purchaser may provide, by requiring the vendor *expressly* to warranty the article." The emphasis in this quotation is mine, not the court's, but the point is unmistakable. "The mentioning the wood, as brazilletto wood in the bill of parcels, and in advertisement some days previous to the sale, did not amount to a warranty to the plaintiffs." Even in 1804 the evidence must show that the seller *intended* to create a warranty. Otherwise, let the buyer beware.

The common law doctrine of *caveat emptor* eventually began to wear away with the passage of time. The process, however, was anything but rapid. Only in 1872 did an authoritative court in New York recognize that the doctrine of *Chandelor v. Lopus* "has long since been exploded, and the case itself is no longer regarded as good law in this country or England." *Hawkins v. Pemberton*, 51 N.Y. 198 (1872). The court went on to remark that "the rule" of *Seixas v. Wood* "has been thoroughly overturned since the courts hold that any positive affirmation or representation as to the character or quality of an article sold may constitute a warranty."

This movement in the direction of greater warranty protection for buyers was furthered by the adoption of the Uniform Sales Act in the earlier years of this century. Section 12 of that Act provided in one subsection that, "Any affirmation of fact or any promise by the seller relating to the goods is an express warranty if the natural tendency of such affirmation or promise is to induce the buyer to purchase the goods, and if the buyer purchases the goods relying thereon." Meanwhile, in other parts of the forest, the notion was developing that even where there was no express language—not an affirmation of fact much less a promise—which the buyer could point to as having influenced his or her purchase, warranty protection might be appropriate. The idea that a seller might warrant the goods' qualities in other ways (what would come to be known by the awkward terms *merchantability* and *fitness for a particular purpose*) was beginning to take hold. Our interest, of course, is in the shape these ideas were eventually to take in Article 2.

Article 2's Scheme for Warranties of Quality

Warranties of quality under Article 2 come in two flavors, *express* and *implied*. This chapter deals with the creation and extent of the express warranties as provided for under §2-313. The following chapter will deal with both the implied warranty of merchantability and the implied warranty of fitness for a particular purpose. As we will see in later parts of the book, if the goods are not as warranted the buyer has a variety of possible responses. He or she may decline to accept the faulty goods, may in some instances revoke an acceptance already made, or may seek money damages for breach of warranty. But all that will come later. For the moment we are concerned only with *when* and *how* buyers can claim that the goods they have purchased are warranted as to quality and beyond that *exactly what* that warranty covers.

It needs to be emphasized at the outset that any time a buyer wants to make an argument based on the goods' failure to be as warranted, it is imperative that his or her argument be made with precision and in detail. I can't stress this enough. It is not sufficient just to wave one's hands about and say that there surely is some warranty of some sort or another floating out there somewhere. The buyer will be expected to state as precisely as possible *what type* of warranty he or she is claiming as part of the contract, *what qualities* it covers, and *how* it was created. What are the *specific facts* in the instant situation that brought *this particular warranty* being relied upon into being?

Once you have finished this and the following chapter, it will be apparent to you how often warranties can overlap. That is, it will often be possible for the buyer in even the simplest fact pattern to claim to be disappointed by the failure of the goods to meet more than one warranty or warranties of more than one type. It is tempting for the law student and also for the practitioner in such situations to end the analysis as soon as one idea pops up that seems to work. This, however, would be a mistake. If a situation allows for the argument that a set of cumulative warranties were created, it is important to at least note each and every one. See §2-317. Why this piling on? For one thing, of course, the skillful advocate is usually well advised to keep as many arrows in the quiver as possible. But there's more to it than this. As you will learn in Chapter 14, the warranties of quality may be (and often are) excluded or modified by the seller in a variety of ways, but the means by which these warranties may be so disclaimed, and the effectiveness of these means, are different for different types of warranties. In particular, it will be much more difficult for a seller effectively to disclaim any warranty that can be successfully characterized as an express warranty, as opposed to an implied warranty. The type of warranty established can make a big difference to the ultimate result. As you work your way through the next couple of chapters, keep alert to all possibilities.

Express Warranties Under Article 2

Section 2-313 is the one place we need look in Article 2 for the rules regarding when and how "express warranties by the seller are created." You should read through that section now. The overall intention of the drafters seems fairly clear. Still, even in a first rough reading you undoubtedly noted some phrases that suggest the kinds of problems we are in for when we actually try to apply the language. The questions that follow will lead you through the issues that have come up under §2-313. There are, as you might expect, a large number of cases decided under this section. Also as you might expect, the results do not quickly (or perhaps ever) give way to any easy generalities. Each decision (even those we may admire) seems so grounded in the facts of the particular case that it will be hard to say much more with assurance than that the questions of when and how an express warranty arises under this section tend to be resolved by the facts as they are presented. This doesn't mean, of course, that there is not plenty to be gained by carefully working through the questions. Section 2-313 is typical of the sort of code provision that is best studied with a mind toward picking up an approach to and an appreciation of the issues that come up and the facts that tend towards one result as opposed to the other, rather than any hard and fast rules. With that said, we proceed.

EXAMPLES

1.   Sal, a dealer in industrial chemicals, receives 20 barrels from a chemical manufacturing company in response to her order for this much of a chemical called blue vitriol. Each barrel is marked "B. Vitriol." Bernard, who uses this chemical in his business, arranges to buy a barrel of it from Sal. His purchase order and the confirmation sent back to him by Sal both refer to "Blue Vitriol." Sal delivers to him one of the 20 barrels, which it turns out actually contains a compound called red vitriol, similar in composition to blue vitriol but inferior in quality.

   a.   Has Sal breached an express warranty?

   b.   Could Sal successfully defend herself by showing she never explicitly said she "guaranteed" or "warranted" that the delivery would be of blue vitriol?

   c.   Could she defend herself by showing she had no intention of assuming responsibility for its being blue vitriol?

   d.   Could she defend herself by showing she had every reason to believe there was blue vitriol in the barrel? That is, she can show that she had never had trouble with mislabelling or misdelivery from this manufacturer before, and that it is not customary for a dealer in her position to open and independently check what is in the barrels it sells to buyers such as Bernard.

   e.   Would your answers be any different if what was delivered was actually *purple* vitriol, a product much more valuable than standard blue vitriol?

2.   Buyer contracts to purchase a stated quantity of "#2 milling wheat" from the seller. Is an express warranty part of the deal? If so, for what?

3.   Betty goes to Carmen's Used Auto Emporium, where she sees a used car which appeals to her. It is marked "1979 Pontiac" on the windshield. She agrees to buy the car from Carmen, and the bill of sale states that

the sale is of a "1979 Pontiac." Betty drives off in the car. Based on each of the following additional facts, determine what express warranties, if any, Betty has gotten from Carmen.

a. First, the baseline: *no* additional facts.

b. Prior to entering into the sales agreement, Carmen told Betty "it has power steering and power brakes."

c. When first examining the car, Betty looked at the odometer and saw that it read 131,257 miles.

d. In the car's glove compartment Betty found the various papers which had been issued to its original owner. Among these were a "Maintenance Log" which indicated that the car had been regularly serviced.

e. The car's windshield born a sticker indicating that it had passed the state's mandatory safety and pollution control inspection for the current year.

f. In the course of negotiations Carmen had said to her, "This is the finest car I've ever had on my lot!"

4.   The Royal Business Machine Corporation sold some 128 plain paper copiers to one Boohler, a dealer in copying machines. In a suit brought by Boohler, the trial court found that the manufacturer had made and breached the following express warranties:

(a) that the models purchased and their components were of high quality;
(b) that experience and testing had shown that the frequency of repairs was very low on such machines and would remain so;
(c) that replacement parts were readily available;
(d) that the cost of maintenance for each machine and cost of supplies was and would remain low, no more than 1/2 cent per copy;
(e) that the machines had been extensively tested and were ready to be marketed;
(f) that experience and reasonable projections had shown that the purchase of these machines by the buyer for lease to his customers would return substantial profits to him;
(g) that the machines were safe and could not cause fires; and
(h) that service calls would be required for the machines on the average of every 7,000 to 9,000 copies, including preventative maintenance calls.

The trial court awarded the buyer some $1,171,216.16 in damages along with substantial attorney's fees. On appeal Royal Business Machine argued that, contrary to what the lower court had found, none of the statements attributed to it were the type of language which created express warranties. As the appellate judge, which of these findings by the trial judge, if any, would you reverse?

5.   Alan, a suburban homeowner, was having trouble with crabgrass on his property. He went to Chuck's Lawn and Garden Supply shop. As he looked over the vast assortment of lawn care products and weedkillers, he confided his problem to Chuck. Chuck pointed to a product called

"Miracle Kill" and said to Alan, "This will do you just fine." When Alan buys the stuff, has he gotten any express warranties from Chuck?

6.   Nuts Incorporated is in the business of selling fresh nuts to processors. It sent a small sample of fresh Malawi peanuts to Snacks International along with an offer to sell such nuts at stated prices. Snacks had the sample fried, oil-roasted, and tested. The results were satisfactory, and Snacks entered into a contract to buy a large amount of these nuts. When the first delivery was put through Snacks's production process, the outcome was a large batch of processed nuts that had a terrible taste and gave off an awful odor. It becomes clear that the nuts are the problem. Unlike those originally sent to the processor, those delivered do not respond favorably to Snacks's process (to put it mildly). Has Nuts breached an express warranty?

7.   Karl goes into Sam's jewelry store intent on buying a watch. Among those out on display is a Chrono SX. Beside it is a display card listing various features. Included on the list is the line "Stop Watch Feature." Karl looks over the display carefully and then buys the watch. Later he discovers that, despite all its dials, read-outs and buttons, there is no way it can operate as a stopwatch. Karl brings the watch back into Sam demanding satisfaction.

      a. Karl would seem to have a clear breach of express warranty argument. Would it make any difference if it turned out that when Sam was trying to make the sale he had made a special point of the Stop Watch Feature to Karl who had said something like, "Oh, I don't care about that. Who needs a stopwatch anyway?"

      b. What would be the result if there had been no discussion at all about this feature at the time of sale, and while the display did mention it, Karl has to admit he never took a look at the card?

      c. Annie comes into Sam's shop. She has been lured in by an advertisement in that day's newspaper which features another watch, the Timola LT, listing among its attributes a "Glow-In-The-Dark Dial." This feature is important to Annie, but it never comes up in her direct discussions with Sam. She buys the watch. Does she have an express warranty for a glowing (or glowable?) dial?

      d.   Another potential customer, Barbara, comes into the store and is shown the Timola LT. She has not seen the ad in the paper, nor does the glowing feature come up in conversation with Sam. She agrees to buy the watch. After he has written up the sale and taken her credit card for payment, and while he is handing over her purchase, she asks him, "By the way, is this one of those watches you can read in the dark?" He answers, "Yes, it has a glow-in-the-dark dial." Barbara takes the watch and walks out of the store. She walks out with the watch, but does she also take with her any express warranty regarding the dial?

      e. That same day a third customer, Carol, buys a Timola LT from Sam. When she makes the purchase she has not yet seen the ad in the newspaper, nor does any mention of this feature come up while she is in the store. That evening at home she finally gets around to reading the paper. She sees the ad. Later that night she finds that the dial on her watch does not in fact glow in the dark. Does she have any claim against Sam?

EXPLANATIONS

1.   This question is inspired by the famous pre-Code case of *Hawkins v. Pemberton,* 51 N.Y. 198 (1872), but you should consider it under §2-313. It should be clear from reading that section that Sal has indeed broken an express warranty that what she sold Bernard would be the chemical blue vitriol. This is a classic sale by description now dealt with under §2-313(1)(b). The description of the goods as "Blue Vitriol" was made "part of the basis of the bargain" between Sal and Bernard and hence "creates an express warranty that the goods shall conform to the description." (The "basis of the bargain" criterion will cause no end of difficulty in some cases, as we'll discuss later on, but there can be no question it is met here.)

None of the factors offered up by Sal makes any difference. The first part of §2-313(2)—the language up to the comma—expressly states that the fact that Sal did not use the exact language of warranty does not matter, nor is it relevant whether or not she had the intention to make such a warranty. She is responsible under the warranty because she made the sale with reference to this description. The fact that she did not, or could not, or customarily would not check before sending a barrel out is irrelevant as well. *She breaches the warranty when the stuff isn't what it is supposed to be.* How or why the mix-up occurred is, of course, something she may want to worry about. The point is, however, that it is *her* problem and not one she has shifted in these circumstances onto Bernard.

Regarding Example 1e, nothing in the analysis would change if what was delivered was the much more valuable purple variety. True, Bernard might in this situation not want to make a stink about the improper delivery, but an express warranty has most definitely been breached by Sal. This serves to remind us that what is injurious about a seller's breaching a warranty of quality is not that he or she has intentionally tried to mislead or defraud the buyer or even that he or she has tendered to the buyer something decidedly worse than what was expected. It is the tender of something *different* from what was contracted for, even if done in total innocence, that is the nature of the wrong.

2.   Clearly a warranty has been made by description just as in the previous Example, and it is a warranty that what is delivered will in fact be "#2 milling wheat." The question, of course, is what exactly that is. How do we determine precisely what is covered by a given description? I would assume that "#2 milling wheat" would have to be what I understand to be the stuff called "wheat," but beyond that I would be pretty much in the dark. Presumably the test in such a situation is something like what a reasonable person in the buyer's position, buying in that particular

market, would expect to be delivered when a contract is made under this description. In the case of *W.A. Davis Realty, Inc. v. Wakelon Agri-Products, Inc.,* 351 S.E.2d 816, 3 U.C.C.2d 507 (N.C. Ct. App. 1987), the buyer, a milling company which produced self-rising flour, bought wheat of this description. The court held that, under the circumstances, among its other protections the buyer had received an express warranty that it would receive wheat that was "grade Number 2 according to U.S. Department of Agriculture standards."

Sometimes the issues involved in a sale by description are trickier than you might expect, as the next Example makes all too clear.

3a. This is easy, at least initially. Carmen warrants to Betty that the item she is purchasing is a 1979 Pontiac. In most cases I think we know what that means, or more specifically, what that would mean to "a reasonable used car buyer." The car is a Pontiac, meaning that it was made by the company that makes Pontiacs and was made by that company to be a Pontiac. Further we take it that the car was made as a Pontiac during the 1979 model year. This seems straightforward enough, but consider the following cases.

The easiest cases are ones of simple erroneous description. In *Best Buick, Inc. v. Welcome,* 18 U.C.C. 75 (Mass. Ct. App. 1975), the defendant gave his old Mercedes Benz as a trade-in when he purchased a new car from the plaintiff dealership. The agreement between the parties referred to the trade-in as a "1970 Mercedes," which is what the defendant believed it to be. He had earlier bought it from another as a 1970 model. When it turned out that it was actually a 1968 Mercedes, the dealership sued for the difference in the trade-in allowance it would have given had the car been correctly identified and the allowance it had in fact given based on the 1970 identification. The defendant was considered in the case to be the seller of the car he traded in, and hence to have given an express warranty that the trade-in was as described. As the court pointed out, the fact that this consumer was innocent of any intent to deceive and had in fact himself been deceived earlier was no defense. "When a seller makes an express warranty which is not true, it is no defense that the seller had acted in good faith without knowledge of the defect." A similar result was reached when a 1976 Cadillac was traded in as a later, 1978 model in *Harney-Morgan Chevrolet-Olds Co. v. Rabin,* 118 Ill. App. 602, 455 N.E.2d 130, 37 U.C.C. 50 (1983).

In *Curry Motor Co., Inc. v. Hasty,* 505 So. 2d 347, 3 U.C.C. 2d 1373 (Ala. 1987), it was the consumer buyer who was able to take advantage of the notion of express warranty. In 1983 he purchased from the seller a truck that was described in the sales pitch and identified in the bill of sale as a "1979 Ford" pick-up. It was, indeed, a Ford pick-up truck and was in large part a 1979 model, but evidence showed that the engine had been replaced with an engine model that was vintage 1970 to 1973. Apparently it is common for dealers in used automobiles to put different components in used cars and trucks to get them in shape for resale. Here the evidence was that this substitution was not made by the seller himself, nor had he any knowledge that the 1979 truck he sold the buyer had an early 1970s engine in it. Still, the court held that it was proper for the jury to conclude that the buyer had received an express warranty that the engine, and not just the body of the truck, was manufactured in the 1979 model year.

Would the result in the *Curry* case have been the same if the evidence had been that the engine was of a 1979 vintage, even if it hadn't been the original engine installed in that particular chassis? That is, could the 1983 buyer of a used "1979 Ford" pick-up argue that he had received an express warranty—based on the model year and name alone—that the car was still basically the same set of pieces that were put together to make up one truck back in 1979? A reasonable buyer would presumably know that over time cars and trucks are repaired and new and replacement parts incorporated into them, but would replacement of the whole engine be too much? If at any time the seller had said that the car "has the original engine," then there would be no problem for the buyer. This would be an express warrant created by the affirmation of fact. The question I pose is whether the buyer could argue this warranty from the year and make description alone.

In *Currier v. Spencer*, 299 Ark. 182, 772 S.W.2d 309, 8 U.C.C.2d 974 (1989), Spencer had been sold what was described as a "one-owner 1984 Datsun 300ZX" as a used car in 1986. Before his check had cleared Spencer experienced troubles with the car and "discovered that the rear one-third had previously been replaced with that of another vehicle and the entire car had been repainted." The court found Currier, the seller, to be in breach of an express warranty. "Currier warranted the car to be a one-owner 1984 Datsun. What Spenser purchased was two-thirds of one car and one-third of another." Compare this case to *Zappanti v. Berge Service Center*, 26 Ariz. App. 398, 549 P.2d 178, 19 U.C.C. 96 (1976). Mr. Zappanti, a man with some experience in auto mechanics, had prior to his purchase considered constructing for himself a "dune buggy." Instead he and his wife decided to purchase the vehicle in dispute from the defendant. The window sticker identified it as a 1969 model, and the bill of sale referred to a "1969 Volkswagen Dunebuggy." After purchase Mr. Zappanti discovered, according to his allegations, that all the parts of the special reconstructed vehicle were from Volkswagen models of years earlier than 1969. It was not disputed that the major components were from models of 1967 and earlier. The defendant seller had identified the dune buggy as a 1969 model because that is how it was described to him when he took it as a trade-in from someone who had registered it in another state, Michigan. It turned out that under Michigan law, since such a vehicle has no model year, it is registered for title purposes as being of the model year in which it was cobbled together out of pieces of other vehicles. Apparently, the same rule would have applied in Arizona, the site of the sale to Zappanti, for registration purposes. Referring to the great deference played in the Code to trade usage and the commercial context of agreements, the court concluded that,

While plaintiffs contend that the affidavits with respect to vehicle title practices are not conclusive as to contractual dealings, plaintiffs have not offered any controverting affidavits reflecting a contrary trade usage, nor have they presented any sound legal or practical basis for holding as a matter of law that the defendant warranted that the components of the vehicle were 1969 components. In view of the material differences between specially constructed vehicles and conventional vehicle models, the absence of any express statements relating to the model year of the components of this vehicle, and in the further absence of any showing of trade usage supporting the position of the plaintiffs, there is no disputed issue of material fact. The summary judgment for defendant must be affirmed.

At least it's not going to be difficult to know what's a Pontiac and what's not. Or so you would think. In *Szajna v. General Motors Corp.*, 115 Ill. 2d 294, 503 N.E.2d 760, 2 U.C.C.2d 1268 (1986), the Illinois Supreme Court held that the designation of a new automobile as a "1976 Pontiac Ventura" alone did not create an express warranty "of the kind or nature of the car's components." Thus, the purchaser of such a car could not recover under a breach of express warranty theory despite the fact that the car he bought had been equipped at the factory with a transmission engineered for a Chevette and not the transmission specifically designed and intended for the 1976 Ventura.

3b. This clearly creates an express warranty that the car does indeed have power steering and power brakes. Betty's authority for this is found in §2-313(1)(a). Carmen's statement was "an affirmation of fact" which "relates to the goods." For the moment we'll assume that it also became "part of the basis of the bargain," even if that phrase will later be shown to be anything but easy to apply (see Example 7).

3c. There are several cases to serve as authority that the odometer reading creates an express warranty that the car has been driven that number of miles and no more, at least where the odometer reading is written into the sales agreement. Once in the bill of sale, it is easy to see this number as "an affirmation of fact or promise" as the section calls for. Would it be enough that Carmen should realize that a potential buyer would look at the car's dashboard itself and take some information from what she sees there? See *Rogers v. Crest Motors, Inc.*, 516 P.2d 445, 13 U.C.C. 1008 (Colo. Ct. App. 1973), which suggests this would suffice.

3d. Logbooks relating to airplanes were found to create express warranties in *Miles v. Kavanaugh*, 350 So. 2d 1090, 22 U.C.C. 911 (Fla. Dist. App. 1977), and *Limited Flying Club, Inc. v. Wood*, 632 F.2d 51, 29 U.C.C. 1497 (8th Cir. 1980). In each case, however, the buyer had been shown the records by the seller. If not an "affirmation of fact," doesn't this constitute a "description of the goods" that will create an express warranty? Should the situation be any different because the buyer found and looked at the maintenance records on her own?

3e. Even if the sticker is never distinctly referred to by the seller, it would seem to be part of the description of or an allegation about the car. After all, the seller may never directly point to the seats as part of the car, but isn't she warranting that they'll be there when it is delivered? In the one case that dealt with an inspection sticker, the court had no trouble finding that it did create an express warranty. The problem for the buyer was how far the warranty extended. The court concluded that "the sticker warrants only that on the date of inspection the car complied with the safety criteria designated by the Department of Revenue. . . . And, since an accident or other circumstance might alter the condition of the vehicle, the sticker could not serve to guarantee that the car would continue to meet those criteria after the date the sticker was issued." *Hummel v. Skyline Dodge, Inc.*, 41 Colo. App. 572, 589 P.2d 73, 26 U.C.C. 46 (1978).

3f. Betty would try to argue that this created an express warranty as "an affirmation of fact or promise" under subsection (1)(a). Carmen, however, would point to the concluding language in subsection (2): "[A]n affirmation merely of the value of the goods or a statement purporting to be merely the seller's opinion or commendation of the goods does not create a warranty." This language was meant by the drafters to continue the doctrine that what is sometimes called mere "seller's language" or "puffing" of the product does not in and of itself create any warranty protection for the buyer. Such language, which a reasonable buyer will presumably understand to mean no more than that the seller is very much in favor of making the sale, is in effect nothing on which the buyer should rely or even take particularly seriously.

In the instant case, the expression that the car is "the finest" ever is just about as good an example of pure puffery as you're likely to find. Or is it? Couldn't Betty make the argument that this is an affirmation or promise that the car is better than others she's been looking over at Carmen's? But the word "finest" is so nebulous that this argument would be hard to sustain. Would you, or anyone you know, make anything out of such a statement uttered by a used car dealer in the course of trying to close a sale?

Of course, making the distinction between language that does create an express warranty of quality and mere puffery is not always this easy, and in some cases it is as much a matter of guesswork as anything in Article 2. Anyone who suggests he or she has a sure-fire method of regularly sorting out mere puffing language from true warranties is, one might suggest, in training for the used car business. Often the question, if it is at all close, is simply left up to the trier of fact, and little can be said except that appellate courts usually give great deference to any decision that gets them off the hook. Just as a sampling involving statements by used car dealers, consider the following two typical cases. In *Crothers v. Cohen*, 384 N.W.2d 562, 1 U.C.C.2d 72 (Minn. Ct. App. 1986), the Minnesota Court of Appeals ruled that the trial court had not erred in submitting to the jury the question of whether an express warranty was created by the statement that a certain 1970 Dodge was a "good runner" made by the salesman to the 16-year-old plaintiff and his friend as they were all looking at the engine and listening to it run. The jury, in a suit to recover for the serious injuries sustained by the buyer when the Dodge went out of control and crashed into a tree on the day after the sale, apparently had no trouble in finding that a warranty had been created by the salesman's words. The Minnesota court let this stand, noting "Statements using the word 'good' in referring to the condition of personal property have been found to create express warranties in a number of cases." Contrast this result to that in *Web Press Services Corp. v. New London Motors, Inc.*, 203 Conn. 342, 525 A.2d 57, 3 U.C.C.2d 1386 (1987). There the Supreme Court of Connecticut held that it was not error for the lower court to conclude that oral statements that a used 1980 Ford Bronco was "excellent," in "mint" and "very good" condition and that it was an "unusual" vehicle all constituted no more than puffery and did not rise to the level of warranty language. Supporting its conclusion the Connecticut Court was able to point to cases in which "[s]tatements to the effect that a truck was in 'good condition' and that a motor was in 'perfect running order' have been held not to create express warranties."

4. The question is based on *Royal Business Machines v. Lorraine Corp.*, 633 F.2d 34, 30 U.C.C. 462 (7th Cir. 1980). The Seventh Circuit held that substantial evidence supported the district court's findings as to items *e, g, h*, and "the maintenance aspect" of *d*, but that as a matter of law *a, b, c, f*, and "the cost of supplies portion" of *d* could not be considered express warranties. Some of these seem fairly easy. Items *a* and *f* are good examples of puffery in its most classic form. The court also found *b* to be a puff, because the imprecise nature of the term *very low* "lacked the specificity of an affirmation of fact upon which a warranty could be predicated." The result is probably correct, but couldn't the buyer have argued that this assurance gave at least some kind of warranty that the frequency of repairs on such machines was lower than for many (most?) plain paper copiers? If the buyer's experience with this brand of copier had been particularly poor, might not assertion *b* stand for something?

The court's explanation for why item *c* and the portion of *d* that asserts that the future cost of supplies would remain low did not create express warranties is worth considering. It held that neither was an assertion "relating to the goods" as is required by §2-313(1)(a). Doesn't the availability of replacement parts for a complicated bit of machinery relate to that machine in just the kind of way that buyers care about and indeed ask about? The relationship criterion of §2-313 must have some purpose, but I'm not sure it's meant to eliminate assertions like that in item *c*. What would be a clear example of something where the lack of relationship would rule out the finding of an express warranty? What about an assertion by the seller that "new government regulations will be issued soon that will mean many more small businesses will need to do copying?" If true, this could make the deal much more attractive to the buyer, and it certainly is an allegation of fact, not mere puffery. But it doesn't seem the kind of information which the buyer would or should rely upon the seller for, nor would the buyer expect the seller to be warranting that it is true. I don't find the allegations in the actual case, at least as to replacement parts, to be in this league. The drafter's choice of language, "relates to the goods," seems to me sufficiently encompassing to include such a statement about replacement parts.

The court in *Royal Business Machine*, by the way, expressed the test it was applying as follows:

> The decisive test for whether a given representation is a warranty or merely an expression of the seller's opinion is whether the seller asserts a fact of which the buyer is ignorant or merely states an opinion or judgment on a matter of which the seller has no special knowledge and on which the buyer may be expected also to have an opinion and to exercise his judgment.

Does this clarify matters? Was the court clearly following its own rule in the actual decisions rendered?

5.   Alan could argue that Chuck has given him an express warranty that the "Miracle Kill" does indeed kill crabgrass, or at least that it destroys it as well as anything else Alan could have bought in the store (or elsewhere?). As you will see in the following chapter, the situation will also give rise to the implied warranty of fitness for a particular purpose, and you might be tempted to wonder why we even bother with it here under the rubric of express warranties. (The answer to *that* question will be apparent in the second chapter to follow, which covers warranty disclaimers.) The implied warranties are much easier to disclaim, so if the stuff fails to have any effect on the crabgrass Alan's ability to establish an express warranty based on the language used here may be crucial to his fate.

6.   Yes. Nuts Incorporated created an express warranty by sample. See §2-313(1)(c) and *Alimenta (U.S.A.), Inc. v. Anheuser-Busch Cos., Inc.*, 803 F.2d 1160, 2 U.C.C.2d 441 (11th Cir. 1986), on which this question is based. Of course there is always the problem of exactly what the warranty was for. Here, presumably, the warranty is that the peanuts delivered would be *like those in the sample*, in that they would fry and roast up in the same way that the sample nuts did. The Court of Appeals quoted with approval a statement by the district court that there was an express warranty "that the peanuts supplied under the contract would conform to the size, appearance, and flavor of the sample peanuts." But assume the sample was hand-picked to contain only nice plump nuts—the kind you'd want to show off to a potential buyer. Does this mean the seller warranted that in the tons that were to be eventually delivered there'd not be a single dried-out dud? I doubt it. On that question I think it would be better to look at any other express warranties about overall

uniformity and quality. Or trade usage could come into play. Failing that we would have to turn to the implied warranty of merchantability, a concern for the next chapter.

As you may have noted, §2-313(1)(c) refers to *models* as well as *samples*. What's the difference? Comment 6 explains that a sample is "actually drawn from the bulk of the goods which is the subject matter of the sale," while a model is "offered for inspection when the subject matter is not at hand and has not been drawn from the bulk of the goods." In *Logan Equipment Corp. v. Simon Ariels, Inc.*, 736 F. Supp. 1188, 12 U.C.C.2d 387 (D. Mass. 1990), the buyer of eight specially manufactured 80-foot boomlifts argued that an express warranty that the lifts would not tip over under certain circumstances had been created by a demonstration of some 42-foot lifts constructed by the seller for another company. The plaintiff buyer apparently characterized its argument as one based on a sample, but this would seem to be a good case for a model if anything. If, for example, the lifts delivered to the buyer had been only 42 feet long, it surely could have been expected to complain. Unfortunately for the plaintiff, it ultimately wasn't a good case on any terms. The court held that differences between the machines demonstrated and those ordered, "as well as [the buyer's] own knowledge that a boomlift's design varies greatly with such characteristics as its boom length and weight," precluded any finding that the demonstration of the 42-foot cranes had in and of itself created any express warranty on the 80-foot units.

If the distinction between samples and models isn't all that clear we are fortunate in that it rarely seems to matter in any individual case. Either can create an express warranty, provided it "is made part of the basis of the bargain." As a full reading of Comment 6 makes clear, it is that last phrase that can cause the problem here, as it does generally for §2-313(1). The remaining questions finally take it on.

7a. If Karl saw the display before he made the purchase there should be no problem in his claiming an express warranty of quality. Would he have to prove, or even make some affirmative allegation, that he would not have bought the watch if he had not been led to believe it had this feature? That's doubtful under the Code. Why should there even be any doubt about this? The answer lies in the cryptic phrase *part of the basis of the bargain* and its history. Prior to adoption of Article 2 the governing law was laid out in the Uniform Sales Act. Section 12 of that Act required that for an affirmation of fact or a promise to create an express warranty it had to be shown that "the natural tendency of such affirmation or promise is to induce the buyer to purchase the goods," and further that "the buyer purchased the goods relying thereon. . . ." This was the classic language of a strict *reliance* requirement, and the courts in applying §12 took it seriously. The language of reliance was left out (purposefully, we are told) of the express warranty provision of Article 2. In its place is the requirement in each of the parts of §2-313(1) that the affirmation, or description, or sample, or whatever it is that is argued to give rise to an express warranty must become or be made a part of "the basis of the bargain." This unquestionably creates a statutory criterion of some sort, but of exactly what sort is anything but clear. The language, and particular that nebulous word "basis," came with no history attached. Over the years since its adoption it is fair to say that neither the courts nor the commentators have come to any agreement exactly what it means.

Is the basis of the bargain test just the reliance criterion in another guise? The drafters apparently thought (or hoped) not. Notice the language in Comment 3:

> No specific intention to make a warranty is necessary if any of these factors is made part of the basis of the bargain. In actual practice affirmations of fact made by a seller about the goods during a bargain are regarded as part of the description of those goods; hence no particular reliance on such statements need be shown in order to weave them into the fabric of the agreement.

Whatever the drafters might have meant by this comment, some writers have concluded that in actual practice the courts are left with little choice in applying the language of the statute itself other than to interpret it as virtually indistinguishable from the fairly strict reliance test of old. Others have found some room for a difference. At the very least it may be that under §2-313 the obligation of the plaintiff buyer to plead and prove actual reliance in a very concrete way has been eliminated, or very much watered down. Once the particular affirmation or model or what-have-you has been in some way brought into the picture during the sales process, the intention of the drafters at least seems to be that it can be assumed that it has become part of the basis of the bargain. I don't think Karl in our question would have much trouble, if any, with this requirement as long as he alleged in some general way that the display card was out and he was aware of it. I doubt he would have to swear on a stack of bibles that he had been looking for a watch with this feature, or that he would have bought something else if the Chrono SX didn't have it. He would probably still be OK if in a deposition he said something like, "Yeah, I probably would have bought it with or without the stopwatch, but I saw the display and it sure did have a lot of nifty features. For that kind of money, and with all those buttons and dials, I certainly figured I'd get a lot of gadgets."

The basis of the bargain test must have some bite to it, however, and we see this when we ask what would happen if at the time of sale Karl made the statement suggested in the Example, that is, that he just couldn't care less about having a stopwatch. One suggestion is that what the basis of the bargain criterion does is shift the burden of proof on the issue of reliance to the seller. And here Sam seems to have the evidence in hand to actually meet, at least initially, a burden of showing that Karl put *no reliance* on this line in the display card. A court would be hard pressed at this point to find for Karl. Perhaps Karl could show that, while he did indeed make this statement, by the time he left the store he had in fact been taken with this feature, or at least had been more impressed with the watch simply because it did have all of these doo-dads in the one package. Would it be fair to Sam to say that to prevail on this criterion he'd have to show that the stopwatch feature was actually a detriment or of absolutely no consequence in making the sale to Karl? I tend to think how such a case would come out would depend as much on how a particular court looked on the whole controversy and on other aspects of the parties' behavior as on anything else. If Karl's position were otherwise sympathetic, the basis of the bargain criterion might well not stand in his way. If it appeared to the court that Karl for entirely other reasons wanted to get out of his deal and was simply latching onto the lack of stopwatch timing as a convenient excuse, the phrase could be found to have much more vitality.

7b. We now consider how a court would handle the case if Karl had made no such disparaging comment about stopwatches, but did have to admit that he never really looked over the display card. Again, there is no easy—or at least no consistent—answer from the cases thus far. There are indeed cases which declare in no uncertain terms that for a buyer to make a claim of express warranty he or she must have at least been *aware* of the affirmation on which it is based prior to entering into the agreement. This does seem a minimal requirement, and even if adopted does not automatically bring into play all of the prior fussiness about full-blown reliance from the earlier law. It could be argued to be a minimal kind of reading of the "basis of the bargain" language. But even this is in doubt. Some courts have found instances that a warranty existed even where the buyer couldn't make a showing of knowledge at the time of purchase. Once again, all is up for grabs, and I tend to think that a lot would depend on the court's general disposition towards Karl's claim. A sympathetic court might take very seriously an argument by Karl that while at the time of purchase he wasn't cognizant of the particular assertion about the stopwatch feature, he had been induced to buy the expensive Chrono SX by the whole aura surrounding it, which certainly included the display card listing lots of impressive features. In this way perhaps the whole card, and all that it said, had become a part of the basis of the bargain and could now be used by Karl to his advantage.

7c. Annie should have the protection of an express warranty. As a matter of fact she does rely on an affirmation in the ad, but I doubt a court would make her prove it in any real way. The basis-of-the-bargain test, whatever it is, has been met here. There are a number of cases finding an express warranty based on statements, or even fair implications from pictures or other material, found in advertisements or sales brochures which were seen by the buyer. This is in keeping with the intention of the drafters. See the language from Comment 3 quoted above.

7d. Barbara will have a problem showing that Sam's statement to her became "part of the basis of the bargain" as is required by §2-313(1)(a).

The criterion must mean something here, and it will be hard for her to argue that whatever it means it is met in a situation where she did not even hear it until after the bargain was struck. But consider what is said in Comment 7:

> The precise time when words of description or affirmation are made or samples are shown is not material. The sole question is whether the language or samples or models are fairly to be regarded as part of the contract. If the language is used after the closing of the deal (as when the buyer when taking delivery asks and receives an additional assurance) the warranty becomes a modification, and need not be supported by consideration if it is otherwise reasonable and in order (Section 2-209).

The directive of this comment is far from indisputable given the statutory language and far from clear in its own right. If the affirmation comes after the bargain is struck, do the writers assert it is directly available to the buyer even given the basis-of-the-bargain test, which seems to be the import of the first sentence, or only because it is a later modification otherwise valid, that is a distinct addition to the contract? In many situations it might not make any difference, but in others it could. For example, if there is an arguably valid warranty disclaimer made part of the initial agreement, such a disclaimer would presumably operate on any term that was itself "a part of the basis of the bargain." It might not have the same effect on a term that was added later. The closing sentences in this comment seem to try to duck the inevitable issue under the statutory criterion, while the first sentence states "precise timing" to be "not material" without explanation.

I think that Barbara can make a good argument that the glow-in-the-dark feature is "part of the basis of the bargain" and hence creates a warranty to her. Of course it assumes that the §2-313(1) criterion and reliance, as conventionally understood, are not identical. Imagine, if you will, what might have happened if Sam's answer to her question had been different. That is, he tells her that the watch she has picked out has no such feature. There is then some likelihood that she might want to call the deal off, explaining the importance to her of being able to read her watch in the dark. Suppose she says that she's going to wait to buy a watch which makes this possible. What would Sam's response be? It's always possible, I guess, that Sam would adamantly refuse to let her change her mind now, giving her a lecture on the sanctity of contract, with its traditional notions of a completed acceptance and all that. In the real world, however, it seems to me at least as likely that Sam will think something like, "That's one deal that got away," take the watch back and rip up the credit card slip. If he does do this his thinking might be that, while he is sure she has already bought the watch and has no legal right to return it, it is simply good business for him to allow her to get away with this. But it's also possible that Sam's attitude is that he really hasn't made a sale until the (at least momentarily) satisfied customer leaves the shop with the item in hand. If that is so, then it doesn't seem to me incorrect to consider his *affirmative* answer to her question as part of the selling language he's put into the mix to nail down the sale and hence as "part of the basis of the bargain."

This argument does at least suggest some meaning for the basis-of-the-bargain test which isn't simply classical reliance in another guise and might actually work for Barbara before a court, although there is no real authority for it as of yet. We look not at the "precise timing" of the contract in the traditional sense of when the formal offer was formally accepted, but rather at when such a deal would "reasonably" seem set and inviolate as parties actually behave in commerce. But see what a slender reed it is. Suppose instead that Barbara had not asked Sam this question. Rather as he was wrapping up her purchase he said something like, "You're really going to be happy you chose this watch. It has all kind of features I didn't even mention. Did I tell you about the glow-in-the-dark dial?" Barbara hears him, thanks him, and leaves the store with her purchase. Does the fact that the seller offered this information gratis mean that she cannot later use it to her advantage? Note that the language of Comment 7 suggests that this would indeed make a difference, as the case I'm now posing is not one in which the buyer "asks and receives an additional assurance."

7e. Here's a case where there has clearly been no reliance, and it would be hard to argue there is anything even close to it. I think Carol would be out of luck. The argument we crafted for Barbara in the previous question might work here as well, but it does seem to be stretching things beyond the breaking point. What if Carol sees the ad two or three weeks later? Would she then be able to act as if she had never purchased the watch? There are a number of cases which contain clear statements to the effect that while an advertisement or a seller's brochure may indeed create an express warranty for the buyer, he or she must at least have seen or been aware of its existence at the time of purchase, and it seems hard to argue with this conclusion. See, for example, *Schmaltz v. Nissen,* 431 N.W.2d 657, 7 U.C.C.2d 1061 (S.Dak. 1988), in which the Supreme Court of South Dakota reasoned that a farmer buying seed could not have received an express warranty based on language found on the bags containing that seed as the language had not been read until delivery, after the sale was completed. "Without having read or even known of this language," the court said, "it is impossible to say this language was part of the basis of the bargain." So much for Comment 7's assertion that timing in such matters is "not material," although to be fair the Comment does say that *precise* timing doesn't matter, and maybe that's all we need.

One final puzzler before we leave the topic of express warranties. Imagine that Sam makes one more sale of the Timola, this time to someone named Darla. Several months later Darla is in his store on an unrelated matter. He says to her, "I see you are wearing that Timola I sold you. I hope you're happy with it. It really is an amazing deal. Did you realize that it's totally waterproof on top of everything else?" The next weekend Darla wears the watch while swimming and it is ruined. The Timola, whatever its other merits, is anything but waterproof. We presume that if a friend had innocently misled her in this way, she wouldn't have any legal cause of action against the friend. Does she have any rights against Sam, the jeweler, who sold it to her initially because he was the one to make the statement albeit much later in time and unrelated to the transaction? Your guess is as good as mine.

13

Implied Warranties of Quality

Introduction to the Implied Warranties

As we saw in the preceding chapter, express warranties become part of the sales contract through some conscious behavior on the part of the seller. In arriving at a deal the seller makes some statement of fact, adopts a particular description of the goods, or makes reference to a model or a sample. In other words, the seller takes some *action* which gives rise in the buyer to some manner of expectation as to the quality of the goods. The implied warranties, on the other hand, arise more out of the seller's *inaction*. Beyond what flows from the seller's explicit words and deeds, other expectations on the part of the buyer about the character of the goods seem to spring naturally from the overall circumstances of the sale (the whole gestalt, if you will) coupled with the seller's doing nothing in the circumstances to disabuse the buyer from these perfectly reasonable beliefs. In the following chapter we will discuss the tools a seller will have at hand (the direct action that he or she may take) to *escape* giving any type of implied warranty if that is his or her intention. Before we go into that, however, we will explore how and when implied warranties arise and become enforceable aspects of a contract for the sale of goods. In essence we are concerned with how the seller's *failure to act* can result in warranty protection for the buyer.

Under Article 2, implied warranties of quality are of two types. The initial challenge is to see what circumstances, what sets of facts, give rise to either or both. Look at §2-314(1). Barring an effective disclaimer or modification (which we've put off for a chapter), a *warranty of merchant-ability* is implied as long as two factual criteria are met. First of all, the transaction must be a contract of sale. As to this requirement, you can refer back to Chapter 1.* The second criterion is that the sale of goods must have been made by "a merchant with respect to goods of that kind." We dealt with Article 2's definition and special treatment of the *merchant* in Chapter 2, which you should review now if you haven't already done so.

That's it. If these two criteria are met then there is a warranty that the goods will be merchantable. Notice the various factors that need *not* be demonstrated in order to bring §2-314 into play. Just as in §2-313, there is no requirement that the seller intended to make any warranty or used any particular language of promise, nor is it relevant whether the seller knew or even could have known of the shortcomings of the goods. Unlike warranties arising under §2-313, however, there is no necessity that the seller use *any* language, samples, or models, or express anything in any way to the buyer. Nor is there any need for the buyer to show reliance on the seller, that anything became "part of the basis of the bargain" between the two, or even that the seller's merchant status played any part in the buyer's decision to take the product.

The issues of greatest concern under this section are by and large not whether a warranty of merchantability was made part of the contract. It's usually fairly obvious when this is so. In the Examples that follow you can assume that there was a sale and that the seller was a merchant. The puzzle will be to figure out as best we can exactly *what* the warranty of merchantability covers. The buyer is guaranteed something, but what exactly is far from self-evident. The drafters made no effort to define *merchantability* or the word *merchantable* in the Code. What help they give is to be found in §2-314(2), which you will want to read in connection with the Examples. This subsection provides not a definition but what is more like a listing of the least, the very minimum, that is and can be expected when purchasing from a merchant. It is not meant to be exhaustive. See Comment 6. As you'll soon discover, the heart of this provision is the right the buyer has to insist that anything bought from a merchant will be at least "fit for the ordinary purposes" for which such stuff is normally used. But what does this mean in actual day-to-day affairs?

The Examples and Explanations also ask you to examine the second type of implied warranty provided for in Article 2. The implied *warranty of fitness for a particular purpose* arises under §2-315. Here the substance of the warranty is at least initially much easier to characterize. If the buyer has a "particular purpose" for which he or she purchases the goods, and if a series of other criteria are met by the facts in the particular case, there is as part of the contract a warranty that the goods will be fit *for that particular purpose*. As to what is a "particular" versus an "ordinary purpose," you should read Comment 2 to this section. But is it all that clear?

---

*Note in addition the language specifying that "the serving for value of food and drink to be consumed either on the premises or elsewhere" is covered by the section. Prior to adoption of the Code this was a big and messy issue in the law of sales, and the drafters wanted to settle it once and for all. See Comment 5.

You should review now the various criteria which §2-315 sets up for anyone wanting to plead and prove this warranty. Notice in particular that it is not a requirement of §2-315 that the seller be a merchant. A casual seller can give this warranty as well as a merchant.

We explore the *when* and the *what,* and even a bit of the *wherefore,* of these implied warranties in the Examples. I think you'll find them particularly interesting. Moreover, if my years of experience with students are any indication, you may well be inspired by this material to think more than you ever have before about all of the purchases you make each day, what you expect will be true when things go right, and what horrible fate awaits you if things go even slightly wrong.

EXAMPLES

1.   Lisa goes into the Springfield Stationery Store, where she finds a display of regular wooden pencils on the front counter. She removes three from the display and places them before the clerk who says, "That'll be $1.50." Lisa pays that amount, takes the pencils, and makes her way home.

a.   Lisa sharpens one of the pencils to a nice neat point. When she starts to do her homework, she discovers that no matter how hard she tries she can't make any marks on her paper with the pencil. Was this pencil merchantable at the time of sale?

b.   Lisa takes the second pencil and sharpens that one. She writes with it for a time, but then the point breaks. Has she a claim that *this* pencil was unmerchantable?

c.   In frustration Lisa decides to do her homework in ink. Writing with a ballpoint pen is fine for a while, but eventually she makes a mistake. She tries to erase her error using the rubber tip on the end of the third of her pencils. It doesn't work. Was this, the third pencil, unmerchantable because the eraser doesn't erase?

d.   Lisa drops the idea of working in pen. She sharpens the third pencil, which writes perfectly well and without any breakage. She gets her homework done with no problem. She continues to use this pencil to do her schoolwork. Later in the week when she is resharpening the pencil she is surprised to discover that the lead in the pencil runs out about half way down its original length, leaving her with only a solid stick of wood painted yellow. Does she have a breach of warranty claim against the stationery store? Would your answer be the same if the lead had disappeared only as she was trying to get use out of the very last bit, say the last one-half inch of the pencil? In other words, how much lead should there be in an ordinary lead pencil?

2.   At the Springfield Quickimart, Marge takes from the shelf a can marked "Peas" and buys the can along with other groceries. At home when she opens the can she discovers it contains nothing but canned corn. It's perfectly safe, nutritious, and tasty corn, but it's just that—corn.

Was this can merchantable? If she chose to, could Marge successfully sue the Quickimart for this grave infraction? If so, what options would Abu, the owner of the Quickimart, have?

3. Bart, a ten-year-old boy, goes into a local variety store. From the candy selection he picks out a package of cinnamon flavored wooden toothpicks marketed under the name "Hot Cinnamon Fire Pix." Later on the playground he is sucking on one of the picks when he falls from the jungle gym, landing face-down on the surface below. The toothpick breaks and punctures his lower lip, leaving him with a scar. Bart sues the owner of the variety store claiming that the toothpick sold to him was unmerchantable. What result?

4. Homer decides to repaint the living room of his home. He goes to the local hardware store where, after looking over the color charts, he buys three cans of No Problemo brand paint, each of which is marked "Interior Egg-Shell White." He paints his walls. When the job is dry he is distressed to find that the area painted with two of the cans is slightly but noticeably darker than the area painted with the third. Either color comes close to that shown on the color chart, and either would satisfy Homer, but they are not the same: The overall effect is just not right. Does Homer have any claim against the store for breach of warranty?

5. Holiday Products Incorporated puts together baskets of fruits, candies, and other goodies, which it buys from various suppliers. It contracts to buy a large number of grapefruit "of size from 6 to 7 inches in diameter" from farmer Jones. When the grapefruit are delivered, Holiday discovers that they are virtually all from six to six and one-quarter inches in size. None is smaller than six inches, but very few are anywhere near seven inches. Has Jones breached the warranty of merchantability?

6. Maria buys a bright red tee-shirt in a local discount store for $2. After several washings she is unhappy because the color of the shirt has faded considerably and it has begun to shrink and lose its shape.

    a. Was the shirt unmerchantable at the time of sale?

    b. Suppose Maria had purchased the tee-shirt for $40 from a classy store ("The Gorge") located in a trendy upscale mall she visited when she went to the big city on her vacation. Was the shirt unmerchantable at the time of sale?

7. In 1990 Mr. Ireland buys a used 1979 Oldsmobile with 82,364 miles on it from Jane's Auto Sales. During the sale, Jane is careful not to make any express warranties about the car's quality. Within weeks of his purchase, the car's engine begins to repeatedly stall, knock, and wheeze. Does Ireland have a claim against Jane for breach of the implied warranty of merchantability?

8. Mrs. Webster, who had been born and brought up in New England, entered the Blue Chip Tea Room, a quaint Boston restaurant located on a wharf overlooking the ocean. She ordered a cup of fish chowder. After taking several spoonfuls she could feel something lodged in her throat.

Later, at Massachusetts General Hospital, a fish bone was found in her throat and removed. Was the chowder as served unmerchantable?

9. Tommy Phillips suffered injury when a chunk of turkey bone got caught in his throat. The bone had been hidden in a bite-sized cube of white turkey meat ladled, along with gravy and peas, onto a mound of mashed potatoes in his high school cafeteria in West Springfield, Massachusetts. Does Tommy have a case against the cafeteria?

10. Harold buys a new aftershave lotion. He liberally splashes it on his face. Within a few minutes his face is covered with a rash and has swollen up considerably. He discovers that the medical term for his condition is *contact dermatitis* and that it was brought on by an allergic reaction to the aftershave. On the basis of this information, can you conclude whether the aftershave as sold was merchantable?

11a.During her vacation in the country Bella goes into a photographic supply store owned by Steve. Showing Steve her camera, she says, "It's supposed to be a beautiful cloudless night tonight, and I'd love to take some pictures of the sky. I'll need some film. What have you got?" Steve takes a roll of Supermax 200 from a shelf and sells it to Bella. Using this film Bella takes a series of pictures, mostly of the night sky, which she has developed when she returns home. The pictures taken during daylight hours come out fine, but none of the nighttime pictures comes out. She then discovers that while Supermax 200 is a perfectly good film for general picture taking, it is not suitable for nighttime photography and certainly not for taking pictures of the stars. Has Steve breached the warranty of merchantability here? What about an implied warranty of fitness for a particular purpose?

   b. Suppose instead that Bella, after commenting on her interest in taking pictures of the stars, had concluded, "I hear that Supermax 200 is a good film. Give me some of that." Does this affect your answer to the previous question?

EXPLANATIONS

1a. Lisa's pencil is not merchantable. To be merchantable goods must be "at least . . . fit for the ordinary purposes for which such goods are used." This language from §2-314(2)(c), while it can't be held up as a code definition of merchantability or even the exclusive criterion, is obviously key to the concept. A pencil that won't make a mark on a piece of regular homework-type paper doesn't meet the standard. It would be different, of course, if Lisa were trying to write on wax paper or on a piece of plastic.

1b. Pencil number two would seem to be merchantable. For goods to be merchantable they need not be perfect or all that the buyer would hope. Of course the pencil would not be merchantable if Lisa could demonstrate that the point repeatedly broke when no more than "ordinary" pencil-pushing forced was applied.

   While it never appears in §2-314, the phrase or notion of *reasonable expectations* is useful, if admittedly fuzzy, in considering questions of merchantability. (We'll see later that it actually has become a term of art in one particular situation, when foodstuffs are involved.) In the field of express warranties we could ask what reasonable expectations were created by the overt actions and words of the seller; now we concentrate on what the buyer can reasonably expect from the goods based solely on the fact that they were purchased from a merchant who deals in goods of that kind. The goods should be what the buyer assumes them to be, what merchants sell when they sell goods of this kind. Pencils are expected to make marks on paper, but pencil points do break now and then. Let's be reasonable. Pencils are pencils. We expect them to do certain things, but they have their limitations, and we have learned to live in this less than perfect world. Lisa is learning the same lesson.

A case which I like in this regard, even if the court managed to decide it without any citation to the Code, is *Fanning v. Lemay,* 38 Ill. 2d 209, 230 N.E.2d 182, 4 U.C.C. 855 (1967). It was a rainy day. Ruth Fanning entered a laundromat intending to do some laundry, wearing a pair of shoes made by the U.S. Rubber Company which she had bought at Montgomery Ward. The asphalt tile floor of the laundromat was wet and slippery. Ms. Fanning slipped and fell to the floor, sustaining serious injuries. She sued, along with other defendants, the manufacturer of her sneakers and the store which sold them to her. Among the counts was one claiming that the shoes were not fit for the ordinary purposes for which they were purchased because the soles became "slippery and dangerous when wet and used upon asphalt tile." The Illinois Supreme Court approved the dismissal of this part of her claim.

> No facts are alleged setting forth any specific defect in the shoes,
> nor are there facts to show that in the respect alleged they
> were any different from shoes ordinarily worn by millions of other
> people. It is a matter of common knowledge that shoes are more likely
> to slip when wet than dry, but this provides no basis for the conclu-
> sion that a particular pair of shoes is dangerous or unsafe.

The court concluded, "The law does not require that common articles such as shoes be accident-proof, or that a manufacturer warn and protect against mishaps in their use." Reason and reasonableness triumphant.

1c. It doesn't seem reasonable to think that the eraser at the end of a pencil will erase a mark made in ink. It should, of course, erase pencil marks. But even here we can't push things too far. Suppose Lisa, using a pencil, makes a mistake in her work and tries to erase it. The eraser at the pencil's end does lift most of the markings from the paper, but it doesn't do so perfectly. There are still faint traces of what she had written, or perhaps more likely an indistinct smudge. The first few times this happens she may be surprised and even upset that the paper is not brought back to its pristine condition, but she's going to have to learn to live with it. Lisa continues to learn her lessons so she can grow up to be a better, more "reasonable" person. (Of course when she grows up to be a successful architect or graphic designer, she will and may reasonably expect more of the costly high-quality pencils, papers, and erasers she uses.)

1d. This is a trick question. There should not be any lead in a lead pencil, if by "lead" we mean the heavy bluish-gray metallic chemical element with atomic weight of 207.21. Even the yellow paint we commonly see on pencils is now expected to be lead-free for health and safety reasons. According to a recent definitive (and highly entertaining) study, the black-ish substance that's inside an American-made pencil of the twentieth century "might be a proprietary mixture of two kinds of graphite, from Sri Lanka and Mexico, clay from Missouri, gums from the Orient, and water from Pennsylvania." Henry Petroski, The Pencil: A History of Design and Circumstance (1992).

So we'll change the question to read how much of what we might call "pencil lead" should there be in your standard variety yellow wooden pencil? My guess is that most people assume the lead goes the whole way through the pencil's seven inches. I know I do. Where this assumption comes from and why I tend to think it a "reasonable" one, I'm not sure. I've never sharpened a pencil down that far. As a matter of fact, as Professor Petroski demonstrates (citing Jane Austen's Emma among other authorities), even well into the nineteenth century the lead of a pencil didn't necessarily extend through its entire length. It was a matter of economy. Graphite was not cheap. Once the pencil got too short it would be difficult to handle, so no one would use it anyway. They would, as I do today, move on to a new pencil.

Would it make sense to go back to these good old days when pencils had less lead in them but were presumably cheaper to some degree? As one who would benefit by spending less on pencils and suffer no countervailing loss, I'd be all for it. Why should I pay for some pencil lead I never get to use? Others who presently work their way through the last little bit of the pencil, and who may even positively enjoy doing so, would object. You begin to see how much is subsumed in this notion of "reasonable" expectations and "ordinary" use. Notice that the issue need not be characterized as some titanic struggle between righteous and demanding buyers and the pennypinching sellers who will always try to get away with giving the consumer as little as possible. What we are really talking about is a balance, an implicit set of trade-offs, between various sets of consumers. When we're dealing with standard off-the-shelf products (just the kind that merchants sell day in and day out), some consumers are going to be paying for features or a higher level of quality than they actually want or need. These people in effect subsidize their neighbors who do take advantage of the added features or appreciate the greater quality. Meanwhile others in the community would be willing to pay *even more* for a product that was distinctly better, but may not be able to find anything like it in the stores. As you continue on, you should keep in mind this notion of balance and trade-offs, not between naturally antagonistic buyers and sellers, but *among various groups of consumers.* It's always in the background, but starts to come to the fore in the food cases and is to be seen most dramatically in the case of atypical reactions or allergies with which we deal in Example 10.

2.   The can was not merchantable. Even if you assume that canned corn is fit for the ordinary purpose for which people buy other canned vegetables, including peas, its contents did not "conform to the promise or affirmations of fact made on the container," which is another thing to look for under §2-314(2)(f). The Quickimart operator is responsible for the breach of warranty. There would be no need for Marge to show that Abu knew the can was mistakenly labelled nor that there was any reason he "should have known" or was negligent in any way. Remember, breach of warranty liability is strict liability. The seller's intentions and state of mind are irrelevant. The thing sold was not what it was supposed to be. End of story, at least as far as Marge is concerned. Of course, if the Quickimart is made to pay Marge for this breach it should itself have a warranty action against whatever dealer supplied it with the mismarked can.

Note also from this example that, while many claims of breach of the warranty of merchantability involve products that end up harmful or downright dangerous to the buyer, this need not be the case. We can assume that canned corn is perfectly good for Marge and her family. The character of the breach is in her surprise or disappointment; what she got wasn't what she reasonably believed she was buying.

3.   No, I didn't make this one up. See *Killeen v. Harmon Grain Products, Inc.*, 11 Mass. App. 20, 413 N.E.2d 767, 30 U.C.C. 862 (1980). In addition to the store, the other defendants in the case were the manufacturer of the Hot Pix, the manager of the variety store, the manager's minor child (who had actually delivered the Pix to the injured child right there on the playground), and a teacher at the school. The appellate court upheld directed verdicts in favor of all defendants. Of interest to us is its holding that there was nothing unmerchantable about a toothpick just because it could splinter in this fashion or because it had a pointy end or two. In fact, as the trial judge pointed out, a consumer would presumably regard a toothpick with no pointed ends as defective rather than the other way around.

Here we see that just as a product doesn't have to be unsafe or harmful to be unmerchantable, a product which does offer the possibility of injury—which is "dangerous" in some fashion—isn't necessarily unmerchantable. In fact some things *must* have sharp edges or dangerous curves if they are to meet the buyer's expectations. A hunting knife would not be merchantable if it didn't come with a pretty sharp blade. A stick of dynamite which couldn't be made to explode under any condition whatsoever might be harmless, but it wouldn't be merchantable.

4.   The three cans of paint sold together were not merchantable. See §2-314(2)(d), requiring that the goods "run, within the variations permitted by the agreement, of even kind, quality and quantity within each unit and among all units involved." I know of no case focusing on this particular language in the section, although it would seem to be important.

Would Homer's case still be good if he had originally bought only two cans of paint and then, finding that he needed more, returned to the hardware store for the third a day or two later? What if he had dawdled so long that a month separated the two purchases?

5.   It appears Jones has breached. See §2-314(2)(b) and Comment 7.

6a. Just because the shirt eventually looks less than brand new doesn't mean it was unmerchantable when sold. But how long should goods wear and how well? How do you react to this—as a reasonable person?

We might take note of the case of *Suminski v. Maine Appliance Warehouse, Inc.,* 602 A.2d 1173, 18 U.C.C.2d 423 (Me. 1992). Paul Suminski bought a brand new television set from the defendant seller for $713.97 in May of 1988. Sometime in June 1989 the set began to turn off by itself, although it would come back on when Suminski clicked it off and then on again. About two months later it would not turn on at all. He contacted the seller whose representative told him that the period of express warranty had run and that the store's only obligation was to give him the name of a repair technician. It did not help matters any that the seller's manager stated that he had been in the appliance business a long time and had never heard of any implied warranty of merchantability. (When Suminski's attorney suggested to the manager that he contact his own attorney to confirm the existence of such a warranty, he promptly hung up.) Be that as it may, the Supreme Judicial Court of Maine held that the buyer had failed to establish a breach of the warranty of merchantability.

> No evidence was presented concerning the specific defect in the product. In some circumstances a breach of the implied warranty of merchantability under the U.C.C. may be established by circumstantial evidence. . . . In the case at bar, however, the television set was in all respects satisfactory during approximately thirteen months after it was purchased. For all that appears in the record, the malfunction at the time may have resulted from a defective switch, repairable at a small cost. We conclude that the sale of a major appliance with a switch that fails more than a year later, cannot support a finding that the entire appliance was unmerchantable when sold.

Was the key fact here that a switch is only a small part of the package? In later language the court suggests this underlies its result. But if the switch had not worked on delivery of the set, so that it could not have been turned on from day one, this would clearly have made the whole set unmerchantable. Isn't it of importance that the problem only cropped up after some time? But then if the picture tube had blown after thirteen months, what should be the result? If you think this would render a TV set unmerchantable, how long *do* you think a picture tube must last?

How long and how well a product can be expected to last must also be considered in light of the use to which it is put and how it is treated. Consider the case of *Hollingsworth v. Queen Carpet, Inc.,* 827 S.W.2d 306, 17 U.C.C.2d 1125 (Tenn. Ct. App. 1991). The plaintiff bought a large quantity of carpeting from the defendant for installation in an apartment complex he was constructing. It was conceded that the carpeting was installed properly, but after something like 18 to 24 months the top part of the carpeting began to unravel and separate from the backing. Technically this is known as *delamination*. In the words of one witness it began to "look like an ol' wrinkly dog." The plaintiff testified that carpeting in his other apartment projects usually had a life expectancy of 10 to 12 years. Other evidence suggested the normal life span of such carpeting to be in the range of at least five to seven years. It did seem something had gone wrong. The defendant seller offered evidence to back up its assertion that the bedraggled state of the carpet was a result of moisture left in it when it had been cleaned by tenants with the Rinse-n-Vac system which could be rented at the local grocery store. As the court sharply noted, the plaintiff offered no expert evidence on the cleaning matter. He rested his case solely on the short length of time the carpet had been useable. A trial court judgment for the plaintiff was reversed. The court of appeals held that the buyer had not met its burden of proof "that it was more probable that the carpet was not fit for its ordinary purpose at the time it was installed rather than that the delamination was caused by excessive moisture." Had you represented the buyer here, what would you have included in your evidentiary case? How hard do you think it would be to meet the burden imposed on the plaintiff here? (Or can you answer that question without knowing more about carpeting in general, carpet cleaning as it is usually carried out in Tennessee, and the Rinse-n-Vac system in particular?)

One additional hypothetical that is certainly worth thinking about is easy enough to state, if slightly unsettling. You buy a pet from a pet store. You give it a name, you give it a home. Later that pet dies. Does this mean it was unmerchantable at the time of sale? See *Bazzini v. Garrant,* 116 Misc. 2d 119, 455 N.Y.S.2d 77, 34 U.C.C. 1550 (1982), the case of the expiring toucan. Unfortunately, the opinion doesn't have a particularly good discussion of the merchantability issue, but it does contain a whole series of truly outrageous puns and some suggestion of what to do if your exotic pet bird suddenly is taken with a seizure. (Hint: Have some Gatorade on hand.)

We return finally to where we began. Did Maria have the right—the *legal* right under the UCC—to expect better of this tee-shirt? Certainly if it had lost all of its color on the very first washing, she would have had a right to complain, but she can't expect it to remain in a like-new condition indefinitely. What would you expect, or rather what *do* you expect, of a $2 tee-shirt?

6b. What you pay for an item surely influences what you expect of it. It seems the notion of merchantability would have to take this into account. Comment 7 says that "[i]n cases of doubt as to what quality is intended, the price at which a merchant closes a contract is an excellent index of the nature and scope of his obligation under this section." So the question now is what Maria could and would reasonably expect *of a $40 tee-shirt?* Why do (reasonable) people sometimes pay more when they could get away with paying less? If you posit that more expensive tee-shirts are desired only because of the added status they afford the owner, then perhaps this shirt doesn't have to wear any better than a cheap one. If, however, you believe that certain shirts can be successfully marketed at higher prices because they are of better materials, made with more care, or made to last longer (or if potential buyers are expected to believe something of the sort), then the amount of wear Maria has a right to expect is that much higher.

7.   The warranty of merchantability applies to the sale of used goods. See Comment 3, which notes however that the seller's obligation is only such as is "appropriate to such goods." How fit must used goods be? As numerous courts have noted, that depends.

> A late model, low mileage car, sold at a premium price, is expected
> to be in far better condition and to last longer than an old,
> high mileage, 'rough' car that is sold for little above scrap value.

Dale v. King Lincoln-Mercury, Inc., 234 Kan. 840, 676 P.2d 744, 38 U.C.C. 35 (1984). As for an affirmative statement of what rightly can be expected, different courts have come up with a variety of formulations, although there doesn't seem to be any real disagreement in substance. The car should be "in reasonably safe condition and substantially free of defects that would render it inoperable." It should "perform up to the level reasonably expected of a car of the same age, mileage, and price." The defects should not be so serious as to "deprive the buyer of the beneficial use of the automobile." In the recent case of *Faulkingham v. Seacoast Subaru, Inc.,* 577 A.2d 772, 13 U.C.C.2d 366 (Me. 1990), the Supreme Judicial Court of Maine refused to overturn a judgment against a seller where the trial judge had found that the car "proved to be unreliable transportation as a commuter vehicle or for the other travel use of the [buyer]."

At the same time a used car is, after all, a used car. As the court noted in *Ireland v. J.L.'s Auto Sales, Inc.,* 151 Misc. 2d 1019, 574 N.Y.S.2d 262, 16 U.C.C.2d 82 (1991) (the case on which this question is based), "no eleven-year-old motor vehicle, having in excess of 82,000 miles, could reasonably be expected to perform without continuous repairs being required." So what do you do with a car that starts to stall and knock? There's no obvious answer. Once again, you are in as good a position as any reasonable person to make the call. The court in *Ireland* did not have to decide. In addition to its other problems, Mr. Ireland's car turned out to have a thoroughly rotten frame which he was informed would not pass state inspection and could never be repaired well enough to do so. The court based its decision on this fact, concluding:

> As to the frame, in considering the extent of merchantability in an
> eleven year old motor vehicle driven in excess of 82,000 miles,
> on which [the seller] declared no guarantee was being given, it
> would be reasonable to expect some rust, but not to such a degree that
> the vehicle would not survive beyond four months.

8. This is the well-known case of *Webster v. Blue Ship Tea Room, Inc.,* 347 Mass. 421, 198 N.E.2d 309, 2 U.C.C. 161 (1964). The cases concerning unwelcome contaminants in food are legion, and don't always make for the most pleasant reading. Prior to the adoption of the Code, a principal question was whether the warranty concept applied to such cases at all. Many states held that, at least when the adulterated dish had been served up in a restaurant, liability was to be based not on a "sale" but on the law pertaining to the rendition of services. Section 2-314 settled at least this question for once and for all. See the concluding sentence of §2-314(1) and Comment 5.

So under the Code any food served up must be merchantable. It must be "fit for the ordinary purposes" for which such food is used, and we know what that means. But we also know that in order for any product to be merchantable it need not be perfect. Even with the adoption of the Code there continues to be legitimate dispute as to what the result should be when faced with a case like that of Mrs. Webster and her fish chowder. The courts are not even in agreement as to what the *test* should be in such situations.

Earlier cases often relied upon a distinction and an analysis (if you can call it that) which came to be referred to as the *natural substance—foreign substance test.* In principle under this approach there is no warranty liability as a matter of law if the injury-causing substance is "natural" to the food, but there is liability and it is indeed automatic if the offending item is something "foreign" or "alien" to the particular foodstuff. This view was most forcefully presented and adopted by California in the case of *Mix v. Ingersoll Candy Co.,* 6 Cal. 2d 674, 59 P.2d 144 (1936), in which the plaintiff had swallowed a fragment of a chicken bone lurking in a restaurant's chicken pot pie. The Supreme Court of California concluded that, "[b]ones which are natural to the type of meat served cannot legitimately be called a foreign substance, and a consumer who eats meat dishes ought to anticipate and be on his guard against the presence of such bones." Under *Mix* foreign substances that would give rise to liability are such things as nails, wires, or ground glass (also presumably beef bones in a chicken pot pie). Coincident with deciding *Mix,* the court held in favor of a plaintiff who swallowed some glass while eating chow mein at a lunch counter. *Goeteen v. Owl Drug Co.,* 6 Cal. 2d 683, 59 P.2d 142 (1936).

So no relief for Mr. Mix, and none for Mrs. Webster had the Massachusetts Supreme Judicial Court in 1964 chosen to follow this approach. But by that time the *Mix* case and the natural-foreign test had come under a good deal of criticism for reasons that you can imagine. After all, there are all kinds of natural things that one would never expect to find in one's soup, just as there may be foreign matter that would come as no great surprise (a grain of sand in the spinach for example). The court in *Webster* chose not to deny relief to Mrs. Webster solely on the quite obvious fact that a fish bone is naturally part of a fish. Instead it engaged in a different analysis and concerned itself with the nature of fish chowder and, more specifically, fish chowder as it is traditionally served in New England and in eateries of the kind where Mrs. Webster sat down to dine. The court asked the question: What would and could reasonably be anticipated of the chowder served to such a consumer in just such a place? Following an extended review of the received definition and history of chowders, complete with a number of traditional recipes including one offered up by Daniel Webster himself, the highest court for the Commonwealth of Massachusetts concluded,

> It is not too much to say that a person sitting down in New England to consume a good New England fish chowder embarks on a gustatory adventure which may entail the removal of some fish bones from his bowl as he proceeds. We are not inclined to tamper with age old recipes by any amendment reflecting the plaintiff's view of the effect of the Uniform Commercial Code.

Thus Mrs. Webster lost her case, but not because of any blanket rule of law about "natural" versus "foreign" substances. As the court remarked,

> [W]e consider that the joys of life in New England include the ready availability of fresh fish chowder. We should be prepared to cope with the hazards of fish bones, the occasional presence of which in chowders is, it seems to us, to be anticipated, and which, in the light of a hallowed tradition, do not impair their fitness or merchantability.

This type of reasoning, if not always so heavily reliant on actual recipes and regional chauvinism, has over the past years increasingly come into the cases. Almost all courts that have had to consider the question recently have implicitly or explicitly declined to follow the rigid natural substance-foreign substance distinction, preferring instead the *reasonable expectations test* for adulterated foods. This test calls for application on a case-by-case basis. It depends on no blanket rules of law, but instead provides that, whether or not the substance causing harm is natural to a food product, liability for a breach of the warranty of merchantability lies whenever the consumer would not reasonably have expected to find the substance in the product.

Slowly but surely this approach is being adopted by virtually every state. See for example *Jackson v. Nestle-Beich, Inc.*, 147 Ill. 2d 408, 589 N.E.2d 547, 17 U.C.C.2d 396 (1992), in which the reasonable expectation test was expressly adopted for Illinois and any lingering support for the *Mix* decision in that state abandoned. Jackson filed suit alleging a breach of warranty when he broke his tooth on a pecan shell embedded in a Katydid (a chocolate-covered pecan and caramel candy manufactured by Nestles). The Supreme Court of Illinois found he was entitled to a trial on the issue of merchantability even though pecan shells are perfectly "natural" to pecans. The manufacturer's argument that a lower court's dismissal of the action was proper under the *Mix* rationale or that at least some distinction should be recognized between natural and foreign impurities was dismissed as not "salutary to our jurisprudence."

The older natural substance-foreign substance test has generally gotten a pretty thorough thumbs-down in recent cases and by virtually all the commentators. Is there any life left to this distinction? That depends where you look. In a series of cases the Louisiana courts have tried to preserve the test in a fashion, or at least to find a middle ground. More importantly, the Supreme Court of California (by a 4 to 3 vote) adopted this so-called *Louisiana approach* in the recent *Mexicali Rose v. Superior Court,* 1 Cal. 4th 617, 822 P.2d 1292, 16 U.C.C.2d 607 (1992). The case involved a one-inch chicken bone which turned up in a chicken enchilada. Under California's *Mix* rule, of course, the plaintiff would have had no relief as a matter of law. The Supreme Court overturned *Mix,* but only part way. What we must now call the *Louisiana-California approach* involves a two-step analysis under which the natural-foreign substance distinction still plays a part. If the substance causing injury was foreign to the food product, then the injured party can state a cause of action in warranty and a reasonable expectation test applies. If, however, the substance was "natural to the preparation of the food served," then the court held, "it can be said that it was reasonably expected by its very nature and the food cannot be determined unfit or defective. A plaintiff in such a case has no cause of action in strict products liability or implied warranty." The plaintiff may, however, in the case of a "natural" impurity seek to prove that negligence in the preparation of the food caused his or her injury.

I think it very doubtful that many other states will follow this Louisiana-California line, much less insist on holding to the unadulterated natural substance-foreign substance distinction. Most commentators appear to agree that a straight reasonable expectation approach is not only the current rule in a majority of jurisdictions but is the wave of the future and a good thing, too. You should, however, be aware of the *Mexicali* decision and its outcome. If you are interested in pursuing the issue of warranty liability for contaminated foodstuff beyond what I've given you here, you would benefit from working your way through that case. Be sure to give plenty of attention to the two separate scathing dissents. You may also want to consult the first California decision to apply the *Mexicali* principles, as the California Court of Appeals wrestled with the question of what contaminants are "natural to the preparation of the food served" in *Kilpatrick v. Superior Court,* 8 Cal. App. 4th 1717, 11 Cal. Rptr. 2d 323, 18 U.C.C.2d 428 (1992). Warning: You might not want to conduct this research right before you plan to go out on the town for a meal.

In what follows we continue to explore the workings of the reasonable expectation test. Perhaps there's not much more to say than that as a reasonable person you should be able to apply it as well as anyone else. We can, however, pick up on an earlier point—a suggested way of contemplating the ramifications of merchantability doctrine. Like any test in which that old devil word "reasonable" takes center stage, what we are talking about is some kind of balancing act. You could think of the balance which must be struck between the seller of the food product and its customers, but there is another way to look at it. As you can see from reviewing the *Webster* language quoted above, the court is in essence striking a balance between the rights of the particular plaintiff and the rights of the community as a whole. Apparently many people like a good hearty fish chowder. Their interests would not be served by a decision that could result in New England fish chowder, even when served in the quaintest of oceanside restaurants, in the words of the defendant's brief "degenerating into an insipid broth containing the mere essence of its former stature as a culinary masterpiece."

We should not make light of the fact that Mrs. Webster was really hurt by that bone in the throat, nor did the Massachusetts Supreme Judicial Court do so. The court was willing to concede that her injury was "not insubstantial" and to sympathize with what it termed her "peculiarly New England injury." Still, think of the consequences if they had ruled in her favor. We can assume that one of three things would have eventually happened. The Blue Ship Tea Room and other places of like kind might have had to charge more for each bowl or cup, to reflect the increased cost of doing business (a kind of built-in fish-bone insurance). That affects each and every one or us, including those who are perfectly capable of working around some bones in the chowder. The other possibility is that restaurants would be greatly pressured to change how they prepared fish chowders, endeavoring to make sure that not even the smallest bone or minimally chunky chunk of any other ingredient made its way into the final mix. The result could be survival not of the fittest or the tastiest, but of the blandest. You just have to think about what airline food is like to appreciate what this would mean. If that's going to be the case we might all be better off if the Tea Room and every other eatery followed a third alternative strategy and simply dropped fish chowders from their menus altogether.

The reasonable expectation test for adulterated foods represents, like all of the law of merchantability when you get down to it, a kind of compromise that lies somewhere between the shoddy and the perfect. It's a compromise between each of us as individuals and where we stand as part of the larger community in which we live—that mass of humanity which looks for a life which is reasonably safe but also reasonably varied and reasonably exciting.

9.   This problem is taken from *Phillips v. Town of West Springfield*, 405 Mass. 411, 540 N.E.2d 1331, 9 U.C.C.2d 535 (1989), decided by the Supreme Judicial Court of Massachusetts as something of a twenty-fifth anniversary celebration of *Webster*. In *Phillips* the court firmly and unequivocally adopted the reasonable expectations test for Massachusetts. The injured schoolboy, it held, was entitled to a trial on "what the reasonable expectations of an ordinary high school student would be concerning the likely presence of a bone in this meal." Putting aside the court's assumption that there is such a thing as a reasonable and ordinary high school student, notice that the court refers to that character's expectations about *this meal*, meaning one slopped over mashed potatoes in a school cafeteria. There seems little doubt that a jury could determine that expectations of any food, even fish chowder, served in a school cafeteria could be different than they would be about a dish nominally the same when served

in the Blue Ship Tea Room. The facts of each case will control. Elsewhere in a footnote the court says, "In particular circumstances, the special knowledge and experience of a plaintiff may have a bearing on the reasonableness of his expectations and his right to recover."

There's fish chowder and then there's fish chowder, and a jury applying the reasonable expectations test is expected to be able to tell the difference. In some extreme cases, of course, a judge may conclude that there is really no issue for a jury. Imagine, for example, the case of even a small bit of bone in a jar of "Baby's First Fish Chowder" marketed for the toddler set.

At the same time there can be instances in which even the most dangerous contaminants will not render a food unmerchantable. See, for instance, *Hohn v. South Shore Service, Inc.,* 141 App. Div. 2d 504, 529 N.Y.S.2d 129, 6 U.C.C.2d 1111 (1988), in which it was held that a supplier of raw pork contaminated with the bacterium causing trichinosis could not be held liable for a breach of warranty. While a distributor impliedly warrants that foods sold are fit for human consumption and merchantable, this warranty does not apply to the wholesomeness of raw pork when it is anticipated the pork will undergo ordinary cooking. Does this result surprise you?

10. We would have to know more about the situation, and even then the answer would be far from clear. The issue over an otherwise harmless product that causes an allergic or idiosyncratic reaction in only some people obviously sets up the merchantability balancing act in its most delicate form. In the cases on the issue a number of factors come into play, but not one of which is decisive. First of all is the question of how many people may be affected. One bit of language that reappears throughout the decisions is the requirement that for a product to be unfit it need not cause harm to every user, but that there must be a "reasonably foreseeable harm to an appreciable number of consumers." What makes up an "appreciable number?" As you would expect, there is no clear line on this. In one early case the likelihood of a reaction in something like 4 to 5 percent of the population was deemed to be enough. *Zirpola v. Adam Hat Stores, Inc.,* 122 N.J.L. 21, 4 A.2d 73 (1939). The distinction is sometimes drawn between this type of situation and a "one-in-a-million" chance of harm that is not likely to compromise merchantability.

The courts will also be concerned with what the manufacturer or seller knew or should have known about the possible allergic reaction. Some allergies are well-known or at least should be known by people incorporating these ingredients into their products. What did the manufacturer put into the aftershave that gave Harold such a problem? Was it a chemical that was generally known to cause this reaction in some people? In some instances it can even be shown that the manufacturer was perfectly aware, in fact had been periodically informed, of adverse reactions. But even if this is so, if such reactions are only reported rarely out of the millions of bottles of aftershave sold, should the product automatically be deemed unmerchantable? Harold might argue that in this case the manufacturer's failure was in not putting any warning on the product, and indeed this might make a difference. There is, however, an obvious downside to requiring a warning on every product sold of each and every conceivable harm that could possibly be associated with its use. A bottle of aftershave loaded down with a detailed listing of possible adverse effects no matter how rare or bizarre—or worse yet accompanied by a lengthy legalistic warning insert—could scare just about anybody off of the product. And those who did take fate into their hands and used the stuff would be so burdened down with information that the number of psychosomatic reactions could well outnumber those which arise from the allergy itself. Warnings of possible known adverse reactions are relevant but cannot be the exclusive factor considered in the allergic reaction situation.

At the other extreme, consider the situation where the manufacturer has no advance warning or even reason to suspect that this particular ingredient would cause such a reaction in anybody. After all, every allergy was once unknown until it was first discovered by someone's getting a rash, feeling queasy, or dropping down dead. Harold's case might just be the first such reaction to surface. Could the manufacturer be made to pay when it had no way of anticipating this problem? Or should we say that the manufacturer was responsible because it incorporated a certain chemical into its product without first testing and proving to its own satisfaction that it was harmless?

Add to the mix the question whether the complaining consumer knew of his or her allergy prior to the problem with the particular product. The courts are clear that at least for people who do know of their own allergies some of the burden of avoiding injury lies with them. A person who knows herself to be allergic to strawberries, for example, would not be heard to complain if she suffers an adverse reaction to some strawberry sherbet. But what should be the result if some strawberry syrup had been snuck in as the secret ingredient of a dish which didn't proclaim itself as having strawberries in it and which would normally not be expected to have anything like berries in it whatsoever? The allergic person could always protect herself by specifically asking if there were any berries in even the most seemingly innocuous dish, thereby either being warned off of the item or gaining protection of an express warranty (or the warranty of fitness for a particular purpose to be discussed below). But can we really expect such diligence of each and every allergy sufferer even when there is nothing to bring the potential problem to light? ("Can you assure me no strawberries were used in making this fish chowder?") On the other hand, if the dish is found to be unfit and the restauranteur liable, the result could well be fewer secret ingredients in restaurant food and less exotic cuisine altogether. Which brings us back to the problem of airline food, and the less said about that the better.

11a. Since the other pictures turned out all right, it appears that the roll of film wasn't defective. It just wasn't a type of film that could capture pictures of the night sky. It's doubtful there has been a breach of the warranty of merchantability. Steve would say that the film was fit for the ordinary purposes, though there's always a question, of course, about what the ordinary purposes are for any particular goods. Maybe the best we can do is revert to our "reasonable expectation" notion. Would you assume that any run-of-the-mill type of photographic film would be serviceable for taking snapshots of the heavens in the deep of night? If someone did make and act on this assumption, would he or she be acting "reasonably?"

It's a very different matter when we are talking about the particular buyer's *particular purpose*. Read Comment 2 to §2-315. For a buyer's purpose to be "particular," take note, it need not be freakish or even especially idiosyncratic. It just has to be particular. In *C. E. Alexander & Sons, Inc. v. DEC International, Inc.,* 112 N.M. 89, 811 P.2d 899, 15 U.C.C.2d 464 (1991), for example, DEC sold some milking equipment to the plaintiff, who installed it in his barn. Use of the system resulted in injury to the plaintiff's cows. The Supreme Court of New Mexico upheld a ruling that there had been sufficient evidence to raise the possibility that the milking equipment had to be fit not only for the ordinary purpose of milking cows but that in addition it had been warranted to be fit for the particular purpose of "milking cows effectively on a double sixteen milk meter system." (The double sixteen is apparently a particular type of production system with which the buyer operated.) And there was evidence that DEC caused the buyer to believe that the equipment involved would meet the requirements of the double sixteen system.

Returning to Bella's case, taking pictures of the stars does seem more like mountain climbing than just walking around on "ordinary ground," to use the comment's example. Bella will argue here that under the circumstances sale of this roll of film created a warranty of fitness for a particular purpose, that is, a warranty that it was fit for photography of the night sky in that part of the world and when used with her camera. To make her case she has to show that Steve had "reason to know" her particular purpose in buying the film and that she was "relying on [Steve's] skill or judgment" to select the right stuff. From the facts I've given you, it seems like Bella will be able to show a warranty arising under §2-315.

As I noted in the introduction to this chapter, in order to find a warranty of fitness for a particular purpose there is no requirement that the seller be an Article 2 merchant. Of course in most instances the kinds of sellers whose "skill or judgment" can be called into play in making the choice of goods are in fact professional sellers of some sort.

A case which illustrates application of §2-315 well is *Klein v. Sears Roebuck & Co.,* 773 F.2d 1421, 41 U.C.C. 1233 (4th Cir. 1985). Soon after their marriage, Steven and Claudia Klein moved into a new home in the suburbs. Claudia's parents came for a visit and offered to buy the newlyweds a riding power lawn mower as a housewarming gift. Steven went to the local Sears with his in-laws where the trio informed the salesman that they had no experience with lawnmowers and that the Kleins' new property was a tract of almost an acre containing numerous hills. The salesman recommended a model in the Sears Craftsman series. A sale was concluded, conditioned however on an inspection of the property at the time of delivery. A few days later the mower was delivered. The salesman inspected the property and pronounced the mower suitable, although he did warn that the mower was to be driven vertically up and down the hills. The next summer, as Stephen was driving the mower vertically up a 19 degree slope, it tipped over backwards. His right hand was cut and seriously injured, which was all the more unfortunate because his injuries made it impossible for him to continue in his profession as a jeweler. He sued Sears. The court of appeals concluded that he had a good cause of action based on the implied warranty of fitness for a particular purpose (here the purpose of mowing his particular hilly bit of land). Compare this result to the earlier case of *Myers v. Montgomery Ward & Co., Inc.*, 253 Md. 282, 252 A.2d 855, 6 U.C.C. 493 (1969). Mr. Myers was hurt when the rotary power mower he had purchased from Montgomery Ward slipped on a sloping part of his property. The court found that this fact alone did not establish any breach of warranty. There was, of course, a warranty of merchantability. However, observed the court, this did not extend to a warranty "that it was fit to cut grass *safely* under all circumstances." And there was nothing in the situation to suggest that anyone connected with the seller had been aware of the slope on Myers' land or any special use to which he would put the mower.

11b. Once Bella herself makes the choice of which film to buy, she presumably has no warranty claim against Steve. Note the last line in Comment 1 to §2-315 which says, "The buyer, of course, must actually be relying on the seller."

What if Bella had mistakenly asked for the Supermax 200 because of some poor advice she had been given by a friend called Frank? She would not as far as I can tell have any legal claim against Frank for her loss. If you take free advice from a friend, I guess, you get what you pay for. If Frank had given the advice in a professional capacity, for example, as a highly paid photographic consultant, then he presumably could be liable. But since his liability would have to arise from breach of a service contract, it's most likely that Bella would have to show negligence on his part, not just that the advice for which she paid turned out to be wrong. Compare this to the seller's potential exposure under §2-315 which is, like all warranty obligation, a matter of strict liability. There is no need on the buyer's part to show that the seller was negligent or "should have known" that the goods involved were not fit for the particular purpose intended.

So if Bella herself specified the type of film it seems she's out of luck. Can't she make an argument that Steve, as someone who specializes in this type of goods and who was after all perfectly aware of what she wanted to do with the film, was under some type of *affirmative obligation* to warn her off of the Supermax 200 if it was so clearly unsuitable? Is there nothing wrong with his making this sale even when he knows she's making a big mistake and will be disappointed with her purchase? Would it make any difference to your response if it were to turn out that Steve did not have on hand any film which would have met her needs, so that by wising her up he would have lost a sale?

Rereading the section and looking at Comment 1, it seems unlikely that a seller would ever have a duty to stand in the way of a purchase the buyer seems intent on making. At least one case, however, suggests that it may not be so simple. And the stakes were high. See *Addis v. Bernardin, Inc.,* 226 Kan. 241, 597 P.2d 250, 27 U.C.C. 80 (1979). Addis was engaged in the production, bottling, and distribution of salad dressing to the wholesale market. Bernardin manufactured jar lids. At a meeting in 1974, Addis advised Hooper, Bernardin's sales representative, that his salad dressings contained both vinegar and salt and that any lids he purchased would have to be compatible with those ingredients. He showed the representative a sample of a lid he was now using, saying he needed a similar product with a "plastisol" lining and a gold lacquer interior. Later Addis called to place an order for lids of this description. Hooper advised him that he would not recommend this type of lid for products containing vinegar and salt. Addis, in the court's words, "insisted that he wanted lids exactly like those he had purchased" from his previous supplier. "In spite of Bernardin's recommendations," Addis ordered 350,000 lids of the type he had described. (Apparently he was hung up on the plastisol part of it.) What Hooper had not explained was that the problem would be the gold lacquer interior — something that was in fact apparently never made clear to Addis until the lawsuit was almost over. As you might expect, there followed a saga of spoiled salad dressing and disgruntled customers. Eventually Addis paid various of his buyers for the spoilage, for an amount claimed by him to be $115,000. The Supreme Court of Kansas held that there was sufficient competent evidence to support the trial court's finding of a breach by Bernardin of a warranty of fitness for a particular purpose.

> Here, although Addis insisted upon ordering white plastisol-lined lids with gold interiors that looked like the lids he had ordered from [his previous supplier], he did not realize he was ordering lids that would be incompatible with his product. . . . Hooper, on the other hand, knew the type of highly acidic product the lids would be used with and failed to explain the difference between the type of lid Addis ordered and the type he thought he was ordering. He allowed Addis to place an order for a lid that was not suitable for his product with only a recommendation against the order. It is clear the seller in this instance had superior knowledge and failed to properly caution the buyer.

Should this case be confined to its facts, or does it stand for a more general principle? If so, how is that principle to be articulated? Is it something compelled by §2-315 or at least consistent with that section? Does it help Bella in the hypothetical I've posed?

14

Disclaimer of Warranties and Limitation of Remedies

Freedom of Contract Revisited

As we saw in the prior chapters, Article 2 goes into some detail over about how warranties of quality arise in a contract for the sale of goods. It's important to appreciate, however, that the drafters expressed no opinion as to whether any precise warranty or degree of warranty protection was appropriate to a specific transaction. That, we have to believe, is up to the parties. A very paltry set of warranties, or none at all, might be just what is called for—called for by the people actually involved—in a given situation. Look again at the general Code deference to freedom of contract as articulated in §1-102(3) and the introductory sentence of Comment 2 to that section. While "obligations of good faith, diligence, reasonableness and care prescribed by" the Code may not be disclaimed by agreement, the warranty obligation is in general open to bargaining by the parties just as are the price term and the delivery date.

There is nothing inherently evil, or unreasonable, or lacking in good faith about the seller's disclaiming responsibility for the good's having any special characteristics or meeting a given level of quality. In fact, Article 2 (in §2-316) instructs the buyer on just how to go about doing this. Likewise, there is nothing intrinsically wrong with the parties' concluding at the time of contracting that the buyer's remedies in the event of a breach will be different from or less than what they otherwise would have been if the matter hadn't been taken up and a different agreement concluded before hand. Contractual modification or limitation of remedy was specifically anticipated and provided for by the drafters in §2-719.

Did the drafters take away with these provisions all they provided the buyer in §§2-313, 2-314 and 2-315?* Have we gone back to the days of "let the buyer beware?" Far from it. The buyer is now if not entirely in the driver's seat at least assured of a role in navigating the way toward the enforceable agreement. Recall that even in the days of caveat emptor it was never the case that a buyer was unalterably barred from securing warranty protection for the goods that he or she purchased. What was true was that there would be no protection *unless* and *until* the buyer made a point of getting it by successfully eliciting special language of promise from the seller. The buyer had to beware, but the wary buyer could (at least in theory) have insisted on warranty protection without which he or she would walk away from the deal. Under the more modern law of warranty and today under Article 2, the seller who carefully follows the rules can choose to lower or virtually eliminate warranty protection in any individual transaction. But the burden will be on the seller to take the initiative and get the buyer's considered agreement (again, at least in theory) if warranty protection is going to fall below the mark set in general by Article 2's provisions. The drafters' only assurance to buyers under this article's scheme is that they are not to be subject to "unexpected or unbargained language of disclaimer" or limitations that come as a "surprise." See Comment 1 to §2-316. See also the introductory paragraph of Comment 1 to §2-719.

It is important to acknowledge that this motif of "freedom of contract" in the Code's treatment of warranties is not just mindless political blather, nor is it a craven surrender to the awesome power that we tend to think of sellers as having in our society (probably because most of us do more buying than selling). Freedom of contract is freedom, and opportunity, for the buyer as well as for the seller. Allowing the parties to agree to a limitation or modification of warranty protection is merely (again, and finally, we say in theory) allowing them to bargain free and uninhibited over one of the terms of the contract. Buyers whose individual circumstances allow them comfortably to take a product with a lesser degree of warranty protection or who are willing to take greater risks to get what they want are able to bargain for the lower price or other positive features which they desire even more. They are not forced to pay for warranty protection that they do not want or need. As one example, consider the individual who is extremely good at automotive repair. He

---

*Exclusion or modification of the warranty of title under §2-312 is dealt with in subsection (2) of that section and was discussed in Chapter 11. Sections 2-316 and 2-719 are applicable only to warranties of quality. The drafters of Article 2A moved these pieces of the puzzle around a bit, but the effect is not radically different. See §2A-214 and the outline in Chapter 17.

or she may even relish buying a clunker for the challenge it represents. There is no sense in making such an accomplished and energetic person pay for a car that is warranted to be like new or close to it. Other buyers may be less energetic, but they are as keenly aware of their own best interests. If I have no intention of ever going scuba diving with my watch on, I would just as soon not pay extra because any watch I might buy is necessarily made so that the manufacturer can warranty it for use down to any number of fathoms. A conscientious buyer should neither be surprised by a lack of warranty protection nor barred from agreeing to such a state of affairs knowingly and in furtherance of his or her own interests. Just one more cheer for freedom of contract.

Freedom of Contract Restrained

Having paid appropriate homage to the principle of freedom of contract, it must be said that in reality as the law now stands no seller should feel confident that he or she has been freed from any and all potential warranty obligation just because the buyer signed a writing containing something to this effect somewhere along the line. First of all, Article 2 in §§2-316 and 2-719 does put *some* restrictions on how, when, and whether the buyer can get out from under the significant warranty obligations imposed by other sections of that article. (Otherwise why this chapter?) As you can imagine, the limitations laid down in these sections can be enforced quite rigorously by a court unsympathetic to the particular seller's way of doing business, especially when a consumer buyer is involved. Furthermore, §1-103 makes clear that other "supplemental" principles of common law such as the doctrines monitoring capacity to contract, fraud, misrepresentation, duress and so on are still available to limit sellers' behavior. Nor should we forget §2-302 setting forth the general Article 2 precept on unconscionability, which may or may not (depending on who you ask) play a part in constraining the seller's ability to disclaim warranties or limit remedies under the Code. (We'll come to this in the Examples and Explanations.)

One overriding issue that you will want to consider as you work your way through the Examples and Explanations is whether the compromise between freedom of contract and what we might loosely label "buyer protection" that the drafters of Article 2 crafted is a workable one. If so, is the balance that has been struck the right one in your view? Or has the seller still too great an opening to force upon the unsuspecting and unprotected buyer results of which you cannot approve? You should be aware that in many states and localities the legislative judgment has been that a buyer (at least the stereotypic consumer buyer) needs and is entitled to a greater measure of protection. A large majority of states have either adopted nonuniform amendments to Article 2's provisions or (more typically) adopted independent consumer protection codes or regulations which go beyond what the Code drafters provided. Note the concluding language to §2-102. The federal government has weighed in as well with

The Magnuson-Moss Warranty-Federal Trade Commission Improvement Act. If you are later confronted with a situation of attempted warranty disclaimer or limitation of remedy in the consumer context, you will I trust check out the effect of your local laws and the Magnuson-Moss act as well as the Article 2 provision on which we focus here. That being said, let's move on to a brief review of these sections before we get into the questions.

Exclusion or Modification of Warranty Under §2-316

To determine whether a particular warranty can be excluded or modified—or as is usually said, *disclaimed*—by the seller, and if so how, it is first of all crucial to have clearly in mind what kind of warranty we are talking about. (I've been warning you about this for a few chapters now.) Is it an express warranty or an implied warranty? If an implied warranty, is it the implied warranty of merchantability or an implied warranty of fitness for a particular purpose? It's going to make a difference.

Any attempt by the seller to out-and-out disclaim an *express* warranty is for all practical purposes ruled out by §2-316(1). Why should the seller be permitted to take away with one hand what was given, an express warranty created by language or other overt intentional behavior, with the other? If the seller does not want to create an express warranty, he or she has only to be careful to avoid doing so by keeping silent, by refraining from using models or samples, and so forth. As you'll see from the first few questions, however, it isn't always this straightforward. For one thing language in the agreement or conduct that purports to negate or limit a warranty may legitimately have the effect of influencing how broadly an express warranty urged by the buyer will be interpreted. After all, §2-316(1) begins with the injunction that, "Words or conduct relevant to the creation of an express warranty and words or conduct tending to negate or limit warranty shall be construed wherever reasonable as consistent with each other." Furthermore, even where the words offered as creating the warranty and the limitation cannot possibly be reconciled, the limitation, if part of an integrated written agreement, can take its toll by virtue of the parol evidence rule. Note the explicit reference in §2-316(1) to §2-202.*

Unlike the case of express warranties, there is nothing in §2-316 which would prohibit or limit the degree to which the *implied warranties* may be disclaimed. Disclaiming implied warranties is perfectly legitimate, as long as it's done properly. And §2-316 tells the fortunate seller just how to go about it! Subsection 2-316(2) gives the method for disclaiming implied warranties by particular language made part of the parties'

---

*If you have not already worked through Chapter 8, this may be a good time to do so.

agreement. Subsection 2-316(3) sets forth other circumstances in which the implied warranties may be found to have been excluded or modified. We saw in the earlier chapters that while an express warranty has to be created by some overt act by the seller, the implied warranties arise from the surrounding circumstances and in light of the seller's failure to act in such a way as to counter the buyer's reasonable expectations. The implied warranties arise, in effect, from *omissions* on the seller's part. The drafters in Section 2-316 were more than happy it would seem to give the seller instructions on how to turn the situation around with some carefully chosen words or deeds.

Finally, you will note in §2-316(4) that this section is intended to link in with the provisions of Article 2 on liquidation of damages and on contractual modification of remedy in §§2-718 and 2-719. The first of these, liquidation, we will leave to the separate chapters on remedies. The second, §2-719, is part of a package with §2-316 and must be dealt with here.

Modification or Limitation of Remedy Under §2-719

Before looking at how the parties may by agreement modify or limit the remedies available under their contract, we have to at least note what remedies would be available if the particular buyer and seller do *not* take advantage of this invitation to "shape their remedies to their particular requirements" (Comment 1 to §2-719). What are the standard off-the-shelf remedies available (here, to the buyer for a breach of warranty) under Article 2? For one thing, of course, if the buyer catches the breach in time he or she may be able to reject the goods on delivery. We deal with the so-called "goods-oriented remedies" of *rejection* and *revocation of acceptance* in the next part of the book. If the goods are accepted and the buyer is seeking monetary damages for a breach of warranty, §2-714 governs. Look at §2-714(2). Note also subsection (3). In the appropriate case the aggrieved buyer is entitled to "incidental and consequential damages." We'll examine these provisions in much more detail in Chapter 29. For the time being it is sufficient to recognize that the buyer who suffers a breach of warranty is fairly well protected by the provisions of Article 2.

Again, it must be emphasized that there is nothing necessarily evil or underhanded about a seller's concluding that he or she would rather not, or cannot afford to, sell at a given price if the full measure of potential liability remains looming over the transaction. If parties can bargain over price and other terms until they arrive at something which suits both of them, they should also be allowed to bargain over the extent of liability and reach their own individualized workable solution on that bit of business as well. While in the Examples and Explanations we will necessarily focus on the restrictions placed on the agreement by subsections (2) and (3) of §2-719, this should not distract you from the main force of the section, which comes earlier on in subsection (1). Subject to the restrictions of the following subsections and to the operation of the preceding section on liquidation of damages,

> the agreement *may* provide for remedies in addition to or in substitution for those provided in this Article and *may* limit or alter the measure of damages recoverable under this Article, as by limiting the buyer's remedies to return of the goods and repayment of the price or to repair and replacement of nonconforming goods and parts.

The emphasis has, of course, been added. But then this is exactly my point.

The restrictions that follow in this section are meant in the words of Comment 1 to insure some base line of protection for the buyer but no more.

> [I]t is the very essence of a sales contract that at least minimum adequate remedies be available. If the parties conclude a contract for sale within this Article they must accept the legal consequence that there be at least a fair quantum of remedy for the obligations or duties outlined in the contract.

As we will see, the section attempts to meet this goal in two ways. Subsection (2) introduces the concept of *failure of essential purpose*. Subsection (3) invokes the principle of *unconscionability* in this special context. There will be plenty of issues to explore under each provision.

Some Questions Remaining

As even this brief introduction should have made clear, the drafters anticipated that sellers will try to protect themselves from an unwanted warranty burden either by disclaimer, which effectively eliminates the warranty altogether, or by extending the warranty but limiting the remedies available for a breach to some level acceptable to the seller. The scheme presupposes that the two types of clauses can be distinguished and calls for different analysis depending on which it is. Attempted disclaimers of warranty are governed by §2-316. If a disclaimer is effective then the fact that the goods are not of a given type or meet a given measure of quality is simply not a breach. If a gem is warranted only to be a zircon, that it is not a diamond should surprise no one and certainly is no grounds for complaint against the seller. If, however, the seller *has* given a warranty but has sought to modify or limit the remedies available to the buyer, then a breach of contract by the seller can occur. It's just that the *remedies* available to the aggrieved buyer may not be all he or she would hope. And such a provision we know to be governed by §2-719.

While the two concepts—disclaimer of warranty and limitation of remedy—are meant in theory to be analytically distinct, I doubt it will shock you to learn that in practice the difference often is hard to make out. The effect of either type of provision on a disappointed, perhaps even a severely injured buyer can be for all practical purposes the same: It will not matter to the buyer who loses out on all meaningful recovery whether §2-316 or §2-719 did the job.

There is another point as well. Sellers are always inventing new language for incorporation into their sales forms, and it has never been hard to come up with a clause which intentionally or otherwise reads as a bit of both disclaimer and limitation of remedy. In which case, what rule or rules do we apply in judging the effectiveness of the provision? This is of particular importance because, as you no doubt already have noticed, the two sections we consider go about their business of policing in such divergent ways. Section 2-316 speaks in the language of procedure. It is a matter of by what *means* disclaimer may be accomplished. The seller may disclaim a large measure of the warranties (indeed, all of the implied warranties) rather simply as long as it is done in the correct form. Section 2-719, on the other hand, is all substance. The governing principles there focus on what outcomes, what *ends*, are to be tolerated as reasonable limitations on the buyer's right to a remedy.

You can immediately appreciate, therefore, some of the unanswered questions which this Code scheme necessarily puts into play. Is there any way for a buyer to argue with any chance of success that a clause written in the form of a disclaimer should be invalidated because of the overall effect it would have, even if all of the procedural niceties of §2-316 have been observed? On the other hand, do the §2-316 criteria or any other mechanistic constraints play any part in consideration of a provision clearly worded as a limitation of remedy? Add to the mix the issue whether the general provision on unconscionability (§2-302) is relevant to these matters at all. We will not want in this chapter for complexity. Nor shall we be astounded to find a number of seemingly fundamental questions on which the commentators and courts have and continue to disagree.

By now you are understandably anxious to get into the Examples and Explanations. We will in just one moment. First, however, there is one preliminary matter which we want to acknowledge, explore, and then put to one side.

A Matter of Timing

Both §2-316 and §2-719 deal with the effect to be given terms incorporated by the parties into their agreement of sale. As such it is important that the particular clause or language at issue actually *be* a part of that agreement. One of the most forceful arguments—in fact the most forceful—that can be made by a buyer whose warranty action seems at worse doomed and at best significantly hampered by language which the seller can point to in one document or the other is that this language, however it might normally be treated by these provisions, was simply not a part of the bargain in the particular case. Most typically the buyer will argue (many times with success) that the language was introduced into the relationship *after* the contract had been entered into. As such it is at best an attempted modification on the seller's part and would be binding on the buyer only if it can be shown that he or she consciously consented to this modification. Not surprisingly courts rarely find an agreement to modify by the buyer in such circumstances. (Of course lack of consideration cannot be used as an argument against the modification because of §2-209(1).) Courts are often predisposed to find against such limitations anyway, and will find very appealing any argument that the clause can simply be disregarded because it is not part of the operative contract between the parties.

This type of argument—the attempted disclaimer was what is sometimes referred to as a *post-contract disclaimer* and hence of no effect whatsoever—often comes up in the consumer context. The language on which the seller relies is found somewhere in the packet of materials, including for example an "Owner's Manual," which came to the buyer only with the actual delivery of the goods. Sometimes it appears for the first time on an invoice which accompanies the goods or as part of a label affixed directly to them. In any case, if the court can rightly conclude that the contract for sale was made at an earlier date and that this language could have been seen by the buyer at or after the time of delivery at the earliest, the seller's argument based on the language can be made simply to disappear.*

In the larger commercial context, language on a seller's standard form that purports to disclaim warranties or limit liability may in the appropriate circumstances fall victim to the Code's treatment of the battle of the forms. It all depends on whose papers initiated the transaction, on what each of the various forms actually said, and on what the parties actually did. But an argument based on §2-207 can, given the right facts, eliminate the language from the parties' agreement altogether—a result devoutly to be wished by the buyer.† In particular, the courts have pretty consistently held that if the buyer's purchase order constituted the offer of contract, then any language in the seller's form that raises for the first time a disclaimer or limitation of liability will be a "material alteration" under §2-207(2)(b) and hence cannot work its way into the contract by that route.

In the Examples that follow we will assume that the language of exclusion, modification, disclaimer, or limitation on which the seller seeks

---

*Of course to be a part of the agreement it is only necessary that the seller show the buyer *could have* been aware of this language at the time the contract was entered into, not that the buyer actually *was* aware of it. The buyer who chooses to enter into a contract of sale without reading what he or she is signing does not later have the luxury of arguing his or her own willful ignorance. As we will see, the drafters' "conspicuousness" requirement seeks to minimize the chances of a buyer's being caught by "surprise," but it can only do so much. The buyer still has to act reasonably, and with reasonable care, to protect his or her own interests.

†On the "battle of the forms" in general, and the Code's well-meaning if flawed attempt to deal with the problem in §2-207, see Chapter 5.

to rely can legitimately be considered a part of the parties' agreement in fact. The issues before us focus on the effect to be given such language or other circumstances, which the seller can argue gives him or her some degree of protection from full-blown warranty obligation under the Code.

EXAMPLES

1. Billows, a manufacturer of women's blouses, contracts to buy a large order of brightly colored silk from Silky Unlimited. Billows receives the silk and makes it into blouses. After manufacture they are sent through a standard washing process during which the color on all of them fades significantly. Billows wants to sue Silky.

a. Billows points to the written contract, which refers to the goods as "Colorfast, Washable Silk." Silky can point to a prominent provision in the same document which reads, "SELLER MAKES NO WARRANTY THAT PRODUCTS SOLD PURSUANT TO THIS CONTRACT WILL RETAIN ORIGINAL COLOR IN PROCESSING, CLEANING OR WASHING." Will Billows's rights against Silky be affected by this language?

b. Suppose instead that the provision in the agreement (which still described the goods as "Colorfast, Washable Silk") had read as follows: "WASH IN COOL WATER ONLY. SELLER MAKES NO WARRANTY THAT PRODUCTS SOLD PURSUANT TO THIS AGREEMENT WILL RETAIN ORIGINAL COLOR IF WASHED AT TEMPERATURES ABOVE 70 DEGREES FAHRENHEIT." Billows's process exposed the material to temperatures of at least 80 degrees. What is your evaluation of Billows's claim under these circumstances?

c. Imagine that, in addition to the circumstances given in Example 1b, Billows could prove that prior to his signing the agreement Silky's salesperson said, "This new stuff is terrific. Even a warm or hot water wash doesn't make it fade one bit." Does this help Billows's case?

2. Worldwide Jars Unlimited produces plastic jars and other containers to order for industry. One of Jars's representatives visits the plant of Peter Piper (a pickle-packing potential plaintiff) in an attempt to get new business. Piper asks her to suggest a kind of plastic jar that would be suitable for a new kind of extra dill pickle he plans to produce. She tells Piper that jars made of her company's "#3 mid-grade" plastic should work well for these purposes. Piper and the representative of Jars sign a contract. The document itself is a standard form of Purchase Memorandum used by Jars for taking orders. The number of jars, their size, the type of plastic from which they are to be made ("#3 mid-grade"), and other relevant terms are all filled into the appropriate blanks on the form. The back of the form contains among a variety of terms the following language in type no larger or darker than that which surrounds it:

EXCEPT AS EXPRESSLY PROVIDED IN THIS PURCHASE MEMORANDUM, SELLER MAKES IN CONNECTION WITH THIS TRANSACTION NO WARRANTIES, EXPRESS OR IMPLIED, INCLUDING BUT NOT LIMITED TO THE IMPLIED WARRANTY OF MERCHANTABILITY.

When the jars arrive Piper packs them with the new extra dills. He soon discovers that many of the jars are cracked or split and that they leak as soon as anything is put into them. Other jars hold tight, but within a couple of days the plastic begins to discolor. Apparently because of its high acid content this particular pickle must be packed in plastic jars of a higher grade plastic than #3 mid-grade (which would be suitable for most foodstuffs including most pickled products).

a. Does Piper have any recourse against Jars because of the leakage problem? Because of the discoloration problem?

b. What if the quoted language was on the front of the form and was printed in red ink?

c. The language was in red ink, but was on the back of the form?

d. The language was in black ink and was on the back of the form, but the front of the form carried a legend in bold red type, "SUBJECT TO TERMS, CONDITIONS AND LIMITATIONS ON THE REVERSE" just above where Peter Piper signed?

e. Assuming that the language of disclaimer was in big, bold, and bright letters right smack on the front of the form, would it influence the outcome if Piper could convincingly demonstrate that he personally did not take notice of the attempted disclaimer until after he had entered into the contract, had received the delivery, and had packed the pickles?

f. What about the converse situation? That is, assume that the disclaimer language was in type no different from any of the other printing on the back of the form but that Piper, a very picky person, had insisted on reading every line of the form before signing it. He noticed the language on the back of the form and objected to the Jars representative. She told him, "Sorry, but I'm not authorized to sell with any change of the form. They insist on this." Piper tells her that he is upset with the idea that they could limit their responsibility this way, but he signs the form anyway as he is in need of the jars. What result here?

3.   Piper's pickle packing business is booming and he decides to expand his plant. He sees an ad placed in an industry newsletter by Simon, who is selling a used labelling machine of a kind with which Piper is familiar and which he believes would meet his needs. Piper journeys to Simon's factory where the machine sits idle in a corner. He agrees to buy it for $12,000. The contract of sale which he signs bears a bold legend on the front stating "MACHINE IS SOLD AS IS." When the machine is delivered to Piper's plant, he plugs it in and flips the "On" switch, but nothing

happens. It turns out that the machine's electrical system is shot and that it will need $1,000 worth of repairs before it can be made operable.

    a. Does Piper have any recourse against Simon for breach of warranty?

    b. Suppose instead that the contract of sale Piper signed with Simon bore no language of disclaimer, but that prior to their signing the document Simon had said to Piper, "Do you want to turn it on and see how it runs?" Piper had replied, "No thanks, I've seen this type before." Does Simon have any warranty liability under these facts?

4.   Betty goes into Selma's Appliance City where she buys a new television set, signing a contract of sale which bears in fine print on the back the following legend:

> In the event that the merchandise sold pursuant to this agreement shall prove defective in any way, seller agrees to repair or replace the product for up to one year at no charge to the buyer.

Betty takes the TV home and plugs it in. A picture appears but she is unable to make it hold steady. Something is seriously wrong with the vertical hold. She takes the set back and says she wants to return it and get her money back. Selma, citing the language on the sales form, says that she will not take the set back, but will agree to take it into her shop for repair. If the vertical hold cannot be repaired, she will replace the set with another of identical make and model.

    a. Betty would prefer to have her money back so that she could go and shop elsewhere. Is she entitled to this as a matter of law?

    b. Would your answer be any different if, instead of being buried in the fine print, the quoted language had been in large bold capital letters on the front of the sales form?

    c. How would you answer the previous question if in addition to being prominently displayed on the front of the form, the provision had included the following sentences:

> IT IS AGREED THAT REPAIR OR REPLACEMENT UNDER THIS PROVISION IS TO BE THE SOLE REMEDY AVAILABLE TO BUYER. UNDER NO CIRCUMSTANCES IS SELLER LIABLE FOR ANY OTHER INJURY OR LOSS SUFFERED BY THE BUYER, INCLUDING BUT NOT LIMITED TO ANY INCIDENTAL OR CONSEQUENTIAL DAMAGES OR DAMAGES RELATING TO INJURY TO PERSON OR PROPERTY SUFFERED BY BUYER AS A RESULT OF ANY DEFECT.

    d. Assume that Selma's limitation language is as prominent and as complete as in 4c above. Once the language is pointed out to her, Betty bends to Selma's will and agrees to leave the TV set for repair. She picks up the repaired set the following week. When she turns it on at home she finds that the problem with the vertical hold has apparently not been fixed, only slightly slowed down. Again, she takes it in to Selma's for repair. When she next gets it back, she finds that while the vertical hold appears to be fine, now the horizontal hold no longer works. This time when she takes it back to Selma's she insists on getting her money back. Selma once again points to the language on her sales form. Who has the better argument now?

5.   Buster buys a toaster from Selma's Appliance City. The contract of sale which he signs includes prominently on the front all of that language which we saw quoted in the immediately preceding Examples. The first time Buster puts some plain white bread into the toaster and pushes down the handle the appliance bursts into flames. Before he can put out the fire Buster is seriously injured and most of his kitchen furniture is reduced to ashes. Buster brings suit arguing that the toaster was obviously unmerchantable. He claims damages both for his personal injury and for the harm caused to his property. Will the language in the contract of sale bar his recovery of any or all of his claimed damages?

6.   Mr. Green owns and operates a private golf course. He contracts to buy a large amount of weedkiller for $835 from Statewide Chemical Providers, Incorporated. The contract of sale which he signs carries the following legend in bold type on the front:

> LIMITATION OF LIABILITY: THE EXCLUSIVE REMEDY OF
> BUYER AND THE LIMIT OF LIABILITY OF STATE-
> WIDE CHEMICAL PROVIDERS, INCORPORATED FOR
> ANY AND ALL LOSSES, INJURIES OR DAMAGES RE-
> SULTING FROM THE USE OR HANDLING OF THIS PROD-
> UCT SHALL BE REPAYMENT OF PURCHASE PRICE.

Green applies the weedkiller to the greens of his course with disastrous results. Many of the greens have to be totally recovered with new sod. In addition, because of the damage Green has to delay the opening of his course and he loses over a month's worth of income. Green sues Statewide for more than $36,000 in damages. Statewide's contends that it should be liable for $835 but no more. Is this argument valid?

7.   Ms. Doe owns and operates a pizza parlor. She contracts to buy a new pizza oven, which will replace her aging equipment, from Ovens of Brooklyn. The contract which she signs includes the following provisions prominently displayed:

> 8.1   LIMITATION OF REMEDY: IN THE EVENT THAT
> ANY OVEN SOLD PURSUANT TO THIS AGREEMENT SHALL
> PROVE DEFECTIVE IN ANY WAY, SELLER AGREES TO RE-
> PAIR OR REPLACE THE PRODUCT AT THE BUYER'S PLACE
> OF BUSINESS FOR UP TO ONE YEAR AT NO CHARGE TO
> THE BUYER. SUCH REPAIR OR REPLACEMENT
> SHALL CONSTITUTE BUYER'S SOLE REMEDY FOR ANY
> BREACH OF WARRANTY.

> 8.2 NO INCIDENTAL OR CONSEQUENTIAL DAM-AGES: BUYER FURTHER AGREES THAT UNDER NO CIRCUMSTANCES SHALL IT HOLD SELLER LIABLE FOR ANY INCIDENTAL OR CONSEQUENTIAL DAMAGES RESULTING FROM ANY BREACH OF THIS AGREEMENT.

The pizza oven delivered to Doe does not work correctly. Doe is forced to close up shop. Over the next two weeks Ovens working diligently is able to get a needed replacement part and makes the necessary repairs.

a. Doe's Pizza Parlor can reopen. Doe is willing to pay for the oven, but claims she has a right to subtract an amount equivalent to her two weeks of lost profits. The president of the oven concern reminds her that she signed an agreement which included clause 8.2 quoted above. Does that clause effectively bar her from getting any lost profits, even if she can prove them with reasonable certainty?

b. Suppose instead that Ovens tries to fix the pizza oven over a period of several weeks, but its efforts are to no avail. Meanwhile, Doe's business remains shut. Eventually Ovens's president agrees to send his employees over to Doe's to pick up the oven and that he will "void her purchase." Doe is willing, in fact anxious, to return the oven but claims that in addition the seller owes her a large amount for the profits she has lost over the long period when her pizza parlor has been closed and will remain closed until she can get another working pizza oven. The president points to clause 8.2 in the agreement which she signed. In this situation, does that clause act as a bar to her claim for lost profits?

8. Bart goes into Selma's Appliance City where he buys an expensive new radio receiver for his stereo system. The contract which he signs bears the following legend in double sized red print directly over the spot where Bart is asked to and does put his signature:

EXCLUSION OF WARRANTIES: BUYER HEREBY ACKNOWL-EDGES THAT ANY AND ALL WARRANTIES, EXPRESS OR IMPLIED, INCLUDING THE IMPLIED WARRANTY OF MER-CHANTABILITY, AND ANY WARRANTY OF FITNESS FOR A PARTICULAR PURPOSE ARE EXCLUDED FROM THIS CON-TRACT AND SHALL NOT APPLY TO THE GOODS SOLD.

Bart takes the receiver home and hooks it up to his stereo. No matter how much he fiddles with it, he is unable to make the receiver work without a loud hum that totally overpowers any music (or public affairs broadcasting) he tunes to. He races back to Selma's and demands relief. She points to the language on the contract he signed and tells him to get out of her store. Does Bart have any remedy against Selma? Would your answer be any different if the problem with the receiver was not a loud hum but (like Buster's toaster in Example 5) that it had burst into flames causing damage to person and property?

EXPLANATIONS

1a. The attempted disclaimer of warranty will not be effective. It's always important to begin by setting out exactly the nature of the warranty being asserted. Billows claims a breach of an express warranty arising under §2-313(1)(b) and based on the description of the goods as "Colorfast, Washable Silk." The goods, Billows argues, were clearly not as warranted. Since Billows's argument relies on an express warranty, we look to §2-316(1). That section does not actually say that an express warranty can *never* be disclaimed, but the effect at least here is pretty much the same. Words argued to negate or limit an express warranty are, subject to the operation of the parol evidence rule which is not a problem here, "inoperative" to the extent that a construction of these words and the words creating the warranty as consistent "is unreasonable." There's no reasonable way, I would argue, to find consistent a seller's assertion that it warrants the goods to be washable and colorfast and at the same time disclaims all warranties to that effect. The expression of warranty wins out. Billows has the full warranty arising from the description of the goods.

1b. Billows's warranty claim is much less likely to succeed here. Silky points to the language in §2-316(1) that says, "Words or conduct relevant to the creation of an express warranty and words or conduct tending to negate or limit warranty shall be construed wherever reasonable as consistent with each other." That may well be the case here. Certainly even the most express of express warranties that a fabric, and particularly silk, is colorfast and washable can't reasonably be taken to mean that it won't lose any of its brilliance no matter how it's washed. Even without the limiting language in Silky's form, would Billows have been reasonable in expecting the product not to fade if he ran it through a process originally created to produce a trendy faded effect on jeans (such as "acid wash")? So the issue—a factual issue that we can't readily resolve without knowing more about what goes in the fabric industry—is whether it is "reasonable" to produce and sell fabric you characterize as "Colorfast, Washable" silk which needs to be washed with this level of care in order to hold its color. If so, then Silky's language is effective and Billows has no breach of warranty claim.

Another way of looking at this result from Silky's point of view is that the language does not really *disclaim* any express warranty but only further explicates it and must be taken into account in establishing the *extent* and *content* of the warranty. Any express warranty, especially one grounded in only a couple of brief words, is open to ambiguity. Section 2-316(1) prevents the out-and-out disclaimer or contradiction by words or conduct of any express warranty given by the seller. It does not interfere in appropriate cases with attempts by sellers to clarify or further explain what warranty they mean to be giving, as long as the meaning eventually arrived at is one which the "reasonable" buyer can be expected to appreciate and which cannot "reasonably" be said to take him or her by surprise.

1c. This helps Billows's case, of course, but it still may not be enough. In particular, Billows's argument based on the salesperson's statement may fall victim to the parol evidence rule. Section 2-202 is explicitly referenced in §2-316(1), and Silky's lawyer would have to be a fool not to invoke it here. See also the first sentence of Comment 2. We will not revisit all the problems and issues which come up in application of §2-202 (for that, see Chapter 8). We know, however, there is a good likelihood that an oral statement made prior to signature of an integration of the agreement (especially where it contradicts the writing which would appear to be the case here) will not be given effect as part of the contractual relationship because of the rule.

2a. Again we begin by getting straight in our own minds what warranty or warranties the buyer is trying to assert. Piper can argue with some force that the failure of the jars to hold liquid without leaking is a breach of the warranty of merchantability arising under §2-314 and that their tendency to discolor is a breach of a warranty of fitness for a particular purpose under §2-315. (This hypothetical is in fact based, if loosely, on the case of *Addis v. Bernardin, Inc.*, 226 Kan. 241, 597 P.2d 250, 27 U.C.C. 80 (1979), which we saw in the last chapter as an intriguing example of the particular purpose warranty as it played out in a commercial setting.)

Whether or not Jars has effectively disclaimed either or both of these warranties by language in the agreement is to be tested by the criteria of §2-316(2). Read that subsection now, carefully, if you have not done so already.

First note that to disclaim the warranty of merchantability arising under §2-314 the language must "mention merchantability." Here Jars's language does just that, so at least that criterion is met. What would be the result if the precise word *merchantability* had not been used? Almost assuredly on that fact alone a court would conclude that the warranty of merchantability was preserved. It's a magic word but it works, and there seems to be nothing that works as well. The courts have been exceptionally picky about what §2-316(2) requires in the way of a "mention" of merchantability, and it's hard to think of any other language or means of referring to *merchantability* which would do the trick other than use of those fifteen letters in that order.

The language which will suffice to disclaim the implied warranty of fitness, as you see from the last sentence of §2-316(2), can be much more general. Jars has probably met the language content requirement here, although wise counsel might be for it to be a bit more detailed if it can be in what it was attempting to accomplish with regard to the fitness warranty.

Jars's problem here is not with the wording of the attempted disclaimer as much as with its failure to make this language "conspicuous." This is, as you see, a requirement of written language if it is to effectively disclaim either the warranty of merchantability or the implied warranty of fitness for a particular purpose. Curiously enough, the subsection does not make it absolutely mandatory that a disclaimer of merchantability be in writing, although it does do so for the disclaimer of the other implied warranty of fitness. The warranty of merchantability can in theory at least be disclaimed by a clear statement agreed to which is entirely oral, as long as it mentions merchantability. Of course, a prudent seller could never feel comfortable relying on such an oral understanding. I can't think offhand of a litigated case where an oral disclaimer was even put into play. We'll stick to writings.

Whether language in a writing is *conspicuous* is governed by the definition of that term in §1-201(10). "A term or clause is conspicuous when it is so written that a reasonable person against whom it is to operate ought to have noticed it." The subsection goes on to give some examples in further elaboration as well as to make the very significant declaration that whether a term is conspicuous or not is a decision for the court. See also the Comment to this subsection. To be conspicuous a term in a writing must be "attention-calling." At least it would be expected to get the attention of a "reasonable" person presented with that writing under those circumstances.

Whether a term is conspicuous in any given situation is not always easy to determine. No precise objective test is available, and the courts tend to look not only at the size of type, its color, and its placement as part of the overall form, but also at any other unique aspects of the situation, including in some instances the sophistication of the party against whom the disclaimer is to operate. Thus it is perfectly possible to conclude that in a commercial context, where what is eventually signed is not a standard form but a long involved typewritten (or more likely word-processed) document over which both parties and their attorneys have labored word by word, each and every clause is conspicuous even though it is set forth in a manner no different from the rest of the text. In preprinted forms, however, the courts insist on something like a "more than slight variation" from the surrounding text as well as prominent placement. Certainly if a court has reason to feel that a seller is just trying to squeak by with a minimal variation, particularly where a consumer buyer is concerned, it is unlikely to find the conspicuousness criterion met.

We explore this more in the following question. For the moment we are faced with language in a preprinted form which is all in capital letters, to be sure, but which is otherwise in noncontrasting type and is on the back. I think that most courts would find, and find without much difficulty, that this failed to be conspicuous.

2b. Once it is on the front all in caps and printed in red ink (assuming that the rest of the form is your standard and uninspired black), a provision should meet the test and be held conspicuous.

2c. Courts have trouble with language on the back of forms and seem always on the ready to take advantage of the conspicuousness requirement of §2-316(2) to make their feelings known. On occasion buyers have asked for a ruling that any disclaimer located on the reverse of a form is inconspicuous as a matter of law. The courts have not bowed to these requests, reasoning rightly that the location of the language is only one of the factors to be considered, but practically a term which is on the back of a preprinted form and not referred to anywhere on the front is unlikely to be held conspicuous.

2d. While it's not an iron-clad cinch, this language on the front of the form located where it was and itself in bold red type probably saves the day for Jars the seller. To be safer, of course, Jars might want to consider putting the disclaimer language itself in bold red and on the front if at all possible.

One factor that has worked against seller in some similar situations is the notion that the *limiting* or *disclaiming* aspect of the provision, not just the provision in some general way, must be conspicuous and attention-calling. This notion quite sensible in light of what §2-316(2) is all about. So, for example, a clause that is headed in big bold letters with something like "YOUR WARRANTY PROTECTION" but which follows through in ordinary type with a disclaimer of those warranties which the buyer would ordinarily have as a matter of law would not do. It is the unfavorable aspect of the language (the bad news) that must be conspicuous. If Jars had referred to the clause on the back with the words "TERMS AND CONDITIONS ON REVERSE," it could easily have run afoul of this type of argument if the court were unsympathetic to Jars or the lawyer for Peter Piper particularly persuasive. Jars is probably safe, however, because it did use the word "LIMITATIONS" as well. Wouldn't this cause you to flip the form over and have a look—or later to curse yourself if you had not?

2e. When if ever Piper actually became aware of the term is immaterial. If the language on the form uses the appropriate language and is undeniably conspicuous then it has its intended effect. Look at Comments 3 and 4. Disclaimer is permitted. If seller can show the contract entered into meets the requirements of §2-316(2), there is no additional requirement that it prove the particular buyer actually *did* see the clause. There have been isolated cases, always in a consumer context as far as I know, in which the court seems to tack on the requirement of actual knowledge on the buyer's part, but you'll have to admit there is nothing in the section to support this idea and it has had no widespread acceptance. If the drafters had wanted to put different criteria in this subsection they were perfectly capable of doing so. Subsection 2-316(2) was intended to give the recipe by which sellers could effectively disclaim any or all of the implied warranties, and if an individual seller follows that recipe he or she is entitled to the full benefit of what is cooked up.

Where does this leave Peter Piper other than with a firm determination never to deal with the Jars company again and kicking himself for his own failure to be more careful in what he signs? Has he no other arguments? As we explore in the very last Example some buyers faced with a seemingly ironclad disclaimer under §2-316(2) have sought to invoke the doctrine of unconscionability. Whether a buyer should have much success with this argument is uncertain at best. In any event, recall that the doctrine of unconscionability begins to take effect almost exclusively where the party invoking it is a consumer or an otherwise downtrodden type. A businessman like Peter Piper, who is expected to sign commercial contracts day in and day out and who should know how to handle himself, will be very unlikely to get any help from the doctrine of unconscionability.

There does remain one other avenue for Piper. If he can show that an *express* warranty was made, at least that the jars would hold pickles without leaking all over the place, then he could argue a breach of this express warranty and the language of limitation would be irrelevant. Perhaps Jars's representative said something like, "Our jars will hold your pickles just right" during the course of the negotiation. But then you see Piper's problem: Will proof of this statement be allowed if a parol evidence challenge is mounted? If the court looks at the contract he signed with Jars as a completely integrated whole (and it's likely that Jars has included a merger clause in the boilerplate somewhere), then Piper may be out of luck. Now for Piper to be successful he would have to show something on the form itself, some language or term, that created an express warranty. Do you, did you, see the argument that just by describing the goods to be sold as "jars" an express warranty was given that each would be a jar, that is a type of container, and as such should contain things like pickles and their accompanying juices? Or is this stretching the notion of express warranty out of all proportion just to get a result for a person, Peter Piper, for whom we may have some sympathy?

2f. The language of §2-316(2) and §1-201(10) would seem to make it undeniable that a disclaimer must genuinely be conspicuous in order to be effective and that actual knowledge by the buyer of a hidden or obscure terms should not make any difference. Most commentators and most courts would, I think, conclude as much. Hence Piper would not be bound by this term even though he *was* aware of it. There have been a few cases that dispute this result, holding or at least implying that an inconspicuous disclaimer can be effective if the seller proves actual knowledge on the buyer's part. See, for example, *Office Supply Co., Inc. v. Basic/Four Corp.,* 538 F. Supp. 776, 34 U.C.C. 857 (E.D. Wis. 1982). At first this conclusion may seem perfectly reasonable. After all, why should the buyer be relieved from a term which the seller could reasonably believe the buyer was aware of and by signing the unamended document implicitly agreeing to? What function is served by a strict rule that is centered entirely on what a reasonable person "ought to" notice? One argument that has been made against results like that in the *Office Supply* case is that it would encourage arguments by sellers, based on very little hard evidence, that this particular buyer did see, or must have seen, or once admitted to having seen what was in the finest of fine print. Professors

White and Summers in their treatise lament a rule which might result in "rewarding the convincing liar." Beyond this, even if we were fully convinced that the buyer did see and appreciate what the seller was trying to do in the fine print, isn't the buyer entitled to rely on what does seem a fairly straightforward reading of the Code? We don't know what Piper was thinking when he signed the form knowing of the offending but inconspicuous clause in it. Perhaps while he was offended by the clause and Jars's attempt to limit its liability in such a drastic way, inside he was really chuckling to himself. The clause, he might have determined, was so obviously inconspicuous that all Jars was doing was deceiving itself. No court in the world would find this provision conspicuous and enforceable under §2-316(2). That being so, he could reasonably have concluded, why bother arguing over it? I think Piper should get the advantage of this reading of §2-316(2) and shouldn't have to play any other games. After all, as we said before, this subsection gives the seller a really quite easy-to-follow recipe for disclaiming implied warranties. If the seller can't conform to a simple recipe, he or she deserves whatever half-baked results follow.

3a. Piper has no claims again Simon for breach of any implied warranty by virtue of the "as is" language to which he agreed and §2-316(3)(a). See Comments 6 and 7. A few issues have arisen with respect to Article 2's treatment of this method of disclaimer, but none would seem to give Piper any workable arguments here. For one thing, what language other than *as is* itself comes within this subpart, that is "in common understanding calls the buyer's attention to the exclusion of warranties and makes plain that there is no implied warranty?" The language of §2-316(3)(a) suggests "with all faults" and Comment 7 adds "as they stand." Beyond this it is hard to think of any other language, at least as a short term of art, that would work. The courts have understandably resisted finding that other phrases of a more ambiguous nature come under this provision. If the seller wants it to be as is, it's best to stick with *as is*.

A second issue is whether the language of *as is* or its equivalent must be conspicuous if it is to be effective. Section 2-316(3)(a) does not contain any such requirement. If the creators of Article 2 had wanted to make this an absolute necessity they certainly would have known how to draft this subpart to get the desired effect. All they had to do is look to the subsection above for a model. On the other hand, what possible reason could they have for leaving out a requirement that the language be conspicuous? A majority of courts have concluded that this omission was just an oversight on the drafters' part, or if not an oversight then an unfortunate dereliction of duty that the courts should feel free to correct, and have required that such a general disclaimer under §2-316(3)(a) be conspicuous. Note how the drafters of Article 2A wrote the equivalent rule in §2A-214(3)(a) and their comment to that section, which seems to say without actually saying it that they thought it prudent to correct a few glitches which have been recognized in the language of §2-316.

A final issue is more substantive. Is there any limit to the use which a seller can make of an *as is* disclaimer? If not, then sellers are given a particularly powerful way of eliminating all implied warranties. A short sentence containing these two words placed conspicuously on the document (and to be sure the buyer's acceptance of that document) is all that stands between a seller and total freedom from liability based on any implied warranty. As a practical matter, the *as is* term isn't used all that often and rarely if ever in the case of new goods, but is this just some kind of transitory self-restraint on the part of people who sell goods, a self-restraint which they at any time could decide to abandon when the going got rough?

It's likely that there is some limit to when and where a general *as is* disclaimer is appropriate and can be found to work as the seller intended, although the limits haven't been tested very well at this point. There is a suggestion in a few cases, most notably in *Gindy Manufacturing Corp. v. Cardinale Trucking Corp.*, 111 N.J. Super. 383, 268 A.2d 345, 7 U.C.C. 1257 (1970), that an *as is* clause will not be effective if placed in a contract for the sale of new goods. Professors White and Summers opine that this type of disclaimer might not be given effect even in the sale of used goods if the buyer is an ordinary consumer unaware of the special "commercial understanding" of this catchphrase had by more sophisticated business types. Some cases do seem to intimate as much. Textual support is found for each of these possible limitations in the introductory language of §2-316(3)(a), "unless circumstances indicate otherwise."

If this disclaimer is effective against Piper in this situation, does he have any other recourse? Again, it would be important if he could show that there was some *express* warranty given which had been breached. Did the seller perhaps say, "It works just fine?" If so, is the writing such that this would be barred by the parol evidence rule? Here I do think it would be pretty hard to argue that a description found in the document created an express warranty that had been breached. True, something like "One Used Labelling Machine" does create a warranty that this machine is designed for and can eventually be made to serve this function, but does it necessarily imply to a reasonable person that the machine is ready to do so at once with no repairs?

3b. Simon would argue that all implied warranties had been disclaimed under §2-316(3)(b), but this argument should fail. Apparently Piper did not examine the machine before entering into the contract. Nor did he "refuse" to make an examination. Simon asked if Piper would like to try the machine, but he did not demand that he do so. See the second paragraph of Comment 8.

4a. The television set given to Betty is not merchantable. As we'll discuss in the later chapters on so-called performance issues she need not accept the set or if she has accepted it may revoke that acceptance. Eventually she *may* be able to get her money back (depending on a lot of things, including whether Selma has a right to cure and whether she does cure). For the moment we are only concerned with whether Betty's rights are affected at all by the quoted language on the back of the form. While Selma as seller does have the right via §2-719(1)(a) to get a buyer's agreement to remedies "in addition to or in substitution for" those provided in Article 2, her attempt here will fail on at least one and maybe two counts. The first, easier point is that the language on the form says nothing about the "repair or replacement" feature being the buyer's *exclusive* remedy under the contract. According to §2-719(1)(b), resort to an additional or substitute remedy "is optional unless the remedy is expressly agreed to be exclusive, in which case it is the sole remedy." Selma's form says nothing about exclusivity and hence Betty has a right to repair or replacement but is not bound to that as her only available remedy. She can pursue any other option open to her under the provisions of Article 2, and this would be true even if this exact language were reproduced in the biggest, boldest print on the front of the form.

4b. Had Selma's form been more carefully drafted in what it said, the effectiveness of the clause would hinge on the other possible infirmity which we can point to here. I think we can assume that the language of limitation in fine print on the back of the form is not conspicuous as that term is used in the Code. The effect of this, however, is far from certain. Does language modifying remedies under §2-719 have to be conspicuous to be effective? The commentators are not in agreement on this, and those decisions we have are likewise divided. In *Insurance Co. of North America v. Automatic Sprinkler Corp.*, 67 Ohio St. 2d 91, 423 N.E.2d 151, 31 U.C.C. 1595 (1981), the Supreme Court of Ohio held that conspicuousness was a prerequisite to an effective modification or limitation of remedy provision. The court commented that the two sections, §2-316 and §2-719, were to be read *"in pari materia"* (translating roughly as "pertaining to the same subject or manner") and concluded that "any other reading of §§2-719 and 2-316(4) would permit inconspicuous provisions excluding or limiting damage recovery to circumvent the protection for buyers in §2-316(2)." The Supreme Court of Virginia, on the other hand, rejected such an argument, stressing that Article 2 explicitly distinguished between modes of disclaiming warranties and limiting remedies in the event of breach and that this distinction had to be respected. *Flintkote Co. v. W. W. Wilkinson, Inc.*, 220 Va. 564, 260 S.E.2d 229, 27 U.C.C. 982 (1979). The two sections do, as we can point out, display great deference one to the other. See §2-316(4). Then see the last sentence of Comment 3 to §2-719.

This issue was again raised in a case before a federal district court applying New York law to a commercial dispute. *American Dredging Co. v. Plaza Petroleum Inc.*, 799 F. Supp. 1335, 18 U.C.C.2d 1101 (E.D.N.Y. 1992). The plaintiff argued that a limitation on consequential damages contained in a listing of "Terms and Conditions" incorporated by reference into a telex setting forth the contract between the parties was unenforceable as a matter of law as it was not conspicuous. The court found this argument without merit.

> Any limitation of remedy is governed by U.C.C. §2-719(3), not U.C.C. §2-316. The issues of disclaimer of warranty and of limitation of remedy are two distinct issues, governed by different requirements. [Citations omitted.] U.C.C. §2-719 provides that parties to a contract may agree to exclude consequential damages upon breach so long as such limitation is not "unconscionable." But, U.C.C. §2-719(3) does not require that the clause be "conspicuous."

The court went on to say that whether the limitation language was conspicuous was, however, a factor to be taken into account in the court's determination of whether the clause was unconscionable as a matter of law. (Recall that unconscionability, like conspicuousness, is expressly made a question for the court under Article 2.)

The court concluded in the *American Dredging* case that the language of limitation, coming as it did in a contract between two sophisticated parties each presumably with some bargaining power, was not unconscionable. Were Betty the consumer buyer forced to make the argument of unconscionability, relying primarily on the placement of the provision in the small print on the reverse of Selma's prepared form and pointing to other indicia of unconscionable behavior by Selma, of course, she might be more successful. As we saw in general with respect to the unconscionability doctrine (in Chapter 9) and as we will soon discuss in the §2-719(3) context, single consumer buyers are much more likely to get somewhere by arguing unconscionability than are commercial parties.

4c. Under this set of facts Selma should have the advantage of her limitation of remedy clause. She has solved the two potential problems with it by making it conspicuous (just in case that is a requirement) and expressly stating it to be the exclusive remedy of the buyer (which is undoubtedly required).

Does Betty have any argument that could potentially defeat this clause? It does not seem so. Once a clause falls within §2-719(1) there are only two ways for a buyer to get around it. Under §2-719(2) she might try to show that the remedy has or would "fail of its essential purpose." What does this mean? Certainly Betty could argue that if she had to live with Selma's offer to repair or replace the TV she'd feel she'd been "failed" in some way. But that is not the idea behind the failure of essential purpose provision. The intention is not to make sure that the buyer gets whatever he or she wants out of life. (As a matter of fact, there will be plenty of times when even the full set of remedies available directly under Article 2's provisions will leave the buyer feeling less than fully satisfied.) Section 2-719(2) starts in effect from the proposition that the parties have agreed to remedies in addition to or in substitution for those provided for in Article 2 and that *those* remedies *as of the time of agreement* are on their face a perfectly reasonable allocation of risks and rewards between two parties each looking out for his or her own interest. (We are *not* talking here about provisions which from their inception are inherently unfair and can be deemed to be unconscionable. This is the subject of the separate subsection (3), which will be discussed and compared shortly.) Look at Comment 1.

> Under this section parties are left free to shape their remedies to their particular requirements and reasonable agreements limiting or modifying remedies are to be given effect.

So we can assume that an exclusive "repair or replace" remedy provision is reasonable at the time of contracting. It would be hard to argue otherwise, as this particular type of modification of remedy is singled out for approval in §2-719(1)(a). There is nothing inherently unfair or improper about the seller's asking for the buyer's agreement to limit his or her potential remedies in this way, and if the buyer does agree this becomes an enforceable aspect of the contract between them.

It may turn out, however, that in some circumstances a clause that is fair and reasonable at the time of contracting fails to do the job intended for it by the parties. "Failure of essential purpose" under §2-719(2) is failure of the essential purpose *of the agreed-to exclusive remedy provision.* When that happens, the provision must be set aside. Note the language in Comment 1 that,

> [U]nder subsection (2), where an apparently fair and reasonable clause *because of circumstances* fails in its purpose or operates to deprive either party of the substantial value of the bargain, it must give way to the general remedy provisions of this Article.

Let's look at the exclusive remedy of repair or replacement of defective goods or parts. What is the "essential purpose" of this remedy? In *Clark v. International Harvester Co.,* 99 Idaho 326, 581 P.2d 784, 25 U.C.C. 91 (1978), the court characterized the purpose of such a provision this way:

> The purpose of the exclusive repair or replacement remedy is to ensure that the purchaser receives a product which conforms to the express warranty [and any applicable implied warranty], i.e., that the product is free from defects, and if the product proves defective within the warranty period the seller is obligated to cure the defect within a reasonable time.

So the essential purpose of the provision in Betty's agreement with Selma is to ensure that Betty ends up with a new TV, working as it is supposed to, but recognizing that even a brand new set may take some reasonable adjustments to get it working just right. That being so, has the limited remedy failed of its essential purpose in our hypothetical? No. If Betty gives Selma the chance to repair and if Selma does so within a reasonably short period of time, Betty does have the benefit of her bargain. (Remember her bargain included her agreeing that Selma would have the chance to make such repairs in lieu of being responsible for breach in other ways.)

We will see a situation where Betty as buyer will be able to effectively argue that there has been a failure of essential purpose in the next question, but for the moment the facts wouldn't support such an argument. And, as we now appreciate, whether there has been a failure of essential purpose under §2-719(2) must always be evaluated in light of the particular circumstances, what exactly has happened to the goods, *subsequent* to the contract's being entered into. The failure of essential purpose doctrine does not judge the clause in the abstract but rather how the clause has or will operate under a specific set of facts.

Contrast this to the unconscionability doctrine as it is invoked in §2-719(3). Whether a provision is unconscionable or not is in theory to be determined not in light of later events but as of the moment of contracting. Unconscionability is the second main line of attack a buyer may follow to get out from under a provision to which he or she has given assent and which expressly provides for an exclusive remedy in substitution for what would otherwise be available under Article 2. We have already explored in Chapter 9 the general doctrine of unconscionability as set forth (albeit with a lot left to the imagination) in §2-302. You should now read §2-719(3) carefully to see how unconscionability works more particularly into the matters we are here discussing. The concern of this subsection seems to be exclusively the possibility that a provision could limit or exclude the buyer's rights to consequential damages in an unconscionable way. In the hypothetical as we now have it, Betty has had no consequential damages nor is she seeking any relief of this nature. Whatever may be the effect of §2-719(3) on this clause once consequential damages do become an issue, it doesn't seem to apply to Betty here. We'll see an appropriate use of this subsection on behalf of one of Selma's customers as we move along, but unconscionability doesn't do anything for Betty under these circumstances.

For the moment it seems fairly safe to say that Selma's clause will be effective under §2-719(1) and that neither doctrine which could under appropriate facts allow the buyer to set aside or limit that clause is available to Betty. Betty is stuck with the exclusive remedy of repair or replacement of the TV set—as she did agree to in signing Selma's form.

4d. Under these circumstances, Betty should be able to win with an argument that the exclusive remedy provision has now failed of its essential purpose. As the court continued in the *Clark* case quoted above,

> If . . . the seller is subsequently unable or unwilling to repair or replace a defective part within a reasonable time, the buyer if left with a defective product—not conforming to the warranty— and the limited remedy has not achieved its purpose. In such circumstances §2-719(2) permits the buyer to pursue the other remedies provided by the UCC if the defect substantially affects the value of the buyer's bargain.

In other words, if Selma was permitted to take one more shot at repair and even if she were successful, Betty would not be left with the substantial benefit of her bargain. She paid for a new TV set. She would end up with a set which has already been patched up a number of times and seems incapable of functioning like a new set should. The repair or replace remedy has failed of its essential purpose.

5. Selma's attempt to avoid consequential damages should fail here, certainly for the personal injury damages and possibly even for the other damages to Buster's property. Buster relies on §2-719(3) and the unconscionability doctrine. While clauses excluding consequential damages are not automatically and irretrievably unconscionable, "limitation of consequential damages for injury to the person in the case of consumer goods is prima facie unconscionable." It is true this is written as if Selma could overcome the presumption, but in all practicality the seller of consumer goods isn't going to have any luck doing so even if he or she has the gall to try. What about the damages to all the stuff in Buster's kitchen? Subsection (3) says that limitation of consequential damages "when the loss is commercial" is not prima facie unconscionable. As a matter of fact, in the general run of cases where both parties were reasonably powerful and supposedly sophisticated commercial entities, the exclusion of consequential commercial damages is upheld with no difficulty. Buster's situation is, of course, different. This portion of his loss was not to the person, but it wasn't "commercial loss" either. Unconscionability will have to be determined, as indeed it always must, by the court's review of all the facts, looking for evidence of what we have termed both *procedural unconscionability* and *substantive unconscionability*. I'd place my bet on Buster here, but perhaps facts not known to us would tip the decision the other way.

6. Statewide would most likely win. This question is based on the case of *Jim Dan, Inc. v. O. M. Scott & Sons Co.*, 785 F. Supp. 1196, 17 U.C.C.2d 788 (W.D. Pa. 1992). The buyer's recovery was limited to return of the purchase price $835. We are dealing here with a substituted remedy not of "repair or replace" but of "return of the good and repayment of the price." Such a substituted remedy is expressly contemplated by §2-719(1)(a). In *Jim Dan* the court first held that the language of this clause expressly stated return of the price to be the exclusive remedy and hence met the requirement of §2-719(1)(b). It then went on to hold that under the circumstances it had not failed of its essential purpose.

> [T]he clause does not fail of its essential purpose because . . . the clause does exactly what it was designed to do: limit the buyer's remedy to the purchase price of the product. [H]erbicides involve latent risks. In fact the herbicide industry often limits its liability to the purchase price of the product. Herbicide manufacturers limit damages because of the uncertainties inherent in the business and because decisions such as planting, cultivation, and harvesting are uniquely within the purchaser's control. Therefore, an herbicide manufacturer's decision to limit damages merely allocates risks among the parties, and [the seller's] exclusive remedy does not fail of its essential purpose. [Citations omitted].

Nor was the clause unconscionable. As the court noted, "a commercial contract will rarely be found unconscionable." Appreciation of the commercial context favored the seller. Such limitations it turns out are common in the herbicide industry. (Recall §2-302(2).) The buyer was not inexperienced in making contracts or in purchasing pesticides, herbicides, and the like. While he had just purchased the golf course, he had previously owned a restaurant, a miniature golf course, and a driving range. Whether or not Jim Dan (as president as Jim Dan, Inc.) may have actually read the clause prior to applying the herbicide, the court concluded, §2-719(3) "should not be used to relieve [the buyer] of the misfortunes of its business practices."

7a. Clause 8.2 should bar Doe from getting anything for her lost profits. The limitation of remedy has not failed of its essential purpose. Doe would have to argue that the exclusion of consequential damages is unconscionable under §2-719(3). That subsection says that limitation of consequential damages "where the loss is commercial is not" prima facie unconscionable. So the matter of unconscionability must be reviewed taking into consideration the particular commercial context and the facts of the individual case. In just about every situation where a court has been confronted with such an argument, the decision has come down in favor of the exclusion. It has proved very hard, if not close to impossible, for a commercial buyer to prove an exclusion clause such as Ovens's 8.2 unconscionable if its effect is to limit recovery for loss of property or other commercial loss. The commentators in general seem to approve of this run of decisions, reasoning that commercial parties should be and under the Code by and large are always free to allocate between themselves all manner of commercial risks.

7b. This question presents a much more difficult issue—in fact one on which the courts are dramatically split. Whether Doe can receive anything for what could be months of lost profits might depend primarily on what jurisdiction she finds herself in. The limited repair or replace remedy has clearly failed of its essential purpose. What is the effect of this, if any, on the companion exclusion of consequential damages provision? Doe as buyer argues that once the limited remedy fails she is entitled to recover any and all of her damages without any limitation established in the agreement. In support she cites the full language of §2-719(2) emphasizing the concluding phrase: "Where circumstances cause an exclusive or limited remedy to fail of its essential purpose, *remedy may be had as provided in this Act*." She points also to the concluding language of Comment 1 to the effect that when an apparently fair and reasonable clause fails of its essential purpose, "it must give way to the general remedy provisions of this Article." The general remedy provisions, and more specifically §2-714(3) and §2-715, allow the buyer to recover consequential damages in the event of a breach of warranty.

The seller, Ovens of Brooklyn, argues that the two contract provisions 8.1 and 8.2 act independently of one another. Even if 8.1 is not enforceable having failed of its essential purpose, 8.2 still thwarts any attempt by Doe to recover consequential damages. After all, why should the buyer come out with *more* than she would have achieved has the limited remedy *not* failed of its essential purpose? Recall that in the previous question we found that she could not recover for loss of profits generally. Of course the buyer can argue that part of the price she paid for signing away her rights to consequential damages in 8.2 was the protection she got in 8.1. The limited repair or replace warranty assured her that "at least minimum adequate remedies" would be available and that there would be "at least a fair quantum of remedy for breach." See Comment 1. When that exclusive remedy failed, she would argue, all bets were off and the only fair thing to do would be to read 8.2 out of the contract as well.

As I mentioned, the courts are terribly split over just this issue. Some have ruled that when a limited remedy fails of its essential purpose then any exclusion of consequential damages found in the same agreement necessarily becomes unenforceable as a matter of law. Other courts have ruled just the opposite: The clauses are independent. They hold that the failure of one is immaterial to how the other should be judged and that an exclusion of consequential damages for commercial loss will therefore survive. A third group of courts have articulated what they refer to as a case-by-case approach. Once the limited remedy fails, whether the exclusion of consequential damages provision should retain its effect is to be judged by a view to the overall "risk allocation package" that the parties entered into. Under this analysis, what factors are to be considered? In this hypothetical I purposefully made the two provisions separately numbered and set apart. More typically they occur together in the same clause or paragraph of the written agreement, often as one run-on sentence. (See the language in Example 4c. Did it strike you as unusual at the time?) Should the way the two clauses were situated on the page affect whether the court considers them dependent or independent in the given case? Is such a "case-by-case" approach workable, or is it just a way of allowing the court to pick winners and losers with few if any guidelines? If you would like to see a recent case or two which review this controversy, you might check out *Smith v. Navistar International Transportation Corp.*, 457 F.2d 1439, 17 U.C.C.2d 84 (7th Cir. 1992), and *Schurtz v. BMW of North America, Inc.*, 814 P.2d 1108, 15 U.C.C.2d 1991 (Utah 1991).

8.   Bart's predicament poses a final problem involving Article 2's treatment of disclaimers and limitations and a particularly difficult one at that. Bart signed the contract containing the clause at time of sale, so he has no argument that it is not part of the enforceable agreement. The clause itself is clearly worded as a disclaimer of warranty, so it must be judged by §2-316 criteria. And under §2-316(2) there seems no argument that it is not effective to disclaim all implied warranties. Selma has met that subsection's stringent requirements—the provision seems superconspicuous—and hence gets the result she intended.

What is Bart to do? Perhaps as we've suggested before he can argue that the description of the goods as a "radio receiver" created an express warranty that there would be no hum, or that it wouldn't burst into flames, but this does seem to be stretching things a bit. A more appealing argument is to confront the situation head-on and argue that this clause cannot have effect because it is unconscionable. The issue—and it's one on which the commentators are split and which the courts rarely have confronted directly—is whether a disclaimer of warranty which meets the standards of §2-316 can nevertheless be deemed unconscionable under the Code and hence unenforceable.

Some courts have suggested that a disclaimer could be unconscionable by virtue of the language of §2-719(3), where the effect of the disclaimer is the equivalent of denying all consequential damages. There are obvious problems with this conclusion, however. Section 2-719 governs provisions that seek to alter or limit remedies. For disclaimer of warranty the place to look is §2-316. The Code's basic structure says that the two types of provisions are to be treated distinctly. See Comment 2 to §2-316, which makes the drafters' intent abundantly clear. See also Comment 3 to §2-719: "The seller in all cases is free to disclaim warranties in the manner provided in Section 2-316." So how can §2-719(3) be applied to what is undeniably a warranty disclaimer?

A different line of argument some courts apparently find appealing is that a warranty disclaimer can be held unconscionable under §2-302. After all, that section is expressed to pertain to "any clause of the contract." But §2-316 does not specifically refer back to §2-302, and an argument can be made that being the more specific provision designed to deal with just such disclaimer clauses it in effect preempts or supersedes the very open-ended §2-302. More to the point, the underlying philosophy of §2-316 is that a buyer is "protected from unexpected and unbargained language of disclaimer by denying effect to such language" through the mechanism of assuring the buyer's chance to see and appreciate any attempted disclaimer of implied warranty. Seller in this case has done everything §2-316(2) tells her she must do to protect the buyer from "surprise." She has followed the course laid out for her by the drafters. How then in all fairness can the result be deemed unconscionable?

The arguments on this issue and the division here run deep. A particularly good treatment of the issue in Professors White and Summer's treatise concludes with the declaration that one of the authors (they don't say which one) finds "dismal" the prospect of courts using §2-302 to police warranty disclaimers that comply with §2-316. Both authors seem to agree that as a matter of practicality once the radio receiver is involved in some dramatic personal injury, a court would be hard pressed to (and probably wouldn't even try) supporting the disclaimer as written. Perhaps one reason the courts have not had to treat this issue more often is that in many states separate consumer protection legislation renders ineffective any attempt to disclaim a basic level of warranty protection in a sale to a consumer purchaser. The question for us here then is whether, if a given state's legislature has chosen *not* to enact such protection, the court may and should read its adoption of the uniform provisions of Article 2 to fill in that gap?

15

The "Privity" Puzzle

Introduction

In discussing warranty law in the preceding chapters, we always stuck close to home. By that I mean we focused exclusively on the two-party transaction and the two immediate parties to that transaction—Buyer and Seller. Seller warrants to Buyer. Buyer, if that warranty is not met, seeks some kind of relief from Seller. All well and good. The problems, however, start multiplying once we allow ourselves even to contemplate the fact that others may be involved. Seller may have bought either the goods themselves or some component part from another, and that person may have in turn bought from someone else even further up the line. The party who has bought may in turn sell the goods, but even if not they can get passed on in some other way. People have been known to give gifts to others or to lend out their belongings for a time. Even if Buyer decides to hold on to the stuff for dear life, his or her use of the goods may affect the lives of a whole host of other people, especially if something goes haywire. A simple breach of a warranty arising out of a single sales transaction can leave an amazingly broad path of destruction.

I will assume that you have had some chance to hear of and explore the rudimentary concept of *privity of contract* sometime in your prior studies. That may have happened in your Contracts course or it may have been in Torts (where privity can take on the role of the all-purpose villain). Recall that individuals are said to be in privity of contract if and only if they are actual parties to the same contract and each directly obligated one to the other by that contract. You may recall as well the age-old teaching which would have it that no one can sue for breach of contract or claim contractual rights against another unless he or she can establish privity with that other party. In the days when this teaching was not only ages-old but still indisputably true, it did make things relatively simple. A right or cause of action arising under warranty was thought to be the very paradigm of contractual obligation. That being so, and if traditional privity doctrine still held sway, the buyer and only the buyer had rights to assert a warranty claim. The buyer could assert that claim only against the buyer's immediate seller.

As you are no doubt aware, things today are nowhere near this cut and dried. The citadel of privity, as the by-now classic metaphor goes, has been breached, shaken to its very foundations, and/or left in rubble, a mere suggestion of its former self. The fact is, however, that chunks of that rubble still lay strewn over the field, and it's all too easy to trip over them. We live in a troubling and unsettled time as far as privity of contract is concerned, and no one (certainly not this author in this chapter) can reasonably expect in a finite space to "clear up" or "solve" the privity puzzle. At best we may be able to select out some of the puzzle pieces and begin to examine how they might fit into the grander scheme of things.

The puzzle pieces on which we'll expend some energy are, not surprisingly given the scope of this book, those which go by the label of warranty and stand governed by Article 2. Under the law as it now stands, however, many situations where we would be tempted to play with these pieces also invite investigation under other companion theories which come from the box marked "tort." Anyone representing a person hurt in some way by a product will naturally have to consider whether liability can be predicated under a negligence theory or via the burgeoning modern doctrine of strict products liability in tort. There's no way around the fact. These pieces don't fit neatly together. There are definite overlaps, or at least there definitely are large areas where two if not three of the concepts apply even if the exact outlines of these overlapping areas are anything *but* definite. The outstanding questions involve not just each doctrine in turn (warranty, negligence, and strict products liability) but how each affects either to expand or contract the reach of the other two. Trying to determine how the interplay works out in any one jurisdiction sometimes seems like a problem in N dimensions, with N being some number significantly larger than three. On top of this, developments in this area are nowhere near uniform across the states. In fact they often seem about as nonuniform as you can get. Any exploration of the field—and particularly one coming at the problem from the point of view of the normally *Uniform* Commercial Code—is bound to be unsettling.

My intention in this chapter, as you've undoubtedly gathered by now, is not to attempt an exhaustive or in-depth study. We will lay out some of the interesting problems that one would come across if one were to dare to fully enter into this exploration. To be fair, the drafters of Article 2 have in §2-318 set forth a trio of alternatives for the states, any one of which once adopted (or as often has happened, adopted with some additional variations) does give definitive answers to *some* questions on how far the reach of warranty protection *minimally* extends in that jurisdiction. That's something. As we'll soon see, however, and as the drafters were only too keen to insist in their commentary, it's only a very limited part of the puzzle.

Comparing and Contrasting

The one thing we can say for certain about the relationship of warranty liability in contract as it relates to negligence and strict product liability in tort is a resounding negative: It is *not* true that in any given factual situation a potential plaintiff's case will necessarily fall into one and only one of the cubbyholes. Depending on the facts, of course, but also depending on the law of the jurisdiction, perhaps one, two, or all three theories may be advanced by an injured party with some hope of success.*
There are instances, of course, in which the courts in some states have ruled that one cause of action need not be extended to cover a particular set of circumstances just *because* those are covered, or more appropriately covered, by one of the other theories. But then there are instances where the logic is just the opposite. Some courts have reasoned that since the reach of these doctrines are matters of sound public policy (as elaborated one way or the other) there is no sense or justification for denying a suit on one theory when it would be allowed under another and where the two would for all intents and purposes seem to work to the same end. So the scope of one theory is extended just *because* of a desire to make it coextensive with the scope of another. No one has ever said the common law doesn't work in mysterious ways.

Make no mistake about it. The choice of which theory or theories a plaintiff is allowed to pursue can make a big difference. (You've had enough law study and badgering by the professorate to appreciate that.) Different causes of action call for proof of different essential elements and hinge on different material facts. A possible claim in negligence against a seller or manufacturer can be everything the plaintiff would wish, but then he or she will have to prove by competent evidence that there actually was negligence on the defendant's part. Breach of warranty and products liability in tort don't require proof of negligence. Each can be established as a matter of strict liability without regard to *how* the breach or defect arose. But then breach of warranty and products liability differ in many other respects. Products liability is premised on the product's being sold by the defendant "in a defective condition unreasonably dangerous to the user or consumer or to his property."† In comparison, goods sold

---

*I know you won't mind that I simplify by ignoring the fact that plaintiffs in these cases are often able to advance other plausible causes of action as well—typically fraud or deceit. You know how aggressive plaintiffs and plaintiffs' attorneys can be. You wouldn't be surprised if there were a claim or counterclaim invoking anything from battery to defamation thrown in as well.
†I'm quoting here from §402A of the Restatement (Second) of Torts. As you have probably seen, this well-known restatement section is a primary source of strict products liability law and has in fact been adopted as a statement of the law in many states. Other states, while adopting the general notion of products liability, have not signed on to §402A in whole or in part but have crafted their own rules. And these rules may have grown out of legislation or common law adjudication or some mixture of both. Fortunately, we are dealing at such a level of generality that none of this need

need not be dangerous to be in breach of warranty (e.g., a perfectly well-made knife with a blue handle which was promised to have a red one). They need not even be "defective" as we ordinarily use that word (e.g., the diamond when a zircon was promised). A claim in tort is usually subject to affirmative defenses such as assumption of risk and contributory or comparative negligence. The buyer's behavior may not come under the same scrutiny and with the same devastating effect if the suit is structured purely as a breach of warranty action.*

What may be recovered under the various theories can differ as well. Actions for strict liability are generally restricted to those seeking recompense for physical injury to the person or to his or her property. Remedies for breach of warranty actions, as we will see in Chapter 29, can be sought for damage beyond personal injury and direct injury to the plaintiff's property. In warranty the plaintiff may recover for the economic loss suffered with the decreased value of the product itself because it failed to live up to expectations. In addition, recovery may be had for so-called consequential damages. For instance, if the buyer's business suffers loss of profits because of the breach, these may be recoverable under a warranty theory. There has been great debate (with no resolution in sight) whether the notion of products liability should be extended to protect affected individuals from such economic losses either direct (to the product itself) or consequential. Things are not all gloomy for the plaintiff forced to sue in tort, of course. Remember that a successful suit in tort may make available a whole measure of damages (including most particularly punitive damages) that are simply not provided for under warranty law and Article 2.

There are what we might think of as procedural differences as well—aware as we always must be that what may be denominated a mere "procedural" point can to a prospective plaintiff spell the difference between ultimate success or ruin. For one thing, there's the statute of limitations. The statute of limitations for actions brought under Article 2 is found in §2-725. Each state will have adopted some other statute for actions in tort in general or for strict liability in particular. The length of the limitation may be greater or less than §2-725's four years, and just as important may begin running at some different point in time altogether. As you can imagine, a large percentage of the cases testing the limits of one theory or another and the potentials for overlap arise as disputes over the relevant statute of limitations and how it is to be applied. Beyond the statute of limitation controversy, there is the question of notice. Section 2-607(3)(a) calls, as we will see in a subsequent chapter, for prompt

---

concern us. You will, I trust, become totally familiar with the law in your jurisdiction when the time is right.

*The same factors may, of course, come into play in determination of what was the "ordinary use" to which the goods were to be put and whether the various criteria of §2-315 were truly met, but courts will not necessarily view these constraints as equivalent to the traditional tort principles which historically have been very harsh on potential plaintiffs.

notice by the buyer of any breach. If notice is not given within a reasonable time the buyer is barred from any and all remedies. There is in general no such draconian notice requirement governing strict liability actions. Finally, recall the complex scheme under Article 2 which allows for (and we might even think encourages) effective disclaimers of warranty and limitations of liability. In a large number of cases these will drastically reduce if not entirely eliminate the breach-of-warranty plaintiff's chance of success. Again we can only speak in general terms, as the law of products liability is anything but uniform across the board, but it can definitely be argued that a disclaimer or a limitation of remedy can have no affect whatsoever on any action brought under that theory.

And then there is *privity*. While the exact extent of *who* may sue *whom* under any state's version of products liability is certainly open to interpretation, revision, and a fair amount of questioning, privity per se has nothing to do with it. The rise of product liability in the United States can to a large extent be viewed as a growing conviction in the minds of commentators and courts that certain controversies would have been better dealt with if the word "privity" had never been invented. Compare this to *breach of warranty,* which is to this day and for better or worse still grounded in the law of contract. Historically, at least, it would have been absolutely essential for a breach of warranty plaintiff to establish privity of contract with the party being sued. Privity of contract was no mere technicality. It was the linchpin—the very heart and soul of the action. As we will see in the Examples and Explanations of this chapter, Article 2 has relaxed this requirement to some degree. Still, matters of privity can't be ignored even in the most modern of warranty actions.

The Vertical and the Horizontal

To make it all the more interesting, privity comes in two types. For a long time now commentators and courts have made the distinction for the purpose of analysis between *vertical privity* and *horizontal privity* concerns. Before we get into either of these varieties, let's start with the two parties who are in *direct privity* any way you look at it, Buyer and Seller. The simplest of diagrams does the trick:

Seller

‖

Buyer

The double line represents a relationship of contract, a purchase and sale.

Vertical privity refers to the possibility that goods may be bought and sold more than once before they come into the hands of the ultimate buyer. Parties are said to be in vertical privity with the buyer if they are part of the chain of distribution which ends with the sale to the buyer.

So, for instance, a manufacturer (Mfr.) may sell the goods to a distributor (Distr.) who then sells to Seller. (Since there are many sales going on, our original Seller is sometimes referred to as this particular Buyer's *immediate seller* with some hope that this will make things clear. Likewise Buyer is referred to as this particular Seller's *immediate buyer*.) To add to the confusion the manufacturer may have purchased a crucial part which later becomes the subject of dispute—and this could be anything from a jet engine to the tiniest screw—from another components manufacturer (Comp. Mfr.). Our vertical chain then looks like this:

The chain of course could be longer or it could be shorter; the main point here is that it is vertical. Should our friend Buyer be injured by a breach of warranty, she may seek to sue any or all above her in the chain of distribution.

As we have said, however, it is not only buyers themselves who may get hurt when there is something wrong with a product. Issues of *horizontal privity* revolve around who other than the ultimate buyer may sue for injuries resulting from some fault with the product. In some instances actual possession of the goods may be passed along (other than by sale) from Buyer to others. Buyer might give what he has purchased as a gift to a relative or loan it to a friend for his or her temporary use. So, for example, Buyer can purchase a car which is then given to a daughter on her successful graduation from law school. (We can all dream.) Or if that isn't in the cards, Buyer might at least allow it to be used by the offspring for an evening or two. Even if Buyer greedily keeps possession of the goods and makes use of them for herself, others can all too easily be affected when things go wrong. If the car breaks down and goes out of control with Buyer at the wheel, serious injury can come to anyone else she's invited along for the drive and even to the totally unrelated bystander who just happens to be in the way when the car comes crashing in his direction.

Our final diagram then looks something like this:

Comp. Mfr.
‖
Mfr.
‖
Distr.
‖
Seller
‖
Buyer _____ X

X is just about anyone who doesn't buy the product but is somehow affected by its use, and by the breach of warranty, after it gets into Buyer's hands. And of course we can't rest comfortable that there will be only one X involved. When troubles come, they oft come in platoons. There could easily be a Y, a Z, and who knows how many others hanging about somewhere horizontally off to the side. Each of these parties when injured may claim some rights not only against Buyer for whatever she may have done to bring on or fail to prevent the injury but also against Seller, based now on whatever warranty was part of the sale from Seller to Buyer. Or X, Y, and Z may try to turn the corner, taking on issues of both horizontal and vertical privity by suing, say, the Distributor who sold to Seller or the Manufacturer even further up the chain but still grounding their actions in warranty theory.

We have come a long way quickly from what we now look back on fondly as the "simple" two-party transaction and disputes between mere buyers and sellers.

Privity Under Article 2

Article 2 deals with the Sale of Goods, of which warranties are a big part. The drafters did not entirely duck the privity problem. Look at §2-318. When initially promulgated in 1962, the Code contained only a single version of this section: that which you now see labelled as "Alternative A." Apparently many state legislatures were uncomfortable with this language and sought to expand the scope of warranty protection beyond what the drafters had offered up. In the hope of averting a flood of totally distinct nonuniform versions of this section, the Permanent Editorial Board in 1966 came up with the trio of alternatives which you now see in the current official version of the Code.*

---

*If the version of the Code with which you are working doesn't have the three alternatives listed in §2-318, it's time to buy a new book. In fact it's way past time. Donate the older version to your library.

As it has turned out the P.E.B.'s strategy was only mildly successful. The states have gone every which way on this. Some states have chosen to simply ignore §2-318 altogether and leave it out of their Article 2. In these states issues of privity as they affect warranty actions are presumably governed by another statute entirely or by a developing common law. Of those 41 states which have adopted some version of §2-318, by far the greatest number have adopted Alternative A. Somewhere in the neighborhood of a half dozen (things are sufficiently confused that not everyone renders the count the same) have opted for Alternative B and a like number for Alternative C. In many of these instances, however, the alternative (whichever one it is) was adopted with variant language particular to the individual state. Even where states adopted identical versions of §2-318, significant differences can exist because as we shall see so much was left for further development by the courts. Interpretations can vary much from state to state.

The lesson is clear: Once the question comes down to the extent of warranty protection in any particular jurisdiction, some research is in order. Check out that jurisdiction's version of §2-318 and read it with an alertness toward any variations that state's legislature might have thought wise to toss in. If you don't find any version of §2-318, or even if you do, check to see if there are any other statutes that may come into play. Research the case law of the jurisdiction to see how the courts have interpreted §2-318 and any other relevant enactment as well as how they may have exercised their common law decisionmaking function to add to or subtract from what you see in the statute books. Finally, *and this is most important,* don't be too surprised if what you eventually end up with doesn't easily resolve itself into one comprehensible whole. When it comes to issues of privity, warranty, and related theories, many jurisdictions are currently in a state of flux. When questions such as these arise, you may well think yourself, in the words of an old saying, "cursed to live in interesting times."

In analyzing the Examples that follow you will have to determine whether the suit being considered will be allowed or blocked by a lack of privity in a variety of situations. In each case you should consider first of all whether the problem presented is one of vertical or horizontal privity. The traditional wisdom is that §2-318 was meant to address issues of *horizontal* privity only, leaving it to the individual jurisdictions' developing common law to sort out matters of vertical privity. See Comment 3. Certainly this is true for any state that has adopted Alternative A. Alternatives B and C leave room for argument that some vertical privity restrictions have been done away with along with allowing recovery by a broader class of horizontal plaintiffs (for lack of a better term). As you read the three alternatives and apply them to the questions which follow, even as you focus on horizontal privity issues, another question will emerge. Any of the three distinct versions says that the seller's warranty "extends" to people beyond his or her immediate buyer. A state's adoption of one or the other of these alternatives indisputably creates a *minimal* extension beyond the immediate parties—a legislatively defined floor, if you will. But does the particular version chosen serve as a *maximum*, that is, a ceiling as well? Some courts have reasoned as much, concluding that if it had been the intention of the legislature to weaken the requirement of horizontal privity still further it could and would have done so by drafting §2-318 differently or by adopting another alternative. Other courts have not felt themselves constrained in this way. The language of §2-318, whatever version, says only that a warranty extends so far, it does not say it cannot extend further when sound public policy justifies the result. The drafters in Comment 3 invite the courts to continue on with the work of fashioning appropriate rules regarding vertical privity. There is no doubt about that. Might they not also be encouraging creative judging along the horizontal axis as well?

EXAMPLES

1.   Buster is adding an enclosed outdoor pavilion to his restaurant, Buster's Beanery. He goes to Selma's Building Supply where he buys a glass door, manufactured by the Makedoor Corporation, of the size and type he needs. He installs the door himself. A few weeks later, during the first rainstorm following installation, it becomes apparent that the seal holding the glass in place is faulty. Water leaks through the door, flooding the pavilion room and ruining much of the furniture Buster has placed there. Buster realizes he must replace the door with one that doesn't leak as soon as possible. He goes back to Selma's, but he finds that store boarded up. Apparently Selma has gone out of the building supply business. He quickly goes to another supplier where he gets a replacement door which he installs.

   a. Can Buster sue Makedoor for the cost of the replacement door? For the damage done to his furniture? For revenue loss during the time the pavilion room cannot be used due to the water damage?

   b. Suppose instead that the problem with the door first becomes apparent not because of leakage but when the glass falls out as Buster is closing the door (gently) for the first time. The glass shatters and Buster is seriously cut up. Can he sue Makedoor under a breach of warranty theory for his injuries?

   c. Would your answer to either of the previous questions be any different if Buster could show that the reason he bought this particular door from Selma was that he had seen an advertisement run by Makedoor for its "Super-Safe, Tight-Sealed" doors in a home and business improvement magazine?

2.   Betty bought a large can of tuna from her local Shophere grocery store, which she used to make a number of tuna salad sandwiches. She left one sandwich at home to be eaten at lunch that day by her five-year-old daughter and another for the college student who had been given a room in Betty's home in exchange for helping her take care of her child. Betty took two other sandwiches to work. When she found herself not that hungry, she gave one of these away to a coworker who had forgotten

his lunch. It turned out that the can of tuna was tainted and each of the people who ate a sandwich became seriously ill. Which, if any, of these people can sue Shophere on a breach of warranty theory?

3.   Burns Construction Company employed Handy as a mechanic. One day while Handy was driving a bolt through a utility pole on his supervisor's directive, the head of the hammer that he was using shattered. Handy was hurt by a piece of flying metal. The hammer had been made by Cooper Industries. Can Handy sue Cooper on a breach of warranty theory?

4.   Doe operates a pizza parlor in a shopping mall. She buys a pizza oven from the manufacturing firm Ovens of Brooklyn. Late one night soon after she buys it, the oven explodes with considerable force.

        a. Jones, a passer-by, is hurt by the flying debris. Can Jones sue Ovens on a breach of warranty theory?

        b. The explosion of Doe's pizza oven is so forceful that it blows out the wall between her shop and that of her neighbor, Flicker, who runs a photography store. Fortunately, since it is late at night no one is in Flicker's store, but a good deal of damage is done to Flicker's equipment. Can Flicker sue Ovens on a breach of warranty theory? Would it make a difference if Flicker did not own the photo store as a sole entrepreneur but had instead sought financial backing from a number of others and incorporated as Flicker & Friends, Inc.?

        c. Suppose that in addition Flicker could show that because of the explosion and the subsequent need for repair his store had to be closed for something like two weeks, during which time he lost a considerable amount of photo developing business that he can never recoup. During those weeks, even his most loyal customers went elsewhere to get their film developed. Could Flicker collect from Ovens for this loss of profit?

        d. Just before the explosion at the shopping mall, Andrew had brought a large number of rolls of film into Flicker's store for developing. These chronicled his recent trip to Outer Mongolia. All of the rolls of film were lost, apparently buried somewhere in the debris. Can Andrew sue Ovens for his loss under a breach of warranty theory with any hope of success?

        e. Would your answer to any of the previous questions involving the exploding pizza oven be any different if it turned out that Doe had purchased a used oven from Ovens of Brooklyn and that the contract she signed contained the statement "OVEN IS SOLD AS IS" in large bold type on the front?

        f. What would be the effect if instead of the "as is" provision, the contract had contained a conspicuous clause that read as follows:

EXTENT OF WARRANTIES: SELLER AGREES TO BE LIABLE TO BUYER FOR ANY BREACH OF WARRANTY. BUYER AGREES THAT UNDER NO CIRCUMSTANCES SHALL SELLER BE HELD LIABLE HEREUNDER FOR ANY HARM CAUSED TO, OR FOR ANY INCIDENTAL OR CONSEQUENTIAL DAMAGES

INCURRED BY, ANY THIRD PERSON OR PERSONS AS A RE-
SULT OF ANY BREACH OF THIS AGREEMENT.

EXPLANATIONS

1a. This problem relates strictly to vertical privity. Makedoor made a sale
to Selma which presumably including a warranty that the door wouldn't
leak like a sieve. Makedoor, however, did not sell directly to Buster. Can
Buster sue Makedoor and if so, for what?

We first ask whether §2-318 in any of its forms extends the right to
sue for breach of warranty in spite of vertical privity problems as a matter
of statutory dictate. The answer would appear to be a clear no. Most
readers have taken it as an act of faith that this section simply doesn't
speak to vertical privity. Possible relaxation of the privity requirement
along the vertical axis has been intentionally left by the drafters and the
legislatures to common law development by the courts. We note the
language in Comment 3, which begins by referring to the first alternative's
extension of warranty protection to some degree along the horizontal
axis. It goes on:

> Beyond this, the section in this form is neutral and is not intended to
> enlarge or restrict the developing case law on whether the seller's
> warranties, given to his buyer who resells, extend to other persons in
> the distributive chain.

There is an argument to be made, however, that if a state's legislature
has adopted either Alternative B or C (and some dozen states or so have
done as much), then this has in effect cut down on the vertical privity
problem. Can't Buster argue that he is a person "who may reasonably
be expected to use, consume or be affected by" the door? Retailers like
Selma buy doors by the dozens for the purpose of resale. But Makedoor
has to know that eventually they'll be used one door at a time by individuals
like Buster. Note that Alternative A contains the phrase "his [that is, the
seller's] buyer" which is absent from either of the two other alternatives.
And the language quoted above from Comment 3 says that the section
in the first alternative form is neutral on vertical privity issues. While there
is reason to believe that the drafters may not have intended as much, a
court eager to extend warranty protection down the line of distribution
may be excused for latching on to its legislature's adoption of either
Alternative B or C as support (if not necessarily a statutory mandate) for
that conclusion. Under our particular fact pattern, of course, Buster would
gain nothing from this argument if his state had adopted only Alternative
B. Section 2-318 even in that version extends warranty rights only to
those seeking to recover for personal injury.

If Buster's jurisdiction has not adopted one of the more expansive
versions of §2-318, or if the courts are not willing to read Alternative C
so broadly, he is not necessarily out of luck. The courts in many states
have concluded that while §2-318 does not extend the right to sue to a
situation such as his, adoption of that section was not intended to *restrict*

the scope of warranty protection either. This much *is* clear from Comment 3. So it is up to the courts to decide the degree to which lack of vertical privity may stand in the way of a breach of warranty action. In many states the answer to this question as it now stands is wrapped up in the type of injury sustained and the relief requested. If the ultimate buyer is suing for personal injury (as Buster will be in the next part of this Example) it's probably true that most states would allow recovery on a breach of warranty theory. Once the injury is all of an economic sort, as it is here, the courts are more divided.

As an example of a case still holding the reins fairly tight on vertical privity, see *Gregory v. Atrium Door & Window Co.,* 106 N.C. App. 142, 415 S.E.2d 574, 18 U.C.C.2d 110 (1992), the case on which this question is loosely based. Doors manufactured by the defendant Atrium Door & Window were purchased by plaintiffs Mr. and Mrs. Gregory from a supplier, the W. R. Jones Co., for installation in their home. The doors quickly began to deteriorate. The Gregorys sued and were awarded a judgment against both the manufacturer and its immediate seller for breach of warranty. Atrium Door sought a reversal based on lack of privity. Atrium Door got its reversal.

> Plaintiffs were in privity of contract with defendant-retailer W. R. Jones Company, from whom they had purchased the doors, but they were not in privity of contract with defendant-manufacturer Atrium Door and Window Company. . . .
> [O]utside exceptions created by [the North Carolina Products Liability Statute], the general rule is that privity is required to assert a claim for a breach of an implied warranty involving only economic loss. [Citations omitted.] The trial court's findings reflect that only economic loss resulted from the alleged breach in the form of malfunctioning and deteriorating doors, along with some water damage to flooring. There is no competent evidence of the privity between defendant Atrium and the plaintiffs required to support the trial court's findings and conclusion as to the alleged breach of these implied warranties. The judgment of the trial court is reversed.

The court did conclude its opinion with the suggestion that perhaps the time had come for a reconsideration of "whether the privity requirement for implied warranties is still good policy." We will have to wait to see whether either the legislature or the Supreme Court of North Carolina takes this recommendation to heart.

See also the language in *American Dredging Co. v. Plaza Petroleum,* 799 F. Supp. 1335, 19 U.C.C.2d 706 (E.D.N.Y. 1992):

> As for implied warranty claims, it is well settled in New York that a claim against a seller for economic loss for breach of an implied warranty of merchantability and/or implied warranty of fitness can be maintained only by those parties with whom the seller is in privity. If there is no seller-buyer relationship or sales contract between the parties, a cause of action based on breach of contract will not lie. [Citations omitted.]

For an example of a state that goes in the opposite direction, see the discussion of Pennsylvania law in *Israel Phoenix Assurance Co., Ltd. v.*

SMS Sutton, Inc., 787 F. Supp. 102, 18 U.C.C.2d 120 (W.D. Pa. 1992).
SMS Sutton sold a replacement main cylinder for a hydraulic extrusion
press to an Israeli company, KLIL Industries. The replacement cylinder,
which had been manufactured by Hodgson Steel, Inc., later malfunc-
tioned on several occasions, each of which temporarily shut down KLIL's
plant. It eventually had to be replaced, causing another shutdown. The
plaintiff insurance company provided coverage for KLIL's losses and in
this action sued both Sutton and Hodgson Steel as KLIL's subrogee,
claiming more than $800,000 in repair costs, replacement costs, and lost
profits as damages. Hodgson sought a summary dismissal of that portion
of the claim against it which relied on asserted breaches of implied warranties of merchantability and fitness for a particular purpose. Hodgson's
request for summary judgment was denied. The federal district court
concluded that privity of contract was not required to state a claim for
breach of implied warranty under existing Pennsylvania case law and that
this was true even where the claim was for purely economic losses of the
type sustained here, including lost profits.

These cases are cited merely as examples. Individual states may have
leading cases on the area, but overall national trends are hard to come
by. With only a little effort you should be able to find jurisdictions which
come down just about anywhere along the spectrum—or are still floating
uncertainly in the void.

If for whatever reason Buster is barred from suing Makedoor, that
does not leave him with no one to sue. He is in direct privity with Selma
and can sue her. No doubt you see the potential problem with that course
of action here: *If* Selma is still in the jurisdiction and available for suit,
and *if* she shut down business not because she went bankrupt but only
because she was tired of the rat race, then a suit is perfectly practical. But
those are two big ifs. Just to conclude this analysis, *if* Selma can be found
and made to pay damages to Buster, you should see that she will in turn
have the right to go against Makedoor, who should make it up to her.

1b. Buster may have more luck going against Makedoor on a breach of
warranty theory once his injuries are of this type. For one thing, if his
state has adopted Alternative B (not to mention C) we now have some
argument that his suit has specific legislative sanction. Even if this is not
so, many if not most state courts have ruled that as a matter of sound
public policy a breach of warranty action may be brought under these
circumstances, whether it is expressly authorized by the Code or not.
Note that the language I quoted earlier from *Atrium Door & Window*
and *American Dredging,* which would have worked against Buster if he
suffered only economic loss, suggest that the same automatic bar would
not necessarily apply where personal injury is involved.

1c. Buster might collect in this situation even if he were only going for
economic losses as in Example 1a. The difference here is that Buster
can make some claim for having relied on an *express* warranty made by
Makedoor. Some courts have said that this actually brings Buster into
privity, or a kind of privity, with the manufacturer. Others conclude not

that privity has been established but that such advertising by the manufacturer, designed to bring in more business and intended to be seen by the ultimate buyer, in effect overcomes or renders moot whatever lack of privity there technically may be. Either way the result is the same—the ultimate buyer can go directly against the manufacturer for breach of the express warranty. For a recent example, you might want to look at *Touchet Valley Grain Growers, Inc. v. Opp & Seibold General Construction, Inc.,* 119 Wash. 2d 334, 831 P.2d 724, 19 U.C.C.2d 1041 (1992). The Washington Supreme Court went beyond the particular express warranties made to the ultimate buyer via advertising materials and its price book, and ruled that the buyer could sue on whatever *implied* warranties could be established based on the totality of the circumstances and the extent of the relationship—even if it wasn't privity of contract—between the manufacturer and the ultimate buyer, Touchet Valley.

> [W]e note that Truss-T [the manufacturer] knew Touchet Valley's identity, its purpose and its requirements for the grain storage building. Truss-T designed the building knowing the specifications were the purchaser's. As was its business practice, Truss-T delivered the components to Touchet Valley's construction site. And, when the first beams buckled, . . . Truss-T joined Opp & Seibold [the intermediate seller] to attempt repairs. [Because of the] sum of this interaction, [Touchet Valley was] the intended beneficiary of Truss-T's implied warranties to Opp & Seibold. Those warranties assured the merchantability of Truss-T's fabricated building and their fitness for Touchet Valley's known particular purpose.

Touchet Valley's warranty claims against Truss-T, based both on express and implied warranty claims, were reinstated.

Would the result of this case necessarily guarantee Buster the right to sue Makedoor for the breach of any warranty under the facts of his purchase? The situation in *Touchet Valley* was unusual and particularly favorable to the distant buyer, but other courts have gone even further and suggested that once a manufacturer advertises and sells its product by brand name in order to "make a market" for those goods, it implicitly extends at least the warranty of merchantability to anyone who buys the goods for their intended use no matter how far down the chain of distribution. As you can imagine, this type of analysis seems to go furthest when the breach of warranty results in personal injury and not just economic loss, but even that has been covered in some instances.

2.   We turn with this question to problems of horizontal privity that *are* addressed by §2-318. Which of these various parties can sue depends, at least initially, on which Alternative Version of that section, or which nonuniform version drafted for a particular state, applies. Betty, of course, is in direct privity with the retailer and can sue no matter what. Her five-year-old's injuries are covered by any version of the section. Alternative A extends protection for personal injuries to "any natural person who is in the family or household of his buyer or who is a guest in his home if it is reasonable to expect that such a person may use, consume or be

affected by the goods." Would this include the college student boarder/mother's helper? I think yes. Such a person is probably a member of Betty's "household." If not, maybe he or she counts as a "guest." Betty's coworker would not be automatically entitled to sue under Alternative A as he or she doesn't fit within the language.

The coworker would, of course, have a much better case if either Alternative B or C were in force. He or she certainly counts as a "natural person" (as opposed to a "something" like a partnership, a trust, or a corporation) and you could argue just about anyone of the sandwich-eating type "may reasonably be expected to use, consume or be affected by" a tainted can of tuna.

Even if Alternative A is applicable, the coworker may still be able to sue on the warranty of merchantability, if the courts in the particular jurisdiction take up his or her cause and choose to extend the reach of warranty protection *horizontally* beyond what is called for by the state's version of §2-318. Some courts have chosen to do so, concluding that §2-318 sets out only the minimal degree to which the bonds of horizontal privity have been relaxed in the jurisdiction and taking the drafters' comments as inviting further extension by the courts along this axis as well as the vertical one. Other courts have not seen or declined the invitation to fool around in the horizontal dimension, reasoning that the legislature's decision to adopt Alternative A instead of one of the other more extensive alternatives speaks to the public policy of the state and is not to be circumvented or second-guessed by common law decisionmaking.

3.   Handy will not be able to sue Cooper if Alternative A is in force and the courts of his state have not extended protection beyond the legislative dictate. This was the result in *Burns v. Cooper Industries, Inc.,* 78 Ohio App. 3d, 605 N.E.2d 395, 20 U.C.C.2d 127 (1992), on which this question is based. Ohio adopted Alternative A of §2-318. The employee did not fall within that version's scope, and as the court noted, "The Ohio General Assembly has declined the express opportunity to enlarge the seller's warranties under the Uniform Commercial Code to a buyer's employee." The employee could not sue the hammer manufacturer on a breach of warranty theory. Since he suffered physical injury, you may be thinking, that shouldn't make much of a difference. He could simply sue on a tort theory of negligence or products liability. Unfortunately for the employee he was unable to demonstrate at trial the existence of any defect in the product at the time it left the manufacturer's possession. In fact, in his brief to the appellate court, he stipulated that there was no physical or chemical defect in the hammer at the time it left the defendant manufacturer's hands. Summary judgment in favor of the manufacturer on all counts was affirmed on appeal. Maybe this was just one of those accidents that just happens. Or maybe the real culprit was the plaintiff's employer who gave him this hammer to undertake this particular task even though a warning placed on the hammer by the manufacturer (although it is unclear what this warning was originally supposed to have said and what difference it possibly could have made) had been obliterated over

time. If this is so, then the employee would be barred from a suit against his employer by the workman's compensation statute. Maybe, after all is said and done, this *was* just one of those things that happens.

Look at Alternative A once again. It shouldn't be hard for you to think up interesting hypotheticals that test the outer limits of that language. Be the law professor you've always wanted to be. Who exactly is in the "family" or "household" of the buyer? Who counts as a "guest in the home"? As a matter of fact, there seem to be very few cases where the courts have been called upon to explicate. Recently, the North Carolina Court of Appeals was presented with an interesting fact pattern. In *Crews v. W.A. Brown & Son, Inc.,* 106 N.C. App. 324, 416 S.E.2d 924 (1992), the Calvary Baptist Church purchased and installed a walk-in freezer that was expressly warranted to have a safety door of the type which could always be opened from the inside. Vicky Ann Buchanan Crews, a thirteen-year-old member of the congregation, was at the Church doing volunteer work when she thought she heard a noise coming from inside the freezer. She went inside to check. The freezer door closed behind her, and because of a malfunction in the safety release she was unable to get out. Ultimately she was rescued, but not before suffering severe frostbite to various parts of her body. The court held that under Alternative A, which had been adopted in North Carolina, neither Vicky Ann nor her mother could sue on a breach of warranty theory.

> Because a church does not have a "family" or a "household" in the ordinary meanings of those terms, Crews cannot be classified as a member of Church's "family" or "household" under N.C.G.S. §25-2-318. . . . Because a church is not a "home" within the ordinary meaning of that term, Church cannot be classified as a "home." Accordingly, because Crews was not in the buyer's "family" or "household," and because she was not a guest in the buyer's "home," N.C.G.S. §25-2-318 does not extend the coverage of Foodcraft's [the seller's] warranties to plaintiffs.

4a. Jones would not have a claim under warranty law against the manufacturer-seller of the oven if the incident occurred in a state which had Alternative A of §2-318, unless the courts of that state had independently extended the scope of warranty protection to a greater degree. If Alternative B or C governed, she would seem to have a good case.

4b. Flicker would not be able to sue under either Alternative A or B because he was not "injured in person" by the breach. While it may turn out that the courts in his jurisdiction have extended the reach of warranty beyond what is expressly provided for in either of those two versions, such extension is less likely in the case of injury other than personal injury. Under Alternative C suit may be brought by anyone "who may reasonably be expected to . . . be affected by the goods and who is injured by breach of warranty." This version does not contain the limitation of the other two that injury be to the person, so Flicker should have a good shot at recover under a warranty theory.

If Alternative C does apply, then the fact that the photo shop is really owned by a corporation will not make any difference. Note that Alternatives A and B speak in terms of "any natural person." Alternative C just says "any person." The omission was intentional. See §1-201(30) for the Code's general definition of *person*. The Code does not define *natural* or *natural person*, but I think we get the point.

4c. Even if Flicker were fortunate enough to have Alternative C behind him, he might not be able to collect for this loss of profits. That alternative does not restrict claims to those for personal injury, and certainly direct injury to property is included, but the courts have not necessarily read even this version of §2-318 as far as to extend to what is referred to as "purely economic loss." If Flicker is fighting his battle under either of the other versions of §2-318, and hence having to convince the court to extend the reach of the warranty on its own volition, he would presumably have an even tougher time getting pure economic loss covered.

4d. I doubt Andrew could recover from Oven no matter what version of §2-318 is in place and regardless of how little the courts of the particular jurisdiction thought of traditional "lack of privity" arguments. This does seem to me to be stretching things just too, too far. But maybe I'm wrong, and you certainly are free to look for cases that would support Andrew's claim here. If you find any, you will, I assume, ask yourself the next question: If Andrew were a professional photographer who had taken these pictures on assignment for a magazine which then had to delay publication or expend more money getting substitute pictures of Outer Mongolia, could the *magazine* sue Ovens of Brooklyn? And so on and so forth. It does make you somewhat nostalgic for the good old days of "no privity, no action," doesn't it?

4e. If Doe bought the oven "as is" and this disclaimer were effective, as it very well may be under §2-316(3)(a), this changes everything. See Comment 1 including the statement that, "To the extent that the contract of sale contains provisions under which warranties are excluded or modified, or remedies for breach are limited, such provisions are equally operative against beneficiaries of warranties under this section." Anyone who's been injured in this whole nasty mess must, if he, she, or it (remember the corporation) is suing on a breach of warranty theory, establish that such a warranty actually does exist as part of the contract between the seller and buyer. If the buyer agreed to take the goods without any or all warranties, this decision affects the rights not just of the buyer but of anyone who would sue through the buyer.

4f. This is not a general disclaimer of warranty or limitation of liability governed by either §2-316 or §2-719, but something else with which the drafters obviously had little patience. The last sentence of §2-318, in whatever version, would render this limitation invalid, at least to the extent which it might possibly bar recovery for injuries to the person. Read Comment 1 in its entirety.

16

Warranties in the Lease of Goods

Expectations of the Reasonable Lessee

The discussion of warranties in the previous chapters focused on what will be expected, and what can be insisted upon, by the buyer of goods. The buyer expects to be getting good title to the property and that the goods will conform to certain standards of quality and value. People who lease goods will likewise have expectations that ought to be met. Lessees do not, of course, think they are getting title to the goods involved, but they do expect that the lessor is the owner of the goods (or at least rightfully holds them) and can legitimately lease them for a period of time to another. The lessee expects the right to use the goods without question and without interference from third parties. Beyond that the lessee will necessarily have expectations, just as the buyer does, about the quality and characteristics of the goods, and will be depending on certain reasonable assumptions about what the goods are made of, how they will perform, how safe they are to use, under what circumstances, and so on.

In other words, a lessee seems as deserving as the buyer of some measure of warranty protection. Do leased goods come complete with warranty, and if so what are that warranty's bounds? There is no doubt that the common law recognizes a measure of express and implied warranty protection for the lessee of personal property. However, as was and remains true in general for questions of law pertaining to the "bailment for hire," while the fundamental principle of warranty covering leased goods is well established it has never been developed in any detail or in a systematic way. As we noted in Chapter 2, the common law's treatment of personal property leases has never progressed beyond a certain rudimentary and murky stage.

It was no surprise then that the adoption of the UCC should have been seen by many as a way out of this murkiness. As was discussed in Chapter 2, courts have in a number of instances and under a variety of rationales applied the provisions of Article 2 to lease agreements. In some large number of these cases, perhaps even the majority, the relevant sections were just those we have been studying in this part, §§2-312 to 2-318, the Article 2 warranty provisions. So even without the adoption of Article 2A in any particular jurisdiction, the warranty provisions of Article 2 can play a significant role in disputes between lessor and lessee when the product causes injury or is otherwise not to the lessee's liking.

Along Comes Article 2A

The adoption of Article 2A in any state should make things much clearer. That article has its own set of warranty provisions that track in many respects those of Article 2 and that apply directly to warranty questions when the parties have entered into a lease of goods. We can review these sections now. In doing so, ignore for the moment any reference to the *finance lease*. This is an animal with which we'll deal in the next section and in the Examples. For the moment we are interested only in the straightforward two-party lease, in which the lessor has some property he or she is leasing to the lessee for some term of years.* As an example, we could think of Larry Lawyer and his rental of a copying machine for a year from an office supply firm. Or his rental of a car or a boat for the weekend. Now check out the following sections from Article 2A, which I've organized not numerically but in the order of the warranty topics as we covered them in the previous chapters.

(1) *Warranties Against Interference and Infringement (§2A-211).* This section is modelled on §2-312 and the buyer's warranty of title, but with some obvious differences. The lessee does not expect to be getting an ownership interest in the goods or actual title. The comment to this section reasserts that what was traditionally referred to as *the warranty of quiet possession* was abolished by Article 2 with respect to sales of goods, even if as we saw in Chapter 11 something very much like it may remain in practice. Here, in the case of leases, the Code expressly retains this warranty of quiet possession. The basic idea is that the lessor warrants that "no person holding a claim or interest that arose from the act or omission of the lessor will be

*Of course, as we discussed in Chapter 2, we must assume that this term is shorter than the anticipated useful economic life of the goods. Otherwise, no matter how the parties have chosen to write up their transaction, they will not have entered into a "lease" for the purposes of the UCC. If the party's deal is in reality a sale coupled with what the Comment to §2A-101 refers to as "a security interest disguised as a lease," then Article 2 governs all warranty questions as well as other sales aspects while Article 9 governs issues relating to the security interest aspect of the transaction.

able to interfere with the lessee's use and enjoyment of the goods for the lease term." Note that the statement of when and how this warranty can be disclaimed, in terms analogous to §2-312(2), has been moved in Article 2A to the general provision on disclaimers and is found in §2A-214(4).

(2) *Express Warranties of Quality (§2A-210)*. As you will notice and the comment confirms, this section tracks virtually word for word §2-313. It has been revised only "to reflect leasing practices and terminology."

(3) *Implied Warranties of Quality (§§2A-212 and 2A-213)*. Again, these track closely §2-314 on the Implied Warranty of Merchantability and §2-315 on the Implied Warranty of Fitness for a Particular Purpose in sales.

(4) *Warranty Disclaimers (§2A-214)*. Compare this to §2-316. It is basically parallel with some minor changes. See the comment to §2A-214. For example, any disclaimer of the warranty of merchantability must be in writing and conspicuous. It will not be effective if exclusively oral, which is at least theoretically possible under §2-316. Exclusion by the use of "as is" or similar language must, under Article 2A, be in writing and conspicuous. This is nowhere stated in §2-316(3)(a), although it was probably intended. These changes in §2A-214 were made by the 2A drafters not so much because they felt that the rules for leases should be different from those governing sales but rather to clear up what was thought to be some less than ideal drafting of §2-316.*

(5) *Modification of Remedies (§2A-503)*. Here we have a pretty close copy of §2-719 with only minor variations. Certain "clarifications" of what is presumably the law under that Article 2 section have been expressly incorporated into §2A-503. See the comments to §2A-503.

(6) *Third-Party Beneficiaries of Warranties (§2A-216)*. The states are given basically the same choice of Alternatives as is found in §2-318.

The "Finance Lease" Under Article 2A

As you could not help noticing from your reading of Article 2A's warranty provisions, the drafters thought special recognition was appropriate for a distinct kind of transaction they refer to as the *finance lease*. What is a finance lease, and why do the rules change when that is what we are dealing with? Actually the drafters of 2A did not themselves first come up with the idea of the finance lease, nor did they coin the term, although

---

*The tinkering in §2A-214 "clarifies existing law by eliminating some overly technical distinctions in Article 2 regarding the form of disclaimer required to exclude or modify various warranties." Huddleston, Old Wine in New Bottles: U.C.C. Article 2A Leases, 39 Ala. L. Rev. 615, 658 (1988).

as we will see they did craft their own definition of the beast which today in application of 2A must necessarily be given its due.

The general set-up of the finance lease is a creature of business necessity and the inventiveness of corporate and commercial lawyers. What makes it distinct is that a finance lease is a *three-party transaction*. Before we get to the finance lease itself we have to think more generally about why and how a third party would come to be invited into a transaction we think of as a game for only two, the purpose of which is the acquisition of goods by one from the other. Initially of course there are the two key players. Some company has or is willing to manufacture some particular item the use of which is desired by another. *A* may simply sell the goods to *B*. In this case no third party need be involved, nor is Article 2A involved. This would be a straightforward sale from *A* to *B* governed by Article 2.

Suppose, however, that *B* (the entity wanting the goods) does not have the kind of cash on hand to pay the full purchase price right up front. *A*, the manufacturer, may agree to sell to *B* on credit, again making for a true Article 2 sale. Manufacturers, however, are not always in the position to extend credit on a single large sale over what could be a period of many years. It is rare they would want to do this even if they could. Their business is making goods and selling them. They depend on large chunks of cash coming into their coffers each and every time some product is shipped out. Manufacturers don't want to get mixed up in the business of extending long-term credit. That is better left to financing institutions.

So here's where the third party comes in. It all has to do with money. This third party, *C* (no surprise) has plenty of cash on hand or can obtain it on very favorable credit terms, and is willing to lend it out to make the deal happen. In general terms, *C*'s role is to provide *B* with financing. He, she, but most typically it (the financing party is almost invariably a corporate actor) is an institution which makes its money by the business of extending credit and is only too happy to do so when the terms are right.

The most straightforward way *C* can become involved is if it lends the money directly to *B*. This allows *B* to make a cash purchase from *A*. The sale from *A* to *B* is again governed by Article 2. The loan from *C* to *B* is governed by the law of contracts and the specific provisions of the loan agreement. To protect itself against the possibility that *B* may one day be unable or unwilling to repay, *C* will typically demand that the item being purchased itself serve as collateral for this loan: *C* takes what is referred to as a *security interest* in whatever has been purchased with the money it advanced. This is meant to insure that while the property itself will be in the hands of and can be used by *B*, should *B* fail to make loan payments to *C* in a timely fashion, *C* will be able to get its hands on the goods (*foreclose*) and recover its value that way. While the sale from *A* to *B* is governed by Article 2, the special relationship between *B* and *C* and the interest which *C* is intended to have in *B*'s property is covered in Article 9 of the UCC. The law pertaining to Article 9 security interests is a topic for an entirely separate (and equally fascinating) part of your studies in commercial law. I have referred before to the course in Secured Transactions. We needn't worry about it here. What's important for the time being is that if *A, B* and *C* go this route, the lease form and Article 2A never come into play.

Another way for the parties to accomplish the same business result is for *C* to buy the goods itself from *A. C* then turns around and itself sells them to *B*, but now on credit terms *B* can handle. Legally now, of course, *C* is the seller of goods, but as you can imagine it will not want to be stuck with all of the responsibilities a seller may have under Article 2, particularly the heavy burdens underlying the warranty provisions. The lawyers for *C* (the financing party) will make sure that *B* agrees to a binding waiver of just about any and all warranty rights it might otherwise have against *C. B* will agree to look solely to *A* (the original seller) for its recompense should there be anything wrong with the goods. Needless to say, an important part of the deal will be for *A* to sign something acknowledging and agreeing to take upon itself this accountability to *B*. Its willingness to do so is not a matter of charity—it wants to make the sale. This deal is structured differently, but the lease form and Article 2A are still nowhere to be seen. But we're getting warmer.

Yet another way that *C*'s money can be used to facilitate *B*'s acquisition from *A* is for *C* to buy the property outright from *A* and then *lease* it for a term to *B. A* gets its price for the sale of the goods immediately. *B* gets the use of the goods and pays over the period of use. Here—finally— we have the foundation for what has become known in the trade and in the legal lingo as the *finance lease*. The financing party is brought into the picture precisely to buy the goods just so that it can rent them out to the ultimate lessee. The financing party is interested solely in financing and is neither the originator of the goods nor their ultimate user.

Much of the time the finance lease is a lease only on paper. In reality it is not a "lease" at all, if by the use of that word we mean (as we discussed in Chapter 2) an arrangement where the lessee obtains the right to use the property for some term of years *shorter* than the property's expected useful life. In a "true lease," remember, it is expected that the property will have some significant residual value after the term is over and the interest in that residual value continues to be held by the lessor. On the other hand, in what may be structured to appear a lease but is not a true lease, the stated lease term will cover what is expected to be the entire useful life of the item. While the documents may read that the lessor will get the subject property back at the end of the lease, for all practical purposes it is anticipated the goods will be worthless by that time. The lessor won't care about them. It plans to be fully compensated for the use of its money by the sum total of the rental over the term of the single lease. The papers may actually read that the lessee has the right to "buy" the goods at the end of the term for some nominal amount, but this just highlights how much of a sham lease we really have here.

Be careful. In the past the commentators and the courts have often applied the term *finance lease* to a situation such as I've just laid out. The parties have in real economic terms simply done a sale from *A* to *B* with *C* providing the (secured) financing. Under the definitional scheme of the Uniform Commercial Code, however, as made clear by the recent revision of §1-201(37) as part of the package along with the proposal of Article 2A, what we have here is *no lease at all!* Look again at the lengthy definition in that subsection and review Chapter 2 if you have any doubts. If the parties, whatever their arcane reasons and however they prepare the documents, have entered into such an arrangement where the "lessee" is in reality simply buying the goods on credit, then the transaction is not treated as a lease for purposes of the Code. Under the UCC there are in effect two transactions: *A* (as seller) makes an Article 2 sale to *B* (as buyer). *C* gets what is referred to in the Comment to §1-201(37) as a "security interest disguised as a lease." This relationship between *C* (as lender and creditor) and *B* (as property owner and debtor) is governed by Article 9, *not* Article 2 and *not* Article 2A.

This point is important because for a transaction to be a *finance lease* under Article 2A as defined in §2A-103(1)(g) it must first and foremost be a lease under the §1-201(37) definition. This is apparent from the definition of *lease* in §2A-103(1)(j) and the comments to either and both of these subsections. So it turns out that many of the transactions which in the recent past and even today may be called "finances leases" by the cognoscenti will really be disguised sales and will *not* be governed by the special provisions for finance leases under Article 2A! It's not clear how many Article 2A finances leases there actually *are* out there, tripartite deals in which the expected economic life of the leased property is shorter than the lease term. Surely there are some, and that is enough of a reason to review the Article 2A treatment of this special case as we will do in a moment.

What then are the rules governing deals structured by the parties as finances leases but which do *not* meet the test of being true leases governed by Article 2A? The answer seems to be that parties who are sophisticated enough to enter into such an arrangement should be clever enough and have available the legal expertise to get for themselves *by individually bargained contract* results substantially similar to those laid out in Article 2A if that is what they do in fact desire. See the second paragraph of the Comment to §2A-103(1)(g): "Unless the lessor is comfortable that the transaction will qualify as a finance lease [under 2A], the lease agreement should include provisions giving the lessor the benefits created by the subset of rules applicable to the transaction that qualifies as a finance lease under this Article."*

---

*You may find this result peculiar, in which case you are not alone. As one writer has noted, the answer may lie in the politics of Code creation:

> rticle 2A's special provisions on "finance leases" are something of an oddity. Originally included in the statute as a sop to industry, these provisions are deliberately narrow in scope. Their impact on the marketplace will depend on whether lessors structure their transactions to invoke the "finance lease" provisions of the new statute. When a lessor qualifies under Article 2A as a *statutory*

We are now ready for a short set of Examples and Explanations. First we'll set up the situation of an Article 2A finance lease and then explore the implications of that characterization for warranty issues. You will be referred back to various sections as you go along.

EXAMPLES

1. Benny wants to open up business as a distributor of fresh fish to local stores and restaurants and realizes he will need a special type of refrigerated truck for his operation. He finds that just the type of truck he needs is manufactured by Acme Refrigerated Incorporated. Acme suggests a certain one of its models (the "Superchill") as having sufficient refrigeration power to keep the temperature in the storage compartment down to what Benny has indicated he will need (below 40 degrees Fahrenheit). Acme is willing to decorate a truck with Benny's logo and sell it to him, but Benny does not have the cash to pay for the expensive vehicle and Acme will not extend him credit. Benny contacts the firm of Cartage Services, which carries on an extensive business selling, renting, and financing the purchase of commercial vehicles in his community. Cartage says it has no suitable refrigerated truck which it could rent to him. A deal is eventually arranged in which Acme will outfit a Superchill and paint it to Benny's specifications. Cartage contracts to buy this truck from Acme. Benny enters into a lease of the truck from Cartage at a monthly rental of $1,000 for a term of six years. Prior to signing this lease Benny is given a copy of the contract of sale entered into by Acme and Cartage. Is the agreement between Benny and Cartage a lease governed by Article 2A? Review §2A-103(1)(j) and, more importantly, §1-201(37). It will help you to know that a truck such as the one involved can be expected to remain in usable condition for between 10 to 12 years. There is a regular market in six-year-old used trucks.

2. Is the agreement between Benny and Cartage a finance lease under Article 2A? See §2A-103(1)(g). Would your answer be different if you

---

finance lessor, the statute basically provides the lessor with *automatic* exemptions from the implied warranties of fitness and merchantability. But a lessor can always structure a lease contract to exclude warranties, making himself a finance lessor *by contract*. When a lessor writes the lease contract to exclude such warranties and, in addition, qualifies as an Article 2A *statutory* finance lessor, he will have two independent grounds for exempting himself from such warranties. The statutory provisions, of course, apply only to "finance leases" that qualify as true leases.

Huddleston, Old Wine in New Bottles: U.C.C. Article 2A-Leases, 39 Ala. L. Rev. 615, 661-662 (1988). Will the finance lessor necessarily have the clout to get the terms it wants in the contract? Don't forget, it is the party with the money to lend. Lenders tend to have the power to insist that a deal (if one is to go forward) should proceed on the basis of their own form of documents. And, as we will see as we review the Article 2A provisions, the lessee will in any event not expect the financer to be in the position to warrant the quality of the goods. The lessee is going to expect to look to the supplier for that in any event.

found out that as part of the agreement Cartage agreed to be responsible for repairs on the truck if and when they became necessary?

3.   Assuming this does qualify as a finance lease, what term does Article 2A use for Acme? How does it refer to the legal relationship between Acme and Cartage? Between Benny and Cartage? See the definitions in §§2A-103(1)(*l*), (x), and (y).

4.   The truck is delivered to Benny and he accepts it. He uses it without complaint for a few months. Then the summer comes. He discovers that no matter how high he turns up the control on the refrigeration unit, the inside of the truck where the fish are kept gets warmer than 40 degrees. In addition the windshield wipers don't work at all the first time he tries to turn them on. Does Benny have any rights against Cartage under his lease contract because of these problems? See §§2A-212 and 2A-213.

5.   Does Benny have any remedy available against *anyone*? See §2A-209.

6.   Can the lessee in Benny's position ever have any warranty rights against the finance lessor? If so when? See §§2A-210 and 2A-211(1).

7.   Even if in the case as it stands Benny has no warranty rights against Cartage, can he at least withhold his monthly rental payments until these defects are cleared up? See §2A-407.

8.   Finally suppose that Benny does bring suit against Acme. The manufacturer is able to point to a disclaimer of warranties conspicuously laid out in the contract of sale it entered into with Cartage. Can this disclaimer have any effect against Benny, who after all was not a party to the sale agreement?

EXPLANATIONS

1.   This arrangement should easily meet the §1-201(37) test for being a true lease. We look, as that subsection tells us to, at the facts of the particular case. We may assume that Benny's obligation is for the full term of six years and not terminable by him, but none of the four factors designated (a) through (d) is present. The term of the lease is not "equal to or greater than the remaining economic life of the goods," Benny is not obligated to renew the lease or become the owner of the truck, nor has he any option whatsoever to become its owner. The rest of §1-201(37) therefore need not concern us, but you should note what is there. The second set of lettered instances, (a) through (e), are meant to counter the results found in some earlier cases which make various factors automatic markers of the untrue lease regardless of the economic reality behind the particular deal. The drafters of this new version of §1-201(37) clearly want a realistic assessment of the facts of each case.

Note also the part denoted (y), which states that the assessment is to be made "with reference to the facts and circumstances at the time the transaction is entered into." Here Cartage must expect to have a used refrigerator truck of some genuine value on its hands at the end of the lease term. What will it do then? It might add this one truck to its rental fleet or it might sell it. It might even find itself selling the used truck to Benny. But if so, the consideration would assuredly not be simply a nominal amount. Cartage is expecting to get some real value out of the truck six years from now.

2.   This should be a finance lease under 2A. As you can see there are three criteria. First of all Benny was the one to select the truck. Cartage did not select the goods, nor did it manufacture or supply them. The principal role of the finance-lessor is to provide the funds. It is not involved with the product itself. Often the lessor is simply a financial institution, something like a bank, which wouldn't know the first thing about trucks or the like, but the fact that here Cartage has more experience and may select or supply other trucks does not matter. See the comment which states that "[a] lessor who is a merchant with respect to goods of the kind subject to the lease may be a lessor under a finance lease."

The second criterion is that "the lessor acquires the goods or the right to possession and use of the goods in connection with the lease." The drafters acknowledge that this "in connection with" requirement will need some later fleshing out by the courts, but there is no doubt it is met by the facts here.

Finally, the lessee must have been given an opportunity to know certain key terms of the supply contract, some "advance notice" as it is said, prior to obligating itself under the lease. Here we are told that Benny was actually given a copy of the agreement between Acme and Cartage prior to his signing the lease, so condition (A) is met. The original version of 2A presented to the states had the mechanism set forth in this (A) as the only way the advance notice could be given. Representatives of finance lessors objected. Among other things it would have meant that for a finance lease to meet the 2A test the lessee would have had to see *all* of the terms of the supply contract, including the price the lessor paid the supplier. Not all finance lessors were happy with that prospect. This accounts for the more limited notice mechanisms provided for in (B) through (D) which were added by the 1990 Amendments.

This would still be a finance lease under 2A even if Cartage did have the repair obligation. See the Comment. "[T]his definition does not restrict the lessor's function to the supply of funds. . . ." And later, "[t]he lessor is not prohibited from possession, maintenance or operation of the goods, as policy does not require such prohibition." If the three criteria of the definition are met, that is enough.

3.   Nothing tricky here. Acme is the *supplier* and its arrangement with Cartage is the *supply contract*. The contract between Benny and Cartage is the *lease contract*.

4.   Benny will not have rights against Cartage. Whatever rights he may have would have to be based on an implied warranty of one sort or another. The failure of the windshield wipers would be a breach of a warranty of merchantability. The truck is in this respect not "fit for the ordinary purposes." The fact that the refrigeration doesn't meet Benny's

particular needs would be a failure of an implied warranty of fitness for a particular purpose. But both §§2A-212 and 213 are clear: The lessor does not give these implied warranties in a finance lease. Benny's relief, as we see in the discussion of the next question, must lie elsewhere.

5.   Benny can go against Acme, the supplier, for the breach of these warranties. This *pass through* under §2A-209(1) of the supplier's warranties (made part of the supply contract as a matter of Article 2 sales law) to the ultimate lessee in a finance lease is, in the language of Comment 1, "self-executing." All Benny need show is that the warranty of merchantability and an implied warranty of fitness for a particular purpose were warranties "in connection with or as part of the supply contract." Could he possibly run into trouble when he tries to show that the supply contract contained, by virtue of §2-315, an implied warranty that the storage compartment would cool down to below 40 degrees? After all, this seems to be a "particular purpose" of Benny's, not Cartage. But I don't see how this could really be held against Benny. Don't forget, if this is an Article 2A finance lease the assumption is that the goods were acquired "in connection with" this particular lease. So if Benny needed the fish to stay this cool and was renting a suitable truck from Cartage, it *was* the finance lessor's particular purpose to obtain a truck that would meet its particular lessee's particular requirements.

Of course the best for Benny would have been to insist that anything this crucial to him be included as an express warranty in the supply contract. He has his right to advance notice of what's in this supply contract, at least as far as warranties are concerned, so he could check that he was getting the protection he needed. Do you see why the alternative mechanisms of §2A-103(1)(g)'s third criterion are written as they are?

6.   The finance lessor can be stuck with warranty liability to its lessee, but it should be able to avoid any such problem by careful handling of the situation. Under §2A-210 the finance lessor *can* make express warranties. This section does not have the automatic exemption for the finance lessor of those creating the implied warranties of quality we just looked at. You can appreciate why the representatives of Cartage will be careful not to make any "affirmation of fact or promise" about the Superchill. That kind of talk they can and will leave to Acme and its representatives.

Even less likely is that Cartage will have to worry about any warranties under §2A-211. Under subsection (2) the finance lessor is automatically protected from any liability "by way of infringement or the like." The finance lessor is not excluded from giving the warranty of quiet possession by subsection (1), but it would be liable only if the other's claim arose from its own act or omission. Cartage will at the time of the deal presumably ask for the appropriate back-up documentation to assure itself that Acme owns the truck and can rightfully sell it.

7.   Benny has to keep making his payments. This is the so-called *hell-or-high-water provision* applicable to the finance lease. It is "so-called" because the lessee is expected to continue sending in those rent checks

come hell or high water. Virtually all finance lease arrangements which have been drafted in the past make this an explicit part of the lease agreement. (Remember it is generally the financing institutions that do the principal drafting when they're lending the money. If you're borrowing money from a bank, you're going to have to live with the bank's forms.) Section 2A-407 is just intended to make this result "self-executing." Read the first comment to this section. Look back to Comment 3 to §2A-209. It tells us that the irrevocable and independent obligation of the lessee is the price it pays for the pass through rights it gains against the supplier under that section.

Notice that the self-executing hell-or-high-water clause is not made a part of any "consumer lease" via §2A-407. For the definition of *consumer lease* see §2A-103(1)(e). What if the parties to a consumer finance lease draft in their own hell-or-high-water clause? Is it enforceable as part of the actual explicit agreement of the parties? Or is it unenforceable as some kind of overreaching by the financing agent in a consumer transaction? The drafters of Article 2A tell us that this section does not address the issue. See Comment 6.

8.   Benny will be stuck with whatever legal effect is given to the disclaimer in the supply contract, as governed by Article 2 principles. His rights against Acme arise from the workings of §2A-209, and that section is clear that whatever rights pass through to the lessee pass through warts and all. See the last phrase of subsection (1) and Comment 1. Again we see the relevance of the advance notice criterion of §2A-103(1)(g)'s definition. If the lessee in the finance lease situation is to be stuck with the effective disclaimers and limitations negotiated by the supplier and agreed to by the lessor, he or she must have an opportunity to know about them before signing the lease.

One final pointer: The drafters stuck into Comments 3 through 5 of §2A-407 a pretty good synopsis of the special rules for finances leases (although why just at that point is not altogether clear). You might want to use those comments to review.

PART THREE

Performance of the Sales Contract

Everything up to this point has been ultimately directed toward answering the most elemental of questions: Have the parties entered into an enforceable contract for the sale of goods? If so, what are the terms of that contract? Now we will assume all that. We will assume that a prospective buyer and a willing seller have entered into an agreement of sale and that their agreement is enforceable under Article 2. Furthermore we will assume that the terms of the contract are settled, unambiguous, and well understood by both of the parties.

This, however, is not the end of the story. Certainly it is not the end for the buyer and seller themselves, who are after all not interested in the contract for its beauty as an abstract legal device. Their needs are not met because as good commercial lawyers we are now able to recite in detail and with all the appropriate flourishes a listing of their manifold legal rights and responsibilities. Once the papers are signed, the hands shaken, or the closing closed, the contracting parties are not unreasonably interested in actually *carrying out* the deal. It is not enough that they can file away the signed papers or hang a picture of the ceremonial handshake on the office wall. Neither the buyer nor the seller can expect to get rich just by sitting back content in the knowledge that a deal has been made and waiting for the money to roll in. The buyer is interested in getting the goods and getting use out of them. The seller is quite naturally interested in getting paid the price. The parties have bargained for the *performance,* not merely the existence, of the contract.

Given that a contract exists and its terms are clear, who must do what, and how and when must it be done? The parties will have to plan and carry out their actions carefully. Each must avoid doing anything that will later leave room for interpretation by the other as a breach of the agreement. But neither can afford to play a purely defensive game. Both buyer and seller must be willing and able to make those moves which put the other under a return obligation. Otherwise the contract will ultimately be of no more value than a stack of papers yellowing in the files or that memorial photograph hanging unnoticed on the wall.

The general obligations of the buyer and seller under the contract of sale are perfectly straightforward. Section 2-301 reads in its entirety as follows:

> The obligation of the seller is to transfer and deliver and that of the buyer is to accept and pay in accordance with the contract.

Obviously more detail is called for, and in fact carrying out these general obligations can be a fairly intricate dance for the parties involved. The chapters in Part III deal with various questions that arise as that dance proceeds to what is, in the vast majority of instances, its successful and satisfying conclusion. In those (we hope) rare instances where the music turns sour or someone trods on somebody else's toes, Article 2 will be there to step in—often to get the parties and the deal back in rhythm, to finish out the dance, or to at least set the ground rules for the unpleasant brawl that ensues.

The sections of Article 2 with which we begin are often referred to in casebooks and other materials as the *TARR provisions*. We are dealing here with the important Code concepts of Tender, Acceptance, Rejection, and Revocation—the principal steps in this dance of performance. To be complete we really should throw into this TARR an **I** for the opening move of **I**dentification of the goods and a **C** for the all-important notion of **C**ure which threads throughout much of the discussion. Each of these steps will be examined in turn and as they relate one to the other. By way of introduction, however, it's helpful to go over the general scheme in its broadest outlines.

First the goods will be *identified* to the contract by some means or another. By this we mean that a particular item or aggregate of items will be segregated from all the other stuff in the universe and marked out as *the* stuff which is the subject of *this particular* sales transaction. That's identification. The next move is typically up to the seller, who is asked to take the lead. The seller must *tender* the goods to the buyer. *Tender* is the action of the seller in delivering or offering up the goods to the buyer purportedly in accordance with the contract. If the tender does indeed meet all of the seller's obligations as set forth in the contract, we will refer to *conforming tender*. Otherwise we have a case of *nonconforming tender*. Either way it's t*ender*, but the consequences are, as you would expect, quite different.

Once the seller has tendered it is up to the buyer to decide whether to follow the seller's lead. He or she will have to respond to tender, either by *accepting* the goods or *rejecting* them.* If the goods are accepted, one set of consequences flows; if the buyer rejects, things take a different course. In some instances when the goods have been accepted the buyer may later attempt to *revoke* his or her earlier acceptance. When the buyer rejects goods (and perhaps when he or she revokes an acceptance), the seller may claim the right to *cure* any nonconformity by making another later tender, this time with the problem or problems cleared up. If cure is attempted, the whole routine starts over again.

We shouldn't forget *payment*. (Undoubtedly the seller would not forgive us if we did.) The seller is entitled to payment for any goods accepted. If there is some problem with the goods, if in some way the seller has failed to meet all of his or her responsibilities under the contract, the buyer's remedy with respect to accepted goods is going to be a cause of action for damages. The buyer will have to keep the goods and pay the contract price, even if he or she may subtract from what is owed some amount corresponding to the injury. Contrast this with the situation where the buyer has rightfully rejected the goods, or having accepted is later able to revoke this acceptance and undo the deed. The buyer is then off the hook. The goods are, except in rare instances, not his or her

---

*Note that in using the word *acceptance* here we are referring to acceptance *of the goods*. Don't confuse this with acceptance of an *offer*, which is part of contract formation process and something else altogether (something with which we dealt in Chapters 4 and 5).

problem at all. Beyond that there is no obligation to pay the price. The buyer can walk away from the whole mess and, if such goods are still needed or desired, simply start afresh with some other supplier. At the same time the buyer retains the right to sue for monetary damages if seller's breach caused greater injury. You can see why the rejection and revocation possibilities—these steps in the dance—are particularly important to the buyer.

Commentators often refer to rejection and revocation as the buyer's *goods-oriented remedies*. This means that they are remedies available to the buyer that can be taken advantage of directly on his or her own initiative and which can quickly and effectively provide needed relief. No intervention by a court—and no involvement with lawyers!—is necessary to accomplish a rejection or a revocation of acceptance. (Of course counseling by a competent commercial attorney may well be advisable. But at least it's not litigation.) Compare this to the case where the buyer is forced to fall back on his or her right to monetary damages as they may be awarded by the courts. (We deal with these in Chapter 29.) Any time the buyer has to look to a court for relief and has to deal with the considerable difficulty of many months (perhaps years) after the fact putting a dollar figure on the consequences of a breach, he or she can expect to encounter additional headaches and heartaches (and legal fees). At the same time, if the availability of the goods-oriented remedies of rejection and revocation are crucial to the buyer, the seller must be alert to the possibility of the buyer's *wrongful* rejection or revocation and ready to take advantage of any right to cure.

There you have it in a nutshell. Of course, plenty fits into that nutshell, accounting for the existence, complexity, and length of the following chapters. As a matter of fact, I don't believe this material is particularly difficult, but you should expect to spend some time working through Chapters 17 through 20 in order. The concluding chapters of this part, Chapters 21 through 24, deal with some special problems of performance. These can be approached in any order as the individual topics come up in your studies.

A very brief note on leases: This Part concentrates on performance of the sale of goods. Just about every section of Article 2 with which we deal in this material has a direct analogy somewhere in Article 2A. With only a few exceptions which I'll note, these sections differ from their Article 2 progenitors only in that they have been revised, in the words of the Article 2A Official Comments, "to reflect leasing practices and terminology." The general concepts and the overall TARR terminology (including the *C* for cure) have been moved over into the field of leases. While there are as yet no great number of reported cases dealing with these Article 2A provisions, it seems reasonable to assume that the courts in applying them will be guided by decisions interpreting Article 2 and the general understanding of performance issues which we discuss here.

17

Identification of Goods and the Seller's Tender

Identification

At the time the parties enter into a binding contract of sale the subject of that sale will often be a particular unique item already in existence. It might very well be sitting right there in front of them. This need not necessarily be the case, however. The goods to be bought and sold may be part of a larger stock held at some distant point by the seller. Or they may not yet even be in existence: Article 2 clearly provides for the contract to sell *future goods*. See §2-105(2). At some time, of course, such future goods will have to come into existence. They may be produced specifically to fulfill the single contract, or again they may just come off the assembly line and eventually be stored as part of a larger batch of goods. If the goods are held in bulk along with their brothers and sisters, there will then have to come a time when they are singled out as individuals. The buyer is expecting to get—and ultimately will get—some particular items, not just the abstract embodiment of goodliness.

The process or event in which an individual item or items become separated out from the whole world of other such articles and are designated as the particular goods "to which the contract refers" is called *identification of goods* under Article 2.* Section 2-501 deals with identifi-

---

*Interestingly enough Article 2A contains no reference to identification.

cation and sets forth the rules for determining when identification has occurred. You can't really find a definition in this section, much as you might want to. As you can see, subsection (1) says in effect only that goods are identified to the contract giving the buyer "a special property interest and an insurable interest" in them "by identification." If this is a definition it's a perfectly circular one, and the section has been criticized on this basis. In practice, the lack of a precise definition isn't of any great problem for us. In fact, the whole notion of identification does not play as great a part in Article 2 performance problems as you initially might expect. Still, there are individual sections in Article 2 which make reference to and depend upon whether the goods have been identified,* and it's worth some study. The first few questions of this chapter will take you through the rules set out at the end of §2-501(1) for determining when identification has occurred.

Note initially that no one party is necessarily responsible for making identification happen. Identification to the extent we understand it is more an event than an activity. It may come about because of action by the seller or the buyer, or simply because the two are thinking along the same lines. Sometimes it just happens as nature takes its course. For example, in some instances a newborn animal is identified to the contract for its sale at the moment of its birth—an event the timing of which neither the seller nor the buyer would claim to control.

Tender and Its Consequences

Tender, as that word is used in Article 2, can like identification be thought of as an event, but it also connotes an action and has the power of a verb. When we do use it as a noun to connote an event, there can be no doubt that (unlike identification) it is an event under the control of one of the two parties. Tender doesn't just happen. It is the seller's responsibility. Unless excused by the buyer's failure to make payment when all or part of the price is due before delivery (§2-511(1)), the seller starts the ball rolling by tendering goods in conformity with the terms of the contract. *What* exactly must be tendered, and *where* and *when* must tender take place? We have to assume that these matters are all covered by the contract of sale, either because of the explicit agreement of the parties, by applicable trade terms, or by virtue of some gap-filling provision of Article 2. (See particularly §§2-307 through 2-309, as covered in Chapter 9.)

Why does the seller tender? That's easy enough to appreciate. Presum-

---

*For instance, see §2-613 on Casualty to Identified Goods or §2-709(2) dealing with the seller's Action for the Price. In point of fact, identification of goods and the buyer's "special property interest" in them from the time of identification has perhaps its greatest importance outside of the scope of Article 2 altogether. You need not worry about this now, but when you study Article 9 security interests, and particularly the criteria for "attachment" of such interests under §9-203(1), you'll see the relevance.

ably the seller wants the transaction to go through to its conclusion, and tender is the seller's way of moving the process forward and forcing the issue. Under Article 2, as in the common law, if both the seller and the buyer become uninterested in actually carrying through with the deal, then it just dies on the vine. The seller will not tender, the buyer will be relieved that this is so or at least not complain, and that will be the end of that. It is up to the parties, the buyer and seller, and not some abstract rule of law or outside authority, to prod the contract of sale along to some resolution or another.

To the seller, tender is crucial because of its consequences. Let's spell those out. It is important (for us and for the parties) to distinguish between tender that conforms to the terms of the contract and tender that is in some way nonconforming. Conforming tender puts the buyer on the spot. Look at the second sentence of §2-507(1). "Tender entitles the seller to acceptance of the goods and to payment according to the terms of the contract." Once the buyer has accepted, he or she will have to pay for the goods at the price contracted for (§2-607(1)). Should the buyer *fail* to accept a conforming tender, the seller has a host of remedies available under the Code. These are set forth starting at §2-703 and will be dealt with in a later chapter. For the moment you can just assume that a wrongful rejection by the buyer gives the seller plenty of options to protect his or her interests.

What of a nonconforming tender? In that event, as we will see in more detail in the chapters to come, the buyer is in the catbird seat. For the moment look at §2-601. With some exceptions to be discussed as we go along, the buyer may react to a tender which "fail[s] in any respect to conform to the contract" by doing just about what he or she wants, including rejecting the whole delivery.

Tender, conforming or otherwise, is the first step in the dance of performance.

The Perfect Tender Rule and the Code

As you are no doubt aware from your Contracts course, contracts for the sale of goods were historically governed by what became known as the *perfect tender rule*. What this meant was that the seller's tender had to be conforming in every respect, it had to be perfect, in order to trigger the buyer's obligation to take and pay for the goods. If the goods were in any way nonconforming (*e.g.*, if there were too few items in the shipment or too many, if any warranty no matter how trivial was not met, or if the delivery was even one day too late or one day too early), the buyer could simply reject with no untoward consequences. And the buyer could usually get away with such a rejection even if the reason for not wanting the goods was in truth unrelated to the nonconformity relied upon to justify rejection.

Presumably you studied this result in Contracts, comparing it to the more flexible notion of *substantial performance* or *material breach* that holds sway in areas of contract law other than the sale of goods. At that time you considered not only the history of the unyielding perfect tender rule for the sale of goods, but some of the arguments that could be made in its favor. Primarily there is the concern that the seller, given a right to insist upon acceptance of a "substantially" conforming tender, might be encouraged to cut corners, thereby foisting upon the buyer something quite different from what he or she was expecting. Beyond that, the common law courts were understandably reluctant to put the buyer in the uncomfortable position of determining at the very moment of delivery as the goods were sitting outside the door whether the seller's breach was "material" or not. A buyer who believed the breach to be material and rejected on that ground would always have to worry about later being second-guessed by a court. An incorrect application of the materiality standard (dare we say a wrong guess?) would find the buyer facing the full range of penalties for breach of contract.

I assume you also had occasion to consider the arguments that have been raised *against* the common law's perfect tender rule, principally the concern that it gave the buyer the opportunity to get out of a deal on the merest pretext and beyond that the whole air of gamesmanship it lent to the performance of contracts for sale. Critics of the perfect tender rule tend to speak of the "rigid" or "formalistic" perfect tender rule, and you know they don't mean any of this as a compliment.

By the time work began on Article 2, criticism of the perfect tender rule had quite generally taken hold, and most commentators probably hoped and expected it not to survive the drafting of the Code. Such was not to be the case, however, as you should convince yourself by referring once again to §2-601. The buyer has the right to reject the whole should the tender of delivery "fail *in any respect* to conform to the contract." Perhaps you think you can eke out some flexibility for the seller by playing around with the word "conform," but look at the definition in §2-106(2). Goods are *conforming* "when they are in accordance with the contract," not when they are "substantially" or "materially" in accordance with the contract. The icing on the cake (for the buyer) is found in the opening sentence of Comment 2 to §2-106. However much one of the goals of the Article 2 drafters was to "modernize the law governing commercial transactions" (§1-102(2)(a)), in this one respect they ended up retaining the most traditional (many would say archaic) of rules.

The language of Article 2 of the Uniform Commercial Code directly incorporates the perfect tender rule for the sale of goods. There's no way around that fact, and with rare exception the courts that have had to consider the question have so concluded.* At the same time there is every reason to believe that the perfect tender rule as it resides in Article 2 is but a shadow of its former self. Various other provisions of the Code,

---

*In fact the only exception seems to be the state of Connecticut. See the discussion in *D. P. Technology Corp. v. Sherwood Tool, Inc.*, 751 F. Supp. 1038, 13 U.C.C.2d 686 (D. Conn. 1990).

some of which we have already considered and some of which are yet to come, are generally seen as working together to virtually gut any "lack-of-perfect-tender"-style argument on which a buyer might try to insist. We can catalog the numerous provisions that work to mitigate the potentially harsh working of the perfect tender rule at this time. Don't worry about the details now. You may, however, want to return to this listing as a review after you have worked through all of Part III on performance issues. For the moment simply note the following:

(1) *§1-203*. A buyer's rejection must be made in good faith. Remember that for an Article 2 merchant good faith requires not only honesty in fact (which is required of all of us) but "reasonable commercial standards of fair dealing in the trade." §2-103(1)(b). The buyer is prohibited from relying dishonestly and, in the case of a merchant, unreasonably on some imperfection in tender which really doesn't matter to him or her simply to get extricated from a deal that now seems undesirable.

(2) *§2-605*. A buyer may not later justify a rejection by pointing to defects on which he or she did not rely at the time of rejection. A buyer is foreclosed from later cooking up a good excuse for a wrongful rejection.

(3) Recall the significance given to trade usage, course of dealing, and course of performance by Article 2. (And see Chapter 7.) These trade terms actually become part of the agreement and hence the contract between the parties. If in a given trade buyers regularly give some leeway to sellers in judging compliance with the contract terms, that measure could also become part of any specific contract within the industry.*

(4) *§2-504*. As we will see in this chapter, some defects in the seller's manner of shipment will be grounds for buyer's rejection "only if material delay or loss ensues."

(5) *§2-601*. The perfect tender standard does not apply to so-called installment contracts. As we'll see in Chapter 22, such sales are governed under Article 2 by a rule of material breach.

(6) *§2-608*. Even if a buyer is given the right to reject for a nonmaterial breach under §2-601, if the buyer does accept and later tries to revoke his or her acceptance, a different standard will apply. See Chapter 20.

(7) Finally, if the buyer does reject, the seller will have in many instances the important *right to cure*. We deal with this in Chapter 19.

---

*So, for example, assume that Seller, a cloth manufacturer, contracted to deliver 10,000 yards of denim to a buyer in the business of making jeans. Assume furthermore that it is customary in the sale of cloth to accept and pay at the contract rate for deliveries which are within five percent of the specified amount. Seller tenders 9,985 yards of denim. Seller can argue that this tender *does* "conform in every respect" with the contract. A contract stated to be for the sale of 10,000 yards of cloth puts upon the seller the obligation to deliver this amount plus or minus five percent. The buyer cannot reject even under the perfect tender rule.

All in all, it is difficult to conceive of a situation arising under the UCC where the seller could unfairly or unreasonably fall victim to the buyer's capricious invocation of the perfect tender rule. With the adoption of Article 2 that rule remains on the books, but its spirit has been severely restrained if not entirely broken by the overall effect of the Code on matters of performance.

The Means of Tender

If tender is an action on the seller's part, we need to inquire exactly what the seller must do to have successfully tendered and by so doing put the burden of response upon the buyer. The key sections here are §§2-503 and 2-504, which you should look over now. *One warning:* You will see various references in these sections and in others we confront in the next few chapters to things like documents of title, bills of lading, and warehouse receipts, negotiable and otherwise. If you have not yet encountered such documents of title, and particularly if you have not yet run into the concept of *negotiability* in your commercial law studies, you should not worry about picking up all the subtleties at the moment. We'll deal with the intricacies of so-called documentary sales in Part VI, and you can wait until then to master the details. For the time being it is enough to think of such a document as something akin to the receipt you get when you take some clothing into the dry cleaners: It serves as evidence of the fact that you've turned the particular garment, be it a skirt or a pair of slacks, over to the cleaners, and beyond that it stands as a kind of record of the service the cleaner is expected to provide. Typically it will note whether there is to be cleaning, pressing, or storage. Finally and most importantly, you will be expected to present the receipt at the cleaners if you want to get your clothing back. *Bills of lading* are documents of title given by commercial carriers when goods are delivered to them, and *warehouse receipts* are (as you might expect) documents given by commercial warehouses; they are indeed more complicated than this, but that's the basic idea and it will serve for the present.

Now back to the two basic sections on tender, §§2-503 and 2-504. As you can see, Article 2 itself does not dictate where tender must take place or in what manner. That is up to the parties. As §2-503(1) makes clear, "The manner, time and place for tender are determined by the agreement and by this Article," that is, by the parties' contract of sale, which is after all just the agreement as interpreted and amplified by the provisions of Article 2.

Tender may take place at the seller's place of business or residence, at the buyer's, or on some neutral territory. The mechanism by which tender is actually carried out is also up to the parties. In many instances the contract will leave the exact method of tender up to the seller, in which case any means will suffice as long as the seller can be said to have suitably "[held] conforming goods at the buyer's disposition and give[n] the buyer any reasonable notification necessary to enable him to take delivery." At other times the parties may have agreed on a single exclusive manner of tender (e.g., "Delivery by United Parcel Service to Buyer's business address on or before February 15"), in which case the seller will have to take the steps contemplated except in the rare circumstance where he or she is excused from doing so by unforeseen circumstances (see §2-614).

So the time, place, and manner of tender is up to the parties. There will be times when the seller tenders directly to the buyer in a face-to-face meeting at the point of sale. Other times the seller will be expected to deliver to the buyer at some distant point by using its own personnel, such as when a department store makes deliveries with its own trucks and drivers. Or the buyer may send its own truck and crew around to pick up the goods from the seller's place of business. In other instances the seller will ship to the buyer via some third-party commercial carrier, like a railroad or an air freight or trucking firm. Finally there will be the situation where the goods are held by the seller in some independent commercial warehouse. (By this we mean a warehouse other than one owned by the seller for the purpose of storing its own stuff. An independent warehouse is one operated by an unrelated party who runs a business storing things for a fee.) The parties might agree that the buyer will pick the goods up from this warehouse, or they could intend that the goods will become buyer's property even as they remain untouched and unmoved in the warehouse.

There obviously are any number of ways that a tender can take place, and hence a number of ways a seller's attempt at tender can go astray. The following Examples and Explanations, after an initial three on identification of goods and §2-501, all deal with when and whether a tender has taken place. They call for application of §§2-503 and 2-504.

EXAMPLES

1a. Arnold Moneybucks goes into Stella's art gallery to view a show of recent works by a contemporary artist. He spots one small painting ("Black on Black") which he decides to buy and enters into a purchase and sale agreement with Stella. The agreement provides that Moneybucks will pick up the painting in a few weeks when the artist's showing is over. At what point does identification of this painting to this contract occur?

b. Arnold then goes on to Bella's gallery, which is showing works by another artist. He sees a lithograph on the wall ("Author at the Keyboard") which he wants for his collection. Bella tells him that the artist has prepared a run of 100 copies of this lithograph, each of which she has in her possession and each of which she hopes to sell. Arnold contracts to buy one, which Bella agrees to deliver to him. When does identification occur in this sale?

c. Suppose instead that Bella has already sold the entire first run of the lithograph. She tells Arnold that the artist is preparing to make a second run of 50 additional copies, and Arnold contracts to buy one of these with delivery to be as soon as possible. When does identification occur?

2.   In February Farmer Jones contracts to sell his entire crop of spring wheat to Agribuyer, Inc., which he expects to plant in late March and harvest during the summer. When does identification occur?

3.   Meanwhile at the farm down the road, Farmer Smith does not contract to sell her crop prior to the growing season. When she harvests her wheat in July, she stores it in her silo. An agent of Agribuyer visits her farm and inspects the wheat in the silo. On behalf of his company he contracts to buy 120,000 bushels of this wheat (about half of what is in the silo) to be delivered over the course of the next five months. When does identification occur under these circumstances?

4a.   Return now to the situation in Example 1. Stella telephones Arnold on a Friday to tell him that the show is ending on that day. She tells him that he can come into the gallery and pick up his painting. Has Stella tendered to Arnold?

      b. Suppose instead that Stella's contract with Arnold provides that she will deliver the painting to him. On Saturday she wraps the painting up, puts it into her delivery van, and drives to the address Arnold has given her. The address turns out to be Arnold's business office in a large office building. No one at the building is willing to accept delivery of the package on behalf of Arnold. Can Stella claim that she has tendered as of this point? If not, what more must she do and how often must she do it?

      c. Assume that "Black on Black" is not a small painting but is in fact rather large. Assume further that Stella has agreed to deliver this monster canvas to Arnold's home, a quaint townhouse in a fashionable part of town. When Stella and her workers arrive with the painting, it soon becomes apparent that there is no way this painting can get through any of the doors into Arnold's house. Stella has to return the painting to her gallery where it now sits. Has she tendered?

5.   Mazie's Department Store, located in Capitol City, contracts to buy six gross of sweaters from Knits Corporation. The contract provides that Knits will ship the sweaters from its manufacturing plant in Boston to Mazie's. Knits arranges for the sweaters to be picked up by Tony's Trucking Service. Tony picks up the cartons and agrees to deliver them to Mazie's, giving Knits a bill of lading covering the sweaters. Knits sends this bill of lading to Mazie along with a notation that she should expect to hear from Tony when the goods have arrived in Capitol City so that she can arrange for delivery to her store.

      a. At this point, has Knits fully performed its tender obligations? Would it affect your answer if you were to learn that the sweaters never arrive in Capitol City and are never delivered to Mazie's?

      b. Would your answer to the previous question change if Knits had turned over only five gross of sweater to Tony's Trucking?

c. What if Knits had shipped the full six gross of sweaters, but had simply placed the bill of lading in its own files and never told Mazie the shipment was coming?

6.   Butterfield Foods, a preparer of frozen dinners, places a large order for freshly caught scrod with Seaside Fish Sellers, located in Boston. Seaside arranges for the fish to be picked up by Tony's Trucking and forwards the bill of lading along with a notification to Butterfield. Unfortunately, Seaside makes no special provision for shipment in a refrigerated truck. Has Seaside effectively tendered?

7.   (You may want to skip this question and §2-503(4) until you have some familiarity with *negotiable* versus *nonnegotiable* documents of title. Or you may forge ahead—it really isn't that difficult.) When Sam moved from his large suburban home to a smaller apartment, he had to put his piano in storage in Willy's Warehouse. At the time of storage, he received a warehouse receipt from Willy and each month was billed a small storage fee. When it becomes apparent that he is never going to find room in his apartment for the piano, Sam contracts to sell it to Dave, who says that he is content that it should remain in the warehouse for the time being. Sam gives Dave the warehouse receipt. Is this enough to constitute tender?

EXPLANATIONS

1a. Identification of the painting to the contract occurs at the time the contract is made. See §2-501(1)(a). In absence of any explicit agreement to the contrary, identification occurs "when the contract is made if it is for the sale of goods already existing and identified." Here again we seem to see *identification* defined, or at least characterized, in a way that relies on use of the word itself. This may be awkward, but there doesn't seem to be any problem here. The particular painting has been identified at the time of the contract of sale in the English language sense of the word. There is one and only one existing object which is being referred to by both the buyer and the seller as they conclude the deal.

1b. In this situation identification cannot occur at the moment of contracting. We are told the item is in existence, but the particular lithograph (out of the 100) which is to be Arnold's has not yet been determined. Subpart (c) certainly doesn't apply, nor does subpart (b), since the lithograph that is eventually to be delivered is already in existence and cannot technically be "future goods" (see §2-105(2)). Under §2-501 the moment of identification must therefore be that which was "explicitly agreed to be the parties." And yet Arnold and Bella never talked the language of identification. As Comment 3 tries to convey, such an agreement need not be explicitly hammered out nor be terribly precise. We have to look here at who will pick out which exact lithograph is going to be delivered to Arnold. If the contract explicitly or implicitly left this up to Bella, then identification would presumably occur when Bella makes the selection. This could be when she takes one lithograph off the pile, wraps it up, and puts Arnold's address on it. Identification could come earlier, for example, if she had immediately gone into her storeroom after concluding the deal with Arnold and put some kind of marker on one of the lithographs saying "Sold to Moneybucks."

In contrast, if the agreement between Bella and Arnold had been that he would sometime come by the gallery and pick out the particular lithograph that was to be his, then identification would occur when he actually made his selection.

Lithographs like this are traditionally numbered to show not only how many were made but what number in the run the particular item was. So, for example, if Arnold's turned out to be the 57th which was prepared by the artist, there would be a marking at the bottom reading 57/100. What if the custom in the sale of such lithographs is for a buyer to get the lowest number, that is, the earliest in the run which is still available? An argument could be made by Arnold that identification of that one particular item would take place immediately upon his contract with Bella. Note the concluding language in Comment 2 to the effect that "the general policy is to resolve all doubts in favor of identification." This has been read by commentators also to favor the earliest possible moment of identification for which an argument can be made.

1c. In the absence of some other agreement, the moment of identification is now governed by subpart (b). At some point Bella will receive the 50 additional prints. Identification occurs when one particular one is "shipped, marked or otherwise designated by [Bella] as the goods to which the contract refers."

What if Arnold had been able to convince Bella, who was able to convince the artist to run off only one additional print especially for him? Once that one copy comes out of the press with Arnold's name written all over it (figuratively not literally), identification may have occurred. Again this is based on a policy favoring early identification. Certainly identification would have occurred by the time the one lithograph arrives in Bella's gallery, even if she is not yet aware of its arrival or made any plans to get it to Arnold.

2. Under subpart (c), identification occurs at the time Jones plants the wheat.

3. From what we have already discussed, particularly in answer to Example 1b, you might think that identification would occur in stages as individual shipments of wheat are taken out of the silo and loaded on trucks destined for Agribuyer. But look at Comment 5, which refers us to subpart (a), implying that identification would occur at the moment of contracting. According to the comment, this hinges on the sale by Smith to Agribuyer of (in what is undoubtedly the clunkiest phrase you'll come across in your studies of Article 2) an "undivided share in an identified fungible bulk." What could this possibly mean? Well, the totality of the grain in Farmer Smith's silo is presumably an "identified fungible bulk," identified in that the parties are referring to a particular hoard of wheat and not just some amount of wheat of a certain type, and a "fungible

bulk" because, well, that's what it is. See §1-201(17) for the definition of *fungible*. *Bulk* is left to your imagination. I think what the drafters meant to be referring to is what I would call (with no great pride of authorship) an *unsegregated* or *not yet isolated* share in an identified fungible bulk. That's what Agribuyer is contracting for, and presumably the drafters want identification to occur as soon as the contract is concluded in such a situation. But then why is this different from the unsegregated lithograph resting neatly in a pile with its 99 identical siblings?

The reasoning behind having a special rule for things like grain in an elevator or oil in a tank really has to do with some consequences of identification with which we are not now concerned. But in any event, is the result in Comment 5 justified in light of the language of §2-501? Look at §2-105(4), which seems to help although it's not clear how. Courts having to consider the question have followed the approach of Comment 5. See, for example, *Great Western Sugar Co. v. Pennant Products, Inc.*, 748 P.2d 1359, 4 U.C.C.2d 1080 (Colo. Ct. App. 1987). Pennant contracted to buy 900,000 pounds of refined beet sugar from Great Western, deliveries to be made at Pennant's request during the fourth quarter of 1980. After Pennant received and paid for 371,500 pounds, it refused to take any more. Pennant was clearly in breach, but the question was one of damages. Great Western sued under §2-709(1)(b) providing for a seller's recovery of the price of "goods identified to the contract" which the seller is unable to resell with reasonable efforts. There was apparently a great sugar glut at the end of 1980 and sellers such as Great Western just couldn't move any of the stuff. Pennant claimed that an award under §2-709(1)(b) was not justified, as the remaining 528,500 pounds of sugar had never been identified to the contract. The Colorado Court of Appeals rejected this argument and followed the suggestion of Comment 5 to §2-501. The court put emphasis on the fact that "[w]ithout question, sugar is a fungible good," and that "at all time [Great Western's] inventory consisted of sufficient excess sugar to supply the remainder of its obligation" under the contract. For more on the same (arguably tedious) subject, see *Apex Oil Co. v. Belcher Co. of New York, Inc.*, 855 F.2d 997, 6 U.C.C.2d 1025 (2d Cir. 1988).

4a. Stella will argue that she has tendered. Section 2-503(1) requires that she "put and hold conforming goods at the buyer's disposition and give the buyer any notification reasonably necessary to enable him to take delivery." But what if her call was at the very end of the business day on Friday? Arnold could argue that tender requires that he have some chance to actually respond. Subpart (a) states that "tender must be at a reasonable hour." If Stella's gallery isn't open over the weekend, it may be that she can't be said to have effectively tendered until some time like the opening of business on Monday.

But what does it matter if she's tendered on Friday or Monday as long as she has in fact tendered? Discussing tender in the abstract is distinctly unsatisfying. If Arnold does come by to pick up the painting within a reasonable time the tender would extend through that time (see the latter part of subpart (a)), and that's all that matters. You have to think of some breakdown in the process in order to make the exact moment of tender relevant and even then it may not be crucial. For example, what if the painting were somehow damaged over the weekend through the fault of neither Arnold or Stella? Who suffers the loss? Such "risk of loss" problems as they are called are dealt with in a separate part of Article 2 with which we deal in later chapters. (As a matter of fact, as you'll see in Chapter 26, the loss in this instance would be on Stella and the technical moment of tender would have nothing to do with it. In other risk of loss cases, however, the moment of tender is considerably more important.)

4b. It's doubtful Stella's action on Saturday would constitute tender. Again we note the language in subpart (a) that "tender must be at a reasonable hour." Stella will have to make a delivery during normal business hours, or at least at some time when it would be reasonable to think that delivery would be accepted. Of course some buyers wouldn't want deliveries, particularly if they may be fairly disruptive, to come during regular business hours. Stella, if she's having any problems, can always contact Arnold and ask when he'd like (or at least tolerate) delivery. Presumably he has to be "reasonable" in what he will allow.

4c. Yes. Her attempt at delivery constitutes tender. See §2-503(1)(b). For the operation of this language in a larger commercial setting, see *Camden Iron & Metal, Inc. v. Bomar Resources, Inc.*, 719 F. Supp. 297, 12 U.C.C.2d 398 (D.N.J. 1989). Camden contracted to sell 23,000 long tons of scrap metal to Bomar. The contract provided that Camden would be responsible for loading and securing the metal aboard a ship to be named by Bomar. Bomar sent a particular vessel, the *Kalli,* and asked that it be loaded with the metal. Witnesses for the plaintiff and defendant alike testified that the *Kalli* was unlike any other vessel they had ever seen. Among other problems, the type of hatches with which it was fitted would have made loading far more difficult and increased the possibility that loading it with the cargo would damage the vessel—damage for which seller Camden would have been potentially liable. As the court noted, "The number and size of the hatches on the *Kalli* materially changed not only the risks that Camden Iron could reasonably have foreseen with respect to damaging the vessel during loading, but the expense involved as well, for a slower loading rate means, ipso facto, a costlier steeve." When Bomar refused to consider getting another ship or agreeing to hold Camden harmless for damage that might be caused to the *Kalli* (which was soon to be scrapped anyway), it had in effect prevented tender. Bomar was held to have breached the contract of sale and required to pay close to one-quarter of a million dollars in damages.

5a. Yes, if we assume that the contract made with Tony's trucking is "reasonable with regard to the nature of the goods and other circumstances of the case." There's no reason to doubt that here. There has been an effective tender, *even if* the sweaters are somehow lost in transit.

The important thing to see in this question initially is that it is governed by §2-503(2), which will lead us to §2-504, and not by §2-503(3). What's the difference? Subsection (2) deals with a *shipment contract*. In such a contract, under the language of §2-504, the seller "is required or authorized to send the goods to the buyer and the contract does not require him to deliver them at a particular destination." That is the seller is obligated to *send the goods off* properly but is not responsible for their actually *getting there*. But someone must be responsible for the goods eventually making their way to their intended destination. In the shipment contract, that responsibility is ultimately the carrier's. Here Knits is responsible to Mazie for getting the goods into the hands of a carrier and effectively arranging for their delivery. *Tony* is responsible to Mazie for carrying through with the delivery. (We'll deal with this type of problem in much more detail in the risk of loss materials of Chapter 26.)

In contrast to the shipment contract the parties can, if they so choose, put the responsibility for successful delivery on the seller by agreeing to a *destination contract*. The rules on tender are then governed by §2-503(3). It is easy to fall into the trap of thinking that just because the seller uses the buyer's address in making the shipment contract ("Deliver to 123 Main Street") it has somehow turned into a destination contract. Indeed the seller will have to use the correct address to meet his or her tender obligation of making a suitable contract of carriage. But use of the destination in this situation is as an instruction to the carrier and not a legal commitment to the buyer. The difference between a shipment contract and a destination contract is like the difference between "I promise to send it to you at your correct address," and "I promise you'll get it." Read Comment 5 to §2-503. It's important to remember that under Article 2 the shipment contract is "regarded as the normal one." Unless the circumstances indicate otherwise, we assume that the parties have entered into a shipment contract. (By way of analogy: Imagine that you told a friend, "I promise I'll call you at home this evening." Would you think you had somehow failed in your duty to your friend if you tried the number several times and always got a busy signal or no answer? How likely is it that you would ever promise more, such as "I promise we'll actually get to talk over the phone this evening?")

If, as in this case, the parties have entered into a shipment contract, then whether the seller has effectively tendered is to be judged by the three criteria of §2-504. Knits seems to have met each of them here.

5b. Knits cannot have effectively tendered if it has not put *conforming* goods into the hands of the carrier. Section 2-504 only uses the term "the goods," but it seems obvious that this has to mean goods conforming to the contract in parallel to §2-503(1).

5c. Here Knits does not tender because it has failed to meet its obligations under paragraphs (b) and (c) of §2-504. You can see why the buyer has a right to expect each of these actions by the seller. The buyer has to know the goods are on their way and by what mode of shipment. Otherwise how could the buyer know where and when to expect the goods and have the ability to get them from the carrier? While the idea of a receipt from the dry cleaner's which I advanced earlier in the text is only a rough approximation of the document of title such as a bill of lading, the approximation will work here. Imagine that a friend agreed to drop some clothes off for you at a cleaners so that you could pick them up later. This friend's actions are of little help to you and could even leave you not knowing where your favorite jacket or skirt was if your friend doesn't tell you which cleaning establishment had the garment and deliver over to you the receipt. You aren't going to be able to get your things back without at least showing the receipt to the cleaner. In most instances it's the same with a bill of lading. The buyer is going to have to display the bill (and in fact will usually have to physically hand it over) to the carrier in order to take delivery. (As I've indicated, there will be plenty more on this in Part VI.)

If you are looking for a case on the importance of paragraph (c), check out *June G. Ashton Interiors v. Stark Carpet Corp.,* 142 Ill. App. 3d 100, 491 N.E.2d 120, 2 U.C.C.2d 74 (1986). Seller promised the buyer that the goods, in this case a shipment of carpeting, would be delivered to the point of pick-up by February 25. There was evidence that they were in that place, a carpet warehouse, by the 26th. Buyer went to the warehouse on the 28th and was willing to accept the carpet in spite of the late delivery. The goods could not be located. Even if they were there, said the court,

> Stark [the seller] had to make the goods physically available to Ashton [the buyer] at the destination so that she could take physical possession of them. This Stark failed to do. . . . Stark argues that its failure to locate the carpeting was due to Ashton's failure to provide proper tagging instructions which were necessary to locate the carpet. However it was Stark's duty to give Ashton any specific instructions which would be necessary for her to take delivery. Stark did not inform Ashton of the importance of the tagging numbers to locate the carpet. Even after Ashton telephoned Stark on February 28, Stark did not inform her of the procedures for locating the carpeting nor of the importance of the tagging identification numbers. Under these circumstances, Stark did not give Ashton the reasonable notice necessary to take delivery.

6.   Seaside may not have effectively tendered. Section 2-504 requires that seller make "such a contract for their transportation as may be reasonable having regard to the nature of the goods and other circumstances of the case." If, as seems very likely, this shipment reasonably called for a refrigerator truck, then Seaside never tendered effectively. What if, perhaps because the fish were themselves packed in ice and the trip was to be quick, buyers and sellers similarly situated would feel comfortable with a nonrefrigerated shipment? Then, of course, Seaside has tendered in this instance.

What if refrigeration would normally be used but the fact that Seaside failed to arrange for it here caused only minor damage to the shipment? Say only five percent of the scrod were at all affected by the heat. Look at the concluding language of §2-504: Failure to make a proper contract under (a), or failure to give proper notification under (c), "is a ground for rejection only if material delay or loss ensues." So if Seaside's failure to ship via a refrigerated truck causes some nonmaterial loss, what result? Butterfield would have to accept the shipment. It could of course when making payment rightfully withhold an amount for the damages it sustained. But that's very different from its having the right to reject the whole shipment. As I mentioned before, this concluding language in §2-504 is one instance where the Code cuts away from what was the very great leverage given the buyer by the traditional perfect tender rule.

Note that the responsibility of the seller under a shipment contract to make a proper contract of carriage does not make the seller a guarantor of the carrier's service or that there will be no trouble along the way. The seller is required to make a reasonable contract of carriage, not a foolproof one. In *Cook Specialty Co. v. Schrlock*, 772 F. Supp. 1532, 16 U.C.C.2d 360 (1991), the seller shipped the goods via R.T.L., also known as Randy's Truck Line, obtaining a certificate of insurance with a face amount of $100,000. The goods, which turned out to be worth something like $28,000, fell off the truck due to Randy's failure to properly secure them and were apparently rendered totally worthless. The buyer was only able to recover $5,000 from Randy, who was otherwise not insured, and sued the seller for the difference. There was held to be no breach by the seller warranting such a recovery. The District Court concluded, "No inference fairly can be drawn from [§2-504] that seller has an obligation to investigate the amount and terms of insurance held by the carrier." Had, however, the buyer's opportunity to recover the full value of the goods from the trucking concern been thwarted not by that company's lack of insurance but rather due to the seller's failure to declare the proper value of the goods when arranging for their shipment, the result could have been different. See the last sentence to Comment 3.

7. Section 2-503(4) deals with goods that are "in the possession of a bailee and are to be delivered without being moved." That's our case here. The contract does not call for Sam to deliver it to Dave from the warehouse or for Dave to pick it up there. So what does §2-503(4) say? The correct analysis depends on whether the warehouse receipt is negotiable or not. If it is negotiable, tender of the receipt is tender of the goods. Here Dave has actually taken delivery of the receipt so there clearly has been tender of the piano. While technically under the language of §2-503(4)(a) Sam could tender in this situation by "procuring acknowledgment" from Willy's Warehouse that Dave has the right to possession, Willy (for his own protection) would not give such an acknowledgment if he had issued a negotiable receipt unless he had knowledge that the receipt had been effectively negotiated over to Dave.

If the warehouse receipt is a nonnegotiable one, the situation is even easier. As you can see by the first part of subpart (b), tender of that receipt or a "written direction" to Willy to deliver the piano to Dave will normally be enough unless Dave objects. If you're finding this difficult, wait if you can until Chapter 32 where all will become clear.

That concludes our initial discussion of tender. Of course tender is important because of the reaction on the buyer's part that must follow. Which brings us to the next chapter.

18

Acceptance or Rejection of Goods

The Buyer Makes a Move

Once the seller has tendered, the next move is up to the buyer. He or she must either accept the goods or reject them. There can be no middle ground, no Code-sanctioned hemming and hawing, and certainly no waiting around. As we will soon see, under Article 2 the seller has a right to expect some response to tender, and if the response isn't a rejection it is by rule of law an acceptance. If the buyer doesn't make a choice within a reasonable time, the law will make one for him or her. So it is up to the buyer, not just in fairness to the seller but for the buyer's own sake, to examine the stuff and make a conscious decision about what to do.

It's important to emphasize at the outset that the buyer has to react to a tender *whether or not* it is conforming tender. If the tender conforms in every respect to the contract, then the buyer has a positive duty to accept the goods (see Comment 3 to §2-602), but this acceptance doesn't happen automatically. Nothing in Article 2 categorically precludes a buyer from rejecting perfectly conforming goods. It can be done. Of course it's a breach by the buyer to do so, but Article 2 is entirely prepared to deal with that eventuality. We deal with remedies in a later part of this book, but for the moment note the introductory phrasing of §2-703.

If seller's tender is nonconforming, the options rightfully open to the buyer are of course greater. But the choice is still up to the buyer, and the fact of a nonconforming tender doesn't eliminate the responsibility for making a decision. The law will not assume a rejection just because the goods aren't as promised. Look again at §2-601. Except in some circumstances with which we deal at other points, if the seller serves up goods which "fail in any respect to conform to the contract" the buyer may do one of a number of things. You shouldn't assume any more than the Code does that a buyer will always want to, or even be able to, reject nonconforming tender. Life is seldom so uncomplicated. Often the buyer will make the decision to accept long before any nonconformity becomes apparent. Even if the buyer *does* notice the problem straightaway at the moment of delivery, remember he or she has been expecting these goods and probably has made plans that hinge on having them available. The buyer may have no choice but to make do with what is at hand. There will be plenty of instances in which the buyer knowing of the nonconformity—and perhaps plenty mad about it—will still choose to accept the goods, using what can be had now and reserving the right to make a claim for damages later when things settle down. Note the subject of §2-714.

At the present we are not concerned with what remedies, principally money damages, a court may later dish out for this or that breach. We are still at the point where the goods have just arrived at the buyer's doorstep. The buyer *may* do one or the other, reject or accept. Each action has its consequences. Let's deal with them in turn.

The Consequences of Rejection

As we've already noted, a *wrongful* rejection, that is, a rejection not authorized by Article 2, is a breach and the buyer stands open to an action under the remedies provisions. What about a rejection that is not "wrongful"? Section 2-601 allows the buyer to reject a nonconforming tender in whole or in appropriate parts. Section 2-602 begins by setting out (with no great detail) the manner of rejection. Assume a *rightful* rejection, that is, one justified by the nature of the tender and that the buyer has carried out with exemplary style. What then? Section 2-602 goes on, along with §§2-603 and 2-604, to tell the buyer what may or must be done with any goods left in his or her possession. As the Examples and Explanations in this chapter will help you explore, there's really not much the buyer is obligated to do after a rightful rejection. A rightful rejection puts the ball back into the seller's court. In most instances the seller is going to have to come and pick up the goods or arrange to get them back. As should be obvious, the seller will have no right to be paid anything for the goods, and is in fact open to a suit for damages. (As a signal ahead be aware that the buyer's damages in the case of a rightful rejection are governed by §2-711.) As we will discuss in the chapter to follow, a seller faced with a rightful rejection, may still have a right to try again under the notion of cure, but then again he or she may not, and in any event cure is not always easy. The buyer will have some minimal responsibility for protecting the goods after a rightful rejection, but the real pressure to deal with the situation is on the seller.

The Consequences of Acceptance

Section 2-607 sets out the effects of an acceptance by the buyer. It is crucial to remember one thing: These consequences follow with respect to any goods the buyer actually does accept *whether or not* those goods conform to the contract, *whether or not* the buyer could have rejected them had he or she chosen to. The buyer by accepting, or by failing to effectively reject (which will turn out to be the same thing), has bought on to this bundle of consequences. Start with the most basic. Under §2-607(1), "The buyer must pay at the contract rate for any goods accepted." That's that. Nothing could be clearer.

Under subsection (2), one result of the act of acceptance is that the buyer has lost forever the opportunity to reject. This may seem obvious, but it's worth pausing over. Once goods are accepted they are accepted. The buyer may in appropriate circumstances have the power later to revoke acceptance, but as we'll discover (in Chapter 20) the right of revocation will not necessarily be as clearcut and uncluttered as may have been the initial right to reject. The buyer who wants to make a clean rejection, taking advantage among other things of the perfect tender language of §2-601, had better do so when the time is ripe.

Skip for a moment to §2-607(4). "The burden is on the buyer to establish any breach with respect to goods accepted." While the section doesn't say so, as you may imagine if goods are rejected the burden will be on the seller to show that at the moment of tender they conformed to the contract and usually in fact that they conformed "in every respect." You've had enough legal training to know how important a procedural point like this can be. Often the main reason the parties fight over whether the buyer can be tagged with having accepted the goods is just because of how significant the placement of this burden can be to the eventual outcome of litigation. We'll see at least one classic case of this in the Examples and Explanations, and you can easily imagine many others.

Finally in our rundown of the principle consequences of acceptance, we focus on §2-607(3)(a). This is an *extremely important* provision of Article 2. So important, in fact, that it deserves its own discussion.

Notification of Breach Under §2-607(3)(a)

Section 2-607(3)(a) is short and to the point. Read it with all the drama you can muster.

> Where a tender has been accepted the buyer *must* within a reasonable time after he discovers or should have discovered *any* breach notify the seller of breach or be barred [read that barred *forever*] from *any* remedy.

The drafters were perfectly clear. The notification requirement applies to any breach and even more significantly lack of notification is a bar to any and every remedy.

As the first paragraph of Comment 4 says, a reason for requiring notification is to defeat what the drafters label "commercial bad faith." They are thinking here of the possibility under some prior law that a buyer could accept goods and make use of them but still, when time came around for payment, have the right to point to some previously undisclosed "problem" with the delivery in order to avoid paying or at least gain some leverage for knocking down the price from what had been agreed. There's no reason to allow, much less encourage, such behavior. But note that despite what the comment says, the actual statutory language "designed to defeat commercial bad faith" makes no reference to the bad faith or the good faith of the buyer. It is all too easy for a perfectly honest buyer, even the "good faith consumer," to be deprived of any and all remedies by virtue of this provision. Of course while the comment on this subsection doesn't mention them, there are other reasons for putting even the buyer operating in perfectly good faith under an obligation to give timely notice as §2-607(3)(a) does. It's a simple matter of fairness to the seller. As we'll see, the seller may have the right to cure a defect under §2-508, but of what use is that right if the seller isn't given prompt notice of the problem? The seller must also have the right to challenge any assertion there's been a breach, and in fact has the right to inspect or test the goods to support this side of the argument (see §2-515), but again these rights wouldn't mean much if the buyer could hold back a claim of breach for any length of time.

The upshot of these concerns was §2-607(3)(a), which in such a draconian form was new to the law of sales when it was included in the Code. No one seems to doubt the basic wisdom and fairness of the provision. At the same time, the stakes are very high and the results can be harsh. The buyer who is found to have waited too long, or who has not given appropriate notice, loses the right to any remedy. Not surprisingly, it is fairly common for an action brought by a buyer against his or her seller to be met at the outset by a challenge under §2-607(3)(a). A successful argument by the seller under this provision throws the buyer out of court and puts an end to the whole matter.

The lesson from a counselling point of view should be apparent: Whenever a buyer experiences any problem with accepted goods, the seller should be notified as soon as possible and with as much specificity as possible about the problem. This notice should make clear that the buyer considers the problem to be a breach of the sales agreement and furthermore that he or she may have to pursue some remedy in light of what is now known about the goods.

From the litigation perspective, several issues can be and have been raised with respect to the application of §2-607(3)(a). First of all is the timeliness of notice. The buyer is given a "reasonable" amount of time. This is presumably a matter of fact in each case, but pity the poor buyer whose situation is not viewed sympathetically by the judge or jury, particularly since the clock started running not just when the breach was discovered but when it "should have been" discovered.

A second question is whether some sort of formal notification is still necessary where buyer can show that the seller should have known and perhaps in fact *did know* of the nonconformity of tender. The simplest situation is one where the seller delivers after the promised delivery date. The seller is as capable as anyone else of reading a calendar and has to know there's been a breach here. Is there any reason for insisting that the buyer give notice of the obvious? In one well-known case, a case involving no small amount of money, it was held that §2-607(3)(a) did in fact require notice in such a situation. In *Eastern Airlines, Inc. v. McDonnell Douglas Corp.*, 532 F.2d 957, 19 U.C.C. 353 (5th Cir. 1976), the court overturned a judgment for approximately $25 million because the question of notice under §2-607 had never been submitted to the jury. McDonnell Douglas sold airplanes to Eastern that were to be delivered on a set schedule. It began to fall behind in its deliveries. Eastern first indicated that it considered the seller to be in breach but later signalled by its actions that it was willing to accept the late deliveries. The appellate court held notice to be necessary, reasoning that the airlines might by its actions have lead McDonnell Douglas to believe that it did not intend to take legal action and that "[t]he purpose of the notice is to advise the seller that he must meet a claim for damages." Other courts have been much more lenient than the Fifth Circuit was here, practically dispensing with the notice requirement when the seller must have known there was a problem. (For all practical purposes, of course, there is no excuse for failing to give notice in any and every situation where it might conceivably be called for.)

The *Eastern Airlines* case also brings out another problem with which the courts have had to wrestle. If notice is required under §2-607(3)(a), exactly how must that notice be given and what must it say? As to *notice* generally, see §1-201(26). Section 2-607(3)(a) does not specify "written notice" as do some other sections of the Code, so it is fair to conclude that notice not in writing will suffice. (It's also fair to conclude that anyone who counsels a buyer that as a practical matter there's no reason to bother with a written notice when oral notice has already been given is just asking for trouble.) But what exactly should the notice say? One court recently confronted with this problem offered a bit of review.

> Section 2-607(3)(a) does not prescribe any form for the required notice. The absence of specific guidelines has forced courts to develop standards for determining what constitutes adequate notice. Some courts have held that almost any complaint will satisfy the requirement. . . . The standard adopted by these courts is known as "the lenient standard of notification." Other courts require the buyer to notify the seller that the buyer considers the seller to be legally in breach. [Citing *Eastern Airlines* as an example]. The standard adopted by these courts is known as the "strict standard of notification."

Southeastern Steel Co. v. W. A. Hunt Construction Co., Inc., 301 S.C. 140, 390 S.E.2d 475, 12 U.C.C.2d 103 (1990). So which is it to be?

Some commentators view (and explicitly or implicitly criticize) the stricter standard as virtually requiring a written communication with the magic word "breach" contained somewhere therein. Which view would the drafters prefer? You can read the second paragraph of Comment 4 to §2-607, but it seems to want to have it both ways. It starts out in a very lenient tone, but closes with language that is less forgiving. In *Southeastern Steel* the South Carolina Court of Appeals—which was not forced to choose since it concluded that the buyer hadn't given adequate notice under either standard—opined that the stricter standard appeared to be the majority view. But then at about the same time as this decision, the Supreme Court of Ohio was declaring that state's rejection of the stricter view. See *Chemtrol Adhesives, Inc. v. American Manufacturers Mutual Insurance Co.,* 42 Ohio St. 3d 40, 537 N.E.2d 624, 9 U.C.C.2d 88 (1989). More recently, in *Arcor, Inc. v. Textron, Inc.,* 960 F.2d 710, 17 U.C.C.2d 475 (7th Cir. 1992), the Seventh Circuit concluded that under Illinois law the more lenient approach would suffice and furthermore that the buyer may be "deemed to have met the notice requirement when the seller has actual knowledge of the product's failure based on the seller's own observations."

A final problem under §2-607(3)(a) (or really a set of problems to which arguably not enough attention has been given) revolves around who has to give notice to whom. When it's a simple two-party transaction, a buyer and a seller, there's no real problem. Suppose, however, that a consumer buyer purchases some product from a retailer which had itself bought (perhaps indirectly through a distributor) from its manufacturer. The consumer is hurt because of some defect in the product and sues the manufacturer claiming a breach of warranty. Can that manufacturer defend under §2-607(3)(a) if timely notice had been given only to the retailer or the distributor? What if the consumer-plaintiff did in fact notify the manufacturer directly but later wants to sue the retailer, which had not initially been given notice? What if the plaintiff is not a buyer at all but some other party who is given the right to pursue a breach of warranty action under the state's particular version of §2-318? Could the manufacturer defend based on the fact that the buyer, not a party to the action, had not given adequate notice? Whatever you may think should be the answer to any of these questions, the courts have had surprisingly few opportunities in the past to explore the issues. Recently a flurry of cases tested these waters, but no clear resolution is yet in sight. About all that we can say with certainty at this point is that as a matter of careful practice a buyer or any prospective plaintiff is well advised to give notice to any and all to whom it might be of any interest whatsoever, practically or legally.

The Modes of Acceptance

As you can see from §2-606(1), the buyer may accept in one of three ways. An *overt acceptance,* in which the buyer "signifies" that he or she will take the goods is covered by subpart (a). Subpart (b) deals with what we might call the *acceptance by omission*. The buyer can also be held to have accepted under subpart (c) if he or she does "any act inconsistent with the seller's ownership" of the goods. Each of these modes of acceptance will be explored in the questions that follow.

You will need to refer to a number of UCC sections before going on to the Examples and Explanations. On the question of when and in what quantities or divisions a buyer may reject, see §2-601. Note also §2-606(2) and the definition of *commercial unit* in §2-105(6). The buyer's rights, if any, to inspect the goods before making a decision are governed by §§2-512 and 2-513. What constitutes acceptance is the subject of §2-606(1). The act of rejection is dealt with, albeit in a cursory fashion, in §2-602(1). Section 2-605 also has something to say on how a buyer who chooses to reject should seize the moment. The buyer's rights and responsibilities with respect to goods in its possession and rightfully rejected are laid out in §2-602(2), which refers you to §§2-603 and 2-604.

EXAMPLES

1. Mazie's Department Store contracts to buy six gross of sweaters from Knits Corporation. Of these, two gross are to be sized medium, two gross large and the rest extra-large. (Mazie has found that no one seems to want this style of sweater in a "small.") The shipment arrives safe and sound in four large packing crates. Inside the cartons the sweaters are plastic-wrapped in bundles of two dozen each.

    a. Mazie discovers that any one bundle contains six sweaters each in the sizes small, medium, large, and extra-large. Mazie has her employees open each bundle. They put the small sweaters to one side of her store room. The other sweaters they arrange by color, putting some directly onto the shelves for sale and the rest in the store room. Has Mazie accepted? If so, *what* has she accepted?

    b. Suppose instead that when Mazie opens the crates she finds that one-fourth of the sweaters are small, but that since the sweaters are grouped by size, all of these small sweaters are wrapped together in nine bundles. Her workers put these nine bundles, still wrapped in their plastic, to one side, and open up the bundles containing the rest of the sweaters. Under these facts, which sweaters if any have been accepted?

2. Bud sees an article about the latest model computer system, the PS/3, in a computer magazine. On January 12, he goes to Sue's Computer Depot. Sue does not have any of this model in her store yet, but is expecting a few shortly. She tells Bud she expects they will sell out quickly, but that she is willing to let him buy one in advance. Bud contracts to buy a PS/3 from Sue. The contract calls for delivery to Bud by February 15. Payment is to be made by Bud in cash, one half by February 1 and

the rest on delivery. By the end of January, Bud has begun to hear rumors that there is a particular infuriating glitch in many of the PS/3's being shipped. Fortunately, it is fairly easy to test for whether a particular machine is subject to the problem. On January 31 Bud calls Sue, who tells him that her shipment of PS/3's has not yet arrived but is due any day. "By the way," she adds, "I haven't gotten your first payment." Bud replies that he has not sent it in and does not want to do so until he has had a chance to see the machine and check whether it is functioning properly. Sue says she wants that money now, and reminds him that there are plenty of other people who would like to buy one of the few models of the new machine.

a. Does Bud have to make the February 1 payment? What could be the consequences if he does not? Would your answer be any different if Sue had told Bud when he called that the machines had in fact just arrived at her store and that she would be opening one up and customizing it to his specifications within the next few days?

b. Assume that Bud does pay half the purchase price in cash to Sue on February 1 but does not get a chance to see, much less to try out, the machine. On February 5 she calls to tell him it is ready for him to pick up. He goes right over to the store. There he finds the machine in a box with his name on it. Sue demands the rest of the money. Bud refuses to give it to her unless he is given the chance to take it out of the box and test it. Sue refuses to let him unpack the machine in the store, and furthermore will not let him take it out of the store until she gets the rest of the price in cash. They are at loggerheads, standing there in the store with the boxed machine between them. The situation could get nasty. You come along, fortuitously carrying your copy of the UCC. How do you advise the two of them?

3. Barney buys a new CD player from Selma's Stereo City. As one of Selma's clerks delivers over to him the player packed in a sealed box, he is asked to and does sign a sales slip underneath a description of the item and the word "ACCEPTED." Later that day when he unpacks the player at his home he immediately notices several large scratches on it. He takes it back to the store and tells Selma he wants his money back or replacement with an undamaged item. Can Selma refuse to take the damaged CD player back based on the paper Barney signed?

4. Joseph Sessa, a Philadelphia beer distributor, owned and raced standardbred horses as a hobby. He contracted to buy the horse "Tarport Conaway" from Gene Riegle, who had a farm in Ohio. Sessa sent Maloney, a personal friend and a knowledgeable horseman, to Ohio to complete the transaction. On March 10 Maloney was given an unlimited opportunity to examine the horse. After observing the horse jogging, he proclaimed Tarport "a fine animal, good and sound." He delivered Sessa's check for the purchase price and arranged for Riegle to send the horse in a van to a designated raceway in Philadelphia. Tarport was picked up by the van

on March 23. He arrived at the raceway at 4:30 A.M. the next day. By 8:00 A.M. he had been examined by a vet and was found to have tendinitis in both of his front legs. After this examination, Sessa called Riegle asking that he take the horse back and return the purchase price. Later, even after the tendinitis cleared up, Tarport was found to suffer from a thrombosis of the left and right iliac arteries, which provide the main blood supply to the hind limbs. On March 29, Sessa again called Riegle and demanded his money back. Was either of Sessa's calls an effective rejection?

5. Finkelstein contracted to buy the pacing horse "Red Carpet" from its owner Gerard Miron for $32,000. He took delivery at 3 P.M. on Monday at the seller's place of business without examining the horse and immediately had it transported to his own barn. The next morning, Finkelstein's trainer discovered that there had been an injury to the horse's leg. By 11:30 A.M. Tuesday Finkelstein called Miron saying he rejected the horse because it was not as warranted. Assuming that a horse that is lame at the time of delivery would not be merchantable, did Finkelstein make an effective rejection?

6a. Mr. Burns purchases a new Chevrolet from Sam's Autos. He picks the car up on February 1 and drives it off the lot. On February 4 he sets off on an extended cross-country trip that he has been planning for some time. About ten miles out of town, the car begins to stall and lurch. Soon it stops completely and will only make grinding noises. He pushes it into a gas station, where a mechanic tells him that the transmission on the car is "shot." He has the car towed back to his home, then he immediately calls Sam and tells him he rejects the auto as defective. Is this an effective rejection?

b. Would it make any difference to your answer to the previous question if it were shown that on February 2 Burns had sent Sam a check for the full purchase price of the auto, which check had been received and deposited by Sam prior to his hearing from Burns on February 4?

c. How would you answer Example 6a if on February 3 Burns had taken the car to an auto customizing shop where he had it decorated with elaborate flames running down the sides and snakes on the hood?

7. Seller contracts to deliver 1,000 "five-inch widgets" to Buyer "on or before March 1." A delivery of 980 widgets arrives at Buyer's plant on February 28. Buyer inspects the shipment.

a. On March 2, Buyer writes to Seller, "I am not happy with the widgets you sent. Some go down to less than 4.8 inches. Please contact me." Has he effectively rejected the shipment?

b. On March 2, Buyer instead writes to Seller, "I reject the widgets, as they do not meet the specifications for five-inch widgets." Seller later sues for the price, arguing that under industry standards the shipments does meet specifications. Her argument appears strong. Can Buyer now defend his rejection on the grounds that the shipment contained too few widgets?

8. Mrs. Bannin orders some drapes for her living room windows from Samantha's House of Window Treatment for a total price of $4,000. The drapes are delivered. The next day Bannin buys and installs the necessary hardware and hangs the drapes. She immediately sees that they hang some five or six inches from the floor instead of the one inch she had planned. She measures the drapes and finds that they are not as long as were called for in her order.

a. She calls Samantha's. When her call is answered by a telephone answering machine, she leaves the message: "I am rejecting the draperies you sent as they are not the right length. Come and pick them up." She takes the drapes down and stores them in a closet. Does she have to do anything more to protect her rights in the situation? In particular, is it necessary for her to arrange somehow to return the drapes to Samantha?

b. Suppose that Samantha writes Bannin telling her to "Have the drapes returned to me. When I get them, I'll send you a check for what I owe you." Is Bannin obligated to follow these instructions?

c. Suppose further that Bannin doesn't follow these instructions, but just keeps the drapes in the closet. Once again she calls Samantha and leaves a message indicating that the seller should pick up the drapes. Several months pass. Samantha is not heard from again. Bannin would like to use her limited closet space for other things. What should she do now?

d. Would your analysis of Mrs. Bannin's situation be any different if, instead of storing the drapes in her closet when she first telephoned her rejection, she had just left them hanging?

EXPLANATIONS

1a. Mazie has accepted under either §2-606(1)(b), by failing to reject in time, or §2-606(1)(c), by her act of putting some of the sweaters out for sale to her customers. We'll look at these methods of acceptance in more detail in questions to follow. For the moment let's focus on exactly what she has accepted.

It appears that Mazie has accepted *all* 864 (that's six gross) of the sweaters *including the small ones*. Step back a bit and first note Mazie's options. What could she have done under §2-601 when the shipment she received was so obviously defective? It was up to her. She could have rejected the entire shipment, accepted it all, or she could have "accept[ed] any commercial unit or units and reject[ed] the rest." Note also §2-606(2), which states, "Acceptance of a part of any commercial unit is acceptance of that entire unit." Finally see Comment 2 to that section.

The question then becomes what is a *commercial unit* under the circumstances, and we turn to the definition of that term in §2-105(6). It all depends on "commercial usage" of course, so we cannot be absolutely sure of anything without a thorough knowledge of the knitwear industry. It seems pretty safe to bet that in sales by the manufacturer no single one of the sweaters is a commercial unit on its own. We can test by asking the question, would Knits have accepted without comment an order for just one sweater, or 863 or 865 of them? Was its price given as an amount per sweater? Highly unlikely. More probably, it customarily deals in some standard multiple, either dozens or two dozens (which is suggested here by the packaging) or by the gross. In any event under these facts Mazie has broken into each and every commercial unit and has accepted them all. This doesn't leave her without a remedy, of course, but she has to pay at the contract rate for all of the stuff accepted—remember the prime directive of §2-607(1)—and will then have to show some actual damage that she can deduct by way of set-off.

It should be clear that while a single sweater is not a commercial unit for the sake of this transaction (a sale by a manufacturer to a retailer), the units can be different in different circumstances. It all depends on commercial usage and the realities of the situation. In any sale by Mazie to one of her retail customers, naturally, each individual sweater *would* be a commercial unit. In fact one way of characterizing the business of retail sales is just this: The retailer's principal reason for being is its willingness to buy things in large commercial units, break up those units and then sell in smaller units, taking of course some measure of compensation for this service and the risks involved.

1b. Mazie here has a good argument that while she has accepted the other sweaters, she has not accepted the small ones. This would depend on her showing that each and every bundle of two dozen was a commercial unit in and of itself. This seems quite possible. What if Knits could show that it usually and customarily dealt in larger units, such as crates of 216 each? (Six gross divided by four equals 216 equals nine bundles.) Then we'd have to inquire further. If the nine bundles she put aside all came out of one crate, she could argue that she has not accepted that crate, only the other three. If the nine bundles of small sweaters had been distributed among the four crates, then by accepting the other sweaters out of each of these crates she's accepted them all.

So the final analysis of this question will depend on facts we don't have, both about how sales are customarily carried out in this industry and about what Mazie and her employees did here. A good exercise is to imagine yourself to be Mazie's attorney. What questions would you ask of her or of others to best represent her in the situation?

As you can see from these two questions, the issue of what is a commercial unit in any situation can be very important. There does not seem to have been much litigation on the point, I would guess because commercial practice is sufficiently clear to the parties (and their attorneys once they've done a good job of investigation) in most instances. A few cases can be noted. In *Axion Corp. v. G.D.C. Leasing Corp.*, 359 Mass. 474, 269 N.E.2d 664, 9 U.C.C. 17 (1971), the contract called for the sale of three valve-testing machines. The buyer acknowledged acceptance of two of the machines but claimed to have rejected the third. The seller argued that the second and third machines, "which were ordered together, delivered together, tested together, and complained of essentially as a unit," constituted a single commercial unit. The court found otherwise:

> The buyer here first ordered one machine separately. Later, after the second and third machines were ordered and delivered together, the seller took the third back separately to work on it. There is no evidence that there was a commercial usage to treat two machines as a single whole or that division of a pair of machines materially impaired their character or value, or that acceptance of one produced a material adverse effect on the other. In these circumstances, it could not be ruled as a matter of law that the two machines constituted a single commercial unit, or that one machine was not a commercial unit.

You can no doubt fool around with the facts here to create a clever hypothetical in which two machines, while physically separate, *do* constitute a single commercial unit. How about a washer/dryer combination bought for the home laundry room? Still probably not good enough. People certainly do consider and sometimes buy one or the other but not both. What about a computer that the maker will consider selling only in conjunction with its own brand of keyboard? Well, you can work out your own hypotheticals.

As one other valve-related example, in *Perkins Pipe & Steel Co., Inc. v. Acme Valve & Fitting Co.*, 2 Ill. App. 3d 338, 276 N.E.2d 355, 10 U.C.C. 127 (1971), the buyer had ordered a bunch of stuff: "two 14-inch steel flanges (the goods in issue), two 8-inch stainless steel flanges, two 6-inch PRV values, one 6-inch steel flanged valve gate valve, and seven used valves. Apparently," the court concluded, "these were five commercial units of valves with the two steel flanges in issue constituting one such unit." The buyer was found to have made an effective rejection of these two valves, this one unit, even while accepting the rest.

Getting away from valves and moving on to animals, note *Texas Imports v. Allday*, 649 S.W.2d 730, 36 U.C.C. 491 (Tex. Ct. App. 1983). The buyer contracted to buy 49 head of cattle. It claimed to have accepted 27 of these cattle, which it found to be healthy, and rejected the remaining 22. The court held this to have been proper. Each cow was a commercial unit. This result seems clearly to be right when you consider that the contract called for 49 of the beasts. If they weren't commercial units one by one, we'd have to posit that the cattle industry deals in groups of seven or seven times seven. Barring a biblical injunction to this effect, I'd not assume it to be commercial custom.

2a. Bud has to make the initial payment and has no right to withhold it pending an inspection. Bud contracted to pay a portion of the price before delivery and before inspection might be possible. Under §2-511(1) payment is a condition to Sue's duty to tender and complete delivery, so if he really wants the computer, he'd better send in that check. He gets no help from §2-512, since at this point there is no reason to think there is necessarily going to be a nonconformity, much less one that now "appears without inspection."

Bud might want to consider using the insecurity mechanism of §2-609 (see Chapter 21), but it's not clear it would do much for him here. First of all, he'll have to show that on the basis of the rumors he has "reasonable grounds" for believing that the computer he's to get would be defective in this particular way. And if Sue is willing to tell him that she'll make sure he gets a good one, isn't that "adequate assurance" under the circumstances? If so, he's back in the position of having to send in his money before he has any right to delivery.

If Sue has received her shipment of the new machines, Bud might be able to argue for a right to inspect prior to payment under §2-513(1) *if* he can show she has already *identified* a particular machine to the contract. But even then, is it "reasonable" to expect that he'd be allowed to come into her shop and play around with the computer before she herself has looked it over and satisfied herself that everything is in order and is ready to make a delivery? In some situations where terribly complex and highly specialized goods are being fabricated to a buyer's specifications, it might be in order for the buyer to make inspections during the course of the seller's manufacturing process, but it seems to me that Bud would be pushing this a bit far if he argued the right to do so here. Consumer buyers often do pay some money, if not all, up front and have to wait until delivery to test out the item.

2b. You advise the two that under §2-513(1), Bud has the right before payment or acceptance to inspect the machine "at any reasonable place and time and in any reasonable manner." So she certainly can't ask him to pay up in cash before he even opens the box. He has the right, at the very least, to be sure that there is a PS/3 in the box. See Comment 1. But does he have the right—right then and there—to take it out, plug it in, and take it for a test drive? Unless there is some special out-of-the-way place at Sue's Computer Depot for him to run through this drill, it doesn't seem to me "reasonable" for him to demand to do it at the store, clogging up her aisles. You may see it differently.

So what's the solution here, other than letting them duke it out? Well, it looks like one of the two will have to give a bit. You might suggest to Sue that she let him take the box out of the store (after a quick peek inside if he insists) in return for a personal check for the amount due. He might go for this as he can always stop payment if the machine turns out to be a dud when he gets to inspect it at home. Or you could suggest to him that he pay the cash, take it home, and really run it through its paces. If it isn't any good, he has all kinds of rights under the Code to reject it then. You could also help by investigating with the two of them, and in light of your own experience, what industry custom suggests here. If the two still can't work it out with all your help, you might just leave them to their own devices, asking as you leave why, if the matter is so important to them, they didn't initially take advantage of the opportunity clearly available under §2-513 to specify before the fact as part of the contract exactly when and how the buyer's inspection could take place.

3.   No. Barney has not "accepted" the goods under §2-606(1), so he has the right to reject under §2-601, and that's exactly what he's doing now. Selma could try to argue that there had been an acceptance under §2-606(1)(a), but you should see why this fails. Even if Selma had been willing to let him open up the box and try out the player right there in the store (and could therefore put up an argument that there had been a reasonable opportunity to inspect), it doesn't make sense to say that his signing as he did "signified" to Selma that "the goods are conforming or that he will take or retain them in spite of their nonconformity." His signature would presumably be evidence against him if he ever tried to claim he hadn't gotten receipt of the package, but that's about it. Remember that the acceptance that we are talking about here is not acceptance of an offer to contract or, as here, what we might call *acknowledgment of delivery*. Section 2-606 deals with *acceptance of the goods* as delivered and under the contract, which is quite a different matter. See Comment 1.

4.   In *Sessa v. Riegle*, 427 F. Supp. 760, 21 U.C.C. 745 (E.D. Pa. 1977), the court held that there had been an acceptance under §2-606(1)(a).

> Sessa accepted Tarport Conaway through his agent Maloney on March 10, 1973. At that time, Maloney was permitted unlimited inspection and both Sessa [via a telephone conversation] and Maloney indicated that Sessa would take the horse.

Having accepted on March 10, any attempt to reject on a later date was doomed to failure (§2-607(2)). Did this mean that Sessa had to be satisfied with a lame horse? No, not necessarily. He would still have recourse (either the right to revoke his acceptance or to seek money damages) if the horse had not conformed to the contract, that is, had been unfit, at the time of seller's tender. Sessa's problem was that having been found to have accepted, he bore the burden of showing the horse to have been injured or ill when it left Riegle's care. Remember §2-607(4). Apparently the type of problems involved can occur in a racehorse for a variety of reasons or simply out of the blue, and it is often difficult if not impossible to determine the cause of the problem much less when it occurred. In fact buyer Sessa offered expert medical testimony, but it was all, in the opinion of the court, nothing more than "conjecture." Sessa was found not to have met his burden of establishing by a preponderance of the evidence that either the tendinitis or the thrombosis was present in the horse on March 23.

5.   Red Carpet figures in the well-known case of *Miron v. Yonkers Raceway, Inc.*, 400 F.2d 112, 5 U.C.C. 673 (2d Cir. 1968). Like the *Sessa* case discussed above, medical testimony was inconclusive on when and how the horse was hurt. So again the crucial issue became the applicability of §2-607(4) and whether the buyer or the seller had the burden of proof on this issue. Buyer had not overtly accepted under §2-606(1)(a), but Miron argued that Finkelstein had accepted by failing to reject after having had "a reasonable opportunity to inspect" Red Carpet. The time between

delivery and the attempted rejection was very short (less than 24 hours), but the court held that an acceptance by omission *had* taken place.

> [W]hat is reasonable depends upon an evaluation of all the circumstances. . . . Finkelstein's own testimony showed that it is customary, when buying a racehorse, to have a veterinarian or trainer examine the horse's legs, and we agree [with the trial judge] that the existence of this custom is very important in determining whether there was a reasonable opportunity to inspect the horse. See Official Comment to UCC §1-204, para 2. We gather from the record that the reason it is customary to examine a racehorse's legs at the time of sale is that a splint bone is rather easily fractured (there was testimony that a fracture could result from the horse kicking itself), and although the judge made no specific findings as to this, we assume that is generally what he had in mind when he pointed out that "a live animal is more prone to rapid change in condition and to injury than is an inanimate object." As we have said, Finkelstein did not have the horse examined either at the place of sale or at his barn later the day of sale. He thus passed up a reasonable opportunity to inspect Red Carpet.

You may want to take the court's suggestion at this time and look at §1-204 and the comments to that section. Notice that the custom shown appears to apply to immediate inspection only of the horse's legs. If there had turned out to be something else wrong with Red Carpet, such as a viral infection, the result could well have been different.

6a. Sam will argue that Burns's attempted rejection came too late, because by February 4 there had been a "reasonable opportunity to inspect" the car, bringing into play §2-606(1)(b). Burns will argue that with a complicated article like an automobile a reasonable period for inspection would have to extend for some time, especially when the type of problem which eventually turns up is one that a typical consumer wouldn't be expected to find on a cursory examination.

Those cases that we have do clearly establish the principle that with an automobile the period of inspection does not end, and the car is not accepted under §2-606(1)(b), just because it has been driven off the dealer's premises by the buyer. The most well-known case involves a very short time and a fairly big problem. In *Zabriskie Chevrolet, Inc. v. Smith*, 99 N.J. Super. 441, 240 A.2d 195, 5 U.C.C. 30 (1968), problems with the buyer's new Chevrolet began to assert themselves within seven-tenths of a mile from the showroom. The buyer was barely able to get his new purchase (eventually travelling in first gear at something like five to ten miles per hour) all the way to his home, about two-and-a-half miles away. Once home the buyer immediately called the distributorship and attempted to reject the car. Later in the course of litigation the seller argued that the buyer had accepted the car by signing the contract and taking possession. The court did not buy this argument.

> To the layman, the complicated mechanisms of today's automobiles are a complete mystery. To have the automobile inspected by

someone with sufficient expertise to disassemble the vehicle in order to discover latent defects before the contract is signed, is assuredly impossible and highly impractical. . . . Consequently, the first few miles of driving become even more significant to the excited new car buyer. This is the buyer's first reasonable opportunity to enjoy his new vehicle to see if it conforms to what it was represented to be and whether he is getting what he bargained for. How long the buyer may drive the car under the guise of inspection of new goods is not an issue in the present case. It is clear that defendant discovered the nonconformity within 7/10 of a mile and minutes after leaving plaintiff's showroom. Certainly this is well within the ambit of "reasonable opportunity to inspect."

So for Burns it's all a matter of reasonable time—a question of fact—and we can't be certain of the result. I tend to think Burns would have the better time of it in front of any judge or jury. Most reasonable people, which has to include judges and jury members, would be understanding if a new car owner hadn't taken his new car out on the open road for a test drive for a few days. Other facts would also play a part: *Had* Burns in fact driven the car very much? Under what conditions? Earlier than the 4th? Had he then experienced anything which should have alerted him to transmission problems?

At the same time it's probably true that if Burns tried to reject on this basis very much later, say two or three weeks after driving the car off the lot, he would have problems. This doesn't mean that he has to be content with a car with a messed up transmission, but his argument under Article 2 will have to be based on something other than a straightforward rejection. As you'll see in a chapter to follow, he may still have the right to revoke his acceptance, which could give him the result he wants. But the route to revocation has its own complications, as you'll discover. At the very least, because the burden of proof will have shifted with acceptance it will be up to Burns to satisfy the court that the transmission was defective on February 1 when tender was made. Contrast this to the rejection situation where Sam, if he wants to argue that Burns was wrongfully rejecting, would himself have to prove that the transmission was perfectly OK when the car was tendered. Given the mysteries of what goes on under the hood and of what can happen to a car over even a few days of hard driving, you can see the significance to Sam of examining as well as he can and rejecting if he is at all tempted to do so as soon as possible.

Just as the actual timing will be an important factor in any assessment of the factual issue, the nature of the defect will presumably be taken into account. Sam the seller's position here would be much stronger if Burns tried to reject on the 4th because he had only then discovered that the door to the glove compartment wouldn't open. What if Burns tried to reject on this basis but earlier on, say early on the morning of the 2nd? Sam might try to argue that Burns had had a reasonable opportunity to inspect, at least for defects of this nature, right there on the lot before he drove the car away. "I told him. Look it over, it's just what you ordered." Should Sam win on this argument? I think not. As a practical matter, does the buyer of a new car go around checking each and every thing that could possibly go wrong, even those which don't require a skilled mechanic to investigate, before taking delivery of the car? (If Sam really did want to get some mileage out of an argument like this, he'd actually have to *demand* Burns make an inspection and even then his position might not be very strong. This is all a matter of §2-316(3)(b) which we met in Chapter 14.)

If Burns were allowed to reject for the faulty glove compartment door—thanks to the perfect tender rule of §2-601—that would not be the end of the story. We deal with the whole doctrine of cure, which may come to Sam the seller's assistance, in the next chapter.

6b. Burns's sending in the check would probably not be in and of itself an acceptance. See Comment 3. Once again it's a question of fact. What really matters here is what the terms of payment had been and why Burns sent the check when he did. If the check constitutes acceptance it would fall under §2-606(1)(a), and we have to inquire whether it "signifies" to Sam anything other than that Burns pays his bills on time. If, for example, the contract had called for payment one day after delivery, then this action couldn't be taken as an acceptance by the seller. If, on the other hand, in order to make the sale Sam had told Burns that he "shouldn't pay for it until you know it's the one you want," then it could be a whole other story.

6c. Sam could hold Burns to have accepted by this flamboyant act under §2-606(1)(c). We normally don't take such liberties with other people's property. Examples of acts that have been held to trigger this provision are the buyer's actually reselling the goods to a third party or running them through its own manufacturing process. In *Mazur Brothers & Jaffe Fish Co., Inc.*, 3 U.C.C. 419 (Vet. Admin. Contract App. Bd. 1965), the seller had delivered a large order of raw shrimp on July 23. On the next day the buyer, a government hospital, cooked the shrimp only to notice an "unwholesome odor" and discoloration. It attempted to reject. The Veterans Administration Contract Appeals Board (which had jurisdiction over the case) ruled:

> Conversion of virtually the entire order of shrimp from a raw to a cooked state in preparation for service to patients far exceeded the testing necessary for inspection purposes. This alteration in the product rendered it incapable of return to [seller] in the condition in which it had been delivered, and in our opinion constituted an act of dominion inconsistent with [seller's] ownership.

A bit of controversy surrounds the application of §2-606(1)(c). Professors White and Summers in their treatise take the position that "use of goods in ignorance of the defective nature of the goods is not as such 'inconsistent' under" that subpart and could never establish acceptance. They are understandably concerned that a buyer not be held to have accepted defective goods when he or she did not even know and had no

316 Part Three. Performance of the Sales Contract

reason to know of the defect. If this reading is correct, then Burns's having the car decorated, even in the elaborate manner which he did, would presumably not affect the analysis of his situation at all. Does this work for you? One problem with this reading of §2-606(1)(c), as has been pointed out, is that reference to "a reasonable opportunity to inspect" the goods—made part of subparts (a) and (b)—is conspicuously missing from (c). For this and other reasons the courts do not necessarily accept the White and Summers approach. Their focus seems more often to be on what is fair to the *buyer* under the circumstances. Note the language in the shrimp case quoted above, the Board's concern for what would end up being returned to the seller, and the markedly different condition it would be in when it came back.

If we do conclude that the decoration of the car absolutely bars a later rejection, can we go further on the seller's behalf and argue that even if it hadn't been so "improved" the fact that the car has been used for four days and driven a considerable number of miles is enough to allow him to invoke §2-606(1)(c) and claim an acceptance? In a word, no. If §2-606(1)(b) and the sections on inspection mean anything, we must conclude that the buyer's use of the goods as they are intended to be used during a period allowing for a reasonable opportunity to inspect cannot be considered action inconsistent with the seller's ownership. It is not inconsistent with the idea that Sam owns an automobile that he is allowing a (still potential) purchaser to drive it around for a period of inspection and testing.

7. No. This is not an effective rejection. We can assume that this letter was sent within a reasonable time as called for by §2-602, but the problem is with what it *says*. The section requires a seasonable notification of rejection, which must actually let the seller know that the buyer is *rejecting* the goods, not just that he or she is unhappy with them or claims there is a breach. This letter would be sufficient for §2-607(3)(a) purposes, but that is another matter. A rejecting buyer does not just claim breach; he or she actually expects the seller to take the goods back. See, for example, *CMI Corp. v. Leemar Steel Co., Inc.*, 733 F.2d 1410, 38 U.C.C. 798 (10th Cir. 1984), holding that notification that the buyer had "a problem" with the goods was not sufficient to effect a rejection.

7b. Buyer has now given a notice of rejection that meets the requirements of §2-602. It turns out, however, that his action may be proven wrongful, as he did not have the right to reject on this basis. Section 2-605 does not allow him to then switch to justifying his rejection on the basis of a nonconformity which he didn't point to initially if that defect was "ascertainable by reasonable inspection" at the time and could have been cured by Seller if she had been notified of it. A delivery that contained too few widgets would seem to fit within this section. The policies behind this section are set forth in Comments 1 and 2.

What if in addition to everything else the shipment had arrived at

Buyer's plant a few days late, say on March 4? He made no complaint at the time but tried to revoke solely on the claimed failure of the widgets to meet specifications. Later when it looks like Seller will be able to show that the widgets were not too small, could Buyer rely on the lateness of delivery to justify his rejection? This was a nonconformity and under §2-601 he would have been able to reject on this basis. Under §2-605 it is also a defect that is easily ascertainable. Buyer knows when something is late as well as the next guy. But lateness is not a defect which it seems could ever be cured (as we'll discuss in the chapter to follow), so §2-605(1)(a) doesn't apply. If Seller hadn't requested in writing a full statement of Buyer's grounds for rejection, §2-605(1)(b) wouldn't apply either. So Buyer might be able to get somewhere with bringing up the late delivery even this far into the proceedings.

There may even be some reason for allowing him to do so. "If the shipment hadn't been late," he may argue, "I would have had more time to figure out how to make use of such stubby (albeit technically conforming) widgets. I didn't complain about the few days before, but now you can see how important they've become." If Seller believes that this argument is just so much hot air, and that the lateness never mattered to Buyer but is only being used by him now in a last ditch attempt to get out of buying some perfectly fine widgets, she can always call into question whether Buyer is acting consistent with his general obligation of good faith. Recall the important triad of §§1-203, 1-201(19) and 2-103(1)(b).

8a. Bannin has made an effective rejection and need do nothing more. The rejection met §2-602(1) as it was within a reasonable time and notice was seasonably given. (*Notice* under §1-201(26) does not require a writing, and §2-602(1) itself speaks only in terms of notice, not written notice as is sometimes explicitly required in other sections of Article 2. So a call should be enough.) Once she has effectively rejected, she has very few obligations. Under §2-602(2)(b), she need only "hold [the goods] with reasonable care at the seller's disposition for a time sufficient to permit the seller to remove them." Storing them in a nice safe closet satisfies this responsibility. Of course she cannot simply throw the drapes out, donate them to charity, or leave them in a pile uncovered in her backyard.

Subpart (c) makes clear that she has no further obligation. Certainly she need not take the time and bother to send the drapes back. While the provisions of §2-602(2), which she is using as a guide, are expressly made subject to the provisions of the two sections that follow, neither makes a difference here nor need concern her. Section 2-603 deals with the limited responsibility to do more which applies to a *merchant* buyer, but Bannin is not a merchant. Section 2-604 just relates certain options which the rightfully rejecting buyer *may* choose to pursue. Nothing in that section is mandatory.

If Samantha, in response to Bannin's message, does come by and ask for the drapes back, must Bannin hand them over? Yes, *unless* she has already paid all or part of the price to Samantha. Until she is repaid this amount (plus any cost of inspection, care, and custody, which here would have to be zero), Bannin would have a security interest in the drapes under §2-711(3) and could refuse to give them up. If Samantha does come through with repayment, then this security interest lapses and Bannin would have to hand over the drapes. So the parties are back to square one—well, not exactly. Remember, rejection of nonconforming tender does not waive other rights of the buyer under the contract. Bannin may still have the right to money damages from Samantha for the seller's failure to meet her contract obligations.

8b. Bannin need not follow these instructions. She can just repeat her demand to Samantha that she come and pick them up. As we've already discovered, no duty to follow such instructions is found in §2-602, and §2-603 doesn't apply as Bannin is not a merchant. Note that even a merchant buyer isn't under an absolute obligation to resell the merchandise on the seller's behalf or ship it back in the general case. The merchant buyer comes under such duties only when the seller itself "has no agent or place of business at the market of rejection," when the buyer has not yet paid for the goods, and (unless the goods are perishable or threaten to rapidly lose their value) when reasonable instructions are given by the seller. And even then, any duty to follow instructions and resell or reship is subject to any rights the buyer may have under §2-711(3) as a result of payments already made.

8c. Under §2-604 (which the comment tells us is not exclusively a merchant's section) it seems Bannin may, if she chooses, after a reasonable time has passed, either store the drapes under Samantha's name and at her expense, reship them to her, or resell them "for Samantha's account." If she did resell them (for what?) she could then subtract what she is owed (any payments made by her not yet refunded plus expenses of the sale) and send the residue on to Samantha.

Beyond following up on one of these options, could Bannin do something else? For instance, if she doesn't hear from Samantha after repeated attempts to contact her, can Bannin just throw the things in the trash or donate them to a local charity? You can make the argument that this would be all right. After all, §2-602(2)(b) only makes her responsible for holding the drapes at Samantha's disposition "for a time sufficient to permit the seller to remove them." Once that time has clearly passed, Bannin can argue she doesn't even have to "hold them with reasonable care." Responsibilities beyond this, she would argue, never applied to her since she is not a merchant. Section 2-604 protects her if she chooses to be nice and take one of the actions listed there, but it doesn't make any of them mandatory.

We might hesitate to advise Bannin she can just toss the drapes, however, because of the problems of what is referred to as improper *post-rejection use* or *exercise of dominion* under §2-602(2)(a), which we explore at some length in response to the next and final question. As a matter of prudence, if Bannin is thinking of ditching the drapes, she should make one final attempt to contact Samantha, in writing this time, warning her of what's in store if she doesn't respond. Better safe than sorry.

8d. Mrs. Bannin should not have any problems if she leaves the drapes up for a few days holding them "at the seller's disposition," but if she just keeps them up indefinitely it could be another story. Section 2-602(2)(a) says that "after rejection any exercise of ownership by the buyer with respect to any commercial unit is wrongful as against the seller." This section does not, of course, say what is the consequence of such "wrongful" behavior, but the courts have looked to §2-606(1)(c) and Comment 4 thereto. A rejection that is followed up by continued use of the goods can turn out to be an ineffective *attempt* to reject and hence an acceptance. Mrs. Bannin's hypothetical situation was inspired by the case of *George v. Fannin,* 67 Ohio App. 3d 703, 588 N.E.2d 195, 17 U.C.C.2d 113 (1990), in which Ms. Jennie Fannin was held to have "waived" her rejection and effectively accepted custom-made draperies by continuing to use them for approximately one year after she first complained of "shoddy" workmanship. Apparently they were still hanging in her home even after she had responded to the seller's suit for the purchase price and filed a counterclaim. The trial court had noted that in addition to "continuing to use [the drapes] despite their inadequacy and non-conformity," Ms. Fannin had not followed up her initial request that the drapes be fixed or taken back and never "request[ed] instructions from [the seller] regarding return of the rejected goods." Given the language of §2-602(b) and (c), was the court right to give apparent weight to these factors?

So it certainly would be a good idea for our Mrs. Bannin to take the drapes down and store them if Samantha doesn't come to pick them up fairly soon. But what if she doesn't have any excess closet space to begin with? And what if, in anticipation of getting the new drapes, she had thrown away her old window treatment? Taking down the too-short drapes immediately would put her in blessed conformity with the Code, but would also leave her with totally bare windows and her neighbors peeking in. (We could suggest that she place a tag on the rejected drapes indicating something to the effect that they were hanging on her windows under protest, but would anyone other than a lawyer find this solution agreeable?)

It may be that the result in the *Fannin* case is more easily explained by the courts' belief that Ms. Fannin was being too persnickety or that by her actions she was actually trying to have her drapes and not pay for them too. In other cases, the courts have been more sympathetic to the consumer buyer who rejects but seems to have no choice but to continue making use of the goods for a time. Take *Garfinkel v. Lehman Floor Covering Co.,* 60 Misc. 2d 73, 302 N.Y.S.2d 167, 6 U.C.C. 915 (1969), for example. On March 8 carpeting was installed in the buyer's home. Immediately he noticed an unsightly condition in the carpet and brought it to the seller's attention. Seller claimed to have fixed the problem, but the condition (unsightly "pressure bands") continued. On April 12, buyer's attorney wrote to the seller rejecting the merchandise and demanding its removal. The seller did not remove the carpeting even after this, and a second certified mailing was made later in August. At the time of trial the carpeting was still on the floor and still apparently looking pretty bad. Seller argued that this continued use barred what the court termed a "rescission" but which we would probably analyze as a flat-out rejection. The court contrasted the language and intention of §2-602 with the result under earlier law.

> The need for this provision of the Uniform Commercial Code has been apparent in this court for some time. Many cases were brought where a merchant delivered defective merchandise, bulky in character, expensive to transport and store. He then left the defective merchandise and refused to remove it. This placed the consumer in a dilemma. If the consumer removes and returns the goods, it is an expensive proposition. He is out of pocket money, in addition to the loss of the purchase price, in exchange for the gamble of recovering some of it by court action. On the other hand, if he retains the merchandise in his home, he loses [under prior law] the right to rescind the contract and the purchase money is gone. In return he has to seek the right to damages for which he will need expensive expert testimony.
>   It is the opinion of the court that one of the beneficial purposes intended by the new commercial code was to put the burden on the merchant when the goods are defective and he is given proper notice of the defect. He delivered the goods and it is fair that he should remove them or let them remain at his peril.

This result under the circumstances seems unquestionably correct. What was the buyer supposed to do with all that carpet, rip it up and leave it in large rolls in the living room? There are, however, other instances of post-rejection use that are more difficult to deal with. Sometimes the question whether to use the goods—even large and bulky goods—may seem more discretionary on the part of the rejecting buyer. A number of cases, not obviously consistent in outcome, have arisen in which the buyer has quickly and unequivocally rejected a car or a mobile home soon after delivery. In theory it's clear what the buyer should do: Don't drive the car. Don't stay one more minute in the mobile home. Either can be parked somewhere safe and locked up tight. But what is the consumer purchaser supposed to do in such a situation? In almost every instance a good deal of money (a stiff down payment if not the entire purchase price) is tied up in the goods. The buyer can't just go out and buy another car or trailer as if the first contract didn't exist, waiting until later to get his or her money back from the original seller. Does the rejecting car buyer have to keep taking taxis in order to avoid "waiving" his or her rejection? Does the mobile home buyer have to camp out in a hotel even if he or she has the money to do so? As I have said, there does not appear to be a consistent hard and fast rule on this. The courts tend to say that the buyer's "reasonable" use is OK, but more than this is not. In other words, each situation is going to be judged on its own merits, and we have to expect that other factors, not just the extent of the use, will come into play.

19

Cure

An Introduction to Cure

Suppose the seller tenders. Suppose further that the buyer has a right to and does reject the goods, citing particular nonconformities in justification of this response. Is that the end of the matter? Maybe, but maybe not. For one thing, in many instances the buyer quite naturally looks to the seller to get things back on track, and the seller may be more than happy to oblige. The buyer still wants or needs the goods promised. He or she sensibly concludes that this particular seller is still either the only potential supplier of just what is wanted or if not the only one then at least that supplier best positioned to quickly and effectively fill the order. Plenty of times a buyer's rightful rejection goes hand in hand with a request that the seller come back soon, but this time with goods conforming to the contract. The buyer still wants to play out this deal with this particular seller. If the seller can and will do so and both parties are eventually satisfied, then all well and good. If the buyer was in fact harmed in some way by the first nonconforming tender—perhaps through some additional but relatively minor expenses occasioned by the delay—then a bit of monetary damages subtracted from the purchase price can make it right.

The Examples that we deal with in this chapter start from a different premise. Suppose that following a rightful rejection the buyer wants nothing more to do with this seller. He or she is either willing to do without the goods altogether or would prefer to procure them elsewhere. Has the seller nothing to say about this? To be more specific, can the seller claim some *right* to a second chance, that is, to a reasonable opportunity to come back to the buyer with a second tender of conforming goods? Or is the typical contract for purchase and sale so fragile a structure that one nonconforming tender automatically and forever puts an end to any obligation on the buyer's part?

In Code terminology, we ask whether the seller has a right to *cure*. One problem we will encounter is that the word "cure" is never defined in the Code, but at least preliminarily the concept is not that difficult to grasp. And there is some history to the term to which we can attend. The possibility of a seller's *right to cure* was not an entirely new innovation with the coming of Article 2. While there was no provision in the Uniform Sales Act similar to §2-508, common law in many states had recognized such a right in the seller at least to some extent. At the same time, it is clear that by including §2-508 and formulating it as they did, the drafters of Article 2 intended to make for a relatively robust and progressive law of cure that went beyond what the common law typically had provided.

Part of the reason for this attitude on the drafters' part has already been suggested. By preserving the perfect tender rule in the language of §2-601, Article 2 set up the possibility of the buyer's using that rule to wriggle out of deals on the merest pretext or for the most minor infraction on the seller's part. One augmentation to the law of sales that the drafters could and did provide to counteract the potential harshness of the perfect tender rule was a clear articulation of the seller's right to cure in many instances. This returns some power to the hands of the seller to deal with sharp practice on the part of the buyer. One of the questions you should consider as you work through this material is whether cure as provided for in Article 2 pushes the balance too far in the opposite direction. Does the Code's treatment of cure put the buyer in the position of having to continue dealing with a breaching seller for a time beyond what is reasonable and fair? How likely is it under §2-508 that a buyer will eventually be made to accept, pay for, and live with goods with which he or she should not in all justice be saddled?

Your views on cure will depend very much on how you read and how you see the courts administering the provisions of §2-508. You should read that section now. (Note also the virtually identical language of §2A-513.) There are some obvious issues that arise. Under what circumstances does the seller have the right to cure? What procedures does the seller have to go through to secure this right? Last but by no means least, what exactly does it mean to "cure" a defective tender? The answer to this last one—what precisely *is* cure other than a four-letter word?—is not at all obvious. You'll have a chance to explore these issues as you work through the following questions.

EXAMPLES

1a. After testing at a hearing clinic, Mr. Riccardi is told that he would be helped by a hearing aid. The Model A-660 Acousticon is recommended to him. He goes to a store owned by Mr. Bartus where an ear mold is fitted to him and he orders the Model A-660, paying cash in advance. The contract provides for delivery by February 15. On February 2 Bartus calls Riccardi and tells him the hearing aid is ready. Riccardi immediately goes to the store, where he sees that the hearing aid is marked as an "Acousticon Model A-665." Bartus tells him that the Model A-660 has been "modified and improved" and that it is now the A-665. Riccardi rejects the hearing aid, saying that he wants only the Model A-660. Bartus says that he is willing to find and sell him a Model A-660 if that is what he really wants, and tells Riccardi that the Model A-660 could be ready by the following week. Riccardi objects. He tells Bartus, "Forget it. Just give me my money back." Does Bartus have to give him his money now? If Bartus does tender a Model A-660 before February 15, what options does Riccardi have?

b. How would your analysis of the previous question differ if Bartus's initial tender of the Model A-665 had been on February 14 and, while he was willing to get Riccardi one of the older models, he could not promise it would be ready before February 21?

c. Suppose that instead of Riccardi's picking up the hearing aid, the parties had agreed that it would be delivered to his home. The Model A-665 is delivered on February 2. Riccardi, seeing that it is not what he ordered, sends it back to Bartus. On February 12 he gets a call from Bartus who explains why he had sent the "new improved" A-665 and offering to immediately deliver either that model once again or a Model A-660 if Riccardi prefers. Either way Riccardi can have delivery by February 15. Riccardi tells Bartus to forget about the whole thing. Bartus claims they still have a contract which he, Bartus, can fully honor. Does Riccardi have to accept and pay for some hearing aid from Bartus or else fear being held liable for a breach? Would it make a difference to your answer if Riccardi could show he had arranged to buy a hearing aid from some other store on February 10?

2. Bert, who is in need of a new refrigerator for his home, goes into Selma's Appliance City on a Thursday. There he contracts to buy a certain model, the Cold Commander, in the color Ivory. Selma agrees to deliver the refrigerator the following Tuesday.

a. As Selma is bringing the boxed refrigerator into his house, Bert notices that the box says that the color is "Avocado." Indeed the refrigerator in the box is a greenish avocado color, not at all the refreshing white which he had expected. Selma says, "It turned out that I didn't have any Ivory in stock, but one will be coming in a couple of days. You can take the Avocado now if you want, and I'll get you the Ivory by next week." Bert says, "No way. Forget about it. I'll get my refrigerator someplace else." (As a matter of fact, that morning Bert had seen an ad for a special sale on the Cold Commander at another appliance store.) Selma says, "That's ridiculous. We have a deal. You'll get the Ivory by next week. I'm holding you to this deal." Who has the better argument under the Code?

b. Change the facts in the following way: The box in which the refrigerator was packaged was clearly labelled "Ivory." When it was opened to reveal an Avocado-colored machine, Selma was as surprised as Bert. Apparently there had been a mix-up at the manufacturer's factory. Selma is extremely apologetic and tells Bert she'll get him an Ivory model "as soon as possible." Can Bert call the deal off under these circumstances?

3.   Betty buys a color television set at Selma's Appliance City. She takes it home in her car. When she takes it out of its box and first turns it on at home, she is disturbed to find that no matter how she fiddles with the controls there is a definite reddish tinge to all of the colors on the screen. She takes the set back to Selma's and asks for her money back.

a. Selma refuses to refund Betty's money, but does offer to immediately give her a new set of identical make and manufacturer. Does Betty have to accept this offer?

b. Instead of offering a new set, Selma says she will take the set into her repair shop and look at it. She says, "It probably just needs a minor adjustment. I'll fix it up and deliver it to you by the day after tomorrow." Betty would still prefer her money back, but can she insist on getting it?

c. Suppose instead that Selma had said, "It looks like there's something wrong with the picture tube. But that can be replaced. Leave it here. I'll make the switch and get you back your set by the day after tomorrow." Does your answer to the question change?

d. Assume that whatever Selma's initial diagnosis, Betty does leave the set for repair. It is returned to her with a note from Selma indicating that only the change of a minor part had been needed. Betty plugs the set in and turns it on. Now all of the colors have a *greenish* hue which can't be eliminated. Betty lugs the set back to Selma who says, "I think I see the problem. One more adjustment should do it." She tells Betty to leave it with her for another repair. Can Betty insist on simply getting her money back *now*? Would your answer be any different if when Betty gets the set back after Selma's initial repair the color is just fine, but there seems to be something wrong with the sound? Selma offers to make this repair. If your answer in either instance is that Betty is legally obligated to let Selma make the additional repair, you can imagine the hypotheticals (the problems and the questions) that would follow.

EXPLANATIONS

1a.   This question is based on the well-known case of *Bartus v. Riccardi,* 55 Misc. 2d 3, 284 N.Y.S.2d 222, 4 U.C.C. 845 (1967), although I've tidied up the facts somewhat for our purposes. In the actual case Riccardi wanted to reject the A-665 because of the sound quality and complained that it gave him a headache. But that doesn't matter. The issue here is not whether Riccardi has a right to reject—of course he does. He is under no obligation to accept something other than what he bargained for. The seller, Bartus, however, has the right to cure under §2-508(1). Here the time for performance has not yet expired, and Bartus immediately notifies Riccardi that he will make a conforming tender by February 15. Under §2-508(1), Riccardi must give Bartus a second chance to make a conforming tender before the promised delivery date. If Bartus does tender a good Model A-660 before February 15, Riccardi's options are no different from those of any buyer facing a conforming tender: accept or face the consequences of a wrongful rejection.

1b. Under these facts Bartus is still probably within his rights if he insists on Riccardi's sticking and buying a Model A-660 from him, but the answer is not as clear-cut. Bartus will have to look to §2-508(2) for his right to cure. This subsection, granting the seller a right to cure even *beyond* the agreed delivery date, is an extension by the drafters beyond where most courts had been willing to take the common law notion of cure. Necessarily there are several criteria which the seller must meet if he or she is going to take advantage of this right. Reread this subsection carefully. First of all, in the instant case did Bartus tender the A-665 with "reasonable grounds to believe" that it would be acceptable (and presumably accepted) by Riccardi? Comment 2 tells us that the purpose of this subsection is to avoid injustice to the seller by reason of a "surprise rejection by the buyer." Assume Bartus was indeed surprised that Riccardi wouldn't take the "new and improved" A-665. Does his surprise seem reasonable to you? It did to the court in the actual case.

> The model delivered to the defendant was a newer and improved version of the model that was actually ordered. Of course, the defendant is entitled to receive the model that he ordered even though it may be an older type. But, under the circumstances the plaintiff had reasonable grounds to believe that the newer model would be accepted by the defendant.

A second criterion is that the seller seasonably notify the buyer of his or her intention to cure. Bartus will have no trouble with that here.

Finally, under §2-508(2) Bartus must show that he offered to make a conforming tender within a "further reasonable time." Bartus had originally promised the hearing aid for February 15. Now Riccardi may have to wait until February 21. Is this extension beyond a "further reasonable time?" I'd argue no. Apparently a hearing aid, which must be made up to a buyer's particular needs, will always take some time to deliver. If Riccardi were to go to another supplier now and order an A-660, it would probably take at least that long for him to get it. Bartus seems to have a good case for the right to cure in this situation.

Notice that if Riccardi does have to accept tender of the Model A-660 on February 21, some days after he was promised it under the contract, and if he can show some monetary damages arising from the lateness, he would have a valid claim against Bartus for breach of the contract of sale. The seller's right to cure does not mean that a later conforming tender is just as good as a perfect tender, only that it must be accepted by the buyer, who is then left a claim for damages for any harm caused by the initial nonconformity of tender.

1c. Bartus has seemingly lost his right to cure here by failing to seasonably notify Riccardi of his intention to supply him with the Model A-660. We don't know exactly when Bartus got the return of the Model A-665, but if he didn't try to contact Riccardi until February 12, it is probably too late. This would be true under the language of the section whether or not Riccardi had acted on the assumption that Bartus didn't care to cure. So Riccardi would not have to accept and pay for anything from Bartus, *and* if he has to pay more for a comparable hearing aid from the other store he should be able to recover the difference in price from Bartus.

2a. Bert has the better argument. This is clearly a defective tender and Selma has no right to cure under either subsection of §2-508. Subsection (1) is applicable only if the time for performance has not yet expired, and she isn't making any offer to cure by the end of the day on which delivery was promised. What about subsection (2)? Here Selma deliberately tendered a green refrigerator when she knew a white one was expected. There's just no way she can argue she had reason to believe that this would be acceptable. If this were to come out any other way, then a seller like Selma could in effect unilaterally extend the time for performance by making some lame tender and offering cure. That certainly isn't within the contemplation of §2-508. Maybe Bert is, in this instance, taking advantage of Selma's nonconforming delivery to get a better deal elsewhere, but that doesn't seem particularly unfair. If Selma wants to hold Bert to the deal the two of them struck, she's going to have to tender better than this.

2b. This Example is meant to explore an important question that still remains about the requirement in §2-508(2) that tender be of that which "seller had reasonable grounds to believe would be acceptable with or without money allowance." Does that include the situation we have here?

We begin with a bit of review. There are a variety of situations where this "reasonable grounds to believe" language becomes relevant. First, there is the case where the seller tenders something he or she knows to be different from what was promised, but which he or she could reasonably expect would not be any less valuable or desirable in the eyes of the buyer. This is our Example 1b, where the seller tenders in all good faith a "new and improved" version of what was promised. It seems clear, and the court in the *Bartus* case concluded, that this meets the criterion.

A somewhat different situation is that in which the seller tenders knowing of some defect in the goods with which the buyer will probably be unhappy, but which the seller wouldn't expect to prompt a rejection because the defect doesn't appear that great or troublesome. If the seller is "reasonable" in this expectation that the buyer won't be a fanatic for details, then the drafters seem to think any rejection would be a "surprise rejection," in the words of Comment 2, and the seller should have the right to cure. That's the whole tenor of that comment. Suppose, for example, that before making delivery Selma did check that the refrigerator was the right color, but she also saw that one of the shelves was bent slightly out of shape. Rather than call off the delivery, she takes the refrigerator to Bert's home and starts to bring it in. As she does so she acknowledges the minor problem with one of the shelves but says she'll bring over a replacement the first thing the next day. True, §2-601 and its incorporation of the perfect tender rule would allow Bert to reject the entire refrigerator. But one of the purposes behind §2-508 in general is to move away from such a rigid and formalistic conception of the sales contract. If, as I think would be true in this slightly bent shelf example, Selma has the right to cure, then even if Bert can reject on this basis it does him little good practically. Selma might have to take the refrigerator back with her out the door, but she will have the right to return with it (now with perfect shelves) the next day and expect an acceptance. Doesn't it just make sense to ask Bert to allow delivery now, even accepting the goods, and accept the cure the next day? (If for some reason the cure is not forthcoming, he can argue for relief under §2-608(1)(a), as we'll see in the next chapter.)

Of course this argument—that the seller would not reasonably expect the buyer to reject a nonconforming tender—only goes so far. It really only works for minor defects, those little annoyances of life with which we are apparently all expected to put up as reasonable men and women. As we saw in Example 2a, the seller cannot reasonably count on the buyer's accepting just about any old thing merely because it's been delivered to his or her door.

So much for review. What each of these previous situations had in common was that the seller was *actually aware* of the nonconformity at the time of tender. In the hypothetical we must now confront, the seller is not herself aware of the nonconformity. Selma will argue for the right to cure under §2-508(2), saying that she had every reason to believe she was tendering just what the contract called for and what Bert expected. She understands Bert wanting to reject the refrigerator when it turns out to be the wrong color, and in fact she doesn't argue against his right to reject, but she claims that the rejection is as much a surprise to her as to anyone and that §2-508(2) gives her the right to cure. Bert argues that this case does not fall within the language of that subsection. How in heaven's name could Selma have "reasonable grounds to believe" he would accept a green refrigerator when he had contracted for a white one?

There has actually been a good deal of debate among the commentators as to whether §2-508(2) allows for cure in such a situation, where the seller apparently has no reason to know that what he or she is delivering is nonconforming in any way. Phrased another way, is cure beyond the contracted time of performance (which is the concern of §2-508(2)) limited to those cases where the seller had "reason to believe" that a particular nonconformity *of which the seller was aware* would not provoke a rejection? Put this way, I find it hard to see why §2-508(2) should be read so narrowly, but not all authorities have seen it this way. In particular, Professor Nordstrom in his treatise on Sales argues against allowing cure when the seller is unaware of the defect. Perhaps it's all in how favorably you look on the whole notion of cure and how easily you think it can get out of control and work oppression on the buyer.

What case law there is on the matter, I think it fair to say, is supportive of Selma's position and a broader reading of the subsection. Particularly important in this regard is the decision of the New York Court of Appeals in *T. W. Oil, Inc. v. Consolidated Edison*, 57 N.Y.2d 574, 443 N.E.2d 932, 457 N.Y.S.2d 458, 35 U.C.C. 12 (1982), which addressed the question directly.

> [W]e are asked . . . to decide whether a seller who, acting in good faith and without knowledge of any defect, tenders noncon-forming goods to a buyer who properly rejects them, may avail itself of the cure provision of subdivision (2) of section 2-508 of the Uniform Commercial Code.

The facts were not in dispute. In January 1974, in the midst of a fuel shortage caused by an oil embargo of certain oil-producing nations, T. W. Oil bought for itself a cargo of fuel oil whose sulfur content was represented to be no higher than 1.0 percent. While the oil was still en route to the United States in the tanker *Khasmin,* T. W. Oil received a certificate from the refinery at which it had been processed stating that the sulfur content was in fact only .52 percent, better than was required. T. W. Oil contracted to sell this oil to Con Ed, a utility company, under a contract describing the oil as having a .5 percent sulfur content. (Both parties acknowledged a trade custom by which contracting parties rounded off specifications of sulfur content at, for instance, 1.0 percent, .5 percent, or .3 percent.) In the course of negotiations, T. W. Oil became aware that Con Ed was authorized to buy and burn oil with a sulfur content of up to 1.0 percent and would even mix oils containing more and less to stay within that figure. This contract with Con Ed called for delivery to take place between January 24 and January 30. The *Khasmin* discharged its oil into Con Ed's storage tanks on January 25. Independent testing reported a sulfur content of .92 percent. Con Ed seasonably and reasonably rejected the tender on February 14. The parties promptly entered into negotiation to adjust the price. By February 20, T. W. Oil had offered a price reduction "roughly responsive" (in the court's words) to the difference in sulfur content. Con Ed, however, although it could have used the oil, "rejected this proposition out of hand. It was insistent on paying no more than the latest prevailing price, which, in the volatile market that then existed, was some 25% below the level which prevailed when it agreed to buy the oil." The next day T. W. Oil offered to cure with a substitute shipment of conforming oil scheduled to arrive within a few days. This too was refused by Con Ed. T .W. Oil resold the oil from the *Khasmin* at a substantial loss. It sued for the difference and was awarded a judgment of $1,385,512.83. The Court of Appeals upheld this award against various challenges by Con Ed, including among others the argument that it was within its rights to refuse both of these offers to cure. The court, applying §2-508(2), found there to have been ample evidence supporting the trial court's determination that under the circum-stances the seller had "reason to believe" the original tender would be acceptable. It had itself purchased the oil under a contract stating it to be .5-percent oil and had a refinery certificate reporting it to have a content within this trade description. Furthermore, the seller knew Con

Ed could burn oil with a content up to 1.0 percent so that, with appropriate price adjustment, the *Khasmin* oil would have been suitable even when it did, to the surprise of both parties, have a content of .92 percent. The court considered, but was not at all sympathetic to, Con Ed's argument (following Professor Nordstrom) that the right to cure under subsection (2) is reserved for those cases where the seller *knowingly* makes a nonconforming tender that it has reason to believe will not be rejected. You can see how if this argument were to have been adopted for New York the result in the instant case would have been to allow Con Ed's escape via the perfect tender route from an unfavorable bargain which (because of intervening changes in the market) it later regretted. The Court's conclusion:

> [I]f seasonable notice be given, a seller [who does not himself have knowledge of any defect] may offer to cure the defect within a reasonable period beyond the time when the contract was to be performed so long as it acted in good faith and with a reasonable expectation that the original goods would be acceptable to the buyer.

Of course, even if you accept the *T. W. Oil* result, you can jiggle the facts around a bit to get some tougher questions. What if, in our hypothetical, it turned out that the previous day Selma had experienced a similar problem with a mislabelled refrigerator which she had herself received in the same delivery from the same manufacturer? Would she be "reasonable" in delivering this one to Bert without first looking inside the box to make sure it was correctly labelled for color? What if the box was such that you could, albeit with some difficulty, get a look at the color of the item inside? Would she still fall within the protection of §2-508(2)?

3a. Betty the buyer's story is loosely based on another well-known case, *Wilson v. Scampoli*, 228 A.2d 848, 4 U.C.C. 178 (D.C. Ct. App. 1967). The first question here is whether Selma has the right to cure at all. The answer would seem to be yes. Even assuming she has to rely on §2-508(2), the analysis of the previous question and the result of *T. W. Oil* put Selma within that provision's reach. In fact the *Wilson* case, decided much earlier than *T. W. Oil*, assumed the same result with no discussion.

> A retail dealer would certainly expect and have reasonable grounds to believe that merchandise like color television sets, new and delivered as crated at the factory, would be acceptable as delivered and that, if defective in some way, he would have the right to substitute a conforming tender.

The real problem in this and the questions that follow is what exactly a seller may do to "cure." What can the seller insist the buyer take as a "conforming delivery"? We start with the easy (or at least the easiest) example. If seller is willing to immediately supply the buyer with identical factory-fresh goods, it's hard to imagine that this wouldn't be a good cure. Of course, as you will always be able to do when discussing cure, you can fairly easily add to the facts and create a hypo where the answer is not so clear-cut. What if Betty does accept this second set and finds the same "reddish tinge" when she takes it home? Can she now storm back into Selma's, drop this second set on the counter and demand her money back? Or will she have to accept a third set and Selma's assurances that her string of bad luck is about to end? What if Selma offers her this third set but agrees to test it out in her store before sending Betty home with it? Would it make any difference to your answer if Betty had by this time read an article in a consumer magazine reporting that this model of color television set has been plagued with color problems? What if when Betty took the second set home and turned it on the color was just fine, *but* there was some problem with the vertical hold which she couldn't clear up? My guess is that with your own experience as a consumer you can easily think of any number of other possibilities and that in fact you were doing so as you worked through these questions.

What you begin to see (and perhaps worry about) is how easily the concept of the right to cure—perfectly understandable as a protection for sellers against harsh and unfair results—has the potential for turning on buyers. If the seller can get away with too much in the name of cure, the buyer may be forced to accept and pay for goods which are not at all as good as he or she contracted for or had the right to expect. The question becomes, of course, what is "too much" for the seller to assert in the name of cure.

As a matter of fact, in *Wilson* the court appeared to assume that substitution of a new set would have been good cure. The problem was that the buyer would have none of this, not even the seller's offer to take the set back for possible repair. On which see the Example that follows.

3b. Betty will probably have a tough time resisting this offer to cure. There is the possibility that only a "minor adjustment" will be made. Selma is offering to have it done promptly and is even offering to deliver it so that Betty doesn't have to make another trek to the store. In *Wilson* the court, having reviewed some earlier cases, declared:

> While these cases provide no mandate to require the buyer to accept patchwork goods or substantially repaired articles in lieu of flawless merchandise, they do indicate that minor repairs or reasonable adjustments are frequently the means by which an imperfect tender may be cured.

This language, or something quite like it, is found in a number of cases, and is a good summary of prevailing thought on the matter. Betty would run a big risk if she refused Selma's offer to make what might turn out to be a minor adjustment at this stage.

3c. Even Betty would probably have to accept cure if it involved only a "minor repair." Once the necessary repair is more involved, she is most likely safe in refusing to accept Selma's offer. A leading case is *Zabriski Chevrolet, Inc. v. Smith*, 99 N.J. Super. 441, 240 A.2d 195, 5 U.C.C. 30 (1968), which we also saw in the previous chapter. Recall that Zabriski sold the Smiths a new 1966 Chevy which began to stall, sputter, and wheeze less than a mile from the dealership. Soon it refused to go into "drive" at all. Mrs. Smith and her husband were barely able to get it back to their house. The next day the seller sent a wrecker to the Smiths' home and brought the Chevy back to his repair shop, where it was determined that the transmission was defective. He replaced it with a transmission from some other vehicle then on his showroom floor, and offered the auto up to the Smiths once again. They refused to take it and asserted their right to cancel the sale. The seller brought suit against Smith, but his action got nowhere. The court held (surprise?) that the auto as delivered to the Smiths was defective. Also, as we saw in the last chapter, the court held that they had not accepted the auto simply by driving it off the lot. What of Zabriski's asserted offer to cure by letting the Smiths have the car with the replaced transmission? The court thought little of this argument as well. Acknowledging that the nature of what will suffice as cure is nowhere laid out in the Code and hence must be judged by the facts of each case, the court was quick to conclude that §2-508 does not "contemplate the tender of a new vehicle with a substituted transmission, not from the factory and of unknown lineage from another vehicle in [seller's] possession." Note also the language in *Wilson* that there is no obligation on the buyer's part to take "patchwork goods or substantially repaired articles."

Would it have mattered to the *Zabriski* court if the seller had shown that the substituted transmission was in fact of the same quality or even better than the transmission originally in the Chevy? What if the seller had evidence to suggest that such a new transmission, specially when individually installed in a dealership's repair department, is actually more likely to be defect-free than a transmission which is installed as one of a great number running down a manufacturer's assembly line? It's at least possible that this is true. (We've all heard the assertion—although I don't know if it is correct—that a broken bone once healed is stronger than it had been before the break.) It's impossible to know of course whether any of this would have made the slightest difference to the result in *Zabriski,* but consider the following language from the opinion:

> For a majority of people the purchase of a new car is a major investment, rationalized by the peace of mind that flows from its dependability and safety. Once their faith is shaken, the vehicle loses not only its real value in their eyes, but becomes an instrument whose integrity is substantially impaired and whose operation is fraught with apprehension. The attempted cure in the present case was ineffective.

This language became the origin of the *shaken faith doctrine* that is the focus of the next question.

3d. We are entering the fringes of what is and what is not *cure* here. Each case necessarily will have to be decided on its own facts, and attempts at further explication tend to fall flat. Some commentators and cases have been taken to suggest that a seller can in any event have at most one chance to cure. If the second tender isn't "perfect," this reasoning goes, then that's it for the seller. It isn't that simple, however. Some goods are very complex, and a few minor adjustments might be perfectly under-standable and to be expected before they work just right. Certainly there's nothing in §2-508 that limits the seller to one attempted cure. And in any event, would the rule apply to a single cure of any one defect as it appears or to one cure overall? Couldn't Selma here claim she did in fact successfully cure the "red tinge" problem? Now there's a second problem, a "greenish hue," which she's also willing to cure.

At the same time, even if the seller is willing and able to clear up every problem that crops up, eventually enough must be enough. Look again at the "shaken faith" language from *Zabriski*. How would you feel about buying a new TV and having to have its color system and its sound system both repaired right at the outset? You could, of course, philosophize about broken bones once healed being all the stronger, but do people really react that way? Eventually the buyer expecting a brand new item is left feeling he or she is being asked to settle for "patched up" goods. The courts, often invoking the language we've seen in *Wilson* and *Zabriski,* have on the shaken faith rationale allowed buyers eventually to reject repeated offers of cure, even if each attempt at cure is in itself successful.

Two other points about cure deserve noting before we exit this chapter. First of all, it has been suggested at times that only "minor" defects can be cured under §2-508. Beside the fact that there is no support in the language of the section for such a proposition, it turns out not to make much sense. Some major defects can be quite easily and successfully cured. A major appliance that is delivered in the wrong color can be quickly replaced by one in the right color and all is right with the world. Some "minor" defects seemingly never can be cured no matter how hard the seller tries. Most of us have had experience with a little grinding noise coming from "somewhere under the hood" that just can't be made to go away. We might as well face the fact. Cure is not a topic that lends itself to bright line rules, much as we might wish that were the case.

A second concluding point: One major question about cure has not been dealt with at all in this chapter. There is much controversy over whether the seller has a right to cure when the buyer is not rejecting the goods but is rather revoking his or her acceptance of them. Naturally enough this must wait for our discussion of revocation of acceptance, which not coincidentally happens to be the topic of the next chapter. We'll have to pick up on cure again at the end of that chapter.

20

Revocation of Acceptance

An Introduction to Revocation

As we've already seen, the buyer's act of acceptance if it occurs is a watershed event in the performance of any sales contract. Not least among the consequences of acceptance is that the buyer may never thereafter reject the goods (§2-607(2)). Once you've accepted, even if you've accepted goods that subsequently turn out to be nothing like what was promised, you are forever barred from rejecting. So what is a buyer to do who has accepted goods only later to find out exactly how defective the stuff is that he or she now holds? One possibility is to look for monetary relief. The buyer will have to pay at the contract rate for the goods accepted, of course, (§2-607(1)), but may be able to subtract from what is owed a significant amount for damages calculated on a breach of warranty theory. See §2-714 and the discussion in Chapter 29. Following this approach leaves the buyer owning and in possession of the goods, albeit having paid less for them than what had originally been called for under the contract. In many instances, keeping the goods at a reduced price may satisfy the buyer as much as he or she could be satisfied given the situation, but there obviously will be times when this result is not anything the buyer would choose to live with. In light of the deficiencies now apparent with the goods, the buyer has no use or desire for them whatsoever and wishes he or she had never accepted at all. Money damages may help a bit, but being told to keep and pay something—anything—for the defective goods is equivalent to rubbing salt in the buyer's wounds. Is there nothing else to be done?

Section 2-607(2) clearly states that the buyer's right to reject is lost forever at the moment of acceptance, but it also contains a tantalizing reference to the possibility that the buyer may, at least under certain conditions, later *revoke acceptance*. The reference is followed up in §2-608 with a full-blown treatment of the buyer's right to revoke acceptance in whole or in part. This chapter deals with that section and with that right. We will get into a series of Examples plumbing the depths of §2-608 in short order, but first a couple of points.

The first question you might have is why if at all this topic deserves a whole section of Article 2, and a whole chapter of this book, of its own. Might not a revocation of acceptance be just a rejection by another name? Article 2 says you can't reject after an acceptance, but you can revoke, so what's the difference? If there is one thing you will see in working through this material, it is that the Code drafters were not just playing with words; they definitely meant for there to be a marked difference in approach to and treatment of a rejection and a revocation. At least in theory, a buyer who accepts is meant to have a harder time justifying a revocation of acceptance than he or she would have had in carrying out a rejection at the first opportunity. This leads to the obvious question of why this should be. As you consider the questions and form your own analysis, you may come to some understanding of why the drafters thought it right to place additional hurdles in the way of the buyer attempting to revoke an acceptance. Without giving away too much of the game, I might initially note one thing: While not invariably true, typically goods that are the subject of an attempted revocation have been in the hands of the buyer for some time. They have seen service, often for a fairly long stretch, and are far from brand-spanking new.

Before going on, let's also note how the situation stands if a buyer does first accept then revoke acceptance and is justified in doing so. What are the consequences, in law and in practice, of a rightful revocation? Almost certainly the goods are at that moment in the buyer's possession. Section 2-608(3) states, "A buyer who so revokes has the same rights and duties with regard to the goods involved as if he had rejected them." We have to refer back to §§2-602 through 2-604. The buyer is under a duty to hold the goods "with reasonable care at the seller's disposition." In some cases, of course, a merchant buyer may in addition be obligated to follow the seller's instructions about returning the goods or disposing of them for the seller's account. Most often, however, the buyer just holds onto them and waits for the seller to come and pick them up. When the seller does come around, is the buyer obligated to hand them over? That depends on the circumstances. If the buyer has made no payments to the seller, he or she must allow the seller to retake possession. But think of a situation in which a buyer has already paid for the goods. She wants to return them—she wants never to see them again—but she also wants to see her money returned. Does she have to let the goods go in exchange for the seller's *promise* to return her payments at some later date? Article 2 provides, in §2-711(3), that the buyer in this instance has a "security interest" in the goods for certain payments made and may "hold such goods" pending repayment by the seller.

We do not treat in this book all the nuances of security interests, but it should be clear that this provision gives an aggrieved buyer some much needed leverage in order to get payments returned.

Say the buyer has chosen to revoke acceptance, the goods are back in the seller's possession, and the buyer has recovered any payments already made. Now at least have we come to the end of the whole sordid affair? No, not if the buyer is also claiming that some additional damage was caused to him or her because of the seller's failure to live up to the contract. The drafters introduced this new term, "revocation of acceptance," primarily to distinguish it from the more traditional concept of *rescission*. If the parties to a contract "rescind" their agreement, this is often taken to mean in effect that both renounce any and all rights under that agreement. The deal is undone. There is no longer any contract to enforce. Distinguish this from the case where the buyer has successfully revoked acceptance of goods under Article 2. The buyer has *not* waived and may still enforce any claim for damages to which he or she is entitled under the terms of the contract and the provisions of the article. See Comment 1 to §2-608. To be fully vindicated, a buyer who has accepted what turn out to be nonconforming goods may, and often will, be perfectly reasonable in first revoking acceptance, getting his or her money back, and then following up with an action on the contract for an appropriate measure of damages. But we leave damages to another time. The questions here all focus on the revocation itself—whether it is permissible, how and when it is to be done, and so on. The answers to all of these are (supposedly) to be found in §2-608.

EXAMPLES

1.   Alice buys a new car from Sam's Auto Sales. The contract calls for the car to be equipped with a special "racing package," which is intended to soup up the engine to a considerable degree. When Alice goes to pick up the car she discovers that the special equipment has not been installed. There is simply the regular engine. Sam tells her the special package is "on order" and that he will be able to install it as soon as it arrives. Alice takes the car on that understanding. Several months later she still hasn't heard from Sam, so she calls him. He tells her that he has since found out that the manufacturer no longer makes any kind of racing package for her model of car. Does she have the right to revoke her acceptance because of this?

2.   Beth also buys a car from Sam. When she picks it up and drives it away it appears from her inspection to be just what she ordered. Two weeks later, she begins to notice that the car is riding much less smoothly. A mechanic tells her that the engine was never mounted properly and that it is beginning to work itself loose from the chassis. The shaking of the engine has already caused serious damage to the basis framework of the car, so that just tightening a few bolts will not solve the problem. Can Beth revoke her acceptance against Sam?

3.   Carol is another buyer from Sam. She ordered a car with a dark blue interior. When she goes to pick it up she discovers the car's interior is a pale blue. She says nothing and drives the car away. The next day she realizes that she really does not like the pale blue as much as the dark. She drives the car back to Sam's, where she insists that he take the car back and refund her money. Is Sam obligated to do as she demands?

4.   Finally, we meet Diana who also buys a car from Sam. Two days after picking the car up from the dealership, she runs over some glass and gets a flat tire. She opens up the covered well in the trunk where the manual tells her the spare tire is to be found. It turns out there is no spare tire in the space. Can she revoke on this basis?

5.   Bailey is searching for a new printer to go with his computer system. He goes to Sylvester's Computer City where he looks at various printers and fiddles around with those on display. He looks at the Phaserjet 1000, which in his fiddling he discovers is even able to print the symbol for the Italian lira (₤) along with all kinds of other quirky characters. He buys the Phaserjet from Sylvester. Two days later, Sylvester delivers a Phaserjet 1000 fresh in a box from the factory to Bailey's home. Bailey sets the printer up and it works perfectly well. Several weeks later he is showing his new printer to a friend (who has suggested that he paid too much for what he got), when he tries to print out a document which includes the lira symbol. This symbol won't print out. He calls Sylvester to complain. Sylvester tells him that manufacturers sometime make minor changes in a model after its introduction and that this is what has happened here. The version of the Phaserjet 1000 which Bailey received was an upgrade from the original version on display and can produce 256 symbols more than could the original. In fact, Sylvester tells Bailey, he is finding that the most recent version of the Phaserjet with its "enhanced character set" helps him sell this particular printer. Several computer magazines have commented favorably about this upgrade of the Phaserjet 1000. Apparently in the alteration the lira got lost in the shuffle.

     a. On these facts can Bailey revoke his acceptance of the printer?

     b. Would your answer to the previous question be any different if it were to turn out that Bailey, as an international financier, had found in the past his correspondence often referring to Italian lira and that he had purposefully checked out the model Phaserjet at Sylvester's for this symbol before making his decision on what to buy? Does it matter to your answer whether Sylvester knew of Bailey's special interest in the lira symbol at the time the sale was made?

6.   Bill buys a mobile home from Trailer-O-Rama of Springfield. The unit, which the contract calls to be equipped with built-in heating and air-conditioning, is delivered to Bill's land and set in place in November. During the winter months the heating unit works with no problems. In May, when the temperature first goes above 80 degrees, Bill turns on the air-conditioning. Air blows out but it is not cold, or even cool.

     a. Bill immediately calls a mechanic to check the air conditioner. It turns out that there is no cooling system at all; behind the air-conditioning panel there is just a hollow space. Can Bill revoke his acceptance of the trailer?

b. Suppose that instead of immediately calling in a mechanic in May, Bill does nothing. By the next day it is cool again. When a heat wave strikes in June he once again turns on the air conditioner. Again it blows only tepid air. Now he checks out the unit and for the first time discovers the lack of a cooling system. Could Bill revoke under this set of facts?

7.   Return to the facts of Example 1. Alice buys a car from Sam which is to be equipped with a special racing package, but several months later it becomes apparent he will never be able to provide this feature.

a. Would it effect her ability to revoke if during the intervening months Alice had repainted the car a different color?

b. Even if Alice had not repainted, could Sam argue against revocation by pointing to the fact that Alice has already subjected the car to several months of hard use? In fact the finish has already been noticeably affected and the tires are considerably worn.

c. Assume that Alice does have the right to revoke her acceptance of the car. She writes Sam a letter which says, "I am terribly upset that the car you've sold to me cannot be furnished as you promised! I expect you to make it up to me in some way." Has she effectively revoked with this letter?

d. Now assume that Alice has a clear right to revoke and further that she does in fact give a clear and unequivocal notice of revocation. What does she do now? Can she continue to drive the car or must she immediately put it in storage?

e. Assume that Alice does continue to drive the car for another two months before Sam is eventually convinced by his lawyer (who is learned in the Code) that he must acknowledge her right to revoke. He offers to take the car back. Alice, who paid cash up front, wants the full purchase price returned. Is Sam obligated to return to her all that she had paid?

8.   Refer back to Example 5b. Bailey, the international financier, rightly revokes acceptance of the Phaserjet printer because it cannot print out the symbol for Italian lira. Soon after he receives the notice of revocation from Bailey, Sylvester makes the following offer: He will send an employee over to Bailey's home to replace a computer chip in the printer. The result will be a Phaserjet just like the one Bailey initially tried out in Sylvester's store. Must Bailey accept this offer, or can he simply ignore it, return the printer, and get his purchase price back?

EXPLANATIONS

1.   Yes, Alice has the right to revoke under §2-608(1)(a). Check that she meets all the criteria. As we saw in Chapter 18, an auto purchaser does not accept the car the minute it is driven off the lot, but in this case enough time has passed to make it hard to argue Alice never accepted.

I think we can assume that the absence of the special equipment is a substantial impairment of the value of the car to her. (Soon we'll see that "substantial impairment" isn't always so clear-cut, but here there seems no real question.) Finally, she accepted the car "on the reasonable assumption that its nonconformity would be cured and it has not been seasonably cured."

So Alice has the *right* to revoke. *How* she must act if she wants to make an effective revocation is another matter, which we pick up again in Example 7. It's important to keep distinct in your mind the difference between a buyer's *having* the right to revoke and his or her *actually having done so*. It's probably fair to assume that in most instances where buyers could legitimately revoke they actually don't but ask instead for some other form of relief—or just forget about the whole thing, living with the problem, grumbling to themselves, and getting that much more cynical about life.

2.   Yes, Beth can revoke, here under §2-608(1)(b). She accepted the car without discovery of the nonconformity and, she'd argue, the acceptance was "reasonably induced . . . by the difficulty of discovery before acceptance." It may be true that a trained mechanic could have spotted the trouble even before he or she drove the car off Sam's lot, but I doubt many car buyers could or do make this thorough an inspection. This type of so-called latent defect is just what subpart (b) is meant to address. Note also that even if the defect were something that *would* normally be spotted by a reasonable buyer making a reasonable inspection at the time of delivery, if the inspection is cut short by the seller's assurances, the buyer will not be barred from revocation. See Comment 3.

3.   No. What Carol wants is to revoke her acceptance, and there is nothing in §2-608(1) that provides her the right to do this. She would have been perfectly within her rights to reject the car at the time of delivery because of the incorrect color, but now that she's accepted it she isn't going to be able to undo the deed. (I'd say it's too late for her to reject on this basis even though only a day had intervened. Any arguments?) So she is going to have to pay for the car and pay at the contract price. Can she argue for a set-off because the car's interior was not the correct color? It's hard to see how, or if so how it will amount to much in the way of money. This just points out once again how important it is for the buyer to take the acceptance/rejection decision seriously. Often there is no turning back.

4.   This is a more difficult case. The question is whether the fact that a spare tire turns out to be missing from a new automobile "substantially impairs" the value of that car to Diana. While in the particular instance she can rightly be annoyed, it is doubtful that this slight defect is a "substantial" nonconformity. This language was put into §2-608(1) with the express purpose of tempering the potential severity of the perfect tender rule, which as we've seen survives at least in form in §2-601 and is operative when the issue is the right to reject. The drafters wanted revocation to be possible when the defects that never get cured (subpart

(a)) or later turn up (subpart (b)) are serious and materially affect the value of the goods to the purchaser. Once the goods have been accepted, minor defects are to be compensated for through monetary damages. So Diana isn't left without a remedy altogether. She can sue for the value of the tire and presumably her consequential damages of having to call a tow truck or whatever, but the lack of the tire does not give her the right to undo the deal and return the car.

There are, as you might expect, a number of cases working over the "substantial impairment" standard, and they don't allow for distillation into a nice neat rule. The easiest cases are those which find (or simply assume) the criterion has been met because there is found to be a major defect and it cannot easily be cured. See, for example, Beth's problem in Example 2. At the other extreme are those situations where the defect is minor (some would say trivial) and can quickly and effectively be cured making the product as good as new. Such would seem to be Diana's case here, where the only nonconformity is the lack of a spare tire. The dealer can send over a spare tire of the type that was to come with the car—and that's that. At least one would think that revocation would not be available here. But consider *Colonial Dodge, Inc. v. Miller,* 420 Mich. 452, 362 N.W.2d 704, 40 U.C.C. 1 (1985), the case that inspired this hypothetical. In April of 1976 Mr. Miller ordered a new Dodge Royal Monaco station wagon equipped with a heavy-duty trailer package with extra-wide tires. He picked it up on May 28. The next day his wife noticed that the new station wagon did not have a spare tire. Mr. Miller notified the dealership the next morning and insisted on having a spare tire. He was told none was then available. He immediately stopped payment on the checks he had tendered to pay for the vehicle and told the dealer that it could be picked up from in front of his home. It turned out that the tires were in short supply due to a labor strike. A tire did become available and was offered to Mr. Miller some months later. Meanwhile the car, which had been left sitting with only a temporary registration outside of Miller's home, had eventually been towed by the police to another dealership. Colonial Dodge sued for the purchase price of the car. The Michigan Court of Appeals determined that there had been a valid acceptance of the car and furthermore that there was no substantial impairment sufficient to justify a revocation of that acceptance. On further appeal (by now eight years have passed), the Michigan Supreme Court reversed. Since the parties had stipulated to the fact of an acceptance, the Supreme Court was left to decide on the revocation issue.

> In order to give effect to the statute, a buyer must show that the nonconformity has a special devaluing effect on him and that the buyer's assessment of it is factually correct. In this case, the defendant's concern with safety is evidenced by the fact that he ordered the special package which included special tires. The defendant's occupation demanded that he travel extensively, sometimes in excess of 150 miles per day on Detroit freeways, and often in the early morning hours. Mr. Miller testified that he was afraid of a tire going flat on a Detroit freeway at 3 A.M. Without a spare, he testified, he would be helpless until morning

business hours. The dangers attendant upon a stranded motorist are common knowledge, and Mr. Miller's fears are not unreasonable. . . .

We hold that under the circumstances the failure to include the spare tire as ordered constituted a substantial impairment in value to Mr. Miller, and that he could properly revoke his acceptance under the U.C.C.

Two members of the court offered separate dissents, which you may want to read. You can decide for yourself with whom you would have voted. Isn't the real problem here that Miller's better claim would have been that he never accepted the car in the first place, but that this argument somehow got stipulated away?

Another set of cases of which you should be aware involve a buyer's attempt to revoke where the defect initially may have seemed trivial but where repeated attempts to cure by the seller prove unsuccessful. In *Capitol Cadillac Olds, Inc. v. Roberts*, 813 S.W.2d 287, 15 U.C.C.2d 1221 (Ky. 1991), for example, the Kentucky Supreme Court was confronted with the case of a Oldsmobile Calais which, when it was stopped on a steep incline and put into park made an annoying "grinding noise." This problem was discovered by the buyers soon after they took possession. During the next six months the car was repeatedly returned to the dealership for repair of this problem but all efforts were unsuccessful. The court ruled that the question of substantial impairment was one best left to the trier of fact and that in the particular case the persistence of the grinding noise, even if it was heard only in unusual circumstances, supported the jury's finding of a revocation. In reaching this conclusion the court quoted with approval the following lines from that well-known New Jersey case we encountered in each of the last two chapters, *Zabriskie Chevrolet, Inc. v. Smith*, 99 N.J. Super. 441, 240 A.2d 195, 5 U.C.C. 30 (1968):

> For a majority of people the purchase of a new car is a major investment, rationalized by the peace of mind that flows from its dependability and safety. Once their faith is shaken, the vehicle loses not only its real value in their eyes, but becomes an instrument whose integrity is substantially impaired and whose operation is fraught with apprehension.

Other courts have cited *Zabriskie* and invoked its shaken faith approach in the revocation context.

Even if the seller *is* able to cure each and every defect as it presents itself, and even if every defect is in and of itself not that significant, the cumulative effect can surely be a substantial impairment of the value of the goods to the perfectly reasonable buyer. After all, there comes a time, as one court has well noted, after which "enough is enough." *Rester v. Morrow*, 491 So. 2d 204, 1 U.C.C.2d 751 (Miss. 1986). For a good review of such cases, which tend to be horror stories of the lemon-from-hell variety, you could look to *East Side Prescription Center, Inc. v. E. P. Fournier Co.*, 585 A.2d 1176, 13 U.C.C.2d 1062 (R.I. 1991).

5a. This strikes me as a case where the admitted nonconformity—recall the printer should conform to the model under §2-313(1)(c)—does not "substantially impair" the printer's value to Bailey. You see the importance of the substantial impairment requirement. Bailey could have refused to accept this printer initially, but he doesn't have the right to revoke now. You should consider, if you have not already done so, why the drafters thought it appropriate to make the standard for revocation different than that for rejection. As I suggested in the introductory material, because revocations generally come much further down the road and after the goods have been in use for some time, they will naturally tend to be much messier. The right of revocation is reserved for the more egregious cases, and those where money damages are not likely to give satisfaction even to the most reasonable of buyers. Is there any value to be served by giving Bailey the right to back out of this purchase just because the printer can't print this one character? Not under these facts. This question is, of course, a set-up for the one that follows.

5b. Revocation should be available here. Bailey will now emphasize that the defect in the printer, whatever may be its importance to others, "substantially impairs its value *to him,*" which is the way the criterion is worded in §2-608(1). The drafters were concerned that incorporating a "substantiality" or "materiality" standard for revocation might work unfairly against some buyers, so they massaged it into giving us something quite novel, something we might be tempted to characterize as an *objective test subjectively applied* or perhaps a *subjective test to be exercised objectively.* Not surprisingly, there is no general consensus as to exactly how this wording is to be given effect, although the disagreements are probably more in shading than in the eventual result. The test seems to be something like whether a "reasonable person" *in the position of and having the particular needs of the buyer* would think the goods *substantially* impaired by the nonconformity. Got that? One court has set the inquiry as follows:

> Whether plaintiff [buyer] proved nonconformities sufficiently serious to justify revocation of acceptance is a two-step inquiry under the code. [T]he value of conforming goods *to the plaintiff* must first be determined. This is a subjective question in the sense that it calls for a consideration of the needs and circumstances of the plaintiff who seeks to revoke; not the needs and circumstances of the average buyer. The second inquiry is whether the nonconformity in fact substantially impairs the value of the goods to the buyer, having in mind his particular needs. This is an objective question in the sense that it calls for evidence of something more than plaintiff's assertion that the nonconformity impaired the value to him; it requires evidence from which it can be inferred that plaintiff's needs were not met because of the nonconformity. In short the nonconformity must *substantially* impair the value of the goods to the plaintiff buyer. The existence of substantial impairment depends upon the facts and circumstances in each case.

Jorgensen v. Pressnall, 274 Or. 285, 545 P.2d 1382, 18 U.C.C. 1206 (1976). One authority refers to §2-608(1) as calling for a "personalized objective test." Call it what you will, it seems to help Bailey here. He does have a subjective, personalized reason for wanting the printer to have a particular feature and for being upset when he discovers that feature to be missing. And I think we all could agree that he is perfectly reasonable in feeling this way, given his situation. He could even bring forward "objective" proof of his individualized situation, such stuff as prior documents produced in the course of his business which require the £ for clarity and testimony of others supporting his assertion that he can expect to need this symbol in the future.

So Bailey has a very strong case for his meeting the standard under these facts. This is not surprising, given that I was able to make up the facts to set out the issue. Not all cases will be so clear. What do you do with a case where you truly believe that the buyer thinks the value of the goods substantially impaired to him or her but this impression seems to you, as a reasonable person, to be based on a misapprehension on the buyer's part? Or how do you respond to the buyer who apparently has no special needs to which attention must be given but is able to satisfy you (with good hard evidence) that he or she has been, is now, and always will be exceptionally picky about what he or she buys? In *Asciolla v. Manter Oldsmobile-Pontiac, Inc.,* 117 N.H. 85, 370 A.2d 270, 21 U.C.C. 112 (1977), the court noted that in the case before it "[t]he record indicate[d] that plaintiff was a particularly prudent and painstaking car buyer and that he had indeed once before refused to accept an automobile from the defendants which merely [?] had a dented fender which had been repaired." Would this buyer, should this buyer, be given a greater latitude in revocation than the ordinary Joe or Jane? The case itself does not actually address the question, since the car involved was among the more lemon-like in the literature and one with which just about any slob would be justifiably dissatisfied.

As to the issue of what Sylvester knew and when did he know it, Comment 2 makes it clear that as far as the drafters were concerned the seller's knowledge or lack of knowledge should play no part in the decision. Do you agree? I know of no case that picks up on the point.

6a. Revocation would seem to be good here. The only issue is whether the attempted revocation took place "within a reasonable time after the buyer discovers or should have discovered the ground for it." See §2-608(2). Even though more than half a year has elapsed, I would say yes, but the seller can argue that Bill "should have discovered" this defect earlier. This is, as are most questions under §2-608, a question of fact, but I wouldn't like to be representing Trailer-O-Rama at trial on this one. Perhaps persuasive counsel could convince a jury that a reasonable person makes more of an inspection and tries out all of the various features of a trailer soon after it is delivered. If Bill is "unreasonable," in that he is too trusting, he might be held to have lost the chance to revoke. He can still go against the seller for damages, of course, but will not be able to return the trailer.

6b. Here Bill has probably lost his right to revoke because of delay in making the revocation. Still, it would be up to the trier of fact. Where an otherwise good case for revocation exists, the courts do not appear to be too strict with this timing requirement. In *Funk v. Montgomery AMC/Jeep/Renault*, 66 Ohio App. 3d 815, 586 N.E.2d 1113, 18 U.C.C.2d 446 (1990), Bev Funk was the buyer of a 1982 Renault who sought to revoke after experiencing problems with the car's air-conditioning for a second consecutive summer. The appellate court reversed a ruling of the trial judge which withheld the question of revocation from the jury on the ground that the attempt to revoke was untimely as a matter of law. What may eventually have made the difference (in this case as in many) is that the reasonable time that the buyer has to revoke is easily affected by how the seller reacts to initial complaints about the goods. As this court said, "the reasonable time requirement must include the time beyond which the seller is attempting to adjust, or cure, the problem." In another representative case, *Mercedes-Benz of North America, Inc. v. Norman Gershman's Things to Wear, Inc.*, 596 A.2d 1358, 16 U.C.C.2d 1076 (Del. 1991), the Supreme Court of Delaware held that revocation could not be held to have been untimely as a matter of law even though it took place 18 months after delivery during which the buyer had put more than 12,600 miles on the car.

> Defendants acknowledge that the time for revocation may be extended "where the delay is prompted either by the seller's attempts to cure the defect, or where the delay was in reliance on the seller's continued assurances that the defect would be successfully repaired." . . . In such instances, revocations occurring two, three, and four years "after purchase and discovery of the nonconformity [have been found reasonable] depending on the number of promises to repair made, the length of time the repairs take, and the buyer's diligence in reporting problems." [Citations omitted.]

See also Comment 4. In our case, if Bill didn't make any initial complaint to the seller in May and just waited around until June, he will not be able to make this kind of "tolling" argument. Even if there is a significant tolling period during which the seller is fooling around and insisting that all will be well, eventually the buyer will have to conclude when enough is enough and make a move. No one is suggesting that the buyer can wait forever.

7a. If Alice had taken this step, she would not be able to revoke. See §2-608(2) and the reference to "substantial change in the condition of the goods which is not caused by their own defects." (Notice, by the way, that this requirement would not bar revocation by Beth the buyer in Example 2. In her case, while there has been a substantial change in the condition of the car it is directly attributable to the car's own defects.)

7b. Sam would like to argue that in this case as well there has been a substantial change in the condition of the goods and he should not be required to take the car back following a revocation. Comment 6 does say that the seller should not be made to take return of goods which have "materially deteriorated except by reason of their own defect." A hard-driving woman like Alice can put a lot of miles on a car in a couple of months. Should the seller be able to get any mileage out of this argument?

Obviously if it were to succeed it could severely cut into the revocation right. At least when the buyer is a consumer and there has been only normal wear and tear for the period the goods have been in his or her hands, I have to doubt whether a court would let this stand in the way of a revocation. In a commercial context where the buyer has had long use of the goods and still could make use of them, but where their condition would make it virtually impossible for the seller to refurbish or resell them to anyone else, the argument has some appeal. Of course in such an instance a court could and would probably avoid the issue altogether by rendering a decision that too much time had passed for a revocation.

7c. Alice's letter probably would be enough to satisfy §2-607(3)(a) (see Chapter 18), but would not be an effective notice of revocation as called for by §2-608(2). As to the mechanism of notice, refer once again to §1-201(26). Section 2-608(2) does not specifically call for "written notice," so an oral notification would do. Alice's problem here is that the content of her letter doesn't make clear she is revoking. See Comment 5. It is not enough that Alice let Sam know that she claims there has been a breach or that she wants some response from him. "While the [notice of revocation] need not be in any particular form and may be implied by conduct, it must inform the seller that the buyer does not want to keep the goods." *Allis-Chalmers Corp. v. Sygitowicz*, 18 Wash. App. 658, 571 P.2d 224, 22 U.C.C. 1151 (1977). To be effective, Alice's letter (or oral notice) should have made clear she did not want to keep the car. To be perfectly safe, she should have told him when and where and on what conditions he was expected to take return of the car.

7d. Section 2-608(3) says that upon revocation the buyer "has the same rights and duties with regard to the goods as if he had rejected them." So we head back to §§2-602 through 2-604. Of particular importance is §2-602(2)(b). Alice is under a duty, subject to her rights under §2-711, to hold the car "with reasonable care at the seller's disposition for a time sufficient to permit the seller to remove [it]." So one thing she could do is just store it in a nice safe place and wait for Sam to make a move. For a case in which the noble buyer actually did put the car in storage, even while continuing to pay insurance on it, see *King v. Taylor Chrysler-Plymouth, Inc.,* 184 Mich. App. 204, 457 N.W.2d 42, 12 U.C.C.2d 686 (1990). But is it always realistic to ask the buyer to act this way? What is Alice supposed to do for transportation in the meantime? If she does continue to drive the car, Sam will also point to §2-608(2)(a) and argue that her use of the car after revocation is "wrongful" against him.

In a large number of cases the seller has argued that the buyer's "continued use" of the goods after a revocation in effect waived the revocation. (Be careful. You should distinguish this argument from what we discussed earlier in Example 7b, that prolonged use *prior to* an attempted revocation somehow makes the remedy of revocation unavailable. The issue here is *post-revocation* use.) Under some circumstances you can imagine this argument of continued use being successful (e.g., if the buyer could have easily set the item aside and avoided having anything more to do with it, but instead kept using it, made no effort to look for an eventual replacement, and so on). But in the typical consumer case where it has come up, the courts have been sympathetic to the predicament in which the revoking buyer is found. Some courts have reasoned that the buyer who retains a security interest in the property under §2-711 is merely taking reasonable steps to protect the value of the property and that interest by, say, continuing to live in and maintain the trailer. Other times the court will conclude that continued use by a consumer who has no financial means to immediately obtain a replacement is not "wrongful" at all, or if it *is* "wrongful," that this does not in and of itself bar a revocation but only gives the seller some rights to a set-off (as we'll discuss in the next question).

Up until recently the cases on "continued use" almost all involved a consumer buyer who had rightfully revoked acceptance of an automobile or a mobile home, big purchases of the sort which your average Joe or Jane can't just set aside in a closet or easily do without. The results, generally supportive of the buyer, were recently summarized in *In re Stem*, 571 So. 2d 1112, 13 U.C.C.2d 1070 (Ala. 1990). In fact, a large proportion of the cases on any and all aspects of revocation involve cars and trailers. This is understandable. These are big ticket items, and when the buyer has a lemon (or thinks so), the stakes can be very high. Nothing seems to satisfy except saying goodbye to the goods for once and for all. The seller, on the other hand, is going to resist losing one large sale and having to take back the massive thing on wheels, which is by now a used car or trailer and rarely in the best of shape.

Recently, however, an interesting new cluster of cases have begun to surface in keeping with the times in which we live. They involve purchases of expensive high-tech equipment by individual doctors or hospitals who then experience continuing problems with what they receive. For instance, in *Romy v. Picker International, Inc.*, 18 U.C.C.2d 771 (E.D. Pa. 1992), Dr. Maurice Romy purchased a Magnetic Resonance Imaging (MRI) system from Picker to be used by his medical partnership. The MRI was delivered to Romy who put it into use, but a new "rampability" option (something to do with hard-core and high tech electronics, it would appear) that had been promised was never delivered. In fact it turned out that no maker of MRI equipment had as of the time of trial produced a "rampable" system for the commercial market. After a seven-day trial, the jury concluded Romy had legitimately revoked and awarded him damages of $2,130,905.00, representing the purchase price plus incidental damages. On appeal the manufacturer argued that the doctor's continued use of the MRI after his having given notice of the nonconformity constituted a waiver of the right to revoke and barred him as a matter of law from that form of relief. The appellate court didn't buy the argument.

> [A] court will annul a revocation and conclude that a reacceptance has occurred only where the buyer's actions with respect to the goods are deemed "unreasonable.". . . The record establishes that Romy's post-revocation use of the MRI was reasonable. The MRI was purchased for the use of Romy and his partnership, UDC, whose main function

is the performance of magnetic imaging tests on patients. MRI equipment is vital to the operation of UDC's business, and without MRI equipment UDC would have had to cease virtually all of its business operations. Had Romy ceased using the Picker MRI system he would have failed to satisfy his duty to mitigate damages. Furthermore, since the MRI equipment had already been installed in UDC's offices, Romy could not easily remove and replace the MRI system. Therefore, the post-revocation use of the MRI was reasonable, and Romy did not waive his right to revoke acceptance of the MRI system.

In a similar vein is *Hospital Computer Systems, Inc. v. Staten Island Hospital*, 788 F. Supp. 1351, 18 U.C.C.2d 140 (D.N.J. 1992). The hospital purchased a custom computer billing and accounting software system from HCS. The system "went live" on January 1, 1986, after which there quickly emerged a series of problems which HCS kept trying to correct. By early 1987 an independent consultant hired by the hospital reported on his conclusion that there was just no way the system's problems could be fully remedied. On June 2, 1987 the hospital's president wrote HCS a letter stating among other things that the hospital had "decided to wipe the slate clean and try another vendorized system" and that it "would like to accomplish a reasonable and orderly transition from HCS to whatever our new system would be." For the next 18 months the hospital continued to use the HCS system and make monthly payments under the contract. During the same time and "unbeknown to HCS" it sought out and implemented a new system. The hospital stopped paying HCS when that new system became operational on February 1, 1989. The district court found that the hospital had effectively revoked in June 1987. Nor did its continued use of the system for 18 months thereafter constitute a waiver of the revocation. The court was urged by HCS to follow an earlier case, *Computerized Radiological Services v. Syntex Corp.*, 786 F.2d 72, 42 U.C.C. 1656 (2d Cir. 1986), in which the Second Circuit had held a radiology group's continued use of a CAT scanner for 22 months following notice to have absolutely barred a revocation. Staten Island Hospital's situation, however, was found to be distinguishable. In *Computerized Radiological Services*, the Second Circuit had put emphasis on the fact that the buyer had failed to search for a replacement for a significant period of time after its attempted revocation. The hospital, on the other hand,

> began almost immediately to search for a replacement system, and, considering the complexity of negotiating for, purchasing, and implementing a customized computer software system, its completion of these tasks within eighteen months could certainly be found by a jury to be reasonable.

This and other matters, the court concluded, were for the jury and would not be disposed of on summary judgment.

7e. The courts that have concluded that such post-revocation or continued use does not bar a revocation then go on to say that the seller should be able to recover from the buyer the "reasonable value" of that use.

How is this value to be measured? If we were to take the difference in market values between a new automobile and one even only a few months old, the measure could be quite high and, it would seem, unfair to Alice. The cases that have had to consider the issue seem to settle on something like the fair market *rental* value of the goods for the period of time they were used by the buyer. But even then, if the seller has been holding on to the full purchase price for this period of time, and accumulating interest, is the calculation complete? In *Erling v. Homera, Inc.,* 298 N.W.2d 478, 30 U.C.C. 181 (N. Dak. 1980), a mobile home case, the Supreme Court of North Dakota remanded for "determination of the reasonable value of use of the home from the date of purchase to date of hearing on remand. The value of the use less interest at the rate of six percent per annum on the purchase price to the date of hearing on remand should be set off against the purchase price."

8. This question is an attempt to frame as clearly as possible an issue on which there is still unresolved debate: Does the seller have any right to cure following a revocation of acceptance? The answer is not obvious. Look at §2-508. This is the sole source in Article 2 of the right to cure and it speaks only of what follows a "rejection." If the drafters had wanted to provide for cure after a "revocation of acceptance," which is clearly a different animal under Article 2, they knew the words and could have included them in this section. There is some Latin maxim or another to the effect that when words are left out of a statute we have to assume this was done intentionally. On the other hand, §2-608(3) says that the buyer who revokes has "the same rights *and duties* with regard to the goods as if he had rejected them." Arguably one of the duties of a rejecting buyer is the duty to allow for and accept cure. But then again §2-608(3) refers to "duties *with respect to the goods.*" Is the duty to cooperate with a possible cure such a duty, or were those five words meant to limit the revoking buyer's responsibilities to keeping and caring for the goods with reasonable care and sending them back to the seller in the rare instances where this is required by §2-603? In short, the language of Article 2 can be read as either repudiating or allowing for the notion of cure following revocation.

If the Code language is not determinative of the issue, that gives us all the more justification for deciding it on "policy" grounds. But again the matter isn't crystal clear. Some authorities focus on the policy inherent in Article 2 that encourages cure and that favors keeping the deal alive and whole if at all possible. They argue that there must be a right to cure after revocation, even if it doesn't allow the seller to string the buyer along forever. For example, see *North River Homes, Inc. v. Bosarge,* 594 So. 2d 1153, 17 U.C.C.2d 121 (Miss. 1992), another mobile home case, which lays out one approach to the problem which is followed in several states:

> Once a consumer has properly notified the seller of his or her intent to revoke acceptance, the seller has a right to cure the alleged defect. This right is not unlimited; that is, Mississippi law does not

permit a seller "to postpone revocation in perpetuity by fixing everything that goes wrong" with the goods. "There comes a time when enough is enough"—when a consumer no longer must tolerate or endure the seller's repeated (though good faith) attempts to cure the defect. [Citations omitted.]

Other courts and authorities place greater stress on the policy allowing for revocation, but restricting it only to the more egregious situations where the buyer has been wronged in a significant way. They then conclude that if a situation is problematic enough to justify the buyer's revocation then it is simply going too far to cut the seller some additional slack in the form of the right to cure. Even in the rejection situation there is legitimate reason to be concerned, as we discussed in the preceding chapter, that an overgenerous reading of the right to cure will overpower the innocent and hapless buyer. Allowing for cure following a fully justified revocation might be just that much worse. In *Gappelberg v. Landrum*, 27 Tex. Sup. J. 260, 666 S.W.2d 88, 37 U.C.C. 1563 (1984), the court reflecting this kind of reasoning stated unequivocally that "once a buyer has properly revoked acceptance of a product, the seller has neither the right to cure by repair or by replacement." And that, we are to take it, is that—at least in Texas. But I'm not so sure.

One reason for the lack of a consensus is that the issue is rarely if ever so neatly set out in the cases as it is in my hypotheticals, whatever a particular court might think. For one thing, in almost all of the cases which have been decided to date the seller *has* actually cured or attempted a cure (often time and time again) before the revocation is made or soon thereafter. But the cure doesn't make matters any better, and the goods continue in a ratty condition. So it is pretty easy to accept the argument, at least in such situations, that if all the criteria for a revocation are met, including "substantial impairment," then giving the seller yet another chance to cure isn't fair to the buyer. The seller has given it his or her best shot and this has been found wanting. Eventually, enough really is enough.

At the other extreme must be those situations where it quickly appears to all involved that cure is still possible and holds out a real chance of success. If this is the case we have to believe that the buyer will almost invariably leap at the prospect—and the problem will rarely if ever appear in the reported cases. If the buyer were to refuse to allow for cure in such a situation, he or she might have difficulty sustaining this position should seller later be forced to bring an action for payment. The court could readily decide that there was after all the right to cure following revocation, but it wouldn't even have to make such a sweeping statement. The issue could be skirted entirely just by concluding that any defect that can easily and effectively be cured cannot by its nature "substantially impair the value" of the goods to this buyer or anyone else. So no revocation was possible in the first place. I'm afraid our friend Bailey the buyer, even if his case came up in Texas and even in light of the language in the *Gappelberg* case, may have to accept Sylvester's offer and learn to live with his Phaserjet.

21

Anticipatory Repudiation and Insecurity

When Trouble Precedes Performance

Look at the first sentence of Comment 1 to §2-609:

> This section rests on the recognition of the fact that the essential purpose of a contract between commercial men is actual performance and they do not bargain merely for a promise, or for a promise plus the right to win a lawsuit and that a continuing sense of reliance and security that the promised performance will be forthcoming when due, is an important feature of the bargain.

Truer words have never been written (even if the comment drafter's syntax and punctuation leave something to be desired). The only question is why these words of wisdom appear *here*, in the commentary to this particular section. They would do just as well, it seems, in explanation of plenty of other sections or in some overall introduction to Article 2 in general. Perhaps, however, the point the drafters were trying to make is particularly relevant to the three sections starting with §2-609 which we are now going to examine.

Consider. If you have a contract with another and that other party actually breaches by not performing when and as due, it's not a pleasant situation. You're probably going to want to do something about it. And you probably have some idea, albeit vague, of what is to be done. You're the injured party. You've been wronged. At the very least you would think to call a lawyer and together with that lawyer look to the remedies provisions of Article 2. A breach is a dramatic event. It demands (or at least allows for) a response, and a response there may very well be. But what about when there's only been a *hint* of a breach or the slightest *suggestion* that one may be in the offing? Perhaps the other who promised you performance at some later date is now hemming and hawing and generally acting disagreeably. He or she may even be threatening to pull out of the deal altogether, offering up either no or merely the lamest of excuses. Still there's time before the grumbler's performance is due, and who knows what the future will bring? Maybe it's all an act or he or she is just having a bad day. Maybe he or she will have still another change of heart.

In this type of situation, is there anything to do besides wait and see what the morrow brings (getting your lawyer on the phone but keeping him or her on one very expensive hold)? As the drafters remind us in their comment, a primary benefit of a contract for sale is the security for the future that it affords to each of the parties. Once that sense of security is threatened, what results is often worse than having no contract at all. If there is anything more worrisome than wondering if you will be able to make a contract on terms that meet your needs, it is having real reason to wonder whether things are going to go according to plan once you've made the desired contract. Sections 2-609 to 2-611 deal with two fundamental concepts that give a party experiencing genuine doubts about the other party's ability or willingness to perform when performance later becomes due something to do about the situation other than just wait and pray and agonize.* It may be slightly awkward but I suggest it is easier to deal with *anticipatory repudiation* as dealt with in §§2-610 and 2-611 and the *insecurity mechanism* of §2-609 in the reverse order from that in which they are given in Article 2. So we start with repudiation.

Anticipatory Repudiation

Section 2-610 lays out the rights of a party, be it a buyer or a seller, when the other party to the contract of sale has repudiated prior to performance. The basic notion of anticipatory repudiation, and the possible responses available to the aggrieved party, should be familiar to you from your study of the common law of contracts. At least in theory the situation is quite straightforward. One party informs the other that he or she is not going to do what was promised. There is a clear articulation that performance as provided for under the contract is no longer to be expected when due. No legitimate excuse is given. The repudiator has not merely hinted that performance may not be forthcoming when the time comes—it was said in no uncertain terms. Section 2-611 goes on to deal with the possibility of a retraction of a repudiation. The first Examples in this chapter ask you to apply these two sections. The problems you will face should come

---

*Look to §§2A-401 through 2A-403 for analogous provisions in Article 2A.

as no surprise. Short of when a party uses some form of the verb "to repudiate" or cites these sections of the Code, how do we know a repudiation when we see or hear one? You'll find the line between a true repudiation, which triggers all kinds of consequences for each of the parties, and mere griping and whining isn't as clear as we might hope. Once we have determined that a repudiation has taken place, what *may* the other party do? Is there anything the nonrepudiating party *must* do? If a contracting party believes the other to have repudiated, but turns out to be mistaken in that belief, what harm is done? (The answer, potentially plenty.) Finally, how and when can a repudiator retract the repudiation, and where does this leave the parties?

Insecurity and Demand for Assurance

Having dealt with the vagaries of repudiation, we will be in a better position to appreciate what is usually referred to as the *insecurity mechanism* provided for in §2-609. Life is not always as uncomplicated as we'd like it to be. The actions and words of others create impressions, but are these to be trusted? What precisely *did* that other person's statement mean? What exactly is going on here? Section 2-609 was meant to go beyond what was available under the common law to establish a means for dealing with (some of) the insecurities and ambiguities of commercial life.

It's important that you think of §2-609 in this way: It is about a process. Despite the first sentence in subsection (1), the value of this section isn't in some general hortatory principle. That first sentence is the one bit of language which really could be done away with without any noticeable effect. The importance of §2-609 to contracting parties is in what follows. The section sets forth a *mechanism*, a procedure that one or the other (or potentially both) of the parties to a sales contract can make use of to clarify the situation. The right conferred on a party by this section is the right to protection *by taking appropriate action*. But action under §2-609 must perforce be guided by that section, and as we will see this Article 2 mechanism can be a trap for the unwary just as it can serve as a boon to the prudent and sober soul.

The later Examples in this chapter will help you work through the various difficulties that come up when one party or the other seeks to take advantage of the §2-609 mechanism. You have by now had enough experience reading the Code that even as you first glance over this section you will immediately sense where problems can arise. What constitutes "reasonable grounds for insecurity"? What must be done to make an effective demand under the section? If a response is forthcoming, how are we to judge if it gives "adequate assurance" of performance? If, as subsection (4) sets out, there is such a thing as a "justified demand" under this section, then we have to recognize that there can be unjustified demands as well. What consequence if any will there be for making an unjustified demand? Is there anything a party can do to protect against misapplication of §2-609 beyond being "reasonable" and following "commercial standards" in every little thing that he or she says and does?

A Special Case: The Buyer's Insolvency

While not dealt with in the Examples and Explanations, we should at least note one other section in Article 2 that may be relevant in deciding what to do when trouble comes calling prior to performance. Section 2-702 gives the seller the right either to refuse delivery except for cash, stop delivery entirely before it occurs, or even in some instances to reclaim goods already delivered in the event of a buyer's insolvency. The operative definition of *insolvency* is that given in §1-201(23). The seller's rights in such a situation are, however, carefully circumscribed and appropriate procedures have to be followed. See §2-705, for example, on stoppage in transit.

We will assume that insolvency of the buyer is not a factor in the following Examples. The buyer could pay if he or she wanted to. But for some reason, or perhaps for no good reason, he or she is refusing to pay when due or otherwise threatening not to follow through on some obligation.

EXAMPLES

1. In January Belle, a clothing manufacturer, contracts to buy a large amount of woolen fabric from Serge's Material Mill. The contract specifies the price as $4 a yard, payable 30 days after Belle receives delivery. The date of delivery is given as March 15.

a. In February Belle receives a letter from Serge that says, "I am sorry that I must rescind our agreement. I hope we can work together in the future." Is this a repudiation under §2-610? If so, what rights does Belle have as of receipt of this letter?

b. Suppose instead that Serge's letter had said, "I am sorry to inform you that delivery isn't going to be until the end of April at the earliest. I wanted to let you know as soon as possible. Other than that, everything's fine." How do you analyze this situation under §2-610? Would your answer be any different if Serge had said that, while he could no longer be sure of delivery by March 15, he could guarantee that the fabric would be delivered no later than March 17?

c. Suppose that Serge had written the following: "The fabric is all ready and you will be getting delivery on March 15 of just what you ordered. However, I really can't let you have it for $4 a yard. I'll have to bill you at $4.15." He does not ask for any response from Belle. Is there any problem with Belle taking this as a repudiation and acting accordingly?

d. What if instead when Serge writes claiming that he will be owed the $4.15 he adds the statement that he will not ship the goods to Belle unless he hears from her acknowledging her duty to pay this increased price? He claims that the price rise is "in conformity with our contract in light of increased cost to me of materials and the custom in this industry of making adjustments in such circumstances." What is the situation here?

2. On Monday Larry agrees to sell Moe his used car, delivery to be made and payment tendered on Friday. On Wednesday, Moe gets a visit from his friend, Curley, who is driving the car. Larry's car! Curley tells Moe that he purchased it from Larry on Tuesday. Is Moe justified in saying there has been an anticipatory repudiation by Larry?

3. Just to make sure we don't suffer any illusions that only sellers can repudiate, let's flip the situation. Let us return to the Belle/Serge contract. Suppose that in February Belle writes to Serge, "I am looking forward to receiving the order on March 15. It turns out that I won't be able to pay for it until May, but don't worry, you'll get your money. You know I'm good for it." What are Serge's options here?

4. In March Betrand, a maker of digital widgets, contracts to buy a large metal stamping machine to be specially manufactured to his order by Stamper Incorporated. The contract calls for delivery by October. On May 5, Betrand writes Stamper saying he no longer needs the machine and "rescinding" his order. Stamper gets this letter on May 10.

    a. Stamper immediately stops the process of customizing the machine to Betrand's specifications. It simply sets the work aside. The President of the company writes back to Betrand, "You have a contract to buy the machine from us. We are readying it for you. Expect to hear from our lawyers." On May 31, Stamper receives another letter from Betrand who says that he has reconsidered and is willing to take the machine. What is the status of the parties at this point? Is Stamper still obligated to deliver the machine in October?

    b. Would your answer to the previous question be any different if Stamper, instead of just putting the work aside, immediately sought and was able to find another buyer (albeit at a lesser price) for the machine? Prior to receipt of Betrand's letter of May 31, it had begun configuring the machine to this new buyer's specifications and had instructed its attorney to begin a suit against Betrand for the difference in price.

5. Arnold Moneybucks enters into a contract to buy a painting from Stella's gallery, with delivery and payment to occur at the end of the gallery's current show. The day after signing the contract, Arnold calls Stella and says that he has decided against buying the painting. Stella responds, "I don't understand it. You were getting a great price. But if that's the way you feel, OK the deal is off." The conversation is at an end. A few minutes later, before Stella has even had the chance to remove the "SOLD" sign from the painting, Arnold again calls Stella saying that he has changed his mind once more. He will take the painting. Is Stella bound to sell it to him at the price originally agreed?

6.   Sunny Toy Manufacturers (Mr. Sunny, President) enters into a contract to sell a large number of talking dolls to Bunny, the owner of a toy store. While Sunny normally does not sell on credit, at Bunny's urging he agrees to do so in her case. The contract finally agreed upon specifies that payment is due within 90 days of delivery.

a.   Prior to shipment Sunny begins to regret that he ever extended credit to Bunny. He writes Bunny requesting that she agree to pay for the dolls upon receipt or in the alternative give a personal guarantee of payment. He gets no response to this request. Is he relieved under §2-609 from his obligation to ship the dolls at the time called for in the contract?

b.   Would your answer to the previous question be any different if the reason Sunny wrote making this request was that at a recent toymakers' convention he had heard reports from a couple of people that Bunny was in trouble financially and had not been paying her bills on time?

c.   How would you respond to the Sunny/Bunny problem if the reason for Sunny's demand was that Bunny was in fact at the time of the writing overdue in a payment to Sunny on a separate contract for the sale of some toy trains? The trains had been delivered a few weeks after the two contracted for the dolls, but Bunny is refusing to pay for the trains, claiming that they were delivered with defective cabooses.

7a.   Betty, an industrialist, contracts to buy a large metal stamping machine from Stamper, Inc. Prior to delivery Betty hears from industry sources that others who have bought similar machines from Stamper are experiencing problems with them. Betty calls Stamper's headquarters and talks directly to the president of the firm. She tells him of her concerns. He replies, "I hear you. Let me check into this and get back to you." Four weeks pass and Betty has not heard a thing. Would she be justified in writing a letter to Stamper canceling the contract and threatening to hold them liable for damages if she is forced to pay more elsewhere for a stamping machine that meets her needs?

b.   Suppose instead that Betty writes to the company explaining her concerns. Within a week she gets back a letter from the president of Stamper. It says, "You have nothing to worry about. I've checked into it and your machine is going to work just fine." That's it. She makes several calls trying to speak to the President, but she never gets through to him and he doesn't return her calls. Does Betty have a right to consider the contract at an end?

EXPLANATIONS

1a.   Serge may think he's "rescinding" the agreement, but absent some special provision in the contract he has no right to call a unilateral end to the deal. This is a repudiation by Serge. The Code does not define *repudiation,* but note Comment 1 to §2-610, which tells us that anticipatory repudiation "centers upon an overt communication of intention or an action which renders performance impossible or demonstrates a clear intention not to continue with performance." In fact Serge's letter is about as blatant a repudiation as you can imagine. One of the principal problems in this area, of course, is that parties rarely make their intentions known in such a pure, unadulterated fashion. Serge's flagrant repudiation, however, does allow us to explore the consequences. What are Belle's options once she's received this communication?

We should note at the outset that there is nothing to stop Belle, if she is so disposed, from letting Serge off the hook here. She could treat his letter as a request that she agree to a *mutual* rescission of the agreement. If she does agree, then the rescission should be valid (see §2-209) and neither party would have any responsibility under the contract. It's doubtful that she's going to want to agree to this, however. More than likely she thinks herself aggrieved by Serge's action, so we must look to what she may do as the *aggrieved party* under §2-610. Under that section she has several options. Subpart (a) says that she may just wait "for a commercially reasonable time" before she makes a move. Maybe Serge will, on his own, recognize the error of his ways and retract his repudiation. If she decides to wait she is under no affirmative obligation to tell him that's what she's doing as long as she is acting in good faith. See Comment 4. As a practical matter, of course, it makes a lot of sense for her to contract him, tell him what she thinks of the situation, and try to convince him to quit this foolishness.

While Belle may want to give Serge some time to reconsider and a second chance to do the right thing, there is no obligation on her part that she do so. Another possibility is for her immediately to take his letter as signalling an end to their agreement and to spring into action. Under (b) she can resort to any remedy she would have for breach. In this case, §2-711 is the section cataloging buyer's remedies in general. We will deal with remedies in great detail in a later chapter, but for the moment note that §2-711 allows for her to "cancel" in addition to pursuing other remedies. *Cancellation* is defined in §2-106(4). In other words, upon a repudiation Belle could immediately declare that the whole deal was off while at the same time retaining her rights to pursue a remedy (typically an action for monetary damages) against Serge for any injury caused her.

Note also that under part (b) Belle does not have to decide to treat his repudiation as a breach immediately or forever lose the chance to do so. She can decide to wait a bit, and she can even tell Serge that she is willing to wait in the hopes that he will reconsider and perform, but when her patience wears thin she may then choose to treat his behavior as a breach and resort to her formidable remedies.

Finally, note the provision in (c) that gives Belle, as the aggrieved party, the right to "suspend [her] own performance in response to the repudiation." (The reference to §2-704 isn't relevant here, as that would come into play only when a buyer repudiates, and even then only in a relatively small number of cases.) The right to suspend your own performance in the face of a repudiation doesn't seem to matter much here, but in other circumstances it could make a great deal of difference. Suppose, for example, that in our situation the contract called for Belle to make a prepayment of 20 percent of the price by March 1. If she doesn't make that payment, could Serge ever argue that *she* actually breached first and that he was therefore, somehow, let off the hook? Obviously the answer should be no. Once he repudiates, her obligation to pay by March 1 is suspended.

So it seems it's pretty much up to Belle how she wants to handle the situation—with one possible exception. While §2-610 never says it in so many words, there's a good argument that the one thing Belle may *not* do is simply ignore the repudiation altogether and act as if it never happened. Suppose she just waits until March 15 without doing anything. She receives no delivery from Serge. She then goes out into the market on March 16 and buys a quantity of woolens to cover, but at a much higher price than the $4 a yard. Perhaps she suffers other losses as well. For instance, because even in the best of circumstances she will now not get delivery of the fabric until some time after March 15, she may suffer decreased profits if her plant must remain idle for a time or if she has to pay overtime to her workers in order to meet her production schedule. Can she sue Serge, holding him responsible for all of these losses? Here, after all, there has been not merely a repudiation but a breach of which she certainly has the right to complain. The problem for Belle here, if she expects to recover every penny of her loss, is that §2-610 says she had the right upon getting the repudiation to wait "a commercially reasonable time" for performance. Depending on the circumstances, a court could easily conclude that waiting the whole way to the promised arrival date was waiting *beyond* a commercially reasonable time. What then? There is nothing in §2-610 to guide us (although you should look at the last sentence in Comment 1), but as we will see when we study buyer's remedies in more detail, there is a strong argument to be made that Belle would not be able to recover by way of damages the full difference in the cost of the fabric, much less the other consequential losses to her such as the amount spent on overtime. It will turn out (in Chapter 29) that this issue is among the most troubling and controversial in the area of remedies under Article 2, and not all authorities are in agreement about what should be the outcome. For the moment it's sufficient for us to note that there is a fairly good argument to be made that Belle, the "aggrieved party" in this case, cannot just wait around forever but must after a "commercially reasonable" length of time acknowledge that the repudiation is going to stick, that she is going to be the victim of a breach some time in the future, and then take action accordingly in an effort to mitigate the damages she will suffer.

1b. When Serge says that delivery is going to come six weeks late, he is repudiating. He is not disavowing the contract (in fact he says he's anxious to perform), but performance will not be as the contract provides. This is a repudiation. Belle may agree to a later delivery date, thus in effect concluding a modification, but she is under no obligation to do so. She may take any of the actions we allowed her in the previous example.

What about the case when Serge tells her something like a month in advance to expect a delay of at most two days? Is this a repudiation? Well, yes, but under §2-610 it turns out we need to explore further. Belle's rights to suspend performance or to treat this as a breach are conditioned on the repudiation being such that the loss of those two days "will substantially impair the value of the contract" to her. Who's to say if two days late is substantial enough? If it is not, what about ten days, or twenty? Comment 3 refers us to how Article 2 deals with similar problems in installment contracts. We will examine this in the next chapter, which will be the better place to ponder over the subtleties of the "substantial impairment" standard. Surely it will come as no surprise if I tell you now that there will be no easy or clear-cut test for when impairment is substantial enough and when it isn't. In our case, Comment 3 asks us to consider whether "material inconvenience or injustice" will result if Belle is made to take the fabric on March 17, given that she can also expect to receive some measure of damages for the lateness. It seems unlikely that the two days are that big of a deal. If Belle does treat this not just as a repudiation but as a repudiation justifying her cancellation of the contract, she runs a terrific risk that a court will later judge that she has made a mountain out of a molehill. If that is the case the court could conclude that her action in canceling for no sufficient reason was itself a repudiation on *her* part.

You can, of course, imagine situations where a statement by the seller that delivery will be a few days late would be enough to trigger all of the buyer's rights under §2-610. What's the use of Christmas trees delivered on December 26? Or consider the case of *Neptune Research & Development, Inc. v. Teknics Industrial Systems, Inc.*, 235 N.J. Super. 522, 563 A.2d 465, 10 U.C.C.2d 107 (1989). The seller of a large specialized manufacturing machine (the Model RC-520 triple access Precision Vertical Machining Center) had originally agreed in April to a mid-June delivery date. Problems ensued and by late August the machine still had not arrived. On August 29, a representative of the buyer visited the seller's place of business and saw the machine which was almost completely assembled. Acting on behalf of the buyer he agreed to take it, on the understanding that it would be ready to be picked up on September 5. On September 3, when the buyer called to make arrangements for the pick-up, he was then told that the machine would be ready on September 9 or 10 at the earliest. At this point the buyer, "fed up" with the course of dealing and claiming to have lost all faith in the seller, canceled the contract. The buyer was held to have been within its rights in treating this final delay as a repudiation justifying cancellation. Normally, the court opined, a delay in delivery of a few days in a complex contract such as this would not be substantial at least where the contract did not make "time of the essence." In fact, the court suggests, the failure to make delivery in mid-June would not necessarily have been a material breach giving the buyer the right to cancel. But the judgment of substantiality has to be made taking into account all of the surrounding circumstances, and eventually enough is enough. The court concluded that,

> Buyer had already waited a long time, seller had not been candid with buyer, and Sule [buyer's president] had good reason to believe that seller would not perform. In essence, the events of August 29 can be viewed as Sule giving seller "one last chance." Seller's failure to call buyer on September 3, as seller had promised to do, could only have deepened buyer's suspicion that seller was not going to perform. In light of these circumstances, [the seller's] unequivocal statement on September 4, that under no circumstances would the machine be ready by the promised delivery date, September 5, was a repudiation going to the essence of the contract.

We'll pick up on another aspect of the *Neptune* case a bit later on.

1c. Serge will claim that he is not repudiating at all. He is continuing to promise his performance, which is the delivery of certain goods just as they were ordered and on the promised date. He is not, he would later claim, repudiating "with respect to any performance [for which he is responsible] not yet due." He finds support in Comment 2:

> Under the language of this section, a demand by one or both parties for more than the contract calls for in the way of counter-performance is not in itself a repudiation nor does it invalidate a plain expression of desire for future performance. However, when under a fair reading it amounts to a statement of intention not to perform except on conditions which go beyond the contract, it becomes a repudiation.

Belle would seem to be taking a big risk by reading what he's said so far as a statement of his intention not to deliver. It would, of course, be different if he begins to make sounds with the clear implication that he isn't going to be shipping the stuff off unless and until he hears from her that she's willing to pay the greater amount. If she doesn't have grounds for taking his letter as a repudiation, what she'll have to do is wait for the delivery, accept it, and then refuse to pay any more than the $4 a yard. What will then happen? Belle has to know that Serge may then sue her for the extra money. She'll win, we assume, but it has to be pretty upsetting for her to have to accept some goods knowing that she's going to have to face a lawsuit (even a frivolous one) some time down the road. If she would prefer to force the issue now, there should be some way she could take advantage of the §2-609 insecurity mechanism. You begin to see the importance of that section when repudiations, or possible repudiations, are not as clear-cut as they were in Example 1a.

1d. It would be very hard, and certainly very risky, for Belle to treat this as a repudiation. Serge does not disavow any aspect of the contract. The problem comes, of course, if Belle disagrees that he has any right under their contract to a price in excess of $4 whatever the circumstances. But a disagreement about the terms of the contract, as long as Serge is acting in good faith, shouldn't be characterized as a repudiation. Serge's argument as to what the contract provides may be wrong, but he certainly isn't saying he is unwilling or unable to perform his obligations under that contract, whatever they turn out to be. At least that's how I would read the language from Comment 2 quoted above. It also seems to me to be the right result. It's a troubling case to say the least when the parties start wrangling even before performance over how to interpret their contract, but I hope that each of them would be wary about declaring the other to have "repudiated" when they recognize that there's an honest dispute. It would be a different matter if Serge's argument for an adjustment in the price was totally frivolous and made in bad faith. (Remember, we are helped here by a definition of good faith under §2-103(1)(b) for merchants that imports reasonable commercial standards.) Assuming good faith on the part of both parties, the situation here seems to be best summed up as one in which neither should yet be encouraged to raise the red flag of repudiation. The Code would encourage them to keep planning for performance according to schedule, assuming things can be worked out if only they keep talking to each other.

2. A repudiation can be found, according to Comment 1 as well as prior law, in "an action that renders performance impossible," which seems to be what we have here. Larry is not going to be able to deliver to Moe on Friday a car that is no longer his to sell. Of course, Larry could argue that it is not literally *impossible* for him to perform on Friday. He could, at least in theory, repurchase the car from Curley on Thursday. That doesn't seem a very convincing argument, and I see no good reason to countenance it here. There will be other situations, of course, when it will be far from clear whether a party's action have actually disabled him or her from performing. Once again, if the other party is at all in doubt about whether to declare a repudiation, the sensible thing would be to go the §2-609 route.

3. This is a repudiation by Belle. Serge could decide it makes sense to treat her letter as a request for a modification of their agreement and go along with the change. If he does not want to do this, Serge's options are all laid out in §2-610: He has the right to suspend performance (that is, he doesn't have to ship the fabric and won't be in breach when it fails to arrive by the 15th); he can immediately treat this as a breach and pursue his remedies as a seller under §2-703; he can wait for a "commercially reasonable time" and hope for a retraction, although after the end of a commercial reasonable time he may be obligated to treat the repudiation as a problem that is not going to go away and react to it as a breach, mitigating his damages as best he can.

4a. The status of the parties at this point is that they have a contract for the purchase and sale of a machine. While there has been a repudiation, there has never really been a breach. Under §2-611 the retraction of the repudiation "reinstates" the contract, "with due excuse and allowance to the aggrieved party for any delay occasioned by the repudiation." Stamper is obligated to deliver the machine, but the date of delivery is moved forward something like a month. Other than that, unless there are other consequences of the delay of which we are not aware, all other terms remain the same.

4b. If this were the case, Betrand would not be able to retract his repudiation as Stamper has "materially changed" its position because of the May 5 letter (§2-611(1)). Stamper may, of course, decide it still wants to sell a machine to Betrand, but it is not obligated to do so and would have the flexibility of negotiating an entirely new contract if it chose. Or it could just tell Betrand to take a hike and keep its lawyer on the case.

5.   No. Stella is not bound to the contract. Arnold has attempted a retraction of his repudiation and can rightly argue that Stella did not materially change her position prior to the retraction. But §2-611 also states that the repudiator has no absolute right to retract if the aggrieved party has "canceled." Under §§2-610 and 2-703(f), Stella had the right to cancel immediately upon hearing the repudiation, and that seems to be what she did. The definition of *cancellation* in §2-106(4) doesn't actually say *how* you cancel, but Stella did say she was calling the whole thing off. Note also that §2-611(1) speaks of cancelling or "otherwise indicating" that you consider the repudiation final. So an *indication,* not any particular formalism or any action taken in reliance, should be enough to frustrate a subsequent attempt by Arnold to retract.

There has actually been very little discussion about how and when a cancellation is executed. The *Neptune* case (remember the Model RC-520 triple access Precision Vertical Machining Center?) seems to be the first (in 1989) to confront the question. The law prior to the Code was unclear, but there was a plausible argument that a retraction was permissible at any time before the other party had suffered some change in position. The court in *Neptune* concluded that §2-611 was to the contrary, at least in the particular instance, commenting:

> [W]e assume that the drafters intentionally used the disjunctive: that is the breaching [don't they mean repudiating?] party loses the right to retract if the nonbreaching party materially changes his position *or* cancels. (Emphasis added.)

The court added to this careful (one might say obvious) reading of the section two other reasons for declining to give effect to the retraction despite the absence of any discernible prejudice against the nonrepudiating party. There is, they noted, a great value to certainty once the nonrepudiating party has had his or her say and means it to be final. In addition the court said it could not ignore, in this instance, the repudiator's "less-than-exemplary conduct" throughout the course of the contract. Could

Arnold Moneybucks distinguish *Neptune* and successfully argue that *his* retraction came in time and should be allowed to have effect? We will have to await further cases, if there are any, beyond *Neptune* exploring this issue, but in light of the "or" in §2-611(1) I don't see why the repudiator should have this argument. If Stella wants to uncancel her cancellation, I think that should be up to her and not forced on her by Arnold's latest change of heart.

6a. No. Use of §2-609 is predicated on a party having "reasonable grounds for insecurity" about performance by the other. This is obviously not a precise requirement, and subsection (2) adds only a bit to our understanding. It should be clear, however, that "reasonable grounds" as that phrase is used here is meant to connote some *change*, or at least an objective reason to suspect change, in the probability that the other party will perform from what would have been true at the time the agreement was entered into. Comment 1 speaks of "either the willingness or the ability of a party to perform materially declin[ing] between the time of contracting and the time of performance." It is not enough that a party like Sunny has second thoughts or himself re-evaluates the risks inherent in the sales agreement, finding greater reason to be edgy. In *Cole v. Melvin,* 441 F. Supp. 193, 22 U.C.C. 1154 (D. S.C. 1977), the court made little of the seller's argument rooted in §2-609.

> The first requirement for application [of §2-609] is that "reasonable grounds for insecurity arise" with respect to the performance of one of the parties. Clearly, the drafters of the code did not intend that one party to a contract can go about demanding security for the performance of the other whenever he gets nervous about a contract. Some reason for demand for assurance must precede the demand. . . . After a search of the transcript, we have nothing . . . which even approaches being a factually established ground for insecurity. Obviously, something prompted Cole [the seller] to ask Melvin if he planned to perform. But, from everything in the record, it appears that Cole was prompted by purely subjective concerns which were not rooted in any objective facts that can now be legally equated with reasonable grounds for insecurity.

Note that if an argument such as Cole's—or Sunny's in our story—were to succeed, §2-609 would be transformed into a means for one party unilaterally to force a revision in the sales contract in his favor, getting some advantage that he hadn't thought it important (or possible) to insist on initially. That's not what the section is about.

If you're looking for a good case where such reasonable grounds unquestionably did exist, you could do no better than *Turntables, Inc. v. Gestetner,* 52 A.D.2d 776, 382 N.Y.S.2d 798, 19 U.C.C. 131 (1976). The court held that the seller had reasonable grounds to be concerned about the buyer's ability to pay, even if he had from the start agreed to a sale on credit and even though the buyer may not in fact have become insolvent as he feared. What warranted the seller's recourse to §2-609?

> The buyer was in arrears in payment for goods already delivered; its "Fifth Avenue Showroom" turned out to be a telephone answering service; its Island Park factory turned out to be someone else's premises, to which the [buyer] did not have a key, and [buyer] did not lease space, had no employees, payroll machinery, or equipment therein; another supplier told [seller] it had been stuck with an unpaid bill of [buyer's]; [buyer] had a bad reputation for performance or payment, etc.

You get the idea. The seller refused to deliver. This nondelivery was held not to be a breach, as the buyer had refused following a written request to give any assurances whatsoever that it would be able to pay.

6b. Comment 3 suggests this would be enough to allow for Sunny's use of the §2-609 mechanism. The comment refers to an "apparently trustworthy source" of information that the other party is not performing his or her contracts. It would therefore be fair to inquire about the people from whom Sunny heard what he heard. But unless rumors of this type are known to be rarely based on anything, Sunny probably has the right to demand "adequate assurance of due performance." See *Clem Perrin Marine Towing, Inc. v. Panama Canal Co.,* 730 F.2d 186, 38 U.C.C. 490 (5th Cir. 1984), for a case that follows this line. What if the rumors are in fact unfounded? Isn't this unfair to Bunny? No, not if you remember that the idea is not that Sunny is automatically able to get out of the contract or unilaterally revise the agreement in his favor. What he *can* do is "demand assurance" from Bunny. If he does not get it within a reasonable time, not in excess of 30 days, he can treat the contract as repudiated by her.

Section 2-609(4) is really the crucial part of the section. The right to demand assurance under subsection (1) gives either party in an appropriate situation the opportunity to force the issue and seek clarification, leading perhaps to a clear-cut and definitive repudiation. The other party can, of course, always short circuit this result by giving adequate assurances if this is possible. If the rumors of her financial trouble are untrue, Bunny should be able to alleviate Sunny's fears by putting him in contact with her other creditors or getting some kind of clean bill of financial health from her bank.

So if Sunny is within his rights in making a demand in this instance, the issue becomes whether the particular demand he is making—that she either pay in cash or give a personal guarantee—is justified. He is not entitled to demand any and everything of her that would make him perfectly comfortable, only *adequate* assurance. Comment 4 goes into some length trying to elaborate what type of demand is justified. Necessarily, the question has to be addressed on a case-by-case basis. Is Bunny a businesswoman of "good repute" or a "known corner-cutter?" What does the application of commercial standards justify here?

You should take time to appreciate the consequences for Sunny if he has legitimate reason to make a demand under §2-609 but makes a demand which in substance is not "justified," perhaps because he demands too much or refuses to be assuaged by what a court later determines to be "reasonable" assurances. If Sunny does respond to his letter in such a fashion and he, still insecure in his own mind but now not justifiably so, continues to refuse delivery of the dolls, *he* will be committing a breach or repudiation. Section 2-609 is meant to offer comfort for the contracting parties, but if either tries to push it too far or demands too much, it can end up blowing up in that party's face.

6c. Does Sunny have reasonable grounds for insecurity in this situation? Under the common law it was generally said that if parties had more than one contract with each other each arrangement worked independently. The breach (or argued breach) of one had no effect on responsibilities under any other. The second paragraph to Comment 3 indicates that this isn't strictly true under this provision of Article 2. A ground for insecurity need *not* arise from or be directly related to the contract in question. (We've already seen that even rumors about how the buyer is treating his other creditors may be enough.) The next paragraph in the comment specifically deals with the situation where the buyer is behind in his account with the seller on other contracts. So if Bunny is behind in payment to Sunny for other purchases and offers no good excuse, Sunny could make a demand for assurance that he will be paid for the dolls. And, what would be important to him, until he got such an assurance he could also suspend his own performance. He would not have to continue preparing the dolls or ship them off until Bunny's account was cleared up or sufficient assurances of payment were arranged.

The situation here is more complex, in that Bunny is arguing that Sunny has not been paid for the trains not because of any financial difficulty on her part but because they were defective. Unless Sunny believes he can establish that Bunny is advancing this claim in bad faith, he would be risking a lot if he puts too much faith in the §2-609 mechanism here or pushes it too aggressively. The fact that she is not paying for goods which she in good faith believes to be defective is not a mark of a "cost-cutter" or of someone who is in any kind of financial difficulty. It's just standard respectable business practice. The court presumably would be careful not to allow invocation of §2-609 to be used as a cudgel to force payment out of a buyer who has legitimate problems with delivered goods by legitimating the seller's threat to withhold unrelated merchandize as it becomes due.

7a. Here it is Betty the buyer who has reasonable grounds for insecurity. See the reference in Comment 3 to the buyer of precision parts who discovers that her seller "is making defective deliveries of such parts to other buyers with similar needs." A case on point is *Creusot-Loire International, Inc. v. Coppus Engineering Corp.,* 585 F. Supp. 45, 39 U.C.C. 186 (S.D.N.Y. 1983).

The problem for Betty here is that she did not make a *written* demand for assurance—her demand was made over the telephone. (Did you catch this?) If anything is certain, it would seem, when the Code calls for a "demand *in writing*" it must really be in writing. Well, maybe nothing is certain. There are a number of cases where the courts have "waived" or "forgiven" a party's failure to put its demand in writing and given effect to a demand under §2-609 despite the fact that it was entirely oral. It is hard to see a justification for this blatant disregard of the Code language other than that the results do seem right. In each case, to be sure, there was no question that the demand was made, even if not in a formal writing, and that the party later held to have repudiated under §2-609(4) well aware of the other's insecurity, the reasonable grounds for that insecurity, and what was being demanded in the way of assurance.

Good practice and common sense, of course, counsel that anyone seeking to use the insecurity mechanism put the demand in writing, make the writing as clear and precise as possible, date it, and get some proof that the other party received it. (Technically, notice does not require this last bit, see §1-201(26), but we're talking good practice and common sense here.)

7b. Here Betty has reasonable grounds and has been careful enough to make a written demand. The question is whether she has received "adequate assurance." Are the president's words alone enough? I would argue not, at least not when coupled with his apparent refusal to give her any more information or even to speak with her. Perhaps she should be grateful for his silence. In *Smith-Scharff Paper Co. v. P. N. Hirsch & Co. Stores, Inc.*, 754 S.W.2d 928, 7 U.C.C.2d 38 (Mo. Ct. App. 1988), a demand for assurance was met with a torrent of words, not all of them friendly. When seller's justified written demand got no response, its president put in a call to the president of the buyer, about which he testified,

> I remember him *yelling at me over the telephone*, that I would have the audacity to question the integrity of their company, that they would honor all commitments, and, historically, they have bent over backwards to honor all of their commitments.

This, the court concluded, "was an unreasonable response to a simple request for assurance." Judgment for seller affirmed.

In our hypothetical, what could the president of Stamper have done, and what would Betty have the right to expect, in the way of adequate assurance? The President should have responded in more detail about what problems they were experiencing if any with the product, whether there was reason to suspect that these problems might affect the machine being made for Betty, and if so what corrective measures were being taken or quality controls instituted. The President could even have offered to let Betty come over and inspect the machinery as it was being fabricated. Certainly he should have returned her calls. The sort of assurances that are called for or which should serve to meet the §2-609 challenge are presumably as varied as the grounds for insecurity that can arise. There is no particular form that assurances must take, and a good business sense should serve as an adequate guide. A buyer or a seller who is justifiably asked to give adequate assurance—and who truly wants to and will be able to perform—should be able to find some way to assuage any reasonable fears of the other party.

22

Installment Sales

The Installment Contract Under Article 2

The term *installment contract* or *installment sale* is familiar from everyday use. For the purposes of analysis under Article 2, however, we defer to the definition in §2-612(1):

> An "installment contract" is one which requires or authorizes delivery of goods in separate lots to be separately accepted, even though the contract contains a clause "each delivery is a separate contract" or its equivalent.

The word *lot* is defined in §2-105(5) to mean

> a parcel or a single article which is the subject matter of a separate sale or delivery, whether or not it is sufficient to perform the contract.

The word *parcel* is itself not terribly clear here. Although this definition of *lot* has never caused a whit of trouble, it might be better if expanded to include not only the parcel and the single article but also something like "a collection of parcels or articles which taken together" are the subject matter of a separate sale or delivery.

In most instances, of course, we know a *lot* when we see one, and in fact there is rarely any great doubt whether a particular contract qualifies as an installment contract. Typically the seller is to make a series of separate deliveries over time and the buyer agrees to pay for each delivery according to some payment plan laid out in the agreement. The contract may call for delivery of specified lots on some predetermined schedule. So, for example, seller may be obligated to deliver 10,000 pounds of a given commodity by the first of the month for each and every month during a period of years. For its part the buyer will be required to accept separately each of the monthly deliveries and pay for them, say by sending seller a check for $500 by the 15th of the following month. In some installment contracts the exact quantities and dates of individual deliveries are not set out in advance. A construction contractor, for example, may contract to buy a total of 8,000 feet of a designated type of pipe from a supplier to be used in a particular building project. The contract will specify that the pipe is to be delivered to the construction site at such times and in such amounts (eventually aggregating to the 8,000 feet) as are called for by the contractor over the period of six months during which construction is to take place. The contract will further provide that when a delivery is made the contractor-buyer must pay for the pipe at a specified price per foot. Payment may be made due on delivery or within some specified period after delivery. Or the contract could call for payment, say, by the 15th of any month for all pipe delivered (no matter the number of deliveries) in the previous month. Any of these arrangements would clearly be an installment contract under §2-612(1) as each *requires* delivery in lots to be separately accepted.

In other circumstances delivery in lots may not be explicitly called for in the contract but may be anticipated nevertheless. As Comment 1 states, the definition in §2-612 is intended to cover, by its use of the word "authorized" in addition to "required," the possibility of a series of separate deliveries "tacitly authorized by the circumstances or by the option of either party." In this regard look back to §2-307. Delivery in lots is *authorized* where "the circumstances give either party the right to make or demand delivery in lots" and furthermore the price, if it can, is to be "apportioned" among the lots. If you have any problem with this result you may want to look at Comment 3 to §2-307 and to our treatment of that section in Chapter 9. (The treatment was brief, but then this section seems to give few people difficulty.) For present purposes, look at Comment 2 to §2-612. It is sufficient for finding an installment contract that the circumstances lend themselves to *delivery and acceptance* in distinct episodes. *Payment* by apportionment may be nice for one or both of the parties involved, but it is not a necessary condition for an installment contract.

Historically, some contracting parties have sought to avoid having their relationship characterized as an installment contract by inserting language in the agreement stating that each delivery is to be considered a separate contract or the like. Practically, of course, it's usually one of the two parties which sticks such language into the boilerplate for its own sinister purposes. As Comment 3 discusses, the definition of §2-612 makes abundantly clear that such "legalistic" language will not have any effect. The "singleness of the document and the negotiations" together with "the sense of the situation" are to control. You should not take from this comment the idea that a contract must necessarily be evidenced by a single piece of paper if it is to be judged an installment contract. In *Cassidy Podell Lynch, Inc. v. Snydergeneral Corp.*, 994 F.2d 1131, 15 U.C.C.2d 1225 (3d Cir. 1991), for example, the buyer contracted to obtain from the seller $350,000 worth of equipment all of which it was to use to meet a single resale commitment. With the seller's blessing the buyer entered 23 distinct purchase orders, the reason being that the seller had a self-imposed ceiling of $15,000 on any individual purchase order.

Despite the multiplicity of papers, the court had no difficulty recognizing this as a single installment contract and applying §2-612 to the controversy between the parties.

It has to be emphasized that the definition of installment contract is just that, a *definition*. There is no language in §2-612(1) that says that an installment contract is such-and-such "unless otherwise agreed" by the parties. Parties are not allowed to vary or contract out of a definition under the Code, even in the very freedom-of-contract-oriented Article 2. Nor may they simply ignore the consequences of that definition. As we will now note, Article 2 sets forth some special rules applicable to installment sales and the buyer and the seller who have entered into what the article deems to be an installment contract will have to play by those rules whether they would agree to them or not.*

Playing by the Rules for Installment Sales

Section 2-612, in subsections (2) and (3) sets forth the special rules which govern the performance of installment sales contracts. The questions that soon follow will explore the workings of these provisions. Read these subsections now. As you can see, the treatment of installment sales is different from the one-shot noninstallment sale in that the perfect tender rule as incorporated into §2-601 does not apply. The right to reject will now hinge on "substantial" nonconformity, which must mean something different than failure to conform "in any respect," the hallmark language of §2-601. (You should refer back to that section and note that it explicitly defers to §2-612 on the governance of installment contracts.) As you work through this material, you will want to consider what might have moved the drafters who otherwise felt committed to the perfect tender rule for sales to abandon that rule in the special circumstance of the installment sale. True, no one is that hot for the perfect tender rule to begin with, but there may be more to the §2-612 result than just the drafters taking every opportunity they could to shoot holes in it. What makes installment sales different, and perhaps particularly unsuited to perfect tender thinking?

Before moving into the questions, we should at least note a couple of other provisions of Article 2 which, while not exclusively applicable to installment sales, can be of particular significance when dealing with such transactions. Section 2-208 (covered in Chapter 7) delineates the effect of any course of performance which arises between the parties to a contract. A course of performance can come up only when there are "repeated occasions for performance by either party," and so necessarily can more easily

---

*In what follows we'll deal exclusively with installment sales under Article 2. You may wish to note, however, the definition of "installment lease contract" in §2A-103(1)(i) and the rules laid out in §2A-510. All is perfectly analogous to what we will see in Article 2.

affect the installment contract relationship. Similarly, modification and waiver as covered in §2-209 (and Chapter 10) can for obvious reasons play a special part when the parties have contracted for repeated performances over time. The longer things go on, the more events of performance in any contract, the greater the chances that a modification or waiver will occur—or at least that one party can make a plausible argument under this type of theory.

The following Examples and Explanations focus not on these sections (each of which has been given the spotlight in preceding chapters) but on subsections (2) and (3) of §2-612, which now take center stage.

EXAMPLES

1. Birmingham Integrated Machines manufactures computers. One of the component parts of the machines it makes is a specific kind of On/Off switch. BIM contracts to buy a total of 600,000 switches (the #GH70) from Switcher International. The contract calls for the delivery of 50,000 switches no later than the 15th day of each month during 1993. BIM is to pay $2 per switch within ten days after delivery. On January 17, Switcher makes its first delivery to BIM. The shipment contains 49,000 of the #GH70 switches. Because it has been careful to keep an ample supply of switches in its own storeroom, BIM does not suffer any production problems on January 15 or 16. The BIM production manager says she does not anticipate needing more than 45,000 or 46,000 switches prior to the middle of February, as the beginning of the year is typically a period of slow production.

   a. May BIM reject the January 17 shipment when it arrives?

   b. Suppose that the delivery made on January 17 had contained only 40,000 of the switches. Could BIM have rejected in that case?

   c. Suppose the January 17 shipment had contained 50,000 switches, but upon inspection it was found that they were all of the wrong type? The purchasing director calls up Switcher and is told that the seller will bring a full load of the correct model switches to BIM within the next two or three days. Could BIM have rejected?

   d. Now suppose instead that Switcher made no delivery whatsoever on January 17. Instead it makes a conforming delivery of 50,000 switches on January 25. On January 21 the production manager had become concerned that she might have to shut down the entire production line for lack of On/Off switches. After consultation among the managers, the purchasing director arranged a contract to buy 50,000 of a similar switch (at $2.25 each) from another manufacturer, Mitch's Switches, which promised delivery of its product on January 27. When the shipment from Switcher International arrives on January 25, is BIM obligated to accept it?

   e. The president of BIM is upset about what has happened and that he has even had to consider the prospect of shutting down production because of a failure in supply of such a rudimentary part. (Mitch has also indicated that he would be willing to supply the needed switches for only $1.90 apiece if he did not have to make delivery on short notice.) May the president simply write to Switcher at the end of January saying that he is canceling their contract because of the lateness of the January delivery? If he did so, what would be the result?

f. Suppose the President does not attempt to cancel the contract in January but only writes to Switcher indicating his annoyance at what has happened. The delivery promised for February 15 does not arrive until February 20. Can BIM now cancel the contract and make other arrangements with Mitch? If not now, when?

2. Seller agrees to sell and Buyer to buy 1,000 large round blue buttons each month during the year 1992. Delivery is to be made by Seller no later than the tenth day of each month. On January 5, Seller makes a delivery which turns out to contain only 900 buttons. Buyer calls Seller to ask what has gone wrong. He doesn't yell; he simply points out the problem. Seller apologizes for the mistake and delivers the additional 100 buttons on January 7. On February 6, Buyer receives a shipment that contains 1,000 *small* round blue buttons. Again Buyer calls, and again Seller apologizes and makes a conforming delivery, now on February 8. In March the delivery arrives on the 7th. It contains the right number of large round buttons, but they are *yellow.* There follows another call, another apology, and another conforming delivery before the 10th of March. When a shipment of 1,000 large *square* blue buttons arrives on April 2, can Buyer reject this shipment? Can he cancel his contract with Seller and buy buttons elsewhere?

3. Buster the building contractor has been awarded a contract to construct an office building. He estimates that he will need something like 200,000 bricks to complete the work. He enters into a contract with Sarah's Building Supply that calls for her to deliver bricks (in commercial units of 10,000) to the job site as requested by Buster. Sarah will bill Buster at $1 apiece for any bricks delivered during a month at the end of that month, and she is to receive payment from Buster by the fifteenth day of the following month. Buster first calls for a load of 30,000 bricks in May. Sarah delivers the bricks and sends him a bill for $30,000 at the end of the month. She is asked to and does deliver a second load of 50,000 on June 5. By June 23 she has still not received any payment from Buster for the May bricks.

a. He calls her and asks for another delivery. Must she make the delivery he is now requesting? Would Sarah be within her rights to cancel the contract at this time following up with a suit for the $80,000 now owed plus her lost profits on the bricks never delivered?

b. What would be the consequence if Sarah immediately brought suit only for the $80,000 now owed her?

c. Suppose that in fact Buster had sent Sarah a check for $30,000 on June 22. This check arrives at Sarah's on the 24th and clears with no problem. Meanwhile, after having been promised this payment, Sarah did deliver an additional 40,000 in late June. She sends him a bill for $90,000 covering the two June deliveries. She receives a check from him on July 24. Sarah calls Buster and tells him that she is not happy with his lateness in payment and that she expects prompt payment in the future. He tells her it will never happen again. Sarah bills Buster for bricks delivered in July, but by August 16 has received no payment from him. Can Sarah cancel the contract now?

    d. Would your answer to the previous question be any different if Sarah had not complained to Buster at all about the late payments in June and July but simply deposited the checks as she received them?

4. Seller and Buyer have entered into a 20-month installment contract, starting with delivery in January 1993, under which Buyer is to make payments by the twentieth day after receiving his monthly delivery. Seller makes the first ten deliveries and receives payment with no problem. After delivery in late November 1993, Buyer calls Seller telling her that he is short of cash and "will not be able to make payment this month." Seller threatens not to make any future deliveries as long as Buyer is behind in his account. Buyer reacts, "You can't do that. If I don't get the stuff from you it will ruin my business and just drive me deeper in the hole. I'm willing to agree that all future deliveries will be for cash. I might even be able to get you a guarantee from my bank that you'll be paid for those future deliveries. You'll just have to wait for the December payment. You'll get it eventually." Seller responds that she considers the contract at an end and will deliver no more stuff to Buyer. Is she within her rights to do this?

EXPLANATIONS

1a. No. BIM may not reject. Under §2-612(2), the buyer may reject an individual installment only if it is nonconforming and "the nonconformity substantially impairs the value of that installment." There are two nonconformities here, the late delivery and the short delivery, but there seems to be no way to argue that either "substantially impairs" the value of the January installment to BIM. A delivery short 1,000 out of the promised 50,000 units could obviously be substantially deficient in many situations, but it doesn't look to be so here. If this were not an installment contract and the right to reject came under §2-601, the perfect tender rule would apply (at least in theory) and Switcher would have faced a legitimate rejection, even if BIM could not have shown and indeed would not have suffered any real hardship because of the sins of this delivery.

    The obvious question is how we are to judge whether a nonconformity "substantially impairs the value of that installment." The equally obvious answer is that there is no set or easy way to make the call. You have presumably studied the doctrine of so-called material breach or substantial performance as it surfaced in the common law of contracts. You saw there that the measure of nonconformity or shortfall that triggers the rule is all a matter of degree and not subject to any bright-line test. If there isn't very much wrong at all with the tender, that's OK. (At least as far as meeting the performance *condition* and triggering the other party's duty to perform everything is OK; the nonbreaching party can always seek damages for breach of the *promise* even for the most minute discrepancy.) If the tender is way off the mark, then that's another story. Too much is too much. The condition on the other party's performance has not been met.

The drafters of Article 2 and the courts applying §2-612 have not been able to do much more with the "materiality" or "substantiality" concept than have the common lawyers. Look at the second paragraph to Comment 4. (Don't worry about defects in documents for the time being.) Does the drafters' list of factors on which the substantiality of a defect turns help? As a matter of fact there has been virtually no litigation over the use of the phrase in subsection (2) of §2-612. Buyers, sellers, and judges seem to know a "nonconformity substantially impairing the value of an installment" when they see one. It will be another matter entirely when we again hit the substantiality measure in subsection (3).

1b. Probably not. A shortfall of 10,000 switches *would* substantially impair the value of the installment to BIM, since it would have to worry about running out of this vital component sometime in February, but it's more than likely that this is a nonconformity *that can be cured*. Under §2-612(2) the rule is clear. Even a substantially nonconforming tender must be accepted if the problem can be cured. Note in Comment 5 that not only must the buyer accept in this instance provided the seller gives "adequate assurance of cure," but it must even be willing to suffer some reasonable minor outlay of time, money, and one would guess effort to make the cure a reality. What would be cure in this instance? One thing that Switcher could do would be to ship the additional 10,000 switches to BIM so that they got there within a couple of weeks. If BIM had a big enough reserve of switches to carry it through four weeks, it might even be enough for Switcher to promise that there would be 60,000 in the February delivery. In other instances, as the comment suggests, the seller may cure simply by allowing a reduction in price to reflect the value of the nonconformity.

1c. This is clearly a substantial nonconformity, but again it seems to be one that can be cured and cure is being offered. So BIM cannot reject this shipment either. The only odd thing here is that under a literal reading of §2-612(2), BIM must actually "accept" this shipment even though it's entirely wrong stuff. What the subsection really means to say here is that the buyer need not either *reject* or *accept* in this situation, but has an obligation to *await the offered cure and then accept that* if it is conforming. It's a minor point of language, and not one which I've ever seen cause any true confusion in the real world.

What if BIM does wait for a new shipment of the correct kind of switch and when it comes in a few days there is some problem with *that* delivery? Could BIM reject for an insubstantial nonconformity? Does it have to allow Switcher another chance to cure? We're quickly into the variety of problems that make the whole concept of cure both interesting and frustrating. (Recall Chapter 19.) And also back into the concern that liberal employment of the cure principle can, especially when coupled with a "substantial impairment" standard for rejection, be so favorable to the seller as to put the buyer at a distinct disadvantage.

1d. BIM may reject the shipment that arrives on January 25 under §2-612(2). While we have no precise way of measuring these things, the lateness here seems unquestionably to have substantially impaired the value of the installment (or rather the value of BIM's having arranged to receive this installment on the 15th), and furthermore the lateness is not curable.

One of the earliest cases on §2-612, and one of the better known, is *Graulich Caterer, Inc. v. Hans Holterbosch, Inc.*, 101 N.J. Super. 61, 243 A.2d 253, 5 U.C.C. 440 (1968). Defendant Holterbosch, an American importer and distributor of Lowenbrau beer, was granted the franchise to operate the Lowenbrau Pavilion at the 1964 World's Fair. He entered into a contract with the plaintiff, a professional catering concern, for daily deliveries of platters of German food which were to be reheated using the then-novel "microwave cooking concept" and thereupon sold to the pavilion's patrons. Initial samples of the meals came out of the microwave in good condition and were apparently of high quality. Following a delayed and muddled opening of the Fair, the buyer first placed a firm order for meals for April 23.

> Upon delivery the members of defendant's organization were stunned by the product and complained immediately that the tendered units did not, in any way, match the contract samples. Rejecting this 955-unit installment as unacceptable, defendant described the food as "bland," unpresentable, tasteless and "just wasn't the type of food we could sell."

The court found that Holterbosch was within his rights in rejecting the April 23 delivery, "since the nonconformity of the tendered goods with the accepted sample was incurable, and thus substantially impaired the value of that installment." What happened next? You'll have to wait for a minute. As is often true when installment contracts are involved, the story didn't end there. We return to *Graulich* soon enough.

1e. It is doubtful that BIM can cancel the entire contract because of the lateness of the first delivery even if it substantially impaired the value of *that installment* to the buyer. The test for whether there is a "breach of the whole" is found in §2-613(3). Does the "non-conformity or default with respect to one or more installments substantially impair[ ] the value of the whole contract" to BIM? While you could say it's anybody's guess once a standard of "substantiality" is to be applied, it seems to me highly unlikely that a problem with the first installment by itself would justify a buyer in treating this as a breach of the whole. Comment 5 isn't any great help here, but do note the first sentence: "Subsection (3) is designed to further the continuance of the contract in the absence of an overt cancellation."

If the president of BIM did use the late January delivery (even if it were a very late one) to justify his cancellation as buyer, he runs a high risk that later, if Switcher claims it was ready, willing, and able to deliver properly from February on, his firm *BIM* will be found to have repudiated the agreement. It's all too easy for a court looking at things after the fact to be persuaded that the party to an installment contract which in the heat of the moment declared the other to be in breach of the whole acted rashly and was itself in breach. The president of BIM is going to have to tread carefully here.

1f. After two successive late deliveries BIM has a much stronger case that taken together there has been a breach of the whole. But who's to say? It's not even clear that BIM has grounds for rejecting this February shipment on the 20th. For that we have to go back to subsection (2). If they can't reject the individual installment under that provision, could they ever say that the cumulative effect was enough under (3)? It seems they should be able to, but there's no clear answer in the language of the section. Switcher can point to the fact that to its credit it came closer this time, being only five days late. Maybe it should be given a final chance to get it right in March and thereafter.

If you do conclude that two late shipments are enough for the buyer to invoke §2-612(3), do they have to be sequential? Suppose the shipment is just fine in February, but then there is late delivery again in March. How do you rule?

For one example of a two-strikes-you're-out result, I refer you back to *Graulich* (the case of the microwave sauerbraten). To continue that story: After the first day's delivery (on April 23) was rejected as just not the type of food the buyer could serve, the buyer and seller conferred on how to make corrections.

> [A second delivery on April 24 was] likewise unacceptable. Of the 2520 units delivered, between 500 and 700 were distributed among the employees and patrons of the exhibit for a fast reaction. The complaints in response to the food were many and varied. Defendant, describing the sources of the unfavorable comment, stated that the sauerbraten was dry and the gravy, pasty and unpalatably "gooey," surrounded rather than enveloped the meat. The knockwurst platter suffered similarly, being dry and comparing unfavorably with the standards established by the samples. Generally, defendant complained that the food was simply not "German food" and as such was unacceptable for the Lowenbrau Pavilion.

Following the failure of this second delivery, the pavilion director quickly sprang into action, converting the microwave set-up to a conventional kitchen using pot burners to successfully prepare food for the duration of the Fair. Peace and the reputation of good German cooking were restored. The court found that under the circumstances the buyer had been justified not only in rejecting the second installment as it had the first, but in canceling the contract altogether.

The second unacceptable delivery and the failure of the plaintiff's additional curative efforts left the defendant in a position for one week without food. Time was critical. Plaintiff knew that platters of maximum quality were required on a daily installment basis. Because of defendant's immediate need for quality food and plaintiff's failure to cure, we find that the nonconformity of the second delivery, projected upon the circumstances of this case, "substantially impair[ed] the value of the whole contract [and resulted in] a breach of the whole."

The result in this case seems easy to live with, but it shouldn't be taken that two nonconforming deliveries, even two in a row, necessarily give the buyer the right to call the deal at an end. In other circumstances the courts have called on the buyer to take a lot more grief without rendering the whole relationship asunder. In *Holiday Manufacturing Co. v. B.A.S.F. Systems, Inc.,* 380 F. Supp. 1096, 15 U.C.C. 820 (D. Neb. 1974), the buyer placed a long-term order for plastic cassettes (the type used in making audiocassettes) with the seller. The contract called for six million pieces in all. About one year after deliveries were to have begun—and after a long string of deliveries (some conforming and some not), notifications, reevaluations, redesigns, and corrections—the buyer attempted to cancel. Deliveries had been consistently late. The buyer could and did point to any number of instances of defects in quality. Was the cancellation justified? The court held that it was not. As to the lateness:

> There is no question that Holiday's cassette manufacturing project was behind schedule and that at no point during the existence of the contract was Holiday delivering five hundred thousand cassettes a month [as had been promised]. However, nowhere in either the correspondence between Holiday and B.A.S.F. or the inter-office correspondence of B.A.S.F. introduced at trial is there any indication whatsoever that B.A.S.F. was seriously concerned with Holiday's delivery delays. . . . The Court concludes that B.A.S.F.'s use of the Holiday sonic-welded cassette was a potentially very profitable business venture and that the delays which occurred in development of this relatively new product by a manufacturer unfamiliar with cassette production were liberally tolerated by B.A.S.F. Certainly B.A.S.F. cannot now be allowed to pursue this course of conduct concerning Holiday's failure to perform the contract on time [that is, continually urging them on to produce an acceptable product], and then be permitted to urge this nonperformance as a justification for canceling the contract.

What of the profusion of quality defects that had come up? The court considered each in turn, concluding that "the issue of whether these . . . substantially impaired the value of the cassette contract to B.A.S.F. is a close one." Looking at all of the evidence, however, the court concluded that B.A.S.F. as buyer was not justified in canceling the contract. Important to the court's determination was the facts that whatever defects (some very substantial in themselves) had been discovered were eventually cured by the manufacturer, even if new problems did then crop up. The court also noted that many months into the agreement, and not long before its attempted cancellation, B.A.S.F. had placed orders with Holiday for additional cassettes "virtually *identical*" (emphasis by the court) to those to be produced under the original contract. B.A.S.F. was held responsible for profits lost by Holiday.

You may want to read the *B.A.S.F.* case in its entirety to get the full flavor of what went on. It's a good example of how complicated and messy the situation can get in a long-term installment contract between two major commercial parties. Whether the decision itself is a good example of the application of §2-612(3) is a matter of opinion. Certainly the result can be questioned. Does the case represent an example of how the "substantiality" requirements of §2-612 could end up putting the buyer very much at the mercy of a seller who keeps pushing and trying and is never ready to give up, even if that seller never quite gets it right? Or is the decision defensible as reflecting an appropriate sensitivity on the part of the court to the fact that in a contract of this nature there are always going to be problems and the possibility of friction? In just about any installment sales agreement in a commercial setting the buyer would, if it wished, be able to generate in time for litigation a list of horribles it has had to endure. Were the courts always to give the buyer the benefit of the doubt in such situations, the result might be to turn this species of installment agreement into one which was for all practical purposes at the option of the buyer, who could always drum up sufficient justification for declaring a "breach of the whole."

2. I believe this is an easy case where the buyer should be able to cancel. Note the language in Comment 6 that reflects the (perfectly reasonable) idea that defects *cumulate* over time. Consider, however, the case of *Bodine Sewer, Inc. v. Eastern Illinois Precast, Inc.,* 143 Ill. App. 3d 920, 493 N.E.2d 705, 1 U.C.C.2d 1480 (1986). The buyer was a construction contractor working on a sewer project. The seller made repeated deliveries of concrete pipe to the buyer's job site. There was no dispute that various installments were nonconforming. Nor did the parties dispute that all of these earlier defective deliveries were cured by the seller's later shipping conforming materials. When one more defective delivery arrived on April 24, the buyer attempted to get out of the contract altogether. Did it have the right to do so? The court said no. This nonconformity, like those before it, could be cured. As for the argument under §2-612(3):

> Where, as here, defective deliveries pursuant to an installment contract are consistently corrected, and the purchaser, during the time for the contract's performance, voices no concerns to the seller with respect to delays occasioned by the defective deliveries, the nonconforming deliveries do not substantially impair the value of the entire contract. [Citing *B.A.S.F.*]

Can this blanket statement possibly be true? If so, our button buyer may still have no grounds for cancellation. Should the result hinge on whether Buyer had yelled and complained during these calls? Even if this series of events did not ever once actually cause him a delay, should he have to live with this situation a day longer? Does Buyer have to put Seller on actual notice that if you have ordered one type of button and you are constantly being delivered an entirely different type there is definitely something wrong?

The actual result in *Bodine Sewer* may be right for all we know. The main lesson I take from the case, however, is how futile (and possibly foolish) it is for a court to come up with general pronouncements when matters of materiality or substantiality of breach are involved. Notice, by the way, that the losing buyer in *Bodine Sewer* apparently tried to make an analogy with the shaken faith doctrine that comes up in connection with issues of cure. (See Chapter 19.) The court didn't seem to see the connection. Do you? If there is something to this idea, it may be undercut by language in Comment 6. You should be able to spot what language I am referring to. Is this part of the comment justified by either the wording (such as it is) or the policies (such as you can imagine them to be) underlying §2-612(3)?

3a. You can see we're now going through the same issues, but here with the *buyer* in breach. In theory the analysis remains the same. Breach is breach and "substantiality" is, in practice if not in theory, to some extent in the mind of the beholder. One missing payment on the part of the buyer would presumably allow the seller to withhold future deliveries until things are cleared up. There is language to this effect in Comment 7. At the same time it seems very unlikely that problems with one payment would automatically allow a seller to call in §2-612(3) and declare a breach of the whole.

What if the payment was not entirely missing but only late? For example, suppose Buster's check had arrived on the 22nd. What if it isn't for the full amount? If Buster pays only $3,000 for the 30,000 bricks, that is presumably a substantial impairment of the value of this payment to Sarah, but what if his check is for $29,000? Does she have to continue delivering as if nothing is the matter? If so, what do you say to $28,000? And so on. Does it matter what his excuse is for the short payment? He could be disputing the quantity or quality of bricks delivered to him in May. Or he could be saying something equivalent to, "Don't think I'd ever be caught paying $1 per brick when it comes right down to it." How much should a court's application of §2-612 be affected by what it believes to be the parties' true motives? Or should all of this be left out of §2-612 analysis and instead disposed of under the separate rubric of good faith? Perhaps I should apologize for this long series of unanswered questions, but after all I am a law professor. And under the circumstances, what would you have me say other than that these certainly are interesting and thought-provoking questions?

3b. On one thing §2-612(3) is clear: If a party brings an action with respect only to past installments, the contract is reinstated. As Comment 6 explains, there was some question about this under prior law and the drafters wanted to settle it one way as opposed to the other.

3c. The defects are certainly beginning to cumulate, and you may well conclude Sarah has sufficient grounds to consider the contract breached as to the whole. Of course, if she does declare a breach of the whole she is taking some risk that she has jumped the gun. Would you be happy having to litigate her case if she did cancel when later it turned out that the August check had been in the mail and arrived on the 17th? If Buster has to go out and buy bricks for a lot more, he's going to seem awfully sympathetic after the fact. What could Sarah be counseled to do now to minimize her risk of being second-guessed (by a court!) in the future? On the insecurity mechanism of §2-609, see the prior chapter.

3d. I hope you see how difficult it would be for Sarah to support any action based on a breach of the whole if she hadn't been complaining about the lateness all along the way. A court disposed to find for Buster would have any number of ways to reach a result favorable to him. Perhaps the parties established a course of dealing (§2-208) that allowed for payment later than the 15th of the month. The written agreement may say that informal variation from what is laid out in the agreement is not to be effective, but we have to be aware of how cavalierly some courts are able to deal with what they consider mere boilerplate. Or perhaps there has been a waiver under §2-209. Neither course of performance nor waiver is free from ambiguity, but that is precisely why Sarah has so much to fear from them. If a court were to apply either of these two doctrines it could rightly say of course that Sarah could reestablish the 15th as the absolute date for payment, but that she could only do so *prospectively* with notice to Buster and only with respect to payments not yet due. Any attempt on her part to cancel immediately under the circumstances would therefore have been unjustified.

A court, of course, would not even have to reach out to these other sections and concepts to find for Buster. It could conclude in a straightforward manner that the cumulative effect of the late payments was not such as "substantially impaired" the value of the contract to Sarah. After all, she was getting her money, and she wasn't even complaining. For a court that followed this route, much to the seller's dismay, see *Flood v. M. P. Clark, Inc.*, 319 F. Supp. 1043, 8 U.C.C. 836 (E.D. Pa. 1970).

4. Was Seller right to consider the contract breached as to the whole? I've set up the facts to highlight a bit of language in Comment 6 to which I alluded earlier.

> Whether the non-conformity in any given installment justifies cancellation as to the future depends, not on whether such non-conformity indicates an intent or likelihood that the future deliveries [or payments?] will also be defective, but whether the non-conformity substantially impairs the value of the whole contract. If only the seller's security in regard to future installments is impaired, he has the right to demand adequate assurances of proper future performance but has not an immediate right to cancel the entire contract.

If this is true then Seller here, assuming that she can be adequately assured of future payments, has no right to cancel. Maybe this is right. After all she's in no worse situation than if she had made a delivery under a one-shot contract and had to wait and/or sue for payment. But what if the amount owed on the one missing payment is a significant portion of the entire purchase price? What if the buyer is "asking" her to wait for more than one payment? Should Seller still have to continue delivering to Buyer as if nothing were wrong? If so, isn't the result that an installment buyer can always in essence extend himself credit at the seller's expense by acting as this buyer has? All the buyer would have to do is be sure not to overreach and to beg indulgence of the seller only for amounts small enough that it wouldn't be worth the seller's energy to sue or try some other drastic action. Meanwhile seller would have to keep making deliveries.

In any event, it seems doubtful to me that in reality anyone or any court could keep this prospective/retrospective distinction that clearly in focus. Where issues of materiality of breach are concerned maybe all we can say is that eventually enough is enough, and hope that our view of what is enough does not differ radically from that of the courts in their wisdom.

One further point to be explored is how §§2-612 and 2-609 interact. It should be clear how the latter may be used in service of someone stuck with an ambiguous situation under the former. But recall that the use of the §2-609 mechanism is always *optional* on the part of any party. In *Cherwell-Ralli, Inc. v. Rytman Grain Co.*, 180 Conn. 714, 433 A.2d 984 (1980), the buyer argued that the seller was not justified in terminating the contract in spite of repeated defaults on its part because it, the seller, had never invoked §2-609. There is no requirement, however, that the seller formally notify the buyer that it is insecure when in such a situation. After all the buyer, who in the instant case had stopped payment on a check, should know perfectly well what could be going on in the seller's mind. As Ellen Peters, a former well-respected UCC professor and now a well-respected judge, opined in *Cherwell-Ralli*:

> [I]f the buyer's conduct is sufficiently egregious, such conduct will, in and of itself, constitute substantial impairment of the value of the whole contract and a present breach of the contract as a whole.

For my money the "sufficiently egregious" rule of thumb is about as good as any you're going to get on the workings of §2-612(3) in general—which makes it an appropriate, if not wholly satisfying, place to stop.

23

Sale on Approval, Sale or Return, and Consignments

Introduction

This chapter deals (briefly) with two special situations, each clearly defined in and governed by Article 2: the *sale on approval* and the *sale or return*. We also have to give a nod to a third species of transaction, the *consignment*, which is nowhere near as easy to pin down. The term "consignment," while well-known in the common law, is nowhere defined in the Code, yet it maddeningly floats in and out of various UCC provisions, in Article 2 and elsewhere. No one seems to doubt that the word's traditional meaning, as well as the common law rules governing consignments, survived the adoption of the Code. So it is basically a common law phenomenon. The practice of consignment, however, regularly interacts with concepts and transactions that are at the very heart of the Code, and it's there that our troubles begin.

There are no Examples and Explanations for this chapter. For one thing, the most interesting problems in this area (if you are interested in this sort of thing) come up in situations that are really beyond the bounds of this book. Consignments, sales on approval, and the sale or return all tend to create particularly dicey problems once third parties get involved (the third parties being in particular any creditors of the consignee or the buyer who has contracted for some right of return). But we're simply not that interested in such third parties. Our focus throughout this book has been and will continue to be on the two-party transaction and on the respective rights of those two parties: the seller and the buyer and

384 Part Three. Performance of the Sales Contract

what they have to do for each other. It will turn out there is nothing particularly tricky in all of this just because we are dealing with the special case of the sale on approval or the sale or return. Article 2 lays out some straightforward rules in §2-327, which we can quickly go over. There has been virtually no litigation or controversy over any part of this section.

In the situation of a consignment, it will turn out we aren't even dealing with a sales transaction at all. The two parties aren't the seller and the buyer but the *consignor* and the *consignee*. Fortunately for us there's little difficulty identifying, then setting to one side, the law that governs their two-party relationship.

I wouldn't want to give the impression that either the realm of commercial transactions in general or the Code in its unique majesty is uninterested in the rights of creditors of buyers or consignees, or creditors of anyone else for that matter. Nothing could be further from the truth. It's just that the rights of such creditors are traditionally dealt with not in the law of sales but in another distinct field of commercial transactions— you may have already been counseled to study "secured transactions" before your law school days are over and you are thrown out into the real world.

The Uniform Commercial Code sets out a grand scheme under which the rights of such creditors are to be determined and balanced against the rights of others not in Article 2, but in Article 9 (not coincidentally entitled the "Secured Transactions" article). Perhaps wisely, perhaps not, the drafters did see fit to throw one fragment of this scheme into §2-326. No one seems to find the result entirely satisfactory. Certainly no professor who has to teach this stuff would dare make such a claim.

Section 2-326 and its relationship to Article 9 is a particularly murky bit of Code business. As you will have gathered, I am doing my best in this volume to duck the problem altogether. It is not simply (or at least not exclusively) a matter of cowardice. As indicated on the cover, this book deals with the law of sales and leases. The law of secured transactions is the subject of another course or will be a separate part of your survey course on Commercial Law. When you do get around to this study, there will be plenty of time for the rights of creditors in any and every situation. Then there will be no avoiding the tangled consignment issues. For present purposes I introduce the consignment concept only with the very limited intention of distinguishing this relationship from the sale on approval and sale or return, which *are* in fact sales and therefore are transactions which we have no desire or reason to avoid. If this discussion also whets your appetite for the exciting world of secured transactions, just think of it as a bonus.

Consignment in the Smallest of Nutshells

A *consignment* is an agency relationship between two parties. It may lead to a sale of goods, but the consignment itself is not a sale. The principal, the *consignor,* delivers the goods to his or her agent, the *consignee,* who endeavors to sell them on the principal's behalf. The consignee may be authorized to conclude the sale to the eventual buyer on any terms which he or she, as an authorized agent of their owner, finds appropriate. Or the consignee may only be authorized to solicit offers that are to be relayed back to the consignor, who will then make any decisions. In any event the law governing the relationship between the consignor and the consignee is clear. It is the law of agency, which you presumably have studied or will study some day, but which you aren't going to be graced with here. Going into no detail whatsoever, the law of agency recognizes that the consignee may by his or her actions enter into a contract binding on the consignor to sell the goods to the ultimate buyer. The consignee is charged under the standard rules of agency to follow any instructions from the consignor and must act with the principal's interests in mind. For his or her pains the consignee will typically get some remuneration from the consignor, most often in this situation a fee based in some fashion on the final price for which the goods are sold.

What's important for our purposes is that the consignee never becomes an owner of the goods, nor is the consignee ever committed to the proposition that the goods can or will be sold. At most the consignee may take on a limited obligation to use some measure of effort in *trying* to sell the goods to another, but even then this is not the real spur to his or her action. The consignee will (perfectly reasonably) try to conclude the sale because it is the one way to get the commission. If a sale is ultimately concluded, it is a sale by the consignor directly to the buyer. The consignee has acted as an agent (sometimes referred to as a *factor*) in arranging the sale, but is not a party to it.

Here is a simple example. Carmen owns and runs an automobile distributorship. She sells new and used cars. Sam has a used car he wants to get rid of. He offers to sell it to Carmen, but she is not confident she'd ever be able to herself find a buyer and so rejects Sam's offer. Carmen does agree to keep the car on her lot and to show it to any buyer who may be interested. The two parties reach an understanding she'll sell it if she can and furthermore on what terms she is authorized to conclude a sale on Sam's behalf. If a buyer is found, the title passes directly from Sam to that lucky soul. Carmen is then responsible for directing the money paid for the car back to Sam, after deducting an agreed upon commission. This commission may be computed as a percentage of the purchase price or as a "margin" due the consignee, any amount paid over some specified figure. In any event, Carmen is agreeing to act as Sam's agent in an attempt to make a sale. It is not within the parties' contemplation that she will ever buy the car, nor that she will be in any way answerable if a buyer can't be found. Carmen assumes no risk other than the time and use of space she invests in trying to make a deal on Sam's behalf. If a buyer does not appear, Sam will eventually have to pick the car up and take it back with him.

Just to make things more confusing, the use of arrangements which are portrayed as consignments but which are really quite different in character has become traditional in a number of industries. For example, consider our friend Carmen. Suppose her main business is selling new cars made by the Zephyr Motor Car Company. Zephyr will deliver a large number of new cars to her lot under a contract that styles itself a consignment. If you believe the documents, the idea is that she will attempt to sell these cars on Zephyr's behalf, and each time she does she will send some money back to the manufacturer. Of course she'll also keep some of the purchase price, which is after all how she makes a living. This arrangement seems very much like the one Carmen had with Sam, but it's really not. Carmen would not take these new cars if she thought it was questionable whether they could or would be sold. One way or another ("Have no mercy on me, I'm practically giving it away.") she anticipates she'll move each and every one of them out of her showroom and into some poor buyer's garage. For all practical purposes the arrangement is more like a sale in bulk by the manufacturer to Carmen with a provision that she can pay for the cars later as she concludes individual sales. Zephyr is extending credit to Carmen, one of its authorized dealers. This is not a true consignment at all. Carmen does in fact take on the responsibility of selling the cars and the attendant risk that this won't happen or that she'll have to sell at a loss. In reality, no matter how the papers signed by Carmen and Zephyr might read, this is a present sale by Zephyr coupled with the manufacturer's retention of a security interest in the cars. Zephyr wants to retain this security interest so that it will have the right to take the cars back in the unlikely (but potentially very troubling) event something goes seriously wrong with Carmen's business, say for example, she goes into bankruptcy.*

The drafters of the Code wanted the substance rather than the form of the transaction to control, so they provided that any "consignment intended as security" would be governed by Article 9 just like any and every other security interest in personal property. See §9-102(2).† A consignment which is not intended as a security interest (what is sometimes called a "true consignment") is not subject to the various provisions of Article 9, but there is a section in that article (§9-114) telling us that this is so and explaining how such consignments interact with actual security interests. All this is a bit of a mess. More to the point, it's a mess that is best left alone until you study Article 9 and all its ramifications.

What remains is the simple proposition that a consignment, at least a "true consignment," is not a sale at all nor does it contemplate a sale by the consignor to the consignee. By contrast, we are led to the sale on approval and the sale or return.

---

*Why would the parties characterize this arrangement as a consignment instead of what it "really" is? The principle object is that it theoretically allows Zephyr to control the price at which any individual car is sold. So-called "resale price maintenance" creates a problem under the antitrust laws, and the consignment mechanism is an attempt to work around this nasty little legal technicality. But any antitrust implications are clearly way, way beyond the bounds of what we are doing here.

†You may see an analogy here to the "lease intended as security" as opposed to the "true lease" and how the Code handles such things as is discussed in Chapter 2.

Two Types of Conditional Sales

Most often when the buyer enters into the sales contract, he or she commits to buy the goods. If they are tendered and conform to the contract the buyer is obligated to take and pay for them. That's what any seller would want out of his or her buyer. There are times, however, when the prospective buyer is wary and it makes for a hard sell. The sale on approval and the sale or return are two practices that have evolved through which a seller may be able to overcome a nervous buyer's resistance. They differ from the consignment in that they contemplate an eventual sale from the seller to the buyer. They are sales contracts. They differ from most sales, however, in that the contract provides some possibility of the buyer's returning the goods to the seller and avoiding the sale, *even if the goods tendered conform to the contract in all respects.*

Traditionally under a sale on approval the idea was that the seller would tender the goods but retain title in them for some time. The buyer had a period to decide whether he or she wanted to become the owner by taking up an option to take title and thereafter pay a specified price for the goods. In contrast under a sale or return title would immediately pass to the buyer, just as it would in an ordinary sale, but it was agreed that the goods could be returned to and title revested in the seller at the buyer's discretion. In either case the buyer seeking to avoid the sale by relying on the special provision might be called upon to justify this action by reference to a detailed standard laid out in the contract or might have a fairly free hand to do so (sometimes depending only on whether the buyer is personally "satisfied" with the goods).* In neither case however could the *seller* later decide after entering into the contract not to go through with the deal. This, if nothing else, distinguishes these types of sales from your typical consignment where the consignor as principal in an agency relationship retains not only title to the goods but has in theory kept to itself some degree of flexibility as to whether to sell and to whom. In an agency relationship, the principal is supposed to have control. You should read Comment 1 to §2-326 at this point, which lays out the basic ideas fairly well.

As we saw in Chapter 11, the drafters of Article 2 tried to downplay the significance of title to goods whenever and wherever they could. In §2-326(1) they distinguish the sale on approval and the sale or return with no reference to title but relying directly on an articulation of contract rights. In such a sales contract the delivered goods "may be returned by the

---

*There is a whole issue as to whether the buyer in exercising such a satisfaction clause has to act "reasonably" or only "honestly" and what this difference might mean. I might as well remark that the definitive article on this kind of arrangement is Brook, Conditions of Personal Satisfaction in the Law of Contracts, 27 N.Y. L. Sch. L. Rev. 103 (1981). You can see by the final sentence of Comment 1 to §2-326 that the drafters of Article 2 took no position on the issue. The same cannot be said for the author of the article, who did take a position even if no courts seem to have later followed (much less noted) it.

buyer even though they conform to the contract." The sale on approval is distinguished from the sale or return not on when title supposedly does or does not pass, but on the intended use of the goods. The contract is a sale on approval if the goods "are delivered primarily for use" and a sale or return if they "are delivered primarily for resale." As we will see, the consequences of characterizing the contract as one or the other, at least as between the seller and buyer themselves, can all under §2-327 be varied by the parties' agreement, so they are not unalterably stuck with one result or the other in any event.

Special Rules Governing Special Sales

Because the sale on approval and the sale or return do have this unique return feature, the relationship of seller to buyer has always had to be treated somewhat differently by the law of sales. Keeping with this tradition certain special rules are laid out in Article 2, although you'll find nothing either very surprising or difficult. The drafters' goal was primarily to clear up any potential confusion that attended these unusual creatures. First of all, look at §2-326(4) and Comment 4 to that section. Any buyer who expects to rely upon any "return" feature of a sales contract had better get it in writing. That much is clear, and the reasons for it should be obvious.

The other "special incidents" of such sales are set forth in §2-327. Risk of loss is a concept that we will address in Part IV. For now simply note that when a contract is a sale on approval the usual risk of loss rules do not apply. From the fact that nothing is said in subsection (2) about risk of loss we can conclude that the usual rules *do* apply unless otherwise agreed when the parties have entered into a sale or return. (You may now want to mark in your copy of the Code the language in §2-509(4) which refers you back to §2-327 for the sale on approval, but don't worry beyond that about risk of loss at present.)

The other parts of §2-327 are fairly straightforward. In the sale on approval the buyer gets to use the goods under §2-327(1)(b) without fear that such use in and of itself will later be construed an acceptance as would normally be true under §2-602. With the sale or return under §2-327(2)(a), the buyer does accept in the regular fashion, but retains the right to return "the whole or any commercial unit of the goods while in substantially their original condition." In either type of sale the buyer must act seasonably, for further elaboration of which we can look to §1-204. Of course in many such deals the parties will in the contract itself specify a time limit within which the buyer must make up its mind. Section 2-327 allows, as we have seen, for such other agreement.

Finally, §2-327(1)(c) and §2-327(2)(b) clear up any confusion about who is responsible for the actual physical return of the goods in the absence of contrary agreement. You can read these provisions and apply them on your own.

Creditors Get the Final Word

While we have now laid out the basic rules covering the relationship between the seller and the buyer in these special situations, it's only fair to say a few words about the interest creditors have in this whole affair. We're talking here about the buyer's creditors, though we can even throw in something about creditors of a consignee.

Why care about the creditors? It's not just to be agreeable, although we have to state at the outset that creditors are perfectly wonderful people who no less than anyone else deserve our attention and our sympathies. A buyer or consignee cares about his or her creditors because it is only the willingness of other people to extend credit which makes it possible to run any kind of even minimally sophisticated commercial enterprise. Others become creditors by advancing needed funds with which goods can be bought or in some cases by actually delivering the goods themselves on the understanding that they will be paid for at a later date. Such creditors expect to be paid as the debts become due, and in the vast majority of instances they are. As an added bit of assurance, however, a creditor may decide it cannot afford to extend credit to an individual unless that individual puts up some collateral to secure the loan. In many instances that collateral is personal property, and we are led inexorably into the field of secured transactions involving personalty and Article 9 of the Code.

It is here that we must leave the discussion for another day and another book. Before we bail out, however, let's take a radically simplified look at the situation. First consider the consignment, using as our example Carmen the auto dealer to whom we've already been introduced. If Carmen is going to borrow money in order to run her business (and there's nothing inherently undignified or unseemly about her doing so; it's a perfectly sound business practice), she's going to have to put up some collateral. What's the one really valuable thing she has? It's the stock of cars on her lot and in her showroom. Typically a dealer like Carmen will get a loan from some party that gets in return, in addition to her promise to make payments as due, a security interest in her inventory. If the creditor is to feel comfortable about making this loan and allowing it to remain outstanding it must have some way of assuring itself that the value of the collateral, the inventory, is at the outset substantially greater than the outstanding debt and that it consistently remains so. To protect itself the creditor will initially send someone to Carmen's and thereafter follow up on a regular basis to actually inspect the inventory, that is, to see what's there and appraise its worth.

Think how a possible consignment fits into this. Suppose that Carmen's creditor sends a representative to the lot who there sees the one car which Sam has left on consignment or the large number of cars which are there purportedly on "consignment" from Zephyr Motors. If this representative has no way of knowing that someone other than Carmen claims ownership of these vehicles he or she could easily be lead to overestimate the value of Carmen's inventory. (Of course Carmen *should* tell the creditor and its people the true facts of the situation, and she may even be bound to do so by language in the loan documents she's signed. But people have been known to put their signature to agreements which they later don't keep. The whole point of the creditor's *independent* verification is to protect itself against the consequences should Carmen turn out to be less than totally up-front in her dealings.) Suppose Carmen gets into financial trouble and is not repaying her debts. She might even go into bankruptcy. The creditor would expect to foreclose and take possession of the inventory. Sam and Zephyr Motors would want simply to come over to Carmen's and drive what they see as their cars away. So the creditor and the consignees are at odds. (It does no good to look to Carmen to straighten it out. She's broke, remember.)

Who wins in such a situation? Well, it's that sort of question which explains why you'll someday have to study Article 9. In brief we can say that in the case of a consignment that is not a "true consignment" but is rather a "consignment intended as a security" (such as Zephyr's), Article 9 governs and the creditor will prevail unless the "consignor" made the kind of filing of its interest provided for under Article 9. In the case of the "true consignment" (such as Sam's), we look to §2-326(3). Not every true consignment is covered, but only those where the consignor delivers goods "to a person for sale and such a person maintains a place of business at which he deals in goods of the kind involved, under the name of a person other than the person making the delivery." An awkward sentence, but you can see it does apply to Sam's situation.* This being so under §2-326(3) the goods are "deemed to be on sale or return." What does this mean? It seems to mean that we then look to subsection (2) of §2-326 to discover that the car is subject to claims of Carmen's creditors as long as the car is in Carmen's possession. We then return to the conclusion of subsection (3) which tells us that Sam could avoid this result, could keep his right to reclaim the car from Carmen's lot not subject to any claim by her creditors, if one of three things is true. As a practical matter very few states have sign laws of the type that are referred to in (a). And how comfortable should any consignor be that he or she would later be able to prove what's called for in (b)? If Sam really wants to be protected against any claims by Carmen's creditors, and if he has been reading up on his UCC, he will know that the wise path is to follow (c) and make a filing of the type provided for under Article 9. This is not required of Sam under Article 9, as it would be for Zephyr which holds

---

*It would not apply to him if he had delivered his car, for example, to a neighbor who was not a car merchant but just an ordinary Joe or Jane who was going to try to sell it for him. But then such a neighbor will not be tempted much less able to use the car as collateral for a personal loan, even if it is sitting right there in his or her garage, since he or she will have no suitable proof of ownership to show to a potential lender.

a true security interest, but it is allowed, and it is Sam's only practical way of feeling secure in his position.*

We return finally to the true sale on approval or sale and return. We know they are different than the consignment for a variety of reasons. They are similar, however, where Carmen's creditors are concerned. Say Carmen purchases some goods in this fashion. Perhaps she buys a duplicating machine for her office under a sale on approval (that is, primarily for use). She also buys a large number of automobiles from a manufacturer on sale or return (for resale). Under either type of contract there will be merchandise at Carmen's place of business which does appear to be her property but which might not (the next time the creditor shows up to see that all the collateral is in apple pie order) be Carmen's at all, its having been returned to its rightful owner. How can the creditor make a loan based on the value of Carmen's property when such a possibility exists? You can see how the Code deals with this problem in §2-326(2).

> Except as provided in subsection (3), goods held on approval are not subject to the claims of the buyer's creditors until acceptance; goods held on sale or return are subject to such claims while in the buyer's possession.

At least the rules are clear. So a creditor who takes a security interest in the autos, or what we would colloquially refer to as an *inventory financer* under Article 9, will be protected as long as those cars remain in Carmen's possession. This last requirement is not trivial, of course, but as you will see when you study secured transactions it's a problem that the inventory financer always has to worry about. Institutions that engage in inventory financing—this is no game for the dilettante—have developed strategies to protect their interests. If on the other hand a creditor loans money and allows Carmen to put up her office equipment as collateral, that creditor can have no interest in the copying machine unless and until she accepts it and the return possibility under the sale on approval has evaporated. Anyone who loans on this type of collateral, the *equipment financer,* should have ways to protect against being left holding nothing but air. The possibility that some of Carmen's equipment has been obtained through a sale on approval does not add appreciably to this creditor's problems. He or she has enough to contend with from the outset. Again, and for the last time, wait for your study of Article 9 and all will become clear.

---

*I would not be surprised, and I don't think you should be terribly upset, if I've lost you by this point. If you have not yet studied security interests under Article 9, this is an awful lot to take in all at once. If you *have* completed a course on Secured Transactions, you should be able to follow, but even then give yourself a bit of a break. It takes a bit of effort to make it all fit into place.

24

Excuse of Performance

Introduction to Excuse Under Article 2

As I noted at the very outset of this part of the book, when you get down to it *performance* of the contract of sale is what the law of sales is all about. Abstract theories and legal constructs are all well and good, but what motivates the parties—the reason they have expended their considerable energies getting to that most blessed of legal states, that which we call contract—is that by entering into such an arrangement each has managed to extract from the other a binding legal commitment. The seller is legally bound to hand over the goods and to stand behind whatever he or she has sold. The buyer is required to take the goods and to pay for them. Should either fail to do what must be done, the other will have the support of the courts in extracting a remedy.

This focus on performance should not strike you as strange. As you saw in your study of the common law of contract, the duty to perform as promised is the very heart of contract law. All else is commentary. If contract is to have meaning there can be no question that you are legally bound to do what you have contracted to do. But then as you also saw in your Contracts course, when push comes to shove (or rather, in light of an "unforeseeable change in circumstances") you can sometimes find authority in the common law under which a contracting party will be let off the hook. The instances will have to be rare of course, but when performance is truly impossible (or at least can be said to be "impossible" as the contract lawyers will use that word) perhaps the law can cut the contractual obligator a little slack.

I am assuming that in your studies you had a chance to become acquainted with the doctrine of Impossibility of Performance, along with its near relatives Impracticability, Frustration of Purpose, and (the ever delightful) Failure of a Mutually Presupposed Condition. I will also assume that when you think back to this material it is not without some discomfort. The instances in which the common law allows excuse of a party from his or her contractual obligation and the theory or theories on which these results are based, other than just doing it when it feels right, are impossible to pin down. No right-thinking person would characterize this as a question to which the common law of contract gives anything like an unambiguous answer. What answers there are purport to hinge on the determination of what is or is not "foreseeable," what the "essence of the contract" is as opposed to its mere "incidents," and so on. Modern theorists throw the discussion over into analysis of "risk allocation" and "minimization of transaction costs," but don't get much farther along. You yourself could be excused for concluding, as any number of learned and level-headed commentators have concluded before you, that the common law of excuse from contract obligation in the event of unforeseen circumstances is about as big a muddle as one could hope to find in a whole lifetime of trying. You may even have seen the case in which, at the end of an opinion that is rightly considered one of the *better* attempts at applying the law of excuse to a contemporary contracts situation, Judge Mulligan of the Second Circuit Court of Appeal concluded as follows:

> Matters involving impossibility or impracticability of performance of contract are concededly vexing and difficult. One is even urged on the allocation of such risks to pray for the "wisdom of Solomon." [Citing Corbin on Contracts]. On the basis of all of the facts, the pertinent authority and further belief in the efficacy of prayer, we affirm.

American Trading and Production Corp. v. Shell International Marine Ltd., 453 F.2d 939 (2d Cir. 1972).

In the course of his opinion in the *American Trading* case, Judge Mulligan noted that the parties had cited the court to §2-615, but he declined to look into that section, reasoning rightly enough that the contract in question was not governed by the Code and that he had enough to deal with in applying the common law. Had he been tempted to follow this lead into the Code, it's doubtful the judge would have found there the answer to his prayers. Article 2 in §§2-613 to 2-615 (and Article 2A for that matter in §§2A-221, 2A-404 to 2A-406) addresses the problem and allows for either a total excuse or a modification of obligation in appropriate circumstances. What circumstances are these? Well, §§2-613 and 2-614 deal with some relatively concrete situations that may not be all that hard to figure out. Section 2-615 is more general and arguably awe-inspiring. Certainly it can be the cause of a good deal more headscratching. The drafters have abandoned reference to "impossibility" and to anything as amorphous as the "essence" of the agreement. Their provision asks us to consider instead the measure of "impracticability" and ponder the "occurrence of a contingency the non-occurrence of which was a basic assumption on which the contract was made." Could this be answer to anyone's prayers?

The purpose of this chapter is not to rehearse all of the arguments you encountered, and the uneasiness you felt, in your study of the various doctrines of excuse under the common law. Our program is much less ambitious. It will be enough for us to see how these ideas work their way through the provisions of Article 2. You should now look over §§2-613 to 2-616. What is the relevance of these provisions to the questions below?

EXAMPLES

1.   Arnold Moneybucks goes into Stella's art gallery where he spots one small painting ("Black on Black") by a contemporary artist which he decides to buy. He enters into a purchase and sale agreement with Stella. The agreement provides that Stella will deliver the art work to Arnold in a few weeks when the gallery's showing is over. The very next day a fire (for which she is totally blameless) sweeps through Stella's gallery that totally destroys this painting along with many others by the artist. Needless to say, Stella does not deliver the painting to Arnold. Can he bring an action against Stella for her failure to perform?

2.   On the same day on which he makes his contract with Stella, Arnold also visits Sheila's gallery in the same building which is showing works by another artist. He sees a lithograph on the wall ("Author at the Keyboard") which he wants for his collection. Sheila tells him that the recently deceased artist had prepared a limited edition of 100 copies of this lithograph, each of which she has in her possession and each of which she hopes to sell. Arnold contracts to buy one, which Sheila agrees to deliver to him within a few days. Before she can do so, the fire (which isn't Sheila's fault either) also damages her gallery. Ninety of the 100 lithographs are destroyed.

   a. Sheila reasons that each of the ten remaining ones will be worth quite a bit more than the original price she had placed on them and the price Arnold had agreed to pay. Is Sheila excused from delivering one of the ten surviving lithographs to Arnold for the original contract price?

   b. Would your answer to the previous question be any different if Sheila could show that prior to the fire she had set aside one of the lithographs, marked it "Sold to Moneybucks," and prepared it for delivery to Arnold—and that this particular piece was one of the 90 destroyed in the fire?

   c. If your answer to either of the two previous questions is that Sheila is still legally bound to perform by delivering one copy of the lithograph to Arnold, how would you deal with the additional fact that prior to the fire Sheila had entered into similar contracts on the same terms to sell one copy of "Author at the Keyboard" to each of 14 other individuals?

3.   Farmer Jones has a crop of tomatoes growing on her land. In April 1992, a representative of Agribusiness, Inc. visits the land and inspects the tender young plants. Together with the farmer, this representative

concludes that the crop should come in at approximately 100,000 pounds of tomatoes. Jones contracts to sell Agribusiness "the crop of California #5 Grade A Tomatoes now growing on her land, anticipated to be approximately 50 tons" at $.55 per pound. In May an unexpected attack of tomato blight hits the area. Jones's farm is particularly hard hit and she is forced to plow under all of her crop. The market price of California #5 Grade A tomatoes soars to over one dollar a pound. Can Agribusiness sue Jones for its damages resulting from her failure to deliver tomatoes?

4.   Suppose that Farmer Green, whose farm Greenacres is next to Jones's, contracted to sell all of his crop to Agribusiness, but in fact did so before he had even planted a crop. The contract signed in February by Green referred to "approximately 50 tons of California #5 Grade A tomatoes which Green intends to plant, grow and harvest upon his property Greenacres during the 1992 growing season." Green's crop is also totally destroyed by the blight. Does Agribusiness have any case against Green for nondelivery?

5.   It turns out that Agribusiness contracted with various growers to buy a total of 50,000 tons of tomatoes when the 1992 tomato crop came in. On the basis of these contracts it entered into a contract to supply Peter's Pizza Corporation with 1,000 tons of tomato paste, with delivery to be spread out over the first six months of 1993. In November 1992, Agribusiness contacts Peter and tells him that it will have to "sharply curtail" its tomato paste deliveries to him "due to the severe shortfall in the California tomato crop occurring in this past growing year." Peter discovers that if he is forced to buy tomato paste elsewhere the cost will be far higher than what he had agreed to with Agribusiness. If Peter does have to pay more for his paste and sues Agribusiness for the difference, does that firm have any defense based on the tomato blight? What other facts would you want to know before attempting an answer to this question?

6.   Buster is building a home. He contracts to buy a large quantity of finished floor tile from Underfoot's Tile Company. The tile Buster selects is made from Pandonian Red marble, a rare material that is found (where else?) in the country of Pandonia. When Underfoot goes to purchase the marble she will need to fill Buster's order, she discovers that a recent outbreak of civil unrest in Pandonia has greatly reduced the amount of marble coming out of the quarries in that troubled country. Pandonian Red marble is still available on the worldwide market, but at a much higher price. If Underfoot is forced to buy the marble to make Buster's tile at the current price, she can expect to make no profit and in fact to lose money on her contract with Buster. Is Underfoot excused from the contract under these circumstances?

7.   In preparation for building his house, Buster also goes to Sarah's Building Supplies where he looks over a large selection of sample doorknobs on display. He picks out one doorknob in a style he likes and contracts to buy a large number from Sarah. This particular knob is manufactured by Hardware Inc., a firm from which Sarah has regularly

obtained supplies in the past. When she tries to contact Hardware to get the doorknobs to fill Buster's order, Sarah is stunned to discover that Hardware's main manufacturing plant has been severely damaged in a recent hurricane. There is no chance they will be able to produce any doorknobs in the foreseeable future, and all of their stock was destroyed. Sarah contacts other doorknob manufacturers, but none has a product at all like the one which Buster has selected. One firm does offer to make up some in the particular pattern, but says that because this would be a special order it would have to charge four to five times what Hardware had charged per doorknob.

    a. Sarah contacts Buster and tells him this story. Is she excused from her contract of sale given what has happened? Would your answer be any different if the reason Hardware would not supply her with the knobs was not that a hurricane had ravaged its plant, but that it had just decided to discontinue that particular style of product since it had not been a big seller?

    b. Suppose Buster makes the contact to buy, and Sarah is able to and does get the knobs from Hardware. However, just as Buster's house is nearing completion a hurricane comes and blows everything that has been built so far down to the ground. The place is rubble. Buster, who had not purchased insurance, finds his plans in ruins. Sarah is ready, willing, and able to deliver the doorknobs. Is Buster obligated to take them and pay the price agreed?

8. Bozzo, who runs a construction business, enters into a contract to buy a large quantity of steel mesh needed for a specific building project from Spang Industries, delivery to be made as called for during the years 1990 through 1992. Spang has no problem delivering what is called for during the first two years. When Bozzo calls for delivery in 1992, however, he is told that this will be impossible as the firm that makes the particular kind of mesh went out of business in late 1991. Bozzo discovers that this manufacturer had been threatening to shut down its operations as early as 1990 and that Spang had been aware of these threats. Bozzo is forced to complete the project with an alternate building technique which avoids the use of the mesh but which costs him more to accomplish. Bozzo sues Spang for his damages. Can the supply firm defend on the basis of §2-615?

9. Seller in Chicago contracts to manufacture and sell a quantity of widgets to Buyer, who is located in Smallville, Indiana. The contract calls for delivery to be made by rail. When manufacture is complete Seller contacts the railroad to arrange for shipment. It discovers that the railroad no longer runs trains to Smallville. Meanwhile Seller has discovered another buyer who is willing to pay much more for these widgets and who is willing to pick them up from Seller's Chicago plant. Can Seller simply ignore its original contract with Buyer? Suppose instead that Seller is more than willing to get the widgets off its hands and arranges for a trucking service to take them to Buyer in Smallville. Can Buyer refuse to take the goods because they did not come by rail?

EXPLANATIONS

1. No. Stella is excused from performing under this contract by §2-613(a). The key is that this contract involved a distinct, already-existing object, that is, delivery was required of "goods identified when the contract [was] made." Had there been no fire and Stella tried to deliver anything other than *this particular painting*, even another one with the same name ("Black on Black #2) to Arnold, he could have rightfully considered this a nonconforming tender. On identification of goods generally, see Chapter 17, which not coincidentally utilizes this same fact set.

So in this situation Stella suffers the loss of the value of the painting itself as a piece of property. This is referred to as the "risk of loss" of the goods and is the subject of the next part of this book. Arnold, of course, would be complaining about the loss of the benefit of his bargain and the loss of a valuable contract interest. If many paintings by this artist have been suddenly destroyed, any one might now be much more valuable than it would have been just days before. But under §2-613, and given the important fact that Stella is in no way responsible for the fire, the contract is avoided, and Arnold will have to bear this loss himself. He cannot successfully sue Stella for nondelivery.

Notice how §2-613(b) would deal with the situation if the painting had not been totally destroyed in the fire but merely scorched. Arnold would then have had the right to inspect the painting and at his option avoid the contract or go through with it at a price reflecting a "due allowance" for the damage. How would this figure be arrived at? Presumably a disinterested appraiser could help out here.

2a. Sheila would not be excused under §2-613 from delivering a copy of this lithograph. Here the contract does not call for goods "identified when the contract is made." Identification was to be by the seller and at some time *after* the contract was entered into. If Sheila is going to have any excuse, it will have to be under §2-615, and her argument there is nowhere near as straightforward. Look at Comment 4 to that section. Sheila could justifiably claim that delivery to Arnold will involve "increased cost" and that the economics of the situation have drastically changed, but has the fire "altered the essential nature" of what she has to do? I doubt she'd be relieved from her obligation in this situation, but like all impossibility (or as Article 2 would say, "impracticability") cases the answer is up for grabs.

2b. If Sheila can't make out an argument under §2-615 for "failure of a presupposed condition," then she's still out of luck. The answer under §2-613 remains the same. No avoidance of the contract. True, in this case Sheila has identified the goods prior to their destruction, but the relevant criterion of this section is not whether the goods were identified at the time of casualty. What is important is whether the nature of the contract required goods which had to be identified at the time of the contract. That was not true in this particular contract, and that has not changed. Sheila should just identify another unsullied copy of the lithograph to her contract with Arnold and deliver that one under the terms of the original agreement.

2c. Now it seems as if Sheila should get some relief, but it's not clear what. Her argument of excuse, if any, would have to come under §2-615. Subpart (b) supports the idea that while she would have to carry through as many contracts as possible, selling all of the ten remaining copies at the original price, she could be excused from her failure to perform on the five other contracts.

What would a "fair and reasonable allocation" look like in this instance? In the typical case where allocation of a lesser amount is called for, the seller is to deliver some quantity of a fungible good and the buyer under any one contract can be allocated some percentage of what he or she had originally contracted to get. But I doubt anyone would want some chopped up portion of a lithograph. Sheila will have to decide on some way of determining who gets the remaining copies. Perhaps she should look at the order in which the contracts were entered into, or the order in which delivery was called for. Perhaps she should hold a lottery and pull names out of a hat.

If she does hold a lottery, would it be permissible for her to include in the drawing not only those 15 people who had like Arnold signed a contract for the lithograph before the fire struck but also the name of her most steady and loyal customer who had bought many works from her before and for whom she had been planning to hold back at least one copy of this lithograph? Look at the language of §2-615(b) and Comment 11. You can see that this language, as well as the procedural language in §2-615(c) and §2-616, is written more with the case of proportional allocation of fungible goods in mind. As a matter of fact, I know of no actual case where the court or a seller for that matter has had to come up with anything like allocation by lottery or on a first-come-first-served basis. Still, that would fit in with the general principle of §2-615(b), and it sure beats the Solomon-like judgment of cutting the lithograph into pieces.

It should be clear that the one thing Sheila *cannot* do is decide which buyers are to get the remaining copies by auctioning them off to the highest bidders. The fire should not be an excuse for a *greater* profit on any item than she had the right to under her contracts.

3. Farmer Jones should be excused from her failure to deliver. Since the crop was identified at the time of the contract and her obligation was to deliver this particular crop §2-613 would seem to be all she needs.

4. Farmer Green should also have a defense to any suit brought by Agribusiness for nondelivery. His excuse will have to be based on §2-615. Looking at this section, there are three principal factors he'll have to establish. First, he will argue that delivery of the tomatoes has become "impracticable" due to the blight. Article 2 uses this term instead of "impossible," which was favored by the common law but which really never meant "impossible" in any event, just "way, way more expensive." See Comment 3.

Green would then have to insist that the tomato blight was "a contingency the nonoccurrence of which was a basic assumption on which the contract was made." Here, the parties (if they had the stomach for it) could argue about how "foreseeable" such an occurrence was—the type of discussion you presumably saw in your earlier studies. No one knows exactly what this condition in §2-615 means, but it seems clear that the drafters at least thought a "local crop failure" caused by something like a disease or drought was enough to trigger the workings of the section. See Comment 4.

Green would also have to show that under the contract he did not "assume a greater obligation." It's possible to argue that Green *did* assume this obligation here. After all, he promised to deliver a crop of tomatoes and when it came time he didn't do it. Courts have generally read this language more narrowly, looking for an express assumption by the contracting party of a *greater* obligation than is typical in the type of contract involved. Green shouldn't have trouble with this criterion unless there's something in the contract like, "Seller agrees to be responsible for delivery in event of tomato blight or other cause of crop failure."

Of course, as in any case, whether any or every one of these three criteria have been met is a question of fact based on the particulars of the situation. As you discovered for the common law doctrine of impossibility, even if you review dozens of cases it's hard to come away with any generalities other than that sometimes the defense works and sometimes it doesn't. Actually, the possibility of excusing the seller of farm products because of crop failure is, at least under the Code, one of the few exceptions where more can be said with some measure of confidence. Look at the first paragraph to Comment 9. Where the seller is a farmer "who has contracted to sell crops to be grown on designated land," he or she may be excused under this section. Of course this comment is just the drafters' opinion, but the courts seem to follow this line with little or no exception. Unless there is some unusual factor here that we're not aware of, for example, if Green was somehow at fault for not protecting his crop from the dreaded tomato blight, he should be excused from performance under this contract.

Imagine instead that the contract Green signs refers only to his obligation to sell "50 tons of California #5 Grade A tomatoes" at a set price and delivery date but makes no mention of his specific land. Green signs this contract assuming he'll grow this much of this type of tomatoes on Greenacres. He plants them, but his crop is wiped out by the blight. What result? Comment 9, by its reference to "designated land," suggests (although it doesn't actually say) that the result would now be different. The courts usually make this distinction and will not allow excuse simply because the seller was a farmer contracting to sell farm products which he or she contemplated growing him or herself. See, for example, *Wickliffe Farms, Inc. v. Owensboro Grain Co.*, 684 S.W.2d 17, 39 U.C.C. 195 (Ky. Ct. App. 1984). The sellers had contracted to sell 35,000 bushels of corn to the buyer. The contract of sale made no reference to the sellers' land. The buyer immediately turned around and resold this corn (which was to come) to a grain exporter at a price that would give it some profit. The sellers' planted corn on their land but a severe drought greatly depleted their harvest. They were able to deliver only 18,718 bushels. The buyer was forced to purchase corn to cover the shortfall at a much higher price and sued the sellers for the difference. The sellers' argument of excuse under §2-615 did not find favor with the court:

> The undisputed admissible material facts before the trial court prove the ordinary "futures contract" of an agreement to buy and sell a quantity of grain at a given price per bushel, to be delivered at a future date. . . . The sellers in such a transaction gamble the market price will not be greater at the time of delivery and the buyers gamble that it will not be lower. All [the buyer] was interested in was buying 35,000 bushels of No. 2 white corn from [the sellers] at $3.70 per bushel and nothing more. Its business was not to speculate either in the weather, crop yield or fluctuation of market price. It guaranteed its profit by selling immediately. [Seller's] only interest was to sell it. It chose to contract to deliver corn at a given price at a future date and it failed to do so.

5. It is unclear whether Agribusiness has any possible defense here under §2-615. I think you have to start with the assumption that any argument for excuse isn't going to work, and that Agribusiness is going to have to answer in a suit for damages. Sellers make money by selling things others want and they take risks as part of their business. Paraphrasing the court in *Wickliffe Farms*, noted above, the buyer's only interest was in buying. Should Peter have to worry about drought or pestilence in other parts of the country?

Agribusiness, on the other hand, based its business decisions on its own dealings in the Sunshine State. It chose to contract to deliver tomato paste at a future date and it failed to do so. Why shouldn't that be the end of the story? An operation like Agribusiness should know enough about the possibility of crop failures occurring at some kind of predictable rate, even if individual instances seem to strike at random, and should be able to do something to guard against being caught off guard with too few tomatoes. For one thing, perhaps it should have avoided contracting with suppliers all in one part of the country or in one growing area. But then again, there must be some situations, some crop failures which are so unexpected and so far-reaching that the entire market is thrown for a loop. Which is it here, and in any event, should that make any difference?

While we professors make a big deal of it in your study of contracts, you should be aware that in general the courts have been unwilling to consider excuse under the doctrine of impossibility or its near relatives, and this reluctance appears to have continued under §2-615. There are a few cases, however, that give Agribusiness some cause for hope in this particular situation. *Cliffstar Corp. v. Riverbend Products, Inc.*, 750 F. Supp. 81, 13 U.C.C.2d 392 (W.D.N.Y. 1990), is the case which inspired this hypothetical. Cliffstar ordered 3.2 million pounds of tomato paste (think of it) from Riverbend. All in all, Riverbend projected that it would produce something like 53 million pounds of paste during the season. Its field department contracted with growers in Arizona and California for 170,000 tons of raw tomatoes. By combining these firm contracts with plans to purchase additional tomatoes on the "spot" market, Riverbend planned to acquire sufficient tomatoes to meet its projections. Weather conditions in Arizona and California resulted in a crop shortage; the combined Arizona and California tomato harvest was about 8.45% less than early season estimates. However, the growers with whom Riverbend had contracted delivered only 95,000-100,000 tons of the 170,000 promised, or about 56-58%. Riverbend chose to allocate the paste it could produce among its customers. Cliffstar was told that it would be allocated only one million pounds of the stuff. Cliffstar demanded its full contract amount and when that wasn't forthcoming brought suit. Riverbend defended its actions and its failure to deliver the full 3.2 million pounds on the basis of §2-615. Cliffstar moved for a summary judgment claiming that there was no genuine issue as to material fact and that it was entitled to a judgment as a matter of law. The court refused to grant summary judgment, holding that there were genuine issues of material fact as to whether the crop shortage and the seller's response to it constituted grounds for excuse under the criteria applicable to a §2-615 argument.

So Agribusiness may be able to get to a jury to argue that the situation in which it found itself was "unforeseeable" and furthermore that this predicament could be said to have rendered its obligation to deliver the full 1,000 tons to Peter "impracticable," whatever that means. How will or should a jury respond? That's anyone's guess, but Agribusiness can also find some encouragement in the result of *Alimenta (U.S.A.), Inc. v. Gibbs Nathaniel (Canada) Ltd.*, 802 F.2d 1362, 2 U.C.C.2d 490 (11th Cir. 1986), in which the Eleventh Circuit affirmed a jury that found grounds for excuse in a similar situation involving devastation of the annual peanut crop through drought. But then of course each case will be judged on its own facts.

It's important to note here that even if Agribusiness can establish a good case of commercial impracticability this does not relieve it from delivering any tomato paste whatsoever to Peter. Under §2-615(b), Agribusiness must "allocate production and deliveries among its customers." The seller is given some latitude in that it may at its option include in the allocation "regular customers not then under contract as well as his own requirements for future manufacture." Any allocation must, however, be "fair and reasonable." In *Cliffstar*, the tomato paste case, the plaintiff also challenged the allocation made to it by Riverbend. Cliffstar argued that any allocation had to treat it "equally," by which it presumably meant on a strictly pro rata basis. Apparently in making its allocation decisions Riverbend had considered such factors as "customer loyalty, past performance, needs, the relationship between Riverbend and the customer, and Riverbend's projections of potential future sales to the customer." The federal district court concluded that, like everything else, the question of whether the seller had acted on a "fair and reasonable basis" was one to be decided on the facts by the jury. Implicit in its decision, however, was the conclusion that a strictly pro rata allocation is not required as a matter of law under §2-615. See also Comment 11.

Finally note the provisions in §2-615(c) and all of §2-616 which set up a procedure for the allocation process. For a case in which the adequacy of notice under §2-615 came into question, see *Red River Commodities, Inc. v. Eidsness*, 459 N.W.2d 805, 13 U.C.C.2d 1076 (N.D. 1990).

6. Civil strife in Pandonia is presumably an unforeseeable occurrence, at least as far as §2-615 is concerned. It's unlikely, however, that Underfoot will have an excuse here. The marble is still available, albeit at a higher price. Note the beginning of Comment 4.

> Increased cost alone does not excuse performance unless the rise in cost is due to some unforeseen contingency which alters the essential nature of the performance. Neither is a rise or collapse in a market in itself a justification, for that is exactly the type of business risk which business contracts made at fixed prices are intended to cover.

This seems pretty unforgiving. Has the "essential nature" of Underfoot's obligation been altered? You are as much of an expert on essentialness of nature as I or anyone else is, but I tend to doubt §2-615 would provide relief here. In point of fact the courts have been very reluctant to give any credence to the impossibility defense under §2-615 where the fundamental problem is just that a seller's own costs have gone up or because completion of the contract could only be done at a loss to the seller.

7a. If §2-615 does offer any hope for a seller based solely on a change in cost, Sarah's case may be the one. Comment 4, which we began to quote in the analysis of the last question, concludes,

> [A] severe shortage of raw materials or of supplies due to a contingency such as war, embargo, local crop failure, unforeseen shutdown of major sources of supply or the like, which either causes a marked increase in cost or altogether prevents the seller from securing supplies necessary to his performance, is within the contemplation of this section.

Sarah's situation does seem to be "severe" and to involve not just an increase in costs but a "marked increase." I would even go so far as to say that it alters the "essential nature" of this agreement. Sarah contracted with the expectation she could directly obtain and then resell standard manufactured goods. If she were now held to perform she'd be in the business of supplying specially manufactured doorknobs, which strikes me as of a different nature altogether. In some cases where the excuse was granted, the costs to seller do not simply rise to where a loss can be foreseen but to some multiple of (4 or 5 times) what was originally contemplated.

I think that if excuse is available to Sarah in this instance, it would be the same whatever reason the manufacturing plant could or would no longer sell her the product (as long as it was not her fault). The unforeseen circumstance here is not the hurricane, it is the total evaporation of the unique source of supply which we have to assume comes as a total surprise to Sarah. See Comment 5.

7b. Can Buster, a buyer, argue excuse based on the failure of a presupposed condition under §2-615? Look again at that section. It speaks only of a possible excuse for the seller. Doesn't this leave Buster out in the cold? Note, however, that Comment 9 to this section anticipates the possibility of excuse of buyer's performance. All the commentators and courts seem to assume that a buyer under the Code might have an argument based on what the common law referred to as frustration of purpose in the appropriate case. If nothing else Buster can cite the court to that old standby §1-103, which allows for supplementation by principles of law and equity not explicitly or implicitly displaced by the provisions of Article 2. While the doctrines of impossibility or frustration aren't specifically mentioned in that section, we are told the listing there is illustrative only, not exhaustive (Comment 3 to §1-103).

8.   I included this question for two reasons. First of all, while the word "fault" nowhere appears in §2-615, it should be evident that for a seller to take advantage of this provision he or she should be able to show that not only was the occurrence unforeseeable but that it could not have been averted through the reasonable care of the seller. Here, once it became aware of the problem, Sprang should have stocked up on the mesh or made some other arrangements to avoid this problem. Bozzo should win. Second, I wanted you to be aware that all the oddball names you run across (even where the seller is an "S" and the buyer a "B") are not solely the product of a fevered imagination. See *Frank B. Bozzo, Inc. v. Electric Weld Division of Fort Pitt Bridge Division of Spang Industries, Inc.*, 28 Pa. Super. 35, 423 A.2d 702, 29 U.C.C. 100 (1980) (in which Bozzo did in fact collect from Spang Industries).

9.   This question focuses us on the special provisions in §2-614 relating to the substitution of another *means* of performance. It should be clear that when delivery by rail becomes commercially impracticable, seller is still obligated to tender via a "commercially reasonable substitute" and buyer is obligated to accept the widgets tendered in this manner. Without knowing more, it is impossible to say for certain whether delivery by truck meets this standard in this instance, but it seems fair to assume that it does unless and until one or the other party explains why this isn't so.

PART FOUR

Risk of Loss

What's true for people is also true for goods. The world is fraught with peril. Thieves will do what they are wont to do—make off with the goods. Clumsy handling can leave them seriously damaged or destroyed altogether. Fires, floods, hurricanes, and the like all take their toll. Sometimes goods simply disappear, leaving forever in doubt what exactly *did* happen to them.

When tragedies such as these occur, it is unfortunate but true that somebody, some legally recognized entity capable of owning property but therefore necessarily also capable of losing it, must suffer the loss. The goods are left worthless or worth less, and someone has either to suffer the loss personally or find another who is obligated to make good for the loss and then go against that person. The person who initially suffers the loss in value of the property is said to bear the *risk of loss* of the goods.

It is important to recognize from the outset that the party bearing the risk of any particular loss need not necessarily end up personally shouldering all of the dire financial consequences. He or she may be able to pass the loss onto another party. If the thief can be caught, the thief should pay. If someone like a carrier or a warehouse owner is legally responsible for the loss or damage, whether because of willful or negligent conduct, then the initial risk bearer will be able to go against that other party. Perhaps most important in many circumstances, the risk bearer may have insurance that covers the loss. That's what insurance is all about. The question of risk of loss, then, is who has to take the time and effort to pursue these other avenues—and who ultimately will be left holding the bag if, when all is said and done, the loss cannot be passed along.

In most situations, of course, the question of who bears the risk of loss of goods is easy to answer: The "owner" of the goods does, and in the vast majority of situations it's not really open to dispute just who that owner is. When the goods are the subject of a contract of sale, however, and are then damaged somewhere along the route of delivery, both Seller and Buyer may find support in the facts for an argument that the risk of loss was on the other at the time of the catastrophic event. Part IV concerns itself with the problems of risk of loss as between Seller and Buyer when the goods were the subject of a contract for sale at the time of the loss.*

The significance of who, between Seller and Buyer, bears the risk is made abundantly clear by Article 2. Subsection 2-709(1) provides in part that Seller can recover from Buyer the price of any goods accepted but also "of any conforming goods lost or damaged within a commercially reasonable time after risk of their loss has passed to the buyer." Once the risk of loss has shifted to Buyer, Seller is entitled to payment of the price.

---

*We do not deal distinctly with risk of loss in the lease of goods. The sections in Article 2A which run roughly parallel to what we'll see in Article 2 are §§2A-219 and 2-220. The rules have been modified by the drafters of 2A to reflect "current practice in lease transactions." See Comment to §2A-219.

If Buyer is to get any relief, it will have to be somewhere else. On the other hand, if at the time of damage or destruction the risk had not yet shifted to Buyer, if it had remained with Seller, then Buyer need not pay the price. Furthermore, unless his or her delivery obligation is excused under some other provision of the Code, Seller may face a successful action for breach if conforming goods are not tendered on time. Between buyers and sellers, let there be no doubt, the question of risk of loss is of more than academic interest.

Prior to the adoption of the Uniform Commercial Code, the question of who bore the risk of loss of goods was dominated by the notion of title. It was said that whoever had the "title" or "property" in the goods at the time of the unfortunate event would bear the risk. This might have made perfect sense, but what it didn't do was explain exactly how the question of title should be decided in a difficult case. The concept of title over property came to have a distinctly amorphous if not downright mystical quality. Adding to the confusion was the fact that this concept and this word, *title,* were invoked in other disputes not directly related to the risk of loss problem. It was said that those who actually understood where title would lay in a difficult situation constituted a very small club. Other commentators were convinced that there really was no way to find consistency or make sense out of the various decisions and that membership in this club, even if available, would be nothing to write home about.

The drafters of the Code made their main contribution to the area by eliminating any reference to title in considering risk of loss problems. Their approach, as we will see, deals with risk of loss directly and on its own terms. While there may be some questions left at the margins by the sections as they were eventually drafted, the general response has been very favorable. Article 2's treatment of risk of loss is among those areas where it has been most successful in establishing rules clear in their application and which generally achieve results in line with the drafters' articulated goals.

One other point deserves attention. Look again at §2-709(1). It gives the Seller the absolute right to recover the full contract price from the Buyer for any goods accepted. If the Buyer can be shown to have made a technical acceptance, as we discussed that important Code concept in Chapter 18, he must pay the price. The distinct question of risk of loss is no longer relevant. We are dealing with a risk of loss problem—and look to those sections of the Code for guidance—when goods are lost or damaged through the fault of neither party *after* their identification to the contract but *prior to* any acceptance on Buyer's part.

Chapter 25 which follows deals with Article 2's basic treatment of risk of loss questions. Chapter 26 explores the rules applicable to situations where the contract of sale requires or authorizes delivery through the agency of a third-party commercial carrier or on site at a commercial warehouse. (We will get into F.O.B., F.A.S., delivery "Ex-Ship," and all that.) We conclude in Chapter 27 with a look at the special rules on risk of loss which come into play when one or the other of the parties, Seller or Buyer, is in breach of the agreement at the time calamity strikes.

25

Basic Treatment

The Article 2 Approach to Risk of Loss

Before looking in detail at the particular sections which deal with risk of loss (§2-509 and §2-510), it is worthwhile to note the basic philosophy behind Article 2's treatment of these problems. There is no need to guess. The first comment to §2-509 states that "the underlying theory of these sections on the risk of loss is the adoption of the contractual approach rather than an arbitrary shifting of the risk with the 'property' in the goods." Language in the third comment, which we will soon see and which the courts are fond of quoting, makes clear that the attempt in these sections is to place the risk on that party who is more likely at the moment of loss to have insurance on the goods. Of course this emphasis on the likelihood of insurance coverage, while admirably pragmatic, involves a kind of circularity. If the risk of loss is placed on the party most likely to have insurance coverage, at least if this approach is well-known to buyers and sellers and regularly followed by the courts, it will presumably lead to that party's actually getting insurance. You tend to insure against those risks you will have to bear.

This circularity, of course, can also be characterized as a glorious harmony between law and practice. More to our purposes, it does serve to emphasize the real reason behind any risk of loss rules. The law serves best when it encourages the parties to face up to the risks of loss before any loss occurs, if that is possible, and protect themselves with an appropriate measure of insurance. To the practicing attorney the message is once again that counseling clients before disaster strikes, especially when the rules of the game are clear, is a lot easier than helping them to pick up the pieces afterwards. While the Examples and Explanations in this and the following chapters will mostly be worded as if the question is which party should bear the unbearable loss, remember that if this party has been attentive to his or her own welfare from the start the real contest in most cases should be which party has to bear the much less onerous burden of having to file an insurance claim and cash the check that should be forthcoming.

Of the two risk of loss sections, §2-509 is undoubtedly the more important and we will concentrate on it first. Before doing so, however, note at least the heading of §2-510. If either seller or buyer is able to substantiate a claim that at the time of the loss the other was in breach, that section is the place to start analysis. We will deal with it as a distinct matter in Chapter 27. For the moment assume that neither party is claiming the other was in breach at the time of the loss, or that if such a claim has been advanced it has failed. How does the Code allocate the loss when there has been no breach?

The rules on risk of loss in the absence of breach are set out in §2-509. Like many Code sections this one is best approached in an order other than that the subsections are written in. Read first §2-509(4). Whatever may be true about the general risk of loss rules arising out of the other parts of this section, the parties are always free—in fact we might say they are encouraged—to vary the results by "contrary agreement."* What must the parties do to make such a special allocation of the risk? The courts have understandably been very strict on this. It would seem that the language relied upon will have to be fairly conspicuous and mention risk of loss specifically. So, for example, in *Hayward v. Postma*, 31 Mich. App. 720, 188 N.W.2d 31, 9 U.C.C. 379 (1971), the court held that what it characterized as "boilerplate language" in a security agreement that spoke only of the buyer's obligation to keep the goods insured at all times was not enough. "Risk of loss," the court noted, "is nowhere mentioned" in the offered clause. In *Commonwealth Propane Co. v. Petrosol International, Inc.*, 818 F.2d 522, 3 U.C.C.2d 1778 (6th Cir. 1987), the court held that a clause that referred only to when "title" to the goods would pass did not reallocate the risk of loss, reasoning quite correctly that the concept of title is no longer the key to risk of loss questions under the Code.

Contrast these cases to *Forest Nursery Co., Inc. v. I.W.S., Inc.*, 141 Misc. 2d 661, 534 N.Y.S.2d 86, 8 U.C.C.2d 923 (1986), where the court found there *was* a sufficient expression of contrary intention. In that situation the only documents that passed between the parties were the seller's invoices. These included the express provision, in italics, of "*No risk to Supplier*," and a large legend at the top of the papers stating, "NOTICE: ALL SHIPMENTS TRAVEL AT RISK AND COST OF PURCHASER." Now that's making it clear.†

---

*It's not worth it here to be worried about the special case of sale on approval, on which generally see Chapter 23.

†Perhaps the most significant application of §2-509(4) is found when the parties explicitly allocate risk of lost through the use in their agreement of so-called trade or delivery terms such as F.O.B., C.I.F., and the like. If these mean nothing to you now, that's perfectly understandable. They figure in the next chapter.

For the moment we will assume that the parties have made no special agreement on risk of loss. Next look briefly at the introductory clauses *only* of subsections (1) and (2) of §2-509. Subsection (1) deals with the case where the goods are to be shipped by a carrier. The second subsection involves goods held by a bailee, which typically means a commercial warehouse, and which are to be delivered without being moved. In either instance the seller is not personally handing over the goods. A third party, such as a shipping company, a common carrier, or a warehouse, is involved in the delivery. These cases deserve special attention and will be the subject of the chapter that follows.

So far, all we've done is eliminate a lot of situations. We aren't dealing with instances where there's been a breach of the sales contract, where the parties have made an explicit allocation of risk of loss, or where the delivery is to be carried out through a third party's actions. What's left? Section 2-509(3), which you should read now.

EXAMPLES

1. Sam's Autorama is a retail automobile dealership. On Friday morning Sam sells a car to one Betty. He gives her the papers she will need to obtain insurance, a certificate of title and plates for the car. She leaves, stating she'll pick up the car the following Monday. Over the weekend the car is destroyed when a fire consumes Sam's business.

  a. Must Betty pay for the car?

  b. Would it make any difference to your answer if Betty had obtained a valid certificate of title under her state's title law on Friday afternoon?

  c. What if you knew Betty had obtained insurance covering the car against all kinds of disasters, including fire, on Friday afternoon?

2. The Sparkle Store, a jewelry retailer, sells a bracelet to Mr. Burns. The store agrees to make some final adjustments to the bracelet and then to deliver it to his home. An employee of the store takes it to Burns's house. When he finds no one at home, he leaves the package containing the bracelet wedged between the screen door and the front door. The package is not there when Burns returns to his home at the end of the day. Must he pay The Sparkle Store for it? Would you think the result will change if the employee had slipped the package through the mail slot in Burns's front door and it had been stolen by a thief who broke into the house before Burns got home?

3a. Janice agrees to sell her old car to a friend, Tom. Tom gives her a check for the price and she offers him the keys. He tells her that he'll have to come around the following day to pick the car up. Before Tom comes to pick up the car on the following day, it is stolen from where it has been parked. Who bears the risk of loss? Would it matter who had possession of the keys overnight?

  b. Suppose instead that when Janice sold the car to Tom they agreed that she would have it until the next day, and that Janice had said, "You can pick it up any time tomorrow. The keys will be here for you." The car is stolen overnight. Who bears the risk? Would it make a difference if Tom had not come until two o'clock in the afternoon on the following day, and the car had been stolen sometime during that morning?

    c. What if Tom had not paid for the car initially but had agreed to pay for it when he picked it up the next day. He never picks it up. A few weeks later the car is stolen from in front of Janice's house. Can Janice successfully sue Tom for the price?

4. Remember Sam from Example 1? As it happens, the fire at Sam's also consumed a trailer parked on the Autorama lot which Sam had been using as his temporary office. A few days before the fire Sam had moved all of his belongings out of the trailer and into a new permanent office that had been built on the site. On Thursday he had entered into a contract of sale for the trailer with one Bill, who had responded to a hand-lettered "FOR SALE" sign Sam had stuck in the window of the trailer. On Thursday, Bill had told Sam that it would take him a few days to come and pick up the trailer. Sam had said, "OK, whenever you want it, it's yours." Who, between Sam and Bill, bore the risk of loss of the trailer when it went up in flames over the weekend?

EXPLANATIONS

1a. No, Betty does not have to pay. Sam bears the risk of loss. Here Sam is clearly a merchant seller of automobiles. Section 2-509(3) says that the risk of such loss in the case of a merchant seller passes to the buyer only upon "receipt of the goods." *Receipt* is obviously the crucial concept here. The Definitional Cross References of the Code lead us to §2-103. We find in §2-103(1)(c) that *receipt* of goods means "taking physical possession of them." Betty has not taken physical possession of the car, so the risk of loss never passes to her.

1b. Whether or not Betty had "title" under her state's law regulating title to motor vehicles would not make a difference. *Receipt of the goods,* as that term is used in Article 2, is still the key. This simply emphasizes that the drafters did not want the concept of title to goods to control risk of loss questions under the Code as it had under earlier, and often more confusing, law.

    This same point is made in a different way in the case of *Hughes v. Al Green, Inc.,* 65 Ohio St. 2d 110, 418 N.E.2d 1355, 31 U.C.C. 890 (1981). In that case Mrs. Hughes, after making a down payment, was allowed to take immediate possession on a Saturday of a car she bought from a dealership. It was agreed she would return it to the dealer the following Monday for the completion of certain new car preparations and the installation of a CB radio. Before leaving the dealership on Saturday she signed a purchase contract and an application for certificate of title among other papers. On her way home, and obviously before she could have obtained legal title under the state's title law, she was involved in a collision. Was she obligated for the remainder of the purchase price? The court had no difficulty finding that she was. She had taken possession of the car, there had been receipt from the merchant seller, and hence the risk had passed to her. Ohio's certificate of title law was simply irrelevant for these purposes.

The Code's justification for the rule based on the taking of possession from a merchant seller is not hard to find. Comment 3 states that

> the underlying theory of this rule is that a merchant who is to make physical delivery at his own place of business continues meanwhile to control the goods and can be expected to insure his interest in them. The buyer, on the other hand, has no control of the goods and it is extremely unlikely that he will carry insurance on the goods not yet in his possession.

Which leads to consideration of our next hypothetical.

1c. Even if Betty had insurance that would cover this loss, the risk of loss is still on Sam if she had not taken possession. The Code's justification for this rule is, according to Comment 3, based partially on who would be most likely to have insurance in the typical case, but the language of the Code makes clear that the result does not depend on who does or does not have insurance *in the particular case*. Similarly, the result would not be affected if for some reason Sam was not insured for the loss of this car. Presumably if Sam did want the risk to shift to Betty on Friday afternoon, and if she was willing to get insurance from that time on to cover the risk, the parties could have shifted the risk by explicit contrary agreement as provided for in §2-509(4). The fact that they happened to have insurance coverage, or in Sam's case failed to have it, would certainly not in and of itself constitute contrary agreement.

An interesting case which tests the limits of this rule as to merchant sellers and which demonstrates how far out these limits run is *Ellis v. Bell Aerospace Corp.*, 315 F. Supp. 221, 7 U.C.C. 918 (D. Or. 1970). Ellis paid Bell Aerospace $102,110, for a new helicopter. The helicopter was ready for delivery in early February, and the contract provided that the buyer would deliver within ten days of its being ready. Ellis asked if he could take delivery later, in March. The seller told him that he didn't have the room to store the helicopter for that length of time and with his acquiescence made arrangements to have it stored at a local airport. The sales contract provided that Ellis was to receive several days of in-flight instruction at the time of delivery. On March 11, he and his wife appeared at the Bell factory and attended ground school. Two days later, while on the first instructional flight with Ellis at the controls and an instructor aboard, the helicopter crashed. Ellis sued to recover the purchase price of the craft and won. The court reasoned that,

> Bell did not, at any time before the helicopter crashed, surrender to Ellis complete dominion and control over the helicopter. The helicopter remained, until it was destroyed, under the practical control of Bell. It

would have continued to remain under Bell's control until Ellis had completed his full five hours of training, a matter of some two or three days.

Thus the risk of loss had not passed even though by the time of the crash Ellis had obtained liability insurance covering the helicopter, had registered it in his name with the Federal Aviation Agency, and had agreed to have it stored at least temporarily with a third party.

One argument that has been made by merchant sellers to avoid the risk which Article 2 puts on them as long as the goods remain on their lots or in their stores is that the buyer in such a case may have actually already taken possession, but then has for some reason left the item in their care in the form of a bailment. This argument, if successful, might conceivably throw the controversy into §2-509(2)(b) and mean the risk had passed to the buyer. Courts faced with such arguments have been quick to decide that subsection (2) was intended to deal only with the situation of goods held by actual *third-party* bailees, particularly warehouses, and that a seller can't turn itself into a bailee so easily. See, e.g., *Caudle v. Sherrard Motor Co.*, 525 S.W.2d 238, 17 U.C.C. 754 (Tex. Civ. App. 1975).

2.   Again we have the case of a merchant seller, only this time delivery by the merchant (not through some third-party carrier) is to be at some place other than its place of business. The rule is still the same. Did the buyer get receipt of the goods? When the package is simply left outside his door, it's pretty clear that he did not and that the risk of loss never passed. The fact that no one seems to know what happened to the bracelet is not important. Somehow it was lost and it is just this kind of loss that the merchant seller must bear until the buyer actually gains possession.

When the package has actually been placed inside Mr. Burns's house, the argument for possession is of course stronger. I doubt, however, the result would be different. True, for a thief to get the bracelet he or she had to get inside the house and that put the bracelet at risk just like all of Mr. Burns's other possessions. But in this context it seems that Mr. Burns would have to have been made aware that he had possession. Note the language in Comment 3 and the *Ellis* case, both quoted above, that emphasizes the consideration of whether actual "control" had gone from the seller to the buyer. It's possible Burns could have guarded against this loss if he at least knew he actually had the jewelry, perhaps by hiding it away where even this thief couldn't find it. If he didn't even know the property's location at the time, it's hard to say he has gotten receipt.

The courts do seem to require that the buyer actually have possession in the sense of some chance to act on or to exercise dominion and control over the goods for risk to pass from the merchant seller. The mere fact that the seller has somehow gotten rid of them is not enough. In *Ron Mead T.V. & Appliance Corp. v. Legendary Homes, Inc.*, 746 P.2d 1163, 6 U.C.C.2d 117 (Okl. Ct. App. 1987), the seller, a retailer of household appliances, was to deliver appliances meant for installation in a new home to the construction site by 5:00 P.M. At five when the appliances had not been delivered the buyer, a builder, closed the house and left for the day. Sometime between 5:00 and 6:30 the seller delivered the appliances. Finding no one there, the deliveryman put them in the unlocked garage. During the night they were stolen. The Oklahoma Court of Appeals, affirming a finding for the buyer that it need not pay, quoted with approval the statement by the trial court that "(t)he act by the deliveryman of placing the goods in an unlocked garage, in a house under construction, and then locking the door did not give the Buyer the opportunity to take physical possession (of them)." In accord is *H & B Chevrolet-Cadillac, Inc. v. Boutell Driveaway, Inc.,* 123 P.L.J. 192, 17 U.C.C. 752 (Pa. Ct. Com. Pl. 1974). There the after-hours delivery of an automobile did not effect receipt, where the car had been driven onto the retailer's lot and the keys slid under the showroom door. Obviously, the merchant seller has to meet a high standard if he or she wants to transfer the risk of loss onto the buyer.

3a. Tom bears the risk. Janice is a nonmerchant seller and the rules in that case are very different. Section 2-509(3) states that in the case of a seller who is not a merchant the risk passes to the buyer on "tender of delivery." When has this occurred? The crucial section here is §2-503 (as we dealt with earlier in Chapter 17). Subsection (4) deals with the case when the goods are in the hands of a bailee and are to be delivered without being moved. That certainly isn't the situation here. We'll deal with sale of goods held by a bailee in the following chapter. We can also put off for the moment the case where delivery is to be tendered through a third-party carrier, which is the concern in §§2-503(2), (3), and (5). That leaves the first subsection as our guiding text. Read it carefully.

Janice was willing to let Tom have the car right away. She offered him the keys. This was tender to him of the car and so he bears the risk of loss from that time on. It really doesn't matter whether he took the keys then and there or left them with her overnight. Even if she kept the keys, if she had made it clear to him that he could have them and drive the car away anytime he wanted, she had made a tender.

Although you may find this result hard to accept, remember the seller here is not a merchant or a professional seller and there's no reason to think she expects to take the risk any longer than she has to. One case makes the point quite well. *Schock v. Ronderos,* 394 N.W.2d 697, 2 U.C.C.2d 1302 (N.D. 1986), involved the sale of a used mobile home by one nonmerchant to another. The buyer appeared at the sellers' property where the mobile home was located and paid the purchase price on a Friday. The buyer received a bill of sale and assurances from the sellers that title to the property would be delivered soon. He then prepared the mobile home for removal, including removal of the skirting around its foundation, certain "tie-downs," and of the foundation blocks. The home was left sitting on its wheels. The buyer intended to take the mobile home off of the sellers' property the following Monday, and the sellers had no objection to its remaining on their property until that time. Later, on Friday evening, it was destroyed by high winds. The Supreme Court of North Dakota affirmed a denial of the buyer's claim for a return of his purchase price. The risk of loss had passed. This was so even though the trailer had apparently still been hooked up to electricity and natural gas connections on the sellers' property at the time of its destruction and some other personal property of the sellers (a piano and davenport) had still been aboard. The court found that tender had occurred, and the risk of loss had passed, as soon as the sellers acquiesced in the buyer's preparing the mobile home for removal. Had he wanted to take it away before Monday, the sellers were apparently willing and able to disconnect the utilities and remove their piano and davenport as soon as requested. The loss was on the buyer. In fact the court affirmed a judgment of $3,080 on a counterclaim by the sellers for their expenses incurred in removing the mobile home (or presumably what was left of it) from their property!

3b. Janice bears the risk if the car is stolen overnight. She is still a nonmerchant seller, but here she wasn't to tender delivery of the car until some time on the following day. So when, exactly, would the risk have passed? It's hard to say exactly. Perhaps the moment is 9:00 A.M. of the next day. Perhaps a bit earlier. Reading §2-503(1) suggests it would be a matter of when Tom could have reasonably understood he had the right to come over, get the keys, and take the car without surprising (annoying?) Janice by his appearance at her door. So the crucial time is not when Tom comes to pick up the car but when he *could have* come to do so. If the car was stolen before that time, of course, the loss isn't his.

3c. Janice would have a hard time collecting the price from Tom. Remember that §2-709 gives her a right to the price "of conforming goods lost or damaged *within a commercially reasonable time after* risk of their loss" has passed to her buyer. Once it should have become apparent to Janice that Tom didn't intend to pick up the car, and she had the opportunity to start protecting or insuring it as she had before, that length of time has presumably passed. The risk reverts to her. Janice can of course sue Tom, but only for the damage caused to her by his failure to buy the car, the lost contract interest, not for the value of the car itself.

4. By now it is clear that if Sam is a merchant for the purposes of §2-509(3) the risk of loss of the trailer would not have passed at the time of the fire. If he is a nonmerchant the risk would have passed. Which is it? Again we see the importance of the merchant classification in Article 2 and how the classification scheme depends not only on the particular seller's business but also on the circumstances in which the question is being asked. We refer back to §2-104(1) and the second comment to that section (as well as to Chapter 3). The comment suggests the test here is whether Sam is a merchant under either the "practices" *or* the "goods" aspect of the definition. Is this so clear? Here, at least, the sale of cars and trailers may not seem so different. But what if the seller were in the business of selling something like flowers and houseplants, which are normally taken out of his or her establishment as soon as they are

bought, and the particular sale involves a used air-conditioning unit which had already been disconnected and was ready to be taken away? This seems miles from the normal business of the seller, even if he or she is a merchant. It is not so clear that the courts would find such a situation to be covered by the merchant seller provision.

26

Delivery Through Independent Third Parties

When the Goods Get Shipped

The situations governed by §2-509(3), as discussed in the previous chapter, all have one thing in common. Delivery of the goods is being made directly by Seller to Buyer. True, Seller's employees might be involved in dropping off the stuff or Buyer's employees might be making a pickup, but since these employees qualify and are acting as agents for their employers, we're still talking about a straight hand-off from one contracting party to another. There are other instances, we know, where delivery is not made directly. The contract may *require* Seller to ship the goods to Buyer via some particular third-party commercial carrier. Even if delivery in a particular manner is not required, it may be *authorized* under the agreement. Seller would be within his or her rights to make delivery via an independent third-party contractor, the kind that gets paid for moving stuff, big or small, from one place to another.

Section 2-509(1) sets forth the risk of loss rules where "the contract requires or authorizes the seller to ship the goods by carrier." Article 2 does not define the word *carrier* used in this subsection, but it is clear that it is to be taken as referring only to an independent third party which transports things from one place to another for profit. See Comment 2 to this section. If delivery is made on Seller's delivery van, or if Buyer sends its own truck around to get the goods, we are *not* in subsection (1). The delivery contemplated in §2-509(1) is made under a separate contract of carriage entered into with a commercial party "engaged in the business of transporting or forwarding goods."*

Look now at §2-509(1). How risk of loss is allocated is clearly governed by whether the particular case fits into subpart (a) or subpart (b). We are dealing here with the distinction between the *shipment contract,* which is the subject of subpart (a), and the *destination contract,* which comes under (b). You should recall this distinction from our discussion of tender in Chapter 17. The parties have entered into a *shipment contract,* when "the seller is required or authorized to send the goods to the buyer and the contract does not require him to deliver them at a particular destination" (§2-504). Seller is responsible for dispatching the goods properly on their way and meeting the other requirements of §2-504. He or she is *not* actually responsible for them getting where they are going. The *destination contract* is different; the Seller "is required to deliver at a particular destination" (§2-503(3)). He or she has an added layer of obligation and takes ultimate responsibility that the goods will get if not literally into Buyer's hands at least to that "particular destination" where Buyer is to take control of them. An important point of Code jurisprudence is found buried to some degree in Comment 5 to §2-503:

> [U]nder this Article the "shipment" contract is regarded as the normal one and the "destination" contract as the variant type. The seller is not obligated to deliver at a named destination and bear the concurrent risk of loss until arrival, unless he has specifically agreed so to deliver or the commercial understanding of the terms used by the parties contemplates such delivery.

If, as this comment says and as the courts seem to have no trouble accepting, the shipment contract is the *normal* one under Article 2, then §2-509(1)(a) is the *normal* risk of loss rule when goods are delivered through a carrier, unless a specific agreement of the parties or the commercial understanding of the language they have used allocates the risk differently and throws the whole matter into subpart (b).

As a matter of fact, commercial buyers and sellers often do allocate the risk explicitly in their agreements. They could do this by explicit use of the words "risk of loss" in conjunction with an agreed to allocation of that risk, but often they do not. Historically the practice developed of allocating the risk of loss, along with the question of who would pay for the carrier's fee and other costs of carriage, as part of the price quotation. The agreement would say something like, "Price of $100 F.O.B. Boston." While this would seem to us laypersons as nothing more than a price quote with some other gibberish thrown in to make it look official, both parties as people engaged in the business would be expected to know

---

*I take this language from the definition of *bill of lading* in §1-201(6). Most, but not all, contracts of carriage of this type will be evidenced by a document which goes by this moniker. We'll reserve a fuller exploration of bills of lading and other so-called documents of title until Part VI.

from this term not only what the price was but also who was to pay the freight and who would bear the risk of loss during shipment. As I say, the system could be Greek to most of us, but in point of fact it worked very well for those concerned. Unfortunately, the courts occasionally got it wrong (see Comment 1 to §2-319), and so the drafters though it best to incorporate these so-called *delivery terms* directly into the statutory scheme. All of us are now made privy to the magical code, and courts kept from "unfortunate" error, just by looking at §§2-319 through 2-322. You should glance at these now. There is, to say the least, no reason for you to try and memorize what they say. The important thing is that you know these sections are there as part of Article 2 and that you can refer to them when the need arises. The need will arise, and you'll get sufficient practice in their use, in some of the Examples that follow.

When the Goods Stay Put

Section §2-509(2) sets out the risk of loss rules where "the goods are held by a bailee to be delivered without being moved." Again, Article 2 does not define *bailee* directly, but it is meant to indicate "a person engaged in the business of storing goods for hire."* The idea behind §2-509(2) is that sometimes Seller will have put goods into storage with an independent commercial warehouse. (We are *not* talking about the case where they are being stored in Seller's own warehouse or where Seller delivers them directly to Buyer's warehouse.) To sell the goods Seller simply agrees to transfer ownership to Buyer. The goods will stay where they are. If all goes well the result, aside from Seller's having been paid the price, is that Buyer will now be the proud owner of the goods as they sit snugly in the warehouse. If something untoward happens to the goods in the midst of this paper transaction—some loss occurs through the fault of neither party—then the risk of loss is governed by subsection (2). Practically, of course, the underlying issue is which party is going to go against the warehouse (which not surprisingly has a duty to care for the goods (see §7-204)) to be made whole or, if the warehouse can prove it is not liable or has effectively limited its liability, must bear the consequence.

There have been a few cases where a merchant seller, seeking to avoid the unfavorable operation of §2-509(3), has argued that under the particular circumstances it had been transformed into a "bailee" by the time of the loss and hence could wedge itself into a more favorable result via §2-509(2). Well-known in this regard is *Caudle v. Sherrard Motor Co.*, 525 S.W.2d 238, 17 U.C.C. 754 (Tex. Civ. App. 1975). In *Caudle*, as in the other cases which have had to deal with this argument, the court found against the seller. The courts have consistently reserved §2-509(2)

---

*Now I'm quoting from §1-201(45) and the definition of *warehouse receipt*. Such a document is, not surprisingly, the receipt issued by a commercial warehouse when it takes in goods for storage. See also the definition of *bailee* in §7-102(1)(a).

for those situations where the goods have been put into the hands of a separate party engaged in the business of storing goods for hire, the commercial bailee. The seller who, as part of doing the deal, agrees to and does store the goods for a time on his or her premises doesn't qualify.

The Examples and Explanations ask you to apply the relevant subsections of §2-509. You'll find that this naturally leads you into other sections, particularly those which set up the criteria for tender (with which we dealt in Chapter 17) as well as those mentioned above which lay out the meaning of the various delivery terms. In answering these questions you may assume, as you did in the previous chapter, that there has been no breach on either Seller's or Buyer's part. We'll deal with the consequences of breach on risk of loss in the chapter to follow.

EXAMPLES

1.   Ben owns and operates an electronics store in Birmingham, Alabama. He regularly places orders with a large audio manufacturer, Stereo Supply, located in Sacramento. In need of some of Stereo's line of speakers, he sends that company a Purchase Order specifying that he wishes to buy five sets of speakers at the price set forth in the Stereo Supply catalog, which he keeps on hand. He receives back a copy of this Purchase Order initialled by someone in Stereo's sales department along with a note telling him that the speakers will be shipped to him via United Pick-Up Services ("UPS"), a well-known delivery service. Neither the catalog nor the Purchase Order makes any mention of the means or cost of shipment nor of the risk of loss. Ben never receives the speakers, but some weeks later receives a bill for them. He calls up Stereo and is informed that the company had indeed upon receiving his order packaged the speakers and delivered them to UPS. That firm now acknowledges that the shipment apparently got lost somewhere in transit.

a. Assuming all this is true, does Ben have to pay the bill received from Stereo Supply?

b. Would your answer be different if Ben could show that his Purchase Order contained a space labelled "Ship To:" which he had filled in with his Birmingham address?

c. What if the Purchase Order had specified that "Seller shall pay freight?"

d. Finally, suppose the Purchase Order had featured in large bold print the language "NOTICE: ALL SHIPMENTS TRAVEL AT THE RISK AND COST OF SUPPLIER." Would this change your analysis?

2.   Mazie's Department Store, located in Capitol City contracts to buy six gross of sweaters from Knits Incorporated which is located in Boston. The price is agreed to as "$1200/gross F.O.B. Boston." Knits delivers the sweaters to Tony's Trucking Service and arranges a contract for their delivery to Mazie. Knits receives a bill of lading from Tony's Trucking, which it immediately mails off to Mazie along with other details of the

shipment. While on route, Tony's truck is sideswiped and falls off a cliff. Fortunately, no one is hurt, but all of the cargo is destroyed.

    a. Who bears the risk of loss of the sweaters?

    b. Would your answer be the same if Knits had never mailed off the bill of lading to Mazie nor otherwise informed her of the shipment?

    c. How would you answer if instead the price term had read "$1340/gross F.O.B. Capitol City?"

    d. What if the price term had read "$1340/gross C.I.F. Capitol City?"

3.   Butterfield Foods, a preparer of frozen dinners, is located in Des Moines. It places a large order for freshly caught scrod with Seaside Fish Sellers in Boston. The contract is "F.O.B. Boston." Seaside delivers the fish to the Midwest and Atlantic Railroad and arranges for their shipment to the railyard in Des Moines. Butterfield is sent notice of this shipment and the bill of lading provided by the railroad. Unfortunately, Seaside neglects to arrange for shipment in refrigerated cars. The fish arrive in Des Moines in an awful state. Does Butterfield have to pay Seaside at the contract rate for the fish?

4.   Seaside also makes a shipment by rail to a buyer in Omaha, this time remembering to pack the fish in ice and arrange for shipment in refrigerated railroad cars. The contract calls for payment "F.O.B. Boston." The fish are delivered to the railroad, which accepts them and furnishes a bill of lading. Notice of the shipment and the bill are sent forthwith to the buyer. The railroad expects to load the fish onto a train bound for Omaha the following day. Overnight a hurricane hits the Boston area causing great damage to the railroad's yards and in particular the crates of fish. They are strewn all over the place. Obviously they have become worthless.

    a. Who bore this risk?

    b. Would your answer be any different if the price term of the contract had read "F.O.B. Cars Boston?"

    c. Seaside makes a third contract to sell fish, this time to a buyer in Fargo, North Dakota. It packs the fish in ice and delivers them to the railroad. Again it makes an appropriate contract for shipment and forwards the necessary documents. The shipment arrives in Fargo where it is off-loaded from the railroad cars. Four days later when Buyer arrives at the railroad yard to make a pick-up, she discovers that thieves have apparently broken into the railroad's facility in Fargo and made off with the fish. If the contract read "F.O.B. Fargo," who bore this risk? What if the contract had read "F.O.B. Buyer's Truck Fargo?"

5.   Seller in Seaport, South Carolina contracts to sell a large metal molding machine to Buyer in Baysville, New York. It is agreed that delivery will be "F.A.S. Gigantic." Seller delivers the machine, properly crated, to the Seaport Pier alongside the *Gigantic* and arranges with that ship's owner for delivery. Notice of this arrangement and the shipping company's

bill of lading are mailed to Buyer. As the crate containing the machine is being loaded onto the ship, a winch breaks and the machine is dropped and severely damaged.

> a. Who bears this risk of loss?
>
> b. What if the contract documents had read "Ex-Ship Gigantic?"

6. A contract signed by both Seller from Seattle and Buyer from Boston reads "$7/ton F.O.B. Boston." It also contains a conspicuous provision stating "Merchandise Travels at Risk To Purchaser." The shipment is damaged somewhere between the coasts. Who bears the risk of loss?

7. Farmer Jones stores a large quantity of wheat at Walter's Wheat Warehouse. She receives a negotiable warehouse receipt from Walter. Jones goes into the big city and to the office of Agribusiness, Inc. A representative of that company agrees to buy all the wheat she has stored. Jones hands over the warehouse receipt. She goes home with a promise that Agribusiness will send her a check in payment within a week. She does not contact Walter. That night Walter's Warehouse is hit by a tornado and all of the wheat is rendered worthless.

> a. Who bears this loss? (For the purposes of this question and the two that follow there is really no need for you to understand the difference between a "negotiable" warehouse receipt and a "nonnegotiable" one. It is enough that you recognize that warehouse receipts come in two varieties, as in fact do bills of lading. Later, after Chapter 31, of course, you will want to come back to these three questions with a deeper understanding of and appreciation for the distinction.)
>
> b. Suppose instead that Jones had received a nonnegotiable warehouse receipt from Walter and that she had not carried this document with her to the city. On Monday she enters into a contract with Agribusiness and agrees to send it the nonnegotiable receipt within three days. When she gets home she immediately sends off the receipt. The receipt arrives in Agribusiness's offices with the Thursday afternoon mail. The tornado comes on Thursday night, wiping out the warehouse and along with it the wheat. Under these facts, who bears the risk of loss?
>
> c. Suppose Jones could show that she stopped by Walter's after she mailed off the receipt and told him that "I've sold the wheat to Agribusiness," to which Walter replied, "OK, I'll note that on my books." Walter makes the notation before the tornado hits. Who now bears the loss?

EXPLANATIONS

1a. Ben must pay for the speakers at the contract price because the risk of loss had passed to him prior to their disappearance. Since the contract is silent as to the risk of loss and no delivery term (like F.O.B. or C.I.F.) was used, the Code's assumption that this was a shipment contract controls. As the comment to §2-503 which was quoted in the introductory text says, the shipment contract is the "normal" one, and there's nothing here to suggest that Ben and Stereo are acting abnormally. This being a shipment contract, we look to §2-509(1)(a). The risk passes to the buyer "when the goods are duly delivered to the carrier." To see what Stereo Supply has to do to "duly deliver to the carrier" and hence pass the risk on, we look to §2-504. Stereo Supply appears here to have met all three of the criteria (a) through (c).

So the risk was on Ben at the time of the loss. He must pay the price. He may of course go against UPS for the loss he suffered, but it is his responsibility, not Stereo Supply's, to pursue the carrier and to prove it liable under some theory. Notice that this is true even though Stereo Supply and not Ben was the one to select the carrier. It is key to the seller's position here that the choice of UPS and the contract of carriage made with that firm were "reasonable having regard to the nature of the goods and the circumstances of the case." Barring any facts not given here, Stereo Supply appears to have lived up to this standard.

1b. The answer should still be the same. Ben bears the loss under this shipment contract. He could try to argue that the "Ship To:" language converted this into a destination contract, but it is doubtful this would succeed. The courts have usually taken the drafters' importuning that the shipment contract is the normal one to heart and have insisted on very explicit language to the contrary in the agreement referring expressly to "risk of loss" or use of a delivery term (such as "F.O.B. destination") which unequivocally denotes a destination contract before they will find the contract to be such and not your standard shipment contract. In particular, in the few instances in which they have been asked to find a destination contract based on language like that here ("Ship to" buyer's location) they have not responded favorably. After all, as the court pointed out in one such case, *Pestana v. Karinol Corp.*, 367 So. 2d 1096, 25 U.C.C. 1306 (Fl. Dist. Ct. App. 1979), sellers who have entered into shipment contracts need to know where to send the stuff just as much as do sellers committed to destination contracts. Either type of agreement is going to have to include the buyer's address, or where he or she wants the goods sent, *somewhere* if the seller isn't to be left guessing.

> A "send to" or "ship to" term is a part of every contract involving the sale of goods where carriage is contemplated and has no significance in determining whether the contract is a shipment or a destination contract for risk of loss purposes. . . . As such, the "send to" term contained in [the instant] contract cannot, without more, convert this into a destination contract.

1c. Ben will still bear the risk. Cost of shipment and risk of loss are distinct aspects of any one contract and need not necessarily be allocated to the same party. This language tells us who is to bear the *cost* of the trip, but it does not refer specifically to the risk of loss. So as to risk of loss the preference for a shipment contract, and an answer like that to Example 1a, still pertains. This is clearly in keeping with the drafters' intention. Reread Comment 5 to §2-503, but this time starting from the very beginning.

1d. Here, finally, is a situation where Ben would not bear the risk of loss. The contract is no longer silent but expressly and unreservedly allocates the risk to the seller during shipment. The parties are always free to allocate the risk of loss as they choose by proper agreement (§2-509(4)), and that is what they have done here. Stereo Supply's only argument would be that it had never agreed to this term, but this shouldn't have much success as it actually initialled the document which conspicuously bore this legend.

So in this case the parties have entered into a destination contract. We look, therefore, to §2-509(1)(b). There is no question that the goods were never tendered at the destination, so the risk of loss never passed from the seller. In some other cases, of course, the issue of tender will be closer. If so we will have §2-503 to guide us. Review subsections (1) and (3) of that section.

2a. Mazie bears the risk. Under §2-319(1) the term F.O.B. (which comes from "free on board" but which really "means" just what this section says it means, no more and no less) is not just a price term but also a delivery term. Here we have "F.O.B. Boston." This is F.O.B. the place of shipment, and so under §2-319(1)(a) marks out a shipment contract. Assuming Knits met all of the criteria of §2-504 (and there's no reason here to doubt it), it bore the risk only until it "put the goods into the possession of the shipper." While the subsection does not explicitly say so, once the seller no longer bears the risk it necessarily must fall, as between the two of them, on the buyer.

2b. The answer here is not perfectly clear. Knits did put the sweaters into the possession of the carrier. But §2-319(1)(a) also refers quite specifically to the seller's duties under §2-504, and these we know include what is required by subpart (c) of that section. Lastly, we note the concluding language of §2-504. It says that a seller's failure to carry out the obligation laid out in (c) is a *ground for rejection* only if "material delay or loss ensues." Is this relevant at all to a risk of loss problem where acceptance or rejection is hardly the issue? Should Mazie bear the risk unless she can show that material delay or loss was a direct result of her not being given notice in this instance? If so, she'd have to show, I suppose, that had she gotten the notice she would have immediately insured these sweaters or that she would have called Tony and importuned him to be even more careful driving than he usually is. Even if the notice had been immediately sent off by Knits, however, it might not have arrived at Mazie's until after the accident had already happened. So Knits might even be able to affirmatively prove that the lack of notice could not have made a bit of difference in any way relating to this loss. If that is so, why could this failure on its part prevent the risk of loss from shifting to the buyer?

In *Rheinberg-Kellerei GmbH v. Vineyard Wine Co., Inc.,* 53 N.C. App. 560, 281 S.E.2d 425, 32 U.C.C. 96 (1981), the parties entered into a shipment contract for the sale of some wine produced in Germany. The wine was delivered to a ship, the *MS Munchen,* on November 29. The first that the buyer learned about the shipment was on or about January 24. Meanwhile, the *MS Munchen* had been lost in the North Atlantic with all hands and cargo on board sometime between December 12 and 22. The trial court found that the risk had remained on the seller because of its failure to give "prompt notice" of the shipment to the buyer. This finding was upheld on appeal.

> The seller is burdened with special responsibilities under a shipment contract because of the nature of the risk of loss being transferred. . . . Where the buyer, upon shipment by seller, assumes the perils involved in carriage, he must have a reasonable opportunity to guard against these risks by independent arrangements with the carrier. The requirement of prompt notification by the seller, as used in [§2-504(c)], must be construed as taking into consideration the need of a buyer to be informed of the shipment in sufficient time for him to take action to protect himself from the risk of damage to or loss of the goods while in transit. . . .
>
> It would not be practical or desirable, however, for the courts to attempt to engraft onto [§2-504] of the U.C.C. a rigid definition of prompt notice. Given the myriad factual situations which arise in business dealings, and keeping in mind the commercial realities, whether the notification has been "prompt" within the meaning of the U.C.C. will have to be determined on a case-by-case basis, under all the circumstances.

This case suggests an answer to the problem we have been looking at—whether the prompt notice of shipment required under §2-504 is an absolute requirement for passage of the risk of loss off of the seller carrying out a shipment contract onto the buyer—but there is still room for doubt. After all the court here stressed the buyer's need to have time to make arrangements to protect itself once it has the loss. And under the particular facts it appears that had the seller given prompt notice the buyer would have known that its wine was aboard the *MS Munchen* some time before she went down. What if that good ship had gone down as soon as she left port, say on November 30? Even if the seller *had* given prompt notice it is unlikely that the buyer would have received this notice until it was too late to matter. If that were the situation, should the seller be able to argue that its failure to give prompt notice was irrelevant to the risk of loss? As far as I can tell, no court has had to directly confront this question.

While it is not perfectly clear from these sections, I would argue that it is a better reading to say that for a seller to shift the loss under a shipment contract it really has to meet the three criteria of §2-504 and take the consequences if it does not, even if its failure to take some step called for by that section does not contribute to the actual loss in any way or otherwise affect how the buyer could have protected itself. There is every reason for encouraging sellers to take their various responsibilities under §2-504 seriously, and making passage of the risk of loss dependent on them certainly is one good way to drive this point home.

2c. This "F.O.B. place of destination" term created a delivery contract. See §2-319(1)(b). The risk remained on Knits until it tendered the goods there, that is Boston, "in the manner provided in this Article (§2-503)." The sweaters never made it to Boston, so they clearly were never tendered there. Knits bore the risk. Notice the price here is more per gross than it was in the shipment contract. That makes sense. Under this type of price term not only has the seller agreed to take the risk of loss during transit, but it has agreed to incur transportation costs as well. Naturally it will have to charge some more. And the buyer, who does not have to bear this risk or expense is usually willing to pay the slightly greater price. (Of course the actual price in dollars and cents no matter what the delivery term is a matter of one-on-one negotiation and follows no logic outside of the law of supply and demand.)

2d. Under §2-320(2) any C.I.F. term creates a shipment contract. See Comment 1. If Knits met all of the criteria of that section (a) through (e) the risk will have passed to Mazie. Here we have an interesting combination. It is a shipment contract, so the risk of loss is on buyer, but the seller agreed to obtain insurance to cover this risk and to bear the cost of this insurance as well as the freight to the stated destination. Of course the price charged the buyer will take into account these costs to seller. See subsection (1).

There is, as you can see, no magic to these various allocations of risks, responsibilities, and costs. It all comes down to each party's knowing what the other is talking about when they use these terms or symbols. Presumably they are able to deal with any allocation as long as it is clearly set out, or more importantly, select the one which best fits their situation at the time of contracting.

3. This is an "F.O.B. place of shipment" contract and the risk of loss during transit would normally be on the buyer. The seller here, however, quite clearly did not meet its §2-504 obligations on shipment, which are referred to in §2-319(1)(a). You get to the same result by recognizing this is a shipment contract and hence is governed by §2-509(1)(a). The seller does not "duly deliver" to a carrier if it does not make an appropriate contract for carriage.

Suppose Seaside did in fact arrange for shipment by refrigerated cars. Unfortunately, the refrigeration system on the cars failed somewhere along the line with the same unsettling results. It would seem that the risk had passed to the buyer Butterfield. That company would quite naturally try to sue the railroad for all the damage caused. Suppose, however, that the contract of carriage arranged for by Seaside contained a clause limiting the railroad's potential liability to a figure far below the value of the fish and that this clause was enforceable under law. Is Butterfield out of luck? No. Now it has another way of arguing that Seaside had never successfully passed the risk along. Look at the concluding sentence of Comment 3 to §2-504.

4a. Butterfield bore the risk. Under §2-319(1)(a) it is sufficient for the risk to pass to buyer that the seller put the goods "in the possession of the carrier." That had been done here.

4b. Under this term the risk remained on Seaside. Look at §2-319(1)(c). The seller's risk continued until it had "loaded the goods on board." That had not happened yet.

4c. If the contract reads "F.O.B. Fargo," the question under §2-319(1)(b) would be whether the goods had been tendered in that city. We consult §2-503. If the buyer could have come and picked them up any time after they were off-loaded, there was tender and the risk had passed. The result would be otherwise, with the risk remaining on the seller, if the term had been "F.O.B. Buyer's Truck Fargo."

5a. "F.A.S. Vessel" is explained by §2-319(2), which you can read and satisfy yourself that under these facts Buyer bore the risk of loss.

5b. Under an "ex-ship" term the risk does not pass to the buyer until "goods leave the ship's tackle or are otherwise properly unloaded" (§2-322(2)(b)). Hence Seller bore the risk of loss.

6.   Buyer would of course argue that since the delivery term was "F.O.B. destination" this was a destination contract. Since the shipment never got to its destination, Buyer would conclude, the risk never shifted to him. Seller, however, can point to an explicit and conspicuous allocation of the risk of loss that puts the risk on Buyer. Seller has the better argument. Remember that where the risk of loss lies and when it switches over is always subject to explicit agreement contrary to the general Article 2 rules we have been reviewing. See §2-509(4) and Comment 5 to that section. Notice also that §2-319(1) begins with that most cherished of all Article 2 phrases: "Unless otherwise agreed." Here, as Seller argues, the parties agreed otherwise and F.O.B. destination does not have the effect on risk of loss it ordinarily would. Freedom of contract reigns supreme.

7a. Agribusiness bears the loss. This case is covered by §2-509(2) as the goods were held by a bailee, Walter's Warehouse, and were to be delivered without being moved. (Who would want to schlep all that wheat from one warehouse to another when the same effect can be had by handing over a document, the warehouse receipt?) The risk passed to the buyer under subpart (a) with its receipt of the negotiable document of title covering the goods.

7b. The risk was probably still on Jones. Since the warehouse receipt is of the non-negotiable variety, subpart (a) is not applicable. Nor for the moment is (b). Under (c) the risk passes to Agribusiness upon its receipt of the non-negotiable document of title "as provided in (4)(b) of Section 2-503." Agribusiness did receive the document prior to the tornado and the loss of the wheat, but look at §2-503(4)(b). It tells us that "risk of loss . . . remains on the seller until the buyer has had a reasonable time to present the document. . . ." Agribusiness could certainly argue that a reasonable time had not passed here. What if the tornado came something like two or three days after the non-negotiable document had been received? The question gets trickier. We (and the parties) have to deal with the troublesome "R" word—*reasonableness.*

At the moment you may not have a good handle on the difference between negotiable and non-negotiable documents of title, but you can see at least one reason why parties might prefer to deal in the former rather than the later. As we'll see in Part VI, dealings in negotiable documents tend overall to be much more certain, crisp, and clean, than are dealings in non-negotiable instruments. What we see here is just one example.

7c. Jones would try to argue that the risk passed based not on §2-509(2)(c), but on subpart (b). Note the three subparts are joined with *or* so risk will pass if any one of the conditions is met. Is Jones right that by the time the big wind struck, Walter had "acknowledged" Agribusiness's right to possession of the goods? This language in the section is imprecise to put it mildly and we get no help from the comments. In *Jason's Foods, Inc. v. Peter Eckrich & Sons, Inc.,* 774 F.2d 214, 41 U.C.C. 1287 (7th Cir. 1985), the seller argued that risk passed under this provision when the bailee acknowledged to it, *to the seller,* that the goods had been transferred to the buyer's name and were now the buyer's property. The court, following the lead of several commentators, concluded otherwise. It held that subpart (b) requires an "acknowledgment" *to the buyer* for risk of loss to pass under this method. Of course, as the court itself acknowledged, this holding still leaves unanswered questions. When exactly does the risk pass under §2-509(2)(b)? Is it when a form of acknowledgment is sent to the buyer by the bailee or when it is received by the buyer? What if the acknowledgment is lost in the mail? What if the buyer becomes aware of the transfer to its name through some other reliable source prior to the acknowledgment? Does the risk pass then? The court in *Jason's Foods* noted these questions but wisely left them for another day as they were not raised by the case before it. So far no other case has come along to further test the waters.

27

When There Has Been a Breach

Introduction

The two previous chapters dealt with risk of loss problems under §2-509. We assumed throughout that there had been no breach or repudiation by either party. Once a breach by either Seller or Buyer has been established, we no longer look to §2-509 for the risk of loss allocation rules but turn instead to §2-510. That much is clear. This section has in fact been the subject of a fair amount of academic criticism. As one court has commented, "It is possible to conjure up a host of hypotheticals leading to seeming perverse results under §2-510. . . . The fact is, however," as the court went on to say, "that those courts considering it have had little difficulty in applying it as written." *Jakowski v. Carole Chevrolet, Inc.,* 180 N.J. Super. 122, 433 A.2d 841, 31 U.C.C. 1615 (1981). In the questions that follow I have tried to take a middle ground, exploring some of the questions left unresolved by the language of §2-510 without getting *too* academically perverse.

EXAMPLES

1. Mazie's Department Store, located in Capitol City, contracts to buy six gross of sweaters from Knits Incorporated, which is located in Boston. The price is agreed to as "$1200/gross F.O.B. Boston." Knits delivers cartons containing 850 sweaters to Tony's Trucking Service and arranges a contract for their delivery to Mazie. Knits receives a bill of lading from Tony's Trucking, which it immediately mails off to Mazie along with other details of the shipment. While on route, Tony's truck is caught in a flood. Many of the sweaters become waterlogged and their colors run. They arrive at Mazie's, but she declines to accept any of them.

a. Who bears the risk of loss?

b. Suppose instead that Knits had delivered a full six gross of sweaters (that's 864) to Tony's, but had failed to notify Mazie of the shipment. The first she knows of it is when the sweaters arrive in their sorry state at her store. She declines to accept any of them. Who bears the risk of loss?

c. Finally, suppose that Knits had delivered 864 sweaters to Tony's Trucking and had in addition given the proper notice to Mazie. Tony drives through rough country and stormy weather, but there is no major flood and his truck is never swamped with water. When the sweaters arrive, Mazie examines them and finds that the colors have run on a good number of them. Tony insists that his truck had stayed watertight throughout the trip and that the sweaters must have been like that to begin with. Mazie telephones Knits and complains that they included in the shipment a number of defective items. She intends to reject the whole shipment. The delivery manager at Knits responds that his records indicate that his firm shipped six gross of sweaters all of which met the contract specifications. He suggests that they must have gotten wet during shipment, whatever Tony may say. Assuming there is significant water damage to some of the sweaters, who bears this risk of loss?

2. Birmingham Integrated Machines, a computer manufacturer, contracts to buy 600,000 switches from Switcher International over the course of a year. Under the contract Switcher is to ship by rail 50,000 switches no later than the tenth day of each month during 1993. The contract gives the price as "$2 per switch F.O.B. Switcher Plant." Switcher delivers 49,000 switches to the railroad for delivery to BIM on January 8. It obtains a bill of lading and sends this bill with a notice of shipment to the buyer. The 49,000 switches are lost in a fire while en route. Who bears this risk of loss, Switcher or BIM?

3. Sam's Autorama is a retail automobile dealership. Sam contracts to sell a car to Betty. The contract provides that the car shall be treated with a special protective undercoating prior to delivery. Betty takes delivery of the car on Monday. On Tuesday she becomes aware that the car has not been given the undercoating as promised. She drives it back to Sam's. Sam acknowledges the problem and tells Betty to leave the car with him so that he can have the undercoating applied within a few days. Betty does leave the car with Sam.

a. That night, before any work is done on it, the car is stolen off of Sam's lot. Who bears the risk of loss for this theft?

b. Suppose instead that Sam does apply the undercoating on Monday afternoon. He telephones Betty and tells her that she can pick her car up at any time. Betty says she will come over the next day. The car is stolen sometime late on Monday night. How does this affect your risk of loss analysis?

c. Suppose that Betty had driven the car for two months prior to becoming aware that it had not been given the undercoating as promised. She returns the car to Sam, who agrees to remedy the defect, but before he can do anything the car is stolen from his lot. Who bears the risk of loss in this situation? Assume that Betty had insured the car against theft from the moment she picked it up at the dealership and that her insurance would cover this loss.

    d. If Betty does collect on her insurance because of this theft, can her insurance company then bring suit against Sam for the amount it has had to pay out?

4.   The wealthy Mr. Burns goes into the Sparkle Store, a jewelry retailer. He spots an emerald tie-pin the setting of which he much admires. He would like to buy such a pin, but only if it has a diamond in it. The owner of the store shows him a diamond of which Burns approves. Burns signs a contract to buy the pin, with the emerald replaced by this diamond, for a price of $25,000. The storeowner agrees to have the pin ready within a week and to call Burns when he can take delivery. The owner puts the diamond in the pin and calls Burns, who tells him, "I've decided I don't want the pin after all. Sorry." The owner puts the pin in her safe, intending to return it to a display case the following day if she can't get Burns to change his mind. That night it is part of a quantity of jewelry that is stolen by a thief or thieves unknown.

    a. Can the owner make Burns pay the $25,000 for the pin?

    b. Would your analysis of the situation in the previous question be any different if the theft had come more than a month after Burns first refused to take delivery of the pin?

EXPLANATIONS

1a. The risk at the time of water damage was on Knits. Since this was an "F.O.B. place of shipment" contract the risk for losses occurring in transit would normally be on the buyer, as we saw in the last chapter. Here, however, Mazie can point to §2-510(1). The tender failed to conform to the contract which called for six gross (864) sweaters. Knits shipped only 850. For the buyer to avoid the risk of loss under §2-510(1) there need not simply be a nonconformity in tender, but a nonconformity such "as to give a right of rejection." Could Mazie have rejected even a perfectly undamaged delivery of 850 units? Barring any other information we have to say yes under the perfect tender language of §2-601. (Knits, of course, might try to establish that the shipment did in fact meet the perfect tender standard of that section, perhaps because of an industry custom or a prior course of dealing. Such an argument may work, but it wouldn't be easy.) Under §2-510(1) the risk remained on the seller Knits "until cure or acceptance." Cure isn't relevant here since the goods were damaged before the buyer had a chance to reject them. And Mazie refused to accept any of the sweaters, as she had the right to do. Knits bears all the loss and is going to have to look to Tony, Tony's insurance, or its own insurance for some relief.

1b. Mazie would again argue under §2-510(1), but in this instance that subsection doesn't apply. Why? Look again at the last sentence in §2-504. Knits' failure to give notification is "a ground for rejection only if material loss or delay ensues." Well there was a subsequent loss, but it appears to be in no way tied to the lack of notice. Comment 6 to this section says that rejection by the buyer is "justified only when the seller's dereliction . . . in fact is followed by material delay or damage." I think what the drafters meant to say is that the seller's failure must at least to some degree have *contributed* to a subsequent delay or damage. If the shipment arrives at the same time and in the same condition it would have even if perfect notice had been sent and there has been no additional burden on the buyer, then I don't think the buyer could ever reject on what then seems like a pure technicality. If that is so, then Knits' failure to give notice in this instance would not in and of itself have been a ground for rejection by Mazie. Now go back to §2-510(1). It does not apply in this case because the nonconformity of tender or delivery, such as it was, did not "give a right of rejection" to Mazie.

Following this line of reasoning, the situation is thrown back into §2-509(2)(a). Fortunately for Mazie, as we saw in the last chapter there is at least one case which stands for the proposition that a seller's failure to give proper notice under §2-504 prevents the risk of loss from passing under a normal shipment contract. *Rheinberg-Kellerei GmbH v. Vineyard Wine Co. Inc.,* 53 N.C. App. 560, 281 S.E.2d 425, 32 U.C.C. 96 (1981). So there is a good chance the risk will be found to have been on Knits, but it's an argument not under §2-510 but rather §2-509.

1c. We really don't know who bears the risk of loss here. This question is designed to drive home the (fairly obvious) point that when a shipment arrives in poor shape it is often very difficult if not impossible to tell exactly what has happened. And when and where the damage occurred is of more than intellectual interest. If the sweaters were in poor condition before they left Knits' plant then Mazie need not accept them, obviously bears no responsibility for this damage (or even any other misfortune that happened to them along the way), and can refuse to pay a penny for them. She may even have a claim for substantial damages because of Knits' failure to perform on its contract. If, on the other hand, the sweaters were in good order when they left the plant but were damaged while in transit, then Mazie bears the risk of loss for this occurrence and must pay for them at the contract rate. Of course the issue here isn't just who has the bother of going against poor Tony, because if Tony has any argument that the sweaters were in bad shape to begin with he may not have to pay anything. It all depends on *what* happened *when,* and that's something even the most careful reading of the Code won't answer for us.

2.   Unless BIM can establish that the shipment of 49,000 switches when 50,000 were promised was a *substantial* nonconformity, it will bear the risk of loss. True the tender was defective, but now it has to be judged under §2-612(2). (See generally Chapter 22.) It may well be that the lack of even a fairly large number of units does not give the buyer the right under that subsection to reject the delivery. If that is so, BIM can't call in §2-510(1) as the nonconformity would not have given it a right to reject. Analyze the situation under §2-509 and you see BIM bears the

risk of loss during shipment. Of course, if Switcher had shipped only, say, 25,000 switches the substantial nonconformity would have given BIM as buyer the right to reject, §2-510(1) would apply, and the risk would have remained on the seller.

3a. Sam bears the risk of loss. This question is based on the *Jakowski* case cited at the beginning of the chapter. The court first ruled that the seller never accepted the car merely by taking possession of it for such a short time. There had been no "reasonable opportunity to inspect" under §2-606. Since there was a clear nonconformity which gave the buyer the right to reject, §2-510(1) applied and the risk remained on the seller until cure or acceptance. The defect had not been cured at the time of the theft nor, of course, had the auto been accepted. Risk of loss remained on seller.

What would have been the result if Sam, after being told of the defect, had told Betty to bring the car in "early next week" for the undercoating and it then had been stolen from Betty's garage over the weekend? The analysis is still the same and Sam bears that risk even though the car was in Betty's possession at the time of the loss. You can see that this risk of loss allocation gives Sam every motivation to get the defect cured and the auto accepted by his buyer as soon as possible.

3b. Sam now has an argument that the risk was on Betty at the time of the theft. Section 2-510(1) says the risk will remain on him until "cure or acceptance." He also can point to the last sentence of Comment 1 which says, "The seller's privilege of cure does not shift the risk, however, until the cure is *completed*." He says cure had been effectively completed as of the close of business on Monday.

Sam's argument is very neat and tidy, but the result just doesn't make sense. Once the cure has been completed and a nondefective car is on Sam's lot waiting to be picked up by Betty, shouldn't the situation be just like that under §2-509(3)? Why should the seller be better off because it has taken him two tries to tender a conforming vehicle? If the analogy to §2-509(3) is right, then because Sam is a merchant the risk would be on him until Betty took receipt, that is, physical possession of the car. I know of no case where the facts are as I have posed them here, but I can't help believing the buyer would win on this one.

3c. Betty bears the risk of loss. After a couple of months it would be pretty hard for her to argue that she had never accepted the car. She could, of course, argue that this substantial nonconformity gave her the right to revoke acceptance. If she can and does rightfully revoke acceptance, the risk of loss is governed by §2-510(2). The buyer can treat the risk of loss as having rested on seller from the beginning only "to the extent of any deficiency of his [or her] effective insurance coverage." Betty has effective insurance coverage for this loss, so the risk which was transferred to her with her acceptance stays with her. Betty's insurance carrier pays for the loss.

3d. No, her insurance company may not go against Sam. See the last part of Comment 3. Under this provision of Article 2 the risk *really was* on Betty at the time of the theft and not on Sam. Betty legally suffered the loss and her insurance made it up. Betty had no rights against Sam, so her insurance carrier does not have any either. If the carrier wants to be reimbursed for its outlay, it is going to have to find the thief and go against him or her.

4a. Burns would have to pay the Sparkle Store for the bauble, but only if this loss was not covered by the store's own insurance. Under §2-510(3)

> Where the buyer as to conforming goods already identified to the contract for sale repudiates or is otherwise in breach before risk of their loss has passed to him, the seller may to the extent of any deficiency in his effective insurance coverage treat the risk of loss as resting on the buyer for a commercially reasonable time.

Here the goods were identified and the buyer repudiated, so the subsection's rule governs. If Sparkle isn't insured for this loss, the risk will be on Burns for a "commercially reasonable time" following his repudiation. The discussion of the next question will delve more deeply into how that phrase should be applied in the situation, but it's doubtful that the time wouldn't run at least for a day or so. Of course this is a diamond, and a court might rule that for a merchant like this to leave such a valuable and thief-tempting object such as this uninsured for even one night was unreasonable. If by the time of the theft it had already been returned to the display case alongside all of the other stuff for sale, it could well be that a court would reason it should have as of that moment been insured just like the rest of her inventory of precious gems.

It's hard to imagine that the seller in this instance, the Sparkle Store, would not have effective insurance coverage for any and all jewelry on its premises regardless of their contract status, but there will be other circumstances where the seller's insurance will not cover and the repudiating buyer must bear the risk. An example that is often cited is *Multiplastics, Inc. v. Arch Industries, Inc.*, 166 Conn. 280, 348 A.2d 618, 14 U.C.C. 573 (1974). Arch Industries contracted to buy 40,000 pounds of brown polystyrene pellets from Multiplastics, agreeing to accept delivery at the rate of 1,000 pounds per day after production of the pellets was complete. Multiplastics produced the pellets but Arch refused to issue release orders that would have signalled the seller to start delivery of the pellets, even after several requests that it do so. On August 18 Multiplastics sent Arch a letter stating that it had already held the pellets in storage for 40 days and that "we cannot warehouse these products indefinitely, and request that you send us shipping instructions." By August 20, and with the help of several phone calls, the seller had gotten the buyer's agreement that it would soon issue the release orders, but in fact it never did so. On September 22 the Multiplastics plant, containing all of the pellets, was destroyed by fire. Its fire insurance did not cover the loss of the pellets. The court concluded that Arch the buyer had been in breach as of the date of the fire. Since it also concluded that a commercially reasonable time had not passed since the breach (see Example 4b), the risk of loss was on the buyer. Multiplastics was entitled to recover the contract price from Arch.

4b. Even if the Sparkle Store did not have insurance covering this loss, it seems pretty clear that "a commercially reasonable time" would have passed and that under §2-510(3) it would have to bear this risk. I think it's fair to say that retail jewelers don't have diamonds hanging around their stores for months without insuring against their loss. At least I hope for their sake that this is so.

In the *Multiplastics* case, as I mentioned above, the court ruled that a commercially reasonable amount of time had not passed between the repudiation or breach, which it took as occurring on August 20, and the loss of the pellets in the fire of September 22.

> The time limitation in [§2-510(3)] is designed to enable the seller to obtain the additional requisite insurance coverage. [T]he trial court found that the defendant repeatedly agreed to transmit delivery instructions and that the pellets were specifically made to fill the defendant's order. Under those circumstances, it was reasonable for the plaintiff to believe that the goods would soon be taken off its hands and so to forgo procuring the needed insurance.

This court suggests that the reason for the time limitation here is to give the seller a chance to get insurance coverage, at least once it becomes apparent that the goods won't be taken off its hands by this particular buyer. Another explanation for the limitation is that it encourages the seller to *try* to get the goods off of its hands by selling them to *someone* even if it isn't this buyer. There's no particularly good reason for the seller simply to hold on to the goods, pining away because this buyer won't take them. Better that he or she should get on with life and reintroduce the goods back into the stream of commerce with no undue delay. With specially manufactured brown polystyrene pellets, of course, there may be reason to hold on to the hope the buyer for whom they were produced will eventually agree to take them. With diamond jewelry, I'd say get it back on display as soon as possible. And again, once it is on display for sale to the general public, it would seem that the risk of its loss has reverted to the seller.

PART FIVE

Remedies

28

Seller's Remedies

This chapter deals with seller's remedies, and the following chapter deals with buyer's. There's no reason for this order except that one of the two topics had to come before the other. You should feel free to take up Chapter 29 first if in your studies you are starting with buyer's remedies, and come back to this one later.

When the Buyer Breaches

Buyers are not necessarily bad people. They do, however, now and then for one reason or another breach or repudiate their contractually binding agreements. What can the individual seller whose rights have been trampled upon in this way do about it? At least the question of where to start looking for answers is easy enough. The drafters of Article 2 provide in §2-703 what they themselves characterize in a comment as "an index section which gathers together in one convenient place all of the various remedies open to a seller for any breach by a buyer." After that kind of billing, it only makes sense for us to start out this chapter by quoting the section in its entirety.

§2-703. Seller's Remedies in General
Where the buyer wrongfully rejects or revokes acceptance of goods or fails to make a payment due on or before a delivery or repudiates with respect to a part or the whole, then with respect to any goods directly affected and, if the breach is of the whole contract (Section 2-612), then also with respect to the whole undelivered balance, the aggrieved seller may

(a) withhold delivery of such goods;
(b) stop delivery by any bailee as hereafter provided (Section 2-705);
(c) proceed under the next section [§2-704] respecting goods still unidentified to the contract;
(d) resell and recover damages as hereafter provided (Section 2-706);
(e) recover damages for nonacceptance (Section 2-708) or in a proper case the price (Section 2-709);
(f) cancel.

It's important to note that the section carries no requirement that the seller pick one and only one of these responses. As Comment 1 explains, "Whether the pursuit of one remedy bars another depends entirely on the facts of the individual case."

Indeed, just about everything depends on the facts of the individual case. What remedy (or remedies) will be at all desirable or of any interest to the seller, which one(s) will be available to him or her under Article 2, and just what result can be expected if any one remedial route is pursued, all depend on the state of things at the time of breach or repudiation and how the story develops as the parties react each to the other. For one thing, what is the condition of the goods at the moment of repudiation or breach? Are they even in existence? If so, have they been identified to the contract? If they do exist, they must exist somewhere. Where, in whose possession, are the goods? Are they held by the seller, the buyer, or some third party like a carrier or a warehouse? And then, of course, there's the question of payment. How much was the buyer supposed to pay and when? How much has been paid as of the time when seller decides to take remedial action? In this chapter we will assume that an agreement between the parties created a valid contract enforceable against the buyer and that the buyer's subsequent actions amounted to a breach or a repudiation of that agreement. Beyond that we have to be open to the full range of situations and possibilities.

To start, we should acknowledge that in some circumstances the most understandable response is for a seller to do nothing. If the seller has not yet produced any goods under the contract or still has all of the goods that have been produced under its control, sometimes the easiest thing is just to take the repudiation or breach as the end of the story and go peddle the goods elsewhere. The options (a) and (f) of §2-703 quoted above support the seller if that is what it chooses to do. A buyer who has repudiated or breached cannot be heard to complain if the goods are not later delivered when, where, and as the contract initially called for. Look at the definition of *cancellation* in §2-106(4). The cancelling seller retains any additional remedies available under the Code, but there's no law that says it must pursue any of them. Sometimes the best course is to forgive if not necessarily forget.* Remember, a buyer may breach a contract in

---

*As a practical matter, of course, an aggrieved seller may have other ways outside of recourse to the legal system, all perfectly legal in themselves, of responding to a

good faith and for perfectly understandable reasons, even if they don't rise to the level of legal excuse. Sellers have been known to show a streak of human kindness and sympathy. On the other hand, a seller can be hopping mad but retain just enough objectivity to recognize that pursuing legal remedy in the particular situation would be fruitless or more trouble than it could possibly be worth. An aggrieved seller will choose between the various options open to it taking into account a whole variety of factors.

There follows a short textual review of two possibilities open to the seller under Article 2 which involve a kind of recapture of the goods, either of which is available only in a narrow range of circumstances. We then turn to the final introductory section and the questions and analysis to the core remedy of monetary damages. We ask, as the seller would no doubt ask us, what must be shown in order to recover a given measure of relief, and (not to beat around the bush) exactly *how much* money are we talking about here?

If you are now studying or primarily interested in only monetary relief (as I would guess would be particularly true for most students in the introductory Contracts course), you should feel free to skip the following two sections of text and go right to the final section introducing the questions.

If Buyer Becomes Insolvent

Article 2 provides the seller with some limited protection in the event of the buyer's insolvency. Look at the definition of *insolvent* given in §1-

---

buyer's breach. Seller may conclude that the breach is sufficiently egregious to warrant never dealing with this particular buyer again, or certainly not giving any special favors in the future. Seller may even have a few choice words that he or she shares with others in the commercial community about how the buyer seems to do business. And would you want to be the buyer applying for membership to the business association or country club on whose board the aggrieved seller sits? There is good reason to believe, as you may have discussed in your Contracts course, that such "extra-judicial" sanctions can have a bigger part to play in how actual business parties think about breach than do the exact requirements of a legal regime like that laid out in Article 2. We'll stick with the legal ramifications of breach, however, which are more than enough for us to handle.

201(23). The buyer's business is going south. There is a good possibility that the seller, if it has sold on general unsecured credit, is never going to get paid or at least not paid anything like the full purchase price for any goods delivered. When all the dust has settled a general creditor may well get something like ten cents on the dollar, and should probably count itself fortunate if it gets that much.* Obviously what the seller would like to do in such a situation, if it finds out about it in time, is to extricate itself from the whole mess by preventing delivery of the goods to the buyer or, if they have already been delivered, simply taking them back.

The buyer's insolvency, of course, is not in and of itself a breach, but it can be just as worrisome to the seller, if not more so. If the seller wants to be overly technical about things, it may be able to turn the events into a breach by invoking the insecurity mechanism of §2-609 and letting things ripen under that section into a repudiation (see Chapter 21). Practically, the smart thing is to move as soon as possible. Section 2-702 outlines the moves that the seller may take. Under §2-705(1), if the goods have not yet been delivered, the seller may upon discovering the buyer's insolvency "refuse delivery except for cash including payment for all goods theretofore delivered under the contract, and stop delivery under this Article." We'll deal with §2-705 and stoppage in transit in the following section.

What if the seller has *already* delivered the goods? Subsection (2) provides some chance that the seller may *reclaim* them, that is, actually take them back. This reclamation right is limited, as you can see. First of all, it applies only when the buyer "has received goods on credit while insolvent." If the buyer becomes insolvent even a short time after receipt of the goods, there is no reclamation right and the seller gets to stand in line with the other people owed cash, waiting for whatever payout eventually comes its way. Secondly, in order to invoke this right, the seller must make demand (except in the very unusual situation where the time limit is waived) within ten days of the buyer's receipt of the goods.

These express statutory criteria would seem stringent enough, but recently a court has added another layer of problem for the seller which hopes to exercise reclamation rights under this section. In *Tate Cheese Co., Inc. v. Crofton and Sons, Inc.*, 139 Bankr. 567, 17 U.C.C.2d 782 (Bankr. M.D. Fla. 1992), the court found that technical compliance with the two timing requirements was not enough under §2-702(2). In addition the seller was responsible for vigorously following up on its reclamation demand and actually getting the stuff back. This decision

---

*If the seller has had the foresight and the bargaining position to sell on so-called secured credit, reserving what is characterized in the U.C.C.'s Article 9 as a purchase money security interest, and is careful to "perfect" that interest, then the chances of coming out of the situation more or less whole will be greatly improved. But this is all for your course in Secured Transactions, and speaks again to why you will want to study that subject sometime soon if you have not already done so.

was undoubtedly influenced by the nature of the goods involved. Tate Cheese Co., the seller, had delivered almost $11,000 worth of cheese to the buyer. As it turned out, the buyer was insolvent at the time of the delivery and the seller made a demand well within the ten days either to be paid immediately or for the return of the cheese. The buyer did not respond. Eight months later the seller had done nothing more to get its cheese back. The bankruptcy court ruled that the time had long passed for the seller to be asserting its reclamation right. "Reclamation," the court stated, "is not a self-executing remedy. . . . It was incumbent on Tate to pursue the reclamation demand through appropriate judicial channels." Further, as the court pointed out:

> Diligent assertion of any reclamation right was particularly important in the instant case. It sought to reclaim cheese which is, of course, a perishable foodstuff. It is incomprehensible to the court that Tate made a written reclamation demand and then just sat on its rights for nearly eight months. . . . Had Tate been interested in regaining possession of the cheese, it should have sought judicial intervention rather than letting almost eight months elapse before pursuing reclamation of its perishable cheese. Tate is asking this court to establish a rule that a reclaiming seller can make a written reclamation demand and then wait for an unlimited period of time before enlisting judicial assistance in regaining possession of the reclamation goods. The court declines to do so under the circumstances of this case.

So, at least according to this decision, the credit seller's right of reclamation begins with an appropriate demand but doesn't end there.

Section 2-702(2) provides reclamation rights only to the seller who has delivered goods on credit. What about the unpaid seller in a *cash* sale? Your first question, perfectly reasonably, is how a cash seller could even end up in this predicament. If the seller sells for cash and is careful enough to inspect the good old American greenbacks handed over at the moment of delivery, what could go wrong? The answer to this riddle has to do with the modern practice of using personal checks in so many situations. Under Article 2 payment by check is perfectly appropriate in the run-of-the-mill cash sale. See §2-511 and the Comments thereto. The unfortunate thing is that sometimes—brace yourself—checks bounce. And we're left with a cash seller who has delivered the goods and yet has not been paid.

While it is not spelled out in so many words in §2-507(2), this subsection is read in conjunction with §2-511 as giving the unpaid cash seller in such a situation a right to reclaim the goods. You see, in §2-507(2) we are told that the buyer's "right to retain" the goods is conditional upon its making the payment due. If the payment is by a check that is dishonored upon presentment at buyer's bank, the buyer has no right to retain the goods as against the seller. Therefore it must follow that the seller can reclaim them. The courts have recognized this reclamation right of the unpaid cash seller. Unfortunately, due in large part to the original language of Comment 3 to §2-507, many times the courts would then go on to import wholesale the requirement for demand within ten days of delivery, which we've seen as part of the statute in §2-702, into the unpaid cash seller situation. The fact that there was no ten-day limit set forth in §2-507 didn't seem to matter. The result was unfortunate, as I say, because in some instances as you can imagine the seller would not become aware that the check had been dishonored and that it wasn't going to be paid until sometime more than ten days after delivery. The upshot was in some situations to deny the unpaid seller any or all right to reclaim the goods for failure to meet a strict ten-day rule found nowhere in the relevant sections. This hardly seemed fair. In March 1990 the Permanent Editorial Board sprang into action with a recommended revision of Comment 3 to §2-507. This should be the version of the Comment you have in your copy of the Code. Read it and see that the P.E.B. now expressly discourages any idea that a "specific time limit" applies to a claim for reclamation made under these circumstances.*

There has actually been a good deal of litigation in recent years involving the reclamation rights of someone who's sold to an insolvent buyer, but there's usually little dispute about whether the seller has such rights against the buyer. Rather, the cases have had to confront how this reclamation right stacks up against rights in the goods which are being asserted by other third parties, each of whom is anxious to get its hands on just about anything of value that the buyer holds as it sinks unceremoniously into bankruptcy. These may include people who claim to have bought the goods or a portion of them from the buyer. They think they should be able to just spirit the goods off and walk away from all the squabbling. Others who may legitimately claim an interest in the same bundle of goods include the trustee in bankruptcy, who is responsible for taking over control of the buyer's assets and using them to pay off debts in a prescribed way, and other creditors who may themselves assert a security interest in the goods which would, if found valid, arguably give them first dibs on the particular chunk of property. It can get to be quite a scene. These interesting issues of just how the seller's reclamation rights arising under Article 2 stack up against other rights asserted in the goods must necessarily wait until you study Article 9 in all of its rousing detail. You should expect the topic to be dealt with in your course on Secured Transactions.

Stoppage in Transit

As we saw in the prior section, a seller who is in the process of delivering goods to a buyer when it discovers the buyer to be insolvent has the right

---

*If you find yourself really getting into this matter, you can look for a copy of P.E.B. Commentary No. 1, dated March 10, 1990, which goes into the problem in more detail and sets forth the P.E.B.'s recommendation. P.E.B. Commentaries are found in many of the massive paperback editions of the Code, one of which you are probably using. If not, your reference librarian should be able to help you find the Commentaries in another Code source book. Happy hunting.

under §2-702(1) to stop delivery of the goods under §2-705. When you look at §2-705(1) you see that the right to stop delivery of goods in the possession of a carrier also extends to the seller who receives a repudiation from the buyer, or who does not receive a payment due before delivery, or who can assert any other right to withhold delivery as long as the seller is careful to stop delivery in "carload, truckload, planeload or larger shipments." (This last criterion was added in sympathy for the carriers. See Comment 1.) Subsection (2) gives a list of events that will serve to terminate the seller's power to stop delivery. Subsection (3) sets forth the procedure which the seller must follow to exercise this option. If a seller has the right to and does properly stop the delivery in midstream this is not the end of the story, of course. The goods are hung up somewhere and the seller is going to have to decide what to do with them and how to proceed further if at all against the buyer. As Comment 6 to this section points out, "After an effective stoppage under this section the seller's rights in the goods are the same as if he had never made a delivery." Seller's rights may be the same, but notice that its practical situation can be all the more trying: The goods are not directly in its possession, but are being held by some carrier or other bailee who is going to be more than anxious to drop them off somewhere, make delivery to someone, collect its fee, and be done with them.

When Seller Goes for the Money

Whether or not the seller has been able to withhold delivery before it even gets started, stop delivery somewhere in transit, or even reclaim goods that were delivered right into the hands of the buyer, just keeping the buyer from possession is not necessarily enough of a remedy for the buyer's repudiation or breach. In many cases it's going to take some amount of money, either voluntarily ceded by the buyer or extracted by judicial process, to make the seller whole. We now turn to the ways in which a seller may seek and be awarded monetary damages under the Code. Article 2 gives a variety of potential measures for seller's damages depending on the facts of the particular case. The first with which we'll deal is the possibility in a limited set of circumstances that the seller can recover the full contract price from the buyer under §2-709. At other times, the seller may resell the goods under §2-706 and, once it has done so, recover a "contract price minus resale price" differential under that section. If seller has no right to the contract price and if there has not been a §2-706 resale, we are next to look at §2-708(1) for the standard measure of damages. You'll recognize here the traditional "contract minus market" measure with which you no doubt dealt in Contracts class. In some cases, as we will see, the seller can argue for a greater measure under the authority of §2-708(2). The seller may also sue for and receive incidental damages in the appropriate circumstances as measured by

§2-710. We'll work our way through these sections in the Examples and Explanations.*

EXAMPLES

1.   Sparkle Plenty owns and operates a jewelry store. Bernie Bigbucks comes into the store and contracts to buy a large emerald ring which she has on display. The contract price is $12,000. It is agreed that Sparkle will have the ring delivered to Bernie's home the next day and that he will pay the full contract price within a week after that. Sparkle has one of her employees deliver the ring as agreed. She hears nothing for the next month, nor does she receive a check from Bernie.

a.   Does she have a valid claim against him for the price of $12,000? Would it make any difference to your answer if it could be shown that the emerald in the ring was not of the size which Sparkle had claimed it to be at the time of sale but actually one-half carat smaller?

b.   Suppose instead that the day after the ring, which is in fact of the correct size, is delivered to Bernie, he calls Sparkle and says, "I have decided against buying the ring. It strikes me as a bit much and it doesn't look good with my new jeans. You can have one of your people come around and pick it up any time that is convenient for you." Would Sparkle be within her rights in just leaving the ring with Bernie and suing him for the full purchase price?

c.   Finally, suppose that the day after Sparkle had the ring delivered, she called Bernie to be sure that he had received and was happy with his purchase. He tells her, "Yes. I have the ring and love it. I'm wearing it right now. I doubt I'll ever take it off." Four days later, however, and before he has made any payment to her, he calls singing a different tune. "I find myself not at all happy with this purchase. I don't want the ring after all. Come and pick it up." In this situation would Sparkle have the right to sue for the price?

2.   Meanwhile, in another part of town, Bernie Bigbucks goes to Sam the tailor and is fitted for a new suit that is to be made to his order. He picks out an expensive green plaid material. Sam is to be paid $1,000 for the completed suit.

a.   Later that day, before Sam has begun work on the suit, Bernie calls and repudiates this agreement. If Sam sues Bernie for the $1,000 price, what result?

b.   Suppose instead that Bernie does not repudiate, but that Sam orders the fabric needed and completes initial work piecing together

---

*Section 2-718(1) allows the parties to a contract of sale to agree to a liquidation of damages provision which will be enforceable in certain but not all circumstances. While in theory this provision could be relevant to a seller's damages as much as to a buyer's, I've somewhat arbitrarily decided to deal with it in the next chapter. Look for it there.

the suit. Bernie comes in for a fitting. He takes one look at himself in the mirror and says, "No, no, this won't do. I don't like the looks of this at all. Forget about it." He rushes out of the store, leaving Sam holding the uncompleted garment. Under these facts can Sam sue Bernie for the full purchase price with any hope of success? What should Sam do with the partially completed green plaid suit for the time being? Would he be within his rights in eventually giving it away to charity, ripping it apart for scraps, or wearing it himself?

3. In early February Arnold Moneybucks contracts to buy an original oil painting ("The Virtues of Capitalism") for $1700 from Stella's art gallery, Arnold's pick-up and payment to come when the artist's showing at Stella's has closed at the end of the month. On February 15, Stella receives a letter from Arnold saying that he no longer "agrees to take the painting."

a. Later that day Stella sells the painting to another of her clients who had previously shown interest in this artist's work for $1,250. Stella sues Arnold for the $450 difference. Does Article 2 make Arnold automatically pay this amount?

b. Suppose instead that Stella had held onto the painting and included it with a group that she presented at auction in March. The painting goes for $1,125 at the auction. Stella sues Arnold for the $1,700 minus $1,125 or $575. What other facts would you want to know in order to determine whether she has the right to this amount?

c. If the painting had instead fetched $1,800 at the art auction, would Arnold have any claim against Stella for $100? Does Arnold have any claim to the painting?

4. At the end of the salmon catching season, one large fishery, Salmons of Seattle, has on hand a great quantity of processed frozen salmon fillets. On August 1 it contracts to sell a large quantity of these fillets to Better Foods of Boise, Idaho for a price of "$2 per pound F.O.B. Boise." Delivery is to be made by rail on or before August 21, and payment is to be made within 30 days of the buyer's receipt. On August 4, before the shipment has been delivered to the railroad, Better Foods contacts Salmons and repudiates the agreement. Additional facts that you may (or may not) need to answer this question follow:

Market price of fillets at Boise on August 1	$2.04
Market price at Seattle on August 1	$1.54
Market price at Boise on August 4	$1.92
Market price at Seattle on August 4	$1.40
Market price at Boise on August 21	$1.14
Market price at Seattle on August 21	$1.00
Cost of shipping from Seattle to Boise	$.05

a. If Salmons sues Better Foods claiming damages under §2-708(1), what amount should it receive?

b. What if instead the price had been agreed to as "$1.98 F.O.B. Seattle?"

c. Assume that the price was "$2 F.O.B. Boise" but that Better Foods did *not* repudiate but instead rejected the shipment for no good reason when it arrived in Boise on August 20. To what would Salmons of Seattle be entitled under §2-708(1)?

d. Continuing on with the situation as in Example 4c, suppose that Better Foods could demonstrate that upon hearing of the rejection Salmons had very quickly been able to arrange sale of the shipment to another buyer, Very Best of Boise, for $1.30 per pound and that Salmons's only additional cost for making this sale was an agency fee of $.03 per pound. Should Salmons still be entitled to sue for and be awarded the amount you calculated in answer to Example 4c? Assuming Better Foods concedes its liability for breach of contract, what argument could it make that Salmons is due less under Article 2?

5. Hacker has a used personal computer, the B.I.M. PS/1, that she plans to replace with a newer model. She posts a "For Sale" notice on a bulletin board at her local laundromat describing the computer and stating an asking price of $400. The notice catches the eye of Billy, who comes to inspect the machine and offers her $350 for it. Hacker accepts this offer. Billy says he will come back the next week with the money. Hacker removes the notice from the laundromat. The following Monday, Billy calls and tells her he has not been able to come up with the money and that he will not be buying the computer. Hacker places a new notice on the bulletin board, again asking $400. A month later Hacker is contacted by someone who has seen her notice and who offers to buy the machine for $350. If Hacker accepts this offer, what rights will she have against Billy? If Hacker doesn't accept this offer, what is her position?

6. Meanwhile, Hacker is looking for that new computer of her dreams. She sees a demonstration model of the brand new H.A.L. Super 2000 at Steve's Computer City. She contracts to buy a Super 2000 for $5,000, which Steve will deliver to her from the first shipment he gets of the new machines from the H.A.L. Corporation. When Steve gets this shipment, he immediately marks one of the boxes containing a single Super 2000 with the label "For Hacker." He contacts Hacker and tells her that the machine is ready for her to pay for and pick up. Hacker tells him that she has decided not to buy the Super 2000, but is instead looking to buy an even newer machine (the G.Z.K. Magnum Pro), which she hears will be coming out on the market soon. Steve takes the box he had marked for Hacker, removes the label, and puts it in his store room. Within two months he has sold this machine to another buyer (Headly) for $5,000.

a. If Steve sues Hacker for breach of her contract to purchase, to what measure of damages is he entitled under Article 2? Assume Steve paid the H.A.L. Corporation $3,200 for this machine. Furthermore, Steve's accountant tells him that based on his past year's business activity his net profit—after taking into account general overhead costs (rent, advertising, salaries, taxes, and so on)—comes out as equal to approximately ten percent of his total sales.

b. Would your answer to the previous question be any different if it were established that the H.A.L. Super 2000 is such a popular computer when it is first introduced that the manufacturer cannot keep up with nationwide demand and has to allocate only so many of the computers to each of its regular distributors? Steve is able to order and receive delivery of only 120 of the Super 2000's during the first year it is produced, all of which he quickly sells.

c. Assume instead that there is a plentiful supply of H.A.L. Super 2000 computers and that Steve can get delivery of as many as he wants. However, you also have the additional fact that Hacker ends up contracting for and taking delivery of a G.Z.K. Magnum Pro from Steve, for which she pays $6,000. Does Steve have any right to substantial damages against Hacker under these facts? What more would you like to know?

7. Nobs Chemical Corporation is a company that buys and sells large quantities of industrial chemicals. It entered into a contract to buy all of its requirements of cumene (a chemical used as an additive to gasoline) from a Brazilian Supplier for the price of $400 a ton. It then went about looking for buyers of cumene in the United States. Nobs contracted to sell 1,000 tons of the chemical to the Koppers Company for delivery in the United States at a price of $540 a ton. Nobs expected to spend approximately $45 per ton transporting the chemical from Brazil to the buyer's place of business. Before Nobs actually purchased any cumene from its supplier for shipment to Koppers, that company repudiated saying that it wanted none of the stuff. At the time of the breach the market price of cumene in the United States had fallen to $265 a ton, and the price continued at this low level up to the time when delivery to Koppers would have been made. Nobs sues Koppers for $275,000 relying upon §2-708(1).

a. Can you see an argument for the defendant buyer that even assuming it was liable for breach it should be liable for less than Nobs is claiming? Should this argument work?

b. Assume that in addition to the facts given above, the Nobs Chemical Corporation is able to show that because of Koppers' repudiation it ended up buying only 3,000 tons of cumene from its Brazilian supplier instead of 4,000. Since the price under its supply contract was determined by its total orders during a calendar year, Nobs had been forced to pay an additional $25 a ton for each of the 3,000 tons it did buy from the supplier for delivery to another of its customers. Can Nobs recover this additional $75,000 ($25 times 3,000) from Koppers in its breach of contract suit?

EXPLANATIONS

1a. Sparkle has a good action for the price against Bernie under §2-709(1)(a). Having received delivery of the goods and not having given a notification of rejection after all this time, Bernie has accepted them.

(Recall §2-606(1)(b) and the lengthy discussion of how acceptance occurs in Chapter 18.) As Comments 2 and 6 to §2-709 make clear, Article 2 treats the action for the price as an extraordinary remedy for the seller, something roughly analogous to specific performance for the buyer, not generally available but limited only to one of three situations. Note also the admonition in §2-703(e) that the seller can recover the price only "in the proper case." The one clearest case is that where the buyer has accepted the goods. (You will recall the prime directive of §2-607(1) that, "The buyer must pay at the contract rate for any goods accepted.")

The second situation where the seller is allowed an action for the price is where the buyer fails to pay the price as it becomes due and conforming goods have been "lost or damaged within a commercially reasonable time after risk of their loss has passed to the buyer." Risk of loss, as you will remember, got a whole part of this book to itself (Part IV) and will not be dealt with here. The third class of cases in which an action for the price may lie are those covered by §2-709(1)(b), which will come up soon enough in questions to follow.

If it were to be shown that the goods were nonconforming, that is, that the emerald was too small, it would *not* change the result—Sparkle could still sue for the price. A buyer is perfectly able to, and often does, accept nonconforming goods intentionally or otherwise. An action for the price lies for any goods accepted, whether they were conforming or nonconforming and whether they *could have been* rejected. If the goods are accepted they must be paid for at the contract rate. Of course, if the ring tendered and accepted did turn out to be nonconforming, and if Bernie still has time to give notice of the nonconformity as required under §2-607(3)(a), then he could make a counterclaim for damages arising from this breach. Any damages proven by Bernie as an aggrieved buyer would be subtracted from what Sparkle is owed on the price, reducing the ultimate award to her, but they do not defeat the basic principle that she is entitled to be pay for the ring and paid according to the contract price.

1b. No. Sparkle can decide not to retake possession of the ring, but she'd be a fool to do so as she will not have an action for the price against Bernie. Here Bernie has attempted rejection and it appears that his actions meets the criteria of §2-602. The rejection may be *wrongful*, in that Bernie had no right to reject and hence by doing so has put himself in breach, but it procedurally fits the bill and hence is considered an *effective* rejection, meaning that it averts an acceptance. In the general case where the goods are effectively rejected and could be resold—and we have to believe this is so of an emerald ring—the seller has no right to sue for the price. The aggrieved seller will have to take back the goods if they are not at the time of rejection in his or her possession and seek a monetary remedy against the buyer via one of the other routes we will explore later. See subsection (3). The justification that is usually given for this result (and which does seem to make a lot of sense) is that even if the seller is the aggrieved party he or she is typically, as someone engaged in the sale of goods of this type, in a better position to make an effective and efficient resale than is the buyer.

1c. The result here is open to dispute. Bernie initially accepted the goods (here under §2-606(1)(a)) and later attempted a revocation of acceptance (under §2-608). There's no doubt that the attempted revocation is not justified in the situation and is *wrongful*; the question is whether it is *effective* and actually works to "undo" the initial acceptance and all the results that flowed therefrom (including triggering the seller's right to an action for the price). As we saw in the discussion of the previous question, the Article 2 drafters plainly contemplated and allowed for a wrongful rejection that is nevertheless effective. But is there such a thing as a wrongful yet effective revocation of acceptance?

Bits and pieces of the Code and Comments can be read to support either side of this debate. Section 2-608(1) gives the conditions under which a buyer "may" revoke his or her acceptance, which suggests that there are times when he or she may not. Saying someone *may not* do something, however, is not the same (careful readers of English will observe) as saying he or she *cannot*. But then §2-607(2) speaks to at least one circumstance in which the buyer actually "cannot" revoke. Returning to §2-709 itself, subsection (3) can be read as anticipating a case of wrongful revocation. It depends on what the word "wrongfully" qualifies: Is it just the immediately following "rejected" or is it the follow- ing phrase "rejected or revoked?" But then Comment 5 to the section says that accepted goods include "only goods as to which there has been no *justified* revocation of acceptance," which suggests that if there has been an attempted revocation which is unjustified or wrongful, then the goods remain accepted and an action for the price would still lie. All in all, the text of Article 2 and the Comments do not resolve the issue.

We can then ask what *policy* would favor. This all depends, of course, on the policy you want to focus on. Some have suggested that there should be room for an effective, albeit wrongful, rejection under Article 2, because after all there definitely is the possibility of an effective wrongful rejection, and the drafters seemed to favor a policy of treating rejections and revocations in a parallel fashion. Note, in this regard, §2-608(3). The wrongful revoker is no more or less a villain than the wrongful rejecter under this view and should be treated no more harshly. Is this persuasive?

Other policies can be teased out of Article 2 which may argue in the other direction. Recall (from Chapter 20) that the drafters made revoca- tion under §2-608 a more difficult road for the buyer than rejection by adding a number of criteria. This suggests they had in mind at least some reason to treat the two possible behaviors (rejection and revocation) differently and, in particular, to discourage (or is that too strong a word?) revocations to some greater extent. If so, there would be no better way of cutting down on the number of wrongful revocations than by having a rule that tells the buyer that if his or her revocation turns out not to meet the substantive as well as procedural criteria of §2-608 it will simply be ineffective. You, as a wrongfully revoking buyer, will still be left with the goods and the obligation to pay the full price for them.

Finally, we can examine the policy behind the unquestioned result in the rejection situation (i.e., that even the wrongfully rejecting buyer is not subject to an action for the price) and see if it works equally well in the revocation case. A number of commentators have made the point that, while the facts in each case will differ, by and large the goods have been in the possession of buyer for a longer period where a revocation is being attempted. They're more like used goods than new goods. If withholding the action for the price in the case of an unjustified rejection is grounded on a belief that generally the seller continues to be in a better position to resell the goods than is the buyer, does the same hold true for goods which have been accepted but for which the buyer is at a later stage trying to revoke? It has been argued that this distinction is reason enough to allow the action for the price to the seller where the buyer unjustifiably revokes even if it is clearly not available where the buyer unjustifiably rejects. Of course, in the particular question we are dealing with this argument may not seem so persuasive. It's one thing to think of new and used goods being very much different and moving in distinct markets in the general context (does the typical hardware store deal in *used* tools and plumbing fixtures?) but it's not so clear that would be true in the case of fine jewelry and gems.

On the question of what the courts have done with the wrongfully revoking buyer and an action for the price, the answer is that few if any cases seem even to acknowledge the problem, much less confront it as squarely as a court would be bound to do if my hypothetical were actually before it. There is, as you will recall, a great deal of "play" for the court on whether what the parties are arguing about should even be analyzed as a rejection or a revocation. And even if the court decides to take it on as a revocation case, there is a good deal of latitude under §2-608 for determining whether in any given situation the revocation was in fact justified and was in fact carried out with procedural precision. Courts, as you are no doubt aware, sometimes get to work around or avoid problems in ways that your typical law student can't.

2a. Sam has no action for the price here. There is no argument that the goods have been accepted or that the risk of loss on them had passed to Bernie, and hence there is nothing for Sam in §2-709(1)(a). Section 2-709(1)(b) requires that the goods be identified to the contract. That hasn't happened here. This exhausts the possibilities for a valid action for the price. Read Comment 6.

Could Sam just order the fabric if he does not already have it on hand and make up the suit? He could then identify the suit to the contract when it was finished and bring an action for the price under §2-709(1)(b). No, not in this situation. To have any argument like this the seller has to proceed under §2-704(2), which you should read now. I can't imagine that making up a green plaid suit to Bernie's measurements (no matter what his shape and size) would be an "exercise of reasonable commercial judgment for the purposes of avoiding loss."

So in this case Sam cannot bring an action for the price. This does not mean, of course, that he has no remedy against Bernie, but it will have to come under another section. The other two sections that provide the seller with a route to money damages are §2-706 and §2-708. Section 2-706 doesn't apply to this case because there can be no resale of a suit that doesn't exist. So Sam will get his remedy under §2-708. How that remedy measures up is the matter of a number of questions later on.

2b. Sam may have an action for the price under §2-709(1)(b). Even if he does no more work on it, he shouldn't have trouble establishing that this particular assemblage of cloth has been identified to his contract with Bernie. Sam would then have to show either that he had been "unable after reasonable efforts" to resell the suit "at a reasonable price" or that "the circumstances reasonably indicate that such an effort would be unavailing."

In a number of cases the results hinged on the court's interpretation and application of this last phrase. It is fair to say that no clear-cut test has emerged. Results may individually strike us as correct, but it always seems to be on a case-by-case basis. For a typical recent case, you may want to look at *Royal Jones & Associates, Inc. v. First Thermal Systems, Inc.*, 566 So. 2d 853, 14 U.C.C.2d 131 (Fla. Dist. Ct. App. 1990). Maybe if the green plaid was green enough and plaid enough Sam could convince a court that any effort to get anyone to even consider purchasing a suit like this would truly be unavailing. If Sam is in any doubt about being able to show this (and here I wouldn't be surprised if a court were skeptical that absolutely no one would be willing to take it off Sam's hands "at a reasonable price"), his better move would be to make some *reasonable* effort to resell it, even if it must be drastically retailored to fit the new buyer and the asking price reduced. If Sam does resell, he should be able to get any loss he suffers because of selling at a lesser price, including the extra incidental cost of the retailoring. If it can't be resold after reasonable efforts, Sam's case for the price is that much stronger. Notice that Sam's continued work on the suit in this situation would presumably be supported by §2-704(2), unlike in the previous question where no work had been done on it prior to the repudiation.

If Sam does bring an action for the price, what should he do with the partially completed suit? As we've just said, he'd be well advised to keep it out in his showroom and continue making reasonable efforts to sell it to someone else. If he can't get himself to do this (for instance, if it is just so hideous that he is reasonably afraid that having it on display could hurt his business) he should still hold onto it if only in storage. See §2-709(2). The idea behind this subsection is presumably that if there is a judgment for the seller and the buyer is going to have to pay the full purchase price anyway, then he or she might decide he wants possession of the goods after all.

Once the buyer has paid a judgment resulting from an action for the price he or she has a right to the goods under the last sentence of subsection (2). Note, however, that in some instances the judgment may be even *greater* than that part of the purchase price which had gone unpaid. Under this section the seller may recover the price "together with any incidental damages under" §2-710. Look at that section now. In most cases a seller's incidental damages suffered when the price is unpaid are, well, incidental. That would seem to be so in Sam's case. If he actually had to store the hideous green-plaid partially-assembled outfit at some place other than his place of business, he could at least get his storage costs.

There are times, of course, when incidental damages do amount to something more. See *Commonwealth Edison Co. v. Allied Chemical Nuclear Products, Inc.*, 684 F. Supp. 1434, 6 U.C.C.2d 380 (N.D. Ill. 1988). Edison had entered into a contract with ACNS under which that company would reprocess spent nuclear fuel for the utility. The court concluded that under the agreement Edison was to be considered the seller and ACNS the buyer of the spent (but hardly harmless) nuclear fuel, which was to be taken for reprocessing from fuel assemblies that had been used in commercial nuclear power plants. ACNS refused to accept delivery of the spent fuel, nor did it make delivery itself of the called-for good usable uranium and plutonium. Edison was forced to store the spent fuel at considerable expense. It sued ACNS under §2-709, asking for the price (the value of the good usable fuel it was to have received under the deal) along with its incidental expenses of storage. ACNS argued that the storage expenses should not have been allowed to Edison as an aggrieved seller, but the court disagreed. As District Judge Aspen noted,

> Although it truly boggles the mind to consider storage costs of 293 million dollars as "incidental," we find that these costs are indeed costs incurred by ACNS's alleged breach to provide [the usable fuel] and take . . . the irradiated [spent] fuel.

If Sam does succeed in getting a judgment in his action for the price and does collect on the judgment, he'll have to finish and then give up the suit if Bernie then wants it. If Bernie *still* doesn't want it, what then? I assume Sam can do pretty much what he wants, including tossing it away or giving it to charity. What if, after he has collected his judgment, Sam wears the strange outfit to a costume ball and (strangely enough) is deluged with offers to buy it? Perhaps green plaid is suddenly fashionable with the hip crowd. It seems he could sell the suit and keep the proceeds. Subsection 2-709(2) speaks only to proceeds of a resale "prior to the collection of the judgment." Is this right? I know of no case where something like this has happened and the buyer who's paid up later brings an action to get some part of his or her payment back.

3.   Arnold may be made to pay the $1,250 difference between the contract price of $1,700 and the resale price of $1,250, but it's far from automatic that this will be so. Stella would sue for this difference invoking §2-706(1), but in order for her to succeed she'd have to establish a number of factors. The resale must be made in good faith and in a commercially reasonable manner. In addition, under subsection (2), "every aspect of the sale including the method, manner, time, place and terms must be commercially reasonable." Finally under subsection (3) where the resale is at a private sale, as it was here, "the seller must give the buyer reasonable notification of his intention to resell." The Code nowhere defines a *private sale* (as opposed to a *public sale*), but Comment 4 indicates that a public sale is a sale at auction and a private sale is anything else. This does seem to be the distinction the drafters wished to make, and the one which is generally accepted.

Will Stella be able to satisfy all these conditions? Even granting her the best of good faith, it may be hard. This will all depend on other facts we don't have, of course. The resale price does seem awfully low, and Stella may have a difficult time establishing that it was reasonable under the circumstances. She'd be in a better position, of course, if she could show that she'd made at least some effort to sell to others at a higher price.

We would have to know more facts, as well, to determine whether Stella met the notice requirement here. As to this, see the first paragraph of Comment 8 and take note of the definition of *notice* in §1-201(26). Subsection 2-706(3) requires only "reasonable notification," not "reasonable written notification," so the requisite notice can be oral. The question has come up in a few cases whether the notice requirement is in effect waived once the seller establishes that the breaching buyer had actually known, or should have known, that the seller was trying to resell, even if this information did not come from the seller directly. There is no clear answer to this. Some courts say that the notice requirement is clear enough from the section and must actually be complied with if the seller is to sue under §2-706. (As we will see, the seller whose claim under this section is unavailing will still have an opportunity to collect under §2-708.) Other courts appear to be somewhat more flexible and if they don't literally waive the notice requirement are willing to find sufficient notice from the totality of the circumstances, not insisting upon proof of a single formal communication which was undeniably "notice" in a conventional sense.

If Stella is able to establish sufficient notice and the other prerequisites to her right to proceed under §2-706(1), she is then entitled to

> the difference between the resale price and the contract price together with any incidental damages allowed under the provisions of this Article (Section 2-710), but less expenses saved in consequence of the buyer's breach.

So the appropriate award under §2-706(1) would be calculated by first taking the $450 difference and then adjusting as necessary. If, for example, Arnold was to have picked up the painting from the gallery but the resale called for Stella to herself arrange and pay for delivery to the new buyer, this extra cost of shipment would be incidental damages for which she could also collect. If, on the other hand, her contract with Arnold had called for delivery of the painting in a certain type of frame, and the resale was of the painting unframed, there would be a certain amount of "expenses saved in consequence of [Arnold's] breach" and he would be entitled to a credit for this amount.

What is the situation if the facts do not support Stella's argument for recovery under §2-706, for example if she hadn't given adequate notice? We deal with these after we consider the second type of resale, the public sale.

3b. You can review §2-706(4) and its various subparts which set forth the numerous criteria for a public resale, which generally means a *sale at auction*. See as well Comment 9. If Stella's resale does meet all these conditions, then again she can collect under §2-706(1) the contract price/ resale price difference adjusted as before for incidental damages she may have suffered and subtracting expenses she may have saved.

If Stella's resale (either the private resale or the one at the auction) does not meet the tests laid out in §2-706(2) through (4), where does that leave her? The simple answer is that she will still have the right to sue under §2-708(1) for the difference between the contract price and the market value of the painting. The problem is, as you can no doubt imagine, that proof of market price can be very difficult, especially for something like an art work. Proof of resale price involves only bringing in a copy of the bill of sale covering the later resale. The price should be evident from that. Proof of market price of some particular goods at a particular time and place can involve estimation, differing expert opinions, and so on. The drafters tried to address these problems with §2-723, which you should look at, but they could only do so much. You see the trade-offs facing the aggrieved seller when the question is whether to pursue a remedy under §2-706 as opposed to §2-708. The amount of recovery should be more certain and more susceptible of proof if she goes the resale route. But in order to protect her rights under §2-706 she has to comply with a series of requirements, including generally a notice requirement, which can take time and effort and which can all too easily be messed up. A suit under §2-708 has no such preconditions. On the other hand, obtaining proof of market price high enough to give her the amount of recovery she thinks she deserves can be a nightmare.

You might reasonably be wondering at this juncture whether a seller who does resell but who for one reason or another does not meet the criteria for recovery under §2-706(1) and is hence forced to prove "market price" under §2-708(1) can at least use the resale price as evidence of that market price. The answer seems to be yes. The actual resale price is evidence, but only evidence, of the market price. The buyer, of course, can be expected to bring in evidence that a correct market price for the goods would have been much higher than the resale price which the seller actually received.

3c. Arnold should have no claim against Stella for the additional $100 she made in the resale. See the first sentence of §2-706(6). There is the possibility that if Stella were to sue him for her incidental damages occasioned by the breach he could argue this $100 as a set-off to those damages. The Code doesn't speak to this, neither authorizing it or ruling it out. It seems reasonable to allow Bernie the set-off, but then Stella will have legal fees in bringing the action thanks to him which she is going to have to take care of without any payment from him. In any event, whether Stella's resale meets all the §2-706 preconditions or not, Arnold will have no claim in the painting as long as the eventual buyer bought in good faith. See §2-706(5).

4a. Under §2-708(1), Salmons is entitled to "the difference between the market price at the time and place for tender and the unpaid contract price together with any incidental damages . . . but less expenses saved in consequence of the buyer's breach." We know the unpaid contract price here is $2 per pound. What was the time and place for tender under this contract? We can look at §2-503 generally as to tender, but once the parties have used a trade term such as F.O.B. to set the price, as Comment 1 to §2-708 reminds us, we have a series of special sections to which we can refer. Under §2-319(1)(b) when the parties have specified a price at "F.O.B. the place of destination," as they have here, the seller in effect tenders at that place, so the time and place of delivery would be in this instance August 21 in Boise. Thus we use the given market price of $1.14 and the market price/unpaid contract price difference is $.86 per pound.

It remains to be considered whether seller had any incidental damages or any expenses saved. The problem does not indicate that there were any incidental damages of the type provided for in §2-710. If Salmons did incur such charges, expenses, or commissions it should speak up now and be prepared to prove them in a court of law. The situation does suggest that Salmons did save on one anticipated expense: the expense of shipping the frozen fillets to Boise. Under an F.O.B. Boise contract, Salmons was to bear the cost of shipment to Boise. So $.05 per pound is to be subtracted from the damages owed Salmons by Better Foods. The final figure under these assumptions is $.81 per pound.

Notice that if the delivery were to have been made much later, say in August of the following year, and if Salmons brought suit right away it is possible (even given the state of our court system) that the damages would have to be measured before the time of tender and hence before the market price could be known. What to do then? See §2-723(1). All of a sudden it seems our focus shifts back to August 4, the date of the repudiation. We'll spend some more time with this section, which can come into play when the breach is the buyer's or the seller's, in the next chapter.

4b. Under §2-319(1)(a), when the price is set "F.O.B. the place of shipment" the tender takes place when and where the goods are put into the possession of the carrier. So the place of tender is Seattle. It's not perfectly clear from the facts what was to be the time (the exact date) of tender, and indeed there may not have been an exact date in mind. The seller was to deliver the frozen fillets to the railroad in Seattle sometime during the middle of August, leaving enough time so they would arrive in Boise by August 21. If Salmons had already scheduled shipment, or if it had a set pattern of when it would ship on a contract such as this, this information would be helpful. Assuming for the moment that it would have shipped on August 4 or soon thereafter, Salmons is entitled to the difference between $1.40 (the market price at the time and place of shipment) and the unpaid price of $1.98, or $.58. Assuming the Seattle market price of frozen fish fillets dropped steadily during the month of August as it appears it did (in other words, that frozen salmon fillets are not the subject of wild speculative market activity), this is the least Salmons can collect. If, for example, it could establish that it would have sent the shipment on its way significantly later in the month—say, August 17, when the price was something like $1.05 in Seattle—and still made the delivery in time, we could advise Salmons to sue for the greater amount of $1.98 minus $1.05, or $.93 a pound.

Again we are assuming that Salmons has no incidental damages to speak of or to sue for. Furthermore, since in an F.O.B. shipment contract the seller does not bear the cost of shipping, but only the expense of "putting [the goods] into the possession of the carrier," Salmons avoided no transportation expense in the situation and nothing would be subtracted from the market price/unpaid contract price differential.

4c. Subsection 2-708(1) treats this situation like that in Example 4a above as to the basic measure of damages. The market price/unpaid contract price difference is likewise $.86 per pound. In the case of a rejection in Boise, however, Salmons really had to pay the shipping expense, and so this amount would not be subtracted from Salmons's damages.

4d. As we said in answer to the previous question, Salmons, the injured seller, will claim damages at $.86 per pound under §2-708(1). Better Foods, however, will argue that an award in this amount would overcompensate Salmons. That company actually resold the goods for a price in excess of the market price, for $1.30 per pound, and it had additional expenses of just $.03 per pound. If damages are measured as in §2-706(1), Salmons could recover (and Better Foods argues would be fully compensated by) just $.73 per pound (this being $2.00 − $1.30 + $.03). We're assuming for the purposes of this question that the fillets sold to Very Best are the very ones that would otherwise have been delivered to Better Foods, and that Salmons would not have made a sale to Very Best had there not been a breach by Better Foods.

The issue, which is one on which major Code commentators disagree most profoundly, is whether an aggrieved seller who actually does cover by reselling the subject goods to another at a price above the provable market price is entitled to no more than the damages it could get under §2-706. Or is the seller in all cases free to choose under which provision, §2-706 or §2-708(1), to proceed and thus free to collect the market/contract differential even though it did resell?

The seller's right to collect under §2-708(1) in such a situation is found, it has been argued, in the language of these sections themselves. Subsection 708(1) says that the market/contract measure of damages is subject to subsection (2), which we'll get to in a while, and to the provisions of one other section (§2-723), but that's it. What it does *not* say is that the seller's damages may be measured this way only when the goods have not been resold. As a matter of fact, some language which could have been read as suggesting as much was actually excised from this subsection during the final phases of the drafting process, which culminated in an Article 2 that all the various interests could support. Note that §2-703(e) says that in the case of a buyer's breach, "the aggrieved seller may . . . recover damages for non-acceptance (Section 2-708) or *in a proper case* the price (Section 2-709)." Can't the placement of this italicized language be read as implying that the drafters didn't intend a seller's use of §2-708 to be limited only to "proper cases" or particular situations? Finally, look at Comment 1 to §2-703.

> This Article rejects any doctrine of election of remedy as a fundamental policy and thus the remedies are essentially cumulative in nature and include all of the available remedies for breach.

The contrary position—that the seller who resells the goods at a higher than market price is entitled to recover only the amount permitted under §2-706 and no more—cannot be so easily fashioned from statutory language. We can, however, look to other principles important to Code interpretation. It has been suggested that for the seller to ignore the resale in a situation like this, and to ask for damages measured under §2-708(1), shows a lack of good faith and hence runs afoul of §1-203. I find this hard to accept. It does seem to be stretching the concept of bad faith more than may be healthy. A more persuasive argument in favor of the buyer's position here has been made by Professors White and Summers in their treatise (§7-7), based primarily on the mitigation principle that is without a doubt firmly embedded in §1-106(1). Look at that subsection. See also the first Comment which informs us that

> compensatory damages are limited to compensation. They do not include consequential or special damages, or penal damages; and the Act elsewhere makes it clear that damages must be minimized. [Citing among other sections §2-706.]

Those who hold the position which would allow Salmons to recover the $.86 per pound (under §2-708(1)) and not just the $.73 (under §2-706) argue that an award including these extra few pennies need not necessarily be seen as overcompensation. Better Foods, after all, did breach, and the trouble and inconvenience which it presumably caused to Salmons of Seattle, which had to scramble to resell the fillets before something untoward happened to them, is sufficient justification for allowing the seller to seek and recover the larger amount. Otherwise the difficulties and the anxiety which the seller was made to suffer might not be sufficiently recognized in the final award. True, the seller can always sue for incidental damages in addition to the resale/contract difference under §2-706, but incidental damages are not always that easy to prove and evaluate in terms of dollars and cents. If all of the sales force at Salmons' Seattle office had to skip lunch one day, or even stay late into the night trying to find a new buyer for these goods, there will probably be no way of actually computing the cost to that company of all the hassle. So, the argument goes, to allow recovery of a little more under §2-708(1) is not undercutting any basic principle of the Code. Rather it is allowing a rough measure of "liquidated damages" for all the inconvenience caused to the seller. To do otherwise, to hold that the seller may recover no more than that to which it is entitled under the strict reading of §2-706, it might be said, would be a cramped and "illiberal" administration of remedies of the type the drafters sought to discourage (now citing §1-106(1) for the seller's purpose).

The issue remains unresolved. White and Summers conclude that a seller should not be permitted to recover more under §2-708(1) than would be available under §2-706 but admit themselves to be "swimming upstream against a heavy current of implication from the comments and the Code history." They even discuss, albeit without enthusiasm, one case that runs against their position. *Wendling v. Puls,* 227 Kan. 780, 610 P.2d 580, 28 U.C.C. 1362 (1980). Perhaps, however, the tide is now turning to make the journey that much easier for these two powerful swimmers. In *Tesoro Petroleum Corp. v. Holborn Oil Co., Ltd.,* 145 Misc. 2d 715, 547 N.Y.S.2d 1012, 10 U.C.C.2d 814 (1989), Judge Lerner of the New York Supreme Court bought the White and Summers analysis and result hook, line, and sinker (to gently change the water-based metaphor). Seller contracted to sell approximately ten million gallons of gasoline to buyer at a price of $1.30 per gallon, having purchased all of this amount only a few days earlier for $1.26 per gallon. Buyer repudiated the agreement. Seller claimed that because of a sudden sharp drop in the price of gasoline, the market value at the time and place of breach was somewhere between $.75 and $.80 per gallon. Seller, for reasons that were never made clear, was able to resell these ten million gallons to another buyer for $1.10 per gallon, but sued for damages measured by the contract price/market price differential. Judge Lerner, in reviewing this controversy and very much under the thrall of White and Summers, concluded that seller was entitled only to damages for the $1.30 minus $1.10 per gallon and no more.

> If plaintiff's damages are measured in accordance with §2-706, it would be receiving the benefit reasonably to be expected when it entered into the alleged contract with the defendant. Granting it the approximately $3,000,000 additional recovery that it seeks would result in a windfall which cannot be said to have been in the contemplation of the parties at the time of their negotiations, and would be inconsistent with the policy of the Code as expressed in §1-106.

Earlier we saw the argument that giving the aggrieved seller a few pennies more might be justified as a way of accounting for the trauma and inconvenience it suffered because of the buyer's breach. A few pennies, maybe, but here is one court at least that finds $3,000,000 additional recovery way more than was necessary to make up for the hassle and potential hurt feelings of an organization like Tesoro Petroleum Corporation.

5.   There is nothing tricky in this question. It's more of a review and a set-up for the questions to follow. The simple answer is that Billy may have breached but it is unlikely that Hacker will be able to get anything out of him. Hacker may decide to sell now for $350, may keep looking for another buyer who's willing to pay more, or may just chuck the whole idea and keep the machine as a memento. In any event, she'll have no right to damages from Billy. Review the possibilities. If she brought an action for the price she'd get nowhere. Section 2-709 allows for such an action only in a limited number of circumstances and none of those is present here. The goods have not been accepted, lost, or damaged. Resale was possible here, so §2-709(1)(b) is no help. If Hacker does resell and sues under §2-706, she'll have to prove that her resale met certain criteria,

and even if she does there seems to be no way she can show a positive measure of damages under that section. (We are assuming that the laundromat doesn't charge anything of significance for the right to post signs.) Finally, look at §2-708(1). There seems to be no way that Hacker could show a market price below $350. It did take some time, but she has eventually been able to find another buyer at $350. The end result seems to be that Hacker should sell to this person and count herself lucky that she actually made the sale at the price she was anticipating. The difficulty, waste of time, and annoyance she has suffered because of Billy's breach are just things she'll have to live with.

In reality, a more difficult question would be what she should do if she is only able to find another buyer at a lower price, like $330. If she doesn't sell, she may only be hurting herself more, as the price of the thing erodes even further with each passing month. If she does sell for this figure, of course, she would be entitled to $20 under the Code. And just what lawyer would take her case? Even if she decided to go after Billy on her own through small claims court, the expenses of travelling to and from the courthouse would probably eat up anything she could hope to win. So much for Hacker as an aggrieved seller and potential plaintiff.

6a. Now we have Hacker as a repudiating buyer and possible defendant. She will argue that while Steve may sue her for her actions, he, Steve, will be entitled to no damages—on the same analysis that was used against her, Hacker, in the previous question. Steve resold the machine which was destined for Hacker at the same price as she had contracted to pay. Ergo, Hacker will argue, Steve suffered no economic loss from the breach. He can try suing under §2-709, §2-706, or §2-708(1), but he'll recover nothing.

Steve, however, will argue that his position as an aggrieved seller is different than hers was. He is what is generally referred to as a *lost-volume seller*. By this we mean that while the goods were resold they were sold to someone who would have bought similar goods from him anyway. This resale was not made possible by the breach. Steve could have made a sale of a Super 2000 to Headly in any event. Steve is hurt in that the total number of sales he will make over the year is *one less* than it would have been if Hacker had not breached. Assuming that each sale means a bit of profit for the seller (which is after all the reason sellers are in business), Steve's profits for the year will be less than they would have been but for the breach. His situation is to be distinguished from that we considered in the previous question: Hacker had one old PS/1 to sell and she ended up selling it. Steve can sell as many of the Super 2000's as he can get willing customers coming through the door. The way Steve sees it he has lost sales volume, lost some of the profit to which he was entitled, and is indeed worse off economically because of Hacker's breach.

Steve finds his remedy in §2-708(2), which is written in a very broad manner but was clearly intended by the drafters to respond to the lost-volume problem. If the facts are as he says they are, Steve will be able to establish that the measure of damages provided in §2-708(1)—zero dollars here—"is inadequate" to put him "in as good a position as performance would have done." That being so, he is entitled to "the profit (including reasonable overhead)" which he would have made from the sale. Look now at Comment 2. Steve's situation is that of a seller of "standard priced goods," so he argues he fits perfectly within subsection (2).

The question then becomes how exactly to measure "the profit (including reasonable overhead)" which he would have made from a completed sale of the Super 2000 to Hacker. No one is terribly happy with the drafter's use of this phrase. Anyone who has ever spent any time studying the principles of accountancy (or who has ever tried to make sense of what an accountant was trying to tell him or her) knows that what counts for "profit" or "reasonable overhead" in any given situation can be a field day for creative numbercrunching. If the case involves significant sums, you can be sure that there will be more than one side to the exciting accounting story.

Take our situation for example. Steve will argue that the profit he lost because of Hacker's breach is measured by the difference of the $3,200 he pays for each machine and the $5,000 he was to receive. He demands $1,800 to put him into the same economic position he would have been in but for the breach. Note that in Comment 2 the drafters say that normally when a loss volume retailer sues the measure would be "list price less cost to the dealer." Another way that Steve would get to this same figure would be to measure "profit (including reasonable overhead)" by the difference of the contract price of sale minus what were to have been his so-called "variable" or "direct" costs in connection with the sale.

Hacker would argue for a lesser amount. After all, Steve's own accountant figures that he makes only something like 10% profit on his overall sales. This, of course, takes into account the fact that he must not only buy the machines from his suppliers, but must pay his salespeople, his rent, his advertising costs and so on. Figuring all this in, he would make a profit of something like $500 on the sale of each H.A.L. Super 2000 during the year. That amount and no more, Hacker will argue, is enough to make up to him for his lost profits.

In this particular example, I think Steve has the stronger position. The section says he is allowed to include his "reasonable overhead" in his profit, whatever that means. As a practical matter, the sale of one computer more or less isn't going to change how much he spends on rent, salaries, and so on. The profit he would have made on one additional sale is more like $1,800. Another way of looking at this is that if his other overhead costs have to be covered by one fewer sale, then each and every other sale that he does carry through to conclusion is just that much less profitable. And all thanks to Hacker's breach.

The courts have shown themselves willing to consider the case of the lost-volume seller like our friend Steve here and to award damages under §2-708(2) pretty much as he would measure them, as contract price minus variable costs. See, for example, the well-known case of *Neri v. Retail Marine Corp.*, 30 N.Y.2d 393, 285 N.E.2d 311, 334 N.Y.S.2d 165, 10 U.C.C. 950 (1972). If, however, the repudiated agreement covered what was to be a very large part of the seller's sales over a given period, so that once it fell through he or she could be expected to economize and cut back on those various overhead items, a more sophisticated calculation of just what is and what is not lost profit "including reasonable overhead" resulting from the breach would be necessary.

In this Example we have focused on the problem of the lost-volume retailer or distributor. Notice that a manufacturer which contracts to fabricate the items it sells can also suffer a lost volume problem and lost profits if a buyer breaches. According to Comment 2, the normal measure of damages in this instance would be "list price less manufacturing cost to the manufacturer." As you can imagine, the lost profits in such a situation are even more difficult to pin down and the parties' competing calculations even more subject to dispute.

6b. The "lost volume" recovery allowed to Steve in the previous problem was predicated, of course, on a showing that he was in fact a lost-volume seller. If, as we now posit, he would have been unable to sell more than 120 of the machines during the year, and if he did sell that many, he has no lost volume and the breach by Hacker didn't harm him. He has no rights under §2-708(2). He's back to recovering nothing from Hacker except perhaps a bit of incidental damages if those can be shown.

Similarly, for a manufacturer to qualify as a lost-volume seller, it would have to establish that its production capacity would have allowed it to produce all of the goods it did sell over the relevant period and *in addition* the amount which it would have sold to the repudiating buyer. If its factory was working to full capacity for the whole time anyway, it suffered no loss of volume and could not proceed using §2-708(2).

6c. Here is another situation where Hacker will be able to argue that Steve is not a lost-volume seller. He may have sold one fewer of one brand of machine because of Hacker's repudiation, but he made another sale (to her) which he otherwise would not have. It all depends on the facts. One thing we'd like to know is whether Steve had an unlimited supply of the Magnum Pro available to him. If not, if he could only have sold a given number because of a short supply of *that* new machine, then the profit he makes on his sale of one to Hacker he would have made anyway and can't be counted in Hacker's favor. We'd then be back to seeing whether Steve lost volume on the Super 2000. If Steve did have unlimited supplies of the two machines, then Hacker's argument that her breach only exchanged one sale for another on Steve's books and didn't cost him any profit has some power to it. Of course, we'd have to know what profit Steve was making on each Magnum Pro he sold. If it is less than $1,800 for some reason, he should at least be able to collect the difference in profits from Hacker.

7a. This Example is based on *Nobs Chemical, U.S.A., Inc. v. Koppers Co. Inc.*, 616 F.2d 212, 28 U.C.C. 1039 (5th Cir. 1980). The first issue presented is whether the seller can elect to recover under §2-708(1) even when the buyer can argue that this would *overcompensate* compared to the measure in §2-708(2). Normally, as we've seen above, the idea behind subsection (2) is that a seller stands the chance of being undercompensated if it is relegated to the market/contract difference of (1) in that it will not ultimately end up with the sum total of profit it had every reason to expect. The seller elects to proceed under (2) because, in the words of that subsection, "the measure of damages provided in subsection (1) is inadequate to put the seller in as good a position as performance would have done." But what if because of the circumstances the measure of (1) is *more than* adequate? Can the *buyer* now insist that the award be determined by the lost profit formula of subsection (2)?

Look at the facts here. Nobs calculates its damages under (1) as $275,000, which is just the $540 contract price minus $265 the market price at the time and place for tender multiplied out by the 1,000 tons. Koppers, however, argues that Nobs expected to make no more than $95,000 profit on the deal even if it had gone through exactly as planned. That firm was committed to buying all its requirements of cumene at $400 per ton. It would have to spend $45 a ton to get it delivered. All to receive the contract price of $540 per ton. You can check that ($540 − $400 − $45) times 1,000 is, sure enough, $95,000. Should Nobs receive substantially more in damages than it ever would have come up with had Koppers not repudiated? (You see why the facts work out as they do here, and why the situation will presumably not be that common. It all results from the seller's being committed to a requirements contract for all of the cumene in which it dealt so that it could not itself take advantage of the tumbling market prices of the stuff.)

So what should be the result under Article 2? Once again we have a kind of dispute like we did in considering whether seller could ever be forced to use §2-708(1) when it would prefer the §2-706 measure (see Example 4d): a dispute between the language of the particular provisions of these sections (subsection (2) states pretty clearly that it's to be used only when the measure of (1) is *inadequate* to get the seller what it wants) with the overriding principle of compensation as articulated in §1-106(1). Once again, as you might expect, Professors White and Summers in their treatise (§7-12) make a strong case for the buyer's being able to restrict the seller to use of §2-708(2) "in those circumstances in which the defendant-buyer can show that §2-708(1) will overcompensate the plaintiff." Once again, a court well disposed to the White and Summers reasoning followed the good professors' lead: the Fifth Circuit determined that the lost profit of $95,000 was all that the seller could recover under the circumstances. In the next edition of their treatise, White and Summers included a discussion of the *Nobs* case, indicating (to no great surprise), "We concur with the court's analysis." Do you?

7b. The second issue in *Nobs* was whether the aggrieved seller could recover the $75,000 loss suffered in this way. Why would there be any doubt? Well, how do we characterize this loss? It seems to be what we will call in the next chapter on buyer's remedies an example of "consequential damages" arising from the repudiation. The problem is that in all the sections we've seen providing for damages to the seller (§§2-706, 2-708, 2-709), there has been reference to something like "incidental damages allowed under the provisions of this Article (§2-710)." We look at §2-710 and sure enough, it allows for the recovery of incidental damages characterized in a certain way. Compare this to §2-715, which applies to suits by an aggrieved buyer. The buyer is entitled to incidental damages and, in the appropriate case, consequential damages. Doesn't this make it perfectly clear that the drafters most certainly did *not* intend for consequential damages to be available to an aggrieved seller? These seem to have been left out intentionally.

Let's turn one more time to White and Summers for advice. Because consequential damages are not explicitly provided the seller, they counsel (in §7-16) that "any lawyer worth his [sic] salt seeks to dress his seller's consequential damages in the clothes of incidental damages so to recover them." What about an argument that consequential damages, brazenly clothed as such, can be awarded a seller-plaintiff under Article 2 in the appropriate situation? Reviewing the cases, White and Summers note that all appellate courts that have ruled on the issue have concluded this is simply not to be. In *Nobs* itself, the Fifth Circuit took this view:

> We believe the trial court was correct in declining to award the plaintiffs the extra $75,000.00. Under UCC 2-708(2), in addition to profit, the seller may recover "incidental damages" and "due allowance for costs reasonably incurred." The code does not provide for recovery of consequential damages by a seller. [Citing §1-106(1).]

We might as well give White and Summers the final word. As to the consistent holdings of courts like that in *Nobs* that consequential damages for a seller are just not part of the Code scheme of things, "We are not so certain of these conclusions. The drafters were far from perfect. . . . It is conceivable that an omission of any reference to a seller's consequential damages is attributable not to any intention to prohibit, but to a failure to contemplate their possibility." Having wrestled so hard with the ins and outs of these remedy provisions, is it that hard for you to conceive that even the drafters may have gotten just a tad confused or absentminded when it got down to the finer points?

29

Buyer's Remedies

When Seller Breaches

Sellers are not necessarily bad people. They do, however, now and then and for one reason or another breach or repudiate their contractually binding agreements. What can the individual buyer whose rights have been trampled on in this way do about it? At least the question of where to start looking for answers is easy enough. The drafters provide in §2-711 an index or summary of the remedies available under Article 2 to the buyer who has been wronged, at least when the situation has not proceeded to the point of the buyer's accepting the goods. Before we even look at that section, however, it is well to remember what we have previously studied about the two so-called goods related remedies which the buyer can and in many cases would be well advised to take advantage of in many situations. When the seller tenders goods that are not as promised, the buyer may reject them. (We gave rejection all the attention it so rightfully deserves in Chapter 18.) Even where the buyer accepts, if the goods are later discovered to be defective there may be the possibility of revoking acceptance under §2-608 (as to which see Chapter 20). Avoiding acceptance is often by far the buyer's best line of defense. Recall, however, that rejection or revocation of the goods is not necessarily the end of the story for the aggrieved buyer. The buyer retains the right to bring an action under the plan laid out in §2-711.* Let's look at the first two subsections:

---

*In the introductory text to the previous chapter, I explored briefly the possibility that in the event of a buyer's breach the seller might choose for perfectly legitimate business or personal reasons not to pursue legal remedy. Sometimes the best response is just to forget about the whole thing and get on with your life, or to rely on other extra-legal (but not illegal) responses to the problem. It should go without saying that even if I don't rehash that whole discussion here the same could equally be true for a buyer trying to decide what reaction is warranted and would best serve his or her purposes in the aftermath of a seller's breach.

(1) Where the seller fails to make delivery or repudiates or the buyer rightfully rejects or justifiably revokes acceptance then with respect to any goods involved, and with respect to the whole if the breach goes to the whole contract (Section 2-612), the buyer may cancel and whether or not he has done so may in addition to recovering so much of the price as has been paid

(a) "cover" and have damages under the next section [Section 2-712] as to all the goods affected whether or not they have been identified to the contract; or

(b) recover damages for non-delivery as provided in this Article (Section 2-713).

(2) Where the seller fails to deliver or repudiates the buyer may also

(a) if the goods have been identified recover them as provided in this Article (Section 2-502); or

(b) in a proper case obtain specific performance or replevy the goods as provided in this Article (Section 2-716).

The one case not covered by this scheme is an important one: that of the damages available to the buyer who has accepted the goods but later claims injury due to a nonconformity. That worthy topic gets a separate section all its own, §2-714, which we'll be taking a look at soon enough.

To get a good handle on what remedies will be available to a buyer in any situation, the key is first to get clearly in mind exactly what that situation is. As in the remedies for the seller (reviewed in the previous chapter), it's all going to depend on the facts of the individual case. Did the goods ever come into existence? If so, were they identified to the contract? Did the seller tender, and if so what was the buyer's response? Were the tendered goods accepted or rejected, and if accepted was that acceptance later "justifiably revoked?" When all the dust had settled, who ended up with the goods and where are they now? Finally, was any payment made by the buyer to the seller and if so how much? In this chapter we are allowed to assume just a few things: (1) that an agreement between the parties created a valid contract enforceable against the seller, and (2) that the seller's subsequent actions amounted to a breach or a repudiation of that agreement. Beyond that we have to be open to the full range of situations and possibilities.

Just as in the previous chapter I gave you leave to skip some textual material on matters involving a party's rights in the event of the other's insolvency, you are free to pass over the following section if that better suits your present study. Go then directly to the section next following, where we again meet up with the buyer going for the goods themselves or for a monetary remedy.

If the Seller Is Insolvent

Article 2 provides special relief in at least some situations where the buyer has not yet received or been shipped the goods but has paid all or a portion of the purchase price shortly before the seller becomes insolvent. The Code definition of when a party has become *insolvent* is given in §1-201(23). The seller's business is in some kind of difficulty. The buyer has paid all or a part of the price and (while the seller's insolvency is not in and of itself a breach) there is the real possibility that the goods will never be shipped or delivered. An insolvent party's creditors will often have the power and the motivation to resist any moves by that party which lessen the amount of valuable stuff over which it has control. The creditors will not want to see goods leaving the seller's plant. From the point of view of the buyer this has to be troubling. It has to wait around for further developments and quite naturally will be in doubt about whether the promised goods are going to be delivered on schedule. Just as important, even if the goods are never delivered the seller, which has been paid part of the purchase price, may well not be in a position financially or legally to return any or all of that payment. The buyer stands a good chance of being left with neither the goods or the money. What it *would* very likely end up with would be a contract claim against the seller for the amount of the payment and perhaps something more as damages of the type we'll talk about for the nondelivery of the goods. But the buyer will be an unsecured, a general creditor for this amount. And we know how unlikely it is, should bankruptcy ensue, that a general creditor will ever see any significant portion of the money it is owed.

Section 2-502 provides the buyer with a right actually to pick up and take away promised goods in the possession of the seller if some payment has been made by buyer and the seller has "become[ ] insolvent within ten days after receipt of the first installment on their price." The buyer recovers the goods and extricates itself from the whole messy situation. There are significant conditions to this right of course. First of all the goods must have already been identified to the contract under §2-501. In addition, the buyer must make and keep open a tender of the unpaid portion of the price. And, of course, this right of recovery only works if the seller has become insolvent within ten days of its receiving the initial payment. Should the buyer have not yet made a payment or if the insolvency occurs after this slender ten-day period, the buyer will have to go elsewhere for relief and may unavoidably end up entangled in the bankruptcy. We turn now to a brief rundown of the general remedies available to the buyer in the event of the seller's breach or repudiation before heading into the questions.

Going for the Goods, Going for the Cash

As we'll explore in the Examples and Explanations, and as presented to us in the index §2-711, the aggrieved buyer will in some circumstances have the chance actually to obtain the goods through judicial process. The possibility of an order for *specific performance*—a contractual remedy to which I trust you were introduced in Contracts—and of *replevy,* a property notion with which you may be less familiar, are covered by §2-716. If the buyer is not able to get the goods for one reason or another or in the very likely situation that it doesn't want them (at least not from this seller) anymore, the remedies then take the form of money damages. The buyer may under §2-712 "cover" by buying the same or similar goods in substitution from someone else and then sue for the difference between what it paid for the goods and what it had expected to pay. Or the buyer can seek damages measured by a market price minus contract price formula under §2-713. If the buyer accepted tender of the goods, this does not, of course, impair its right to proceed against the seller for any damages suffered because the delivered goods are not as promised. See the concluding language of §2-607(2). The assessment of damages with respect to accepted goods is governed by §2-714. To each of the measures we will consider may be added so-called incidental or consequential damages as set forth in §2-715 if the facts allow.

One final point: If the buyer is entitled to some measure of money damages, how does it collect? When the buyer has paid the full purchase price and is left with no goods in hand, there is little to be done if the seller does not or cannot make voluntary amends but to bring a lawsuit, get a judgment, and enforce that judgment for all it is worth in any way possible. Sometimes, however, the buyer will have an easier road to recovery. In the event that the buyer has accepted the goods but not yet paid the full purchase price on them, any damages to which it is legally entitled may be deducted from what it has yet to pay under §2-717. If the buyer has rightfully rejected or justifiably revoked acceptance and the goods are in its possession, then §2-711(3) offers some help. The buyer has a security interest in the goods to the extent of any payment it has made or any expenses it has incurred in relation to its handling of the goods (not however for any other damages it may be claiming), so it need not release them back into the custody of the seller unless and until its payment has been returned and its expenses recompensed. Should this amount not be forthcoming, it may eventually resell the goods and try to get its money that way. As to any other damages it may have suffered, the buyer will have to proceed along other lines. See Comment 3 to §2-711.

We now bring all these sections (and a couple of others to which I'll direct you) to bear on our usual array of examples, explanations, and oddball characters.

EXAMPLES

1. In early February Arnold Moneybucks contracts to buy an original oil painting ("The Evils of Socialism") for $1,500 from Stella's art gallery. Arnold will pick up and pay for the painting when the artist's showing at Stella's has closed at the end of the month. On February 15, Arnold

receives a letter from Stella saying that she has decided against selling him the painting, that she has herself fallen in love with it, and that she will be keeping it in her private collection. Arnold realizes all the more how much he himself is enamored of this work. Does he have the right to obtain a court order making Stella deliver the work to him?

2. Seller in Seattle contracts to deliver ten tons of noodles to Buyer in Boise. It is agreed that the goods will be shipped by rail under a nonnegotiable bill of lading consigning the goods to Seller's agent in Boise. When the shipment arrives in Boise the railroad is to notify Buyer, who will then make payment to Seller's agent. This agent will then in turn produce a delivery order directed to the railroad authorizing delivery to Buyer. The goods arrive and the Buyer is notified. Seller has instructed his agent, however, that the shipment not be turned over to Buyer but that instead it be put into storage in Boise for possible sale to another buyer at a higher price. Does the Buyer have the right to get these noodles?

3. Buster contracted to buy a new refrigerator, the Penguin Deluxe, for $1,000 plus a $50 delivery fee from Selma's Appliance City. The refrigerator was to come in the Penguin appliance line's Avocado color, which Buster had picked to blend in with his kitchen decor. Selma's delivery crew arrived at Buster's with a large box marked "Penguin Deluxe/Avocado," but when the box was opened it turned out that the machine inside was a burnt orange. Buster rejected the refrigerator on the spot and the delivery crew took it back to Selma's. Later that day Selma called Buster to apologize for the error, which apparently resulted from some problem at the manufacturer's plant. Unfortunately, Selma explained to Buster, she doesn't have any of the refrigerators in the right color in stock and when she contacted the manufacturer she was told that it no longer made the Penguin Deluxe in that color. "I'm sorry," Selma concludes, "but you're not going to be able to get what you want." That weekend Buster goes to several of the town's other appliance stores. At the fourth store he visits he finds they have one remaining Penguin Deluxe in the Avocado color. He contracts to buy this machine (which this store will deliver free of charge) for $1,200.

a. What rights does Buster have against Selma's Appliance City?

b. Would it make any difference to your answer if Selma could show that there was one appliance store in town at which Buster never checked that would have sold him just the refrigerator he wanted for only $1,050?

c. How would you respond if it turned out that the refrigerator Buster eventually bought and had delivered was equipped with a special automatic ice cube and crushed ice feature that had not been included in the machine Buster originally contracted to buy from Selma?

4. Marinara Incorporated is a large producer of tomato sauces. It contracts with a garlic distributor, Cloves and Sons, for the delivery of 600 pounds of fresh #1 garlic at $2 per pound, delivery to be made on April 1 to Marinara's plant. On April 1 Cloves & Sons brings around several

crates of garlic. Marinara's purchasing director discovers that the garlic in these crates is only of #2 quality, and in addition isn't all that fresh. The purchasing director rejects the delivery. A month later, when Marinara's stock of garlic is running low, the purchasing director buys 600 pounds of #1 garlic from another distributor for the then-market price of $3.50 per pound. (The market price of garlic has been rising steadily since the end of the summer due to an unexpectedly poor garlic harvest.) Should Marinara Incorporated have any difficulty in collecting the $1.50 difference per pound from Cloves & Sons?

5.   At the end of the salmon catching season, one large fishery, Salmons of Seattle, has on hand a great stock of processed frozen salmon and other fish fillets. On August 1 it contracts to sell a large quantity of salmon fillets to Better Foods, a food wholesaler in Boise, Idaho for a price of "$2 per pound F.O.B. Boise." Delivery is to be made by railroad on or before August 21, and payment is to be made within 30 days of the buyer's receipt. On August 4, Salmons delivers some crates marked for Better Foods to the railroad with instructions that these be delivered to Boise, where that firm will take delivery. When a representative of Better Foods goes to the Boise railyard on August 21, she quickly discovers that the crates contain not salmon but less valuable haddock fillets. She rejects the shipment. The following prices may (or may not) help you answer the questions.

Market price of fillets at Boise on August 1	$2.04
Market price at Seattle on August 1	$1.97
Market price at Boise on August 4	$2.16
Market price at Seattle on August 4	$2.09
Market price at Boise on August 21	$3.00
Market price at Seattle on August 21	$2.97
Cost of shipping from Seattle to Boise	$.05

a. If Better Foods seeks to recover damages based on §2-713, how much should it be awarded per pound?

b. What would Better Foods be awarded if instead the price had been agreed to as "$1.98 F.O.B. Seattle?"

c. Suppose that Salmons contracted for $1.98 F.O.B. Seattle, but never makes any shipment to Boise at all. Better Foods only becomes aware of this when its representative contacts the railroad on April 21 and asks when would be a convenient time to pick up the shipment she has been told to expect. She is told the railroad has not received any shipment from Salmons intended for Better Foods. She contacts Salmons and that firm admits it never made the shipment. If Better Foods sues Salmons asking for recovery under §2-713, to how much is it entitled?

6.   On May 1 Seller contracts to deliver wheat directly to Buyer's plant on or before December 15 for $1.00 per bushel. On June 1 Seller contacts Buyer and repudiates its contract. Buyer investigates the supply of wheat it has on hand and its anticipated needs and decides it can do without

the wheat contracted for from Seller. In January it sues Seller for damages under §2-713. It is able to show that the market price for such wheat in its vicinity on December 15 was $1.83 a bushel. Seller acknowledges that the market price of wheat had been steadily rising over the later part of the year, but points out that it was only $1.05 on June 1 when it had told Buyer not to expect delivery. What amount should Buyer be awarded under §2-713?

7.   Marinara Incorporated, the tomato sauce manufacturer, contracts to buy a large amount of oregano from Herb, a spice and herb distributor, for $15 a pound. Delivery is to be made to Marinara's plant on or before May 15. By May 15 no shipment of oregano has arrived. The market price for oregano in the vicinity of Marinara's plant is $18 per pound. The Marinara purchasing director contacts a spice merchant who has been trying to attract the saucemaker's business and is willing to sell him the needed quantity of oregano for $17 a pound. The purchasing director makes the purchase on Marinara's behalf. Marinara's legal department then brings suit against Herb claiming damages in the amount of $3 per pound under §2-713. Is Marinara entitled to this amount?

8.   Barbara buys a watch, the Chronos Masterwork 660, from Sam's Jewelry store. She pays $3,200 for the watch, which at the time of purchase was marked with a prominent label as being "18 carat gold." A few months later she shows it to a friend who is in the jewelry business who informs her that what she has gotten is not the 18-carat-gold version of the Masterwork, which in fact has been selling in most stores for $3,500, but only a gold-plated model. This model, the Masterwork 460, is a perfectly good watch, but can be had in the stores for something like $800.

    a. If Barbara decides to keep the watch and to sue Sam for damages, to what amount is she entitled?

    b. To what amount would she be entitled assuming all the facts remain the same except that the Masterwork 660 has been selling in most of the major stores for something like $2,800?

9.   Dominic Doe buys a new pizza oven for his pizza parlor from Ovens of Brooklyn. The purchase price is $10,500. Soon after the oven is delivered it becomes apparent that its temperature control is not functioning properly. Doe contacts the seller but Ovens refuses to make repairs, claiming that the oven is just fine. He then calls Crafty, a repair person with whom he has had good experience in the past. Crafty tells him that the control clearly is faulty, but she is quickly able to find a control that will work in that brand of oven and installs it. The oven now works perfectly well, but Crafty tells Doe that since she has had to install a used part there is no telling how long it will hold out and that "it's merely a patch-up job, though it should hold you for a while."

    a. Crafty charges Doe $1,200 for parts and labor. Doe brings suit against Ovens of Brooklyn. To how much is he entitled?

    b. Suppose instead that after Crafty installs the replacement control (still for $1,200) she tells Doe that she was able to find and install a brand new part and that in fact, "what you've got in there now is really much better than that control they had in there to begin with. When these ovens go, it's usually the temperature control that's the problem, so you can bet this oven's going to last you much longer with this new control." To how much is Doe entitled under these facts?

10. Buyer and Seller contract for the purchase and sale of 10,000 yards of carpeting. Buyer takes delivery of the carpeting at his store, but as soon as he inspects the first roll, it is immediately apparent that it is not what he ordered. Buyer calls Seller and rejects the goods. Seller says she will arrange to have this carpeting picked up and the correct carpeting delivered, but that this will necessarily take a few weeks. Having only limited floorspace, Buyer arranges to have the carpeting taken away and stored by a local warehouse, paying $200 for this service. Seller delivers the correct shipment to Buyer and collects the incorrect shipment from the warehouse. Seller accepts the second shipment as conforming with the contract in quality and amount, even though it has arrived some two weeks after the promised delivery date. Buyer now is to pay for the carpeting. What amount or amounts can he legitimately subtract from the purchase price under §2-717?

11. Assume that Dominic Doe, from Example 9 above, is able to show that because of the problem with the pizza oven he has had to close down his shop for a period of four days, Thursday through Sunday. Normally he would not be open on Sunday, but as it happened he had agreed to be open for a special private pizza party for which he was to receive $1,000. Does this information add to the amount to which he is entitled from Ovens of Brooklyn, and if so by how much? What other information would you need to more fully evaluate the situation?

12. Charlie, a professional musician, inherits one million dollars from a distant relative. Having been advised that a good investment would be to purchase a small business for himself, he uses the million to buy a company named Garden Seating Incorporated, which has been in operation for some years and which he is able to convince himself has a good, steady business making lawn furniture (marketed under the name "Nettie Chairs" and such) that it sells to garden stores and similar retailers. On behalf of Garden Seating he contracts to buy a large supply of plastic webbing from Webber and Company for use in making lawn chairs. The finished chairs are delivered to various buyers around the country. It soon becomes apparent that there is something wrong with the chairs and particularly the webbing, since there are several reports of people sitting in the chairs and falling right through. Fortunately, no one is hurt, but Garden Seating immediately issues a recall of all of the chairs. It turns out that the plastic webbing was clearly defective and not as warranted, in that it became brittle after only a few months. Charlie concludes that owning and running a small business is not what it was cracked up to be. He looks around for someone to buy Garden Seating from him, just as he had bought it only a few months before from the previous owner,

but no one will give him more than $500,000 for the business. All of the prospective purchasers point out that the lawn chair fiasco has seriously damaged the reputation of the company. (One late night talkshow host went through more than a week of "I'd rather sit in a Nettie Chair" jokes.) Charlie decides that he'll have to hold onto the company, as he could not bear thinking he lost that much money in business in such a short time and particularly when it wasn't his fault. He resolves to sue Webber & Company for all of the harm they have caused the company. To what will Garden Seating be entitled?

13. Bertha Moneybucks is considering the purchase of a large pleasure boat from Maryland Marine Sales. She is satisfied that the price quoted, $34,000, is a good one for the boat in question, but is very concerned that she won't get the boat in time for the prime boating season even though the seller is willing to promise delivery by May 1. In order to make the sale, the president of M.M.S. writes into the contract the following provision:

> Seller promises to deliver the boat as provided for herein on or before May 1. In recognition of the distress and inconvenience which will be caused Buyer should delivery be delayed, it is agreed that the price to be paid by Buyer is to be reduced by $100 for each day delivery may be delayed beyond May 1.

The boat is not delivered until June 15. Is Bertha entitled to deduct $4,500 from the purchase price of the boat? See §2-718(1).

14. Sam contracts to buy Dave's used car for $3,000. He gives Dave $800 as a down-payment on the car. The next day he calls Dave and tells him that the money he was counting on to complete the deal would not be coming his way and he is going to have to back out of the deal. Dave tells him, "That's all right. These things happen." Two weeks later when Sam next sees Dave he asks for his $800 back. Dave tells him that fortunately he was able to sell the car to someone else for $3,100, but that he has no intention of returning to Sam his money. "I said it was all right, that I wasn't going to hold you to the deal or sue you or anything," explains Dave, "but you certainly can't expect to get your money back. After all, it was you who backed out. I was ready to sell to you." Sam decides not to get into a fight with Dave right there on the street, but now he is wondering: Is there any way he can legally recover his $800? Look at §2-718(2) and (3).

EXPLANATIONS

1.   Arnold will probably be able to get his hands on the artwork itself, but the question of whether he has *the right* to relief of this nature is more in doubt. First consider an argument by Arnold that he should be awarded specific performance of the contract under §2-716(1). I am assuming that you have studied the history and nature of this equitable remedy in Contracts. If so, surely you remember that while a court may

exercise its equitable powers to give such relief, whether or not it does so is always discretionary on the court's part. That is in the nature of equity and specific performance. Note that §2-716(1) and (2) both carefully use the word *may* and not *must, shall, will,* or anything of the sort.

Comment 1 to this section tells us that:

> The present section continues in general prior policy as to specific performance and injunction against breach. However, without intending to impair in any way the exercise of the court's sound discretion in the matter, this Article seeks to further a more liberal attitude than some courts have shown in connection with the specific performance of contracts of sale.

You can see how the drafters sought to effectuate this more liberal approach in the language of the section itself. Notice that there is no mention of the traditional requirement that before the court will consider granting specific performance it be established that "no adequate remedy at law" is available to the plaintiff. The section doesn't even require that the goods be in existence or identified to the contract. The only statutory requirement is that the goods be "unique" or that "other proper circumstances" be shown.

In Arnold's case it seems likely that he will prevail and be awarded specific performance as the artwork is "unique" in the most conventional sense in which equity would use this term. Note, however, in Comment 2 that the drafters hoped to be introducing along with this section (albeit through the Comments) a "new concept of what are 'unique' goods" for this purpose. "The test of uniqueness under this section must be made in terms of the total situation which characterizes the contract." Add to this the suggestion in §2-716(1) that specific performance may (and again we have to stress *may*) be granted in "other proper circumstances," and you have the go-ahead for some fairly creative use of the equitable power. Unfortunately, the drafters gave little indication about what this last phrase was meant to entail other than that "inability to cover is strong evidence" of such circumstances, whatever they may be. A critic could ask what this language in §2-716(1) adds other than to remind us that the court's discretion is always, well, within the discretion of the court.

It would be fair to say that even under this new section there has not been any wild expansion in the courts' willingness to grant specific performance when it comes to sale of goods. The traditional attitude that this is an exceptional remedy and one to be used sparingly and with discretion has suffered no fundamental rethinking. If the goods are not something pretty special but can be replaced through normal channels, the court is not going to be tempted into specific performance. However, a number of opinions have indeed taken the expanded and more liberal focus on "commercial feasibility of replacement" to heart as the drafters had hoped. Most notably these have been where the seller and buyer have entered into a long-term relationship for the continuing supply of some type of fuel or other natural resource. In such a situation the buyer could, of course, with enough time and energy and laying out enough money make substitute arrangements to replace a supply that is abruptly cut off. It could then sue for whatever damage had been done. The courts recognize, however, that the disruption of the buyer's business, not to mention the inconvenience caused to others down the chain of distribution, could be enormous and at the same time difficult to evaluate with any certainty. Specific performance of the supply contract has been granted, although in most such cases whether the court has done so by an expanded reading of "unique" or through reliance on the "other proper circumstances" language has been left unclear. Whatever the reason, the result as far as the particular case is concerned has been just as the buyer would have wished. Unfortunately for us, we have to wait for future developments to get any real guidance about what substance if any this phrase "other proper circumstances" has, other than as a grand catch-all.

Before we leave Arnold's dilemma, there is one more question: If for some reason Arnold were afraid that the court might in its discretion refuse to award him specific performance, could he invoke the right to replevin under §2-716(3) to reach the same outcome? Notice that if a case comes within the criteria of that subsection, replevin is a matter of right and not (as is true with specific performance) a discretionary remedy within the power of the court to grant or withhold. You may not be as familiar with replevin as you are with specific performance—at least it is much less likely that you would have spent time on it in Contracts. That's because under the common law replevin is not a contractual notion or remedy at all, but a *property* concept. Traditionally, replevin is available if it is established that the defendant is wrongfully holding onto property that is rightfully the plaintiff's. The key to an action in replevin has always been the showing that the "title" to the goods in question rightfully resides in the plaintiff. The drafters of Article 2, of course, did everything they could to play down the whole notion of title as it might apply to the law of sale, so their provision on replevin makes no reference to that concept. Instead they require a showing that the goods have been identified to the contract and "cover is reasonably unavailable." See Comment 3, which says this about replevin and not much more. It would seem Arnold could avail himself of this provision, but then it's very unlikely that he would have to given the strength of his argument for specific performance even under traditional doctrine. There has been very little action whatsoever under §2-716(3), and it's hard to come up with any obvious situation, other than that of the following question, where its invocation would add much to an argument based on specific performance alone. Perhaps the amazing ability of the real world to come up with fact patterns even beyond the invention of law professors will eventually reveal a special part to play for subsection (3), but if so only time will tell.

2. This is a situation of shipment under reservation under §2-505 and Buyer should be able to recover the noodles under replevin and §2-716(3). Buyer will, of course, have to pay the purchase price to get the noodles, which is what the language about "satisfaction of the [seller's]

security interest in them" is all about. Here at least is one instance in which replevin would work for a buyer even though specific performance is highly unlikely. How unique can noodles be? And yet you can understand why Buyer would find it highly preferable simply to pay for and get this particular shipment of noodles rather than having to worry about cover, incidental expenses, proof of market price or anything like that. Buyer is able to pay for the noodles, get the noodles, and get on with its business. Case closed.

3a. Buster should be able to recover $150 from Selma. Under §2-712(1) he is entitled if he chooses to "cover"

> by making in good faith and without unreasonable delay any reasonable purchase of or contract to purchase goods in substitution
> for those due from the seller.

That's just what Buster did here. There certainly was no unreasonable delay and under the circumstances this seems like a reasonable purchase. Further, we have no cause to doubt Buster's good faith especially as he is to be held only to the lesser standard imposed on the nonmerchant. See Comment 4.

The pay-off for Buster comes in subsection (2), since he is entitled to recover as damages the difference between the cost of cover ($1,200) and the contract price ($1,000) together with any consequential or incidental damages "but less expenses saved in consequence of the seller's breach." Here he saved $50 by not having to pay for delivery under the substitute contract, so the final figure is $150 due and payable by Selma.

We are assuming that Buster had no consequential or incidental damages here. If there were any, he should come forward and prove them. Incidental damages under §2-715(1) could include any "commercially reasonable charges, expenses or commissions in connection with effecting cover." Unfortunately, if all that Buster suffered in order to effect cover was more than a little annoyance and a lost weekend spent touring the local appliance stores, it is unlikely he could get anything for this since no dollar figure attaches to his time and inconvenience. As to consequential damages, again we are told of nothing. If he did have such, say for example he was forced by the breach to go for a few days without a refrigerator at all and some frozen food had to be tossed out, then this amount should be added in as well, as long as it could be demonstrated that he had done all that he could have been reasonably expected to do to avoid this consequential loss. Note the last part of §2-715(2)(a).

3b. Buster's recovery should not be affected by the fact that there was, somewhere in town, a store where he could have made cheaper cover. See Comment 2:

> The test of proper cover is whether at the time and place the buyer acted in good faith and in a reasonable manner, and it is immaterial that hindsight may later prove that the method of cover used was not the cheapest or most effective.

But what if Selma wanted to show that the place where the cheaper cover was available was the one big discount store in town which is generally known to have the lowest prices around? Could she argue that Buster's failure to even check at this store made for an unreasonable if not bad faith search for what he needed? Perhaps, but don't forget that Buster originally bought from Selma, so he might very well be able to demonstrate that for one reason or another he chooses not to shop at a place just because it's the cheapest. Even if Buster *had* been aware that there was a place where he could have covered more cheaply, that does not necessarily make his purchase at $1,200 from a store he trusts more or which is thought to give better service an unreasonable purchase.

An interesting case on the cover minus contract measure is *Laredo Hides Co., Inc. v. H & H Meat Products Co., Inc.*, 513 S.W.2d 210, 16 U.C.C. 78 (Tex. Civ. App. 1974), for it demonstrates how much leeway a court can allow a buyer doing its best to cover under difficult circumstances. The buyer sued for seller's breach of its agreement to sell all of its output of cattle hides during March to December 1972. Delivery was to be made at least twice a month. When the seller breached and eventually repudiated the agreement the buyer was forced to go into the open market for hides and make substitute purchases. The court awarded buyer the cost of cover minus the contract price even though the cover purchases "had to be made periodically throughout 1972 since Laredo Hides had no storage facilities, and the hides would decompose if allowed to age," and even though the market price for hides was steadily increasing during the period in question.

3c. Selma will argue that by getting a better machine Buster will receive a windfall if she is made to pay the full $150 previously calculated. Recall that under §1-106 the purpose of all of these remedy provisions is to compensate the plaintiff but no more. I doubt Selma's argument would get very far here. If it were to work, her breach would be in effect forcing Buster to pay for a feature which he never wanted and for all we know finds undesirable. Even if he comes to love the icemaker, I'd still let him keep it without worrying about a little too much in damages levied against Selma.

In some other situations however this factor—cover with goods of markedly better quality—might reasonably be taken into account in lessening the eventual damage award. Suppose the buyer is a commercial party which buys goods for resale, that is, a retailer or distributor. When it does not receive the ordered goods from the seller it makes cover by buying the only available goods of that type, but ones which are of a higher quality. The buyer has no trouble selling these substituted goods and in fact because of their quality is able to get a higher price for them and make more of a profit that it has anticipated. Under those circumstances it could well be argued by the breaching seller that the buyer's damages should be reduced by the amount of this increase in its resale profits.

482   Part Five. Remedies

4.   It's doubtful that Marinara is going to be able to collect the $1.50 per pound. The seller will argue that the purchase was made with unreasonable delay especially considering what was going on in the volatile garlic market. Marinara will not be able to collect damages under §2-712. It will instead have to argue for damages based on §2-713 and it is likely that it will get far less under that section. We move onto how §2-713 works with the next Explanation.

5a.   If the seller sues for recovery measured under §2-713 the two initial questions to be answered are as of what date and at what place is the market price to be determined. Subsection (1) tells us that we are to use the market price "at the time the buyer learned of the breach." That phrase will give us trouble in a different circumstance later on, but for the present it seems clear that the date Better Foods learned of the breach on August 21. Subsection (2) says that "Market price is to be determined as of the place for tender or, in the cases of rejection after arrival or revocation of acceptance, as of the place of arrival." Here we have a rejection after the goods have arrived in Boise, so the relevant market is Boise. The market price on August 21 in Boise was $3.00. The contract price was $2.00. Better Foods is entitled to damages to the tune of $1.00 per pound.

Section 2-713 also provides, of course, for the aggrieved buyer's recovery of incidental or consequential damages as well as a deduction for any expenses saved by the buyer in consequence of the seller's breach. Here there are no incidental or consequential damages, or at least none that we know of. Did Better Foods save anything because of the breach? It appears not. This contract was F.O.B. Boise. Salmons of Seattle was to pay for the transportation and we assume has done so. So Better Foods was to incur no expense for transportation to begin with. Barring any additional facts of which we are not now aware, the $1.00 is all that Better Foods is entitled to under §2-713, and it's an amount that should make that buyer whole in an economic sense.

5b.   The date when the buyer learned of the breach remains the same, August 21. The place of arrival, which is the relevant market since this was a shipment rejected, is still Boise. So we subtract the contract price of $1.98 from the market contract price of $3.00 and get $1.02. It appears that Better Foods will get more under this scenario, but wait: Better Foods has under this price term also taken upon itself the cost of transportation of $.05 per pound. If it still must pay the carrier then it can get a recovery of $1.02 per pound from Salmons, but it ends up with only a total of $.97 in pocket. If, on the other hand, under the arrangement with the railroad Better Foods is not liable for the shipping cost when it rejects the goods, then it is off the hook in that respect. But the §2-713 measure of damages must be decreased by the expenses saved in consequence of Salmon's breach. Better Foods would not have to pay the railroad anything but could only recover $.97 from Salmons. All this is simply a result, as you can see, of the price of "$1.98 F.O.B. Seattle" actually being a less attractive price than "$2.00 F.O.B. Boise" when the cost of transportation between the two cities is $.05 per pound.

5d. The time that the buyer learned of the breach remains the same, August 21. What is the relevant market? Under §2-713(2), because this is not a case of rejection upon arrival or revocation of acceptance, the place to pick is the *place for tender.* Unfortunately, Article 2 nowhere specifies exactly where the place for tender is either in the general case or, more importantly for our purposes, in a shipment contract such as this. In a destination contract it seems unavoidable that the place for tender is the actual destination. There's some greater question in a shipment contract. Looking at §§2-503(2) and 2-504 together, however, it seems fair to conclude that the drafters would want us to take the place where the goods are loaded on board and the seller completes its duties under the shipment contract as the place of tender in this situation.

So Better Food's damages are to be measured initially as $2.97 minus $1.98 or $.99 per pound. From this must be subtracted the $.05 per pound transportation cost which the buyer will not have to pay because no stuff was ever shipped at all. Better Foods collects $.94 per pound.

6. This Example presents how to measure damages under §2-713 in light of an anticipatory repudiation. This issue has caused a great deal of controversy, and there is no general agreement by the authorities. The problem is that §2-713 says that the time at which market price is to be determined is "the time the buyer learned of the breach." That section also refers us to §2-723, which is supposed to help out but which really doesn't. Look at §2-723(1). It states a rule to be applied when the action based on repudiation comes to trial before the time for performance. So arguably it has no part to play in our particular hypo. If anything it may be an evil influence. Notice that the drafters here use the phrase "when the aggrieved party learned *of the repudiation.*" If nothing else this reminds us that the drafters usually are careful to distinguish "breach" and "repudiation" to mean different events. A repudiation signals a breach may be in the offing, but it is not a breach in and of itself. It may be turned into a breach given the passage of time, or the nonrepudiating party may choose to treat it as a breach, but then it also may be retracted so that no breach can ever be said to have occurred (§2-611). If a repudiation does ripen into a breach, typically the breach would come at least some time after the repudiation. But when? Is the nonrepudiating party ever *required* to treat the repudiation as the other party's last word on the subject and accept the repudiation as a breach? If so, that innocent victim could then be held to some obligation to take steps to mitigate prior to the initially promised date of performance. Look carefully at §2-610. It says that the nonrepudiating party *may* "for a commercially reasonable time await performance by the repudiating party." What it never says is that this party *must* do anything, and in particular it never says what untoward consequences the nonrepudiating party will be made to face if after the end of this "commercially reasonable time" it does nothing

other than keep on waiting—waiting perhaps still in the hope that the repudiator will see the error of its ways, or waiting to bring a suit when it gets around to it, or when it thinks the circumstances will get it the biggest damage award.

We seem to have strayed very far from §2-713, but when we return to that section we find a whole new level of problem in that section's directive that the time "when the buyer learned of the breach" be used to ascertain the correct market price. Since the adoption of Article 2, analysts have argued over at least three different readings which could be given this language in the repudiation case such as we have here. As a matter of fact we should give a nod to one casebook editor, Professor Corman, who has been able to come up with a *fourth* possibility, but as it is we are teetering on the brink of overload. It will be enough for us to discuss the three traditional contestants for the post of "the time when the buyer learns of the breach." Each has something to say for it and each has its problems. Let's take each in turn.

One suggestion is that buyer's market damages should be measured with respect to the market value of wheat as of the time the buyer *learned of the repudiation*. At least the date in question would usually be easy to assess in most instances. In our case the date would be June 1 and the damages would be $.05 per bushel. The problem with this proposal is that the drafters refer in §2-713(1) to the time the buyer learned of the *breach*, and as we know *breach* and *repudiation* are just not the same thing under Article 2, not just technically but as a matter of practice. There is no language in §2-713 that calls for or even really supports this result. And if this were the correct reading of §2-713, look what it would say to Buyer. You have just received a repudiation. The Code in §2-610 understands that you deserve some time to react. You may decide to cover, and even then you may cover in one of a number of ways. If you do decide to cover, under §2-712 you can be sure that you will have a reasonable time to do so. If, however, it later turns out that you decide not to cover you will be stuck with a remedy measured as of the moment this problem was first put before you. In a rising market as we have here it almost seems as if it could cost you something if you don't cover. And you certainly will suffer if you do cover and a court later decides you took too long to do so. Perhaps the best thing for a buyer in this situation is to elect immediately to treat the repudiation as a breach and to cover as soon as possible. But this, as we've said, doesn't seem to square with what is said in §2-610(a). Besides which it almost seems to penalize the buyer who is willing to cut the seller a little slack and give it some time to consider retracting its repudiation. It's hard to imagine that this is what the drafters would have intended. Professors White and Summers give this problem a good going-over in their treatise (§6-7) in spite of the fact (or perhaps because) it involves making one's way through in their words "an impossible legal thicket" of Code sections. As to this approach—reading "learned of the breach" as equivalent to "learned of the repudiation"—they report, "Sad to say . . . a majority of the courts who have faced this issue have adopted this obvious, if pedestrian, interpretation of the 'learned of the breach' language." So much for approach number one.

A second candidate for the honors of "the time when the buyer learns of the breach" in this situation is equally easy to reckon. We take the actual date of delivery (the date that is when delivery had initially been promised but does not arrive) to do the market minus contract calculation. This is in fact how the problem was usually dealt with by the common law. In our hypothetical the date would be December 15 and the measure of damages a whopping $.83 a bushel. Technically this may be the easiest result to reconcile with the language of Article 2. Whatever is true of the repudiation, we reason, the breach doesn't actually occur until the date when delivery is not made as promised. So the buyer can't "learn of" the breach until that moment. Also, §2-723(1) is respected because that subsection is stated to apply only when an action is brought before the scheduled time for performance. But then we can have second thoughts. Why should Buyer here get the $.83 per bushel in damages where it would have been entitled, under the clear mandate of §2-723(1), to only $.05 if had sued on December 1 instead of during the following January? What purpose would there be in the drafters' allowing for such an increase in damages principally because the suit was delayed?

Finally we come to the third and final contender: It has been argued that the appropriate time to set the market price on which the buyer can recover is the date, whatever it is, at the end of that "commercially reasonable time" given to the buyer to await performance under §2-610(a). One problem here, of course, is that we don't know exactly what that date is. The Code at other points does refer to "commercially reasonable this" or "commercially reasonable that" in any number of places, but it seems particularly tricky to apply this kind of language to judge when something *should have* happened when the whole problem is that nothing *did* happen. And what was supposed to happen anyway? Section 2-610, as we have noted before, says only that the buyer may await performance for such a length of time, but it doesn't say anything about the buyer having to do anything once that time has run. Why can't the buyer just go on waiting and waiting if that is its considered choice? Comment 1 says that if the nonrepudiating party "awaits performance beyond a commercially reasonable time he cannot recover resulting damages which he should have avoided," but that seems to beg the question here. If the buyer eventually decides never to purchase other goods in substitution, that is, not to cover, what does it mean to say that it shouldn't be entitled to resulting damages it could have avoided? In our case, should Buyer sue asking for the full $.87, and if we argue (along with Seller) under this interpretation that this is somehow an inappropriate amount, what are we telling Buyer it should have done to avoid running up the damages that high? We certainly can't be saying it should have covered even when it had no desire to do so. Section 2-712 makes cover totally optional for the buyer. Perhaps all we end up saying is that Buyer could have avoided seeking damages of $.87 per bushel by instructing its attorneys not to be so greedy and to ask instead for another, lower figure.

In spite of all the problems with reading §2-712 and §2-610 together in this way, a number of commentators have concluded that this is indeed what the drafters would have preferred in this situation and what should be done. First we come to some conclusion about when a commercially reasonable party in Buyer's position would have realized that Seller in repudiating meant what it said and would not be changing its mind. We must settle on the date when such a reasonable buyer would wake up and smell the coffee so to speak and resign itself to the fact that it wasn't going to get any wheat from this Seller in December. Having come to rest on some date some time after June 1 but presumably before December 15, we take the market value of wheat in Buyer's locale on that date and toss it into the §2-713 formula.

It may indeed be that this middle road is the one the drafters would have preferred in the situation. That turns out to be the conclusion of a number of commentators who have looked at the problem and a goodly number of courts. See, for instance, the discussion in *Cosden Oil v. Karl O. Helm Aktiengellschaft*, 736 F.2d 1064, 38 U.C.C. 1645 (5th Cir. 1984). It's only fair to point out, however, that the drafters didn't draft a statute which made it easy to reach this result. White and Summers conclude that the preferred interpretation is to stick with the common law result of measuring the damages as of the time set for delivery:

> Pre-Code common law, the Restatement (First) of Contracts, and the Uniform Sales Act all permitted the buyer in an anticipatory repudiation case to recover the contract-market differential at the date for performance. Before we permit the drafters to upset such uniform and firmly entrenched doctrine, we can rightfully ask for at least a sentence or two of comment and more explicit statutory language than "learned of the breach."

Perhaps the best we can do when all is said and done is to quote the court in the *Cosden Oil* case which observed in a footnote: "The only area of unanimous agreement among those who have studied the Code provisions relevant to this problem is that they are not consistent, present problems in interpretation, and invite amendment." Amen to that.

7.   This Example presents a second of the great controversies involving application of §2-713: Is the buyer free to sue for the market minus contract measure of damages when it did in fact cover and covered at below the market price? Marinara argues for $3 per pound as the difference to which it is entitled under §2-713. Herb claims that since that company was able to buy the oregano it needed for $17 it was only damaged to the tune of $2 per pound and can be fully compensated by an award of that amount. What result?

Again there is a difference of opinion among the experts. One side relies upon a strict reading of §2-713 which simply says that the aggrieved buyer is entitled to recover in this fashion. It doesn't say that the aggrieved buyer, in the event it should not cover, can get this much. Note also that §2-711 (the font of all wisdom about buyer's remedies) has a nice and simple *or* between subparts (1)(a) and (1)(b). Another argument for this position goes beyond the text. If the buyer makes many purchases of similar stuff over a period of time at a variety of prices, it may be possible for the breaching seller to point to just about any of these purchases, and in particular one at a price near to or even lower than the contract price, and characterize it as the buyer's "cover" to replace what the seller didn't deliver. Seller, it is feared, might be able to wriggle its way out of paying damages for its breach just because the buyer had made other advantageous purchases of the same product some time after seller's breach or repudiation. The problem might not seem so acute in the hypothetical we are considering, at least if we assume that Marinara usually buys only a given amount of oregano during any one year. If, however, the buyer is someone who regularly trades in goods and who will normally order as much as it can from whomever it can if the price is right, the potential for seller's abuse of a contrary interpretation is significantly greater.

Those who would limit Marinara to $2 per pound here, and in general limit the buyer who covers to damages as measured by §2-712 even if (especially if) §2-713 would produce a heftier sum, point first of all to the general policy enunciated in §1-106 that Code remedies are to be applied for the purpose of giving the wronged party adequate compensation but, they would emphasize, no more than is necessary for this purpose. Note also the last comment to §2-713:

> The present section provides a remedy which is completely alternative to cover under the preceding section and applies *only when and to the extent that the buyer has not covered.*

This is only a comment, true, but shouldn't it be given some weight in deciding the issue? And to the argument which we saw earlier, that the breaching seller should not be given the option of deciding for the buyer which if any of its purchases of like goods served as cover, the response is that this is just a matter of proof with which the courts can and will deal should it become necessary.

There are surprisingly few cases which have had to come to grips with the issue here. If there is anything like a better or more accepted result it would probably be that in favor of the breaching seller, at least in a case like we have here where the fact of cover and the cover price seem not fairly in dispute.

8a. Barbara has accepted the watch and paid for it at the contract rate. The question here is how much she can recover from the buyer for a very blatant breach of warranty. With respect to accepted goods we look to §2-714. Before we do so, however, we want to remind ourselves once again about the importance of §2-607(3)(a). Now is as good a time as any to look at that subpart one more time. Having done so you are entitled to move on to §2-714(1).

> [The buyer of accepted goods] may recover as damages for any
> non-conformity of tender the loss resulting in the ordinary course of
> events from the seller's breach as are determined in any manner
> which is reasonable.

That's a very general statement. Read on to subsection (2).

> The measure of damages for breach of warranty is the difference
> at the time and place of acceptance between the value of the goods
> accepted and the value they would have had if they had been as
> warranted, unless special circumstances show proximate dam-
> ages of a different amount.

This fits Barbara's situation exactly. The value of the watch she accepted
was at the time of sale approximately $800. The value which the watch
would have had if it had been as warranted was $3,500. Barbara is entitled
to $2,700 in damages. Notice that at the time of purchase Barbara had
not only been expecting the higher quality watch, but she could reasonably
have thought that she was getting a bargain, at something like $300 off
of the standard price. The $2,700 recovery, measured as it is by the true
value of *what she was promised* and not by the purchase price, gets her
the economic equivalent of everything she was promised including the
benefit of her bargain.

8b. If the value of what she bought would have been $2,800 if it were
as promised, then she is entitled to recover $2,000, which is just $2,800
minus the actual value of what she got ($800). She ends up with a total
value of $2,800: $2,000 in cash and $800 in watch. Recall that she
originally paid Sam $3,200. She still seems to come out behind by $400
and indeed she does, but the reason for this is that she initially made a
bad bargain with Sam. She agreed to and did pay $3,200 for a watch
worth only something like $2,800. Assuming he didn't put a gun to her
head, Sam is not responsible for this loss. He is responsible in the contract,
and by the measure of damages he will be made to pay, for her getting
what she was promised by him and that is $2,800 in value, however you
slice it up.

9a. If Crafty had been able to repair the oven so that it was just as good
as new, it would be fairly easy to say that the difference between the
oven as promised and as delivered was $1,200. The courts have in many
instances used the cost of repair as a measure of damages for nonconformity of accepted goods, and that seems an appropriate measure here. The
interesting issue here is how to deal with the fact that the oven even as
repaired is not as good as it was warranted to be by the seller. If Doe can
establish by some credible evidence how much less the oven is worth as
a patched-up job than it would be worth new and as warranted, he should
be able to add this difference onto the cost of repair to get the full measure
of his recovery. The value of the oven as warranted might not be that
hard to establish. If nothing else the purchase price of $10,500 would
seem to be good evidence of that value. His difficulty will be in coming
up with a figure for the value of the oven now as imperfectly repaired.

Perhaps he can find a person who specializes in appraising used pizza ovens who would be willing to give it a shot.

9b. Here we have the even more interesting question of what to do under §2-714 where the nonconformity is repaired and the end result is a product *even better* than the buyer ever had a right to expect under the warranty. Doe argues for $1,200, the cost of repair, but now the oven manufacturer argues that some of that expense went into improving the oven which will work to Doe's benefit and that the heightened value of the oven should be subtracted from what it as a breaching seller has to pay in damages. What do you think of this? Perhaps if Ovens can come up with a very sound figure representing the increase in value over what Doe was first promised, it should get somewhere with this argument, but I can't say that I'm terribly concerned about Doe's being "overcompensated" in this way. Others would differ.

10. Buyer should be able to subtract the "loss resulting in the ordinary cost of events" due to Seller's late delivery "as determined in any manner which is reasonable." How exactly Buyer is going to put a figure on the effect of this delay is not at all clear, and maybe it will not be able to do so, but at least §2-714(1) leaves no doubt he is entitled to try. Note also the final part to Comment 1 to §1-106.

> [The Code] reject[s] any doctrine that damages must be calculable with mathematical accuracy. Compensatory damages are often at best approximate: they have to be proved with whatever definiteness and accuracy the facts permit, but no more.

So good luck to Buyer as he tries to prove the damage caused to him by the two-week delay.

An interesting case to consider in connection with the damages that can be caused by late delivery is *Franklin Grain & Supply Co. v. Ingram,* 44 Ill. App. 3d 740, 358 N.E.2d 922, 21 U.C.C. 53 (1976). The defendant contracted to sell and apply fertilizer to the plaintiff farmer's crop. The fertilizer was applied after the time called for by the agreement, too late in fact to be of any benefit to the crops. When the seller sued for payment, the buyer counterclaimed for the damages caused by the delay. An award to the buyer for damages was upheld on appeal, the appellate court concluding:

> Though there is some uncertainty about evidence of loss of yield, complicated by many factors such as weather, date of fertilizing, and other matters, we cannot say that the trial court's decision that [buyer] had been damaged to the extent of five bushels per acre is against the manifest weight of the evidence. Testimony of adjoining and nearby farmers regarding their use or non-use of fertilizer and their yields furnished sufficient evidence to support the court's findings regarding damages.

Buyer should have no trouble getting reimbursed for the $200 paid to the local warehouse to hold on to the rejected goods. This would be a classic case of incidental damages under §2-715(1) to which he is entitled in addition to any other damage he may have suffered (§2-714(3)).

Note in general that for the wronged buyer to recover for incidental damages under §2-715(1) only three criteria need be met. The expenses need to have been actually incurred, they must be "reasonable" in amount, and they must represent "expense incident to the delay or other breach."

11. Doe would claim his lost profits for the five-day period as consequential damages under §2-715(2). The criteria for award of consequential damages are more extensive than those we just saw for incidental damages under the same section. The damages need to have been actually suffered, of course, and in addition they need to be reasonably certain of calculation. As to this last point, see Comment 4. There is also the requirement that they "result from the seller's breach," that is, a causation element. Beyond that there are two criteria in subpart (a) each of which should sound familiar to you. First of all, loss such as Doe is claiming here must result "from general or particular requirements and needs of which the seller at the time of contracting had reason to know." If this sounds like that old standby from Contracts, the rule of *Hadley v. Baxendale,* well that's just what it is. I won't repeat here all that I might about that doctrine, as you are no doubt perfectly familiar and comfortable with it. (Note in passing Comment 2's pronouncement that the *tacit agreement test* that was offered up at one time as a refinement of *Hadley* has been explicitly rejected by the drafters of Article 2.) The final requirement is that the items claimed as consequential damages "could not [have been] reasonably prevented by cover or otherwise." Here we have the traditional mitigation principle of the common law incorporated into the Code.

So it's not at all clear whether Doe can get any or all of his lost profits under the circumstances. Certainly the courts have shown themselves willing to accept loss profits caused by a seller's breach as includable consequential damages, but each of the criteria will have to be met. We would want to know, for starters, how much profit Doe makes on a typical day and how well he can back up this figure. It would also be important to know whether Ovens had any reason to know, at the time the contract was entered into, that he was going to be open that particular Sunday for the private party. Or would it be enough if Doe could show that Ovens was aware that he sometimes served private parties on Sundays? This is the kind of question, you'll remember, that made *Hadley v. Baxendale* so much fun. Also it will be important to explore whether Doe could have reasonably prevented this loss of profit "by cover or otherwise." It seems unlikely that cover would have been available quickly enough to make a difference, but maybe there was some other way Doe could have prevented or lessened his losses over these five days. It's all in the facts.

The range of items that can and have been considered as legitimate consequential damages is, not surprisingly, very broad. Where a breach of warranty results in injury to a person or property, §2-715(2)(b) makes extra sure that these things are included, the only criterion being that the injury was proximately caused by the breach. Consequential damages have been awarded when the buyer has lost profit from an anticipated resale or has been made to pay damages to or entered into a settlement with other third parties adversely affected by the goods. Consequential damages are where and as you find them. On the question of what effect is to be given a provision in the contract of sale purporting to limit or modify what the buyer can recover for consequential damages, see §2-719(3) and the discussion of that section in Chapter 14.

12. Garden Seating has lost whatever profits it was expecting to make from the sale of lawn chairs during the current season. It should be able to collect that either under the rubric of general damages under §2-714(1) or as consequential damages under §2-715(2). Webber had every reason to know of Garden Seating's requirements for that year, and it does not appear there was anything which the furniture manufacturer could have done to avoid this loss. If anything, the prompt recall may well have saved someone from getting seriously hurt and suing for personal injury. The more interesting question is that presented by the fact that the company seems to have lost so much of its value as a going concern because of what has happened. A term that you will hear in connection with this type of thing is a *loss of commercial good will* or simply *good will*. Garden Seating had over time built up a valuable reputation for the Nettie Chair and that reputation was worth something to the company. Now a good portion of that precious reputation seems to be lying in ruins, all thanks to the breach by Webber and Company. Another way of looking at this loss of good will is to think of it as some reflection, imprecise although it may be, of the loss of profits for some years into the future which can be expected until the public forgets about what has happened or until Garden Seating can reestablish its profitability, perhaps by starting to make chairs under another name entirely and slowly building up some good will under this new name. Either will take time and during this time Garden Seating's profits can be expected to suffer.

There is no reason in theory why loss of good will should not be recoverable as foreseeable consequential damages just as lost profits in the current year are. The problem is one of proof. Courts in the past have been very leery of any argument that loss of good will could be valued with any kind certainty or at least not the certainty required to underlie an award of damages. This attitude, however, seems to be changing. A number of recent decisions have allowed for recovery of this type of damage as long as the plaintiff could prove a measure of lost good will with reasonable certainty. For an example, see *AM/PM Franchise Association v. Atlantic Richfield Co.*, 526 Pa. 110, 584 A.2d 915, 14 U.C.C.2d 11 (1990), which is particularly interesting in that it overruled a series of earlier Pennsylvania cases that had been read as declaring that loss of good will could never be recovered in such a situation. With the new trend in the cases and with what does seem like some very strong evidence of loss of good will, Garden Machines should be able to recover something from Webber and Company on this argument. Of course they should be ready to confront a battery of experts for the defendant ready to testify that the apparent loss in value of the company could and should be attributed to just about any other factor than the minor problem with the webbing.

13. Yes, Bertha should be able to deduct the $100 for each day late. The language of this subsection of §2-718 will look familiar to you. It's the basic notion which you should have studied in Contracts: A so-called liquidated damages clause is enforceable while what is characterized as a penalty clause is not. I hope you went over the basic idea in Contracts and have secure in your mind how the courts, and here the Code, will make the distinction. See also Comment 1 to this section. Unless M.M.S. can make the argument that $100 a day is an "unreasonably large" amount, Bertha should have her boat, late but for a lesser price. This figure doesn't seem unreasonably large to me. Certainly if the boat where a day or two late, a subtraction of $100 or $200 wouldn't seem inappropriate. Maybe it's because I don't sell boats for a living.

14. This question is unique in this chapter because Sam the buyer is also the breacher. Certainly a man who's breached a contract can't go after the other fellow for contract damages, can he? No, he can't, but under §2-718(2) the drafters have allowed for the breaching (or, we have to assume, the repudiating) buyer's getting some measure of relief under the theory of restitution. Assuming there was no liquidated damage provision in the contract, Sam is entitled to any amount by which his payment exceeds the smaller of 20 percent of the value of the total performance, which in this case equals $600, or the flat sum of $500. So Sam has the right under this subsection to get $300 back. Dave has the right to keep $500 of the down-payment as a kind of statutory liquidated damage sum. See Comment 2. Notice that under subsection (3) even this $300 sum is subject to offset if Dave could show any damages resulting from Sam's breach. Assuming that Dave is not a lost-volume seller and given that he has sold the used car for more than the initial contract price, there probably will be no such offsetting damages. Which raises one final point for consideration: What if Dave had resold for $2,400, thereby suffering damage of $600? A literal reading of §2-718 seems to unmistakenly say that Sam should not get a penny of his down-payment back. The amount to which he is entitled under subsection (2) is, as we have seen, only $300. Subtract $600 actual damages from that under (3) and you see that Sam should consider himself lucky that he's not being asked to come up with even more money. But if the subtraction provided for in subsection (2) is intended to work as a kind of statutory liquidated damages provision, shouldn't it fall away once real damages have been proven? In other words, here Dave actually suffered $600 damage from the breach; if he

got to keep that amount and had to return only $200 of the down-payment, isn't he perfectly compensated? It seems likely that the drafters meant this to be the effect of these two subsections working in tandem. Unfortunately, that isn't what they wrote.

30

Remedies in Lease Transactions

Introduction

There are no Examples to be analyzed or agonized over in this chapter. Rather I will try to give a brief explanation of the remedy provisions of Article 2A as they exist in the most recent, the 1990 Official Version.* This abbreviated treatment is justified I believe, for two reasons. First of all, as you will quickly discover, the basic structure of the remedy provisions follows fairly closely that of Article 2. The remedies available to lessors and lessees under 2A are by and large meant to be analogous to those available to buyers and sellers under Article 2. Certainly the underlying philosophy is the same. See the reference to the goal of putting the lessee "in as good a position as if the lessor had fully performed the lease agreement" but no better in Comment 2 to §2A-508 and the perfectly parallel language characterizing lessor's remedies in Comment 4 to §2A-523.

Secondly, the drafters of 2A have been particularly generous with their Official Comments to these sections. There has in fact been criticism of what is said by some to be an attempt to "legislate by comment," but the overall result has been to make the reader's task (and mine) that much

---

*On Article 2A and its recent history, please see Chapter 2 and the "History" portion of the Comment to §2A-101. Be sure, before you try to work through this chapter that your copy of the Code does say it is the *1990* Official Version. Many of the changes made by the Standby Committee through the 1990 Amendments to 2A (promulgated in the hope of assuring the article's "rapid and uniform" adoption by the states) were in these remedy provisions, the original 1987 versions of which were the subject of a good deal of criticism and debate. It remains to be seen how well the 2A drafters did on their second pass through these issues.

easier. I will try to go through the list of available remedies, basically following the order in which we met the analogous provisions covering the sale of goods. In some instances only a few words have been changed, the only purpose being, in a phrase found repeatedly in the comments to 2A, revision "to reflect leasing practices and terminology." Sometimes pieces of the puzzle have been moved around a bit, but the overall effect is basically the same. In those cases where the fact of a lease or traditional leasing practices called for a notably different approach or introduction of an entirely new level of complexity (as we'll see, for instance with the concept of *present value*), we'll stop and note the difference.

There is one overriding difference between traditional practice in sales and that in lease transactions which seems to inform and run through-out these provisions. The drafters of 2A worked under the assumption that the parties to a lease transaction, at least a long-term commercial lease, were more likely than were the parties to a sale to include in the lease contract itself by explicit agreement terms or conditions relating to the remedies to be had by one or the other, the lessor or the lessee, in the event of a default. (Note from the outset this one semantic distinction: In sales we tend to speak of a *breach,* in leases it's a *default.*) Article 2, as we know, allows the parties, with some notable exceptions, to contract around its provisions or "otherwise agree" to just about anything they want. The same commitment to freedom of contract is apparent in 2A. The difference may come more in practice. In actual fact, lessors and lessees appear much more likely than sellers and buyers actually to take the opportunity in their contract documents to spell out what will happen in such-and-such an event. At least the drafters of 2A thought this was so and worked to accommodate this type of thing. See the "Damages" portion of the Comment to §2A-101 and Comment 1 to §2A-503.

One significant addition in Article 2A is seen right away in §2A-501 which introduces the Default provisions. Subsection (1) states that: "Whether the lessor or lessee is in default under a lease contract is deter-mined by the lease agreement and this Article." This language has no precedent in Article 2. For sales, a breach occurs when a breach occurs and we know all about this from the article itself. Leases, as we have just noted, are more likely to have express provisions drafted and agreed to by the parties—often very lengthy and prodigiously detailed—spelling out in no uncertain terms "the events of default." In this respect the documents evidencing lease agreements often look more like security agreements drafted for the purpose of creating and making clear the parties rights under an Article 9 security agreement. Note that the uniform statutory source for §2A-501 is not from Article 2 at all. Rather it is §9-501. If you have already studied Article 9, you will be able to appreciate this point. If you have not yet studied Secured Transactions, do not fear. The drafters of 2A for better or worse decided to model their work on Article 2 for the most part. See the "Statutory Analogue" discussion in Comment 1 to §2A-101. For our purposes, this decision was clearly for the better, as it allows us to review the 2A remedy provisions by tracking those we've already seen in studying Article 2.

Modification of Remedy and Liquidation

Section 2A-503 governs the modification or impairment of rights and remedies under 2A. As you read through this provision, everything will seem more than vaguely familiar. Subsections (1) through (3) come directly from §2-719, the 2A drafters pausing only to rewrite to reflect lease terminology and to make explicit some things which they find implicit in the sales section. Subsection (4) is, as the comment tells us, a revision of §2-701, but contains no change of great import.

We pass on to §2A-504, which should look even more familiar. Liquidation of damages is governed by rules borrowed from §2-718 with a touch of §2-719(2) thrown in. The drafters have, however, allowed for greater flexibility in some respects. Section 2A-504 covers the situation of a default (just as §2-718 deals with a breach) but also "any other act or omission." It allows for liquidation by the use of "a formula," not just "an amount." Liquidation under §2A-504 does not require proof of a situation in which there can be expected to be "difficulties of proof of loss" and "the inconvenience or nonfeasibility of otherwise obtaining an adequate remedy," as does §2-718(1). For other changes, indeed for a short course on the subject, see the comment to this section.

Lessee's "Goods Related" Remedies

We discussed the buyer's so-called goods related remedies of rejection and revocation of acceptance, with the attendant issues of cure and all the rest, in an earlier part of the book in the context of performance. Article 2A moves these topics from its Part 4 on Performance to Part 5 on Default. Otherwise the terminology and the treatment remains virtually identical. Section 2A-509 provides in its first subsection for the lessee's right to accept or reject the goods or to accept only some commercial units upon an improper delivery, just like §2-601. It even adopts the "fails in any respect" perfect tender language of that section. The procedure for rejection is found in §2A-509(2), which tracks §2-602(1).

The *installment lease contract* is defined in §2A-103(1)(i), which is a steal from §2-612(1). The provisions governing such a lease contract found in §2A-510 track the rest of §2-612 just as slavishly.

The general duties of any lessee with respect to rightfully rejected goods are listed in §2A-512, which has as its source parts of §§2-602 and 2-604. The special rules applicable to a merchant lessee upon rightful rejection are given in §2A-511, which follows §2-603 and one part of §2-706.

The doctrine of cure coming out of §2A-513 is the same, terminology aside, as cure in §2-508. Similarly, §2A-514 tracks §2-605 and §2A-515 on acceptance follows §2-606. Section 2A-516 on the effects of acceptance generally follows the similar section, §2-607, in Article 2. Some changes have been made to reflect the special situation of the finance lease (on which see Chapter 17) and the consumer lease, which is defined in §2A-103(1)(e). Neither special situation need detain us here.

You are no doubt beginning to get the picture of how Article 2A relates to Article 2. Imitation, after all, is the sincerest form of flattery—and, the drafters must have hoped, uniformity. To wrap up this section, we note that §2A-517 deals with revocation of acceptance. Here again we have no trouble divining the source for the general provisions. It is §2-608.

Lessor's Remedies

Look at §2A-523(1). The style, and quite a bit of the substance, should be familiar. This is an index provision, listing the remedies available to the lessor if the lessee "wrongfully rejects or revokes acceptance of the goods or fails to make a payment when due or repudiates with respect to a part of the whole." It is analogous to §2-703 which catalogs the seller's remedies in the event of a buyer's breach. Subsection (2) of §2A-523 gives the lessor's rights should it not exercise a right or obtain a remedy to which it is entitled under the first subsection. See Comment 19 for further explanation. Subsection (3) was necessary because a lessee may be in default of the lease contract in ways not enumerated in subsection (1). The lessee, for example, may be obligated under the terms of the lease to keep the goods in good repair or to have them protected by a given level of insurance coverage. These provisions are important to the lessor, who is expecting to get the goods back at the end of the lease term in decent condition. Should the lessee fail to meet its obligations under such a provision of the lease agreement, it will be a default, but not one of the sort which automatically triggers the provisions of subsection (1). The lessor will look to subsection (3) for its rights under the circumstances. See Comment 20.

In reviewing the various options open to the lessor under §2-523(1) and the sections that follow, you should be able to make use of what you know about seller's remedies under Article 2 as we covered them in Chapter 28. If you want a bit more practice, the drafters of 2A have conveniently included discussion of a lengthy hypothetical in Comments 5 through 18(!) to this section. We'll move on to the sections themselves.

First we run into §2A-524 on the Lessor's Right to Identify Goods to the Lease Contract, which is nothing new. It comes directly from §2-704.

The next section, §2A-525, does slow us down a bit. Subsection (1) is a revised version of §2-702 (with which we are familiar), but (2) and (3) have no counterparts in Article 2. Their source is, in fact, §9-503. Here we *do* have a code difference between 2 and 2A reflecting an important practical distinction between sales and leases. When the seller sells goods it parts with them forever. If it is not paid it will have various means of trying to get some money out of the buyer, but it cannot simply take the goods back. If the seller is selling on credit and does want this manner of protection, if it wants to have the right to come and retake the goods if it is not paid as it has been promised, it must look for a mechanism beyond the bounds of Article 2. The seller finds this mechanism in the *purchase money security interest* allowed for and governed by Article 9. *If*—and it's a big *if*—the seller does secure for itself such a security interest, and *if* it protects that interest appropriately, it will have the right under §9-503 to repossess the goods (which are now referred to also as the *collateral*) upon a default by the buyer. But in general, we should be clear the Article 2 seller has no such right.

The lessor under Article 2A is working under a different set of assumptions. Given that we are dealing with a true lease, which we must if we are working within the scope of 2A,* the lessor has from the very start always assumed that it would continue to be the owner of the goods. Further it continues to assume that it will get the goods back at some time in the future. As long as the rent is paid, the lessee has the use of the goods. If the rent isn't paid, it is a fine old tradition in the law of leases, both of real property and of goods, that the lessor will be able to retake possession earlier than the end of the term. If you don't pay the rent on your house or apartment, you may eventually expect to be locked out with your stuff on the street. If you don't keep up with the rental payments on that car or that boat, you may find the lessor has taken it back to the lot or the showroom. Section 2A-525 reflects this facet of leasing. As the comments elucidate, this section was included in 2A "to codify the lessor's common law right to protect the lessor's reversionary interest in the goods."

With that out of the way, we can look once again at §2A-523(1) and sketch out the parallels between the monetary relief afforded the lessor and that which are available to an aggrieved seller under Article 2. The aggrieved lessor may go after the lessee for cash in one of three ways: "In the proper case" it may bring an action for rent under §2A-529. If the lessor covers by disposing of the goods either through another substitute lease or through a sale, it may seek damages on a contract minus cover measure (§2A-527). Finally, it may seek damages under a contract minus market theory (§2A-528(1)), or where the situation warrants for lost profits (§2A-528(2)). All this is very much in keeping with the basic remedies for sellers under Article 2, with only a few changes worthy of note.

We saw in a previous chapter that the seller's action for the price is available in only a limited number of circumstances. So too for the lessor's action for the rent under §2A-529. In fact it is even less likely to be available. Like the seller, the lessor can sue the lessee for the rent where the goods have been lost or damaged after the risk of loss has passed to the other party or where they cannot be disposed of in some way at a reasonable price. Unlike the seller, however, the lessor does not usually

---

*On the importance of this strange term, the *true lease,* and the scope of 2A in general, see Chapter 2.

have a right to this type of relief just because the goods have been accepted. The lessor can sue for the rent only with respect to "goods accepted by the lessee and not repossessed by or tendered to the lessor." If the lessor has taken the goods back, or if the lessee is willing to let the lessor take them back, then the lessor is going to have to be the one to try to arrange some disposition of the goods that minimizes the damages the lessee can be made to pay. The reasoning behind this further narrowing of the right to collect directly the amount of the rent following a default is set forth in Comment 1.

Notice what the lessor can collect under this type of action should it be available. Section 2A-529 gives lessor the right to

> (i) accrued and unpaid rent as of the date of entry of judgment in favor of the lessor, (ii) the present value as of the same date of the rent for the then remaining lease term of the lease agreement, and (iii) any incidental damages allowed under Section 2A-530, less expenses saved in consequence of the lessee's default.

The new concept here—new to the Code, that is, not to the world of finance—is that of *present value*. The idea is not difficult. Suppose a lessor was going to get rent of $100 a month, over time, for the remaining two years on the lease. A simple calculation tells us that the rent yet to come in is $2,400. But this calculation is *too* simple. It ignores the very basic principle that cash in hand today, which could be put in the bank and begin immediately earning interest, is inherently worth more than the same amount which is to be collected at some time in the future. Another way of looking at it is that if I had $2,400 today, I could place it in an interest-bearing account, take out $100 each month for the next two years and still have some money in the account at the end of that period. Even a perfectly guaranteed income stream of $100 each month for the next 24 months is worth less than $2,400 today. There is some amount *less* than $2,400 which is the economic equivalent of the right to that income stream over that period of time *assuming* some particular rate of interest. This is the present value of that income stream, or those anticipated payments over time. Given a periodic payment amount, the number of periods and an assumed or agreed upon interest rate, it is a matter of mathematics (more often now a matter of consulting an available table or cranking up a calculator) to find the equivalent present value.

You can see why the present value concept comes into play in remedies calculations once we are talking about leases. Typically the lessor is to get its money over time. If for some reason it is entitled to a judgment, that judgment is calculated as a lump sum. Our system doesn't traditionally award plaintiffs the right to receive bits and pieces of a judgment over time. So lease remedies must necessarily, if they are to be fair to the lessee and not overly compensate the lessor, take into account the present value concept. Hence the definition of *present value* for Article 2A purposes in §2A-103(1)(u):

> "Present value" means the amount as of a date certain of one or more sums payable in the future, discounted to the date certain. The

discount is determined by the interest rate specified by the parties
if the rate was not manifestly unreasonable at the time the
transaction was entered into; otherwise, the discount is determined
by a commercially reasonable rate that takes into account the facts and
circumstances of each case at the time the transaction was entered
into.

See also the comment to this definition. Once you have the concept of
present value firmly in place, there isn't that much that is new or challenging about the monetary remedies in Article 2A.

See, for example, the working of the "cover" minus contract measure
in §2A-527(2). The basic calculation when the goods have been relet is
the subtraction of the present value of what will be made by way of cover
from the present value of the original lease. For the lessor to be entitled
to this amount the substitute or cover lease must be made "in good faith
and in a commercially reasonable manner." Furthermore, the lessor must
be able to establish that the new lease agreement is "substantially similar
to the original lease agreement." The drafters of 2A recognized that this
test of "substantial similarity" might be difficult in some instances. Unlike
resales, where typically what the seller gives in the cover contract will be
pretty much what it was to give to the breaching buyer, lease contracts
may differ in many ways which can make direct comparison tricky. The
drafters provided us with a lengthy set of comments, Comments 4 to 7,
on the substantial similarity issue. Note first of all, in Comment 4, that
whether the new lease agreement is substantially similar to the original
is to be decided on a case-by-case basis. Note further, in the following
comment, that even if there are significant differences between the two
leases this does not necessarily rule out recovery under this section:

> If the differences between the original lease and the new lease can
> be easily valued, it would be appropriate for a court to find
> that the new lease is substantially similar to the old lease, adjust
> the difference in the rent between the two leases to take account
> of the differences, and award damages under this section.

This comment concludes with a helpful example which you may want to
look at.

The third measure of damages to which a lessor may refer is the
standard contract minus market value, here given in §2A-528. This is
substantially the same as §2-708(1) at which we have looked, revised
here to take into account the present value problem. (On the proof of
market value see §2A-507.) Like its Article 2 precursor, §2A-528 has a
second part which gives the lost-volume lessor the right to calculate its
damages in a way analogous to the lost-volume seller's rights under §2-
708(2). Note that §2A-530 provides for the lessor's incidental damages
in virtually the same language as we saw in §2-710 with regard to the
seller.

Article 2A does provide for damages in one situation which Article
2 had no need to consider. Look at §2A-532. If the lessee returns the
goods in a damaged condition or in worse shape than is permitted under

the lease agreement, the lessor must necessarily have a right to recover for this injury, and it does.

Lessee's Remedies

Since we have already explored the concept of present value as it is used in Article 2A as well as the notion of the "substantially similar" lease, there is nothing that should keep us from taking on the lessee's remedies under Article 2A at a particularly brisk pace. Section 2A-508 serves as an index. Subsection (3) is new (see Comment 4) and covers a default by the lessor that does not deprive the lessee of the goods and which is not so serious as to justify a rejection of the goods or a revocation of acceptance. For example, suppose the lessor has agreed in the lease to keep the leased goods in good repair or to provide regular tune-ups and it fails to do so. The lessee should be able to get this work done elsewhere and sue for the cost of this work.

We have already discussed the lessee's so-called goods-oriented remedies of §§2A-509 to 2A-517. Section 2A-518 provides for the lessee who does not get the goods or who has to reject them to "cover" in one form or another and sue for the difference between what it would have had to spend and what it must now pay on the substitute contract. Once again there is the criterion that the substituted agreement be "substantially similar" to the original lease and a set of comments (3 to 7) which try to flesh out this concept. And once again the calculation of damages must take into account the present value aspect of this type of transaction.

An award of damages based on the market minus contract measure is provided for in §2A-519, again taking into account present values. Subsection 2A-519(4) gives the measure of damages if the lessee's complaint is a breach of warranty, in terms reminiscent of §2-714. Section 2A-520 sets out the concepts of incidental and consequential damages of the lessee in terms basically those of §2-715. Section 2A-521 on the lessee's limited rights actually to obtain withheld goods in an action for specific performance or under the right of replevin tracks §2-716. Finally, note the lessee's right to the goods on the lessor's insolvency under §2A-522.

PART SIX

Documentary Transactions

In all that's gone before you have been advised to skip over the various references running throughout Article 2 to *documents* or *documents of title.* We are now ready to confront these terms head on. A document of title under the Code is, to be sure, a *document* in the ordinary sense in which we use the word. It's a piece of paper with writing all over it all right. But it is not just any old piece of paper which happens to have been generated in connection with a commercial transaction. The world, and the commercial world especially, is piled high with paper. As defined in §1-201(15), a *document of title* is a highly specialized affair:

> [A document] which in the regular course of business or financing is treated as adequately evidencing that the person in possession of it is entitled to receive, hold and dispose of the document and the goods it covers. . . . To be a document of title a document must purport to be issued by or addressed to a bailee and purport to cover goods in the bailee's possession which are either identified or are fungible portions of an identified mass.

Documents of title—the two most important of which are the bill of lading provided by a carrier and the warehouse receipt given by a warehouse company—are papers issued by commercial bailees upon their receipt of goods. In this respect they are like the piece of paper you get from the dry cleaner or the laundry when you turn over your clothes to them for a time. They serve as receipts, as evidence of what goods were handed over, when and where. But true documents of title are much more than this. Typically there is language on the document itself that sets forth the terms of the contract of bailment itself. Bills of lading and warehouse receipts don't look like the slip of paper you get at the dry cleaner. They are among the most detailed, and boilerplate-laden, of the various papers which business people deal on a regular day-to-day basis. You have to wonder how many people, if any, have ever read through all of the provisions on one of these things. Of course if everyone did read them regularly, commerce as we know it would grind pretty much to a halt. (This is not to say that savvy business people don't know what they're getting into when they deal in standard documents of title, only that the standardization resulting either from law or custom is what makes the whole system work.)

Beyond its function as a receipt and as the memorial of the bailment contract, a document of title can have a third and very significant function. This will be so if and only if the document is of a special type, what is referred to as a *negotiable* document of title. When and whether a document is negotiable, and if so what the consequences of this will be, become a large part of the story of documentary transactions as that story unfolds in the following two chapters. This is not the place to try a shorthand explanation, even if one could be given. In trying to convey the sense if not any of the particulars of negotiability of documents of title, writers tend (perfectly understandably in my opinion) towards the metaphysical. A negotiable document of title is "a kind of legal substitute for the goods themselves," or "embodies the right to the goods held by the bailee" or is "the physical embodiment of the concept of title to the goods." All very interesting as you will see.

To close this introduction let me suggest another angle from which you will want to view the whole subject of documents of title and documentary transactions. These things have a purpose and perform a function. Documents of title are not new to the Code nor were they invented the other day just so that we'd have some special way to refer to a set of papers. The concepts being explored in what follows have grown up over a long period of time in response to the felt needs of the business community. They serve as the means of accomplishing certain very important goals which otherwise could be attained, if at all, only with much more bother and expense. The idea that trading in goods, the buying and selling that goes on every day, can in many instances be handled much more efficiently by moving around and dealing with pieces of paper (no matter how wordy) which "substitute for" or "embody" the goods themselves has a long and noble history. Today as much as at any time in the past the system works and in the vast majority of cases works well and to the benefit of all involved. In that small minority of cases where the system breaks down, of course, the law will be expected to step in. In the two chapters which follow we will, being who we are, give due attention to how the law parses out the responsibility when something goes wrong. This should not distract us, however, from the main lines of the story that is to emerge, the highly efficient and downright clever system that has been devised over time to keep the wheels of commerce turning and turning as well as they do.

31

Bailment Basics and Documents of Title

Moving Stuff Around

If any one thing is central to the sale of goods in the minds of the parties, it is that ownership of the stuff must actually be passed on from the seller to the buyer. Most often (although not always, as we'll see later in this chapter) this calls for a transfer of possession. The stuff has to move from the seller's possession to the buyer's. This can be done in a variety of ways. If the goods are the kind of thing that one person can handle, there can be a direct hand-off from one party to the other. Even if the goods are bulky, they may be directly transferred. Seller could make a delivery using its own facilities, such as its own delivery van and crew, or the buyer may have the means for making a pick-up, say by sending its own truck and burly employees around to the seller's place of business to collect whatever is waiting for them.

Often enough, however, the means of getting the goods from one place to another involve use of an independent third party, a commercial carrier. One or the other of the parties will have to pay for the carrier's services, of course, but that is not our concern here. We're interested in the mechanics of the procedure itself—how the goods are handled.

To start things off, the seller will deliver some goods over to the carrier, which issues a bill of lading in return. Note the definition of *bill of lading* in §1-201(6):

> "Bill of lading" means a document evidencing the receipt of goods for shipment issued by a person engaged in the business of transporting or forwarding goods, and includes an airbill.

Further note the terms that can now be used to identify each of the parties as defined in §7-102: The carrier is a *bailee* and also the *issuer* of the bill. The seller in this instance is the *consignor* (colloquially *the bailor* or more often *the shipper*). Who is the *consignee?* That depends. In many cases the goods will be consigned directly to the buyer at their ultimate destination. In others, as we will discover, the seller reserves some control over the goods (typically to insure payment before they are actually handed over) by consigning them to itself or to some other person who is to act on the seller's behalf. In some instances, in fact, the seller will have no choice but to consign the goods in this way, since the identity of the party to whom they will ultimately be delivered will not even be known at the time of shipment. Imagine that seller in Seattle has a load of fresh fish that she intends to sell in Des Moines. She knows of several potential buyers in that city and is confident that one will take the fish. To speed things up she can ship the fish to Des Moines consigning them to herself or perhaps to a representative of hers in the destination city. As the fish make their way into the heartland, she contacts the various potential buyers. By the time the shipment has arrived in Des Moines, she will have found a buyer and she or her agent can take the proper steps to see that the shipment is delivered to that party. What those appropriate steps are, of course, and who is responsible if there is a slip-up are things we will need to consider.

Putting Stuff in Storage

Stuff can get bulky. It takes up a lot of room. If the seller does not have its own storage facilities, it may choose to deliver the goods over to someone who does and who will store them for a fee. Section 7-102(1)(h) defines a *warehouseman* as "a person engaged in the business of storing goods for hire." When the goods are received the warehouseman will issue a document called a *warehouse receipt.* Check out §1-201(45). Be careful here: The definitions apply only to warehouses owned and operated by independent third parties. If the seller stores the stuff in its own warehouse building and makes its own deliveries out of this warehouse, as many do, then no document of the type we are talking about here will be issued and any tender or delivery will not be in the form of a documentary transaction. It is not the fact of a building called a warehouse that is of first importance to us here, but the introduction of a new person *engaged in the business* of storing goods for hire.

The definitions which we saw before in §7-102 apply to this situation as well. The warehouseman is also a *bailee.* The seller who puts the goods in storage is the *consignor.* It's not at all unusual for the seller to make itself the *consignee* as well. The seller puts the goods in storage and departs with the right to retrieve them whenever it wants and a document to prove it. Of course what the seller wants is to sell the goods. When it does so, and when it has gotten the payment it has a right to, it will take certain steps to make the buyer the *person entitled* to retrieve the goods. The buyer goes and picks them up. All ends happily.

You can see how the independence of the warehouseman is the key to the workings of this system. The buyer must have confidence that the goods will be there and in the condition described when he or she arrives to take possession. You begin to see as well why the mechanism arose (what we'll speak of as *negotiability*) to make these warehouse receipts themselves something more than just the paper that they were written on. As I mentioned in the introduction to this part, we begin to think of negotiable warehouse receipts (or negotiable bills of lading for that matter) as something like a metaphor for the goods themselves. They "embody in a physical form the title to the goods" or serve as a kind of "legal substitute" for the goods themselves. To the extent that the receipt can *become* for all intents and purposes equivalent to the goods themselves, cumbersome dealings in the goods can be carried out with a high level of confidence and a lot less inconvenience by moving around the documents, all the while letting the goods remain where they are.

This whole concept—that paper can be made to substitute for valuable assets in a very tangible way—shouldn't be unfamiliar to you, at least not if you ever pay for things by check. You are able to transfer bits and pieces of your wealth, to the extent you have any, by initially handing it over to a trusted independent institution (the bank) and then dealing in pieces of paper which "represent" or "embody" the right of the holder to go to the bank and get an equivalent amount of cold hard cash.* People will take these pieces of paper from you (your checks) where they might not take just an I.O.U. scribbled on the back of a napkin or envelope because checks are *negotiable* instruments and subject to special rules under the law and the Code. (But this is all for your study of the field of Commercial Paper, or as it's now often called, Payment Systems. For the moment I'm just trying to invoke a comparison which you might find helpful.)

One difference between your paying by personal check and the seller's delivering by handing over a negotiable warehouse receipt has to be appreciated, however. The person who takes a check runs the risk that when it is presented you will not have enough funds in the account to cover it. The buyer of a negotiable warehouse receipt should not have to worry about running an analogous risk. Certain particular identified goods, or a given amount of some fungible commodity, has been put in storage to generate the receipt, and if the warehouse is conducting its business properly those goods should still be there when the person entitled to pick them up comes calling. Of course this all depends on a clear understanding of who is entitled to retrieve the goods in any situation and on the warehouseman's careful observance of the rules. We will soon explore the rules, and the liability of a warehouseman who fails to follow

---

*And then again, what is this cold hard cash but dollar bills and the like, still another example of paper which has somehow been transformed—by a clear common understanding of what possession of the paper means to ourselves and others and a high degree of confidence that the law will support this understanding—into the very physical embodiment of wealth? When was the last time you carried your wealth around with you as nuggets of gold or silver or asked to be paid in kind for a job well done?

them. For now be sure you have the basic scheme and terms well under control.

Using Stuff as Collateral

So we see that one way or another the owner of goods (in our case a seller, but the system is not necessarily limited to this situation) has the ability to deliver over the goods to an independent bailee and get in exchange a paper embodiment of those goods. This certainly is handy. The goods, or at least the value they hold in our world of private property, is made easier to deal with, to move from place to place, to have and to hold. One aspect of this system for compacting bulky goods into nice neat reasonably sized packets of paper of which you should be aware is the importance such documents play in the use of goods, that is, of material wealth, as collateral under common commercial practices.

You probably have picked up from one source or another, inside or outside of law school, the basic idea behind what we loosely term *collateral*. Perhaps there is a mortgage on a house or other real property you own. If you have ever borrowed money to buy a car or the like you most likely had to give a lien on the car to whoever was loaning the money. *Mortgage* is the term used for a transaction that gives a creditor an interest in the debtor's real property as collateral to help secure payment of some loan or other outstanding obligation of the debtor. What was historically denoted the *lien* or the *chattel mortgage,* and which may still be referred to as such, today is more correctly called the *Article 9 security interest.* The basic idea remains the same. It is an interest given by a debtor in some personal property he or she owns to a creditor as collateral for some obligation. (If you have not already studied Article 9 security interests in great detail, I trust you will do so soon enough, when you take a course that covers Article 9 or, as the field is called, Secured Transactions. Although this is not the place to get into all of the detail you'll see then, it is a good time to at least introduce the special way that security interests in documents of title fit into the overall scheme.)

When you study Secured Transactions you will find out that an important (arguably the most important) thing that a creditor has to be sure of when obtaining a security interest in his or her debtor's property is that this interest becomes *perfected,* meaning in brief that the security interest will be good against competing third parties who might later make a claim on the goods and also will still be good if the debtor goes into bankruptcy. This is, to be sure, far too sketchy an explanation, but *something* must be left for your study of Secured Transactions. In any event, the problem will arise as to how a creditor is to perfect a security interest in someone else's property. One way which you will learn about is by making a proper filing, filling it out in the proper way, and depositing it in the proper official filing office or offices.

Another way that the security interest can be perfected is for the creditor actually to take temporary possession of the property and hold onto it until the debtor has paid off the obligation or is willing to put other property into the creditor's possession in substitution. The creditor who makes loans on this basis, taking what you will call a security interest perfected by possession, will want to make sure that it (typically a bank or similar institution) always has in its possession collateral of the debtor's at least equal in value to the amount of the loan still outstanding. If that is so and if the debtor does not repay the lender will have recourse against the property, one way or another, taking the value out of the property on hand and returning whatever is left over to the debtor.

A simple example is what was historically called a *pawn*. Say you own a small ruby ring worth $1,000. You are in need of some immediate cash, but no one will loan you any significant amount of money on your word alone. Nothing personal, lenders are just that way. What if you don't repay the loan and when the lender comes looking for you (or suing) you are nowhere to be found? What if, even if you can be found and are terribly sorry and are doing everything humanly possible to make good on your debts, you just don't have the money at the moment? Lenders tend to want collateral to lessen their worries about such things. Fortunately, we postulated that you had a valuable ruby ring. You can borrow some amount less than $1,000 but still fairly hefty on the collateral of the ring. Of course the lender will want you to leave the ring in pawn, in his or her possession, until you have repaid. If you do not repay when you are supposed to, the person holding the ring in pawn will have the right to sell it to another and keep whatever amount is still owed him or her out of the proceeds of sale. That's in theory what is happening when you see all those rings, saxophones, and banjos up for sale in the pawnbroker's window.

So far so good, if what you have of value is small and compact like a ruby ring. But what if your wealth at the moment consists primarily of two railroad cars of barley? That's certainly valuable (more valuable in fact than many a ruby ring) but who's going to take it in pawn? Most banks and other lending institutions will find it difficult enough to take a ring or other piece of jewelry as collateral. Their files are built to hold papers, not awkward three dimensional objects. Maybe you could find a conventional lender that would agree to take jewelry as collateral, but there's no way you are going to use all of that barley, fresh and wholesome though it may be, as collateral in this fashion.

Fortunately, there is a way to work through this dilemma. You take all of this grain over to a reputable commercial warehouse that specializes in storing grain. You turn it over to the warehouseman, getting in exchange a negotiable warehouse receipt. As you walk away, you feel your load significantly lightened. You are no longer the proud possessor of two railroad cars of barley, but hold instead a warehouse receipt that is for all intents and purposes valuable in the same way this much barley is (allowing for the relatively minor fee which will have to be paid the warehouse for its services). Now you can take this paper to a bank. The bank may not want to buy the receipt—what would it want with the right to all this barley?—but it may be willing to lend you money with this document playing the part of collateral. And the bank can easily perfect its interest in the collateral just by taking physical possession of the receipt. Much easier than taking possession of all that barley. And as long as the bank feels comfortable that the receipt represents goods actually delivered to a reputable warehouse and as long as the warehouse does not allow the grain to lose value unexpectedly or to be spirited off by someone who has no right to it, the bank can rest assured that its control over the documents of title makes its collateral secure.

As I said at the beginning of this section, we will not be concerned here with this separate and important role documents of title play as tools in commercial financing. We'll stick to their role in performance of the sales agreement. Still, you should be aware that much of what you will study here, in particular about the responsibilities of the bailee to hold the goods with care and to surrender them up only to the appropriate party, is of importance to the financing function as well as in sales. Indeed, if you were to study documents of title in any more detail many if not most of the major cases you would read would arise in this context rather than in the area of sales law itself. If you do not have a basic understanding of documents of title and how they work when you get into your course on Secured Transactions, expect to be asked to pick it up at the time. All the more reason for continuing as we do.

The Applicable Law

In our brief run-through of the rights and responsibilities of carriers and warehouses, we'll regularly cite to Article 7 of the Uniform Commercial Code. That is after all the part of the Code adopted uniformly by the states which deals with Documents of Title (see §7-101), those who issue them, and those who deal in them. In practicality, however, Article 7 governs relatively few such situations. Look at §7-103. Any applicable federal treaty or statute as well as any statute or regulation adopted by the particular state will elbow Article 7 out of the picture.

The federal government has passed a number of statutes regulating carriers in interstate commerce. Most especially there is the Federal Bills of Lading Act, which is also called the Pomerence Act of 1916, 49 U.S.C. §§81 et seq., but a number of other federal statutes also regulate aspects of carriage by sea. As a result, Article 7's application is necessarily reduced by these federal enactments to covering intrastate shipments and those shipments made into a particular state from outside the country. Interstate shipments or shipments originating in the United States and destined for a foreign location are all going to be subject to federal law. Beyond that, most of the carriers themselves are regulated in all sorts of ways by the Interstate Commerce Commission or the Federal Aviation Agency under their respective enabling statutes. International shipments by air are subject to the Warsaw Convention of 1929. The Department of Agriculture licenses and regulates warehouses storing agricultural products.

In addition many states have passed legislation or promulgated regulations relating to carriage within the bounds of the state or to warehouses operating there. All this is very interesting—and potentially very overwhelming—but fortunately for our present purposes we don't have to worry about all these other rules of law. With respect to the basics of documents of title and documentary transactions, the rules wherever found are pretty much the same as we will see them in Article 7. We can study Article 7 without worrying about all of the minor details that may work differently under this federal statute or that state regulation. Our study is only at the first level of difficulty. I trust that if you ever have reason to look more deeply into a situation involving carriers or warehouses or the like you will have a basic familiarity with what the issues might be because of what you see here. I also trust that you will be careful to identify the exact legal regime under which the particular controversy has to be assessed and not assume Article 7 applies just because it's so very near at hand in your copy of the Uniform Commercial Code.

Negotiability and Negotiation

Here's a basic fact to remember: Every document of title will necessarily be either *negotiable* or *non-negotiable*. The difference will be crucial. How do we know which is which? Look at §7-104. Under subsection (1) a warehouse receipt, bill of lading or other document of title is negotiable "if by its terms the goods are to be delivered to bearer or to the order of a named person" or "where recognized in overseas trade, if it runs to a named person or assigns." Don't worry about this second part, but look again at §7-104(1)(a). A document of title is negotiable if it uses certain words that are referred to as *words of negotiability*. The document will either say that the goods are to be delivered "to bearer" or "to the order of" such and such a named person. That's it. It's magic. If some certain magic words (which acquired their magic not on my say-so or that of the drafters but by virtue of centuries of recognized and precise use by commercial parties) are on the document, it is negotiable. Otherwise, the document is non-negotiable. See subsection (2).* So it's the wording that makes the difference. Practically in the United States we are aided by the fact that issuers of either bills of lading or warehouse receipts tend to put nice big legends "NEGOTIABLE" or "NON-NE-GOTIABLE" on the various forms they use. Also it's of no small significance that the Interstate Commerce Commission requires of carriers under its jurisdiction that negotiable (sometimes referred to as *order*) bills of

---

*It will obviously be of help at this point if you have studied the concepts of negotiability and negotiation in the case of negotiable *instruments* (notes and drafts) under Articles 3. If you have studied in that area, you should be pretty well familiar with what goes for negotiable documents of title. The primary difference is that collecting on an instrument gets you some money, and collecting on a document gets you some particular goods held by the bailee.

lading be printed on yellow paper. Non-negotiable (or so-called *straight*) bills must be printed on white paper.

In any event, the important point is that it will be possible to determine whether a document of title is negotiable or non-negotiable from an examination of the item itself, that is, from looking at the face of the document. People in commerce regard and handle the two types differently, as indeed they must for reasons we will see, and it is crucial that it be possible to know without question what type of bill or receipt you have in front of you without having to make further inquiry of anyone. The document must speak for itself. If it did not, people could not deal with them as they do and as they have to if the great rivers of commerce are to flow as sweetly and majestically as we know they do.

Beyond knowing what type of document a particular bill or receipt is, it should be possible from inspection to know just who is entitled to get what goods held by what bailee—all from the paper itself. You know the bailee by the fact that the issuer must sign the document in one form or another. You know what goods are concerned since the document will describe the goods, or at least the packages containing them. See §7-202 on the form of warehouse receipt in particular.

How can you know as of any particular time exactly *who* is entitled to get the goods from the bailee, the carrier, or the warehouse? Look at §7-403(1). Briefly put, the bailee must deliver, with very few available excuses (even though it looks like a long list as set forth in this subsection, it really gives the bailee very little room to maneuver), to "a person entitled under the document." Who might that be? It depends on whether the document is non-negotiable or negotiable, and in the latter case, on knowing a bit about negotiability, how negotiable documents are passed from hand to hand, and with what effect. Look at §7-403(4). Start with the non-negotiable document. The person entitled under the document is the person to whom delivery is to be made "by the terms of or pursuant to written instructions under" the document. A non-negotiable document will either say that delivery is to be made to Joan Jones at a particular location or upon her instruction given in a form as specified by the document. In the latter case Joan Jones is expected later to issue directions to the bailee, often using a kind of paper termed a *delivery order* which specifies that some or all of the goods held under the document are to be delivered to, say, Richard Roe.* If the delivery order is good, and that is to be judged by whether it complies with the criteria set forth in the initial bill or receipt itself, then Richard is the person entitled under the non-negotiable document.

In the case of a negotiable document, the person entitled under §7-403(4) is the *holder* of the document. Look at §1-201(20): " 'Holder' with respect to a document of title means the person in possession [of the document] if the goods are deliverable to bearer or to the order of

---

*And just to make it more interesting, delivery orders themselves can be either negotiable or non-negotiable.

the person in possession." We're getting warmer, but there still remains the question of what it means for the goods to be deliverable "to bearer" or to "the order of" a person. Such is the mystery of negotiability and negotiation. Recall that for a document to be negotiable it must initially be issued with one of the words of negotiability. It will either say that the goods are deliverable "to bearer" or deliverable "to the order of Debra Doe" or another named individual. So each document starts out in life as either a bearer document (the first case) or an order document (the second situation), and initially the goods are deliverable just as it says. If the document of title is in bearer form, then with only some slight exceptions that we're not going to worry about here, whoever has possession of it (certainly if he or she has possession rightfully) is by that fact alone the "holder" and is entitled to delivery of the goods. In the case of the order document, Debra Doe is initially the person entitled to the goods. Of course she can pass on this right to receive the goods to others, but she won't be able to do it just by notifying the bailee with something like a delivery order of the type which would do with the non-negotiable document. She executes her order that someone else be entitled to the goods, in effect, by *negotiating* the document over to that particular person. Negotiation is an act that has to be done in a particular way. You can look at §7-501 now, but if it threatens to overwhelm don't worry about it. The basic idea is not *that* difficult. If the document is in bearer form (either because it was initially issued as a bearer document or has later become one by a holder's indorsement in blank or "to bearer") then negotiation involves nothing more than delivery to another. If the document is in order form at the time the holder wants to negotiate it to another, he or she must *indorse* it (that is, sign his or her name somewhere on the document) and then deliver it over. Either way the person who takes delivery, say Manny Moe, is now the holder. He may be holding a bearer document or, if it was negotiated to him with an indorsement "deliver to Manny Moe," he will be a holder of an order instrument made out to his order.

And so it goes. A negotiable document of title may be negotiated many times, passing from hand to hand. Barring some skullduggery along the way (theft or forgery), it passes from holder to holder, and at any given moment the "person entitled to delivery" of the goods should be unambiguously and easily ascertainable from a good look at the document itself.

What is especially important is that the actual physical possession of the negotiable document is all important. With only rare exception, possession of the negotiable document will be necessary, though not in all cases sufficient, to give anybody the right to pick up the goods and carry them away. The negotiable document of title is not just an interesting piece of paper that acts as a receipt from the bailee, nor is it just an important piece of evidence that would be helpful in resolving any dispute as to who is entitled to get the goods. The negotiable document is—and here we are forced into metaphor to get the full flavor of it—*a physical embodiment of the right to get the goods,* the very essence of title to the goods captured in a tangible form. The negotiable document represents and stands in for the goods in some way that is, I admit it, hard to capture in words. Hopefully, as you work your way through the material to follow and the Examples and Explanations the cumulative effect will do what mere words alone cannot.

There is one additional difference between the negotiable and non-negotiable document of title that must be mentioned. That has to do with what defenses will be available when a person seemingly entitled under the rules we have seen comes calling for the goods. *If* the bill of lading or warehouse receipt is negotiable and *if* the person presenting it has acquired the document through what is termed *due negotiation,* then that person will have the right to the goods with only a very limited set of exceptions. Many defenses which would have defeated the rights of the original bailor, for example, will not be of any effect against the party who holds through due negotiation.* Compare (or at least acknowledge) the existence of §§7-502 and 7-503. What makes for that special something, "due negotiation"? See §7-501(4). Boiling it down, what makes negotiable documents special in this regard is that the transferee who takes under certain circumstances (those of due negotiation) may end up with rights to the document and rights to the goods it covers *greater than* the rights of the person who transferred to him or her. As a general matter under the law a person can normally not pass on to another greater rights in any property than he or she has to begin with. But when the special words of negotiability come into the picture, either with respect to negotiable instruments or as here with negotiable documents of title, the normal rules don't necessarily apply. One more example of the extraordinary things we have to get used to when we're dealing with negotiable documents.

A Recapitulation of Some Issues in the Law of Sales

In all of the previous chapters we pretty much put to one side any reference to documents of title in the myriad Article 2 sections we looked at. This is no time to start all over from scratch. Still, now that we have documents in hand, so to speak, it seems only fitting to take at least a short look back to what has gone before, but now noting how documents of title fit into the picture. This review is in no sense intended to be exhaustive. Think of it as a reprise of some of the highlights of the law of sales,

---

*Again, for those who have studied Commercial Paper, this idea should seem very familiar. It is the Article 7 analog, albeit with some minor variation, of the "holder in due course" of a negotiable instrument under Article 3. If you haven't studied Article 3 yet, all of this may be more than you can reasonably expect yourself to handle right now. If that's the case, try at least to familiarize yourself with only the basic outline of what you see here.

now concentrating on one particular strain within the full orchestral arrangement, that melody carried by documents of title.

Gap Fillers:

Look at §2-308(c). Unless otherwise agreed, "documents of title may be delivered through customary banking channels." That's nice to know. We'll get a sense of how customary banking channels handle these documents on behalf of the parties in the next chapter. When is the buyer to make payment in a documentary transaction? Unless otherwise agreed, the default rules are given in §2-310(b) and (c). See also §2-319(4) and §2-320(4). On the special question of whether the buyer can insist on the right to inspect the goods themselves before being obligated for payment, see §2-513(3)(b) and Comment 5 to that section. (We're getting into some pretty fine points here, I grant you, but I thought I'd at least set out these provisions.)

Passage of Title:

We've previously seen how the whole concept of title is downplayed in Article 2. In the event there should ever be a question of when title has "passed" as between the buyer and seller in a documentary transaction, however, see §§2-401(2) and (3)(a).

Tender of Goods:

Now we're getting into some meatier matters. Remember that the basic rules on tender are to be found in §2-503 and §2-504. Look more particularly at §2-503(3), (4) and (5) and also Comment 7 to that section. When the parties have entered into what we term a *shipment contract,* §2-504(b) becomes important. To appropriately tender the seller must

> obtain and promptly deliver or tender in due form any document
> necessary to enable the buyer to take possession of the goods
> or otherwise required by the agreement or by usage of trade.

It is not enough for the seller to deliver the goods to the carrier and send them on their way. If it is required or customary in the situation, he or she will have to obtain a proper bill in a form which would allow the buyer to take delivery from the carrier of lading and send *that* on its way to the buyer. Otherwise the buyer couldn't get possession of the goods, and we have to say that tender has not been made. Note that the leeway given to a seller by the last sentence to §2-504 does *not* apply to this particular requirement. See also Comment 4 to this section.

Risk of Loss:

Risk of loss when the goods are being shipped by a commercial carrier is governed, we know, by §2-509(1). While there is no mention here of documents of title, recall the central role the documents play in tender under a shipment contract per §2-504 as mentioned above. If goods are held in a warehouse and are to be delivered to the buyer without their being taken from that warehouse, §2-509(2) governs. Notice the different results depending on whether the goods were stored under a negotiable or a non-negotiable warehouse receipt. If the receipt is non-negotiable, you have to look back to §2-503(4)(b) to get the full story.

The Heavy Responsibilities of the Bailee

As you can see from what has gone before, the whole notion of dealing with documents of title (mere pieces of paper) as things of value in their own right necessarily depends on the people involved having a high degree of confidence that the goods which the documents represent are what the papers say they are. Furthermore, a deal in paper of this type must presuppose that the goods are *where* the paper says they are and that they can be obtained without difficulty by whomever a reading of the paper establishes as the person to whom delivery is to be made. People have to be able to examine the documents and know who has what rights under them from an examination of the paper itself. Beyond that there has to be reason to believe that those rights will be observed by all others involved and not least of all by the bailee now holding the goods. Turning over good money in exchange for a document of title only makes sense if you can be sure that you'll be able to get the goods on which the document was written without any undue hassle, or that someone else would in turn buy the document from you because of the unambiguous value it represents. No one is interested in buying a pig in a poke, as the saying goes.

If you or I were to issue a document which we called a bill of lading or warehouse receipt, it would be a big surprise if anyone took it very seriously. That's assuming of course that you are not someone "engaged in the business of transporting or forwarding goods" or "storing goods for hire," as I know I am not. Recall the definitions in §1-201(6) and (45). Professional bailees, commercial carriers and warehouses, issue these documents, and the documents gain credence in the trade by virtue of their taking on the duties inherent in the contract of bailment. The whole system works because the bailee is known to have taken on a measure of accountability for the goods and can be made to answer if it fails to live up to its responsibilities.

The questions that follow are designed to get you acquainted with the basic rules under which a commercial bailee who goes into the business of taking and holding goods for hire must live. There is a lot going on here, and we won't be covering everything that could go wrong or that is covered by Article 7. You should, however, get a feeling for the basics.

Roughly, as you'll see, the responsibilities of the commercial bailee fall into three main categories. First of all, the bailee will be responsible for when and how it creates and issues the document of title itself. If the document purports to cover goods that aren't as described or which aren't where the document says, other innocent parties can get hurt and will have an argument that their predicament is at least partly the bailee's responsibility. On bills of lading, you will want to look at §7-301. On warehouse receipts, see §7-203. We are talking here about what is generally referred to as the sin of *misdescription* or *improper issue* of the documents.

Secondly, the bailee is, as you would expect, responsible for holding the goods and protecting them. See §§7-204 and 7-309, which deal with problems of loss or injury to the goods while in the bailee's custody. Notice that in both the bailee is obligated to "exercise the degree of care in relation to the goods which a reasonably careful man would exercise under like circumstances." If issues arise about the bailee's care and handling of goods in its charge, a negligence standard is to be applied.

Finally, the bailee is responsible for surrendering the goods only to the proper party. On problems of *misdelivery* see §§7-403 and 7-404. When misdelivery is the issue, as you will discover, the bailee's responsibilities are not to be measured by a standard of negligence but by the more exacting rules set forth in the relevant sections. A bailee who turns over the goods to the wrong person will be liable in conversion just as if the bailee had taken the goods for itself. See §7-601(2).

EXAMPLES

In reality Article 7 would not govern many of the situations which follow, as goods will be crossing state lines with impunity. For purposes of analysis, however, consider these questions as they would be answered under Article 7.

1. Sarah in Seattle contracts to sell to Buddy in Boston 1,000 widgets for $2,000. The contract calls for her to ship the goods to Buddy, the parties anticipating that shipment will be made by one of several commercial trucking concerns that operate between their two cities. Buddy agrees to pay for the widgets upon receipt of the bill of lading covering their shipment. Sarah packs a large crate with widgets and delivers it to Carry's Trucking Company and arranges for its delivery to Buddy. Sarah receives from Carry a straight (non-negotiable) bill of lading, which describes the goods as "1,000 widgets." Sarah sends this bill to Buddy, who immediately sends her a check for $2,000 by return mail. A week later Carry's agent notifies Buddy of the shipment's arrival in Boston. Buddy picks up the crate. When he opens it he finds that it contains only 400 widgets.

   a. Buddy tries to contact Sarah, but her phone has been disconnected. Apparently she has gone out of business, quitting Seattle without any warning and without leaving a forwarding address. He also finds out that before her disappearance she had cashed his check for $2000. Does Buddy have any rights against Carry's Trucking?

   b. Suppose that before her disappearance Sarah had delivered another large crate to Carry's Trucking, this time taking back an order (negotiable) bill of lading describing the goods as "1,000 widgets" and calling for their delivery "to the order of Sammy" in Boise. Sarah sends the bill of lading on to her friend Sammy, who is a dealer in industrial merchandise in Boise. He contacts Betty, a Boise businesswoman, who he knows is interested in obtaining some widgets. Betty agrees to buy the 1,000 widgets making their way to Boise. She gives Sammy a certified check for the agreed purchase price of $2,000, in return for the bill of lading, which Sammy negotiates over to her by signing his name on the front under the legend "deliver to Betty." Betty contacts Carry's agent in Boise who tells her that the shipment has arrived. She picks up the crate, handing over the bill as she picks up delivery. It turns out the crate contains only 200 widgets. Sammy is nowhere to be found, having apparently vanished along with his friend Sarah. Does Betty have any rights against Carry's Trucking?

c. Would your answer to the previous question be the same if the bill of lading Betty had bought from Sammy was a non-negotiable bill?

d. In either situation—Buddy's or Betty's—would your answer be any different if the bill of lading involved had described the shipments as "one crate said to contain 1,000 widgets?"

2. Laurel is an employee of Carry's Trucking Company. Unfortunately, she is not the most honest of people. One evening, after everyone else has gone home for the day, she takes one of Carry's negotiable bill of lading forms and prepares a phony bill indicating that a shipment of 10 tons of tomato sauce had been shipped from Seattle to Boston "to the order of Hardy." She sends the bill to her friend Hardy a wholesale food broker in Boston, who sells the (entirely fictional) tomato paste to the Boston Pasta Works by negotiating the bill over in exchange for a check. The check clears. Laurel and Hardy both disappear, presumably starting life over somewhere in the middle of the country with the Pasta company's money.

a. Does the Pasta company have any recourse against Carry?

b. Would it make any difference to your answer if the bill of lading had borne the language "shipper's weight, load and count?" See Comment 3 to §7-301.

c. How would you answer this question if instead of being a wholesale dealer in foodstuffs Hardy had been a used car salesman or a professor of law? See the definition of *due negotiation* in §7-501(4).

3. Owen is the owner of an expensive piano worth $15,000. He is concerned that it will be damaged during the renovation of his house, so he has it delivered to Walter's Warehouse. He receives a non-negotiable warehouse receipt naming himself as the person to whom the piano should be delivered upon demand. Several months later a fire starts in a chemical plant located a few blocks from Walter's Warehouse. In spite of the best efforts of the fire department, the fire quickly spreads through the

neighborhood and eventually consumes most of the warehouse before it can be brought under control.

a. There is no evidence that the warehouse had been built or maintained in an improper manner and it seems unlikely that any normal building, even one built to serve as a warehouse, would have been able to withstand the blaze. Owen's piano is destroyed in the fire. Can he recover the value of the piano from Walter?

b. Assume instead that the fire started in Walter's warehouse when one of Walter's watchmen fell asleep on the job, allowing a lit cigarette to fall to the wooden floor of the warehouse. In this situation, does Owen have any rights against Walter?

c. Would your answer to the immediately preceding question be affected if the warehouse receipt issued by Walter covering the piano contained a provision limiting Walter's liability in the event of any damage to the piano to $5,000?

d. What if the warehouse receipt had instead contained a provision stating that the consignee agreed that Walter's Warehouse would not be responsible for any damage whatsoever to the goods, even if caused by its own negligence? See §1-102(3).

4. Stan in Savannah contracts to sell 15,000 yards of cloth to Bill in Butte. Stan, expecting to receive payment from Bill in a day or two, delivers the cloth to the Rickety Railroad and contracts for its delivery to the railroad yard in Butte. He receives a straight bill of lading which specifies the consignment is made to Bill in Butte, giving Bill's telephone number and address. When the shipment arrives, a railroad employee calls Bill. Bill drives a truck over to the railyard, identifies himself and is given the goods. Bill is dissatisfied with the cloth and refuses to pay for it.

a. Does Stan have an action against the railroad under the circumstances?

b. Suppose instead that the straight bill of lading obtained by Stan consigned the goods to *Stan* in Butte, but specified "Notification on arrival to Bill" at his telephone number. Bill is told of the delivery and comes and picks up the cloth. He does not pay Stan the contract price. If Stan goes against the railroad in this situation, what result?

c. Stan contracts to sell a separate order of 22,000 yards of his cloth to Bertha in Birmingham. The cloth is delivered to the Rickety Railroad with instructions that it be delivered to Birmingham, notice to be given to Bertha upon arrival. Stan obtains a negotiable bill of lading made out "to the order of Sy." Sy is an agent of Stan's who works in Alabama. Stan forwards the bill to Sy with the instruction that it is not to be turned over to Bertha until Sy has received a cashier's check made out to Stan for the purchase price. Bertha never obtains the bill, but upon hearing of the shipment's arrival goes to the railyard where she is allowed to take possession of the cloth. If Stan never gets his money from Bertha, can he hold the railroad responsible?

d. Suppose instead that Sy endorses the bill over to Bertha in exchange for a personal check. Bertha immediately takes the bill to the railyard where she surrenders it and is given in return the shipment of cloth. Bertha's check bounces and by the time Stan becomes aware of the fact she is apparently on the road to insolvency. There is no way Stan is going to get his money out of Bertha. Can he get relief by suing the railroad?

e. Suppose Sy receives the bill of lading (negotiable and made out "to the order of Sy") and immediately signs the back of it. He makes arrangements with Bertha to come to her place of business and exchange the bill for the cashier's check. On his way to Bertha's, Sy is robbed of his briefcase into which he had placed the bill. By the time Sy checks with the railroad he is informed that someone was allowed to take delivery of the shipment of cloth, surrendering in exchange the bill of lading. Is there any way Stan can hold the railroad liable in this situation?

f. Suppose that Sy had not signed the bill of lading before he put it into his briefcase. He intended to sign it over to Bertha only when he got to her office and confirmed that she was ready to complete the deal. The thief gets away with the bill, forges Sy's signature to it, and then picks up the cloth from the railroad. Who (other than the thief if he or she can be caught) is responsible for this loss?

5. Farmer Jones delivers her entire crop of winter wheat to Wheatly's Grain Warehouse. She takes in exchange a negotiable warehouse receipt covering the grain and made out to her order. Later she agrees to sell the warehouse receipt to Aggie, a commodities dealer who trades in wheat and other farm products in her area. Aggie gives a cashier's check for the price ($42,500) to Jones who negotiates the warehouse receipt over to the order of Aggie. Aggie presents the receipt at the warehouse and is given all of the wheat covered by the receipt. An employee at the warehouse notes the delivery on a log in his office but does not ask for or take possession of the receipt. Aggie then negotiates the receipt over to one Baker, who pays $43,000 for it. Baker goes to Wheatly's warehouse to pick up his grain only to find that it is not there. Aggie has vanished from the scene. Does Baker have anywhere else to turn to recover for his loss?

6. Before he took off on a year-long round-the-world tour, Taylor delivered several pieces of valuable statuary that normally resided on the gardens of his estate to the Acme Warehouse, taking a non-negotiable warehouse receipt in exchange. When he returned he called the warehouse to arrange for his pick-up of the statues, only to be told that the warehouse could not locate them anywhere in it's facility. No one at Acme Warehouse has any idea what happened to them. They have just vanished. In order to hold the warehouse responsible, will Taylor have to demonstrate that it was negligent in some way and that this negligence resulted in the statues being lost? If the receipt Taylor signed had contained a provision

limiting the warehouse's potential liability to a figure less than the value of the statues, will this provision be effective to limit the amount Taylor can recover?

EXPLANATIONS

1a. Yes. See §7-301. Buddy is "a consignee of a non-negotiable bill who has given value in good faith" in exchange for a bill "relying . . . upon the description therein of the goods." As such he may recover from the issuer, Carry's Trucking, "damages caused by the . . . misdescription of the goods." The carrier here is guilty of the sin of *misdescription* and will be made to pay. You can see that Buddy allowed himself to be separated from some of his hard-earned money because of the trust he put in the document created by Carry's Trucking. That firm earns money by transporting goods *and* by issuing bills of lading in the proper manner on which people can rely. When it makes a mistake, it pays.

1b. Yes. Betty has rights against Carry's Trucking equivalent to Buddy's, because she appears to be a "holder to whom a negotiable bill has been duly negotiated," who is also protected by §7-301. You can check out Betty's status. As we've already noted, the holder of such a document is, under §1-201(20), "the person in possession [of the document] if the goods are deliverable to bearer or to the order of the person in possession." The bill was initially created an order bill running to the order of Sammy. Sammy negotiated it over so that it ran to the order of Betty who was also in possession. Was the bill *duly negotiated* over to Betty under the criteria of §7-501(4)? Unless we hear any different, it's only fair to assume that she purchased the bill in good faith "without notice of any defense against or claim to it on the part of any person." She gave "value." Unless it is established that the negotiation "was not in the regular course of business"—and Sammy here does appear to deal in such stuff—the bill was duly negotiated to Betty. On this last criterion, you should look at the lengthy but helpful first comment to §7-501.

1c. No. If Betty had bought a non-negotiable bill from Sammy she would not fit within the provisions of §7-301 and not have rights against the carrier for misdescription. This is just one reason why savvy commercial parties will not turn over good money for non-negotiable bills in the same way they might for negotiable ones. Taking a non-negotiable bill is, as this and any other number of possible examples would show, inherently riskier than taking a negotiable one. In the real world and for all practical purposes, trading in bills of lading as if they were the goods themselves is limited to negotiable bills.

1d. Carry's Trucking could effectively prevent its being held responsible for misdescription under §7-301 by such language. Read the latter part of subsection (1), beginning with the words *except that.* The further subsections, which you may want to look over quickly, lay out the more detailed rules of when and to what extent the carrier can relieve itself from responsibility for the description of the goods.

2a. Yes. Under §7-301(1), the carrier is responsible to the appropriate parties for *non-receipt* as well as the misdescription of the goods. Here, the Pasta Company is the holder of a bill that it has taken by due negotiation. See also Comment 3 to this section, which states in no uncertain terms that, "The issuer is liable on documents issued by an agent, contrary to instructions of his principal, without receiving goods." Laurel is, as we said, not the most honest of people. Unfortunately for Carry's Trucking, that company took her on as an employee and let her have access to its negotiable bill of lading forms. You can see why a firm like Carry's will normally be sure to keep careful track of the forms it uses as well as keep an eye on those who have access to them. The employer will have to bear the loss here just as if Laurel had stolen from or misused her position at the firm in some other way.

2b. The last sentence of Comment 3 says the answer is no. "No disclaimer of this liability [for issue by an agent contrary to instructions without receiving goods] is permitted since it is not a matter either of the care of the goods or their description."

2c. The Pasta company would not be able to hold the railroad liable if Hardy was not someone regularly engaging in this type of sale. It would be a holder of the bill, but not a holder to whom it had been duly negotiated and as such would not have the protection of §7-301(1).

The preceding questions all focused on the responsibility taken on by a carrier for the bills of lading it issues under §7-309. You should note the analogous provision §7-203 covering warehouses and their issuance of warehouse receipts.

3a. It's unlikely that Owen would be able to collect anything from the warehouse company. Under §7-204(1), the warehouseman is liable

> for damages for loss of or injury to the goods caused by his failure to exercise such care in regard to them as a reasonably careful man would exercise under like circumstances but unless otherwise agreed he is not liable for damages which could not have been avoided by the exercise of such care.

Absent some special agreement, the warehouse is not an insurer of the goods, but is responsible for their loss or damage only if it results from its own negligence. In the story as it's given, it seems unlikely that Owen could show any negligence on the part of Walter's Warehouse and so Owen has no rights against that concern. See also §7-403(1)(b). Walter's obligation to deliver the piano back to Owen is excused by "loss or destruction of the goods for which the bailee is not liable."

3b. Here Walter's Warehouse would be liable for the loss because the fire was the result of the negligence of one of its employees.

3c. See subsection (2) of §7-204. Such a limitation of liability is permissible, but would be effective only if Owen had been given the opportunity when he stored the piano or within a reasonable time thereafter to in effect declare the piano's greater value and contract for a higher level of protection, paying some additional cost to do so.

Note that §7-309 contains provisions on bills of lading analogous to those we've just relied upon in §7-204 covering warehouse receipts.

3d. Section 1-102(3) has been taken to mean what it says. The bailee, be it a warehouse or a carrier, may not contractually disclaim any and all liability for the results of its own negligence.

4a. No. The railroad did nothing wrong here. Under §7-403(1), the bailee must deliver the goods to "a person entitled under the document," with only a few exceptions of which none would seem to apply here. The key question in such a case is, who is a person entitled under the document, and on that we have to look at §7-403(4). When the goods are shipped under a non-negotiable document, as here, the proper party is "the person to whom delivery is to be made by the terms of or pursuant to written instructions under" the straight bill of lading. The straight bill called for delivery to Bill, and that's just what the railroad did.

4b. Under this set of facts, the railroad is responsible to Stan for the sin of misdelivery. Again we have a straight or non-negotiable bill, but here the person entitled under the bill was Stan. Delivery could only be made to Stan or pursuant to his written instruction given according to the terms of the bill, that is, pursuant to a delivery order signed by him directing delivery to someone else. Misdelivery by the railroad is a breach of its contract of carriage entered into with Stan and also conversion of Stan's property. The railroad can be made to pay.

The railroad may want to argue that the notation on the bill about contacting Bill when the goods arrived in Butte somehow makes Bill a person entitled to take delivery, but this argument won't work. This language doesn't say that the goods should be delivered to Bill, only that he should be made aware of their arrival. The idea is that once he is aware that the stuff has arrived in Butte, he is going to want to get Stan to make out that delivery order and present it to the railroad so that he, Bill, can take delivery. And Stan in turn will be able to insist, if that is the nature of the contract of sale, that he be paid in cash before he does issue the delivery order. By allowing Bill to get possession of the goods before he has paid for them the railroad has put Stan in the position in which he now finds himself and which he particularly wanted to and thought he had avoided by consigning the goods to himself. This process is what is generally referred to as *shipment under reservation* and is perfectly legitimate as long as the buyer has agreed to it in the contract for sale. See §2-505.

4c. Yes. Here is another example of the railroad's making an improper surrender of the goods for which it is liable both in breach of contract and on the theory of conversion. The negotiable bill of lading was made out "to the order of Sy." Looking once again to §7-403(4), we see that the person entitled under the document—and hence the person to whom delivery must be made under subsection (1)—is the "holder" of the bill. Sy is the holder of the bill under §1-201(20). Sy is still holding it. He will take it over to the railroad and demand the goods. When they are not forthcoming, Stan (for whom Sy was acting as an agent) has rights as a result of the carrier's nondelivery to him.

4d. No. The railroad did nothing wrong here. By indorsing the bill and handing it over to Bertha, Sy was *negotiating* the bill to her. See §7-501(1). She becomes the holder per §1-201(20) and hence had the right to pick up the goods from the issuer, here the Rickety Railroad. If Stan has the right to complain of anyone's behavior, it is Sy's. What was he thinking? He was directed to turn over the bill, which was in effect like turning over the valuable goods themselves, only upon receipt of a cashier's check. This would have assured Stan of payment. Sy blew it by not following his principal's instructions and instead accepting a personal check.

4e. Here we have another case of Sy's actions turning out to haunt Stan. The railroad made a proper delivery. When Sy signed the bill of lading in blank he turned it into a *bearer document*. The thief or whoever got his or her hands on it could and did become the holder as someone in possession of a bearer document. Look once again at §1-201(20). The railroad was obligated to deliver to the holder of the negotiable bill of lading and that is what it did. It all comes from the nature of a bearer document. In this respect the bearer bill which Sy was so nonchalantly carrying around in his briefcase was like a one-hundred-dollar bill that he might also have had tucked away there. These things are legally his property. If the thief or thieves can be caught, they can of course be made to give restitution to Sy of anything valuable they stole from him. That would include the value of the one-hundred-dollar bill and the bearer bill of lading. But a stolen bearer document, like stolen money, can be used by the thief profitably. The lesson here is not hard to grasp: Just as you try not to carry around too much cash as you go about your daily business, you shouldn't carry around more bearer instruments or documents than you can afford to lose. This is especially so when it is so easy to avoid doing so.

4f. The railroad made an improper delivery in this situation and will be responsible for the loss. When the bill was stolen it was an order document running to Sy's order. It could only have been turned into a bearer document or into an order document running to someone else's order by Sy's indorsement, that is his authorized signature. So whoever picked up the cloth was not legally a holder. The railroad surrendered the goods to someone not legally entitled and will have to take the consequences. All of this follows from some very basic principles of the law of negotiable instruments. The party who takes a negotiable instrument (or in this case a negotiable document of title) from a forger relying upon the forgery to get what he or she wants is the one left holding the bag when the forgery is discovered. The idea is that the person who took from the forger, here the railroad, was in the best position to protect itself—by insisting on proper ID and by checking the signature purporting to be that of Sy carefully.

5.   Baker should be able to hold Wheatly liable for his loss. Look at §7-

403(3). The warehouse had the right to insist that the negotiable receipt be surrendered to it in exchange for the goods, and it should have done so. Its failure to take and cancel the document resulted in its being "liable to any person to whom the document is duly negotiated." It appears Baker did take by due negotiation. Section 7-501(4) again. He paid value and such an amount that would have given him no reason to think there was anything wrong with the bill or to suggest that he took in bad faith. Beyond that he took in the regular course of business. Wheatly's employee made a mistake and the warehouse is responsible.

6.   The issue here is what section, and what theory of liability, is applicable when the goods just vanish with neither party able to establish what has happened to them. The warehouse will argue that the appropriate place to look is §7-203 which outlines it's duty of care and allows for it effectively to limit its liability contractually. The bailor, Taylor here, argues that this is a situation which comes under §7-403. He'll present the warehouse receipt and when the warehouse necessarily fails to make the called-for delivery he has an action against it for a breach of contract and on the theory of conversion. To win, Taylor will argue, he need not show or even allege a lack of due care; nondelivery, he argues is enough.

The courts have sided with the bailor on this question. Nondelivery of goods by the bailee when nothing more is known about what happened to them amounts to conversion and is to be dealt with in that fashion. Following along that line, the bailee's limitation of liability, while it might be effective if the action brought against it sounded in negligence, cannot be effective when the argument is conversion. See *National Resources Trading, Inc. v. Trans Freight Lines,* 766 F.2d 65, 41 U.C.C. 948 (2d Cir. 1985); *I.C.C. Metals, Inc. v. Municipal Warehouse Co.,* 50 N.Y.2d 657, 409 N.E.2d 849, 431 N.Y.S.2d 372, 29 U.C.C. 217 (1980).

32

"Payment Against Documents"

Making the Swap

The essence of the sales contract is that the buyer is to get the goods and the seller is to be paid for them. It's a swap. If the goods are the sort which can be handled by the buyer and seller themselves, or by their employees, and if it is possible for the two sides to meet face-to-face, there's really not much of a trick to setting up the exchange. If the contract does not call for either party to extend credit to the other, then all that happens is that the two actually *do* meet someplace (it can be the seller's place of business, the buyer's, or some other mutually acceptable spot) and make the trade. The buyer gets the goods and the seller gets the payment.

Performance of the contract is not that much more complicated if credit is involved. If it has been agreed that the buyer is to extend credit to the seller, that is, to prepay for the goods, the buyer will make payment and once its check has cleared the seller feels free to tender directly to the buyer. If on the other hand it is the seller which has contracted to sell on credit, it tenders at the time and place called for in the agreement and then expects (and in the vast majority of cases receives simply as a matter of course) payment when payment is due.

There can, of course, be problems of performance even under these most simple of scenarios. We've already dealt with the possible problems and the Code's methods for sorting them out in plenty of detail, primarily in Chapters 17 to 24. In this chapter we focus on a method devised within the commercial community for performance of the sales contract when the parties are separated by some distance, the goods are to be delivered by a commercial carrier, *and furthermore* neither buyer nor seller is of the mind to extend credit to the other. The seller doesn't want the buyer to get its hands on the goods or any kind of control over them unless and until it has handed over a sufficiently certain form of payment for them. The buyer is unwilling or unable to make payment without firm assurance that it will without question get the goods. Neither party wants to let go of what it has of value without getting something of real value in exchange. No one is buying (or selling) the right to bring a lawsuit. It all could lead to a stalemate of enormous proportions were it not for that most ingenious solution: the routine known as *payment against documents.*

Notice that if one of the two parties is willing to extend credit to the other, nothing as fancy as payment against documents is necessary even if the goods have to be sent a distance. If the buyer is willing to prepay for the goods, for example, and contracts to do so, then there is no great problem. We already have the necessary mechanism in place with the theory and practice of documents of title which we considered in the preceding chapter. The buyer sends the seller a check in payment. When the check clears the seller feels free to send the goods on their way to the buyer under a bill of lading. It may either be a straight bill with consignment made directly to the buyer or a negotiable order bill of lading, in which case the seller endorses the bill over to the buyer before sending it off. In either case the buyer should have no trouble getting possession of the goods when they arrive at their destination. If, on the other hand, the seller is willing to extend credit (and many sellers do extend credit to major buyers or regular customers without anyone's questioning their business sense), the timing is reversed. The seller ships the goods under a bill which allows the buyer to take possession. The buyer makes payment by the prescribed means and in the time called for. That is that.

The distinct problem with which we now deal comes up because in many situations the parties are separated by considerable distance and cannot easily themselves get together to make a simultaneous swap of the goods and the payment. At the same time neither is willing to extend credit to the other. One possible way around this dilemma presents itself if the seller has a trusted agent operating in the buyer's vicinity. The seller can ship the goods under a bill of lading made out in some way to give this agent control over the goods, such as an order bill made out to the agent's order. As the goods make their way by carrier to the buyer's city, the bill is also on its way, having been sent by the seller to its agent. The agent is instructed to negotiate the bill over to the buyer only upon the agent's receipt of the price in cash. This agent and the buyer can now arrange for a simultaneous exchange of the bill for cash or its equivalent. The agent then delivers the payment to his or her principal, the seller. The buyer has a good bill of lading, now negotiated over to its order, which will allow it to pick up the goods from the carrier when they arrive in its city. The seller is protected by the trustworthiness of its agent and that agent's ability to follow instructions carefully. The buyer is protected by the fact that it is being asked to surrender cash only in exchange for a negotiable bill of lading on which it can rely.* In a similar fashion, of course, the parties could work a simultaneous exchange of the necessary bill of lading for payment through the buyer's trusted agent, authorized and able to dispense cash or its equivalent, working in the seller's city. Often enough, however, neither party has an agent in the other's locality. The solution, as we will see in this chapter, is devilishly clever. One party, typically the seller, will in effect use a bank—a nice trustworthy bank—in the buyer's city as its agent to handle the documents and make the all-important simultaneous exchange. Before we get to see exactly how this is done, however, we need to add one more piece to the puzzle, and so we introduce the documentary draft.

The Documentary Draft

A draft is a piece of paper, but it is not just any old piece of paper. It is a *negotiable instrument* under Article 3 of the Uniform Commercial Code. I trust that you already have or will at some time in the future study negotiable instruments under Article 3 and the bank collection mechanism of Article 4 in all their mesmerizing detail. These are things not to be missed. For our purposes, we'll need only the brief version and only those aspects of the Code relating to documentary drafts. When you study §§3-103 and 3-104 in detail, you'll come away with the following understanding: The *draft* is by its nature a very simple piece of paper. It must state an unconditional order to pay a fixed amount of money, the order being made by a party designated the *drawer* to a party called the *drawee*. The draft will state that the money is payable by the drawee on demand or at a definite time and finally that it is payable "to bearer" or "to the order of" some named individual.† Those words of negotiability, bearer and order language, will work their same magic when a draft is concerned as we had a chance to see in connection with negotiable bills of lading. They make apparent from the face of the document that the draft is

---

*It has probably already occurred to you that the story just related is in essence what was going on in Example 4 in the previous chapter, where Stan the seller was counting on Sy his trusted agent in Birmingham, Alabama. The fact that Sy had so many problems as the hypotheticals played out shouldn't be taken as evidence that the seller's use of its own agent in this fashion is not in the vast majority of cases a perfectly workable approach.

†Most of us are familiar with that particular kind of draft which goes by the name of the *check*. See §3-104(f). When you write up a check, you as drawer are *ordering* your bank, the drawee, to pay to the holder of the check the amount of money specified upon the holder's presentment of the check and on demand. When the bank must carry out this order, when it is justified in not doing so, and what responsibility it will have for failing in its duties—all this is a large part of the area of commercial law which historically went by the title "Bills and Notes," then turned into "Commercial Paper," and is just now transmogrifying into "Payment Systems." We're not going into any of that here, where we'll stick with documentary drafts.

negotiable, and allow us to know the rules by which the draft can be *negotiated* from one person to another.* Finally, if a draft is negotiable and if it gets into the hands of a certain type of party, someone who qualifies to be called a *holder in due course*, that party holds it free from many of the defenses (and in particular the standard contract defenses of nondelivery, failure of consideration and the like) that make savvy commercial customers so unwilling to take mere non-negotiable instruments and the assignment of contract rights as worth anything more than the paper they are written on.† Major commercial players with money to spend or money to lend will be willing in the right circumstances to part with funds in exchange for negotiable instruments, including the negotiable draft, where any other piece of paper just wouldn't do no matter how many signatures, seals, and acknowledgments it brandished.

So the draft is very important to the whole scheme of things. And yet it has to say very little. A sample of what a form of draft might look like before it is filled in is no more than what Figure 1 looks like. In the story we are soon to relate, we'll have the seller fill out just such a form. One more point before that story can begin: The type of a draft with which we are concerned in this situation is what is called a *documentary draft*. See §4-104(a)(6). It is not the form of the draft itself which gives it this distinction, but rather the role it plays and the company it keeps. It is a draft that travels along with a set of documents and is to be paid or accepted (as we will use that word) by the drawee in exchange for the drawee's getting those documents. You'll see how this works in the section to follow. For the moment also note that we have all of a sudden jumped into Article 4. This article is the part of the Code which deals with banks and how money, checks, drafts, and other papers all move merrily around the country in what is referred to as *customary banking channels*.†† In particular, as we proceed we'll need to consult §4-501 and the sections following on the Collection of Documentary Drafts. For that matter, a full understanding of the law behind payment against documents involves more than just dabbling in Articles 2, 3, and 7 as well. (The Article 7

---

*Those rules are fundamentally the same as those we've already seen in the last chapter with respect to the appropriate procedure for negotiating a negotiable document of title.

†Who qualifies as a holder in due course under Article 3 is set forth in §3-302. The idea, if not every detail, is essentially the same as the special status given under the law of documents of title to the not very elegantly tagged "holder to whom a negotiable document of title has been duly negotiated" encountered in §7-502.

††Again, if you have ever written a check on your bank, sent it via the mails to someone who deposits it in an account somewhere half-way across the county, found your account decreased by the exact amount within a few days and gotten the canceled check in the mail from your bank not long thereafter—well, you must have figured there was some method for getting all of this done *somehow* even if you have never known the details. Again, I urge you to take Payment Systems and learn the mysteries behind all this. In the present chapter, of course, we're not dealing with the check-collection system but rather another major role that the banks play, providing a mechanism for collection on documentary drafts.

Figure 1

stuff we basically took care of in the previous chapter, which I have to assume you went over carefully.) Article 9 can get involved too, but not in ways we'll see here. We have to draw the line somewhere. The story we are about to set forth has enough going on as is.

The Basic Story of a Sale Made "Payment Against Documents"

In this section I want to lay out the basic scheme, the story of a typical contract of sale which calls for payment against documents. We'll assume each step of the way that things go just as they should. Later, as no doubt you were expecting, I'll have a few questions for you involving situations where something starts to go wrong (or at least arguably so). For the time being, however, we'll ignore the potential for conflict (even if we are students of the law) and assume at least initially that things run smoothly. The story I have to tell (which you must appreciate is not of my devising but only a retelling of what has gone on in the mighty world of commerce for some time now and which we can expect to continue into the foreseeable future as long as deals have to be dealt with) is to be told in eight episodes. As we move through these episodes you may want to refer back to Figure 2, which covers it all. Granted, you might not believe it now, but then you haven't heard my story.

Episode One: Seller and Buyer Make the Contract of Sale

The whole thing starts, of course, when a seller and a buyer enter into a contract for the sale of some particular goods. As part of their agreement they will necessarily specify—or leave to trade usage, course of dealing, or incorporation through one of Article 2's gap-filling provisions—when and how payment is to be made by the buyer. Under Article 2 there is no prescribed language that the parties must use to set up this payment-against-documents pattern for payment and delivery. One convention is for the agreement actually to invoke the words "payment against documents" followed by any other details necessary to fully specify the responsibilities of each party. In the story we'll follow here the parties may have used instead the words, "sight draft against bill of lading," the import of which you'll appreciate when you see what is in store. In any event, the important point is that the legal contract calls for this mechanism to be used because the parties themselves agreed to it in language that is sufficiently clear to them and to others in the trade. Note also that if the price term agreed to by the parties is quoted with one of the delivery terms F.O.B. vessel, F.A.S., C.I.F., or C. & F., then it is assumed unless otherwise agreed that the contract calls for payment against documents.

The Numbers Below Refer to the Episodes
in the "Payment Against Sight Draft" Story

Figure 2

See §2-319(4), Comment 4 to that section, and §2-320(4) and its Comment 12. The other delivery terms, such as F.O.B., do not suffice to specify a contract for payment against documents.* So there you have it. Episode One is complete. The parties have contracted to go down this particular road.

Episode Two: Seller's Delivery to Carrier and Receipt of Bill

Performance is now under way. Some employee of the seller takes the goods to the place of business of a carrier. In our case we'll assume it's a railroad operating out of seller's city, Sellersburg, U.S.A. On behalf of the seller this employee will "put the goods in the possession of such a carrier and make such a contract for their transportation as may be reasonable having regard to the nature of the goods and other circumstances." This comes from criterion (a) of §2-504 on shipment by seller, with which you are no doubt familiar. You also know that in (b) the seller is told to obtain "in due form any document necessary to enable the buyer to obtain possession of the goods or otherwise required by the nature of the agreement." In this situation what is required by the agreement is seller's obtaining a negotiable bill of lading covering the goods, which is by custom most often made out *to the order of the seller*. Why would the bill be made out like this? Again, you'll have to wait until the story unfolds to see why this works in the situation, and wait until the Examples and Explanations to see what difficulties might arise if the bill were made out any other way. For the moment, assume that that's how the bill is made out.

We might also ask the question exactly what form the bill of lading has to take. Is it enough that it describes the goods as "one carton said to contain 3,000 widgets" or must it state flat out that the carrier is taking responsibility for the shipment's containing "3,000 widgets in working order?" The answer is that the bill must be as the parties have agreed. Sometimes the specification will come from the dickered terms of writings which the parties have signed, sometimes it's to be found in some boilerplate on one or the other's standard form, and sometimes it is all understood because of an applicable trade usage. Look over the last part of Comment 7 to §2-503. See also §7-509.

The goods are on their way by rail to buyer's city, Buyeropolis. The seller's employee returns to seller's place of business with the bill of lading firmly in hand.

---

*If you are not familiar with delivery terms such as these, I wouldn't worry about it now, although you may want to refer back to Chapter 26. The point here is really a minor one in the grand scheme of things.

Episode Three: Seller Creates a Draft on Buyer

Once the bill is returned to seller's shop, this employee or someone else takes the next step by drawing up a draft on buyer. Recall the sample form we saw above. Now filled out for these purposes it looks like that in Figure 3. The drawer is the seller. The drawee is the buyer. The seller is ordering the buyer to pay a given amount, the price, "to the order of seller." That makes sense. In its present state the only party who could collect on the draft would be the seller itself. So the buyer is to pay the seller. When is payment to be made? In the instant case the draft has been made out as a *sight draft.* The seller-drawer is ordering the buyer-drawee to pay the amount stated as soon as it is presented with the draft—as soon as it "sees" the instrument itself. The seller has made out a sight draft because we stipulated that what was called for in this particular contract. The payment term was "sight draft against bill of lading." (In other situations the parties may have agreed that the buyer would have some additional time after having been confronted with the draft to come up with the payment. We'll explore the use of the *time draft* as a variant on our theme in the section following this one.)

$6000.00	Nov. 20, 1993
Amount	Date

TO: Buyer Inc.
　　　　Buyer

　　Buyeropolis, U.S.A.

At Sight   Pay to the Order of   Seller Corp.
(At sight or time)   (Payee)

Six thousand   dollars and   no   cents.

Seller Corp.
Seller

Authorized Signature

Figure 3

Episode Four: The Seller's Tender Through "Customary Banking Channels"

The seller is now ready to tender. Look at §2-503(5). The seller enters this draft and its accompanying documents into "customary banking channels" through one of its employee's taking the whole package of paper to the appropriate office of some bank in its city (Sellersberg Bank & Trust). Typically this will be a bank with which the seller has already established a working relationship, but in theory any bank with a commercial banking department will do. At the bank the seller's employee endorses the draft and the bill of lading (both of which currently read "to the order of Seller" recall) by placing his or her authorized signature on each. The indorsements may run in a variety of ways, depending on exactly how the details of the transaction are to play out, but one common scheme would be for the seller to have the bill indorsed in blank (that is "to Bearer") and the draft as "Pay to Sellersberg Bank & Trust." Let's assume that's what is done here.*

The indorsed bill, the indorsed draft, and whatever other documents may be called for by the contract of sale are handed over to the proper person at the bank. In addition the seller's agent signs and the bank is given a form of instruction, sometimes called a *collection memo* or a *collection letter,* which specifies just what the bank is supposed to *do* with this packet of papers it has been given.

Episode Five: The Papers Make Their Way to the Presenting Bank

The documentary draft and the documents it accompanies having been entered into banking channels and the proper instructions having been given to Sellersberg Bank, the whole set of papers are now on their way to a bank in Buyeropolis which will carry out the next steps in the procedure. See §4-501. To which bank in that fair city are they sent? Normally the buyer will during the course of negotiations specify which bank should be used, typically one with which the buyer has some ongoing business relationship, and explicitly or not this will have been made part of the agreement between the parties. The instructions given to the people at Sellersberg Bank & Trust will then tell them to which bank the papers

---

*You may be worried that as valuable an item as this negotiable bill of lading has been turned into a bearer document. As we saw in the last chapter, it's risky dealing with a negotiable instrument or document in bearer form, for if it gets into the wrong hands there could be trouble. Here, however, the document while now in bearer form is in a matter of seconds to enter those "customary banking channels." Banks are, we hope, accustomed to holding on to and keeping secure valuable bits of paper. If the bill is lost or misappropriated from this point on, the seller should be able to hold one of the banks involved responsible.

are to be forwarded. If for some reason the buyer has not specified which bank is to be called upon to make presentment, the Sellersberg Bank would be justified in forwarding the documents to any reputable bank in that city with the facilities for handling this type of business.

How exactly this packet of papers makes its way from Sellersberg Bank to the particular bank in buyer's city (Buyeropolis Federal) is a matter of some complexity. Article 4 deals in no small detail with how banks are to carry out their responsibilities in getting all of these things from one place to another in the "customary fashion." Fortunately for us we don't have to worry about these things. It's enough to know that the documents do arrive in a packet at Buyeropolis Federal along with the instructions on what to do with them. In this grand scheme of things, Buyeropolis Federal is referred to as the *presenting bank* (§4-105(6)).*

So as the goods make their way to a railyard or depot in the buyer's city via the railroad, the important papers are similarly on their way but going through customary banking channels and destined to arrive on the desk of someone in the offices of Buyeropolis Federal who will know what to do with them.† The scene of our drama now necessarily shifts to Buyeropolis, where the buyer is about to meet the documents.

Episode 6: Presentment to Buyer and Buyer's Payment on the Draft

The draft and its accompanying documents have arrived at Buyeropolis Federal, the presenting bank. The bank knows to whom it must present the draft because that party, here the buyer, is named as the drawee on the draft. The bank presents the item either by sending a written notice to the buyer (see §4-212(a)) or by making a phone call. (On *presentment* in general, see §3-501. Since this is a sight draft we would refer to presentment for payment. Presentment for acceptance of a draft is dealt with below. On the time that the buyer has to respond to presentment, see §3-502(c).) A representative of the buyer comes down to the bank and inspects the documents to be sure they are what is called for in the contract. This representative will then, on behalf of the buyer, either *honor*

---

*Just in case you were worried, rest assured that the presenting bank as well as the bank which initially takes the draft from the seller, which is termed the *depositary bank,* will get some small remuneration for the services they are rendering here or at least will find it worth their while for some reason. If the bank does something like this as a courtesy to either the seller or the buyer it is presumably because that party is a valued customer from which they will get their reward one way or another.

†You might wonder how this whole system can work if the goods are sent by some particularly speedy means, say for instance by air. Even the fairly fast customary banking channels described here may create a snag in the system if the goods can be expected to arrive before the papers, and the buyer wants to get its hands on them as soon as possible. For explanation of a method worked out to deal with this problem, see the comment to §7-305.

or *dishonor* the draft. In the case of a sight draft like we have here, honoring the draft means paying it in cash or its equivalent. The seller's representative may actually bring the proper amount of cash to the bank, but more likely the buyer has an account at Buyeropolis Federal and can authorize payment from that account. The bank will immediately transfer funds out of that account, so that the draft is paid. (The buyer's not paying on sight would amount to a dishonor, but since we're assuming for the moment that everything is running just fine, we won't worry about that here.) Upon payment the buyer has the right to all of the accompanying documents (§4-503). The buyer's representative goes away from the bank with the bill of lading covering the goods, indorsed you'll recall in blank.

Episode Seven: The Buyer Gets the Goods

With a negotiable bill of lading covering the goods and indorsed in blank in hand, the buyer should have no difficulty getting possession of the goods from the carrier as soon as they arrive in Buyeropolis. The bill typically calls for notification of the buyer when the goods have arrived, or the buyer can just keep calling the railroad and making a pest of itself until it is told the goods are there. The buyer sends some of its workforce over to the railroad yard with instructions to surrender the negotiable bill in exchange for getting the goods the bill represents. The buyer gets the goods.

Episode Eight: The Seller Gets Its Payment

The buyer's having paid on the draft, there is now an amount of money equivalent to the purchase price in the hands of Buyeropolis Federal. That bank holds this money in effect as an agent for the seller which had sent the draft for presentment. Buyeropolis Federal is responsible for remitting this amount back along the banking network to the bank which initially sent it the draft for collection, that is, Sellersberg Bank & Trust. Once there the money can be picked up by the seller. Most likely the seller has an account at this bank and so the bank will immediately credit its account with the amount of the collected draft. The money is now parked in this account and available for the seller to use as it sees fit. Our story, both on the buyer's end and on the seller's has reached its expected and hoped for conclusion.

Some Variations

What was outlined above was, of course, just one version of the story. Parties with slightly different needs can and often do arrange for variations to meet those needs. So, for example, it has to be appreciated that in the story as originally told the seller sends off the goods and the documentary draft and then has to wait some time until it gets its payment. The documents must move forward in the bank collection chain, the buyer is given at least a few days to pay, and then the payment must move back along the chain before the seller's bank makes the funds available for the seller to draw upon.* One way that the seller can get the use of this money (or at least a good percentage of it) more quickly is if it arranges with its bank to *discount* the draft at the time it is handed over to that bank for collection. In effect seller's bank buys the draft from the seller, paying slightly less than the face amount to take into account the interest which it is losing by giving up the money right away in effect financing the transaction during the period of collection and also to reflect the small risk that there will be some difficulty making collection on the draft. The seller immediately gets to take advantage of the value of the goods it has shipped. The seller's bank gets repaid by retaining for itself the proceeds of the draft collection process. What should happen if the draft is not paid for some reason? The seller's bank will be disappointed but not without remedy. Under the Code the bank has retained a security interest in the goods themselves and could always get its money that way. In addition, the seller as drawer of the draft could in some circumstances be held liable because of the dishonor. The seller's bank in buying the draft at a discount does take on some extra risk by becoming a party in its own right, but this risk is typically small and something that the bank can handle. Practically, if the buyer fails to take the goods, it will be in the mutual interests of the seller and its bank to find someone who does want them and complete a sale to that party as soon as possible.

Another variation occurs because the parties anticipate that the buyer may not be able to pay the draft outright when it is presented. The buyer may be expecting to pay for the goods with the proceeds of its own resale to others down the line. It will need some time to pay, some credit, so that it has sufficient time to resell or otherwise come up with the cash. The seller and buyer may in this case contract not for payment against documents as we have been considering but rather for what we could call *acceptance against documents*. The draft which is prepared by the seller and accompanies the documents is not a sight draft as we saw above but rather a *time draft*. It calls not for payment "on sight" but for payment some number of days (typically 30, 60, or 90) "after sight." The draft

---

*You may have experienced a similar problem in dealing with your own bank account. You deposit a check in that account but it will be several days, sometimes quite a few, before the amount of this check is available to you. Often this is of no great concern, but at other times it may be a real inconvenience. You can appreciate why the seller may find this aspect of the story as originally told difficult to live with.

and its accompanying documents are forwarded for collection just as we saw before. The presenting bank, however, does not present the draft for payment but rather makes a presentation for acceptance. *Acceptance* of an Article 3 negotiable draft occurs when the drawee, here the buyer, signs the draft and by so doing agrees to pay the draft according to its terms when it is later presented for payment. See §3-409(a) and §3-413. The signed, accepted draft is kept in the possession of the presenting bank. The documents are then, at the time of acceptance, released to the buyer. See again §4-503. The buyer has the right and all the means to get the goods.

What happens to the accepted draft? That depends. It may work its way back the collection chain and into the hands of the seller. When the time comes around for payment the seller can itself present the draft to the buyer, now making a presentation for payment, and expect to get the money. It can again make use of the bank collection mechanism to make a presentment in a city far from its own base of operations. If the seller does in fact take back the draft and wait for payment it is of course extending credit to the buyer for this period of time. Fortunately for the seller awaiting payment on an accepted negotiable draft is not the same thing as waiting for payment on a mere contract promise. If the buyer does not pay up when it is supposed to, the seller will have a decidedly easier time proceeding on the draft than if it had simply extended credit under the contract by agreeing to send the documents directly to the buyer and take payment by check at some later date.

In actuality the seller may not itself wait around to collect on the accepted time draft. Such an item, a time draft on a buyer which has been accepted by the buyer, is referred to as a *trade acceptance*. Trade acceptances are themselves marketable and the seller may as soon as it gets it hands on the accepted draft discount this item to some other party. We now have a situation in which the seller gets its money fairly quickly and yet the buyer has some time to make payment. The party which takes up the trade acceptance is now in the position of extending credit to the buyer, and will itself get some benefit (by paying a discount for the draft) for the pleasure of so doing.

While trade acceptances may have a market, there can still be some resistance to purchasing them. After all the buyer may not be able to pay up when the draft becomes due. One further variation is for the buyer to arrange for the draft to be presented to, accepted and paid by a bank of some repute. If buyer's bank is willing to extend to the buyer what is referred to as *acceptance credit*, then the seller will make the draft out to this bank not to the buyer as drawee. The draft is again forwarded to this bank along with the documents. The buyer's bank now accepts the time draft in its own name and returns it to the seller's bank for delivery to the seller. A time draft which is drawn on a bank and which is accepted by that bank is known as a *banker's acceptance*. Since banks are even more likely than buyers to pay up on their obligations as they become due, the banker's acceptance is a particularly formidable and valuable piece of paper. The seller (or the seller's bank if it has already released funds upon the deposit of the documentary draft) will have no trouble turning the banker's acceptance into cold hard cash through a ready market for such items.

As Problems Arise

The storyline given above assumed that every part of the transaction from beginning to end went like clockwork. In the vast majority of cases, we have to believe, this will in fact be just what happens. Given the multitude of such transactions which take place every day, however, problems are bound to crop up from time to time. When they do the law, that is our old ally the Uniform Commercial Code, is there to straighten things out and to sort out who owes what to whom, as you'll see when you work through the questions that follow. I'm not suggesting that this set of questions takes care of *every* conceivable controversy that could arise, but there should be more than enough here to get you thinking and to make you appreciate (more than you may have ever thought possible back when you first took up this book) that the Code is there by your side, your friend through strife and through storm.

EXAMPLES

All the questions in the chapter involve a single transaction. Selma, Brown and Company, a publisher of law books operating out of Seattle, contracts to sell two thousand copies of a certain book (I'll let you guess which) to Byers, a textbook distributor in Buffalo. The contract specifies that delivery is to be made to Byers via the Transamerica Railroad and calls for payment to be made "sight draft against bill of lading." Consider the following problems that could come up:

1.   Selma, the president of the publishing company, decides to take personal responsibility for carrying out this transaction. She picks up 40 cartons from the company's warehouse, each of which is supposed to contain 50 copies of the book, and delivers them to the Seattle railroad yard. There she hands them over to an agent of the Transamerica Railroad, receiving in return a negotiable bill of lading made out to the order of Byers. She takes the bill back to her office, where she finds a faxed communication that has just been received from Byers. He is repudiating the deal. Selma figures she will have her attorneys look into what action she can bring against Byers soon enough, but for the moment she is more interested in what to do about the books. There's a hot market for this particular book, and she's sure she can find another buyer for them. Can she simply go back to the Railroad and get the books returned if they have not yet left Seattle? Should she just look for another buyer in the Buffalo area and when she finds one notify Transamerica to have the cartons delivered to that individual instead of to Byers? See §2-705 and

§7-303. Do you see why it might have made more sense for Selma to have the bill made out to the order of her company, which would then actually be the holder of the bill up to the very minute when she delivers it over to her bank along with the draft for collection?

2. Let's start again. Selma does have a bill of lading, describing the goods as "40 cartons each said to contain 50 copies of" the book in question made out to the order of Selma, Brown and Company. She takes it back to her office, where there is no message of repudiation from Byers. In fact Byers has sent a fax asking whether the goods have been shipped yet. Selma has a fax sent to Byers telling him that, yes, the goods have been delivered to the railroad and should be on their way to Buffalo. Has Selma tendered at this point? Recall §§2-503(3) and 2-504.

3. Selma makes out a draft directed to Byers as drawee ordering him to pay "to the order of Selma, Brown and Company" the agreed purchase price "on sight." She delivers this draft along with the bill of lading to the bank with which her company does the principal part of its banking business, the Seattle Bank of Commerce. She endorses the bill in blank and the draft "Pay to Seattle Bank of Commerce." Along with these two papers she gives the bank a form of instructions which directs it to arrange for the collection of the draft through the Buffalo Merchants Bank. (This bank had been suggested by Byers as the one through which presentment should be made.) Under a discounting arrangement with Selma, Brown the Seattle Bank immediately credits that company's account with an amount less than, but only slightly less than, the face value of the draft. Selma leaves the bank. Has her company tendered as of this moment? Assuming the contract price was stated "F.O.B. Seattle," has she done all that is required to pass the risk of loss of the books over to Byers should something happen to them in transit?

4. If the draft and its accompanying bill of lading were to languish around the offices of the Seattle Bank of Commerce for, say, a week or so, would that bank be in any trouble (other than that it might anger an important client and lose some business)? See §4-501. See also §§4-202 and 4-204(a).

5. Suppose the people at Seattle Bank and Trust do send the documentary draft along to the Buffalo Merchants Bank through customary banking channels by the end of the day on which Selma delivers it for collection. It reaches the Buffalo bank two days later. An officer of this bank puts it in a pile of things to do and doesn't get around to dealing with it for three days. Is this bank now in trouble? To whom is it responsible?

6. Suppose the Buffalo bank does immediately send Byers by registered mail a notification of the arrival of the documentary draft. The post office receipt indicates that Byers received this notification on a Monday. It is now Friday and Byers has not come to the bank to make payment. Has the draft been dishonored? See §4-212. In the case of dishonor what is the Buffalo bank supposed to do? See §§4-503 and 4-504. When the Seattle bank receives notice of the dishonor, what are its responsibilities? See §4-501.

7. Selma is informed of the dishonor. What are the various actions that she might take under the circumstances? If she does authorize her company's attorneys to commence a law suit against Byers, what theory of legal liability will those attorneys have to work with? What remedies will be available? See §§2-503(5)(b) and 2-703.

8. Suppose instead that as soon as Byers receives the notification from the Buffalo bank he heads right down to the bank's offices. He gives the bank a personal check for the amount called for by the draft written on another Buffalo area bank. The bank officer handling the transaction gives him the bill of lading. The goods arrive in Buffalo the next day, and Byers takes the bill of lading to the railroad yard where he is given the forty cartons. The railroad asks for and receives the bill of lading which it cancels and puts in its files. If the check written by Byers bounces and if Byers can't ever be found to make good on this check, who takes the loss? See §4-503 again as well as §§4-202 and 4-213(a)(1).

9. Suppose instead that the Buffalo bank is wise enough not to take a personal check in payment of the draft. Byers leaves the bank without the bill of lading. The next day when he is notified by the railroad that this shipment has come in he goes to the railroad yard. There he is able to convince a railroad employee that it is "just a technicality" which keeps him from having the bill of lading and that he surely would be getting it the next day. Since Byers had a truck and several employees with him all ready to take the goods off of the railroad's hands, this employee lets him take the cartons. Can the railroad be in any trouble because of what has happened? Who might sue the railroad and on what theory? Recall §7-403.

10. Assume again that Byers goes to the Buffalo bank to pay on the draft but that this time in fact he has a certified check for the necessary amount. He tells the bank officer that he would like to inspect the cartons when they arrive before paying the draft. Does he have the right to do so? See §2-513(3)(b).

11. Byers, refused the right to inspect the goods, gives the bank officer the certified check anyway and is given the bill of lading in return. He takes it to the railyard where he surrenders it in exchange for the 40 cartons. When he gets back to his warehouse he opens the first of the cartons and quickly finds that many of the books are faulty. In fact a whole series of pages in the middle are blank. Does Byers have the right to reject the shipment or is it too late? See §2-512(2). What rights does he have here?

12. Suppose when Byers takes the bill to the railyard a representative of Transamerica Railroad tells him that the boxes have as far as she can determine simply vanished. Can buyer get his money back from the Buffalo bank? Does he have any rights against Selma, Brown? Where will he have to look for recompense? Recall §7-403 and all that we dealt with in the last chapter.

13. Suppose that the railroad is able to make a delivery but that it delivers only 36 cartons or that it delivers 40 cartons a good number of which are in obviously damaged condition. Who does Byers go against and on what theory?

14. Finally, suppose that the railroad is able to and does deliver 40 cartons all of which seem to be in fine condition and each of which had been marked by the publisher as containing exactly 50 copies of that certain book. At his warehouse Byers opens the cartons and discovers all of them contain a totally different book than the one he had ordered. He tries to contact Selma, Brown but it appears that company has gone out of business, Selma having left Seattle with whatever money she could get her hands on. Can Byers sue the railroad for failing to deliver what it was supposed to? If not, what might he do differently next time he orders from a publisher in order to avoid ever again being in the situation he now finds himself in, that is, having paid a lot of money for some books he does not want?

EXPLANATIONS

1. Selma cannot just go back to the railroad and get the goods back that easily. Section 2-705 gives her the right to stop delivery but in the case of repudiation by the buyer this can only be done by the "carload, truckload, plane or larger shipments of express or freight." This probably will not cover Selma here. See Comment 1 on why this qualification was put into §2-705. But Selma's concern isn't that the books will somehow be delivered to Byers without his paying for them. She's quite able to protect herself against that eventuality just by holding onto the bill. What she wants is to be able to redirect the goods to some other willing purchaser. Look at §7-303. Delivery may be diverted to someone else but in the case of shipment under a negotiable bill of lading only on instructions from the holder of the negotiable bill. Since the bill has been made out to the order of *Byers*, Selma is in physical possession of it but is not the holder. If she could get Byers's signature on the bill, then she'd be the holder, but he may not be in the frame of mind to oblige her so readily and anyway he's a long way away. The goods are in a kind of limbo. What Selma may have to do is allow the whole collection process to go forward and then, when Byers dishonors the draft as we assume he will, pick up from that point. That's a lot to go through, however, when Byers has already repudiated. So you can see that to retain some measure of flexibility sellers like Selma are well advised to have the negotiable bills made out to their order and then sign and negotiate them later. As indeed we have Selma doing in the questions that follow.

2. Tender in such a contract requires the tender of the documents and that occurs only when they are offered up (by the presenting bank) through the customary banking channels (§2-503(5)). So she hasn't tendered yet just by sending the goods on their way. She's working at it though.

3.   Selma still hasn't tendered. As we said, that moment will come only when the documents are tendered in Buffalo. Under an F.O.B. place of shipment contract, however, she has done enough to shift the risk of loss from this moment forward onto the buyer. Recall §2-509(1)(a) and the seller's obligations under §2-504. Subpart (b) of that section says that the seller must obtain and "promptly deliver or tender" the documents. It appears that this is met if the seller promptly forwards the documents via the channels through which the buyer expects to get them. See Comment 5.

4.   Banks which are in the business of making collection for parties such as our seller are expected to do what they are instructed to do and to do it with ordinary care. Note in §4-201 that the banks involved in the collection process act as agents or sub-agents for the owner of the draft. Under §4-501 the Seattle bank was obligated to "present or [in this case] send the draft and accompanying documents for presentment." The bank was a collecting bank under §4-105(5) and as such had to exercise ordinary care in sending the item for presentment (§4-202(a)(1)). See also subsection (b). (You'll learn about the bank's "midnight deadline" when you study Payment Systems.) The Seattle bank was also responsible under §4-204 for sending the item

> by a reasonably prompt method taking into consideration relevant instructions, the nature of the item, and the number of those items on hand, the cost of collection involved, and the method generally used by it or others to present those items.

So we'd have to know something about industry practice here. It seems pretty clear, however, that letting this kind of item sit around for a week would be a lack of ordinary care.

5.   The Buffalo bank acts as an agent for the seller (or the Seattle Bank where as here that bank has actually purchased the draft) and is also a collecting bank under Article 4. So it too is responsible for exercising ordinary care in making presentment under §4-202. If the Buffalo bank just lets the draft sit for this long, it would be in trouble.

6.   The bank made a proper presentment for payment under §4-212(a). The draft has been dishonored by Byers since he did not make payment in response to this presentment within three days. That's §4-212(b). On dishonor in general, you can look to §3-502(c).
    Once it knows of the dishonor, the presenting bank in Buffalo must

> use diligence and good faith to ascertain the reason for the dishonor, must notify its transferor [here the Seattle bank] of the dishonor and of the results of its efforts to ascertain the reasons therefor, and must request instructions.

It then must follow "any reasonable instructions received." The bank will have the right to receive expenses incurred in following any instructions. Furthermore, if it does request instructions about what to do with the goods but does not receive any within a reasonable time the Buffalo bank may take action on its own and "store, sell or otherwise deal with the goods in any reasonable manner" under §4-504. Again, it will have the right to its reasonable expenses.

Once the Seattle Bank receives notice of the dishonor it must "seasonably" notify Selma of what has happened under §4-501. Notice it must do so even if, as if true here, it had discounted the draft and Selma's company has already received the cash it's going to get from the sale. The reason for this requirement is given in the comment.

7.   Selma, having been notified of the dishonor, may well be required under its agreement with the Seattle bank to take back responsibility for the goods. One way or another either that bank or more likely Selma is going to look for another customer for the goods in the Buffalo area. If one can be found then the Buffalo bank, which as you recall is awaiting instructions on what to do, can be instructed to deliver over the bearer bill of lading to that new individual upon receipt of cash or its equivalent. At least that's ideally what will happen to the goods.

If Selma has been forced to resell at a lower price, or if her company has other damages because of what Byers has done, it will want to proceed against Byers on the contract of sale as a breaching buyer. Section 2-503(5)(b) specifically says that she may do so. This dishonor on the draft constitutes non-acceptance or rejection of the goods. Selma has all of her rights against Byers that arise under §2-703, on which see all of Chapter 28.

8.   The presenting bank, Buffalo Merchants, will be responsible for the loss. It was authorized to deliver up the bill of lading only upon payment (§4-503). If it allows Byers to have the bill without getting cash or its equivalent in return it is going to take the responsibility. A personal check, as we all know, is not the equivalent of cash for these purposes. If Byers could ever be found, he could be held liable on the draft he presumably signed. Or because of the check he bounced. If he could be found with the goods he could eventually be made to give them back. See §2-507(2) and Comment 2 to that section. The whole point, of course, is that Selma contracted to sell on "sight draft against bill of lading," just because that was supposed to eliminate her worry about ever having to pursue Byers in any of these ways. Buffalo Merchants's mistake, a lack of ordinary care under §4-202, makes it liable for the damages that flow from that mistake.

9.   Here the Buffalo bank has done nothing wrong, but the railroad's agent at the Buffalo railyard has made a mistake for which the railroad will be responsible. The Buffalo bank which has the bill in hand might on instruction either continue to hold it, negotiate it to another or send it back to the Seattle bank which might in turn send it to Selma. Eventually someone who qualifies as a "holder" under the §1-201(20) definition would bring an action against the railroad for misdelivery, relying on §7-403(1), as we talked about in the last chapter.

10. Byers has no right to inspect the goods under §2-513(3)(b). See Comment 5. Of course he has the right to inspect *the documents* to be

sure they are what he is entitled to under the contract before he pays on the draft, but that is a different matter.

11. Byers has paid for and received the bill of lading. He's used the bill of lading to take possession of the goods. Under §2-512(2) his payment did not constitute an acceptance of the goods and did not in any way impair his right to reject them. He still has a reasonable time under §2-602 to reject the goods by a seasonable notification to Selma. As to his possible remedies, see §2-711 and all of Chapter 29 as it pertains to rejected goods in the buyer's possession.

12. Byers has no right to get any money back from the Buffalo bank. That bank has made only a very limited warranty to him under §7-508 and nothing here indicates it did anything in breach of that warranty. Nor has Byers any rights against Selma. Her company as seller did all that it was supposed to as far as we can tell. It delivered the goods to the carrier and got and forwarded a proper bill of lading. Again the key is the duty of the carrier under §7-403. Byers as the holder of the bill can hold the railroad responsible for not delivering as it is charged to do.

13. Once again Byers goes against the railroad either for misdelivery of four of the cartons or for damage to some of them. Either way the railroad will most likely be liable as we saw in the last chapter. There's the slight chance that the railroad could show the damage was nothing that could be traced to its lack of due care—maybe the railroad car was swamped by a precedent-setting flood—but even then the carrier would probably still be liable. In all likelihood either the railroad agreed to be liable up to some figure closely approximating the worth of the goods or the buyer and seller arranged in their contract for insurance to cover such loss. As we said in answer to Example 3 above, however, as between the seller and buyer the risk of loss would fall on the buyer here. Byers would have to pursue the railroad or the insurance carrier to get compensation.

You see here why it is important that the railroad's agent in Seattle act carefully in handling the transaction on the railroad's behalf. He or she was responsible for issuing a bill of lading that described the goods as "40 cartons each said to contain" such and such a book. If there weren't 40 cartons to begin with, the agent should have been aware of it and should have refused to issue the bill with that language. If the cartons had marks of damage on them when they were delivered to the railyard in Seattle, the agent should have made sure that the bill prominently noted their condition. As it is, it's going to be very hard for the railroad to argue that it got the goods in any shape other than what the bill indicates. And in any event this is nothing that Byers as a holder of the bill would have to worry about. He has a right to get what the bill calls for.

14. The railroad has no potential liability here. What was delivered was just what the bill described, "40 cartons each said to contain" that particular most remarkable book. Byers has all kinds of rights against Selma, of course, but who knows what that will ever get him.

What might he do in the future to avoid repetition of such a catastrophe? Well, as you can imagine, one lesson is that he should try to restrict his dealings to established publishers of only the highest reputation, not fly-by-nights like Selma, Brown and Company. Beyond that, he could of course have insisted, if Selma would only deal in terms of a "sight draft against documents," that the bill of lading under which the shipment was to travel specify something like "inspection by buyer allowed," which would have given him a right to inspect the goods before making payment. Or he could have bargained for the right to be presented with a bill of lading that actually described the goods in more detail, say "2,000 copies of a book known as Sales & Leases: Examples and Explanations." But would it be easy to find a carrier willing to issue a bill in this form? Maybe if you paid the railroad enough it would do about anything, but practically that business won't issue such a bill unless it has had a chance to open up every carton, count all the books, and so on. The railroad isn't going to want to do this.

One way around this dilemma is for Byers to insist that the documents accompanying the draft include an inspection certificate issued by some independent trustworthy third party (an arm of the American Booksellers Association?). This inspection certificate would indicate that a representative of this agency had inspected the cargo during the packing and that the cartons do contain what they say they contain. If the contract called for such an inspection and such an inspection certificate, then Byers would not be under an obligation to pay on the draft and take up the bill of lading unless the draft were accompanied as well by such a certificate. And he would have the right to inspect *the certificate* before paying on the draft. I doubt such an inspection procedure has ever been used in a transaction like we have here, for the sale of books no matter how precious they might be. This technique of third party inspection is, however, used in a variety of situations, for instance the sale of large amounts of commodities sold in bulk.

One final point: Should either Selma or Byers intend to bring an action against the other on the contract of sale, she or he should be sure to observe the provisions of §2-725, the Statute of Limitations in Contracts for Sale. This provision is applicable to all Article 2 transactions, of course, and not just documentary transactions. It seemed to me, however, that §2-725, being the very last section in Article 2, was as good a place as any to end a book that started back at Chapter One with the very first section, §2-101. And with that I take my leave.

Table of U.C.C. Sections

§1-102 89-90, 96, 109, 120, 219, 286, 525
§1-103 44, 86, 117, 120, 221
§1-106 461
§1-201(3) 88, 100, 119, 158
§1-201(6) 507
§1-201(9) 171
§1-201(10) 234-236
§1-201(11) 88, 101, 119, 158
§1-201(15) 504
§1-201(17) 293
§1-201(19) 142, 170
§1-201(20) 514, 526
§1-201(23) 354, 444, 471
§1-201(26) 80, 303, 317, 457
§1-201(27) 80
§1-201(30) 265
§1-201(32) 166
§1-201(33) 166, 170
§1-201(37) 6, 31-34, 272, 274-275
§1-201(39) 49, 79
§1-201(42) 87
§1-201(44) 170
§1-201(45) 421, 508
§1-201(46) 79, 100
§1-203 142, 287
§1-204 313
§1-205 89-97, 107-111
§1-206 72
§2-101 3, 162
§2-102 3-17, 21-28, 140, 221
§2-103(1)(b) 142, 170, 287
§2-103(1)(c) 412
§2-104(1) 35-42, 81, 142, 147, 416
§2-104(3) 36
§2-105(1) 8, 10-17
§2-105(2) 10, 283, 291
§2-105(5) 135, 369
§2-105(6) 305, 308-310
§2-106(1) 4, 163
§2-106(2) 286
§2-106(4) 357, 442
§2-107 8, 17
§2-201 42, 71-86, 102, 152
§2-202 99-117, 119-120, 222
§2-204 43-47, 126, 130
§2-205 47, 49-50
§2-206 47, 50-52

§2-207 53-69, 126, 226
§2-208 90-91, 95-97, 111, 149, 156, 381
§2-209 115, 139-156, 381
§2-301 139-140, 158, 280
§2-302 120-126, 221, 225, 246
§2-304(1) 129
§2-305 130-131
§2-306(1) 131
§2-307 135-136, 370
§2-308 136, 517
§2-309 135-136
§2-310 136, 517
§2-311 136-137
§2-312 164, 173-178
§2-313 116, 154, 179-198, 200, 232
§2-314 17, 36, 38, 199-200, 203-215, 233
§2-315 200-201, 215-218
§2-316 219-227, 232-238, 245-247, 265
§2-317 182
§2-318 250, 255-265
§2-319 426, 428-429, 459, 517
§2-320 428, 517
§2-322 429
§2-326 383-384, 387-391
§2-327 388
§2-401 162-164, 517
§2-403 163-164, 166-173
§2-501 283-284, 291-293, 471
§2-502 471
§2-503 288-289, 293-295, 415-416, 420, 426-429, 517
§2-503(4) 297-298, 429, 518
§2-503(5) 546-547
§2-504 287-289, 295-297, 420, 425-429, 517, 535, 546
§2-505 479
§2-507 136, 285, 445-446, 547
§2-508 323-334, 349
§2-509 409-417
§2-509(1) 411, 419-429, 517-518, 546
§2-509(2) 411, 421-422, 429-430, 434, 518
§2-509(3) 411-417, 419, 435
§2-509(4) 410
§2-510 431-437

§2-511	136, 284, 310
§2-512	310, 548
§2-513	311, 517, 548
§2-601	285-288, 299-300, 324
§2-602	300, 316-321, 346, 452, 548
§2-603	317, 346
§2-604	317-318, 346
§2-605	287, 317
§2-606	304-305, 308-316
§2-607	285, 301
§2-607(1)	301, 309
§2-607(2)	301, 312, 335
§2-607(3)(a)	252, 301-304, 487
§2-607(4)	301, 312
§2-607(5)	176
§2-608	287, 335-350, 453-454
§2-609	311, 351-354, 363-367, 382
§2-610	352-353, 356-361, 483-486
§2-611	352, 361-363
§2-612	369-382, 434
§2-613	394, 398-399
§2-614	394, 404
§2-615	139, 394, 398-404
§2-616	402
§2-702	354, 444-446
§2-703	441-443, 547
§2-704	454-455
§2-705	354, 446-447, 545
§2-706	456-458
§2-708(1)	458-463
§2-708(2)	463-466
§2-709	406-407, 416, 451-455
§2-710	455-456, 466-467
§2-711	318, 336, 346-347, 357, 469-470, 548
§2-712	480-482, 487
§2-713	482-487
§2-714	174, 223, 487-490
§2-715	174, 480, 490-492
§2-716(1), (2)	477-479
§2-716(3)	479-480
§2-718(1)	448, 492
§2-718(2), (3)	492-493
§2-719	219-221, 223-227, 238-247
§2-723	459, 483-485
§2-725	4, 26-28, 67, 252, 550
§2A-101	495-496
§2A-102	30-34
§2A-103(1)(e)	277, 498
§2A-103(1)(g)	272, 275-277
§2A-103(1)(i)	371, 497
§2A-103(1)(j)	30, 272
§2A-103(1)(l)	275
§2A-103(1)(t)	35
§2A-103(1)(u)	500-501
§2A-103(1)(x)	275
§2A-103(1)(y)	275
§2A-103(3)	35

§2A-108	121
§2A-204	45
§2A-205	47
§2A-206	47
§2A-207	90
§2A-208	139
§2A-209	276-277
§2A-210	269, 276
§2A-211	268-269, 276
§2A-212	269, 275-276
§2A-213	269, 275-276
§2A-214	220, 269
§2A-216	269
§2A-219	406
§2A-220	406
§2A-221	394
§2A-404	394
§2A-406	394
§2A-407	276-277
§2A-501	496
§2A-503	269, 497
§2A-504	497
§2A-508	495, 502
§2A-509	497
§2A-510	371, 497
§2A-511	497
§2A-512	497
§2A-513	324, 497
§2A-514	497
§2A-515	497
§2A-516	497
§2A-517	498
§2A-518	502
§2A-519	502
§2A-520	502
§2A-521	502
§2A-522	502
§2A-523	495, 498-499
§2A-524	498
§2A-525	498-499
§2A-527	499, 501
§2A-528	499, 501
§2A-529	499-500
§2A-530	501
§2A-532	501
§3-103	531
§3-104	531
§3-302	532
§3-409	541
§3-413	541
§3-501	538
§3-502	538, 548
§4-104	532
§4-105	538, 546
§4-201	546
§4-202	546, 548
§4-204	546
§4-212	538, 548

§4-501	537, 546-547	§7-309	524-525
§4-503	539, 541, 547	§7-403	514, 525-527, 548
§4-504	547	§7-501	515, 523, 527
§7-101	512	§7-509	535
§7-102	421, 507-508	§8-319	72
§7-103	512	§9-102(2)	386
§7-104	513	§9-114	386
§7-202	514	§9-203	72, 284
§7-203	524, 527	§9-501	496
§7-204	524-525	§9-503	498-499
§7-301	523-524	§10-102	7
§7-303	545	§10-103	7
§7-305	538		

Index

Acceptance of contract offer. *See* Offer and
    Acceptance
Acceptance or rejection of goods
    generally, 299-321
    commercial units, 308-310
    consequences of acceptance, 301
    consequences of rejection, 300
    inspection, 310-311
    modes of acceptance, 304-305, 312-321
    post-rejection use, 318-321
Acceptance of goods. *See* Acceptance or
    Rejection of Goods
Anticipatory repudiation, 352-353, 356-363
Article 2
    applied to leases, 20-28
    scope, 3-17
Article 2A. *See also* Leases
    history, 28-30
    scope, 30-34
"As is." *See* Modification or Limitation of
    Warranties

Bailment. *See* Documents of Title
"Battle of the forms." *See* Offer and Acceptance
Bill of lading. *See* Documents of Title
Buyer's remedies. *See also* Modification or
    Limitation of Warranties
    generally, 469-493
    anticipatory repudiation, 483-486
    breach of warranty, 487-489
    consequential damages, 490-492
    incidental damages, 489-490
    liquidated damages, 492
    money damages, 471-472, 480-493
    notification of breach, 301-304
    replevin, 479-480
    restitution, 492-493
    seller's insolvency, 471
    specific performance, 477-479

Commercial units, 308-310
Consignments, 384-386, 389-391
Contract formation. *See* Offer and Acceptance
Course of dealing. *See* Trade Terms
Course of performance. *See* Trade Terms

Cure
    generally, 323-334
    following revocation, 349-350

Destination contract. *See* Risk of Loss
Disclaimer of warranties. *See* Modification or
    Limitation of Warranties
Documents of title. *See also* Payment Against
    Documents
    generally, 504-527
    applicable law, 512-513
    bailee's responsibilities, 518-527
    bill of lading, 507-508
    documentary sales, 516-527
    negotiability, 513-516
    use as collateral, 510-512
    warehouse receipt, 508-510

Excuse of performance, 393-404
Express warranties. *See* Warranties of Quality

Failure of essential purpose. *See* Modification or
    Limitation of Warranties
Fitness Warranty. *See* Warranties of Quality
F.O.B. *See* Risk of Loss
Future goods, 10-11

"Gap fillers," 126-137
Goods, 8-17

"Hybrid transactions," 11-17

Identification of goods, 283-284, 291-293
Implied warranties. *See* Warranties of Quality
Impracticability. *See* Excuse of Performance
Insecurity, 353-354, 363-367
Insolvency
    buyer's insolvency, 443-446
    seller's insolvency, 471
Inspection, 310-311
Installment sales, 369-382

Leases. *See also* Article 2A
  application of Article 2, 20-28
  distinguished from sale, 30-34
  finance lease, 269-277
  remedies, 495-502
  warranties, 267-277

Merchantability. *See* Warranties of Quality
Merchants, 35-42
Modification and waiver, 139-160. *See also* Modification or Limitation of Warranties
Modification or limitation of warranties
  generally, 219-247
  "as is," 237-238
  conspicuousness, 233-235
  disclaimer of warranties, 222-223, 232-238
  failure of essential purpose, 240-245
  limitation of remedies, 223-224, 238-245
  time of agreement, 225-227
  unconscionability, 243-247

Notification of breach, 301-304

Offer. *See* Offer and Acceptance
Offer and acceptance
  generally, 43-69
  basics, 43-52
  "Battle of the forms," 53-69
  firm offers, 49-50
  open terms, 130

Parol evidence rule
  generally, 99-117
  effect on trade terms, 107-111
  effect on oral agreement, 111-117
  writing as integration, 101-104
Payment against documents, 529-550
Perfect tender rule. *See* Tender
Privity. *See* Warranties of Quality

Rejection of contract offer. *See* Offer and Acceptance
Rejection of goods. *See* Acceptance or Rejection of Goods
Remedies. *See* Buyer's Remedies; Modification or Limitation of Warranties; Remedies in Leases; Seller's Remedies
Remedies in leases, 495-502
Requirements contracts, 131-135
Revocation of acceptance, 335-350
Risk of loss
  generally, 406-437
  agreement as to, 410-411

destination contract, 295, 419-421, 426-429
effect of breach on, 431-437
F.O.B., 426-429
merchant sale, 412-415
nonmerchant sale, 415-417
shipment contract, 295, 419-421, 424-429
warehoused goods, 421-422, 429-430

Sale on approval, 383-384, 387-391
Sale or return, 383-384, 387-391
Seller's remedies
  generally, 441-467
  action for the price, 451-456
  buyer's insolvency, 443-446
  consequential damages, 466-467
  incidental damages, 466-467
  lost-volume seller, 463-465
  money damages, 447-448, 451-467
  stoppage in transit, 446-447
Shipment contract. *See* Risk of Loss
Statute of Frauds
  generally, 71-86
  admissions exception, 82-83
  and modifications, 152-154
  merchants exception, 79-81
  partial payment exception, 84-85
  promissory estoppel, 85-86
  specially manufactured goods, 81-82
  writing satisfying, 77-79

Tender
  generally, 284-289, 293-298
  delivery in lots, 135-136, 369-371
  destination contract, 295
  means of tender, 288-289, 293-298
  perfect tender rule, 285-288
  place for tender, 136
  shipment contract, 295
  time of tender, 136
Title
  generally, 161-178
  concept of title, 161-162
  disclaiming warranty, 177-178
  passing title, 163-164, 166-173
  warranty in lease, 268-269
  warranty in sale, 164, 173-178
Trade terms, 87-97. *See also* Parol Evidence Rule

Unconscionability
  generally, 120-126
  limitation of remedies, 243-247
Usage of Trade. *See* Trade Terms

Waiver. *See* Modification and Waiver
Warehouse receipt. *See* Documents of Title
Warranties in leases, 267-277
Warranties of quality. *See also* Buyer's Remedies;
  Modification or Limitation of Warranties
  express warranties, 179-198
  implied warranties generally, 199-218
  privity, 249-265

warranty of fitness, 200-201, 215-218
warranty of merchantability, 199-200, 203-
  215
Warranty of fitness. *See* Warranties of Quality
Warranty of merchantability. *See* Warranties of
  Quality
Warranty of title. *See* Title